A compilation of evaluations
appearing in *Reference Books
Bulletin*, September 1, 1988 –
August 1989

Prepared by the
American Library Association,
Reference Books Bulletin
Editorial Board
Edited by Sandy Whiteley
Compiled by Penny Spokes

AMERICAN LIBRARY ASSOCIATION
Chicago and London 1989

Cover design by Ellen Pettengell

Composed by ALA Books/Publishing Services on a BestInfo Wave-4 pre-press system and output on a NEC 890 Laser printer in Times Roman. Display type, Bodoni Book, composed by Pearson Typographers.

Printed on 50-pound Finch Opaque, a pH-neutral stock, and bound in 10-point Carolina cover stock by First Impression, Inc.

The paper used in this publication meets the minimum requirements of American National Standard for Information Sciences--Permanence of Paper for Printed Library Materials, ANSI Z39.48-1984.

Copyright © 1988, 1989 by the American Library Association

Permission to quote any review in full or in part must be obtained from the Office of Rights and Permissions of the American Library Association.

Permission to quote a review in full will be granted only to the publisher of the work reviewed.

Library of Congress Catalog Card Number 73-159565

International Standard Book Number 0-8389-3379-3
International Standard Serial Number 8755-0962

Printed in the United States of America.

CONTENTS

Preface v
Reference Books Bulletin Editorial Board vii
Alumni ix
Omnibus Articles 1
    Medical Reference Tools for the Layperson 1
    1988 Annual Encyclopedia Update 5
    Reference Tools for Literary Criticism: A Selected Guide 14
    Selected Reference Sources on Gardening 18
    Sports Reference Books 21
    Telephone Books as Reference Sources 24
Featured Reviews and Reviews 29
    Generalities 29
    Philosophy, Psychology, Religion 54
    Social Sciences 59
    Business, Economics 67
    Law, Public Administration, Social Problems and Services 75
    Education, Communication, Customs 84
    Language 91
    Science 100
    Medicine, Health 109
    Technology, Management 115
    Fine Arts, Decorative Arts 123
    Music 132
    Performing Arts, Recreation 140
    Literature 149
    Geography 163
    Biography, Genealogy 173
    History 178
Subject Index 193
Index to Type of Material 203
Title Index 207

PREFACE

The *Reference Books Bulletin* Editorial Board is pleased to offer this twenty-first annual cumulation of reviews published in *Reference Books Bulletin*. *Reference Books Bulletin* is published twice a month (monthly in July and August) within BOOKLIST.

The most distinctive characteristic of *Reference Books Bulletin*—one learned by library school students all over the country—is that reviews are produced by a committee: the *Reference Books Bulletin* Editorial Board. The Board, a subcommittee of ALA's Publishing Committee, consists of 25 librarians from school, public, and academic libraries in the United States and Canada, representing a wide variety of professional and personal interests. The Board's chair and *RBB* editor decide together which of the approximately 1,000 items submitted per year will be reviewed in the pages of *RBB*. English-language reference materials in any form suitable for school and small to medium-size public and academic libraries are considered. After the chair and editor decide that a book will be reviewed, a review copy is forwarded to the Board member or alumnus reviewer (one who is no longer an active Board member but continues to write several reviews per year) to write the evaluation. When the Board member submits the draft review, the editor circulates it for comments to the chair and Board members who serve as "readers." The editor then revises the review, taking into consideration readers' comments, sometimes negotiating compromises about comparisons of sources or choices of words with the wisdom of Solomon and the tact of Emily Post. The final draft of each review is approved by the *RBB* chair and the reviewer. This unique committee approach ensures that each review is scrutinized by an interdisciplinary group of critics, each providing a different perspective.

Besides the 436 reviews of individual reference sources, this year's cumulation offers six subject-oriented, collective reviews of reference items ranging from sports to telephone directories. Like the reviews for individual sources, these omnibus articles can be used to develop collections; they can also be used to polish reference skills in the areas covered.

The Board appreciates very much our superb editor, Sandy Whiteley, and her staff at ALA, Penny Spokes, Brenda Barrera, and Jill Sidoti. I wish to thank the Pennsylvania State University Libraries for providing space and resources needed to carry out the responsibilities of the chair and also my assistant, Lee Carpenter, who organized and carried out with utmost efficiency the logistic complexities inherent to the review process.

CHRISTINE A. WHITTINGTON
Chair, 1988–89

REFERENCE BOOKS BULLETIN EDITORIAL BOARD

CHRISTINE A. WHITTINGTON, Reference Librarian, Pattee Library, Pennsylvania State University, University Park, Pennsylvania, Chair

HILDA ARNOLD, Circulation-Extension Librarian, Great Falls Public Library, Great Falls, Montana

BARBARA M. BIBEL, Reference Librarian, Science, Business, and Sociology Department, Oakland Public Library, Oakland, California

CHRISTINE BULSON, Head of Reference and Associate Librarian, Milne Library, State University of New York at Oneonta, New York

BRIAN E. COUTTS, Coordinator of Collection Development, Helm-Cravens Library, Western Kentucky University, Bowling Green, Kentucky

CAROLE C. DEILY, Reference Librarian, Plano Public Library System, Plano, Texas

PAUL M. DUCKWORTH, Reference Department Manager, Springfield-Greene County Library, Springfield, Missouri

MARIE ELLIS, English and American Literature Bibliographer, History and Humanities Department, University of Georgia Libraries, Athens, Georgia

GARY GOLDEN, Director, Camden Arts and Science Library, Rutgers University, Camden, New Jersey

SUSAN GOODEN, Librarian, Concord High School, Wilmington, Delaware

LUCY BJÖRKLUND HARPER, Portland Campus Librarian, Health Science Library, Linfield College, Good Samaritan Hospital and Medical Center, Portland, Oregon

CLARA G. HOOVER, Librarian, Millard South High School, Omaha, Nebraska

NANCY HUNTLEY, Assistant Director, Lincoln Library, Springfield, Illinois

JOAN W. JENSEN, Head of Reference Department, Homer Babbidge Library, University of Connecticut, Storrs, Connecticut

RASHELLE KARP, Assistant Professor, College of Library Science, Clarion University of Pennsylvania, Clarion, Pennsylvania

ABBIE VESTAL LANDRY, Head of Reference Division, Watson Library, Northwestern State University, Natchitoches, Louisiana

ARTHUR A. LICHTENSTEIN, Head of Reference and Access Services, Owen D. Young Library, St. Lawrence University, Canton, New York

JUDITH YANKIELUN LIND, Director, Roseland Free Public Library, Roseland, New Jersey

SUZANNE MUNDY, Head of Children's Division, Tufts Library, Weymouth, Massachusetts

MARY ELLEN QUINN, Director of Collection Development, Chicago Public Library, Chicago, Illinois

MARTIN D. SUGDEN, Reference Librarian, Business, Science, and Industry Department, Jacksonville Public Library, Jacksonville, Florida

TERRI TOMCHYSHYN, Director of Professional Development, Canadian Library Association, Ottawa, Ontario, Canada

JIM WALSH, Government Publications and Microforms Librarian, O'Neill Library, Boston College, Chestnut Hill, Massachusetts

BOBBI WALTERS, New Orleans, Louisiana

DAVID B. WELLS, Head of Reference Department, Las Vegas/Clark County Library District, Las Vegas, Nevada

ALUMNI

James D. Anderson, Associate Dean and Professor, School of Communication, Information and Library Studies, Rutgers University, New Brunswick, New Jersey

Douglas G. Birdsall, Associate Director of Libraries, Texas Tech University, Lubbock, Texas

Pamela S. Bradigan, Head of Reference Services, Ohio State University Health Sciences Library, Columbus, Ohio

Frances Neel Cheney, Nashville, Tennessee

Frances Evelyn Corcoran, IMC Coordinator, School District 62, Des Plaines, Illinois

Milton H. Crouch, Assistant Director for Reader Services, Bailey-Howe Library, University of Vermont, Burlington, Vermont

Donald G. Davis, Jr., Professor, Graduate School of Library and Information Science, University of Texas at Austin

Winifred F. Dean, Reference/Bibliographer Social Sciences, Cleveland State University Library, Cleveland, Ohio

Jack Forman, Reference/Bibliographic Services Librarian, Mesa College Library, San Diego, California

Charles L. Gilreath, Head of Central Reference Department, University of Arizona Library, Tucson, Arizona

Ruth M. Hadlow, Head of Children's Literature Department, Cleveland Public Library, Cleveland, Ohio

Vincent J. Jennings, Documents and Map Librarian, Hofstra University Library, Hempstead, New York

Donald J. Kenney, Head of General Reference Department, University Libraries, Virginia Polytechnic Institute and State University, Blacksburg, Virginia

Martin A. Kesselman, Coordinator of Online and Instructional Services, Library of Science and Medicine, Rutgers University, Piscataway, New Jersey

Donald Krummel, Professor, Graduate School of Library and Information Science, University of Illinois at Urbana

John C. Larsen, Baltimore, Maryland

Lauren K. Lee, Collection Management Officer, Atlanta-Fulton Public Library, Atlanta, Georgia

H. Robert Malinowsky, Associate Professor/Bibliographer of Science and Engineering, University of Illinois at Chicago

Josephine McSweeney, Professor and Reference Librarian, Pratt Institute Library, Brooklyn, New York

Arthur S. Meyers, Director, Hammond Public Library, Hammond, Indiana

J. B. Post, Print and Picture Curator, Free Library of Philadelphia, Philadelphia, Pennsylvania

Margaret C. Power, Department Head and Reference Librarian, Depaul University Library, Chicago, Illinois

James R. Rettig, Assistant University Librarian for Reference and Information Services, Earl Gregg Swem Library, College of William and Mary, Williamsburg, Virginia

Stewart P. Schneider, Associate Professor, Graduate School of Library and Information Studies, University of Rhode Island, Kingston, Rhode Island

David A. Tyckoson, Information Services Librarian, Parks Library, Iowa State University, Ames, Iowa

Wiley J. Williams, Chapel Hill, North Carolina

A. Virginia Witucke, Regional Librarian, Central Michigan University, Fairfax, Virginia

Raymund F. Wood, Encino, California

OMNIBUS ARTICLES

MEDICAL REFERENCE TOOLS FOR THE LAYPERSON

This list selectively identifies key reference materials on diseases, drugs, physicians, health facilities, and other personal health concerns. It emphasizes authoritative materials that can be used by the general public. It complements and updates the annotated list, "General Consumer Health Reference Books" [*RBB* F 1 85].

Many of the books below are written for health professionals, but because substantial gaps exist in both the subject coverage and currency of medical materials for the general public, librarians must rely on them to meet the health information needs of the library patron. For libraries that can afford medical textbooks, additional core materials can be identified in two articles by Alfred N. Brandon and Dorothy R. Hill in the *Bulletin of the Medical Library Association*: "Selected List of Books and Journals for the Small Medical Library" (April 1987; 75(2):133–65) and "Selected List of Books and Journals in Allied Health Sciences" (October 1986; 74(4):353–73).

DICTIONARIES

Dictionary of Medical Syndromes. By Sergio I. Magalini and Euclide Scrascia. 2d ed. Lippincott, 1981. hardcover $59.50 (0-397-50503-5).

The authors define hundreds of medical syndromes like floppy infant syndrome or Down's syndrome. Unlike most medical textbooks, information about each syndrome is given in the sequence of events that occurs when a patient seeks medical care: synonyms, symptoms, signs, etiology, pathology, diagnostic procedures, therapy, and prognosis, plus a brief authoritative bibliography for additional information. Libraries should also consider the *Dictionary of Medical Eponyms* (Parthenon Publishing Group, 1987). It does not include as much information or a bibliography; however, it does provide names of syndromes coined since 1980.

Dorland's Illustrated Medical Dictionary. 27th ed. Saunders, 1988. hardcover $38.95 (0-7216-3154-1). [*RSBR* F 15 81]

The recognized standard for defining medical terminology among health-science professionals, this dictionary is used by the National Library of Medicine when establishing medical subject headings. It is an up-to-date source and attempts to show preference for properly constructed and unambiguous terms. While most terms are listed alphabetically, those consisting of two or more words are given as subentries under the noun in medical dictionary tradition. For example, *Down's syndrome* is a subentry under *syndrome*. Numerous tables and charts are included, such as laboratory values, a temperature conversion chart, and weights and measures.

Encyclopedia and Dictionary of Medicine, Nursing, and Allied Health. By Benjamin F. Miller and Claire Brackman Keane. 4th ed. Saunders, 1987. hardcover deluxe binding $24.95 (0-7216-1815-4); hardcover economy binding $19.95 (0-03-011507-8).

This dictionary strives to provide "authoritative vocabulary for students and learners of all ages and degrees in the nursing and paramedical sciences." It strongly emphasizes patient education. Many of the entries addressing the disease process and patient care management are long and encyclopedic in nature. Helpful appendixes include tables and charts on topics like body weight, laboratory reference values, and recommended daily dietary allowances. Most commonly compared with *Taber's Cyclopedic Medical Dictionary*, this volume presently is more comprehensive and up-to-date.

Logan's Medical and Scientific Abbreviations. By Carolynn M. Logan and M. Katherine Rice. Lippincott, 1987. paper $22.50 (0-397-54589-4).

This is a comprehensive list of thousands of shortened forms of medical and other scientific terms. It includes acronyms, initialisms, abbreviations, symbols, and Latin terms. The most complete and easily read compendium of medical abbreviations.

DIRECTORIES

ABMS Compendium of Certified Medical Specialists. 7v. 2d ed. American Board of Medical Specialties, 1 Rotary Center, Ste. 805, Evanston, IL 60201-4889, 1988. hardcover $240, including June 1989 supplement (0-934277-12-5; ISSN 0884-1543). [*RBB* My 15 87]

This biographical directory authorized by all 23 medical specialty boards is published every two years. The information on certification and recertification is provided by specialty boards; general biographical information is obtained from individual physicians. Separate sections are available for each specialty. Entries are arranged by physician's name and include year of certification, birth date and place, medical school and year graduated, internships and residencies, current professional status and/or academic appointment, professional association memberships, address, and telephone number. A geographic index accompanies each specialty and subspeciality section, and volume 7 is a master alphabetical index of all specialists. A probable replacement in libraries for the *Directory of Medical Specialists* (Marquis Who's Who), which according to *ABMS*, is missing newly certified diplomates in anesthesiology, radiology, emergency medicine, and thoracic surgery.

American Hospital Association Guide to the Health Care Field. American Hospital Association, 1988. paper $150 (0-87258-452-6; ISSN 0094-8969).

For over 40 years, the American Hospital Association has annually surveyed U.S. hospitals and summarized the results in this volume and a second publication, *Hospital Statistics*. The *Guide* is a geographic directory of hospitals providing address, telephone number, administrator, and codes for facilities such as CT scanner or neonatal intensive-care unit. Hospitals are also classed with regard to type of control, service provided, and length of stay. Brief statistics are given on the number of beds, admissions, percent occupancy, births, number of personnel, and payroll. The scope of this tool has recently been expanded to include information on health maintenance organizations, hospices, multihospital systems, freestanding surgery centers, and substance-abuse programs. Also new are state and metropolitan hospital distribution maps.

American Medical Directory. 4v. 31st ed. American Medical Association, 535 N. Dearborn St., Chicago, IL 60610, 1988. hardcover $450 (0-89970-322-4).

Based upon the AMA's Physicians Masterfile, this is the most comprehensive biographical directory of U.S. physicians. The AMA begins tracking physicians as soon as they enter U.S. medical schools, and tracks foreign medical graduates when they begin accredited residencies in the U.S. The primary entry for each physician lists local address, medical school, year of license, primary and secondary self-designated practice specialty, type of practice, American specialty board certifications, and recognition awards. Arranged geographically by state and then by city, an index volume lists name and specialty codes for cross-reference to the geographic volumes.

Directory of Nursing Homes: A State-by-State Listing of Facilities and Services. 3d ed. Ed. by Sam Mongeau. Oryx, 1988. paper $195 (0-89774-414-4). [*RBB* D 15 83]

This directory of over 17,000 state-licensed long-term-care facilities gives address, telephone number, number of beds, levels of care, and names of administrators. Entries may include facilities and activities, type of ownership, languages spoken, number of staff, and admission requirements. The facilities are organized by state and by city. Indexes include one of nursing home names and another by religious/fraternal/maternal affiliation.

Medical and Health Information Directory. 3v. 4th ed. Gale, 1988. hardcover $440 (0-8103-2519-5). [*RBB* My 1 86]

According to Gale, this edition identifies "more than 40,000 associations, . . . research centers, hospitals, clinics, treatment centers, education programs, publications, audiovisuals, data banks, libraries, and information services." Sources of information include other Gale directories, federal and state government documents, materials from national organizations (e.g., Federation of American Health Systems), and questionnaires. All entries include addresses, most have telephone numbers, and several chapters have descriptive annotations. Volumes are arranged by topic with arrangement varying within a chapter: most are organized by name, subject, or geographic location. The new edition provides a single name and keyword index in each volume.

DRUG HANDBOOKS

Handbook of Nonprescription Drugs. 8th ed. American Pharmaceutical Association, 2215 Constitution Ave. NW, Washington, DC 20037, 1986. hardcover $70 (0-917330-54-4).

Designed to assist pharmacists in advising patients about the use of nonprescription drugs, the *Handbook* is widely used by both health professionals and consumers. An advisory committee of the American Pharmaceutical Association developed content guidelines for each chapter and appointed authors and panels of pharmacists, physicians, dentists, podiatrists, and dietitians, who reviewed each chapter. Organized by product categories such as laxatives or personal-care products, each chapter contains the following information: conditions considered for self-medication, etiology of the conditions, signs and symptoms, assessment criteria, primary pharmacologic agents contained in the products, rationale for label warnings, considerations in product selection, and practical patient advice. Perhaps most helpful for quick reference are the product tables that accompany each chapter. Because of its unique organization and unbiased viewpoint, this is a vital reference tool on nonprescription drugs.

The Merck Index: An Encyclopedia of Chemicals, Drugs, and Biologicals. 10th ed. Merck & Co., Inc., P.O. Box 2000, Rahway, NJ 07065, 1983. hardcover $28.50 (0-911910-27-1).

Composed of concise articles on chemical compounds or groups of compounds with references to reviews and original research literature, *The Merck Index* provides information on more than 10,000 chemicals and drugs marketed worldwide. The tenth edition was expanded to include information on chemical biochemistry, pharmacology, toxicology, and metabolism. New environmental and agricultural information has also been added. Entries include physical data such as molecular weight and formula, structure, toxicity data, patent information, biological and pharmacological information, plus over 100 pages of chemical tables. Entries are listed by number with a variety of indexes: a formula index, a cross-index of names (generic, chemical, trade, experimental, and drug codes), and a *Chemical Abstracts* name and registry-number index. Updates to this work are available online through BRS.

Physicians' Desk Reference. 43d ed. [available Jan. 1989] Medical Economics Books, 680 Kinderkamack Rd., Oradell, NJ 07649, 1989. annual. hardcover $41.95 (0-87489-700-9).

This annual handbook of prescription drugs is intended primarily for physicians but is well known by the general public. The *PDR* is composed of drug descriptions provided by drug manufacturers, including color photographs of capsules and tablets for product identification. Over 2,500 pharmaceuticals are described as to indications and usage, dosage, administration, description, clinical pharmacology, supply, warnings, contraindications, adverse reactions, overdosage, and precautions. Information is in the same language as the approved labeling included with each product when it is sold to a patient. The *PDR* also has emergency telephone numbers for drug manufacturers and poison control centers. Indexes provide access by product name, product category, and generic and chemical name. Because the *PDR* is intended for physicians, it uses technical terminology and emphasizes information often irrelevant to the general public. Adverse reactions are often listed without an indication of the likely frequency or severity of the reactions, a point of confusion among the public. Because of its name recognition and color photographs, most libraries will still want a copy for the reference collection.

Physicians' Desk Reference for Nonprescription Drugs. 9th ed. Medical Economics Books, 1988. hardcover $23.95 (0-87489-846-3).

Like the product information for prescription drugs, entries include active ingredients, indications, actions, warnings, drug interaction, precautions, symptoms and treatment of overdosage, and dosage and administration. Again all information is provided by the drug manufacturer. Entries are arranged by manufacturer with multiple indexes by active ingredients, product category, and product name. An appendix of educational materials is also included. This is a more current complement to the *Handbook of Nonprescription Drugs*.

USP DI: United States Pharmacopeia Dispensing Information. 2v. 8th ed. United States Pharmacopeial Convention, P.O. Box 2248, Rockville, MD 20852, 1988. hardcover $115 (0-913595-24-1).

Prepared by the organization that sets the official standards of strength, purity, packaging, and labeling for medical products, this series provides information on the correct use of medicine. Volume 1, *Drug Information for the Health Care Professional*, includes chemistry, pharmacology, precautions, side effects, patient guidelines, and dosage information. Volume 2, *Advice for the Patient*, corresponds directly to the entries in the professional sections, supplements the patient consultation guidelines, and features information in lay language and larger type. Both volumes have bimonthly updates. The series has a variety of useful appendixes, including a drug product-identification directory with illustrations of tablets and capsules, pregnancy and breastfeeding precautions, and a new section on veterinary medicines. Drug entries are listed by official or other established generic names. Indexes include official name, category of use, brand names, nonproprietary names, and indications. While the *Advice for the Patient* volume is available from Consumer Reports Books as *United States Pharmacopeia Drug Information for the Consumer* [*RBB* S 15 87], many libraries will want the more complete *USP DI*, which serves both health-professional and consumer interests and is updated more frequently.

MANUALS AND HANDBOOKS

American Cancer Society Cancer Book: Prevention, Detection, Diagnosis, Treatment, Rehabilitation, Cure. 1st ed. Ed. by Arthur I. Holleb and others. Doubleday, 1986. hardcover $24.95 (0-385-17847-6). [BKL Je 1 86]

In this book, the American Cancer Society hopes "readers will find the knowledge and encouragement to help them cope with cancer and assume an active role in protecting themselves and loved ones against the disease." Written by leading cancer specialists, each chapter is devoted to a specific aspect of cancer. Included is advice about specific forms of cancer, recent medical advances, methods of prevention, and suggestions for living with the disease.

The American Medical Association Family Medical Guide. Rev. ed. Random House, 1987. hardcover $29.95 (0-394-55582-1). [RBB Ja 1 84]

Part of the AMA Home Health Library, this handbook was produced to promote preventive care in the general public. Self-diagnosis charts help the reader decide whether an ache or pain is simply a temporary annoyance or something more serious that requires prompt medical attention. The book is organized in four parts: "The Healthy Body" emphasizes good health habits and physical fitness; "Symptoms and Self-Diagnosis" provides charts by sex and age to help readers assess their individual condition; "Diseases and Other Disorders" has chapters on specific areas like eye disorders and behavioral and emotional problems; and "Caring for the Sick" provides suggestions on how to choose a family physician, information about hospital services, and care for the sick at home. There are subject and drug indexes.

Columbia University College of Physicians and Surgeons Complete Home Medical Guide. 1st ed. Crown, 1985. hardcover $39.95 (0-517-55842-4).

Organized in eight sections, this guide by Columbia University physicians covers important health basics like what to do until the doctor comes, how the body works, maintaining personal health, disease treatment, and drug usage. There are additional sections on poison control centers and keeping medical records, as well as an atlas of the major organ systems.

Control of Communicable Diseases in Man: An Official Report of the American Public Health Association. 14th ed. American Public Health Association, 1015 15th St. NW, Washington, DC 20005, 1985. paper $9 (0-87553-130-X).

Aimed at health professionals, this handbook prepares them to recognize a specific disease, manage patients, and ensure the disease does not spread and also describes preventive measures, epidemic measures, disaster implications, and international reporting measures. Its global coverage makes it a good source for rare diseases as well as current information on inactive diseases like smallpox. Individual entries include the description of the disease and infectious agent, occurrence, reservoir, transmission, incubation period, communicability, susceptibility, and resistance. Diseases are listed alphabetically with additional access through a detailed subject index. A glossary defines concepts like *endemic*, *host*, and *isolation*.

Current Medical Diagnosis and Treatment, 1988. Ed. by Steven A. Schroeder and others. Appleton & Lange, 1988. hardcover $32.50 (0-8385-1344-1).

This medical handbook is "designed to function as the complete physician's single most useful source of information about adult medicine." It covers over 1,000 diseases and disorders and all aspects of internal medicine. Developed by organ system, the first three chapters cover patient care; chapters 4–19 describe diseases and their treatment; chapter 20 is on nutrition; chapters 21–28 cover infectious diseases and antimicrobial therapy; and the final chapters (29–33) cover special topics like genetics and immunologic disorders. Individual disease entries follow the patient-care process, covering diagnosis, clinical findings, complications, treatment, prognosis, and bibliography. Sections on normal values, CPR, and emergency treatment of airway obstruction append the volume. While the intended audience is the health professional, many people find *CMDT*'s format and writing style helpful. Similiar handbooks useful in general library collections are *Current Pediatric Diagnosis and Treatment*, *Current Surgical Diagnosis and Treatment*, *Current Obstetric and Gynecologic Diagnosis and Treatment*.

Diagnostic and Statistical Manual of Mental Disorders DSM-III-R. 3d ed. American Psychiatric Press, 1987. hardcover $39.95 (0-89042-018-1); paper $29.95 (0-89042-019-X).

DSM-III-R describes mental disorders and defines a common language, diagnostic criteria, and classification of mental disorders for use in the U.S. Entries describe symptoms, associated features, age at onset, familial pattern, course, prevalence, sex ratio, and predisposing factors. The content is written and reviewed by committees of mental health professionals. It is organized by major categories like sleep disorders, schizophrenia, and adjustment disorders. An index references disorder names, symptoms (dry mouth or irritable mood), and diagnosis (identity disorder or pyromania). While designed for the mental health professional, entries are more descriptive and clinical than most medical or psychiatric dictionaries.

Handbook of Poisoning: Prevention, Diagnosis & Treatment. 12th ed. By Robert H. Dreisbach and William O. Robertson. Appleton & Lange, 1987. $16.50 paper (0-8385-3643-3).

This handbook covers a broad spectrum of health hazards found in agriculture, industry, medicine, the home, and the plant and animal kingdoms. Special sections include a checklist of household poisons and first-aid measures for poisoning. The index provides access by brand name for insecticides and medicines.

Health Information for International Travel. By Health and Human Services Dept., Centers for Disease Control. Govt. Print. Off., 1987. paper $4.75 (Stock #017-023-00177-9).

This annual publication provides up-to-date and comprehensive information on immunization requirements for international travel. Indexes provide access by subject and country.

The Patient's Guide to Medical Tests. 3d ed. By Cathey Pinckney and Edward R. Pinckney. Facts On File, 1986. hardcover $21.95 (0-8160-1292-X); paper $12.95 (0-8160-1593-7). [RBB F 1 87]

This dictionary of diagnostic tests informs readers about test procedures, helps them identify appropriate questions regarding proposed medical tests, and encourages patients to refuse unnecessary testing. The 1,063 tests are described with an increased emphasis on risk factors and test accuracy and significance since the 1982 edition. Written by a librarian and a physician, entries describe how tests function, when they should be performed, normal and abnormal values, discomfort, cost, where they are performed, and accuracy and significance.

Professional Guide to Diseases. 2d ed. Springhouse Corp., 1987. hardcover $26.95 (0-87434-035-7).

Each entry for the 600 diseases included reviews normal functions, defines the disease (often including incidence and prognosis), and gives a brief summary of causes and pathophysiology, signs and symptoms, diagnosis (summarizing clinical findings and medical tests), and treatment. The first six chapters deal with disorders that affect the entire body such as genetic abnormalities and trauma; the remaining 15 chapters describe conditions that affect a specific body system, such as respiratory or neurologic disorders. Charts, anatomical drawings, and other illustrations amplify the text.

Surgery on File. By the Diagram Group. Facts On File, 1988–89. loose-leaf.

This new loose-leaf series provides patient information on important medical and surgical procedures. Each procedure has a two- to four-page illustrated entry that explains the procedure and why it is performed. Like other "On File" titles, pages can be easily removed and photocopied. Currently available are *General Surgery* (0-8160-1774-3, $75) and *Obstetrics and Gynecology* (0-8160-1768-9, $75). Forthcoming titles include *Pediatrics*; *Orthopedics and Trauma Surgery*; and *Eye, Ear, Nose, and Throat Surgery*.

STATISTICS

Cancer Facts and Figures. American Cancer Society, 1988. single copy free from local ACS unit.

Based upon data gathered by the National Cancer Institute and the National Center for Health Statistics, this booklet reflects current trends in cancer incidence, mortality, and survival rates. Statistics are presented by major site, such as lung cancer, as well as by age and race.

Health, United States, 1987. By Health and Human Services Dept., Public Health Service. Govt. Print. Off., 1988. paper $13 (Stock #017-022-01032-1).

This is the twelfth annual report on the health status of the U.S. The report is divided into two parts: the first shows health status trends such as the probability of surviving to age 65 and the incidence of suicide, and the second includes 119 tables on health status and determinants, utilization of health resources, and health-care resources and expenditures. Data in the tables cover seven years. Access to the statistics is by a guide to the tables that serves as an index to the data and enables users to find statistics that cross-classify concepts such as birth rates and race.

MEDICAL EDUCATION

AAMC Curriculum Directory. Association of American Medical Colleges, 1 Dupont Cir. NW, Ste. 200, Washington, DC 20036. annual. paper $12.50. [*RBB* F 1 87]

AAMC Directory of American Medical Education. Association of American Medical Colleges. annual. paper $12.50. [*RBB* F 1 87]

Medical School Admission Requirements: United States and Canada. Association of American Medical Colleges. annual. paper $12.50. [*RBB* F 1 87]

These volumes provide information for persons interested in medical education. The first describes the curriculum of the individual schools, the second lists primary educators, administrators, and facilities of medical schools, and the third explores the nature of medical education, the process of applying to medical school, and the individual requirements for medical schools. All volumes are arranged geographically.

Admission Requirements of U.S. and Canadian Dental Schools. American Association of Dental Schools, 1625 Massachusetts Ave. NW, Washington, DC 20036. annual. paper $20. [*RBB* F 1 87]

More than a listing of admission requirements, this volume is a guide to obtaining a dental education. It includes basic information on dentistry as a career and how to plan for a dental education, plus descriptions of the various dental programs. Like most directories in this section, it is arranged by state.

Allied Health Education Directory. 16th ed. Ed. by William R. Burrows and Hannah L. Hedrick. American Medical Association, 1988. paper $27.95 (0-89970-312-7; ISSN 0194-3766). [*RBB* N 15 88]

A directory of programs accredited by the AMA Committee on Allied Health Education and Accreditation, describing occupations, employment characteristics, education programs, and contacts for more information. The descriptive section is followed by an alphabetical listing of accredited programs by state and city. Information on programs includes address, program director, medical director, class size, tuition, and date of next accreditation review.

Guide to Programs in Nursing in Four-Year Colleges and Universities: Baccalaureate and Graduate Programs in the United States and Canada. Ed. by Barbara K. Redman and Linda K. Amos. Macmillan, 1987. hardcover $90 (0-02-901490-5). [*RBB* Je 1 87]

Listing 592 institutions that offer B.S. or graduate degrees in nursing, this book gives detailed information on nursing faculty and their research interests, student life, admission requirements, and continuing education programs. In addition to an institution index, there is an index by level of degree.

State Approved Schools of Nursing—R.N. National League for Nursing, 10 Columbus Cir., New York, NY 10019, 1988. annual. paper $18.95.

State Approved Schools of Nursing—L.P.N./L.V.N. National League for Nursing. annual. paper $18.95.

The data in these two comprehensive directories were identified during annual surveys of nursing schools. For each school, the following information is included: address, telephone number, director, accreditation, state board approval, financial support, and administrative control, as well as number of admissions, enrollments, and graduations. Newly opened programs and those that have recently closed are listed at the end of the directory. The R.N. directory includes a separate listing of programs designed exclusively for R.N.s completing baccalaureate degrees.

PHYSICIAN AND MEDICAL FACILITY EVALUATIONS

The Best Hospitals in America. 1st ed. By Linda Sunshine and John W. Wright. Holt, 1987. hardcover $22.95 (0-8050-0583-8). [BKL N 15 87]

According to the author, this is the "first comprehensive guide to the services offered at the most prestigious medical institutions in the nation." Its purpose is to provide the background patients and their families need to choose a hospital. The book is based upon recommendations of physicians and supported by information from government sources, professional and popular publications, and interviews with more than 150 hospitals. Entries include a summary emphasizing the services the facility is most well known for; a comprehensive list of specialties; a statistical profile including data on the number of beds, average patient stay, and emergency room visits; well-known specialists; admission policy; room charges; and average cost per patient stay. Indexes include names of medical professionals and subjects.

The Best in Medicine: Where to Get the Finest Health Care for You and Your Family. By Herbert J. Dietrich and Virginia H. Biddle. Harmony Books, 1986. paper $12.95 (0-517-55966-8).

The authors state their purpose, "based on our own observations and reports of knowledgeable sources, is to provide a guide to centers of treatment for the patient who is seeking the best possible care that can be given to his specific ailment." They list medical centers selected by doctors, medical professors, hospital administrators, and scientific researchers based on a questionnaire sent to 10 representatives in each of 25 specialty categories. Each person was asked to list for his or her own specialty 10 hospitals of outstanding excellence and three areas of specific expertise within that specialty for each hospital chosen. The book is organized by subjects like transplants, cancer, or pediatrics. Entries include a general overview of the specialty and a geographic listing of recommended medical centers.

Consumers' Guide to Hospitals. Consumers Checkbook, 806 15th St. NW, Ste. 925, Washington, DC 20005, 1988. paper $10.

Advertised as "a starting point for anyone needing to select a hospital for medical care," this directory lists nearly 6,000 acute-care hospitals and gives key factors affecting quality such as size, nature of hospital ownership, advanced teaching programs for doctors, and university affiliation. Death-rate information drawn from a federal government study of Medicare patients is also included. Introductory chapters advise consumers on how to interact with their doctors in the choice of a hospital, how to get the best-quality care a hospital has to offer, and how to keep down the costs of hospital care.

Health Care U.S.A. 1st ed. By Jean Carper. Prentice-Hall Press, 1987. hardcover $35 (0-13-609686-7); paper $19.95 (0-13-609694-8). [*RBB* O 15 87]

This directory is a list of medical centers, clinics, support groups, publications, and individual physicians specializing in areas such as AIDS, cystic fibrosis, hemophilia, lung diseases, and sickle cell anemia. Each subject area has the following information: cause, symptoms, diagnosis, and treatment; where to find treatment; some leading specialists and treatment centers; and research, organizations, books, and free materials. According to the author, this book's "list of specialists was not arbitrarily compiled by the author or by a small select group of physicians or other experts. The lists of centers, physicians and other health care professionals included in each chapter came from established respected medical sources such as physicians' professional associations, medical accreditation bodies, voluntary health associations and government agencies."

INDEXES

Consumer Health and Nutrition Index. Ed. by Alan Rees. Oryx, 1985– quarterly. paper $79.50/yr. (ISSN 0883-1963). [*RBB* Mr 15 86]

This subject index to periodical literature provides "access to top articles in health and general magazines and newsletters that are written for the layperson...[It is] designed to help consumers and librarians locate information on subjects such as nutrition, particular diseases, drugs, exercise, and other areas of concern." Periodicals indexed here are affordable to libraries, address practical health-care concerns, and allow for a number of orientations and viewpoints. They have been selected with special effort to provide coverage of the disabled, women's health, vegetarianism, alternative health care, and natural health products. The 80 periodicals include newsletters from medical centers, research-based publications like *Nutrition Today*, publications of national health organizations, and alternative journals like *Prevention*. General-interest magazines like *Good Housekeeping* are also selectively indexed. Citations are enhanced with short annotations. A separate section contains book and audiovisual reviews. Subject headings are based upon the National Library of Medicine's Medical Subject Headings, altered and amplified to meet the needs of lay users.

Cumulative Index to Nursing and Allied Health Literature. Glendale Adventist Medical Center, P.O. Box 871, Glendale, CA 91209, 1961– .bimonthly with hardcover annual cumulation. $180/yr. (ISSN 0146-5554).

CINAHL is a "comprehensive and authoritative index to current periodical literature for nurses, allied health professionals, and others interested in health care issues." Approximately 300 nursing, allied-health, and health-related journals are indexed for inclusion. Also included are pertinent articles from 2,600 biomedical journals from *Index Medicus* as well as relevant material from popular journals. Entries include supplementary phrases when the title is not definitive, descriptors like *care study* or *research*, and an indication of bibliographic references. A thesaurus similiar to the MESH vocabulary but enhanced to better reflect nursing and allied-health literature is used. *CINAHL* is available on both DIALOG and BRS. Abstracts are available for approximately 40 core nursing journals since 1986 in the online database.

Bobbi Walters, a resident of New Orleans, was until this fall a reference librarian at the Thousand Oaks Public Library in Thousand Oaks, California. She has also been a reference librarian at the University of California–Los Angeles Biomedical Library and an intern at the Southern Illinois University School of Medicine Library. She was president of the ALA Junior Members Round Table in 1986–87 and has been a member of the *RBB* Editorial Board since 1987.

1988 ANNUAL ENCYCLOPEDIA UPDATE

This fifth annual encyclopedia summary updates last year's article, which appeared in the November 1, 1987, issue of BOOKLIST/*Reference Books Bulletin*. (Last year's reviews are also available, along with an introductory essay, in the pamphlet *Purchasing an Encyclopedia: 12 Points to Consider*, which can be ordered from ALA Publishing Services for $4.95.) This "update" analyzes the revision done in the 1988 editions of the 10 continuously revised encyclopedias published in the U.S. (A new set, *Children's Britannica*, will be reviewed in a forthcoming issue of *RBB*.) The Board looked particularly for changes in purpose, arrangement, content, general quality, and currentness. If a more extensive review of the encyclopedia has been published in *RBB* within the last several years, the date of that review follows the imprint. For the convenience of our readers, a quantitative statistical summary appears in this article.

Continuous revision is a system by which an encyclopedia publisher revises a certain amount of the set each year, rather than issuing new editions periodically. (*The New Encyclopaedia Britannica* is the only one of these sets that has numbered editions, though it too is continuously revised.) Continuous revision is unique to U.S. encyclopedia publishing; European encyclopedias, for instance, are still issued periodically in new editions. On the average, changes are made on about 10 to 20 percent of the pages in a U.S. set every year, though some sets also undertake less frequent major revisions where as many as 25 to 70 percent of all pages will have some revision. Each year, articles on topics never covered before in a separate entry are added to an encyclopedia ("new articles"), some articles from the previous year's set are replaced with totally new articles on the same subject, often by a new author ("rewritten articles"), and many articles are revised. Revision can range from the addition of a death date in a biography to the addition of several paragraphs on the latest political developments in an article on a country to even more substantial changes.

The continuous revision program has its strengths and weaknesses. Major changes can be made each year on a small part of a set and minor changes can be made on a lot of articles, but normally economics dictate that not everything can be updated in one year. Adding or lengthening an article generally means that an equal amount of text must be cut, ideally from the same page to keep recomposition costs as low as possible. It is easy to insert brief facts, but space constraints

Encyclopedia Summary Chart 1988

Encyclopedia	Approx. No. of Entries; Excl. Cross-References	No. of Pages	Approx. No. of Illus.	Consumer Price	School and Library Price 1988	School and Library Price 1989
Academic American Encyclopedia 21v.	28,700	9,776	16,730	$855 + shipping & handling	$600 + shipping & handling	$660 + shipping & handling
Collier's Encyclopedia 24v.	25,000	19,750	17,600	$1,399.50; $1,699.50 with Collier's Home Educational Program	$849 + $20 shipping & handling	$899 + $20 shipping & handling
Compton's Encyclopedia and Fact-Index 26v.	4,900 + 34,000 Fact-Index entries	10,450	22,500	$699; $949 with deluxe binding; + shipping	$539; $510 for two or more sets; + shipping	Same as 1988
The Encyclopedia Americana 30v.	52,000	26,965	22,732	$1,255 + shipping & handling	$880 + shipping & handling	$995 + shipping & handling
Funk & Wagnalls New Encyclopedia 29v.	25,000	13,024	9,156	$135.81 during Fall 1988–Spring 1989	$140	Same as 1988
Merit Students Encyclopedia 20v.	21,000	12,300	20,000	$1,399.50; $1,699.50 with Merit Students Home Educational Program	$559 + $16 shipping & handling	$579 + $16 shipping & handling
The New Book of Knowledge 21v.	4,352 + 4,650 Dictionary Index entries	10,556	22,700	$815 + shipping & handling	$549.50 + shipping & handling	$625
The New Encyclopaedia Britannica 32v.	64,950 in *Micropaedia*, 680 in *Macropaedia*	32,135	22,948	$1,399	$1,069 + shipping & handling	Same as 1988
New Standard Encyclopedia 17v.	17,351	10,164	12,000	$699.50	$499.50 + $20 shipping & handling	Same as 1988
The World Book Encyclopedia 22v.	18,000	14,048	29,000	$549–$799 (depending on choice of binding)	$549 + shipping & handling	Same as 1988

sometimes hamper the addition of material that would interpret these facts, and therefore some entries lack a context in which the reader can judge their significance. The editorial process for many encyclopedias today is computerized, making it even easier to update entries. However, page layout is still expensive to change, so there continue to be budgetary constraints on the addition of new articles and the lengthening of existing ones. The result is an inevitable unevenness in revision that is more pronounced in some sets than in others.

American libraries are fortunate to have so many encyclopedias to choose among—especially since libraries make up less than 10 percent of the market for general encyclopedias—because these sets have different strengths and in many ways complement each other.

Academic American Encyclopedia. 21v. Bernard S. Cayne, editorial director; K. Anne Ranson, editor in chief. Grolier Inc., Sherman Turnpike, Danbury, CT 06816, 1988. (last full review in *RSBR*, July 1, 1981)

Academic American Encyclopedia (*AAE*) is the most recently developed encyclopedia reviewed here, having first appeared in 1980. *AAE* presents, in specific entries, a broad spectrum of up-to-date information to meet the needs of adults and students from high school through college and presents the information accurately, objectively, and concisely. It is published by Grolier Incorporated, the largest U.S.-based publisher of encyclopedias worldwide, publishers of *The New Book of Knowledge* and *Encyclopedia Americana*. Grolier also markets a consumer edition of this set under the name *Lexicon Universal Encyclopedia*. The binding of the consumer edition is much less sturdy and is not acceptable for use in schools or libraries.

Because of its relatively recent creation date and the constant and thorough revision process, *AAE* continues to be one of the most up-to-date encyclopedias published. Its articles concentrate on providing short, factual information rather than lengthy analytical material: it has the smallest number of pages of any of the encyclopedias reviewed here, but one of the largest number of entries—ranking behind only *The New Encyclopaedia Britannica* and the *Encyclopedia Americana*. On the average, each page contains three articles. The short-entry format is useful when searching for basic factual information like a statistic or brief biography, but it is not as helpful when comprehensive background material is needed, for example, information on a country or historical event. As the name *Academic American* implies, the editors attempt to reflect the current curricula of American schools and colleges. As new developments in educational practices and interests occur, the set is updated to reflect those developments. Over one-fourth of all of the pages in the 1988 edition have had some revision; 98 new subjects are included, 213 articles have been completely rewritten, and 3,007 articles have received minor changes. This is twice the number of pages revised last year.

This year, the editors have concentrated on updating articles on medicine, space exploration, sound recording and reproduction, and music. Each of these areas has been updated to include recent advances in technology and add material on the contributions of other nations and cultures to the field. Other new and revised articles cover a wide range of topics, including *Gulf War*, *Fantasy (Literature)*, *Homelessness*, *Lyme Disease*, *Superconductivity*, *Card Games*, and the nations of Africa. *AAE* is the only one of the sets reviewed in this issue to have entries on surrogate motherhood and desktop publishing. Brief biographies remain one of the strengths of *AAE*, comprising over 35 percent of the total number of entries. New biographies for 1988 include Alan Greenspan, Diana Ross, Kiri Te Kanewa, Jonas Savimbi, Martin Scorsese, and Ted Turner, most of whom are not represented in any other encyclopedia. Like all biographies in *AAE*, these entries provide a one- or two-paragraph description of the person's life and impact on society. In the revised articles, most of the changes involve information of a statistical nature, such as population, economic indicators, or election results. Several late-breaking news events were also incorporated into the text of some entries, including the stock market crash, the Tamil-Sinhalese conflict in Sri Lanka, and the signing of the arms control treaty. Seventy-five percent of *AAE*'s entries are signed, and a list of contributors with their credentials is given at the beginning of volume 1.

AAE continues to try to remain free of social and political biases. Its recent heritage means that it is not burdened with outdated language incorporating an ethnic or gender bias, and new articles are written to present the facts without taking sides on the issues. Articles on potentially controversial topics, such as *Gulf War*, *Religious Broadcasting*, *AIDS*, and *Pit Bull*, present information describing all aspects of the subject without editorializing.

One of the areas in which *AAE* continues to excel is in the quality and quantity of its illustrations. The 1988 edition contains over 16,700 illustrations, occupying approximately one-third of the total page space of the encyclopedia. This is an increase of over 100 from the 1987 edition. Approximately three-quarters of all illustrations are in color. Because this set has a shorter history than the others reviewed, it does not have a legacy of outdated photographs and illustrations. The index of the work has increased slightly in size to accommodate the new entries and uses the same format as in past years, providing both detailed and broad subject access to the set. It includes access points not only to the encyclopedia entries but to all illustrations, maps, and bibliographies.

AAE is the only encyclopedia available in multiple electronic formats as well as in a printed version. The entire text of this encyclopedia may be accessed online through commercial vendors, on laser videodisc, or on CD-ROM. In each case, the user may search any relevant portions of the text with standard Boolean search techniques. The illustrations are not available in the current electronic formats, but the publisher is investigating additional technologies as they become available. An experimental version combining text, video, and audio information on compact disc–interactive is under development.

Academic American Encyclopedia remains one of the most up-to-date and attractive encyclopedias. With its concentration on breadth of coverage rather than depth of analysis, it serves a different purpose than the other adult encyclopedias. As long as Grolier maintains its aggressive revision and updating programs, it will remain one of the premier English-language encyclopedias for high school and college students as well as adults.

Collier's Encyclopedia: With Bibliography and Index. 24v. William D. Halsey, editorial director; Bernard Johnston, editor in chief. Macmillan Educational Co., 866 Third Ave., New York, NY 10022, 1988. (last full review in *RBB*, September 1, 1983)

Collier's Encyclopedia traces its antecedents back to a one-volume 1882 compendium. The current 24-volume format was first published between 1949 and 1951. Now published by Macmillan, *Collier's* has established a reputation as a scholarly set for adult readers and for students at the high school and college levels. Over the years it has maintained a high level of accuracy and objectivity in a readable, well-designed format. Contributors are recognized authorities in their fields, and nearly all articles are signed. Approximately 5,000 advisers and contributors, as well as editors, are listed at the front of volume 1, and brief credentials are given for each. There are 53 new contributors to this edition.

The 1988 edition of *Collier's* does not represent a change in editorial policy or physical appearance. Although there are numerous short articles, broad subject coverage is favored, for example, the new entries for *Drama* and *Conservation of Wildlife*. Typically encyclopedias append bibliographies to long articles; however, *Collier's* has a separate 200-page bibliography in volume 24. This is in a classified arrangement, and each of its 11,500 entries is indexed by subject in the set's index, found in the same volume. In recent years *Collier's* also began adding bibliographies to the conclusion of major new articles; however, this year the trend seems to have abated, for none of the new entries have bibliographies and, of the rewritten articles, only *Dreams* and *Meteorology and Climatology* have had them added. It can be argued that a separate bibliography can be an effective guide to related reading, but many readers will be unaware of its location.

Illustrations account for 20 percent of *Collier's* space, and 10 percent of these are in color. It is noteworthy that in this edition the number of new illustrations (176) has approximately doubled from that added in the 1985 and 1986 sets, with a significant increase in four-color reproductions. The rewritten and expanded article *Museums* has 21 new illustrations, and *Morocco* has been reillustrated with 12 new photographs. The use of opaque paper prevents bleeding from the reverse side, enabling illustrations to be placed within the text or immediately adjacent to it. Maps are also placed with relevant articles, rather than in separate sections. There are numerous uses of color transparency overlays, e.g., in the articles on protective coloration in nature and the Acropolis.

A distinctive feature of *Collier's* has been the comprehensiveness of its index (400,000 entries), which provides access to articles as well as to the bibliography, illustrations, and geographic information on maps; 1,936 pages of revisions in this edition necessitated over 16,000 line changes in the index. *Collier's* also continues its exemplary standards for binding, typography, and page makeup. The set is inviting to read and is physically durable.

There are 39 new articles in *Collier's* 1988 edition, down from 54 to 68 articles in the previous three years. Biographical treatments account for 24 of these entries, with English, American, Israeli, and Canadian literary figures making up over half of this total. Only six of the new articles exceed one column in length, with the longest being *Drama* and *Minerals and Mineralogy* at $8^1/2$ pages each. The *Drama* contributor surveys the genre from ancient times through the work of Sam Shepard; the article has neither illustrations nor a bibliography, but cross-references direct the reader to additional articles, e.g., *Theater*, *Chinese Drama*, and *Melodrama*. *Minerals and Mineralogy*, written by a Harvard mineralogist, replaces two separate articles; it doubles the number of pages and increases illustrations from zero to 13 photographs, drawings, and charts.

Other new articles include *Star Wars* (SDI), *Steroid*, *Insulin*, and *Theory of Communication*. In an unusual juxtaposition, the new article *Artificial Intelligence and Human Intelligence* follows the existing article *Artificial Intelligence* and qualifies the first article's content by a philosophical and semantic approach to the subject. New contributors have rewritten 29 existing articles, down from 52 rewritten articles in the 1987 edition. Building on its strength in area studies, *Collier's* has doubled the length of the *Mozambique* article (14 pages). Coverage now includes the troubles that have beset this country since independence in 1975: periodic droughts, floods, and the continuing war waged on its economy by South Africa. The *Dream* article now addresses post-Freudian theories at greater length, and *Interest* has been expanded from two paragraphs to a three-page historical treatment of the subject from the economics of classical times to those of the present. Significant changes have also been made in the articles *Gynecology* (which now includes sociocultural issues such as abortion, malpractice, artificial insemination, and AIDS); *Middle East*; *Palestine*; *Museum*; and *Cousteau, Jacques-Yves*, among others. In a check for currency, *Collier's* notes the discoveries (*Superconductivity*) of Müller and Bednorz in Zurich during late 1986. Updated information and minor revisions involve 919 articles, a number comparable to that in recent *Collier's* editions. (See the review of Macmillan's *Merit Students Encyclopedia*, below, concerning use of the same text as *Collier's* in some articles, as well as instances of questionable objectivity, e.g., *Reagan, Ronald*.)

Collier's Encyclopedia remains one of the largest and most prestigious adult general encyclopedias. The number of new and rewritten articles in the 1988 edition is down from recent years, but attention to new illustrations, some in color, is a praiseworthy trend. *Collier's* editors present perceptive coverage and analysis, not simply facts, and its style is both readable and literate. It continues to be a sound purchase for high school, college, and public libraries, as well as the home.

Compton's Encyclopedia and Fact-Index. 26v. Dale Good, editor. Compton's Learning Co., div. of Encyclopaedia Britannica, Inc., 310 S. Michigan Ave., Chicago, IL 60604, 1988.

Compton's Encyclopedia was first introduced in 1922 as an encyclopedia designed for young people. From the outset, it maintained an annual program of continuous revision, though not always at a consistent rate. *Compton's* lays claim to being the first "pictured" encyclopedia, and over the years has become known for its "Fact-Index" (containing capsule articles), a set of pertinent questions prefacing each volume, and the fact summaries accompanying articles on major countries and geographic areas. *Compton's* still emphasizes practical and curriculum-related information and focuses on readers from age nine through high school.

This was a year of extensive revision. One-fifth of the articles—mostly in the *H, M, N, 0, S, W, X, Y,* and *Z* volumes—were reworked. This edition contains 471 new articles, 348 extensively revised or rewritten articles, 100 articles with minor revision, and 118 new "Fact-Index" capsules. Also included are 1,226 new illustrations and 60 new maps. Bibliographies were updated only if the accompanying articles were revised.

The "Fact-Index" found at the end of each volume serves as the index to that volume and related articles in other volumes. It also provides short entries for topics not covered in the main text. The last volume is a compilation of all the "Fact-Indexes." The "Fact-Index" pages are now printed on the same paper stock as the text. *Compton's* continues to remove references to the "Fact-Index" from the text; three-fourths of the boxes with references to the "Fact-Index" have been eliminated. The editorial consultants and contributors, with their credentials and the titles of their articles, are listed at the beginning of the first volume. Generally articles are not signed, with the exception of those that are three or more pages long; their contributors' names and credentials are provided in boxes at the beginning of articles.

The special features at the beginning of revised volumes are especially noteworthy. The "Exploring Volume . . ." pages have attractive color photographs with questions to which answers can be found in the text. Each letter begins with an extremely handsome three-fourths page graphic of the letter accompanied by text and a diagram describing its history.

Notable features throughout the revised articles include more current and more color photographs, more up-to-date statistics and bibliographies, the use of nonsexist language, the addition of metric equivalents, and especially good graphics. The revised articles on U.S. and foreign cities contain more recent statistics and new photographs. The articles on U.S. states have the same photographs—mostly historical and tourist attractions—as in earlier editions. Many of these photographs are outdated. The attractive and more informative fact summaries have been extended to two pages. Bibliographies have been updated. The state profiles showing photographs of famous people have been eliminated from revised articles.

Articles on foreign countries vary in the extent of their revision and include new photographs and updated statistics and bibliographies. *Mexico, North America, Norway,* and *Nepal* are among those completely rewritten. *Zimbabwe* is now listed under *Z* with cross-references from *Rhodesia* in the "Fact-Index."

The deaths of famous persons who died in the first eight months of 1987 are noted. A brief definition of *glasnost* appears in the "Fact-Index." Recent advances in superconductors are described briefly in *Electronics,* and there is the "Fact-Index" entry *Superconductivity.* A sampling of new articles shows that *Home Appliances* includes microwave ovens and smoke detectors; *Video Recording* mentions camcorders and videodiscs; and *Microprocessor,* which was only mentioned briefly under *Automation* in earlier editions, has excellent graphics. However, surrogate mothers and the arms limitations talks are not mentioned. Relatively limited information on his presidency is found in the article *Reagan, Ronald.*

Nursing is greatly improved, more concise, and uses nonsexist language. As an example, the caption "She hands the surgeon the instruments he uses" has been changed to "A surgical nurse readies instruments for use by the surgeon." The photographs are current, though none shows a male nurse. The article *Medicine* has been rewritten in nonsexist language, but there is only one new photograph in this article; none of the pictures shows a female doctor. Much of *Shoes* is rewritten with new photographs, graphics, and data recognizing Brazil, Spain, Italy, and Great Britain as surpassing the U.S. in the production of leather shoes. *Newspaper* has new photographs of computer terminals and modern printing processes.

Some topics of high interest to young adults are still almost ignored. AIDS and Alzheimer's disease are defined in the "Fact-Index" but barely mentioned in the text of other articles. Cocaine and marijuana are briefly mentioned in *Drugs* and *Drug Abuse,* but crack is not. Bar mitzvah rates one sentence in *Judaism. Skateboarding* is not found in the index, but is mentioned briefly in *Skates.*

Compton's contains many well-written and well-illustrated articles. Most of its revisions are noteworthy; however, many other articles are still outdated. *Russia* has statistics on education comparing 1927 and 1965 and on economics comparing 1928 and 1962. Although this article has a current picture of Mikhail Gorbachev as general secretary of the Communist party, many of the other photographs do little to portray a balanced image of modern Russia. The first photograph is a blue-tinted night photo of the Kremlin that fails to reveal its beauty. The photograph of a Russian woman bears the caption "This Russian woman from Khar'kov is smiling to show how proud she is of her new teeth. They are made of stainless steel." The photographs accompanying *Vocations* are sex-stereotyped. The population figures given in *Sweden* and *Switzerland* are from 1970.

Public libraries and school libraries that own several encyclopedias may consider *Compton's* as an optional purchase. However, the editors need to continue the intensified revision program of the last several years before *Compton's* will suffice as the only encyclopedia for home or library use.

The Encyclopedia Americana. International ed. 30v. Bernard S. Cayne, editorial director; David T. Holland, editor in chief. Grolier Inc., Sherman Turnpike, Danbury, CT 06816, 1988. (last full review in *RBB,* December 1, 1983)

The first multivolume encyclopedia created and published in the U.S., *The Encyclopedia Americana* has been published for more than 150 years. It took its current 30-volume form in the edition published between 1918 and 1920. It has been published by Grolier since 1945.

Since 1936, *Americana* has followed the industry's practice of continuous revision, each year targeting some subject areas for major revision and others for updating with changes of fact that can easily be incorporated by the substitution or addition of a few lines. The Board has generally given *Americana* good marks for currency, but its record in this regard reflects the strengths and weaknesses of the continuous revision process. For example, in its review of the 1987 edition, the Board pointed out datedness in the set's coverage of African countries. This has been remedied in the 1988 edition with a major revision of the 67-page article *Africa* (with new sections added on critical topics such as environmental concerns and the emergence of modern economic systems) and revision of the articles *South Africa, Angola,* and those on other African nations. New articles have been added on subjects such as *Turing, Alan* and *Strategic Defense Initiative.* The articles *AIDS, Clothing Industry,* and entries for eight geologic periods have been completely rewritten. On the other hand, that part of the article *Colleges and Universities* treating the history of higher education stops in the 1960s. The history of the Court in the article *Supreme Court of the United States* trails off in the mid-1970s. The lengthy article *Sound Recording* makes no mention of compact discs. And the article *Drug Addictions and Abuse* implies that PCP ("angel dust") is the latest trend in drug abuse; it fails to mention crack, a far more common problem today.

Americana abounds with examples of how matters of fact have been successfully updated. For example, it notes the appointment in 1987 of C. William Verity, Jr., as secretary of commerce; it records the death of Alf Landon on October 12, 1987; and it mentions the Reagan administration's desire to sell CONRAIL. However, while it is easy to insert brief facts such as death dates, space constraints often hamper more extensive revision. For example, the article on Gorbachev discusses his economic reform program in just a single sentence—without mentioning either *glasnost* or *perestroika*. The history section of the article on the USSR summarizes the Gorbachev era in two sentences. In short, the editors manage to squeeze the facts in but sometimes lack space to provide a context in which a reader can judge their significance. In reporting facts, *Americana* has consistently earned high marks for accuracy; the 1988 edition continues this tradition of reliability. Balance is preserved in articles on controversial topics.

Americana combines long survey articles with short, specific-entry articles. Some of the latter treat individual literary works, musical compositions, and works of visual art. Many of the long survey articles, such as those on each state and Canadian province, include a brief table of contents to help a reader zero in on a particular aspect of a topic. Forty-one articles, including *Aerodynamics, Ballet, Dog, Insurance,* and *Textile,* include glossaries of technical terms. *Americana* is rather sparing in its use of *see* and *see also* references in its main body. Fortunately, the 353,000-entry index, comprising the whole of the final volume, provides ready, accurate access to its contents by volume and page number. Index entries subdivide broad and complex topics into narrow topics and note illustrations.

The long articles are signed by their authors, a distinguished group of authorities, and many of the 52,000 articles include bibliographies. Bibliographies are very current, most citing items from the mid-1980s. While the general level of revision in the 1988 edition of *Americana* is consistent with previous years, more than 5,000 bibliographies were updated for this edition, a major accomplishment.

Americana has been criticized for dark pictures and sparing use of color. The editors are working on this, in 1988 alone having replaced or added 185 illustrations, half of them in four-color. A number of the remaining black-and-white pictures are too dark, and others, while not misinforming, are clearly tired and out of date—for instance, photographs of the skylines of Philadelphia and Milwaukee.

Along with its thorough coverage of geographic topics of North America and its survey articles on each of the centuries of the common era, *Americana* has justly been renowned for its strong coverage of scientific and technical topics. The 1988 edition sustains these reputations, though the article *Superconductivity* has not been updated with the latest findings. Drawings accompanying many articles on technical topics complement and amplify on the clear text. These articles, typifying the entire set, are written at a level appropriate for adults, high school students, and advanced junior high students.

This year's revision program touched 6,271 of *Americana*'s 52,000 articles and 5,489 of its 26,965 pages. While this compares favorably with the amount of revision done in the other large adult encyclopedias, there are still areas that need attention to keep up with the rapid pace of change. *Americana* remains a reliable and balanced source for adults and young adults seeking information on a wide range of subjects and will continue to be useful in academic, high school, and public libraries.

Funk & Wagnalls New Encyclopedia. 29v. Leon L. Bram, editorial director; Norma H. Dickey, editor in chief. Funk & Wagnalls, Inc., 70 Hilltop Rd., Ramsey NJ 07446, 1988. (last full review in *RBB*, December 15, 1983)

With its spring 1988 revisions, *Funk & Wagnalls New Encyclopedia* keeps up the momentum of its long publishing history. The publisher initiated *Funk & Wagnalls Standard Encyclopedia* in 1912; in 1931 it began a continuous revision program and took its present title; 1983 brought another total revision, and updates continue twice yearly. The set is unique in that it is distributed through supermarkets on "book-a-week" programs. Schools and libraries can acquire it only from the publisher. Designed for use by junior and senior high school students as well as adults, its 25,000 articles are accurate, well illustrated, and easy to read.

The set is in 28 text volumes with volume 29 serving as the index. Lettering on the spine can be confusing, for only five letters designate the beginning and end of a volume, and there are 10 times where the same five letters both end one volume and begin the next; for example, *AMERI* ends volume 1 and begins volume 2. Thirty-six percent of the illustrations are in color. The paper is not glossy, so color illustrations are not spectacular but are pleasing. (One particularly striking exception, however, is the handsome new color illustration for *Glacier*.) Illustrations are sometimes bled to the edges or into the gutters, and margins are narrow. Rebinding could be a problem, but the set is sturdily bound.

Volume 1 has a four-page detailed guide to the use of the encyclopedia, which is then condensed into one page in each of the other volumes. Bibliographies make up the last half of volume 28; while a brief list of topics gives an overview of the classified arrangement, main access is provided by *see* references at the end of over 2,800 articles. There are 1,255 subject reading lists and 322 biography reading lists. Two additional special helps, primarily for students, are the newly revised articles found just before the bibliographies, "How to Use the Library," describing online catalogs and computer-assisted research (as well as more traditional library access and materials), and "How to Write a Term Paper," discussing the use of word processors (as well as index cards).

F&WNE has always had distinguished contributors and editors, and this continues; several new consultants and contributors were noted by the Board. Most articles are signed by initials, and volume 1 includes a list identifying them.

Articles range from brief identifications of a few lines to many pages; the average article is less than two pages. This year there are revisions on almost 3,700 pages representing new articles, illustrations, and bibliographies as well as updates and revisions to existing articles and tables, etc. Over 11,500 pages have now been revised since 1983. As before, room for new articles has been made by condensing articles nearby or by omitting illustrations, bleeding them to the edges, or by cropping them. Of the 43 new articles, most are in the sciences (e.g., *Amyotrophic Lateral Sclerosis, Blackout, Celestial Sphere*), and four of the seven new biographies are for scientists; but other subjects are also represented (e.g., *Information Science, Justice System Improvement Act Agencies*). Chernobyl now has its own entry.

Articles with extensive revisions include *Acquired Immune Deficiency Syndrome* (although the controversial mandatory testing issue is not mentioned), *Anorexia Nervosa, Burn, Cancer, Geochemistry, Malnutrition,* and *Satellite, Artificial. Cocaine* now states the possibility of death from overdose and mentions crack. *Photography* devotes a whole column to the new autofocus cameras and has replaced a black-and-white illustration of a disk camera with a color illustration showing part of the electronic circuit board of an autofocus model. *Deep Sea Exploration* and *Titanic Disaster* both mention the finding of the *Titanic* and its exploration, and the latter notes the controversial salvage expedition and its display in 1987 in Paris. Death dates for 1987 were added for Jean Anouilh, Fred Astaire, Henry Ford II, and Bayard Rustin, among others. Margaret Thatcher's reelection for an unprecedented third term is mentioned both in her biography and under *Woman Suffrage,* while under *Great Britain* the June 1987 election results for the Conservatives are given. *Glasnost* is mentioned in the USSR article but is not listed in the index. Lewis Powell's retirement from the Supreme Court is noted in his biography but not under *Supreme Court*. Over 100 country articles have been updated, giving new foreign exchange rates and economic statistics, population updates, new elections, political events, etc. *South Korea,* for example, mentions student demonstrations and the 1987 constitution and December elections; *Switzerland* tells of the 1986 chemical release into the Rhine River; the two military coups in *Fiji,* following the 1987 election, are noted; so too is the fact that the president of *Burundi* was deposed. *Finland, Syria,* and *Thailand* are three of the country articles updated with many changes.

A major focus of this year's revisions was on science, and in addition to the many new articles, over 150 others in the field received attention. Many tables accompanying articles were also updated, including those for the Indianapolis 500 race (under *Automobile Racing*), brought up to 1987 from 1984, and heavyweight boxing champions brought up to August 1987 from 1983. The *America's Cup* table now includes the 1987 victory of *Stars and Stripes* over *Kookaburra III*. Art and literature sections were also updated, examples being new information on Wole Soyinka in *African Literature* and mention of the Russian publication of *Dr. Zhivago* in *Russian Literature*.

The bibliography section was another major area of revision this year, and, in addition to 16 new biography reading lists, many others were updated extensively. The total number of titles was increased by some 200 in addition to many hundreds of replacements, new editions, and imprints. Also this year, many more references are made from articles to the bibliographies, so the usefulness of this part of the set will be enhanced. Last year's "Update" mentioned that the article on Nietzsche referred to a bibliography that was nonexistent; that has now been rectified.

A few current topics not found in the spring 1988 printing were mention of surrogate motherhood; the nonstop, around-the-world flight of the experimental aircraft *Voyager*; the October 1987 stock market crash; and the insider stock trading scandals. The many changes, additions, new illustrations—many black-and-white pictures replaced by color—do very much, however, to keep the set up-to-date and attractive.

While *Funk & Wagnalls New Encyclopedia* is not as scholarly and comprehensive as the largest encyclopedias, it presents information on people, places, and things in a straightforward manner, covers all fields of knowledge, and remains quite current. The extensive science revisions this year bolster its depth and coverage of these areas. For its intended audience it provides excellent value for the money, and it can be a practical purchase for libraries.

Merit Students Encyclopedia. 20v. Willam D. Halsey, editorial director; Bernard Johnston, editor in chief. Macmillan Educational Co., 866 Third Ave., New York, NY 10022, 1988. (last full review in *RBB*, September 15, 1983)

Merit Students Encyclopedia was first published in 1967 by Crowell-Collier Education Corporation (now Macmillan Educational Company). Intended to support the curricular needs of students and teachers of the fifth grade through high school and based on analysis of curricular material from all U.S. states and Canada, its stated purpose is to focus on "educational and informational demands brought about by the changes that have taken place in our society and our schools since the advent of the space age." *Merit* also addresses the noncurricular interests of children in this age group by including articles on sports, careers, hobbies, and organizations of interest to them, such as *Girl Scouts* and *Junior Achievement, Inc.* While much of the content was written specifically for this set, some articles are shortened, simplified versions of entries from Macmillan's other encyclopedia, *Collier's*.

Merit was developed with the assistance of advisory boards of prominent librarians in the U.S. and nine other countries, nearly all of whom are now either retired or deceased. A board of special editors, mostly academics with distinguished careers in U.S. institutions, assisted in the preparation of articles and bibliographies and reviewed articles in their areas of expertise. Nearly all of *Merit*'s articles are written or reviewed (indicated by an asterisk) by subject specialists who are listed, with their credentials, in the last volume of the set. The 1988 edition of *Merit* includes 46 new contributors, including many from top academic and research institutions. Several of the shorter new articles are unsigned, e.g., *Leonids, Ventilation,* and *Tasmanian Devil.*

The arrangement of *Merit* is unchanged from previous editions. The 20-volume set contains approximately 21,000 entries, 12,300 pages, and 20,000 illustrations. An accurate and thorough 140,000-item index is included in the last volume. The 1988 edition includes 40 new entries, ranging from short, straightforward articles on minerals (*Moonstone, Tanzanite*) and art galleries (*Getty Museum, Walters Art Gallery*) to the lengthiest of the new articles, *Star Wars*, occupying 2½ pages. Poets, including Stevie Smith, Joseph Brodsky, and Seamus Heaney, are well represented among the new subjects. An additional 14 articles have been completely rewritten (*Superconductivity, Persian Gulf War*) and 412 more revised or updated.

The currency of articles on countries and newsmakers is generally good. The article on Mikhail Gorbachev now includes discussion of the concepts of *glasnost* and *perestroika*, and the adoption of new constitutions in Haiti, the Philippines, and South Korea is reported in the articles on those countries. The October 1987 stock market crash is discussed within the articles *Reagan, Ronald* and *United States, History of the.* Deaths noted include those of James Baldwin and Rudolf Hess. A number of articles on less newsworthy topics have been updated to reflect new developments in research. *Dinosaurs* now uses the name *Apatosaurus* rather than the previously accepted *Brontosaurus*, discusses the theory that an asteroid or supernova may have led to the dinosaurs' extinction, and includes two new books in its bibliography. The article *Man* reflects discoveries in Ethiopia in the 1980s of the oldest known australopithecine remains and has been rewritten to reflect current theory that Neanderthal man was of the same species as modern man.

This year, 72 new illustrations have been added to *Merit* and 39 maps revised and updated. The percentage of space occupied by illustrations remains 25 percent. The 32 new four-color illustrations mostly depict artwork (paintings by Fragonard and Giotto), architecture (the Cathedral of Florence), and animals (*Lobster, Sea Anemone*). These reproduce better on the flat paper used in the set than landscape and other outdoor photographs, which tend to appear too pale. Many of the new black-and-white illustrations respond to the problem noted in previous reviews of out-of-date photographs reflecting racial and sexual stereotypes of their period or, at least, presenting outdated styles of hair and dress. New photographs include a female attorney addressing a jury (*Law*) and greater representation of minorities. Unfortunately, many older photographs remain. For example, the five photographs illustrating the article *Future Farmers of America* show a total of 35 boys sporting haircuts from the 1950s and include no girls or minorities. Among the eight photographs illustrating *Sports*, only one (tennis) shows women. Nevertheless, *Merit* is attempting to rectify the bias reflected in these older photographs, and the Board hopes this effort will continue in future editions. *Merit* has deservedly been praised for its drawings and photographs of animals, historical illustrations and reproductions, charts, graphs, and color overlays, and this illustrative material enhances the set's attractiveness to children.

Bibliographies of books for further study accompany approximately 1,000 (5 percent) of the articles. Longer articles (e.g., *Animal, Insect*) frequently contain separate lists of books appropriate for younger readers; shorter bibliographies are annotated to note the appropriateness of books for this age group. Some shorter articles include recommendations for further reading within the text of the article, and others refer the reader to professional associations for more information. Bibliographies revised in this edition contain a high percentage of books published in the 1980s. Some articles, such as *Fashion* and *Home Economics*, contain bibliographies with books no more recent than the 1960s or early 1970s. Surprisingly, considering young people's interest in AIDS, the article *Acquired Immune Deficiency Syndrome (AIDS)* includes no suggestions for further reading.

Merit adheres to a philosophy of treating controversial issues in "an honest and reasonable manner." Articles on topics such as *Sex Education, Vegetarianism,* and *Animal Experimentation* present different viewpoints in a fair, unbiased manner. Two articles concern the Board, however, because of the transparency of their authors' viewpoints. The author of the clearly written article *Star Wars*, a professor of peace studies at the University of Hawaii, concludes that the Star Wars program "can only make the already dangerous arms race even more dangerous. A major task of arms control negotiation should be to halt Star Wars research and development—and especially development—on either side." A more objective statement on the same issue is provided in the article *United States, History of the*, which states that "Reagan announced plans for developing a space-based ballistic missile defense system . . . that many felt would intensify the arms race." Similar problems appear in the 1988 article *Reagan, Ronald*. It states that "Reagan's chief function was as a media figure, 'the great communicator,' " and that the Iran-contra scandal "made a mockery of Reagan's hands-off management style." It also states, "Reagan was often poorly informed about facts, and he delegated much of his work to his staff. He disappeared from Washington for weeks at a time to vacation at his ranch in California. Sometimes he fell asleep at Cabinet meetings." (These remarks also appear in the articles in *Collier's*; the *Star Wars* article is by the same author, the *Reagan* article by a different person.)

The 1988 edition of *Merit Students Encyclopedia* incorporates consistent updating and an effective attempt to enhance the currency of the set by replacing outdated photographs with more recent ones. Despite the exceptions noted, articles are generally authoritative and balanced. *Merit* is a relatively inexpensive and attractive purchase for school and public libraries.

The New Book of Knowledge. 21v. Bernard S. Cayne, editorial director; Jean E. Reynolds, editor in chief. Grolier Inc., Sherman Turnpike, Danbury, CT 06816, 1988. (last full review in *RBB*, March 15, 1988)

In 1966, the first edition of the alphabetically arranged *New Book of Knowledge* (*NBK*) replaced the topically arranged *Book of Knowledge*, which had been published since 1910. *NBK* is organized and designed to be particularly useful in meeting elementary children's curriculum and out-of-school needs for information. While language, style, and format are geared primarily to the needs and interests of elementary school children, the set can be used with younger children under parental guidance, and junior high age readers can benefit from its good basic introduction to a wide variety of subjects. In addition to entries for general knowledge, there are such entries as *Book Reports and Reviews*, samplings from the works of well-known authors, and how-to-do-it articles on sports, hobbies, and crafts.

Prepared by educators and subject specialists, *NBK* has added 67 new authors, consultants, reviewers, and advisers in its 1988 edition. Among these are C. Everett Koop, surgeon general of the U.S. (*Smoking*); Mort Walker, cartoonist (*Cartooning*); Chuck Pezzaro, professional bowler (*Bowling*); and Eugene T. Maleska (*Crossword Puzzles*).

Two kinds of articles appear in *NBK*: articles in the body of the text and brief entries called "Dictionary Index" articles, which appear in the index section of each volume. This edition reflects the publisher's policy of fulfilling the ever-changing and expanding reference needs of today's children. Thirty-five new subjects have been added. Among them are *Cabinet of the United States*; *Caldecott, Randolph*; *Castles*; *Clowns*; *Credit Cards*; *El Paso*; *Nashville*; *Watercolor*; and *Zhao Ziyang*. There are 400 replacement and revised articles. This required the addition of over 870 new graphics. In addition there are 121 new "Dictionary Index" articles.

Updating is evident throughout the set, for example, the 1987 death dates added to many biographies, Anthony Kennedy's appointment as a new Supreme Court justice, the appointment of Ann Dore McLaughlin as secretary of labor, the Reagan-Gorbachev arms-reduction talks, sports fact boxes, and children's book awards. Under *Dinosaurs*, the *Brontosaurus* is now rightly referred to as *Apatosaurus*.

Body, Human remains a long survey article; however, for more detail the following separate articles have been added in 1988: *Circulatory System*, *Nervous System*, and *Skeletal System*. Space exploration now makes it advisable to have separate articles on the planets. *Earth* and *Mars* were separate in the past. This edition sees the addition of *Neptune* and *Uranus*, with plans for separate entries on the remaining planets to follow. The editors indicate that the rudimentary reference skills and decline in general knowledge among many children necessitated some changes from a broad-entry philosophy to one of breaking down major subjects into smaller components. For example, the entire Crustacean group, which used to be discussed in one article, now has four separate articles: *Crustaceans*, *Shrimp*, *Lobster*, and *Crab*.

Coverage in *Diseases* was reexamined, resulting in the complete rewriting of the majority of the 33-page article, with major revision of the remainder. *AIDS* has been moved from the "Dictionary Index" to fuller coverage under *Diseases*. Fuller treatment has been given also to such illnesses as Alzheimer's, Reye's syndrome, bulimia, and anorexia nervosa. The graphics, too, have been updated.

Two new glossaries were added for the 1988 edition: *Computers* (43 entries) and *Cooking* (38 entries). Among the new "quick-reference" materials added are a box naming all 88 star constellations by their Latin and English names; a table of all the administrative divisions of China (giving both the traditional Wade-Giles and the new pinyin spellings); a table of the 13 departments of the executive branch of the U.S. government, including the year that each was created; and a chart showing Canada's provinces and territories (capital, area, population, and the date of joining the confederation).

Because of revisions, new articles, and rearrangement of some areas, the 1988 *C* volume was completely restripped (i.e., the layout totally redone), enlarging it by 16 pages. The opening page of volumes *A* through *M* shows a new format in the article on the letter of the alphabet. A new feature is the panel along the side of each opening page indicating the many ways in which the letter can be represented, e.g., Morse Code, the manual alphabet. Volumes *N* through *Z* will be completed for the 1989 edition of *NBK*. Informative new opening designs have been added for the presidential biographies. These include a color portrait of the president, the presidential signature, and two fact summaries.

"Wonder questions" can be found throughout the set, set off in boxes within the appropriate articles. Among the 1988 contributions are "Why must lobsters be cooked alive?" "Why don't most clowns speak?" "Why are some coins grooved around the edges?"

Of the 121 new "Dictionary Index" articles, 72 are biographical. Examples of new entries are *Babbitt, Bruce*; *Fundamentalism*; *Glasnost*; *Grizimek, Bernard*; *Hart, Gary*; *Infomercial*; *Kwanzaa*; *Pit Bull*; *Sexual Harassment*; *Space Camp*; *Telemarketing*; *UZ*; *Wallyball*; and *Winfrey, Oprah*. The "Dictionary Index" contains brief biographies for all state governors, and the one for Michael Dukakis has been updated to note his candidacy for the 1988 Democratic presidential nomination.

Eleven new maps were added. Significant ones include a street map of Boston, two historical maps for Canada, and a map of the U.S. during the Civil War. Fifty-nine maps were revised. About one-third of the page space in *NBK* is devoted to illustrations. Print throughout is clear and easy to read.

NBK has indexes at the end of each volume and a cumulative index volume. The indexes are easily accessible to children. Index references to illustrations say "picture" instead of the common, but less clear to children, "illus." *See also* references appear at the end of some articles.

Bibliographies appear in a separate paperbound volume entitled *Home and School Reading and Study Guides*. The first section is a selected list of books for children at all reading levels, primary to advanced (kindergarten through ninth grade and up). Selections are sound and up-to-date. There are no references to this supplementary volume in the encyclopedia itself. Directed at parent and teacher, the *Study Guides*, a separate unit, suggest ways in which children can be helped in learning situations at home and with schoolwork. Included here are listings of hobbies and leisure activities, literary selections, projects, and experiments that can be found in *NBK*.

With its 1988 revision, *The New Book of Knowledge* sustains the high standard of reliability, accessibility, currentness, and attractiveness that enable it to effectively meet the reference needs of elementary school children.

The New Encyclopaedia Britannica. 32v. 15th ed. Philip W. Goetz, editor in chief. Encyclopaedia Britannica, Inc., 310 S. Michigan Ave., Chicago, IL 60604, 1988. (last full review in *RBB*, November 15, 1985)

The New Encyclopaedia Britannica combines scholarship and tradition with a contemporary focus to sustain its reputation. Its long history spans 220 years, the first edition having been published in 1768 in Edinburgh as a three volume "dictionary of arts and sciences." Published in America since 1901, *Britannica* is now in its fifteenth edition and is annually revised. The fifteenth edition was first published in 1974, with contributions from over 4,000 scholars from more than 131 countries. Called *Britannica 3*, it had a unique, three-part self-indexing arrangement that was controversial. The major sections (the *Micropaedia* and *Macropaedia*) offered concise entries contrasted with lengthy articles. When, in 1985, a two-volume *Index* was added and significant changes were made in the organization of the set, some of the earlier criticisms were answered, and information in the encyclopedia became much more accessible.

Britannica is structured around a detailed classification scheme contained in the one-volume *Propaedia*. This can be used as a study guide, providing lists of the specific articles and related biographies found in the other volumes of the encyclopedia. The 12-volume *Micropaedia* is a quick-reference resource containing about 66,000 relatively short, unsigned, factual articles. It has more than 15,000 illustrations, usually small but clear, about half of which are in color. The *Macropaedia*, in 17 volumes, provides "knowledge in depth"— comprehensive articles on 580 broad subjects and 100 biographies. Authors of *Macropaedia* articles are identified in the *Propaedia* and were selected because they are authorities in their fields. In addition to its more than 8,000 illustrations (generally larger than those found in the *Micropaedia*), the *Macropaedia* includes 162 color-insert plates. The *Index* provides in-depth access to the rest of the set. The annual *Britannica World Data* is now an important component of *Britannica*. Since 1985 it has been bound with the *Britannica Book of the Year* and given to first-time purchasers of the set. Its blue pages present current "geographic, demographic, economic, and financial data" for 220 countries and dependencies of the world to complement and update information found elsewhere in the encyclopedia. *The New Encyclopaedia Britannica* has a more intricate structure than other encyclopedias, but the sections are linked to one another through abundant cross-references, guiding phrases, and the *Index*.

The improvements that made the restructured 1985 *Britannica* notable are being maintained through a strong revision program. Approximately 20 percent of the text (5,982 pages from every section of the encyclopedia) have been changed for the 1988 printing. Substantial revisions have been made to 102 articles in the *Macropaedia* (26 of which have new texts), and information on countries has been updated. One hundred eighty-six articles have been added to the *Micropaedia*, and revisions have been made to 886 entries. Adjustments have been made in the *Propaedia*, and the *Index* has increased by 47 pages and now has a total of 419,436 entries. New or revised illustrations total 560, a net gain of 36, including new flag plates in the *Micropaedia*.

Macropaedia articles with new texts cover all disciplines. They are current and have up-to-date bibliographies. Subjects range from *Atmosphere* and *Subatomic Particles* to *Dance, The Art of* and *Yiddish Literature*. *Computer Science* has been added to complement the existing article *Computers* in order to reflect developments in that area. A valid criticism that too many articles in *Britannica* had been left unchanged since 1974 continues to be addressed systematically. *Mental Disorders and Their Treatment*, for example, is a clearly written, comprehensive treatment of the subject current enough to include comment on homelessness in relation to deinstitutionalization, as well as the latest advances in drug therapy. Its bibliography features works published within the last five years, as compared with the 1960s for the superseded article. *Viruses* includes information on retroviruses, including the AIDS retrovirus. *Britannica* has a deserved reputation for scholarliness, and this is particularly evident in the bibliographic essays that support articles in the *Macropaedia*. The *Macropaedia* also features detailed biographies of 100 persons selected for inclusion because they profoundly influenced world history. Those for Darwin, Freud, Michelangelo, Picasso, and Rembrandt have been rewritten for the 1988 printing, each by a contemporary scholar.

In the *Micropaedia*, biographies for a fascinating variety of men and women have been added (114) or updated (267). Geography, science, and medicine are also strongly represented among new or revised items. Political and other organizations are the focus of 25 new and many revised entries for such bodies as the American Bar Association, OXFAM, the Greens, and the Communist Party of the Soviet Union.

Britannica does not add bibliographies to *Micropaedia* articles, apart from some biographical entries. Revisions in *Macropaedia* articles usually require changes in the *Micropaedia* (for example, *Anxiety*, *Chlorpromazine*, and *Psychoneurosis* all relate to the new article *Mental Disorders* in the *Macropaedia*). Another reference source in the *Micropaedia* is the 64-page "Sporting Record," a feature not found in other encyclopedias. In one place it provides significant information, statistical tables, and photographs for 38 professional and amateur sports that are international in character or that attract a large national following. For the 1988 printing this section has been thoroughly redesigned and revised, with all new illustrations. (Articles on individual sports can also be found throughout the *Micropaedia*.)

The necessity for looking in more than one place to secure information in *Britannica* can be demonstrated by the *Macropaedia* article *Rembrandt*. It is an excellent text, accompanied by a comprehensive list of works and current annotated bibliography, but it includes only one black-and-white illustration. Using the *Index* it is possible to locate two more plates—part of the color inserts that accompany the *Macropaedia* articles

Painting, The Art of and *Western Painting, The History of*—and one further Rembrandt reproduction with the article *Bistre* in the *Micropaedia*. By comparison, biographies of artists in other encyclopedias may not be as well documented, but their texts are effectively illustrated by generous reproductions found adjacent to the articles.

The *Britannica World Data* annual is a work that can stand alone and compete favorably with other reference sources. It clearly presents for each country an enormous amount of current data, then provides "Comparative National Statistics" by topic in tabular form. However, because of the existence of the annual, only limited statistical information is given in the set itself, and references are made to the annual, with the result that libraries owning *Britannica* will need to have a subscription to the yearbook.

The New Encyclopaedia Britannica is a unique work that continues to improve through a balanced revision program. The concise, colorful articles in the *Micropaedia*, the substantial coverage of major subjects from all areas of knowledge in the *Macropaedia*, and the supporting *Propaedia*, *Index*, and *Britannica World Data* combine to offer an attractive alternative to other major encyclopedias arranged in a more conventional fashion.

New Standard Encyclopedia. 17v. Douglas W. Downey, editor. Standard Educational Corp., 200 W. Monroe, Chicago, IL, 60606, 1988. (last full review in *RBB*, October 1, 1987)

Now in its ninety-third printing, the *New Standard Encyclopedia* first appeared in 1910. Since its inception the set has undergone several name changes and has been expanded from 5 to 17 volumes. Intended for use by readers as young as 9 or 10 years of age for school assignments, and by adults for everyday use, the set gives general information in clear, straightforward language without many details. The unsigned articles are written by the editorial staff and checked for accuracy by authorities in appropriate fields. These authorities are listed in volume 1, and their positions or affiliations indicate that they are knowledgeable in their fields.

New Standard follows a policy of continuous revision with 10 to 30 percent of its pages open for revision every year. In this printing 25 percent of the pages were revised. There are 60 new articles; 22 were extensively revised; 76 were rewritten and 1,172 updated. In addition, 199 bibliographies were updated; 68 maps were revised, one added and one recompiled. New articles include *Acid Rain, Aspartame, Carbon Cycle, Fox Hunting, LSD, Federated States of Micronesia, Numerology, Political Action Committee, Weight Control, Weightlessness*, and *Wind Shear*. Some individuals included for the first time are Woody Allen, Corazon Aquino, A. J. Foyt, Philip Johnson, Dorothea Lange, Louis L'Amour, Rupert Murdoch, and Pinchas Zukerman. Major revisions were done on the articles *Nuclear Energy, Nuclear Physics, Railways, Rome* (the city), *Rome and the Roman Empire, National Parks, Nigeria, World War I, World War II*, and *Washington, D.C.* Death dates of famous people have been added if they occurred before July 1987.

Entries in *New Standard* are specific and result in many articles that give brief treatment, with an average of 1½ entries per page. Articles are long when the subject warrants, however (*Banks and Banking, Black Americans,* and *Petroleum* range from 8 to 17 pages). Instead of an index volume, the set provides self-indexing in which many *see* references are inserted in the main alphabetical sequence of the encyclopedia. *See also* and *for further information see* references are given at the ends of articles. This works well for the brief entries on specific topics, but sometimes information within a long entry is hard to locate. Pronunciation is given for difficult words (a pronunciation guide is at the front of each volume), and foreign place-names are given in both English and the language of the country (*Venice, Venezia*), or in some cases the common name and the formal name (*Syria, Syrian Arab Republic*). Glossaries of terms used in specialized fields, such as architecture and space exploration, are provided.

Photographs, drawings, diagrams, charts, tables, and maps supplement the text. Many of the drawings, such as those of bees, amphibians, fruits, etc., are especially colorful and attractive. The article *Planet* would benefit from the addition of a drawing. Most diagrams are very clear; for instance, the parts of an elevator and the anatomy of a fish. Maps are easy to use; county boundaries are outlined in color on maps of the U.S. states. This edition is printed on a different type of paper, which the editors deem superior for illustrations; colors reproduce well. Bibliographies appended to about 1,000 of the 17,000 entries suggest additional reading and are divided into adult and juvenile titles.

Much of the material in *New Standard* is appropriate for school reports. Articles on U.S. states are especially good and include many photographs, as well as the feature "Interesting Places in . . ." (also given for Canadian provinces). As has been noted in past reviews by the Board, coverage of basic factual information is a strength of this set. Information on how things work (*Gasoline Engine, Piano, Television*) is clearly presented. Articles on U.S. presidents give thorough coverage and include a picture of the president, his signature, and sidebars noting a chronology of his life and information about the the state of the U.S. and the world during his administration. Most articles on animals, flowers, and other nature topics are accompanied by color photographs. Science, agriculture, history, and sports are all well covered, though the article *Superconductivity* is out-of-date. The article *Painting* is well illustrated with works of art and includes a guide to other reproductions of artwork throughout the set. The arts in general are well represented in *New Standard*, with the seven-page article *Dance* and the 11-page article *Theater*, for example.

Up-to-date medical information is given in *AIDS*, but there is no discussion of its epidemic proportions or of the AIDS testing controversy. The article *Cocaine* also includes mention of crack. There is no information on surrogate mothers, the homeless, or the Strategic Defense Initiative. In general, *New Standard* does not address social problems or controversial issues in much detail. Two articles in need of revision and new photographs are *Prison* and *Library*.

For the benefit of prospective tourists, armchair travelers, and students, the treatment of the history, art, and geography of many foreign countries and cities is well done (*Mexico, France, China, Venice*). Recent foreign political developments receive little treatment, however. For instance, there is no comment on present hostilities in Peru or currency devaluation in Mexico. In the article *International Trade* no information is given for the 1980s. Under *Iran* the last date mentioned is 1982. Some country articles, *Nicaragua*, for instance, were found to be current, however. *New Standard*'s continuous revision program for updating information is generally satisfactory.

New Standard has traditionally been a set purchased for use in the home. It has the advantage of clarity and brevity, which should allow students—and less serious readers—to finish reading before they feel overwhelmed by the amount of material provided. *New Standard Encyclopedia* continues to be a reliable source of current, concise treatments of a broad range of topics of interest to North American readers from the middle grades through the adult level. Its emphasis is on factual information, and it presents that information accurately and objectively.

The World Book Encyclopedia. 22v. William H. Nault, publisher; Robert O. Zeleny, editor in chief; A. Richard Harmet, executive editor. World Book, Inc., 510 Merchandise Mart Plaza, Chicago, IL 60654, 1988. (last full review in *RBB*, February 1, 1984)

The World Book Encyclopedia, first published in 1917, appears in 1988 with a new and contemporary look. This traditionally reliable encyclopedia has now undergone its fourth major revision, the first such overhaul in 25 years. While retaining its eight-member advisory board of scholars and specialists, the list of 3,000 contributors has significantly changed. There are 840 new contributors, many of them professors, professionals, reporters, or editors. A similar number of them were dropped, presumably now replaced by more active experts. All articles are signed and the contributors listed, with their articles, in volume 1.

Designed to meet the needs of elementary school, middle school, and high school students, *World Book* also serves well as a general reference source for homes and libraries. It provides roughly 18,000 articles alphabetically arranged in 21 volumes. Volume 22 has an index with over 150,000 entries and more than 200 reading and study guides. Within the main set there are 7,800 cross-references. The articles themselves vary in length and difficulty but frequently include lists of related articles, an outline, study questions, and bibliographies divided by reading level. The physical format changed this year with every page reset in a new typeface (World Book Modern), ragged right margins, and guide words and page numbers together at the top. The result is a more attractive page that is easier to read.

Another major feature of the revision is the dramatic increase in the use of color. Of the 29,000 illustrations (approximately one-third of the space), 24,000 are now in color (compared with 14,000 in 1987). Black-and-white illustrations are now used only when they are more appropriate (e.g., reproductions of black-and-white photographs taken before the advent of color photography). Examples of this changeover to color can be found in the illustrations for *Coati* and *Coaxial Cable*, while updated illustrations include photographs of the *Queen Elizabeth II* after its renovation in 1986 and 1987 (in the article *Ship*) and a fashion designer using computer graphics (in *Clothing*). Sixty-nine countries have new four-color maps, leaving Vatican City the only country without such a map. The new articles in 1988 number more than 70. The trends seem to be articles on Supreme Court cases (*Baker v. Carr, Plessy v. Ferguson, Roe v. Wade*); current events and issues (*Strategic Defense Initiative, Nuclear Winter, Homelessness*); biographies (*Turing, Alan; Wiesel, Elie; Merton, Thomas; Jordan, Michael*); sports (*Luge, Martial Arts*); speculative science (*Antigravity, Extraterrestrial Intelligence*); birds (*Bee-Eater, Manakin, Oilbird*); and monkeys (*Colobus, Langur, Titi*). The article *Nuclear Weapon* is particularly strong, with six pages of information on what nuclear weapons are, how they work, the issues relating to their control, and a bibliography of works written between 1984 and 1986. In addition to the new articles, there are 45 new bibliographies appended to articles, for example, *Marketing, Northwest Territory,* and *Personality*.

Nearly 1,000 entries were completely revised, most by new authors. *Alcoholism* has been expanded to include more information on the types of alcoholism, while *Child Abuse* has added a mention of growing concerns over sexual abuse. Religious topics received attention this year, with revised articles for *Altar, Ecclesiastes, Lazarus, Lucifer, Mark, Methuselah,* and *Polytheism*. The article *God* was refocused from its formerly Christian emphasis to an article including the sections "Cosmic Gods," "Personal Gods," "Gods of Nature," and "Ideas about God." On the geographic front, *Mountain* is now considerably longer, with more illustrations and a revised bibliography, including a 1986 title. Several articles listed as completely revised did not seem much changed (*Classicism, Cosmetics*).

Another 6,500 articles were partially revised. All states and provinces got new, attractive full-color fact spreads, with symbols, information on land and climate, population, government, important dates, economy, and sources of information. There is also a new inset for each, with interesting facts (e.g., *California* includes the tallest known tree in the world, and the highest temperature ever recorded in the

U.S.). The U.S. presidents articles also got a new design for their opening spreads: portrait, preceding and succeeding presidents, vice president, signature, and important events during their administration. The final part of the layout, "The World of . . . ," includes such events as Three Mile Island for Carter, and the publication of *Silent Spring* for Kennedy.

General updating included the long-overdue retitling of *Russia* to *Union of Soviet Socialist Republics* and moving it to the *U* volume. *Cottage Industry* is no longer just a historical article; it now mentions the use of computers at home. Events of 1987 that received coverage include the tanker escorts in the Persian Gulf; Gary Hart's off-again, on-again campaign; and Gorbachev's concepts of *glasnost* and *perestroika*. The October 1987 stock market crash is covered, but earlier insider trading scandals are not. There is no mention of the controversy over the Supreme Court nominations, the various evangelist scandals, or surrogate mothers. The FDA's approval of AZT for AIDS is noted, but not the controversy over AIDS testing. The "Today" section for countries has been updated for some but not all countries. *Egypt* has a new paragraph on Mubarak, *Finland* mentions Kekkonen's death, the *United States* articles include U.S.-Soviet negotiations on intermediate-range nuclear missiles and the Iran-contra affair.

Notable deaths during the previous year are acknowledged—Alf Landon, John Huston, Harold Washington, for instance. Various statistics have been updated since the previous edition. The leading petroleum producers and the 50 leading U.S. manufacturers are 1986 figures, while the crime statistics are now from 1985. *Forest Products*, however, still has statistics from 1976 to 1982.

World Book staff reviewed 600 of the 1,800 bibliographies and revised them as necessary. Five post-1980 titles were added to *Journalism*, and five 1984–86 titles to *Vietnam War*. The resources list for *Laser* seems to have been revised in reverse. The 1987 edition had titles from 1979, 1982, and 1983. The new edition suggests titles from 1972, 1973, and 1979. The reading and study guide on black Americans in the index volume is in need of revision, with the latest given title dating from 1981.

This $7 million revision, called by World Book the "most sweeping and comprehensive revision in over 25 years," updated 71 percent of the text pages as well as changed the type and graphics of the whole set. Thus the changes were more than just cosmetic. *World Book*, always one of the leading general encyclopedias, has strengthened its position even more in the home, school, and library markets. It continues to be authoritative, comprehensive, well organized, and readable, and now the packaging makes it all the more attractive.

REFERENCE TOOLS FOR LITERARY CRITICISM: A SELECTED GUIDE

In the area of literary criticism, librarians are faced with an almost dizzying array of choices to satisfy the requirements of users who need to consult critical material. This review is written for libraries where access to a wide range of original criticism in scholarly books and journals is neither feasible nor even desirable. Its purpose is to sort out those reference tools that serve to introduce students and general readers to literary criticism. The review discusses several kinds of tools: surveys and digests, compilations that reprint criticism, and biobibliographic sources that include critical comment.

SURVEYS AND DIGESTS

Magill Books/Salem Press

Salem Press dominates this category of literary criticism materials with its various sets edited by Frank N. Magill. The original *Masterplots*, published almost 40 years ago and updated through 1976 by the *Survey of Contemporary Literature* (12v., 1977, $350), was a boon for students and a bane to librarians and teachers because it contained little more than plot summaries. Since 1976, however, the original *Masterplots* concept has evolved to provide more in the way of analysis, while retaining its accessible format. First came *Masterplots: Definitive Revised Edition*, which added critical essays to the plot summaries contained in the original set. Then came *Masterplots II*, covering titles not treated in the original set and also eliminating the plot digests. Salem Press also publishes the Critical Survey series, which is arranged by author rather than title. Taken altogether, the different Salem Press/Magill sets provide useful introductions to authors and their works and serve as a gateway to literary appreciation.

Masterplots: Definitive Revised Edition. 12v. Ed. by Frank N. Magill. 1976. $425 (0-89356-025-1). [*RSBR* D 15 77]

This set presents 2,010 plot digests of works from 4000 B.C. to the middle of the twentieth century. They are preceded by ready-reference data on author, type of work, setting, and principal characters and are followed by evaluative essays. The set is augmented by *1300 Critical Evaluations of Selected Novels and Plays* (4v., 1978, $175) and updated by *Magill's Literary Annual* (2v., $65). It has also been repackaged into smaller sets that cover literature by nationality: *Masterplots: Revised Category Edition American Fiction Series* (3v., 1985, $120); *Masterplots: Revised Category Edition British Fiction Series* (3v., 1985, $120); and *Masterplots: Revised Category Edition European Fiction Series* (3v., 1986, $120). Except for minor changes, these three sets reproduce the plot digests and critical essays found in the 12-volume set, so libraries in which one set of *Masterplots* is sufficient can afford to skip the revised-category editions.

MASTERPLOTS II SERIES. The different sets that make up *Masterplots II* augment the original *Masterplots* by presenting works not covered within any other *Masterplots* collection. Coverage ranges from the middle of the nineteenth century to the late 1980s. Major authors, such as Tolstoy and Balzac, are discussed in terms of relatively minor works because their best-known titles are covered in the earlier *Masterplots* set. Added authors reflect the increasing attention paid to the work of women writers, black writers, and contemporary authors from such areas as Latin America. This series retains the familiar *Masterplots* ready-reference summaries but drops the plot digests in favor of longer interpretive essays. The discussions adhere to the same convenient format, covering plot development, characterization, major themes, critical context, and sources for further study. *Masterplots II* follows the lead of the revised-category editions of *Masterplots* by grouping literary works by nationality and also by genre. Salem Press is planning to add a *Masterplots II: Nonfiction Series* and a *Masterplots II: Drama Series* to the series listed here:

Masterplots II: American Fiction Series. 4v. 1986. $300 (0-89356-456-7). [*RBB* O 15 86] Includes authors from Latin America.

Masterplots II: British and Commonwealth Fiction Series. 4v. 1987. $300 (0-89356-468-0). [*RBB* Ja 15 88]

Masterplots II: Short Story Series. 6v. 1986. $400 (0-89356-461-3). [*RBB* S 1 87]

Masterplots II: World Fiction Series. 4v. 1988. $300 (0-89356-473-7).

CRITICAL SURVEY SERIES. The Critical Survey series, which began in 1981, takes the interpretive aspect of *Masterplots II* a step further. Each set is arranged by author rather than title, allowing the contributors to discuss a writer's creative development and examine individual works within the context of an entire career. Like other Magill titles, the Critical Surveys have a standardized format: a list of principal works within the genre, a brief discussion of the writer's contribution to other literary forms, an assessment of major achievements, a biography, an analysis of major works in the genre, a selected list of major publications in other forms, and a short bibliography of secondary sources. The articles, which average about 10 pages, are clearly written for students needing a basic introduction to authors and their work. Each set in the series includes comprehensive indexing and one or more volumes of essays that discuss the literary genre from a historical, national, or thematic perspective. Four supplements, published in 1987, add writers not previously surveyed and also provide updated information on death dates, recent achievements, and literary awards and prizes. Sets within the Critical Survey series complement and augment one another, just as this series is complemented and augmented by *Masterplots* and *Masterplots II*. For instance, for fullest coverage of Charles Dickens, a student would want to consult not only the *Critical Survey of Long Fiction* but also the *Critical Survey of Short Fiction* for an analysis of Dickens' contributions to the short story form. The student might also consult *Masterplots* and *Masterplots II* for a fuller discussion of individual titles. *Bleak House*, a major work, receives scant attention in *Critical Survey of Long Fiction* but is given a two-page treatment in *Masterplots II*. Titles in the series are as follows:

Critical Survey of Drama: English Language Series. 6v. 1985. $350 (0-89356-375-7). [*RBB* My 1 86]

Critical Survey of Drama: Foreign Language Series. 6v. 1986. $350 (0-89356-382-X). [*RBB* Mr 1 87]

Critical Survey of Long Fiction: English Language Series. 8v. 1983. $375 (0-89356-359-5). [*RBB* S 1 84]

Critical Survey of Long Fiction: Foreign Language Series. 5v. 1984. $275 (0-89356-369-2).

Critical Survey of Poetry: English Language Series. 8v. 1982. $375 (0-89356-340-4). [*RBB* N 1 83]

Critical Survey of Poetry: Foreign Language Series. 5v. 1984. $275 (0-89356-350-1). [*RBB* Ap 15 85]

Critical Survey of Short Fiction. 7v. 1981. $330 (0-89356-210-6).

In addition to the Masterplots and Critical Survey series, Salem Press publishes *Survey of Modern Fantasy Literature* (5v., 1983, $275) and *Survey of Science Fiction Literature* (5v., 1979, $250). Both follow the uniform *Masterplots II* format and discuss the genres by title, covering in each case around 500 classic and modern works.

Beacham Publishing

Salem Press' only rival in providing convenient access to plot summaries and explication is Beacham Publishing, which recently released *Beacham's Popular Fiction in America, 1950–1986* (edited by Walton Beacham, 4v., 1986, $249 [*RBB* Je 1 87]) and *Popular World Fiction, 1900–Present* (edited by Walton Beacham and Suzanne Niemeyer, 4v., 1987, $249 [*RBB* My 15 88]). Arranged alphabetically by author, articles in each set cover life and work, publishing history, and critical and popular reception and examine one or more individual titles in terms of social issues, themes, techniques, literary precedents, and adaptations. Beacham's main criteria for including authors are that their work must be best-selling and reflect social concerns. Though many writers are found in both series, Beacham extends the coverage of Magill by providing introductions to such authors as Sidney Sheldon and John Jakes.

Scribner

The Scribner's Writers Series is another survey-type reference series. This series began with *American Writers*, a collection of 156 critical essays, over half of which were originally pamphlets published by the University of Minnesota Press. *British Writers* is a revision and expansion of monographs first published in the British Council series Writers and Their Work. Scribner has added other sets, all based on the *American Writers* concept: collections of essays that provide critical introductions to a writer's life and work, but no biographical sketches or plot summaries. The essays are written by distinguished scholars and are more scholarly than those found in the Magill sets. Titles in the Scribner's Writers Series are as follows:

American Writers. 4v. and supplements 1 (2v.) and 2 (2v.). Ed. by Leonard Unger and A. Walton Litz. 1974–81. $545 (0-684-17322-0). [*RSBR* Jl 15 75]

Ancient Writers: Greece and Rome. 2v. Ed. by T. James Luce. 1982. $140 (0-684-16595-3). [*RSBR* Ag 83]

British Writers. 8v. and supplement. Ed. by Ian Scott-Kilvert. 1979–87. $545 (0-684-18253-X). [*RSBR* Je 15 82]

European Writers. 9v. Ed. by George Stade. 1983–89. various prices per volume. [*RBB* S 15 84] (Four final volumes, covering the twentieth century, plus an index volume are in preparation.)

Science Fiction Writers. Ed. by E. F. Blieler. 1982. $75 (0-684-16740-9). [*RSBR* Ap 15 83]

Supernatural Fiction Writers. 2v. Ed. by E. F. Blieler. 1984. $140 (0-684-17808-7). [*RBB* Ja 1 86]

Writers for Children. Ed. by Jane Bingham. 1987. $90 (0-684-18165-7). [*RBB* Mr 15 88]

A three-volume set, *Latin American Writers* ($225), is to be published in the fall of 1989. In preparation for 1990 publication are *Black American Writers* and *Modern American Women Writers*, each one volume.

COMPILATIONS OF REPRINTS OF CRITICISM

The old Moulton's *Library of Literary Criticism*, published in 1901–05 and reprinted by Peter Smith in 1959, set a standard for another type of literary criticism reference work, one that reprints samples of critical reception from a variety of sources. Such compilations provide a spectrum of opinion absent from the Magill sets and offer a way to gauge changes in an author's reputation over the years. They serve as both encyclopedias of critical comment for students in introductory literature courses and as indexes to literary criticism for students who wish to consult original sources. There are three important reference collections of literary criticism: the Library of Literary Criticism that evolved from the original Moulton's and is now published by Ungar, the Chelsea House Library of Literary Criticism, and Gale's Literary

Criticism series. It is worth noting that there are also several monographic series in which each volume is devoted to collecting the criticism on a single author or work. The G. K. Hall Critical Essays and the Chelsea House Modern Critical Interpretations and Modern Critical Views are such series.

Ungar's Library of Literary Criticism

All titles in this series from Ungar follow a uniform structure, arranging authors alphabetically and providing selected quotations of criticism for each. The critical material is arranged chronologically and is excerpted from letters, books, newspapers, periodicals, and other sources. The brief biographical notes that appeared in the earlier sets are dropped in more recent publications. An abridged and updated version of the original Moulton's was published by Ungar in 1966. This four-volume set adds some authors not found in the original and deletes others. Coverage is from *Beowulf* to 1914. Other titles in the Library of Literary Criticism series are as follows:

The Critical Temper: A Survey of Modern Criticism on English and American Literature from the Beginnings to the Twentieth Century. 3v. and 2 supplements. Ed. by Martin Tucker and others. 1969–89. v.1–3, $180 (0-8044-3303-8); supplement 1, $65 (0-8044-3307-0); supplement 2 [available June 1989], $75 (0-8264-0435-9). [*RSBR* My 1 81]

Updates the original Moulton's by providing excerpts of twentieth-century criticism.

Modern American Literature. 3v. and 2 supplements. Ed. by Dorothy Nyren Curley and others. 1969–85. v.1–3, $225 (0-8044-3046-2); supplement 1, $75 (0-8044-3050-0); supplement 2, $75 (0-8044-3265-1). [*RSBR* Mr 1 77]

Expands the original Moulton's by providing samples of criticism of modern American writers.

Modern British Literature. 3v. and 2 supplements. Ed. by Ruth Z. Temple and Martin Tucker. 1966–85. v.1–3, $225 (0-8044-3275-9); supplement 1, $75 (0-8044-3279-1); supplement 2, $75 (0-8044-3140-X). [*RSBR* Jl 15 66, Jl 1 76]

Expands the original Moulton's by providing samples of criticism of modern British authors.

The Library of Literary Criticism has broadened its scope over the years to include world literature. Additions to the series include compilations on *Modern Commonwealth Literature* (1977, $60), *Modern French Literature* (2v., 1977, $120), *Modern German Literature* (2v., 1972, $130), *Modern Latin American Literature* (2v., 1975, $120), *Modern Romance Literatures* (1967, $60), *Modern Slavic Literatures: Russian Literature* (1972, $60), *Modern Irish Literature* (1988, $95), *Modern Spanish and Portuguese Literatures* (1988, $85), and *Modern Arabic Literature* (1987, $75). All of these compilations follow the standard Moulton's format. Recently, Ungar published the first genre-oriented set in the Library of Literary Criticism series: *Major Modern Dramatists* (edited by Rita Stein and others, $150 [*RBB* O 15 86]). Volume 1, published in 1984, covers American, British, Irish, German, Austrian, and Swiss playwrights. Volume 2, which appeared in 1986, includes playwrights from other European countries. Some of the critical material is available here in English for the first time. Most of the authors are also covered in the language-oriented volumes of the Library of Literary Criticism, although the critical excerpts have been expanded.

Chelsea House Library of Literary Criticism

This series, under the editorial direction of the distinguished critic Harold Bloom, covers the entire range of British and American literature from earliest times to the present. Its arrangement, borrowed from the old Moulton's, provides a brief biography and extracts of criticism divided into personal recollections, general assessments, and comments on particular works. There is considerable duplication of authors covered between this and Ungar's Library of Literary Criticism. Surprisingly, however, there is little duplication of criticism reprinted. Both series offer 11 excerpts from nineteenth-century criticism on *Jane Eyre*, for example, but only three of the excerpts are duplicates. A comparison of the two series shows a difference in editorial philosophy. Excerpts in the Ungar sets are freely edited, while Bloom tries to retain the flavor of the original by making fewer changes, even allowing idiosyncratic punctuation to stand. Excerpts in the Ungar series are very brief, while Bloom makes a point of offering complete texts as well as extracts. The Chelsea House article on Charlotte Brontë, for example, has eight full essays in addition to extracts. By supplementing extracts—which are taken out of context—with full texts, the Chelsea House sets provide more in-depth treatments. Biographical essays and accompanying portraits help give a fuller picture of each author.

The New Moulton's Library of Literary Criticism: British and American Literature to 1904. 11v. Ed. by Harold Bloom. 1985–88. $55/vol. (0-87754-778-5). [*RBB* O 15 86]

Bloom updated the original Moulton's by adding some authors and deleting others who are no longer studied. Coverage begins with *Beowulf* and ends with Kate Chopin. Extracts are drawn from critical material published up to 1904. The concluding volume of this and all the other sets in the series contains bibliographies and an index. *The Major Authors Edition of the New Moulton's Library of Literary Criticism* (5v., 1985–88, $60/vol.) reprints articles on more important authors, often exactly as they appear in the parent set. *The Critical Perspective* (10v., 1985–88, $55/vol.) provides twentieth-century criticism on the authors covered in *New Moulton's*. *Twentieth-Century American Literature* (8v., 1985–87, $60/vol.) and *Twentieth-Century British Literature* (6v., 1985–87, $60/vol.) expand *New Moulton's* by providing coverage of modern authors and their work.

Gale's Literary Criticism Series

Gale publishes several series that allow students to study the critical reception given to authors of all nationalities, genres, and periods. Volumes follow a similar format and include, in addition to extracts of criticism in chronological order, a portrait of the author, a biographical and critical introduction written by Gale's editors, a list of principal works by the author, and a selected bibliography of works about the author. Some of the extracts run to several pages and are preceded by a brief identification of the critic and the context from which the criticism has been excerpted. Cumulative author indexes in each new volume provide access to information in the entire series. Gale's policy of frequent and regular revision makes its information the most current but also makes the series cumbersome to use. For example, a student would need to consult six separate volumes of *Contemporary Literary Criticism* for fullest coverage of Chinua Achebe. Gale's publishing policy also means that the Gale Literary Criticism series can be prohibitively expensive for some libraries that would have to commit significant amounts of their budgets to maintain standing orders.

The Literary Criticism series share with the Ungar Library of Literary Criticism an international range and exceed the Bloom series published by Chelsea House in depth of coverage. There are 38 extracts and 12 complete essays on Jane Austen in Bloom's *New Moulton's* and eight additional full-length essays in *The Critical Perspective*. Gale's *Nineteenth Century Literature Criticism* has almost 40 extracts of Jane Austen criticism in volume 1 and 34 extracts in volume 13. Some of the appraisals extracted in *Nineteenth Century Literature Criticism*, such as Archbishop Whatley's essay published in the *Quarterly Review* in 1812, and W. F. Pollock's comments published in *Fraser's Magazine* in 1860, are printed in full in *New Moulton's*. In general, there is not much duplication of criticism between the two series. Of the eight essays on Jane Austen appearing in Bloom's *Critical Perspective*, only one is extracted in Gale. Some of Austen's most interesting contemporary critics, such as the controversial Marvin Mudrick and the pioneers of feminist criticism, Sandra M. Gilbert and Susan Gubar, are quoted in *Nineteenth Century Literature Criticism* but are absent from Bloom. Sets in Gale's Literary Criticism series are as follows:

Contemporary Literary Criticism. 1973– . $95/vol. [*RSBR* S 1 79]

Covers novelists, playwrights, short story writers, poets, mystery and science-fiction writers, nonfiction writers, and screenwriters who are still living or who have died since 1959. Some volumes are devoted to special topics. Volume 12, for instance, covers authors for young adults. More than 50 volumes have been published so far.

Children's Literature Review. Ed. by Gerard J. Senick. 1976– . $84/vol. (ISSN 0362-4145). [*RBB* Je 15 86]

Like *Contemporary Literary Criticism*, but covers authors and illustrators of books for children, preschool to high school.

Classical and Medieval Literature Criticism. 1988– . $85/vol. [*RBB* My 15 88]

Covers authors who lived from antiquity through 1399. Unlike most of the other Literary Criticism series, this one includes sections on specific works as well as authors.

Literature Criticism from 1400–1800. 1984– . $95/vol. [*RBB* Ja 15 85]

Covers authors who died between 1400 and 1799.

Nineteenth Century Literature Criticism. 1982– . $95/vol. [*RSBR* D 15 82]

Covers authors who died between 1800 and 1899.

Shakespearean Criticism. 1984– . $95/vol. [*RBB* Mr 15 85]

Short Story Criticism. 1987– . $70/vol. [*RBB* My 15 88]

Twentieth Century Literary Criticism. 1978– . $95/vol. [*RBB* My 1 86]

Covers authors who died between 1900 and 1960.

BIOBIBLIOGRAPHIC SOURCES

Though not, strictly speaking, critical sources, works in this category can provide students with varying degrees of interpretive material. Several series are discussed briefly here in terms of their critical content.

Gale

Dictionary of Literary Biography. 1978– . $95/vol.

The goal of this ever-expanding series, which is rapidly approaching its hundredth volume, is to provide "career biographies tracing the development of the author's canon and the evolution of his reputation." DLB is a useful supplement to the literary criticism sources because it helps put writers and their work into perspective. The scope of DLB is very broad; recent volumes include *Nineteenth Century Literary Critics and Scholars, 1880–1900*; *British Mystery Writers, 1860–1919*; *Canadian Writers since 1960*; and *French Novelists, 1930–1960*. At $95 per volume, the entire DLB is a luxury for all but the largest libraries; fortunately, libraries can pick and choose among the various volumes to round out their literary reference collections. To meet the needs of smaller libraries, Gale began in 1988 to publish the *Concise Dictionary of American Literary Biography* (6v., $60/vol. or $290/set). When completed later this year, this set will reprint unabridged articles on around 200 of the 2,300 American authors covered in the parent set. The articles are updated to include discussion of works published since the original DLB entry was written.

St. Martin's/St. James

These titles in a series originally published by British Macmillan are familiar to most librarians:

Contemporary Dramatists. 4th ed. Ed. D. L. Kirkpatrick and James Vinson. St. James, 1988. $85 (0-912289-62-7). [*RBB* D 1 88]

Contemporary Novelists. 4th ed. Ed. by D. L. Kirkpatrick. St. Martin's, 1986. $70 (0-312-16731-8). [*RBB* Ap 1 87]

Great Writers of the English Language. 3v. Ed. by James Vinson. St. Martin's, 1979. $160/set. [*RSBR* S 1 80]

Twentieth-Century Children's Writers. 2d ed. Ed. by D. L. Kirkpatrick. St. Martin's, 1983. $75 (0-312-82414-9). [*RSBR* O 15 79]

Twentieth-Century Crime and Mystery Writers. 2d ed. Ed. by John M. Reilly. St. Martin's, 1985. $75 (0-312-82418-1). [*RSBR* Je 1 81]

Rights to these titles tend to change hands, so that *Twentieth-Century Science-Fiction Writers* (2d ed., edited by Curtis C. Smith, $85 [*RBB* Mr 15 87]) and *Twentieth-Century Romance and Historical Fiction* (2d ed., formerly *Twentieth-Century Romance and Gothic Writers*, edited by Leslie Henderson, $85, available September 1989 [*RBB* D 15 83]) are currently published by St. James, and *Twentieth-Century Western Writers* (edited by James Vinson and D. L. Kirkpatrick, $75 [*RBB* Ja 15 84]) is published by Gale. Entries provide who's who–type biographical information, a list of publications, and short, signed critical essays. The value of the essays is best exemplified by A. O. J. Cockshut's comments on Charles Dickens in *Great Writers of the English Language*: "There is no space here to chart his development in detail."

Wilson Author Series

Beginning with *American Authors, 1600–1900* (1938), this biographical series now consists of 10 volumes, covering writers from 800 B.C. to 1980. Early volumes, which have not been revised, contain scanty analysis that tends to reflect the tastes of another age or the idiosyncrasies of the contributor. In later volumes, the editors have made an effort to expand critical content and make it a summation of opinion rather than an original analysis. Typical phrases in the essay on P. D. James in *World Authors, 1975–1980* are "James thinks of herself as" and "what one critic calls" and "In an article in the *New York Times*." The Wilson Author series is very broad in scope, covering not only creative writers but scientists, journalists, philosophers, and authors from many other fields:

American Authors, 1600–1900. Ed. by Stanley J. Kunitz and Howard Haycraft. 1938. $48 (0-8242-0001-2).

British Authors before 1800. Ed. by Stanley J. Kunitz and Howard Haycraft. 1952. $38 (0-8242-0006-3).

British Authors of the Nineteenth Century. Ed. by Stanley J. Kunitz and Howard Haycraft. 1936. $40 (0-8242-0007-1).

European Authors, 1000–1900. Ed. by Stanley J. Kunitz and Vineta Colby. 1967. $53 (0-8242-0013-6).

Greek and Latin Authors, 800 B.C.–A.D. 1000. By Michael Grant. 1980. $46 (0-8242-0640-1).

Twentieth Century Authors. Ed. by Stanley J. Kunitz and Howard Haycraft. 1942. $68 (0-8242-0049-7).

Twentieth Century Authors: First Supplement. Ed. by Stanley J. Kunitz. 1955. $58 (0-8242-0050-0).

World Authors, 1950–1970. Ed. by John Wakeman. 1975. $90 (0-8242-0429-0).

World Authors, 1970–1975. Ed. by John Wakeman. 1980. $73 (0-8242-0641-X).

World Authors, 1975–1980. Ed. by Vineta Colby. 1985. $73 (0-8242-0715-7).

* * *

Such a wealth of material makes it difficult for librarians to make acquisitions decisions. There is a good deal of duplication in literary criticism reference sources, but not so much that some sets can be safely ignored by large libraries that aim to provide full coverage of the field. Academic libraries, in particular, need to offer a range of sources. High school and public libraries should choose carefully from among the available options. Some titles published by St. Martin's/St. James and Wilson are considered standards and belong on the shelves of most libraries. Academic libraries will want the Scribner series. High school libraries and public libraries serving high school students need the Magill sets, but they are shortchanging their patrons if they don't offer access to reprints of criticism. Among the compilations of reprints of criticism, Gale's Literary Criticism series is superior to Ungar's Library of Literary Criticism in terms of currency and depth of coverage. But Ungar provides access to national literatures missing from Gale. The Chelsea House Library of Literary Criticism is an attractive series for American and British literature, but, except for the full-length essays, does not really distinguish itself from Gale. On the other hand, unless currency is a priority, titles from the Ungar Library of Literary Criticism or the Chelsea House Library of Literary Criticism can be considered as less expensive alternatives to maintaining standing orders for all the Gale series.

Mary Ellen Quinn is the director of collection development for the Chicago Public Library where she has been on staff since 1979. She has been a member of the *RBB* Editorial Board since 1986, is a member of the Collection Development Policies Committee of the CODES section of RASD, and also reviews fiction for the Adult Books section of BOOKLIST.

SELECTED REFERENCE SOURCES ON GARDENING

Gardening books are of perennial interest to public library patrons. Reading about gardening is not limited to particular seasons, as there is usually interest in planning next year's garden or gardening indoors. To help meet the needs of gardeners, libraries should have resources in their reference as well as their circulating collections. The list below emphasizes current general resources appropriate for large public libraries. Smaller public libraries, and even academic libraries, may wish to have some of these titles as well.

Because of the enormous amount of literature on gardening, this list should not be considered comprehensive. Instead, it is a sampling of some of the best works available, with an emphasis on books dealing with the selection and growing of plants outside and inside the home. A few directories of botanical gardens and arboretums where cultivated plants can be viewed firsthand have also been included. Books on the uses of plants, such as those dealing with herbal medicine, or on the natural history of plants, have been excluded, as have books on specific plants, such as cacti or roses, and those of only regional interest.

GENERAL COMPREHENSIVE WORKS

America's Garden Book. Rev. ed. By James and Louise Bush-Brown. Scribner, 1980. 819p. hardcover $30 (0-684-16270-9).

Published since 1939 and now revised by the New York Botanical Garden, this comprehensive work covers garden design, plant selection, special habitats (e.g., rock gardens), cultural methods and practices, and indoor gardening. There are lists and tables of plants throughout, such as those on deciduous trees with information on hardiness zones, height, soil requirements, and blooms and fruit, and others for shrubs, perennials, and annuals. Black-and-white and color photographs are used throughout. Lists of plant societies, a glossary, and an index are included.

Dictionary of Gardening: A Practical and Scientific Encyclopaedia of Horticulture. 4v. 2d ed. Ed. by Fred J. Chittenden. Oxford, 1956. hardcover $275 (0-19-869106-8).

Dictionary of Gardening Supplement. Ed. by Patrick M. Synge. Oxford, 1969. 554p. hardcover $74 (0-19-869116-5).

Although the emphasis in this encyclopedic dictionary is on the inclusion of every plant suitable for cultivation in Britain (both outdoors and under glass), there is much here for U.S. audiences concerning indoor gardening and plants for temperate climates. Each genus listed includes an extensive history and information on species, hybrids, and cultivation. Many general entries on botanical and horticultural terms and techniques are accompanied by lists of references. Apart from some line drawings, few illustrations are provided.

Hortus Third: A Concise Dictionary of Plants Cultivated in the United States and Canada. Comp. by Liberty Hyde Bailey and Ethel Zoe Bailey. Macmillan, 1976. 1,290p. hardcover $135 (0-02-505470-8).

Hortus Third is based on several publications published since 1900, including the *Cyclopedia of American Horticulture*, earlier editions of *Hortus*, and the *Manual of Cultivated Plants*. This comprehensive dictionary of plants cultivated in the continental U.S., Canada, Puerto Rico, and Hawaii contains entries for almost 300 families and more than 3,000 genera and 20,000 species. Entries include synonyms, common names, and information on use, culture, and hardiness zones. Drawings accompany most of the family descriptions. General articles on important crops, a glossary of botanical terms, and an index of common names are also featured.

The New York Botanical Garden Illustrated Encyclopedia of Horticulture. 10v. Ed. by Thomas H. Everett. Garland, 1981–82. hardcover $240 (0-686-82042-8). [*RBB* S 15 83]

This beautiful work provides comprehensive coverage of the field of horticulture in the U.S. and Canada, is geared toward the general gardener, and uses nontechnical language. There are approximately 7,000 entries, including more than 20,000 species and varieties of plants, and covering subjects such as bonsai, famous botanical gardens, pest control, and plants of the Bible. Extensive cross-references are widely used. Plant entries include descriptions, uses, and cultivation. In addition to black-and-white photographs, each volume includes several pages of colorplates. The preface contains a classified list of general subjects.

Wyman's Gardening Encyclopedia. 2d ed. Ed. by Donald Wyman. Macmillan, 1986. 1,221p. hardcover $50 (0-02-632070-3). [*RSBR* S 15 77]

Wyman's standard encyclopedic dictionary treats plants, methods of cultivation, fertilizers, pesticides, etc. More than 9,500 plants are listed, and species are rated for hardiness in major U.S. zones. A table of contents refers users to such topics as air layering, bonsai, hydroponics, biblical plants, plants for growing under fluorescent lights, and poisonous plants. Black-and-white and color photographs are included.

BIBLIOGRAPHIES/INDEXES

Farm and Garden Index. Bell & Howell, 1978– . quarterly. paper $170/yr. (ISSN 0193-8487).

Approximately 100 agriculture- and horticulture-related periodicals are indexed, covering both popular and research areas. Two indexes are provided, one by subject and the other by author or named person. Both indexes include complete article citations.

Gardening: A Guide to the Literature. By Richard T. Isaacson. Garland, 1985. 198p. hardcover $22 (0-8240-9019-5). [*RBB* Je 15 86]

Sections in this guide include reference books, books on topics such as landscape design, ornamental gardening plants, gardening practices and problems, and miscellaneous garden topics like horticultural therapy or photography. Entries are annotated, and books within each section are ranked by usefulness, with best books listed first. Also included are an annotated section on periodicals, a list of publications of societies, and a list of libraries and book dealers specializing in gardening. Title and subject indexes.

Gardener's Index for . . . CompuDex Press, P.O. Box 27041, Kansas City, MO 64110, 1987– . annual. paper $12 (ISSN 0897-5175). [*RBB* S 15 88]

This is an annual index to six of the most widely read gardening magazines: *American Horticulturist*, *Flower and Garden*, *Garden*, *Horticulture*, *National Gardening*, and *Rodale's Organic Gardening*. The main subject-guide section has articles arranged by major subject with a very brief descriptive phrase. A detailed subject index includes all named species with notations on article emphasis, cultural information, and photographs and illustrations.

BOTANICAL GARDENS

Gardens of North America and Hawaii: A Traveler's Guide. By Irene Jacob and Walter Jacob. Timber Press, 1986. 368p. hardcover $24.95 (0-88192-017-7).

Arranged by state, this directory provides information on approximately 1,400 gardens, conservatories, and arboretums. A rating system is used to highlight important gardens, and symbols are used to denote special plantings. Each entry includes a brief description, address, telephone number, hours, admission charges, and access for the disabled. Indexes by place-names and garden names.

The Traveler's Guide to American Gardens. Rev. ed. Ed. by Mary Helen Ray and Robert P. Nicholls. Univ. of North Carolina, 1988. 375p. hardcover $22.50 (0-8078-1787-2); paper $9.95 (0-8078-4214-1). [*RBB* F 15 89]

Gardens were selected for this *Guide* if they had historic importance or unique or significant features and nonprofit status. Entries for gardens are arranged by state and city, and for each, there are brief descriptions. Superior and must-see gardens are noted by one or two stars.

DIRECTORIES

The Gardener's Book of Sources. By William Bryant Logan. Viking/Penguin, 1988. 271p. hardcover $24.95 (0-670-81223-4); paper $12.95 (0-14-046761-0). [BKL Je 1 88]

Over 1,000 sources on home gardening are included, consisting of companies, books, magazines, societies, and individuals. Categories include general sources, annuals and perennials, trees and shrubs, wildflowers and native plants, vegetables and herbs, tools and supplies, furniture, and landscape architecture. All entries are critically annotated, providing information on catalogs, services, etc. Also included are a listing of horticultural booksellers, a directory of book publishers, and an alphabetical index of sources.

Gardening by Mail: A Source Book. 2d ed. By Barbara J. Barton. Tusker Press, P.O. Box 1338, Sebastopol, CA 95473, 1987. 336p. paper $18.50 (0-937633-02-X). [*RBB* Ap 15 88]

Several types of gardening services are reflected in this directory, which includes descriptions, addresses, telephone numbers for each entry, and several indexes. Included are more than 1,200 nurseries and seed companies in the U.S. and Canada with indexes by plant name and geographic location, more than 300 garden suppliers with a product index, entries for horticultural societies with an index by specialty, listings of horticultural libraries and horticultural magazines, and an annotated bibliography of gardening books.

The Mail Order Gardener. By Hal Morgan. Harper/Perennial, 1988. 287p. hardcover $27.95 (0-06-055113-5); paper $12.95 (0-06-096241-0).

Offering more than 1,500 mail-order sources for seeds, tools, and garden accessories—most U.S., some foreign—these annotated entries are arranged by type of plant and include address, telephone number, and cost, if any, for catalogs. *See* references are used throughout. There are also annotated sections on companies that offer horticultural tours, societies and organizations, and magazines. Index of company/organization names.

North American Horticulture: A Reference Guide. Comp. by the American Horticultural Society. Scribner, 1982. 367p. o.p. [*RBB* O 1 83]

This comprehensive directory includes organizations and societies, nomenclature authorities, U.S. government programs, pesticide regulations, educational programs, libraries, herbaria, public gardens, major horticultural awards, and major flower shows. In addition to a bibliography of suggested books and periodicals, a miscellaneous section lists the biggest U.S. trees, U.S. state trees and flowers, and world-record vegetables, fruits, and flowers. The index is made up of subjects and names of organizations, and the preface provides a history of American horticulture.

GARDENING PROBLEMS

The Encyclopedia of Natural Insect & Disease Control. Ed. by Roger B. Yepsen. Rodale, 1984. 490p. hardcover $24.95 (0-87857-488-3).

The emphasis here is on protecting garden plants without the use of toxic chemicals. Most entries are by plant name, providing descriptions of major pests, diseases, and controls. Control measures discussed include interplanting with herbs or flowers that keep pests away, taking advantage of pests' life cycles, selecting resistant varieties, and using biological controls.

The Ortho Problem Solver. 2d ed. Ed. by Michael Smith. Ortho Information Services, 1984. 1,040p. hardcover $179.95 (0-89721-032-8).

Excellent color photographs and many points of access make this book valuable. Included is information on solving plant problems; on groups of plants such as lawns and fruit and nut trees; on household pests, weeds, plant diseases, insects, and soil; and on cultural and climate problems. All sections are color coded. Specific Ortho products or generics are recommended. Concluding the volume are an appendix with tables of plants appropriate for various conditions and susceptible or resistant to various problems and a directory of county cooperative extension offices. The third edition will be available in October 1989.

Rodale's Garden Insect, Disease & Weed Identification Guide. By Miranda Smith and Anna Carr. Rodale, 1988. 328p. hardcover $21.95 (0-87857-758-0); paper $15.95 (0-87857-759-9) [BKL Ag 88]

Several keys and charts are provided for easy identification of insect, pest, and weed problems. Entries include drawings and descriptions of their damage, life cycles, range, host plants, and prevention and control. Additional aids include a color-photograph section and a glossary of terms. Bibliography and index.

INDOOR GARDENING

Exotica, Series 4 International: Pictorial Cyclopedia of Exotic Plants from Tropical and Near-Tropical Regions. 2v. 12th ed. By Alfred Byrd Graf. Roehrs Co., P.O. Box 125, East Rutherford, NJ 07073, 1985. 2,606p. hardcover $187 (0-911266-20-8).

Here is a beautiful and authoritative work on the identification and cultural requirements of house and greenhouse plants or, in warm climates, patio and outdoor plants. Of the 16,300 outstanding photographs, approximately 400 are in color. Volume 2 includes descriptions for each plant with symbols as to cultural requirements. It also has an index of common names and a botanic index to genera illustrated. *Tropica* (3d ed., 1986, $125) by the same author is very similar except that it includes fewer species, but all of its 7,000 photographs are in color. Abridged versions of *Exotica* are also available as *Exotic Plant Manual* (5th ed., 1978, $37.50) and *Exotic House Plants* (10th ed., 1976, $8.95).

The Good Housekeeping Encyclopedia of House Plants. By Rob Herwig. Morrow, 1984. 288p. hardcover $19.95 (0-688-03321-0).

A major portion of this resource is a plant dictionary of approximately 1,500 species. Plant entries, many with color photographs, include a description with information on origin, cultural requirements, and diseases. Symbols are used throughout for quick information on lighting, temperature, watering, humidity, and soil-acidity requirements. Also included are general discussions on topics such as greenhouse gardening, hydroponics, windowsill gardening, plant propagation, and pest control. There are useful listings of plants by such categories as full sun, low temperatures, or tolerance of dry air. Subject and name index.

The RHS Encyclopedia of House Plants: Including Greenhouse Plants. By Kenneth A. Beckett. Salem House, 1987. 492p. hardcover $34.95 (0-88162-285-0). [RBB N 15 87]

Compiled by the Royal Horticultural Society, this *Encyclopedia* includes chapters on the natural history of houseplants; how to choose and buy plants; plant cultivation, maintenance, and propagation; and pests and diseases. Next, the "A to Z of Houseplants," arranged by genus, gives descriptions and cultural requirements for nearly 1,000 species, accompanied by color illustrations. A brief glossary of botanical terms and an index of common names are appended.

OUTDOOR GARDENING

The Complete Handbook of Garden Plants. By Michael Wright. Facts On File, 1984. 544p. hardcover $22.95 (0-8719-6632-8). [RBB Mr 1 85]

Here is a comprehensive guide to the identification and description of more than 9,000 species and varieties of garden plants, other than fruits and vegetables, in cultivation in temperate zones throughout the world. Entries are divided by type—trees and shrubs, rock plants, water plants, and so on. Separate articles for each major botanical family follow, with numerous watercolor illustrations included. Plant descriptions present cultural information as well as the best varieties to grow. There is also a glossary and index of botanical and common names.

The Encyclopedia of Organic Gardening. Rev. ed. By the staff of Organic Gardening Magazine. Rodale, 1978. 1,236p. hardcover $34.95 (0-87857-351-8). [RSBR Mr 1 79]

With more than 2,000 entries, this one-volume source covers the entire spectrum of horticulture (including greenhouse gardening) from an organic and practical point of view. There are entries for groups of plants by common name as well as for various gardening techniques such as composting. Among the special features are numerous *see* and *see also* references and tables in several of the entries (for instance, companion planting and insect control). No index.

Flowering Trees and Shrubs. By Richard Bird. Barron's, 1989. 160p. hardcover $24.95 (0-8120-5970-0).

This A–Z directory of over 950 varieties of trees and shrubs is illustrated with 80 pages of four-color photographs and botanically correct drawings. Each descriptive entry presents information on some of the newest cultivars and cross-breeds along with facts about shape, height, flowering period, and color of leaf and flower, concluding with advice on planting, pruning, sun and soil requirements, and propagation.

The Gardener's Index of Plants & Flowers. By John Brookes and others. Macmillan, 1987. 272p. hardcover $24.95 (0-02-516690-5); paper $14.95 (0-02-049100-X). [RBB S 1 87]

Charts are used to provide quick information on the characteristics and cultivation of more than 4,000 popular garden plants. Arranged into eight categories—trees; shrubs; perennials; succulents; annuals and biennials; bulbs, corms, and tubers; water plants; and climbing plants—they provide data on plant height, flowering season, color, soil, and other cultural requirements. Introductory chapters cover how to plan and plant a garden. A directory of nurseries and seed companies and an index of common and scientific names are included.

Growing and Propagating Wild Flowers. By Harry R. Phillips. Univ. of North Carolina, 1985. 331p. hardcover $24.95 (0-8078-1648-5); paper $14.95 (0-8078-4131-5). [BKL Ag 85]

There has been increased interest in gardening with native plants over the past several years. This book provides general sections on cultivating and propagating native plants and specific information on growing selected wildflowers, carnivorous plants, and ferns. Each plant entry contains a description, drawings, and information on fruit and seed collection, propagation, cultivation, and uses in the garden. The appendix comprises sections on how to organize a plant rescue, charts of blooming dates and production timetables, a guide to recommended literature, a glossary, and an index.

Know It and Grow It II: A Guide to the Identification and Use of Landscape Plants. By Carl E. Whitcomb. Lacebark Publications, Rte. 5, P.O. Box 174, Stillwater, OK 74074, 1985. 739p. hardcover $35 (0-9613109-0-1).

Entries on plants are divided into five main sections: "Deciduous Trees," "Deciduous Shrubs and Vines," "Broadleaf Evergreens," "Ground Covers," and "Coniferous Evergreen Trees and Shrubs." Each one-page entry has information on size, form, exposure, leaves, stem, flowers, fruit, color, propagation, culture, pests, and cultivars. On the page opposite each entry is a map highlighting hardiness zones as well as photographs of the plant, its leaves, and branches. A glossary, a tabular plant-selection guide providing information on features such as fall color or pest problems, and indexes by common names and scientific names are appended.

National Wildflower Research Center's Wildflower Handbook. Texas Monthly Press, 1989. 337p. paper $9.95 (0-87719-167-0).

Information is provided on how to buy seed in bulk, when to plant, seeding methods, and (through charts) what to plant. Charts provide information on wildflower origin, life cycle (e.g., perennial), exposure, site preference, and seeding rates. There are also bibliographies of books arranged geographically. Most of the book is devoted to a directory of information sources and wildflower seed and native plants sources. Information services include nonprofit organizations, landscape architecture firms, botanical gardens and arboretums, and state agencies. Entries are arranged by state and city and include address, telephone number, brief description, publications, and notation of purpose, research, and public programs. The second listing of nurseries and seed companies, also arranged geographically, includes information on wildflower seed offered and propagation methods used.

Marty Kesselman is information services librarian at the Library of Science and Medicine, Rutgers University. He was a member of the *RBB* Board from 1980 to 1984. He has also compiled "Microcomputers and Software: Selected Resources" [*RBB* Ja 1 87] and "General Consumer Health Reference Books: A Selected Annotated List" [*RBB* F 1 85]. ALA recently published *End-User Searching: Services and Providers*, which he coauthored.

SPORTS REFERENCE BOOKS

Sports reference books are consulted more to satisfy a fan's curiosity or settle a bet than for scholarly research. These books vary in scope, format, and content. Most are popularly written and filled with tables of statistics. They can provide information for high school students writing research papers, but they are also popular for recreational reading.

This bibliography is a representative selection, not a comprehensive list. Dictionaries, statistical compilations, handbooks, and directories were considered rather than historical studies and how-to books. Bibliographies, indexes, and out-of-print titles are not included. The bibliography is divided into two sections: books covering multiple sports and books on individual sports. Several sports are not included because the standard reference books on them are out of print. *The Ring Record Book and Boxing Encyclopedia*, *USTA Official Encyclopedia of Tennis*, and *The American Encyclopedia of Soccer* are often-consulted titles that would have been listed if they were in print.

Sporting News, Barron's, and Guinness annually publish many sports handbooks that are popular but often small and that disappear from libraries. Serious sports fans may want to purchase these paperbacks at local bookstores. Also not covered here are publications by and about local collegiate and professional sports organizations. Books on the Fighting Irish of Notre Dame, the Nebraska Cornhuskers, Washington Redskins, Los Angeles Dodgers, Chicago Cubs, Boston Celtics, etc., can be purchased from local bookstores and sports stores.

BOOKS COVERING MULTIPLE SPORTS

Biographical

Biographical Dictionary of American Sports: Baseball. Ed. by David L. Porter. Greenwood, 1987. 713p. hardcover $75 (0-313-23771-9). [*RBB* N 15 87]

Biographical Dictionary of American Sports: Football. Ed. by David L. Porter. Greenwood, 1988. 786p. hardcover $75 (0-313-25771-X). [*RBB* N 15 87]

Biographical Dictionary of American Sports: Outdoor Sports. Ed. by David L. Porter. Greenwood, 1988. 728p. hardcover $75 (0-313-26260-8). [*RBB* Ja 15 89]

Biographical Dictionary of American Sports: Basketball and Other Indoor Sports. Ed. by David L. Porter. Greenwood, 1989. 776p. hardcover $85 (0-313-26261-9).

One of the best sources of biographical information on players, managers, umpires, and sports announcers and writers. The 200- to 900-word entries are balanced between living and deceased persons with about half the living persons still active in their sport. Personal and career information is included. The biographees are arranged alphabetically within each sport. Each volume has several appendixes and indexes.

Dictionaries/Encyclopedias

Encyclopedia of Physical Education, Fitness and Sports. 4v. Ed. by Thomas K. Cureton. American Alliance for Health, Physical Education, Recreation, & Dance, 1977–85. v.1: Philosophy, Programs, and History, o.p.; v.2: Training, Environment, Nutrition, and Fitness, o.p.; v.3: Sports, Dance, and Related Activities, o.p.; v.4: Human Performance: Efficiency and Improvements in Sports, Exercise, and Fitness, hardcover $49.95 (0-88314-293-7).

Provides academic treatment of all aspects of health, physical fitness, physical education, and sports. Chapters are written by contributing editors and include the history and growth of individual sports. Index in each volume.

The Language of Sport. By Tim Considine. Facts On File, 1983 (c1982). 355p. hardcover $17.95 (0-87196-653-0). [*RBB* N 15 83]

Easy-to-understand and fun-to-read definitions are given for 5,000 terms. A two- to three-page historical sketch of each sport precedes the definitions, which are arranged alphabetically within each sport. Terms such as *jam*, *in*, and *hole* that are used in several sports are defined for each. Many cross-references. Detailed index.

The Oxford Companion to World Sports and Games. Ed. by John Arlott. Oxford, 1975. 1,143p. hardcover $35 (0-19-211538-3).

Though dated, this comprehensive, alphabetically arranged volume provides long historical essays on individual sports and shorter entries for athletes and teams. Diagrams of courts and playing fields are provided. The sketch on football includes several variations: American, association, and Winchester College. Many cross-references. No index.

Webster's Sports Dictionary. Merriam-Webster, 1976. 512p. hardcover $10.95 (0-87779-067-1).

Also dated, this volume defines 7,000 commonly used sports terms and often puzzling slang words. Individual sports, team sports, and recreational activities are covered. Multiple definitions are provided for terms used in more than one sport, such as *double* in baseball, bowling, cricket, curling, fencing, fishing, and jai alai. Illustrated. Many cross-references.

Directories

The Directory of Athletic Scholarships. By Alan Green. Facts On File, 1987. 343p. hardcover $29.95 (0-8160-1549-X); paper $15.95 (0-8160-1550-3). [*RBB* S 1 87]

Except for a short discussion of the recruiting process, this book is an index to scholarships available for four-year and two-year colleges. The sections include school, sport, state, and conference indexes. Address, telephone number, enrollment, athletic director, sports-information director, and a listing of men's and women's sports are given for each college.

Masters Guide to Sport Camps: National Edition. Ed. by Carol J. Bast and others. Masters Press; dist. by Little, Brown, 1987. 1,064p. paper $24.95 (0-940279-00-2). [*RBB* Jl 87]

This directory of U.S. summer camps for elementary, junior high, and senior high athletes provides information on camp programs, staff, location, dates, cost, and application process. The book is divided into regions with sports listed alphabetically within each region. Regional editions are also available.

The National Directory of College Athletics, 1988–1989 (Men's Edition). By the National Association of Collegiate Directors of Athletics. Ray Franks Publishing Ranch, P.O. Box 7068, Amarillo, TX 79114, 1988. paper $15 (ISSN 0738-2758).

The National Directory of College Athletics, 1988–1989 (Women's Edition). By the National Association of Collegiate Directors of Athletics. Ray Franks Publishing Ranch, 1988. paper $11 (ISSN 0739-1226).

Includes college records for NCAA, NCIA, NJCAA, NCCAA, and CACC schools, and also athletic conferences and tournaments. Provides address, telephone number, enrollment, colors, nickname, stadium and fieldhouse, college president, athletic director, sports-information director, and coaches, as well as football and basketball season records. Lots of advertising. College, advertiser, and product indexes.

The Sports Address Book. Ed. by Scott Callis. Pocket, 1988. 294p. paper $6.95 (0-671-64771-7). [*RBB* N 15 88]

Provides 5,000 addresses for anything related to sports: athletes, teams, organizations, conferences, gifts, camps, publications, halls of fame, International Olympic Committees, sporting-goods manufacturers, agents, media, and sports-medicine clinics. The addresses for players are usually agent or business addresses rather than home addresses. No index.

Sports Market Place. Ed. by Richard A. Lipsey. Sportsguide, P.O. Box 1417, Princeton, NJ 08542, 1989. 700p. paper $135 with midyear supplement (ISSN 0277-0296). [*RBB* Mr 15 86]

Provides addresses, telephone numbers, and names of executives for professional teams, amateur associations, governing bodies, media, promoters, apparel and equipment suppliers, and manufacturers. Many cross-references. Several indexes: product, brand name, trade name, executive, geographic, and master index.

Miscellaneous

Facts and Dates of American Sports. By Gorton Carruth and Eugene Ehrlich. Harper/Perennial, 1988. 373p. hardcover $27 (0-06-055124-0); paper $12.95 (0-06-096271-2).

This is a chronological listing of sports highlights from 1540 to January 1987. Very short descriptions of events are interspersed with biographical sketches of noted sports personalities. A 70-page index includes persons, sports, and events.

From A-Train to Yogi: The Fan's Book of Sports Nicknames. By Chuck Wielgus and others. Harper/Perennial, 1987. 192p. paper $7.95 (0-06-096163-5).

This enjoyable volume is more than just a dictionary of athletes' nicknames; it also explains how people acquired them. The book follows no particular arrangement; however, a nickname index and a real-name index make it easy to use.

Guinness Sports Record Book, 1988–89. Ed. by David A. Boehm. Sterling, 1988. 256p. hardcover $16.95 (0-8069-6811-7); paper $10.95 (0-8069-6810-9). [*RBB* S 15 88]

Similar to many other Guinness record books, this annual covers popular and lesser-known sports as well as games and pastimes. Some sports list only all-time record holders; others have a complete list of past winners. Brief historical coverage is given to several sports. Black-and-white action photos. Detailed index.

National Collegiate Championships, 1987–1988. National Collegiate Athletic Association, P.O. Box 1906, Mission, KS 66201, 1988. 543p. paper $16 (ISSN 0190-4329).

Published annually. Provides a brief chronological history of NCAA championship series. Lists of men's and women's championships are given for all NCAA divisions with the exception of I-A football. Results of conference and regional championships are also included. Team standings and all-tournament teams are listed. No index.

Sports. By Tim Hammond. Knopf; dist. by Random, 1988. 63p. paper $12.95 (0-394-89616-5).

Young people as well as adults will enjoy this book because of its proliferation of color photographs and drawings of all kinds of items associated with sports: balls, gloves, headgear, masks, shoes, uniforms, and playing fields and courts. Especially noteworthy are the explanations of how many types of balls are made. Index.

The World Sports Record Atlas. Comp. by David Emery and Stan Greenberg. Facts On File, 1986. 192p. hardcover $19.95 (0-8160-1378-0); paper $12.95 (0-8160-1579-1). [*RBB* F 1 87]

The records of 42 sports events are highlighted. Because of the British slant, baseball and football are covered only briefly, and basketball is not even included. Track and field are heavily emphasized. The introductory comments are oversimplified and misleading. Loosely organized. No index.

Olympic Games

The Complete Book of the Olympics. Rev. ed. By David Wallechinsky. Penguin, 1988. 680p. paper $12.95 (0-14-010771-1).

Provides complete final results for every event, even discontinued ones, of the winter and summer Olympics through 1984. The results and statistics are interspersed with profiles of athletes and descriptions of special incidents. Black-and-white photographs. No index.

Olympic Games: The Records. By Stan Greenberg. Guinness Superlatives; dist. by Sterling, 1988. 176p. hardcover $17.95 (0-85112-897-1).

In typical Guinness format this book provides lists of gold, silver, and bronze medal winners for each event of every Olympics from 776 B.C. to A.D. 1988. Each year begins with narrative highlights of both the summer and winter Olympics. A few of the best all-time Olympic heroes are profiled in depth. Black-and-white photographs. Index.

The Olympic Record Book. By Bill Mallon. Garland, 1988. 522p. hardcover $68 (0-8240-2948-8).

This overpriced volume is simply a listing of records from the beginning of the Olympics through 1984. Loosely organized, the sections include overall Olympic records, summer records, winter records, records by sport, records by nation, and records by Olympic games. Each record includes the person, country, and year. No index.

Quotations

Dictionary of Sports Quotations. Comp. by Barry Liddle. Routledge & Kegan Paul; dist. by Routledge, Chapman & Hall, 1987. 210p. hardcover $24.95 (0-7102-0785-9).

Arranged by broad topics identified in the table of contents, these quotations cover all aspects of sports. The originator of the quotation is identified but not a printed source. The book has subject and author indexes.

Sports Quotations: Maxims, Quips and Pronouncements for Writers and Fans. Ed. by Andrew J. Maikovich. McFarland, 1984. 168p. hardcover $18.95 (0-89950-100-1).

These 1,782 quotations are arranged by 22 broad topics that are listed in the table of contents. The name of the speaker and that person's sport are given following the quote. Baseball and football receive the most coverage. Minor sports and recreations are also included. Detailed index.

Rules

Official Rules of Sports and Games, 1988–89. Ed. by Reginald Moore. W. Heinemann Ltd.; dist. by David & Charles, 1988 (c1987). 852p. hardcover $29.95 (0-434-98062-5). [*RBB* N 1 83]

The rules of 26 sports are provided by their British associations. Baseball and American football are not included. The differences between British rules and international or North American rules are explained.

The Rule Book: The Authoritative, Up-to-Date, Illustrated Guide to the Regulations, History, and Object of All Major Sports. By the Diagram Group. St. Martin's, 1983. 430p. paper $9.95 (0-312-69576-4).

Of much more appeal to American sports enthusiasts, this volume covers 55 Olympic, major, and some minor sports. Rules are given for playing and scoring. Color diagrams of playing fields, courts, and courses are found on every page. The sports are arranged alphabetically. No index.

BOOKS ON INDIVIDUAL SPORTS

Baseball

The Baseball Encyclopedia: The Complete and Official Record of Major League Baseball. 7th ed. Ed. by Joseph L. Reichler. Macmillan, 1988. 2,875p. hardcover $45 (0-02-579030-7).

This is the most comprehensive statistical source on all aspects of baseball from 1876 through the 1987 World Series. It includes a chronological listing of teams and players; pitching, batting, and fielding statistics; and lists of lifetime and single-season record holders. Also included are special achievements and awards; player, manager, and pitcher registers; all-time leaders; and information on trades, World Series, playoff games, and All Star Games. The appendixes include "Sources," "Decisions of Special Baseball Records Committee," and "Major Changes in Playing and Scoring Rules." No index.

The Bill James Historical Baseball Abstract. Rev. ed. By Bill James. Random/Villard, 1988. 723p. paper $15.95 (0-394-75805-6).

Based on his annual *Bill James Baseball Abstract*, this volume presents statistics on baseball from the 1870s through the 1980s. An introductory essay highlights each decade and includes nicknames, news stories, and most admirable superstar. Statistical information and records follow. A glossary of terms is provided. Index.

The Dickson Dictionary of Baseball. By Paul Dickson. Facts On File, 1989. 464p. hardcover $35 (0-8160-1741-7).

Definitions are given for nearly 5,000 terms and phrases, official and slang, associated with baseball. In addition to providing multiple definitions, this *Dictionary* also gives the origin and etymology of most terms, how the terms are used outside of baseball, special-context usage, and cross-references. Frequently the terms are cited in their original quotations, complete with dates and sources. An enjoyable source of baseball terminology, this work includes 250 black-and-white photographs. It concludes with a thorough bibliography.

The Sports Encyclopedia: Baseball. 9th ed. By David S. Neft and Richard M. Cohen. St. Martin's, 1989. 640p. paper $16.95 (0-312-02644-7). [*RBB* Ap 1 86]

Facts and statistics are given for American and National League baseball through 1988. The book is chronologically arranged with a narrative summary and statistics for each year. No index.

Basketball

The Basketball Abstract. By Dave Heeren. Prentice Hall Press, 1988. 232p. paper $12.95 (0-13-069170-4).

This book does for professional basketball what *Bill James Baseball Abstract* does for professional baseball. The author explains how his TENDEX rating system developed and the formula used to determine each player's TENDEX rating. Using this system, he identifies the best all-time players in several categories and evaluates the top players in each NBA franchise for the 1987–88 season. The last section of the book contains statistical charts for 63 categories. No index.

Football

College Football Records: Division I-A and the Ivy League, 1869–1984. By Robert Baldwin. McFarland, 1987. 198p. hardcover $25.95 (0-89950-246-6). [*RBB* Ap 15 88]

Information on 111 teams is arranged alphabetically within each athletic conference, followed by a list of independent colleges. Although the book is mostly a list of each school's record, other items noted are nickname, colors, location, stadium name and size, first year of football, year in which the school entered the conference, number of conference champions, total overall record, total conference record, and overall bowl record. College and university index.

The Official NFL Encyclopedia. 4th ed. By Beau Riffenburgh. NAL, 1986. 544p. hardcover $39.95 (0-453-00524-1). [*RBB* Mr 1 87]

This book is the most comprehensive collection of information and statistics on professional football through the 1985 season and 1986 draft. A season-by-season narrative is given for each team, along with statistics on individual records and awards. Besides rosters of players and coaches, information is given on the Super Bowl, playoffs, and halls of fame. No index.

The Sports Encyclopedia: Pro Football, the Modern Era, 1960 through 1987. 6th ed. By David S. Neft and Richard M. Cohen. St. Martin's, 1988. 624p. paper $15.95 (0-312-02289-1).

A companion to *The Sports Encyclopedia: Pro Football, the Early Years* (2d ed., Sports Bookshelf, P.O. Box 746, Ridgefield, CT 06877, 1987, 0-932070-01-9, $23.50 + $5 postage and handling, prepaid only), this book provides complete statistical records on professional football from 1960 to 1987. Because of the merger of the AFL and NFL in 1970, the book is divided into two sections: 1960–69 and 1970–present. Although there are short discussions of an era or a team, most of the information is statistical. Chronologically arranged. No index.

Golf

The Golf Digest Almanac, 1989. Golf Digest/Tennis; dist. by Random, 1989. 512p. paper $9.95 (0-8129-1830-4).

Following a detailed table of contents, this volume provides tournament schedules; lists of winners and all-time money winners; lists of men, women, and senior amateurs and professionals; information on college, junior, and international golf; as well as state and club champions. Brief biographical sketches are given for professional golfers. Information is given on equipment and selected courses. The almanac concludes with the complete rules of golf. No index.

Golf Rules in Pictures. Rev. ed. By the U. S. Golf Association. Putnam/Perigee, 1988. 87p. paper $6.95 (0-399-51438-4).

Revised frequently, this guide answers many questions as it explains the regulations. Line drawings illustrate the rules, and definitions and golf etiquette are explained. The USGA Rules of Golf are reproduced in the last section. Although there is a detailed table of contents, there is no index.

Horse Racing

The American Racing Manual. Daily Racing Form, 10 Lake Dr., Hightstown, NJ 08520, 1988. 1,936p. hardcover $60.

The first section provides general information, both historical and current, on horse racing. The second emphasizes earnings and records. Outstanding horses of the twentieth century are profiled. Information is given on race tracks, sales, breeding, track officials, and historical events. No index.

Ice Hockey

The Complete Encyclopedia of Hockey. 3d ed. Ed. by Zander Hollander and Hal Bock. NAL, 1983. 466p. hardcover $24.95 (0-453-00449-0).

This volume provides historical and statistical information on professional hockey players and teams. Also included is a chapter on amateur and collegiate hockey. Index.

The Hockey Encyclopedia: The Complete Record of Professional Ice Hockey. By Stan Fischler and Shirley Walton Fischler. Macmillan, 1983. 720p. hardcover $24.95 (0-02-538400-7).

The emphasis here is on statistics, but awards and achievements are also highlighted. The book includes a player register, goaltender register, and coaching register. Year-by-year finishes of all NHL and WHA teams and players are provided. No index.

Martial Arts

Martial Arts: Traditions, History, People. By John Corcoran and Emil Farkas. W. H. Smith/Gallery Books, 1983. hardcover $17.95 (0-8317-5805-8).

This fascinating volume provides a chronologically arranged historical account of martial arts. Coverage is given to many countries. There are many illustrations, a bibliography, and an index.

Track and Field

The Olympic Games: Complete Track and Field Results 1896–1988. By Barry J. Hugman and Peter Arnold. Facts On File, 1988. hardcover $40 (0-8160-2120-1).

The authors provide narrative highlights of track and field events of each Olympics as well as complete alphabetical lists of all competitors with each person's country, event, round, heat, place, time, distance, and medal. Biographical sketches and black-and-white photographs are provided for each Olympics. The narrative highlights and biographical sketches make this source far more than just a compilation of statistics. Chronologically arranged with a short bibliography. No index.

Running from A to Z. By Cliff Temple. Stanley Paul; dist. by David & Charles, 1987. 184p. hardcover $29.95 (0-09-166410-1).

A variety of information about running—events, people, training hints, equipment, and records—can be found in this dictionary. Although there are biographical sketches of several running greats, there are none for Bill Rodgers, Frank Shorter, Grete Waitz, or Joan Benoit Samuelson. The Olympics are omitted. Overall, the coverage is broad; however, the information just skims the surface. No index.

Clara Hoover, librarian at Millard South High School in Omaha, Nebraska, has been a member of the *Reference Books Bulletin* Editorial Board since 1987. She also chairs the committee that selects the recipient of the American Association of School Librarians/Baker & Taylor Distinguished Service Award.

TELEPHONE BOOKS AS REFERENCE SOURCES

Telephone directories of major United States cities may be available for your use at local libraries.
—*Greater Atlanta White Pages, 1987/1988*

At midnight on December 31, 1983, one of the biggest changes in American telecommunications history took place. As a result of a long court battle, AT&T was forced to break up its virtual monopoly on telephone service. Ma Bell, the only telephone company that most users had ever known, ceased to exist. In its place, seven distinct regional companies were formed to provide similar local services using the equipment and networks that AT&T had established.

For the consumer, this breakup has resulted in competition for long-distance business. For libraries, it has had an unforeseen and expensive result: charges for telephone directories. In the past, the telephone company provided libraries with the telephone books of their choice at no charge. There was a public relations benefit in this policy, while at the same time it reduced the load on directory assistance. When directory assistance became a fee-based service in many places, even more patrons turned to their local libraries for telephone information. (However, many phone companies that charge for directory assistance will now give addresses and zip codes as well as telephone numbers.)

It is difficult to predict exactly what any individual library will have to pay for telephone directories, quite apart from the number of directories it wishes to obtain. Each regional company distributes free copies of directories within its own region but charges for the directories published by the other regional companies. To obtain all of the directories for cities of over 100,000 population, a library would need to spend between $3,000 and $5,000. Due to the uneven distribution of large cities in the U.S., a library in the Northeast will tend to pay less than a library in the West. For the purposes of this review, all prices have been derived from the U.S. West "Directory and Price Information." Prices for these materials change constantly and are included here for comparative purposes only.

Telephone books have always been considered one of the primary sources for local information. Librarians traditionally use these directories to find names, addresses, and telephone numbers of persons and businesses around the nation and the world. However, many telephone books provide additional reference information about the communities they cover, ranging from street maps to shopping guides to local history. The purpose of this review is to critically evaluate telephone books as reference sources, using the same criteria used in evaluating commercial reference tools: content, format, and price. The number of telephone directories available to consumers continues to escalate. In addition to the seven regional telephone companies, many independent systems are still in existence, especially in rural areas. On top of this, the regional companies are required to make their lists of names, addresses, and phone numbers available to anyone who wishes to purchase that information. Thus, competing firms publish alternative directories, especially in the lucrative yellow-pages advertising business. Several of the regional phone companies are even publishing competing yellow pages in other regions. Foreign-language phone books and yellow pages for children and senior citizens have appeared. Obviously, with an estimated sum of more than 200 telephone directory publishers already in business, publishing a wide variety of directories, a comprehensive review of these directories is impossible. Therefore, this review will be restricted to the directories published by the seven regional companies and to *Phonefiche*, a microfiche reprint service for telephone directories.

Because most libraries are likely to purchase telephone books for major cities, and because the books in each region contain the same types of information, I have concentrated on examining the phone books for the largest cities. However, I have also included prices for telephone books for smaller cities and towns for comparative purposes.

In all these directories, entries are listed alphabetically on a word-by-word basis. Numbers file as if spelled out when they are the first word in an entry (*31 Flavors* would fall between *Thirst Quencher* and *Thrifty Rent-a-Car*), but they file at the end of the alphabet when they appear later in the name (*Motel 6* files after *Motel XYZ*). Hyphenated names file as if the second part of the surname were actually the first name, e.g., *Smith-Jones* is located between *Smith, John* and *Smith, Karl*. Perhaps the most serious problem is that some entries file under the article instead of under the first significant word. *El Patio Restaurant* is filed under *E*, *La Boutique* under *L*, and *The Car Wash* under *T*.

AMERITECH

Ameritech is the regional telephone company for the states of Illinois, Indiana, Michigan, Ohio, and Wisconsin. Ameritech's white pages vary in organization from city to city. Some have a single alphabetical listing of all entries, others contain separate directories for business and residential numbers. Some large cities have two sets of yellow-page directories, one aimed at consumers and one aimed at businesses. Most directories have a separate set of blue pages devoted to government agencies, although a few list city, local, and federal government numbers under the appropriate headings within the business section of the directory. All large cities have indexes to the subject headings in the yellow pages.

In addition to the main body of the directory, each Ameritech telephone book provides additional reference information. Specific local information is contained in a separate "Infopages" section that contains detailed street maps of the cities and towns covered by the directory, transportation information, calendars of cultural and sporting events, information on colleges and universities, and some small business information. The Infopages are compiled with the assistance of the local Chamber of Commerce and other community organizations. In addition, some basic consumer health, automobile, and income tax information is occasionally provided. A state zip-code directory, toll-free information and assistance numbers, and senior citizen information are also usually included in this section. Complete directories (white and yellow pages) for the two largest cities, Chicago and Detroit, cost $57.60 and $42.80, respectively. The cost is higher if a library also purchases directories for the suburban areas. For example, complete coverage of the Chicago metropolitan area is available at $97.60. Smaller cities have correspondingly smaller price tags. Madison, Wisconsin, is available at $11.15, and Springfield, Ohio, at $5.60.

BELL ATLANTIC

Bell Atlantic is the regional telephone company for Delaware, the District of Columbia, Maryland, New Jersey, Pennsylvania, Virginia, and West Virginia. The white pages from this company are organized into a single alphabetical sequence of business and residential numbers, with a separate government blue-pages section. The yellow pages for large cities are published in two volumes, one for consumers and one for businesses.

The yellow pages contain most of the information about the area. Two sections of information are provided: a glossy, full-color, illustrated "City Showcase" and a standard yellow-pages introduction. The "City Showcase" contains information on transportation, tourist attractions, theaters and sporting events, calendars of activities, parks and recreation, community services, and regional tourist sites. This section is very useful for the visitor or newcomer to the city. The "regular" yellow-pages introduction includes a subject index, some brief consumer information tips, zip codes, volunteer services, information on long-distance services, and a special business customer guide.

Directories for Washington, D.C., and Philadelphia cost $37.40 and $44.40, respectively. Wilmington, Delaware, and Wheeling, West Virginia, cost $23.60 and $12.20, respectively, and Altoona, Pennsylvania, costs $4.95.

BELL SOUTH

Telephone service in the southeastern part of the country is conducted through Bell South, which covers the states of Alabama, Florida, Georgia, Kentucky, Mississippi, Louisiana, North Carolina, South Carolina, and Tennessee. The white pages of most of Bell South's directories have separate business, residential, and government sections.

As with the other regional companies, the yellow pages contain most of the local information. The "Community Information Pages" in the beginning of the yellow pages provide a history of the city, information for newcomers, tourist attractions, a calendar of events, and a list of special services for senior citizens. Seating charts and calendars are provided for theaters and sporting events. Maps of the city, information on public transportation, and zip-code directories are also included in this section. While many of city guides present only the positive side of each city, the Miami directory mentions the riots that took place in the early 1980s. This type of material is quite unusual in what is essentially a promotional tool for the city.

At least one of Bell South's directories has a very different organization than other phone books. The Miami directory is divided into two volumes, one of which provides both white pages and yellow pages from *A* to *L* and the other, these sections from *M* to *Z*. This forces libraries to have both volumes available in order to have a complete set of either the white or yellow pages. Prices of Bell South directories are equivalent to most other telephone directories. Atlanta and Miami are available for $26.75 and $30.90, respectively. Louisville, Kentucky, is $16.50 and Knoxville, Tennessee, is $8.40.

NYNEX

NYNEX is the regional telephone company for New York and New England (Connecticut, Maine, Massachusetts, New Hampshire, Rhode Island, and Vermont). NYNEX directories cover some of the most urban areas of the nation. They are organized in an integrated format. One alphabetical sequence covers both business and residential listings in the white pages, and only one edition of the yellow pages is published, providing both business and consumer information. The only distinct section is a set of blue pages for government offices, which is included in the same volume as the white pages.

Local information is provided in a supplement to the yellow pages called "The NYNEX Yellow Pages Guide to the . . . Area." This full-color, illustrated section provides facts and history for each city. Specific information is given on tourist sites, parks and recreation activities, transportation, sporting and cultural events (including seating charts for theaters and stadiums), a calendar of festivals and other activities, restaurant and nightclub information, shopping areas, and zip and area codes.

Telephone books for New York City are divided by borough. Manhattan alone costs $23.85, and the entire city is available for $92.25. Boston costs $20.75, Hartford is $23.90; Portland, Maine, is $6.15; and Bennington, Vermont, is $3.60.

PACIFIC BELL

Pacific Bell was formed from the merger of Pacific Telephone and Nevada Bell and covers only the states of California and Nevada. Although this company covers the smallest number of states, its population base—and resulting number of telephone directories—is quite large. The white pages of each Pacific Bell directory contain a single, integrated alphabetical listing of residential and business numbers, with a separate set of blue pages for government entries. The yellow pages are similarly combined into a single volume.

Pacific Bell includes the majority of the local information in the yellow pages. For each city, a wealth of tourist and local material is provided, including a calendar of local events; lists of shopping areas, nightclubs, and tourist sites; theaters and sports stadiums, including seating charts; transit, airport, and highway information; city maps; zip codes; and hospitals and community services. Special local business information is also provided, including calendars of trade shows, business resources, and maps of air-freight terminals and port facilities. Each directory contains approximately 50 pages of local information, which is more than directories published by other regional companies.

In addition to the local information, each of the Pacific Bell yellow pages includes three indexes. Along with a standard subject index to the yellow pages, special consumer and business subject-search indexes are provided. Each of these subject-search indexes covers a specific topic area, such as automotive or office supplies, and directs the user to the appropriate subject headings in the directory through the use of both text and illustrations. With this index, someone who is unfamiliar with the anatomy of an automobile could still use the pictures and be directed to the appropriate subject headings for purchasing the necessary parts or services. Pacific Bell is the only company that includes this feature in their directories.

Since Pacific Bell includes more information in each directory than the other publishers, the price of its directories is also correspondingly higher. For Los Angeles and San Francisco, the prices are $76 and $40.55, respectively. Obtaining suburban directories will raise the price significantly. To purchase directories for the entire Los Angeles area costs $214.70. Las Vegas costs $18.80, and the entire rest of the state of Nevada is available at $17.60.

SOUTHWESTERN BELL

Southwestern Bell is the regional company covering the states of Arkansas, Kansas, Missouri, Oklahoma, and Texas. Southwestern Bell directories are similar to those above, but they do have some minor differences. All Southwestern Bell directories have divided business and residential sections in the white pages but only a single volume of yellow pages. All government listings are included in a separate section of blue pages included in the business portion of the white pages.

A full-color glossy spread in the beginning of the yellow pages contains information on shopping, museums, theaters, parks and recreation activities, and major tourist attractions in each city. Advertising of local attractions, hotels, and restaurants is also contained in this section. Entertainment information includes seating charts of the major theaters and sports centers. In this section, additional information is also provided on zip codes, community services, utilities, and voter registration. Color photographs and maps add appeal. In addition to the yellow pages and the introduction to the city, a set of green pages at the end of each directory provides even more local information. A subject index to the yellow pages comprises the majority of this section, but guides to products and services, businesses open 24 hours per day, and Better Business Bureau members are provided, along with community information such as churches and health-care institutions and city street maps.

One problem with Southwestern Bell directories is the lack of a comprehensive table of contents or index for the various types of information contained in the yellow pages. Because there is no cross-referencing from the full-color to the green and the yellow pages, the reader needs to know in advance which section is most likely to contain the necessary information. The user needs to consult the yellow pages for the name of a business, the color pages for its zip code, and the green pages for a map of its location. Cross-references in the table of contents would solve this problem.

Houston and St. Louis cost $45.40 and $21.60, respectively. Little Rock costs $8, and a small town, such as Stillwater, Oklahoma, is $2.40.

U.S. WEST

U.S. West has the largest geographic region of any of the seven telephone companies, covering Arizona, Colorado, Idaho, Iowa, Montana, Nebraska, New Mexico, North Dakota, Oregon, South Dakota, Utah, Washington, and Wyoming. It is also the most rural of all of the seven regionals and includes very few large cities. U.S. West Direct, publisher of all telephone directories for U.S. West, organizes each of the white pages into separate residential, business, and government sections. Yellow pages for the largest cities appear in two volumes divided alphabetically.

In its yellow pages, U.S. West uses a full-color section labeled "Easy Reference Guide" to present local information. Maps, zip codes, and information on city history and services, public transportation, parks and recreation, sporting events, colleges and universities, local events, and tourist sites are all presented in this attractive and readable supplement. An index to the yellow-pages subject headings is also included as an appendix. U.S. West is the only directory publisher that cross-indexes from the regular table of contents to the "Easy Reference Guide." A user looking for a city map or zip codes is led directly to the local information. U.S. West telephone books have more cross-references than those of the other regionals.

Directories for Phoenix and Denver cost $23.20 and $24, respectively. Omaha, Nebraska, costs $9.60 and Gallup, New Mexico, costs $5.60.

PHONEFICHE

Phonefiche, a set of telephone directories on microfiche available from University Microfilms, is the only nationwide alternative to the purchase of telephone directories from the regional telephone companies. All of the information contained in the original directory is reproduced on diazo microfiche, including the white pages, yellow pages, indexes, and community guides. This set reproduces rather than restructures the information contained in each directory and does not solve any of the organizational problems of the directories themselves. The microfiche is produced and distributed soon after the paper directory is printed, so there is very little delay in receiving the information in this format. A library may subscribe to *Phonefiche* in any one of several categories, or it may select cities or states on an individual basis. Prices currently range from $310 for all directories for cities over 1,500,000 in population to $1,650 for cities of greater than 150,000 population to $6,640 for all directories covered by the program. This final category is roughly equivalent to the combined total price of all of the directories published by the regional telephone companies.

Phonefiche offers three distinct advantages over the paper telephone books. The first advantage is in space savings. An entire nation of microfiche directories occupies the same physical space as only a few paper directories. The microfiche format also allows libraries to keep older editions of telephone directories if they so desire, and obviates the need for binding heavily used directories. Currently, most libraries discard older editions due to space problems and damage from heavy usage.

The second advantage of *Phonefiche* is that all of the telephone books come from one source with a single subscription and payment. The categories provided by University Microfilms make ordering telephone directories on microfiche very easy. With paper copies, libraries need to order new editions as they are published because not all regional telephone companies currently take standing orders.

The final benefit of *Phonefiche* is one of cost: although its initial cost is slightly higher than ordering the same directories in paper and a microfiche reader must be available, the labor required in the upkeep of the collection is much less intensive. Because paper telephone books are published throughout the year, they require constant processing and updating. With *Phonefiche*, all that is required is to file the new fiche and remove the old. When labor costs are included in a cost comparison, *Phonefiche* will be less expensive than paper directories.

However, patron and librarian resistance to the use of microfiche needs to be considered. It takes longer to locate a telephone number or address on fiche than it does in paper. Since large communities often require several microfiche for one directory, browsing through a telephone book is difficult when using *Phonefiche*. Many libraries purchase a combination of *Phonefiche* and selected popular paper directories.

***

Telephone directories are still important sources of local information for library reference collections. However, they have some major organizational and indexing problems that would not be tolerated in commercial reference tools. Although each directory on its own is relatively inexpensive, the cumulative cost of providing information for the entire nation is quite high. Lobbying efforts to restore free distribution of telephone directories have already been successful in the state of California, where the California Institute of Libraries lobbied the California Public Utilities Commission to continue to provide free directories to libraries in that state, and in New York and New England, where libraries served by NYNEX lobbied to restore free provision of phone books from the phone companies outside their region. Efforts by other regional or national library associations might accomplish the same result in other parts of the country or even on a national basis. Since phone companies are advertising that libraries provide access to telephone directories (as the quotation at the beginning of this review indicates), they should be willing to furnish libraries with the materials necessary to provide this service.

David Tyckoson, compiler of "Telephone Books as Reference Sources," is information services librarian at the Iowa State University Library. He was a member of the *RBB* Editorial Board from 1984 to 1988. Tyckoson also compiled the *RBB* lists "United States Government Guides" [F 1 88] and "Guides to Graduate Study" [F 1 87].

FEATURED REVIEWS AND REVIEWS

GENERALITIES

World of Winners: A Current and Historical Perspective on Awards and Their Winners. 1st ed. Ed. by Gita Siegman and Cynthia Russell Spomer. Gale, 1989. 977p. indexes. hardcover $60 (0-8103-0665-4; ISSN 1041-3529).

001.44 Rewards (Prizes, etc.)—Directories I Rewards (Prizes, etc.)—U.S.—Directories I Rewards (Prizes, etc.)—Canada—Directories [BKL]

World of Winners supplements Gale's *Awards, Honors, and Prizes* by listing and indexing "more than 75,000 recipients" of "almost 2,000" of the 16,000 to 18,000 awards described in *Awards, Honors, and Prizes*. Selection criteria include "the most important and most interesting awards, ... the most significant awards, ... awards that are representative of major fields of endeavor, ... and awards of popular interest that are frequently cited in the media." Most of the awards are still offered, and retrospective coverage extends back as far as 90 years for the Olympic Games and 60 years for the Academy Awards. "Generally, a complete historical record of winners has been given ... with winners listed from the most recent to the first recipient." The definition of *award* is broad, including even election to the presidency of the United States! The listing of its winners goes back to 1788.

According to the preface, sources for data included questionnaires sent to award sponsors, news reports, telephone interviews, announcements, and "original research," but the particular sources used to document individual awards are not indicated. Awards are listed alphabetically by name of award or awarding body within 12 broad categories: "Arts and Letters"; "Business, Management, and Marketing"; "Design and Architecture"; "Health and Medicine"; "Humanities, Education, and Library Science"; "Lifestyles" (a catchall category for beauty, fashion, and a single award for cooking); "Live Performance"; "Mass Media"; "Music"; "Public Affairs"; "Science, Engineering, and Technology"; and "Sports and Hobbies."

Under each award are occasional notes on the history of the award, followed by recipients—with affiliation and/or country when known—in reverse chronological order. For many recipients, brief notes indicate the achievement that resulted in the award. Three indexes complement the main listing of awards: an organization index to the award sponsors, a winners index to recipients, and an awards index to the names and subjects of awards. The organization and award indexes include cross-references from English names to actual vernacular names. In the winners index, there has been no attempt to standardize names, so that, to cite the example given in the preface, there are separate entries for *Clay, Cassius* and *Ali, Muhammad* and for *Aaron, Hank* and *Aaron, Henry*.

Subject access to awards is minimal. The table of contents lists the 12 broad subject categories and under each one lists more specific categories; e.g., under "Sports and Hobbies" are "Automobile Racing, Baseball, Basketball, Biking, Bowling," etc., but the actual awards are not arranged within these categories. The awards index claims to cite "subject keywords within the award name," but this is done very sparingly and inconsistently, and there is no attempt to link related subjects. The National Academy of Sciences Award in Applied Mathematics and Numerical Analysis is listed only under *National*.

The National Baseball Hall of Fame is listed under *National* and *Hall of Fame*, but not under *Baseball*. On the other hand, the National Music Theater Awards are listed under *Music* and *National*, but not *Theater*, and the Norbert Wiener Prize in Applied Mathematics is listed under *Mathematics* as well as *Wiener*. There are no subject cross-references linking equivalent terms; for instance, there are entries under both *Automobile* and *Car*, with no linking reference. This is a large, heavy volume; the binding appears to be inadequate for a book of this size.

The main purpose of *World of Winners* is to index the winners of the world's principal awards, and this it does fairly well. It does less well in providing access to awards by subject, but the companion Gale work *Awards, Honors, and Prizes* would be a more appropriate and comprehensive source for information on awards in any case.

International Encyclopedia of Communications. 4v. Ed. by Erik Barnouw and others. Oxford, 1989. bibliog. index. hardcover $350 (0-19-504994-2).

001.51'0321 Communication—Dictionaries [CIP] 88-18132

The complex, highly interdisciplinary field of communications is rapidly evolving due to constant technological innovations. The difficulties and challenges inherent in this process may be why the field has heretofore lacked a comprehensive subject encyclopedia. This void has now been filled by the four-volume *International Encyclopedia of Communications (IEC)*, a cooperative publishing venture undertaken by the Annenberg School of Communications at the University of Pennsylvania and Oxford University Press. In preparation for six years, this collaborative project drew on the expertise of an impressive array of international scholars and experts who served as editors, editorial advisers, and contributors under the direction of editor-in-chief Erik Barnouw, professor emeritus of drama, Columbia University. As Barnouw indicates in the preface, the term *communications* encompasses "all ways in which information, ideas, and attitudes pass among individuals, groups, nations, and generations." Intended for college students and educated laypersons as well as scholars and professionals, *IEC* attempts "to define, reflect, summarize, and explain the field in an accessible, comprehensive, and authoritative way."

Arranged alphabetically word by word, the 569 articles range in length from 500 to 4,000 words. The articles are signed, and a list of contributors in volume 4 notes their professional affiliations and the titles of the entries they wrote. The editor's commitment to creating a work of international scope is reflected in this list, which includes more than 450 scholars and other specialists from 29 countries. Also evident in this list is the wide range of disciplines involved in studying various aspects of the field of communications. Among the subject areas represented are anthropology, art, drama, education, history, journalism, law, linguistics, literature, music, philosophy, political science, psychology, religion, and sociology. Thus, it is not surprising that perhaps the most impressive feature of *IEC* is the diversity of the topics treated. Some articles are devoted to subjects pertaining to the history of communication (e.g., *Colonization, Egyptian Hieroglyphs,*

Silk Road), while others discuss customs or social interactions that further communication (e.g., *Festival, Food, Gossip*) and institutions involved in the communication process (e.g., *Library, Museum, School*). Visual art forms and the performing arts are covered (e.g., *Photography, Sculpture, Acting, Dance*), as are literature and other written forms of communication (e.g., *Poetry, Literary Canon, Newsletter, Spy Fiction*). Among other categories treated are the mass media, popular culture, communication technologies, nonverbal forms of communication, animal communication, and research methodologies used by communication scholars. In addition, approximately 130 articles are devoted to individuals who made significant contributions to some area of communication (e.g., *Confucius*; *Hitchcock, Alfred*; *Piaget, Jean*; *Webster, Noah*). Although most of the individuals covered are deceased, some living persons born prior to 1920 are also included. While biographical information on these subjects is generally available in other reference sources, *IEC* articles offer a different perspective on their careers by concentrating on those aspects of their work that contributed to either the development of, or current knowledge about, communication. For example, the article *Darwin, Charles* emphasizes the significance of his observations regarding animal signaling and human gestures and facial expressions.

While the general arrangement is alphabetical by article title, in some cases several articles are grouped together under a topical heading for easier access. For example, the entry *Children* actually consists of four separately authored articles dealing with children and communication: *Development of Communication, Development of Symbolization, Use of Media*, and *Media Effects*. Additional access to related articles is provided by a network of cross-references that greatly facilitates the use of the set. These references indicate links in a variety of ways: by capitalizing an entire word or phrase within the text of an entry to indicate that a term has a separate entry, by frequently including *see* and *see also* references within the body of articles, and by providing *see also* references at the end of articles.

Concluding each article is a brief bibliography that provides suggestions for further reading. Although some foreign-language monographs and articles are cited, most of the references are to sources in English. The majority of these bibliographies include citations from the 1980s, and a number cite publications as recent as 1987. However, some of the articles dealing with technology do not have citations as current as might be expected. For example, the most recent sources cited in the articles *Satellite* and *Microelectronics* were published in 1984. In fact, the generally skimpy coverage of recent developments in communication technologies is a disappointing aspect of *IEC*. The set contains no mention of high-definition television, telefacsimile transmission, or the burgeoning books-on-tape industry, and it gives only very brief treatment of computer graphics and video games. This weakness is apparently a reflection of the editorial decision to concentrate on long-range patterns and processes in order to prevent the encyclopedia from becoming obsolete too quickly. Curiously, the only other serious omissions noted involved communication and the visually-and hearing-impaired. Although separate articles are devoted to *Keller, Helen* and *Sign Language*, there is no article or even an index entry for *Braille*. In addition, while references to *blindness* and *deafness* appear in the index, these subjects receive only peripheral treatment. In a work of this scope, main articles addressing the historical development of communication mechanisms for the blind and the deaf would seem appropriate.

However, an area of even greater concern is that, while the articles are authoritative and generally well written, the level of erudition of some of the entries may render them incomprehensible to all but specialists. This seems to be the case particularly with articles that discuss theories and concepts. The following sentence from the article *Attitudes* illustrates this problem: "In the case of expectancy-value attitudes, a molecular attitude might be represented as interrelated networks of individual belief-times-evaluation products; alternatively, attitude might be conceptualized as substructures of beliefs and evaluations organized as indicators of higher-order expectancy-value latent variables."

If a prize were awarded for most attractive reference work of the year, *IEC* would surely be a top contender. Printed in two colors on acid-free paper, the text is arranged two columns to a page. Article headers, page numbers, and page headers are printed in reddish-brown ink, which is also used to highlight certain parts of entries and graphics. More than 1,100 illustrations, including photographs, maps, charts, tables, and line drawings, enhance the text. While most of these were taken from other sources, some were prepared especially for *IEC*. Preceding each section of the alphabet is a tinted page that displays the next letter and reproduces part of the description of the letter from *The Oxford English Dictionary*. The separately paged volumes, averaging about 480 pages each, are attractively bound, and the volume number and the first four letters of the beginning and ending articles appear prominently on the spine. Colorful endpapers in a marbled motif add a touch of elegance.

Volume 4 includes both a topical guide and a traditional index. The topical guide provides a useful overview of the contents of *IEC* by grouping article titles into 30 broad categories, such as *Advertising and Public Relations, Computer Era, Government Regulation, Nonverbal Communication*, and *Theater*. The detailed index contains more than 15,000 entries for topics, titles, individuals, and organizations. Titles are further identified in parentheses by format or genre (e.g., *book, film, journal, comic strip*). References note volume number and pagination, with an asterisk following the pagination indicating a main article. Illustrative material is not represented in the index.

The *International Encyclopedia of Communications* is a significant scholarly achievement. Its broad and authoritative coverage of the multifaceted aspects of communication provides a synthesis of ideas and concepts that span many disciplines. While a number of the topics treated are also covered by other subject encyclopedias and even by general encyclopedias, *IEC* offers a unique perspective by viewing events, places, organizations, social processes, and other factors in relation to their contribution to or influence on the evolution of communication. Although its sometimes pedantic language may deter some elements of its intended audience, this fine work is recommended for academic and large public libraries. It will be an essential purchase for institutions that support graduate programs in journalism and mass communication.

National Directory of Bulletin Board Systems, 1988/1989. Ed. by Ric Manning. Meckler, 1988. 108p. paper $39.95 (0-88736-351-2; ISSN 0884-9536).
004 Computer bulletin boards—Directories [OCLC] 86-647246

Computer hobbyists with a personal computer and modem are often in search of free or limited-fee bulletin-board systems (BBS). To communicate and share files with other enthusiasts, they need a bulletin board that is compatible with their type of personal computer. This *Directory* attempts to fill the need of locating BBS by listing a cross-section of several thousand bulletin boards accessible by various types of personal computers.

It is organized alphabetically by type of computer: Amiga, Apple II, Atari ST, Commodore 64/128, IBM, and Macintosh. Under each computer are the communications software packages used by the bulletin boards. For example, under IBM there is listed *FidoNet, Galacticomm, GT Powercom, InfoHost, PC Board, RBBS-PC, Bread Board System*, and *Wildcat!* Each communications package has a three- to nine-paragraph explanation. Included in this explanation are the price of the software, searching commands, and other important protocols. Then the bulletin boards using the particular software are listed, arranged either by area code or by state.

A look in more detail at one package will show exactly what this *Directory* can accomplish. For example, the *PC Board* bulletin-board package is used for IBM-compatible computers. This section begins with the name of the developer of the software, a short introduction, the purchase price, and a reproduction of the menu one sees when signing onto a bulletin board using this software. This is followed by a list of the bulletin boards arranged by area code. Foreign boards are included. For each bulletin board there is the telephone number, hours of operation, SYSOP name (i.e., who runs the board), modem used, and telecommunications speed (1200, 2400, 4800, or 9600 baud). If the board has a specialized purpose (e.g., medical, astronomy, desktop publishing), it is noted. However, a purpose is not listed for most boards because they attempt to be general and thus contain as many different files as possible. The format for this section is an exact copy of what one finds in a file on any *PC Board* BBS that lists other bulletin boards. Therefore, it is safe to assume that the author downloaded this list from his favorite BBS.

Three of the six bulletin boards looked for were included, and the information about them was accurate. The boards not included are somewhat specialized (they were RACHEL, Greenpeace, and Economic Bulletin Board) and may have been omitted for that reason. There is no index and no rationale for inclusion or exclusion of any specific BBS. This work is limited to bulletin boards and does not include online sources like CompuServe, Source, BRS, VuText, etc. *The Computer Phone Book* [*RBB* D 1 86] does not include as many bulletin boards. Bulletin boards go out of business fairly rapidly and new ones are born every day. Therefore, a 1986 imprint is very out of date, and even a 1988 imprint like this *Directory* is somewhat dated. To keep current about bulletin boards, all one has to do is join any BBS and download its file of other boards. One problem a novice computer user has is finding that first BBS to dial up. One way is to contact a local computer club, another would be to use this *Directory*. Libraries asked by patrons for low-cost or free systems they can dial up will find this *Directory* useful.

McGraw-Hill Personal Computer Programming Encyclopedia: Languages and Operating Systems. 2d ed. Ed. by William J. Birnes and others. McGraw-Hill, 1989. 752p. bibliog. index. hardcover $95 (0-07-005393-6).

004.16 Microcomputers—Programming I Programming languages (Electronic computers) II Operating systems (Computers) [OCLC] 88-8410

This handbook for users of personal computers has been updated to reflect the introduction of new hardware and software since the 1985 edition. It opens with 13 essays on special applications such as local area networks, microcomputers in libraries, artificial intelligence, computer-aided design, desktop publishing, and graphics. These are written for the layperson; the remainder of the book requires some knowledge of programming.

The essays are followed by four- to eight-page discussions of 17 microprocessors (Motorola, Intel, etc.), 28 high-level programming languages (COBOL, Pascal), 9 software command languages (*dBase II*, *Lotus 1-2-3*), and 12 operating systems (MS-DOS, CP/M, etc.). The major portion of the *Encyclopedia* is devoted to programming languages. Functions, commands, course codes, and special features are explained. There is a good review of a language's historical development along with practical hints on getting started using it. An explanation of a language's working vocabulary is the larger part of these entries.

The best feature of the work—for those users able to make practical use of it—continues to be the "Index of High-Level Language Keywords." It serves as a cross-reference to all the programming languages in the *Encyclopedia*, enabling users to find definitions for the major keywords used in a program's vocabulary and translate statements used in BASIC, ZBASIC, and COMAL, for example, into corresponding statements in Fortran, LISP, and SNOBOL.

A glossary of an estimated 1,700 terms is another useful feature. These definitions are intended for beginning programmers and compare favorably with those given in Alan Freedman's *Computer Glossary for Everyone* (Computer Language Co., 1983), a helpful dictionary intended for laypersons. A subject index and an updated bibliography containing complete citations to books and manuals are additional features.

This *Encyclopedia* should receive heavy use in high school, public, and academic libraries that serve users who design and write programs for personal computers.

American Reference Books Annual, 1988. v.19. Ed. by Bohdan S. Wynar. Libraries Unlimited, 1988. 761p. indexes. hardcover $70 (0-87287-681-0; ISSN 0065-9959).

011.02 Reference books—Bibliography [OCLC]

One of the staple sources for reference reviews and evaluations is now in its nineteenth edition. *American Reference Books Annual, 1988* (*ARBA*) contains extended reviews of 1,809 English-language reference materials. The annual is arranged in four parts: "General Reference Works," "Social Sciences," "Humanities," and "Science and Technology." The signed reviews are written by librarians and college faculty. As in any book with 300 contributors, there is some unevenness in the reviews, and some would benefit from more careful editing. As noted in our previous review [*RSBR* Je 1 83], the evaluations are comprehensive and "range in size from a paragraph to several pages." Also noted in that review, *ARBA* is not as current as one might wish: the nineteenth edition covers 1987 and some 1986 publications. What it lacks in timeliness it makes up for in comparative evaluations, including citations to reviews in 17 other publications ranging from BOOKLIST to *Wilson Library Bulletin*.

This edition has some changes from previous ones. Coverage of Canadian reference books has been expanded, with the intention to provide as complete coverage of them as of works published in the U.S. Second, library-science sources that are not reference works are now reviewed in a separate publication, *Library and Information Science Annual*. Third, the author-title index has been separated from the subject index.

Still going strong after 19 years, *ARBA* is a comprehensive source of critical reviews by knowledgeable reviewers. This perennial favorite is a must purchase for all academic and most public libraries.

Reference Books for Young Readers: Authoritative Evaluations of Encyclopedias, Atlases, and Dictionaries. Ed. by Marion Sader. Bowker, 1988. 615p. bibliog. illus. index. hardcover $49.95 (0-8352-2366-3).

011'.02 Children's reference books—Bibliography I Libraries, Children's—Book lists II Libraries, Young people's—Book lists [CIP] 87-38234

This introductory volume in Bowker's Buying Guide series is designed for librarians who provide reference services to young readers, preschool through high school, to aid in selection. A companion volume covering reference books for adults will be published this fall. Approximately 200 encyclopedias, atlases, and dictionaries and wordbooks as well as large-print reference works are given descriptive and evaluative reviews here. Included are several online encyclopedias (one of which is no longer available) and sets in other formats. Chosen for inclusion were works published in the U.S. and available for purchase as of August 1987. As a result of this cutoff date, the second edition of *The Random House Dictionary of the English Language* is not reviewed. Some of the encyclopedias reviewed are 1987 sets; others are 1986 editions. Three librarian-consultants selected works for inclusion, set the criteria, and reviewed the essays and reviews prepared by close to 30 librarians and subject specialists who are identified with current affiliations in the front matter.

The text is divided into five sections, described in the prefatory "Using This Book." The introductory section includes chapters on the history of general reference books, especially for young readers; criteria for choosing reference works; a survey of public and elementary librarians ranking various tools; and a chapter consisting of comparative charts that display key information on the works reviewed. Parts 2 to 4 contain detailed evaluations of encyclopedias, atlases, and dictionaries and wordbooks. Each section begins with a "What to Look for..." chapter that details the criteria used to judge the particular type of work, defining such concepts as *scope*, *currency*, and *clarity* and indicating what subjects were used in evaluating each of the works. For example, the subjects reviewed for accuracy in each encyclopedia include *Henry the Navigator*, *Bill of Rights*, *Brain*, and *Saturn*. Each individual review follows an outline that begins with summary data, "Facts at a Glance," then covers general criteria and those specific to the type of work, such as scale and projections for atlases. Attention is given to special features, and a summary discussion follows the review. Facsimile pages in black and white are included for selected encyclopedias and dictionaries, providing another indication of a work's appropriateness or ease of use. The final section, part 5, considers large-print reference works suitable for the visually impaired in the same categories. Some of these are large-print versions of works reviewed earlier, and so are treated only briefly, with a reference made to the entire review in one of the other sections. (As with all the cross-references that appear in the text, page numbers would facilitate use.) Newly appearing titles are accorded a full review. The reviews of these reference titles are very comprehensive and detailed, showing that the works have been examined closely. Concrete examples are given for each criterion discussed, and comparisons made with other similar works reviewed. Reviews are critical, and there is no hesitation to give a qualified recommendation or a complete pan. There is also a section that quotes from other reviews. Because the reviews are so extensive, the summary paragraph is important. The largest chapter is on dictionaries and wordbooks, with over 100 reviews. This should be helpful to those selecting dictionaries, since so many are published, with widely varying quality and authority, and many titles sound so similiar. The statement that the name *Webster* is out of copyright and used by publishers for dictionaries of widely varying quality and authority is found in one of the first introductory chapters. It would be better placed or bear repeating in the chapter on what to look for in dictionaries. The reviews themselves do indicate authority and whether the name *Webster* in the title is an abuse of the lexicographer's name.

Appended are a select bibliography on the different types of works evaluated and a publishers list. The name-subject-title index lists all titles mentioned in the guide (useful since reference works are published in many versions with slight name changes), with small caps indicating those with full reviews. Another supplementary feature of this work is the glossaries that appear at the end of the "What to Look for ... chapters, defining such terms as *conic projection*, *citation*, *colloquial*, *denotation*, and *vendor*. Other buying guides that can be compared with this title are Kister's *Best Encyclopedias* (Oryx, 1986) and guides to the literature such as *Reference Books for Children* (Scarecrow, 1981) or *Guide to Reference Books for School Media Centers* (Libraries Unlimited, 1986). The latter two are more comprehensive guides to reference works for children, covering all types of titles more concisely. Comparing Kister's work to the encyclopedia section in the Bowker guide, we find the coverage remarkably similar for the scope Bowker defines (in print and published in the U.S.). Kister also reviews out-of-print and foreign encyclopedias. The Bowker discussion of adult encyclopedias such as *Americana* focuses, of course, more on their suitability for younger users. If a criticism can be made of *Reference Books for Young Readers*, it might be that there is almost too much information in each review. Also, the 18 pages on the history of reference books seems unlikely to be used outside a library science class, although this guide would provide useful training for librarians in how to do a rigorous review of a reference work.

This handsomely produced work will be useful to librarians selecting for younger readers and can also be helpful to parents wanting guidance for home purchases.

Spanish-Language Reference Books: An Annotated Bibliography. Comp. by Bibliotecas para la Gente Reference Committee. Chicano Studies Library Publications Unit, 3404 Dwinelle Hall, University of California at Berkeley, Berkeley, CA 94720, 1989. 45p. index. paper $10 (0-918520-15-0).
011'.02 Reference books, Spanish—Bibliography [CIP] 88-39932

This bibliography was compiled by a group of library professionals concerned with serving the Spanish-speaking population. It is an annotated list that will help librarians find reference sources for Spanish-speaking patrons.

The 117 works included are drawn from the collections held in the libraries of the compilers. They are arranged by broad subject area: "General Reference," "Library Science," "Religion," "Folklore & Customs," "Economics & Business," etc. Typical titles include a family medical dictionary, Amy Vanderbilt, and a Chilton auto-repair manual in Spanish. Each entry is annotated with a detailed description of the work and its strengths and weaknesses. ISBNs and prices are included if available, but the latter should be used as an estimate since the prices of foreign materials change constantly. An index of names and titles appears at the end.

This bibliography is not exhaustive, but it does provide materials that will fill many needs. In some cases, the sources do not meet the standards of English-language tools available in the same subject areas. Many are out of date, and some may be out of print. The California Vehicle Code, for example, is from 1970. Often, however, the sources are the only Spanish-language ones available on a given topic. When working with foreign-language tools, one often has to deal with poor indexing, inferior binding, and high prices.

Librarians responsible for reference and/or collection-development services in the Spanish language will find this bibliography extremely useful. It evaluates many sources covering a wide range of subjects. The books included are those actually used by the librarians who compiled it. Since all the prefatory material and annotations are in English, it can be used by librarians with little or no knowledge of Spanish. *Spanish-Language Reference Books* is worth far more than its $10 price tag. It is a unique source that belongs in all collections serving Hispanic communities.

Ulrich's International Periodicals Directory, 1988–89: Now Including Irregular Serials & Annuals. 3v. 27th ed. Bowker, 1988. indexes. hardcover $279.95 (0-8352-2563-1; ISSN 0000-0175).
011.34 Periodicals—Directories [OCLC] 32-16320

With this twenty-seventh edition, *Ulrich's International Periodicals Directory*, long a standard reference source, has changed significantly. First and foremost, it has merged with its companion, *Irregular Serials and Annuals*, to become a three-volume set covering both periodicals and other serials. This new set is about $30 cheaper than the two titles were when ordered last year. Secondly, there are several new entry elements—Library of Congress classification number, CODEN, CD-ROM availability, and brief descriptions of selected titles. The look has changed somewhat as well. There are alphabetic guides on the page edges, flags indicating new titles, and a larger typeface for main entries. Finally, the updating service, which becomes more and more important as print sources compete with online and CD-ROM equivalents, has changed yet again. It is now called *Ulrich's Update* and comes free with the set on a quarterly basis. There is another related publication, the bimonthly *Ulrich's News* (not seen by *RBB*).

This edition contains 108,000 titles, 6,700 of which are listed for the first time. Another 65,000 entries have been updated since the publication of last year's editions of the two directories. The stated exclusions to the *Directory* include daily and local newspapers, membership directories, and comic books.

Periodicals and other serials appear together in the main body of the work, the two-volume classified list of subjects. Within a subject, they are listed alphabetically. Volume 3 combines features that previously appeared in both directories ("Serials Available Online," "Vendor Listing/Serials Online," "Cessations," "Index to Publications of International Organizations," "Title Index") and brings one index over from *Irregular Serials and Annuals*—the ISSN index.

With these changes, *Ulrich's* has become more like its recent competitor, EBSCO's *Serials Directory* [*RBB* Mr 15 87]. Both are now three-volume sets combining periodicals with other serials. Entry elements are also becoming more alike. *The Serials Directory* still has a slight edge in number of entries (118,000 in the third edition) and seems to have improved since the first edition by filling in more entry elements for each title. The prices of the two are within $10 of each other.

Combining the two Bowker directories into one should provide a definite convenience factor for librarians. In addition, the other improvements should enhance *Ulrich's* long-standing reputation as an authoritative source for serials information.

Illustration Index VI: 1982–1986. By Marsha C. Appel. Scarecrow, 1988. 531p. hardcover $42.50 (0-8108-2146-X).

011'.37 Pictures—Indexes [CIP] 88-18207

The purpose of this index is to serve as a guide to illustrations in nine U.S. magazines. The list includes *National Geographic, Life, Sports Illustrated, American Heritage, Natural History, Ebony,* and *Travel/Holiday*. Appel states in the preface that the journals "were chosen for their richness of illustration and for the availability of back issues in libraries." Magazines indexed in this volume have been indexed in previous volumes. This sixth edition of the *Illustration Index* is the third one to be compiled by Appel.

Each entry under a subject includes journal title, volume number, pagination, date of publication, type of illustration (usually a photograph but also maps, drawings, etc.), color or black-and-white note, and a code for illustration size—full page, half page, etc.

Subjects are wide ranging; places, people, medicine, all kinds of sports, animals, and technical topics are covered. *See* references are plentiful and helpful. The preface states that there are 17,000 individual subject headings with over 35,000 entries. The book is in a straight alphabetical arrangement that is simple to use. The directions are easily understood.

This is a serviceable, functional index. It is worth purchasing if a library wants to update previous volumes, which extend coverage back to 1950. Public and school libraries that are often asked for pictures will find this a useful reference work.

Variety's Complete Home Video Directory, 1988. 1st ed. Bowker, 1988– .annual. 852p. indexes. paper $129.95 (0-8352-2500-3; ISSN 0000-1015).

011.37 Video tapes—Catalogs [BKL]

With *Variety's Complete Home Video Directory,* Bowker adds another format to its "in print" family. The *Directory* is a fairly comprehensive listing of videocassettes available for purchase by consumers and video retailers. Libraries with video collections should also find it useful. This first annual issue contains information on over 25,000 items from more than 1,200 producers and distributors. According to the preface, this information was gathered by 20 editors through telephone and mail inquiries. The connection to *Variety* is not made clear in the introductory portion of the directory. Bowker does state, however, that it provides quarterly updates containing similar information on new releases, each of which is cumulative, replacing the previous update. The second update, covering July–September 1988, has just been published. It includes 5,000 new titles plus 7,000 titles from the first update published in April. The arrangement is the same as the annual volume, except that there is an additional index giving title and order information for the videos new to this update. Apparently, there is also a separate directory for "adult" videos, available to subscribers upon request.

The body of the *Directory* is the alphabetical listing by title. The entries generally contain the dates of theatrical and video release, genre, running time, and a brief annotation. Some examples of annotations: "*The Color Purple*—A Southern sharecropper's daughter in the early days of this century moves from despair to personal triumph"; "*How to Windsurf with Murray Willet*—Covers the sport of windsurfing from basic rig assembly to advanced wind maneuvering. Proper form & technique & safety are stressed throughout." Other information includes availability of closed-captioning, MPAA rating, awards won, language, and series. And for those video buffs horrified by colorization, the hue is listed also. The final portion of the entry is dedicated to order information and includes the producer or distributor, suggested list price, format (VHS or Beta), and order numbers. In actuality, the entries vary in terms of completeness. For example, *The Seven Samurai* entry contains all of the applicable information, but *Seniors,* on the opposite page, has only title, running time, producer, format, order number, and price.

There are five indexes to the title listings. The first, the genre index, includes such headings as *Comedy, Opera, Young Adult, Foreign* (followed by the country), and *How-To* (followed by the activity). Then follows an alphabetical listing of titles available with closed-captions and another index by key cast members and directors. The awards index includes not only Academy Awards, but also British Academy Awards and Cannes International Film Festival, Directors Guild of America, Golden Globe, and New York Film Critics Circle awards. The final two sections are listings of companies providing videos or video services. The first contains approximately 1,300 producers and distributors. The latter lists services and supplies ranging from public relations and consulting to cases and display racks. This section has an alphabetical portion and a classified portion for the 300 companies represented. The format of the book, an oversized paperback with fold-out divider tabs, is somewhat awkward to use and may not hold up through a year of heavy use.

Variety's Complete Home Video Directory is the first comprehensive directory available for identifying home videocassettes for purchase. Most libraries have probably been using dealer catalogs for this purpose and should welcome this compilation from many producers and suppliers. It will not replace catalogs but supplement them, and it makes it possible to identify particular productions. It overlaps to some extent with *Video Source Book* (9th ed., Gale, 1987), but this latter title is aimed at the educational market. While *Variety's Complete Home Video Directory* is not limited to theatrical releases, it does not emphasize educational videos. This source is recommended for libraries with active video collections.

The Video Source Book, 1989. 10th ed. Ed. by David J. Weiner. Gale, 1988. 2,471p. hardcover indexes. $199, including two supplements (0-8103-4258-8; ISSN 0748-0881).

011'.37 Video recordings—Catalogs—Periodicals ‖ Video recordings—Indexes [OCLC]

The Video Source Book, formerly distributed by Gale Research, is now also edited and published by them. The tenth edition includes listings for over 54,000 video programs in five formats (VHS, Beta, Laserdisc, 8mm, and $^3/_4$ U-matic). Compiled from catalogs and press releases, it covers videos available for programming and home use.

The format is basically unchanged from the former edition. After a user guide, two pages of new releases, and a key to entry elements, the alphabetical program listings begin. Each entry contains up to 25 elements including date, running time, hue, cast/host, awards, and a brief description. Each title is also assigned one of eight main categories (e.g., *Business/Industry, Children's/Juvenile, Movies/Entertainment*) and one or more of 420 subject categories (e.g., *Drama, Marriage, Physics*). To aid those planning programs or broadcasts, the entries note restrictions on the use of the video, number of programs in series, acquisition information (purchase, loan, rental, etc.), producer, distributor, MPAA rating, intended audience, and purpose (e.g., teacher education, instruction, entertainment). According to the preface, prices are not included due to the fact that they are "subject to constant change."

The listings are followed by a main-category index that shows that *General Interest/Education, Movies/Entertainment,* and *Health/Science* are the largest categories. There is also an index by video subject category. To show how this two-tiered system works, a program called "Conversational German" can be found under *General Interest/Education* in the main-category index and under *Languages—Instruction* in the subject index. A cast index lists 410 actors, actresses, and directors. This is not an index of all people cited in entries, only those "readers are likely to look for." There are smaller indexes that list videodiscs, 8mm, and closed-captioned titles. A final list gives the addresses and telephone numbers of the producers and distributors of the listed titles. Two free supplements are issued to purchasers in February and June.

The Video Source Book is the most comprehensive listing of available video programs. The less expensive *Variety's Complete Home Video Directory* [RBB O 15 88] has a comparable number of titles for the home market and does include price information, but *The Video Source Book* also has thousands of technical, scientific, and medical titles. It has more specific subject categories and more formats than does *Variety's*. Both sources can serve the needs of libraries seeking information on videos aimed at home use, but *The Video Source Book* provides the broader coverage needed by those using videos in schools, the workplace, and broadcasting.

According to the publisher, the tenth edition of *The Video Source Book* has about 3,800 new videos. Libraries owning the ninth edition (1987) will need to decide how often they need to replace this useful source. Libraries just beginning video collections may want to rely on the selective lists in *Video for Libraries* [RBB Ap 15 89].

The Art of Children's Picture Books: A Selective Reference Guide. Sylvia S. Marantz and Kenneth A. Marantz. Garland, 1988. 165p. bibliog. indexes. hardcover $27 (0-8240-2745-0).

011.62 Reference books—Picture-books for children—Bibliography II Reference books—Children's literature—Bibliography I Reference books—Illustrated books, Children's—Bibliography I Picture-books for children—History—Bibliography I Children's literature—History and criticism—Bibliography [CIP] 88-1704

Black Authors and Illustrators of Children's Books: A Biographical Dictionary. By Barbara Rollock. Garland, 1988. 130p. bibliog. illus. hardcover $25 (0-8240-8580-9).

011'.62 Children's literature—Black authors—Bio-bibliography I Children's literature, American—Afro-American authors—Bio-bibliography II Afro-American authors—Biography—Dictionaries I Authors, Black—Biography—Dictionaries I Artists, Black—Biography—Dictionaries [CIP] 87-25748

A librarian and a professor of art education have compiled *The Art of Children's Picture Books*, a carefully selected bibliography of books, articles, papers, and audiovisuals through 1987. An insightful introduction considers the factors that make a picture book more a visual art object than a piece of literature.

The bibliography is in six parts: "History of Children's Picture Books"; "How a Picture Book Is Made"; "Criticism of Children's Picture Books"; "Artists Anthologized"; "Books, Articles, and Audiovisual Materials on Individual Picture Book Artists"; and "Guides and Aids to Further Research." Part 7 lists institutions that have collections of material on picture books and artists.

The 451 entries give full bibliographic data, with a brief annotation of contents. The volume concludes with artist, author-editor-compiler, and title indexes. Artists covered range from Randolph Caldecott and Kate Greenaway to Chris Van Allsburg.

The Art of Children's Picture Books will be a useful reference work for public libraries and for universities and colleges where there is interest in children's literature or programs in art education and illustration.

In her introduction to *Black Artists and Illustrators of Children's Books*, Rollock, former coordinator of children's services for the New York Public Library, indicates the need for material that "can provide an integral study of the black creative presence in children's books." Her intention, therefore, is "to provide those ill-informed or curious about the subject with a single reference volume in which the works of black authors and artists are recognized in relation to their particular contributions to children's literature."

The biographees live or work in this country, Africa, Canada, or Great Britain and have all been published in the U.S. People now deceased have been included if they lived in the twentieth century. Some authors or artists are listed even if they chose not to use black themes, e.g., Donald Crews. Rollock states the only exclusions are those authors, writing primarily for adults, who have written only one book for children (e.g., James Baldwin, Owen Dodson, and Pearl Bailey), though Gwendolyn Brooks, Charles Chesnutt, Countee Cullen, and others are listed with just one children's book.

Following a list of bibliographic sources, the dictionary is arranged alphabetically by name. One hundred fifteen sketches are included, most of them for authors. Entries ranges from a couple of sentences that sometimes sound as if they were taken from book-jacket copy to slightly over a page and are strictly biographical, not critical. A selected bibliography of the person's works appears at the end of each entry. Out-of-print titles are designated; however, more titles could have been so marked. Small black-and-white photographs of 31 artists and writers, plus some black-and-white photographs of dust jackets of books, are found in two inserts.

Although more complete information on 69 of the authors and illustrators in this book can be found in Gale's *Something about the Author*, *Black Authors and Illustrators of Children's Books* will be of interest to children, parents, teachers, and librarians who need to identify black authors and illustrators for children.

Books for Children to Read Alone: A Guide for Parents and Librarians. By George Wilson and Joyce Moss. Bowker, 1988. 184p. indexes. hardcover $32.95 (0-8352-2346-9).

011'.62 Children's literature—Bibliography I Children—Books and reading [CIP] 88-10430

This is an ideal reference source to help parents and librarians reinforce good reading habits in children prekindergarten through third grade. Educators Wilson and Moss discovered that of the 2,500 books published yearly for this age range, more books are written to be read to the child than for the child to read alone. Children who have been read to most of their lives are eager to practice for themselves. Rather than create frustration in this endeavor, a wise parent or librarian should be alert to those books best suited for solitary reading.

Books for Children to Read Alone is divided into seven chapters, beginning with wordless or nearly wordless books and continuing by intervals of half a grade through the second half of third grade. The introductory chapter explains how the more than 350 titles published between the early 1950s and 1985 were chosen by the authors. Each entry has an annotation that briefly describes the story, comments on the illustrations, and identifies genre (e.g., nonfiction, mystery, fantasy) and subject (ducks, family life, friendship). Any awards won by the book are noted. Each chapter begins with a list of the books divided into *Easy*, *Average*, and *Challenging* categories. There is an appendix that lists books by series plus indexes by subject, author, title, and readability level.

This invaluable reference tool should be on the shelf of every elementary school and public library.

Books for the Gifted Child. v.2. By Paula Hauser and Gail A. Nelson. Bowker, 1988. 244p. indexes. hardcover $32.95 (0-8352-2467-8).

011'.62 Gifted children—Books and reading I Children's literature—Bibliography [CIP] 79-27431

This volume carries forward the principles of the 1980 volume by Barbara H. Baskin and Karen H. Harris [BKL Ja 15 81]. Like the first volume, it is directed toward librarians, teachers, parents, and others working with gifted children, preschool through grade six. The authors hope that this bibliography will serve as "a resource of cognitively challenging books recommended for intellectually gifted youngsters."

Part 1, "Reading and the Gifted Child," considers the definitions of giftedness, the characteristics of gifted children, the need for guidance, and the importance of literature in various categories—picture books, fiction, nonfiction, poetry, folklore, and biography.

Part 2, "A Selected Guide to Intellectually Challenging Books," consists of lengthy annotations for 195 juvenile books, published from 1981 to 1987, considered appropriate for gifted children, from prereading through beginning, intermediate, and advanced readers (these latter terms are fully explained). The entries, with full bibliographic information, are arranged by the author's surname. The insightful annotations summarize the book and then discuss the features that make the title appropriate for gifted children. Occasionally quotations are included to give a feel for an author's particular style.

Title selection was based on the following: (1) appropriate form and content wherein the language is sufficiently complex to call on gifted readers' abilities to deal with abstractions, ambiguities, and other reasoning tasks, and (2) an interface of text and illustrations. The work is indexed by title, level, and subject.

Books for the Gifted Child, volume 2, is a valuable resource for those interested in meeting the reading needs of gifted children, ages 3 to 12.

Introducing Bookplots 3: A Book Talk Guide for Use with Readers Ages 8–12. By Diana L. Spirt. Bowker, 1988. 352p. indexes. hardcover $39.95 (0-8352-2345-0).

011'.62 Children's literature—Stories, plots, etc. ‖ Children's literature—Book reviews ‖ Children—Books and reading ‖ Book talks [CIP] 87-37513

This is a sequel to the author's *Introducing Books* (1970) and *Introducing More Books* (1978) and includes books published from 1979 to 1986. The title of this volume is different because it has joined the larger "plot" series that Bowker produces with titles such as *Juniorplots 3* [RBB Je 1 88]. It is designed to help persons engaged in reading guidance for middle-grade children to create booktalks, select books to read aloud, or design bibliographies especially for this age group.

The selection process began with at least three reputable reviewing sources recommending the title. The book was then read or reread by Spirt. "The final criterion, however, although subjective, involved personal reading and the relationship of the title to the developmental goal."

The book begins with a reading ladder listing the titles covered in each chapter by range of difficulty. The book is arranged by "developmental goals for middle childhood" that also serve as chapter headings: "Getting Along in the Family," "Making Friends," "Developing Values," "Understanding Physical and Emotional Problems," "Forming a View of the World," "Respecting Living Creatures," "Understanding Social Problems," "Identifying Adult Roles," and "Appreciating Books." Each of the entries for the 81 featured titles includes paragraphs on plot summary, thematic analysis, discussion materials, and related materials. The latter two areas list a substantial number of audiovisual and print materials related to the topic.

For ease in accessing information in the text, there are three indexes and a source directory for the materials suggested. The indexes include an index to biographical sources for the authors and illustrators, a title/author/illustrator index, and a subject index that categorizes titles under types of literature, geographic locations, and topics like *friendship* and *survival*.

Spirt's previous books have proven of value to teachers, librarians, and parents involved in reading selection and guidance. "Too often children in the middle years are left to struggle on their own to find engaging books, and frequently they turn away from reading to more easily accessible but less rewarding and sustaining pastimes." Public, school, and academic libraries supporting schools of education should include this title in their collections.

Primaryplots: A Book Talk Guide for Use with Readers Ages 4–8. By Rebecca L. Thomas. Bowker, 1989. 392p. indexes. $29.95 (0-8352-2514-3).
011'.62 Children's literature—Stories, plots, etc. ‖ Libraries, Children's—Activity programs ‖ Children—Books and reading ‖ Book talks [CIP] 88-34054

This title complements others in Bowker's series of booktalk guides: *Seniorplots: A Book Talk Guide for Use with Readers Ages 15–18* [RBB My 1 89]; *Juniorplots 3: A Book Talk Guide for Use with Readers Ages 12–16* (1987 [RBB Je 1 88]); and *Introducing Bookplots 3: A Book Talk Guide for Use with Readers Ages 8–12* [RBB S 1 88].

Created to serve as a guide to picture and early-reading books published between 1983 and 1987, this work features 150 titles. The author notes in the introduction that "in order to focus on high quality materials, the 'best books' and 'notable' lists from standard reviewing and evaluation sources were consulted, including *School Library Journal*'s 'Best Books,' . . . BOOKLIST's 'Editor's Choices,' and 'notable trade books' selected by various science and social studies committees. *Children's Catalog*, 15th edition and supplements . . . were also consulted." These recommended titles have been arranged into eight categories with headings such as "Developing a Positive Self-Image," "Finding the Humor in Picture Books," "Exploring the Past," "Analyzing Illustrations," and "Focusing on Folktales."

Each entry includes bibliographic information, grade-level use as well as suggested reading level, plot summary, thematic material, booktalk material and activities, audiovisual adaptations, related titles, and citations to sources of additional information about the author and illustrator. The book has four indexes: author, title, illustrator, and subject.

Primaryplots was designed to suggest recent titles to teachers and librarians for booktalks and book-related activities for children in grades K–3. It readily provides program-planning assistance. Parents and teachers will find this title a valuable tool, as will students of children's literature. Veteran children's librarians will be familiar with most of the books but will appreciate information on AV adaptations, related titles, and access to the books by subject.

The Reader's Adviser: A Layman's Guide to Literature. 6v. 13th ed. Ed. by Barbara A. Chernow and George A. Vallasi. Bowker, 1986–88. indexes. hardcover $375/set or $75/vol. (v.1: 0-8352-2145-8; v.2: 0-8352-2146-6; v.3: 0-8352-2147-4; v.4: 0-8352-2148-2; v.5: 0-8352-2149-0; v.6: 0-8352-2315-9; ISSN 0094-5943).
016 Bibliography—Best books ‖ Literature—Bio-bibliography ‖ Reference books—Bibliography ‖ Booksellers and bookselling—Bibliography [BKL]

The dozen years since publication of the twelfth edition of *The Reader's Adviser* have seen a burgeoning of publications in all fields, but especially in the social sciences, the pure sciences, and areas of technology. In recognition of this growth, the thirteenth edition of this long-standard work has grown to six volumes—five volumes of text and a general-index volume. Begun in 1921 as *The Bookman's Manual*, a tool to aid booksellers, the work has long since been adopted by library staff seeking help in collection building and readers' advisory services. Despite its increasing bulk, *The Reader's Adviser* continues its main goal of identifying the "best" books appropriate for the English-speaking layperson.

The first two volumes of the new edition follow the plan of the twelfth edition. Volume 1 covers American and British fiction, poetry, essays, literary biography, bibliography, and reference. Volume 2 covers American and British drama and world literatures in English translation. Volumes 3 through 5 reflect the most change from the previous edition, having all grown out of the third volume of the twelfth edition. Volume 3 covers social science, history, and the arts. Volume 4 is devoted to philosophy and religion, and volume 5 covers science, technology, and medicine. Each of the text volumes contains its own name, title, and subject indexes. Volume 6 merges all these indexes and includes a directory of publishers as well.

Under the general editorship of Chernow and Vallasi, the set represents the work of 98 volume or chapter editors, almost all of whom are professors, librarians, or graduate students. The general organization followed is to lead the reader from general works on a topic to more specific treatments. Each chapter, therefore, begins with a three- to four-page introduction followed by listings of general treatises and reference books, works tracing historical or critical trends, and anthologies. The general sections are then usually followed by listings of works by and about individuals prominent in the field. In this edition these sections are arranged alphabetically, but in the front matter of each volume is a chapter-by-chapter chronology of individually treated authors to assist those readers who wish to approach the literature from that perspective. Each entry for a major author contains brief (100 to 250 words) introductory remarks about the author and his or her significance in the field.

Bibliographic entries cite author, title, publisher, date of publication, and price. Where an out-of-print book has been included because of its significance to the field, that fact is noted. Many entries also contain brief annotations, although the number and quality of annotations vary widely from volume to volume. In the volumes dealing with belles lettres (1 and 2), annotations are usually restricted to general works and collections. Volumes covering other areas of inquiry typically include informative annotations for all entries. The extent of these annotations varies from the relatively unenlightening "probing and insightful book" to meatier fare of one or two sentences characterizing the content or significance of a given work.

Least changed in the new edition, volumes 1 and 2 are principally updates to the twelfth edition. Not surprisingly, there are few changes in the selection of authors covered in chapters dealing with earlier periods of British and American literature, that literary corpus being well established and slow to change. A number of authors of more recent note, such as John Irving, Stevie Smith, Beth Henley, and Toni

Morrison, have been added to the appropriate chapters on modern American and British literature. The creation of a separate chapter on Commonwealth authors has provided an opportunity for including many more authors from Canada, Australia, and New Zealand. Other Commonwealth writers are covered in separate chapters on African, Caribbean, and Indian Subcontinental literatures. Chapters in volume 2 on world literatures in translation show considerable editing and reorganization. The chapter on French literature, for example, has been considerably pared, with several French-speaking African authors moved to the chapter on African literature and many modern French writers dropped from this edition altogether. No author in the French literature chapter in this edition was born since 1928, even though younger writers are mentioned in the introduction and nine younger writers were included in the twelfth edition.

The twelfth edition's third volume covered religion, philosophy, the social sciences, and the natural sciences in 1,034 pages. In this edition that coverage has been expanded to 2,306 pages in three separate volumes. The new volume 3 contains thoroughly revised and expanded chapters on general reference, biography, history, and social-science disciplines like anthropology, political science, economics, and psychology. The chapters on folklore and humor and travel and exploration literature have been updated. Separate chapters on music and dance and the mass media have been created out of the twelfth edition's chapter on the lively arts. This expanded coverage of dance is a welcome improvement over the earlier edition, allowing for greater coverage of major dancers and choreographers. "Music" is effectively a new chapter, having been covered for the most part in the earlier edition by a brief section on opera. In this edition one finds a solid listing of major reference titles and surveys of music plus an interesting, eclectic selection of entries for individual composers and performers, ranging from Bach and Louis Armstrong to Webern and Iannis Xenakis. A new 35-page chapter on art and architecture contains, in addition to a representative listing of major encyclopedic works in this field, entries for 34 landmark artists and architects from the Italian Renaissance to modern America.

The new volume 4 expands coverage of philosophy and world religions by over 500 pages. What had been covered in three chapters in the twelfth edition is now reorganized into 14 chapters, which allows for much fuller introductory remarks and the inclusion of many additional important writers. In the chapter on Greek and Roman philosophy, for example, one finds a listing for Xenophon as a philosopher, whereas in the twelfth edition only his historical writings were treated. The new chapter on Islamic religion and philosophy highlights a dozen Islamic writers, while only the works of Muhammad were listed in the previous edition. The editors have devoted seven chapters to the development of Western philosophy; three chapters to religion and philosophy of ancient times and the East, where the subjects have never been easily divided; and three chapters to Judaism and the development of Christianity. Separate chapters on biblical studies and on "Minority Religions and Contemporary Religious Movements" complete the volume.

Volume 5 provides a similar major expansion of coverage for science, technology, and medicine, devoting 722 pages and 20 chapters to topics formerly covered cursorily in just one chapter of under 100 pages. In addition to the expected chapters on subjects like chemistry, physics, and earth sciences, the editors treat information and computer science, statistics and probability, and energy. The four pages devoted to medicine and health in the twelfth edition have been expanded to 156 pages, covering general medicine and health, illness and disease, and clinical psychology and psychiatry. Two chapters have been added covering philosophical and ethical aspects of science as well as pseudoscience (e.g., creationism and paranormal phenomena), topics likely to be of interest to lay readers.

This new edition is more pleasant to read than earlier editions. The typeface used is much larger, and the pages are not so cramped in appearance. The tables of contents are detailed enough to allow quick reference to major sections and subsections of the work, and the indexes appear to be accurate. The combined index of volume 6 is especially helpful in light of the fact that many authors are listed in more than one volume. The use of boldface type in the index makes it easy for the reader to identify authors who have received major treatment.

At $75 per volume, this is not an inexpensive purchase. Libraries that cannot afford to buy the entire set at once may want to consider starting with the most changed volumes, 3 through 5; however, libraries that purchase the entire set will receive the index volume at no additional cost. This well-crafted and greatly expanded set is worthy of consideration by libraries of all sizes that provide reference and readers' advisory service to an adult population or that need to build general adult collections.

The Humanities: A Selective Guide to Information Sources. 3d ed. By Ron Blazek and Elizabeth Aversa. Libraries Unlimited, 1988. 382p. bibliog. indexes. hardcover $36 (0-87287-558-X); paper $23 (0-87287-594-6).

016.0160013 Bibliography—Bibliography—Humanities I Humanities—Bibliography I Reference books—Humanities—Bibliography I Humanities—Information services—Directories [CIP] 87-33907

This is a revision of A. Robert Rogers' standard guide to the humanities, last updated in 1979. After Rogers' death in 1985, library educators Blazek and Aversa assumed editorial control of this long-needed revision, which reflects changes through October 1987.

As defined originally by Rogers, the humanities include philosophy, religion (and mythology and folklore), the visual arts (painting, drawing, architecture, sculpture, and a variety of applied and decorative arts such as photography and fashion), the performing arts (music, drama, dance, film, radio and TV, and video), and language and literature. History is considered a social science and therefore outside this book's scope.

In the 1979 edition, Rogers used two chapters to cover each of the disciplines—one chapter dealing with accessing information in that particular field and the second detailing the most important sources. The new editors have retained this format. They have also eliminated most of the periodical entries included by Rogers in order to limit the sources to reference tools. This new edition includes 973 entries compared with 1,200 in the second—a decrease largely the result of eliminating periodical entries.

The odd-numbered chapters consist of narratives on information access in the different subjects covered. Each of these chapters begins with a working definition of the discipline and a delineation of some of the major subdivisions within the field. Utilizing available use studies, the authors then provide a profile of the sort of person most likely to use the information and the way the information would be used. This is followed by a discussion of how the information is organized, how computers are employed in the field, and what the major professional associations and special collections are in the discipline.

The even-numbered chapters contain classified annotated lists of sources organized alphabetically by title within each subsection. After basic bibliographic information, annotations averaging 135 words describe and evaluate the sources listed. Appropriate cross-references are noted at the end of the annotations.

The book concludes with an author-title index to the sources chapters, citing both entries themselves and important books noted in the annotations. In this index, all titles available online are asterisked. A separate subject index tells where broad subjects are found in the book. While the author-title index succeeds in helping the reader, the subject index is little more than an alphabetical index to the table of contents. It would have been more useful to have compiled a more specific subject index citing subjects such as *rock music*, *Islam*, and *photography*.

There are some important humanities reference sources published in 1987 not included here, probably because of the cutoff date (e.g., the *Film Review Index* and the second edition of *The Random House Dictionary*). In addition, Macmillan's new multivolume *Encyclopedia of Religion* is entered incorrectly under Christian encyclopedias rather than general religion encyclopedias.

Overall, however, the choice of entries is excellent, the classification is accurate, and the annotations are informative. Especially useful in this new edition is the updated information on computerized data access in each field. Together with William Webb's *Sources of Information in the Social Sciences* (2d ed., ALA, 1986), which complements this guide, the third edition of *The Humanities* is a must for four-year college and university libraries as well as medium-sized and large public libraries. Many community college libraries, smaller public libraries, and school libraries will probably find Sheehy's *Guide to Reference Books* (10th ed.) sufficient for their needs.

Computer-Readable Databases: A Directory and Data Sourcebook. 5th ed. Ed. by Kathleen Young Marcaccio and Janice A. DeMaggio. Gale, 1989. annual. 1,188p. indexes. paper $160 (0-8103-2775-9; ISSN 0271-4477).

025.04 Information storage and retreival systems—Directories [BKL]

This fifth edition is now published by Gale, the third publisher since the work's inception in 1976 (the Board reviewed the fourth edition [*RBB* Ap 15 86]). Martha Williams is no longer editor, but she wrote the excellent introduction, "The State of Databases Today." This new edition is in one volume and includes more than 4,200 databases, an increase of 1,400 over the previous one. Covered are "all publicly available electronic databases, including online and transactional, CD-ROM, bulletin boards, offline files available for batch processing, and databases on magnetic tape and diskette."

The book is in the standard Gale format. The six main sections are "Database Profiles," "Database Producers," "Database Vendors," "CD-ROM Product Index," a subject index, and a master index.

The largest and most important section contains the profiles of the databases. Arrangement is alphabetical, and each entry is sequentially numbered. The previous edition's problem of not ignoring lead articles when alphabetizing has been corrected. Features new to this edition are complete address, telephone number, fax and telex numbers, and contact person for each database. In addition, each entry includes general description, type of database (e.g., textual, numeric), language, time period covered, file size, and update frequency. Other areas covered are subject, data elements, database availability (e.g., online with vendor name, CD-ROM, magnetic tape, batch, etc.), and print/microform products.

The next two sections list database producers and database vendors. The producer record includes address, telephone number, names of the databases it produces, and their numbers in the profile section, allowing easy access to the descriptions. The vendor section also includes address and telephone number along with the databases each brokers and the numbers of those databases in the profile section.

The last three sections are the indexes. The CD-ROM product index is new to this edition. It is alphabetical by title. The subject index has 672 subject terms and cross-references. The last index is the master index of names, acronyms, variant and former names, keywords within a name, corresponding or related print and microform products, and database producers and vendors. Indexing each entry in this manner insures ease of retrieval through multiple access points.

There are several other database directories on the market. A comparable one is the *Directory of Online Databases* by Cuadra Associates. There is much overlap in database listings between these two directories, but the Gale title has several hundred more names than Cuadra. In addition, Cuadra's coverage is limited to online interactive databases available to the public and accessible through a vendor. Therefore, *Hail Bibliography*, which is in the Gale directory, is not listed in Cuadra because searching can be done only through the database producer. There are also no CD-ROM products in Cuadra. One major advantage to Cuadra is that quarterly updates are included in the purchase price of $175. *Computer-Readable Databases* is an annual that is updated quarterly only in the online version on DIALOG. With the rapid growth of CD-ROMs and other databases, this print version will become outdated well before the year is over. Even with this shortcoming, librarians doing a lot of online searching could easily justify purchasing both directories.

Women in LC's Terms: A Thesaurus of Library of Congress Subject Headings Relating to Women. By Ruth Dickstein and others. Oryx, 1988. 221p. hardcover $28.50 (0-89774-444-6).

025.4'93054 Subject headings—Women I Subject headings, Library of Congress [CIP] 87-34766

Library resources on women can be difficult to identify because of the interdisciplinary nature of women's studies. By providing a list of subject headings relating to women taken from the ninth edition of the *Library of Congress Subject Headings* (1983) along with headings that begin with *women* from the tenth edition, this book offers the potential of vastly improved access to library collections. It complements *A Women's Thesaurus: An Index of Language Used to Describe and Locate Information by and about Women* (Harper, 1987 [*RBB* D 15 87]), another key source for identifying women's studies terminology, because the latter work intentionally excludes LC headings. *Women in LC's Terms* is not concerned with criticizing the appropriateness of the subject headings (although the authors state that they do not necessarily accept them); it simply pulls them out from *LCSH* into a thesaurus that will serve both those who catalog resources and those who seek to use them.

The extent of the list (more than 3,500 headings are included) and its carefully stated rationale and methodology reflect a high level of dedication on the part of its compilers to improving research in women's studies. Four primary types of headings were identified: gender specific to women (*Girls, Housewives, Motherhood*); aspects of women's lives (*Parenting, Equal pay for equal work*); sexual and medical terms (*Abortion, Osteoporosis*); and groups (*Single parents, Homosexuals*). Proper names are not included. The first chapter lists all the headings in one alphabet. In 11 subsequent chapters the selected terms are listed again, arranged under broad subjects such as "International Women," "Social Science and Culture," or "Economics and Employment" (the same topics, incidentally, as those used in *A Women's Thesaurus*). Each chapter has an explanatory introduction. Chapter lengths vary, and some terms may appear in more than one place.

Women in LC's Terms is intended to be used in conjunction with *LCSH*, and the conventions of *LCSH* need to be understood if the review title is to be properly exploited. Single examples of "pattern headings" from which other similar headings can be created are provided throughout, but for information about relationships between terms, the user is directed to definitions in *LCSH*. Free-floating subdivisions appear at the beginning of each chapter and are cumulated in appendix 1, but they are not as a rule included in the lists. The exception is the heading *Women*, which is fully expanded. Other appendixes are "Free-Floating Subdivisions Used under Classes of Persons," "Subdivision Pattern Headings for Names of Individual Authors," and "Free-Floating Subdivisions Used under Names of Persons." Appendix 5 provides a list of Library of Congress call numbers that relate to women and women's issues.

This book is a definitive guide in its field, providing an opportunity for superior cataloging of women's studies materials. It also reveals for the first time the wide variety of terms in *LCSH* that apply to women. It has the potential for assisting researchers to identify far more resources for women's studies if it is made available for use in conjunction with catalogs or bibliographies arranged by Library of Congress subject headings. Since the eleventh edition of *LCSH* has been announced for this fall, the Board encourages the compilers to find a way to update the material in this book to include the new headings added.

Video for Libraries: Special Interest Video for Small and Medium-Sized Public Libraries. Ed. by Sally Mason and James Scholtz. ALA, 1988. 163p. index. paper $14.50 (0-8389-0498-X).

026.02517'82 Libraries—Special collections—Video recordings I Public libraries—Collection development I Video recordings—Catalogs [CIP] 88-22235

As videos have become increasingly popular and important sources for entertainment and education, librarians have been faced with sorting through the seemingly endless number of advertisements for the more than 50,000 videos currently on the market. While a number of catalogs exist for feature films and nonfiction films (e.g., *The Video Source Book* [*RBB* Ap 15 89]), collection development can be difficult. Finally, small and medium-sized public libraries have an authoritative list of recommended videos. Included in this volume are 1,000 titles selected on the basis of superior content, production quality, currency, and patron demand. Mason is director of Video and Special Projects at the American Library Association and the director of the ALA-Carnegie Project, and Scholtz is a consultant for audiovisual services for the Northern Illinois Library System.

The introduction states that criteria for inclusion were the film's authenticity, utilization, content, and technical qualities. Contributing editors submitted listings of recommended titles from which the editors worked. Arranged by subject in Dewey Decimal main class numbers and then alphabetically by title, this buying guide includes a mixture of both inexpensive tapes as well as very expensive productions. Typical entries include producer, date of production, distributor, running time, price, Library of Congress subject headings, and availability of public performance rights. Videos especially appropriate for young adults are noted with a symbol. Brief annotations highlight the uniqueness of each film. A separate list of videos for children is arranged by title. There are cross-references between the two lists as well as a comprehensive title index.

A short introductory chapter discusses feature films on video in public libraries, notes videotape guides, and lists recommended titles in various categories including a basic collection, classic foreign films, camp classics and erotic films, and classic silent films. Appendixes list videos for professional viewing and give addresses for producers and distributors, wholesalers, and retailers.

This buying guide is highly recommended for all public libraries with video collections, especially those just beginning to build them.

Directory of American Libraries with Genealogy or Local History Collections. Comp. by P. William Filby. Scholarly Resources Inc., 1988. 319p. index. hardcover $75 (0-8420-2286-4).

026.973'025 Genealogical libraries—U.S.—Directories I Historical libraries—U.S.—Directories II Genealogy—Library resources—U.S.—Directories II Local history—Library resources—U.S.—Directories II U.S.—Genealogy—Library resources—Directories [CIP] 87-37109

Filby, a former librarian and compiler of several genealogy reference works (*Passenger & Immigration Lists Index, Philadelphia Naturalization Records*), has crafted this work from the 1,500 responses to a questionnaire mailed to 4,000 libraries in the U.S. and Canada. In the introduction, he explains "there is a substantial need for a publication that will offer genealogists, historians, librarians, and those individuals seeking their family history information on where genealogy and local history collections are located, what they contain, and how they may be accessed."

The mailing list was compiled from the *American Library Directory* and *Meyer's Directory of Genealogical Societies in the U.S.A. and Canada* (by that author, 1986) as well as other R. R. Bowker mailing lists, professional periodicals, and suggestions from individuals. Filby consulted with "several prominent genealogists" in creating a two-part questionnaire. A sample appears following the table of contents and again on the inside back cover.

Arranged by state or province, the directory offers basic information about each library and its genealogical or local history collections. Information includes days and hours open to the public, name of contact person, number of books held (by language), number of manuscripts and microfilm reels, geographic areas covered, whether staff will answer questions by telephone or letter, whether a qualified genealogist is on the staff, fees, lending regulations for books and microforms, whether a published guide or an unpublished index to collections exists, if a list of professionals willing to do research for a fee is available, and if the collection is on OCLC or RLIN. Entries conclude with notes on which of 26 standard sets and 9 periodicals are owned by the library (e.g., *Biography and Genealogy Master Index, D.A.R. Lineage Books, The American Genealogist, Canadian Genealogist*). This is followed by "Libraries Not Holding Genealogy or Local History Collections," a list of institutions that responded to the questionnaire as not holding these materials. It seems unlikely that the Chicago Historical Society Library, Georgia Genealogical Society, Alaska Historical Society, and Historical Society of Michigan do not contain any genealogical or local history materials. The "Index of Libraries with Significant Out-of-State Collections" indexes libraries holding material from other states, U.S. regions and ethnic groups, Canada, and foreign countries. Libraries possessing only materials for their own state are not listed in the index.

While libraries typically own various lists of state and local historical and genealogical societies, there is no other source that comes close in offering researchers so much information. Nevertheless, the poor response to the survey seriously hinders the usefulness of this work. Did approximately 2,500 libraries neglect to respond because the library did not possess appropriate materials, or for other reasons? It is the compiler's hope that many more libraries will be added if there is a second edition. Also, while a sample of the questionnaire is located in two places, the key to abbreviations appears only with the questionnaire following the table of contents.

In spite of this, this title will find an audience in large public libraries, historical society libraries, and others having genealogical or local history collections.

General Reference Books for Adults: Authoritative Evaluations of Encyclopedias, Atlases, and Dictionaries. Ed. by Marion Sader. Bowker, 1988. 614p. bibliog. illus. index. hardcover $69.95 (0-8352-2393-0).

028.1'2 Reference books—Reviews I Encyclopedias and dictionaries—Reviews I Atlases—Reviews [CIP] 88-10054

This second volume in Bowker's Buying Guide series is designed to provide a tool both for collection development and for answering patrons' questions about general reference works. Approximately 215 in-print (as of April 1, 1988) encyclopedias, dictionaries and wordbooks, and atlases are comprehensively evaluated. Large-print reference works in these categories are also reviewed. The format is the same as the first title in the series, *Reference Books for Young Readers* [*RBB* S 1 88].

The first of the five sections contains introductory material: an initial chapter on the history of reference books (somewhat rewritten but essentially the same as in *RBYR*); a chapter on criteria for choosing reference books; results from a survey of public, academic, and special librarians rating general reference books; and charts comparing features of the titles reviewed. The core of the work is the chapters that review individual titles in the three categories. Each section starts out with a "what to look for. . ." chapter that describes the criteria used for evaluating titles, the structure that the reviews will take, and a glossary of terms. Each individual review follows an outline that begins with summary information, followed by discussion of elements such as scope, authority, clarity, objectivity, and special features. Criteria specific to each type of work, such as scale and projection for atlases, are also treated. Facsimile pages are included for many of the encyclopedias and dictionaries. The "Other Opinions" feature is sometimes included to give digests of reviews from other reviewing media.

Reviews are comprehensive and follow the outline in the "what to look for" chapter, often checking the same feature or article in each title to make a comparison. Reviews are evaluative and do not hesitate to point out both strengths and weaknesses or to compare works for suitability to various purposes. Useful to librarians are the reviews of a title in all formats: paper, online, or CD-ROM. A bibliography and index conclude the book, along with a list of publishers and their addresses.

In comparing it with *RBYR*, there is some overlap of titles covered, especially in the very standard works. For instance, in the atlas section, each volume reviews seven Rand McNally atlases, four of them appearing in both guides. Sometimes the reviews have been revised to reflect the different emphasis of the buying guide, but some of them are virtually identical to those appearing in *RBYR*. The dictionary section is the most changed, with the addition of reviews of etymological, synonym and antonym, and usage dictionaries.

While the standard guides to reference books offer little evaluation, and specialized sources such as Kister's *Best Encyclopedias* [BKL D 15 86], *Dictionary Buying Guide* (now more than 10 years old [RBB S 1 78]), and *Kister's Atlas Buying Guide* [RBB D 15 84] offer in-depth treatment, this Bowker work pulls a lot of information together in one source. So much information could be almost a drawback, although one can rely on the comparative charts and summaries for a faster look at a title. Potential users will include library science students (for whom it will be essential reading), selectors, and reference librarians who will find it helpful for patrons wanting evaluative comparison of reference books or sets.

Young Adult Book Review Index, 1987. Ed. by Barbara Beach and Beverly Anne Baer. Gale, 1988. annual. 451p. indexes. hardcover $85 (0-8103-4373-8; ISSN 0897-7402).

028.162'016 Young adult literature—Book reviews—Indexes II Books—Reviews—Indexes [BKL]

Young Adult Book Review Index, 1987 (*YABRI*) is the first volume in an annual series intended to provide access to young adult book reviews listed in *Book Review Index*. *YABRI* identifies 16,000 reviews of 6,300 books from 303 periodicals. These reviews all appeared in 1987 or late 1986 issues. Reviews are cited from periodicals specifically associated with young adult services (*Voice of Youth Advocates, School Library Journal, Kliatt Young Adult Paperback Book Guide*) and from periodicals that review all types of books (*New York Times Book Review, Time, Atlantic Monthly,* BOOKLIST). The editors state that they included titles recommended for young persons aged 11 to 17 but recognize that there is no single definition that sets age limits for young adults. The entries include adult titles that might be of interest to young adults, e.g., Toni Morrison's *Beloved*, as well as titles written specifically for young adults. Approximately 13 percent of the titles are also cited in *Children's Book Review Index, 1987* [RBB F 1 77], another Gale spin-off of *Book Review Index*.

Books are arranged alphabetically by the last name of the author or editor or by title main entry. Each entry also gives the illustrator, abbreviated title of the reviewing source, date, volume, and page number. If appropriate, a letter code appears with the citation; *c* denotes books for children as well as young adults, *a* marks books of interest to both adults and young adults, *r* indicates reference books, and *p* identifies periodicals. Audio books are listed as "audio version." A list of abbreviations for the periodicals indexed appears on the front and back endpapers. Following the introduction is a list of publications indexed with bibliographic information: full title, ISSN, frequency of publication, and publisher's address. *YABRI* has two special indexes: an illustrator index and a title index. The introduction explains editorial policies and provides simple instructions on how to use *YABRI*.

Although the citations will be useful for librarians working with young people, as in the parent set, some data have not been included. Publishers, copyright dates, and pagination are not given for the books cited. No indication is given of the length or scope of the reviews. The editors occasionally list articles that discuss multiple titles. For instance, 10 titles are listed for Richard Peck, but only one or two are new books. The rest have been published over the last 10 years. Six of these were mentioned in one *Top of the News* article discussing his writing.

YABRI will be useful to librarians working with young adults, but the high cost for each annual volume may prohibit its purchase by all but the largest public and school libraries. *YABRI* will be a welcome addition in academic libraries where young adult literature is part of the college curriculum, though libraries subscribing to the parent title may want to continue to rely on it.

Children's Literature Awards and Winners: A Directory of Prizes, Authors, and Illustrators. 2d. ed. By Dolores Blythe Jones. Neal-Schuman; dist. by Gale, 1988. 671p. bibliog. indexes. hardcover $92 (0-8103-2741-4; ISSN 0749-3096).

028.5 Children's literature, English—Awards—Directories I Children's literature, American—Awards—Directories II Literary prizes—Directories [OCLC] 84-643512

Children's Literature Awards and Winners, second edition, updates and augments the first edition published in 1983 [RBB Ap 15 84] and the 1984 *Supplement*. It describes awards granted for excellence in children's literature in English-speaking countries and lists winners. International awards are included if they can be awarded to an author or illustrator from an English-speaking country or to a book written in English. Discontinued awards are included.

The new edition lists 211 awards compared with 144 entries in the first edition. More than 5,000 titles and almost 7,000 authors and illustrators are included. The preface indicates that the basic information was compiled from responses to questionnaires sent to all organizations listed in the first edition and its supplement, as well as to newly identified agencies.

Part 1, "Directory of Awards," is arranged alphabetically by award name. Entries include the name and address of the awarding body, the scope and guidelines for the award, and a chronology of winners and runners-up, with full bibliographic data. Award listings are up-to-date as of 1987 or 1988. Part 2, "Authors and Illustrators," is arranged alphabetically by personal name, listing their books and the awards won. Part 3, "Selected Bibliography," lists books, articles, reports, and dissertations relevant to all aspects of children's book awards. There are 39 added entries since the 1983 edition. This section should be of value to researchers as a starting point for further inquiry.

Part 4 contains four indexes, three of which are new to this edition. In addition to the award index, there are subject, author/illustrator, and title indexes. The Board criticized the lack of a title index in the first edition, so we are glad to see one here. Better print, headings in dark type, and guide words at the tops of pages also help to make the directory more usable. While expensive, *Children's Literature Awards and Winners* is an accurate and comprehensive directory for large collections of children's literature. The Children's Book Council's *Children's Books: Awards & Prizes* [RBB N 1 86] lists fewer awards and is not as current. It is out of print, but the publisher plans to issue a revised edition.

High Interest Easy Reading: For Junior and Senior High School Students. 5th ed. By Dorothy Matthews and others. National Council of Teachers of English, 1111 Kenyon Rd., Urbana, IL 61801, 1988. 115p. indexes. paper $6.25 (0-8141-2096-2).

028.5'35 High interest-low vocabulary books—Bibliography I Junior high school libraries—Book lists I High school libraries—Book lists [CIP] 88-1430

This guide continues to be a helpful and standard work for all librarians and language arts teachers serving junior and senior high students. Compiled to be used by young adults themselves, it is designed for browsing, too, since the concise but descriptive annotations speak directly to students. Meant for the reluctant—rather than the disabled—reader, annotations include plot summaries and characters' ages, making each title sound appealing. This edition was revised by a committee of the National Council of Teachers of English and includes more than 350 titles (no "classics" or "required reading"), mostly from 1984–86, making it an entirely new list. The "Afterword to the Teacher" states, "Our working definition of a 'good' book was one that is not only well written but that has recognizable power for gaining and holding a young person's interest." Books are grouped in 23 categories, including "Real People," "Wartime," "Ghosts," and "Ethnic Experiences." A few are listed in two categories, but this repetition is useful rather than annoying. Lots of nonfiction is included, which may encourage students to consider reading less popular books. Author and title indexes and a directory of publishers are provided.

While this book is only about one-tenth the size of Gale's *High-Interest Books for Teens* [RBB Ag 88] and lists some of the same titles, as a group the books listed here seem much more in tune with the interests of young adults. The only problem for libraries will be having enough of these books on hand for borrowers!

Academic American Encyclopedia. 21v. Ed. by Bernard S. Cayne and K. Anne Ranson. Grolier Inc., 1988. bibliog. illus. maps. $850 retail; $600 to schools and libraries.

031 Encyclopedias and dictionaries [OCLC] 87-17594

Nine years ago, a new encyclopedia first appeared on the U.S. market. The goals of the set were to provide quick access to definitive factual information, provide readily intelligible overviews without requiring the reader to grasp intricate subtleties or wade through drawn-out historical analysis, provide a starting point for further research by directing the reader to more specialized primary and secondary sources, and enable the reader to recognize concepts by providing as many color maps and illustrations as possible. These lofty ambitions remain today as the goals of *Academic American Encyclopedia* (*AAE*). In its first review of this work [*RSBR* Jl 1 81], the Board praised the set for its accuracy, objectivity, and conciseness. The bibliographies and illustrations were also rated highly. In our annual encyclopedia updates, the Board has suggested that this encyclopedia has become one of the standard American sets. The purpose of this review is to provide a thorough analysis of changes in *AAE* through the 1988 edition.

1. HISTORY OF PUBLICATION. *Academic American Encyclopedia* was originally published in 1980 by the Aretê Publishing Company, a subsidiary of a Dutch publishing conglomerate, and was unique in that it was sold to consumers through bookstores. Grolier, publisher of *The Encyclopedia Americana* and *The New Book of Knowledge*, purchased publication, marketing, and distribution rights in 1982 (after which it was no longer sold through retail outlets) and since 1985 has owned the entire set outright. Dating back to only 1980, *AAE* is the newest English-language encyclopedia on the market. It has been continuously revised each year in an attempt to enhance its recent origin. Since Grolier has been responsible for the work, an average of 175 new or replacement articles have been added each year, 175 have received major revisions, and 10 times as many have received some minor changes.

2. AUTHORITY. In terms of the authorship of the encyclopedia, *Academic* is a very appropriate name. The publishers claim that over 95 percent of the articles are written by scholars outside of the editorial staff. Over 2,250 scholars have contributed to the current edition. Of these authors, over 80 percent are college or university faculty members. Government, museum, and association employees are the next most prominent group and represent slightly less than 10 percent of all contributors. Five percent are writers, journalists, or editors, 3 percent are from business and industry, and approximately 2 percent are retired or have a status that cannot be identified from the information provided. All material submitted by outside writers is reviewed by the editorial staff and checked for factual accuracy, balance of treatment, and possible biases. Several layers of review are reported by the publisher, including verifying facts in several large research libraries, such as the New York Public Library, Princeton University, and Columbia University. When articles written by outside contributors get extensive revision, the attribution line is removed. An example of this policy is in the article *Cicely*, where the 1988 edition includes somewhat expanded text and no signature, whereas the 1980 edition included a signature and different text. A random survey revealed that slightly more than 60 percent of all of the articles are signed by contributors. While this rate may appear low compared with some other sets, almost every unsigned article consisted of a brief entry of only one or two paragraphs. All of the more substantial articles in the survey were signed.

The persons contributing to *AAE* have not changed significantly over the past nine years. In a comparison of a sample of the contributors to the original edition with those in the 1988 edition, approximately 15 percent of the names were found to be new. While this demonstrates that the editors are soliciting new authors, 85 percent of the contributors have not changed since 1980. Listing contributors who are either no longer working in the position indicated or who are deceased is a problem that plagues most encyclopedias and is one area where *AAE* has a distinct advantage due to its shorter history. However, the editors need to continue to replace contributors, or this advantage will slowly be eroded.

In addition to the outside contributors, an editorial staff of 35 is responsible for selecting new articles for inclusion and carrying out revisions to the existing material. This group has turned over almost entirely from the much larger editorial team that compiled the 1980 set, though the current editor in chief, K. Anne Ranson, was a member of the original editorial staff. The contributions of the compilers of the first edition are still credited by listing their names in the preface. This is appropriate in that much material from the first edition still appears in the 1988 version. The current editorial team includes staff who have worked on almost every other major English-language encyclopedia.

3. SCOPE AND TREATMENT. While the editors claim that this set is suitable for everyone from elementary school students through adults, the Board feels that it is actually written at a higher reading level. The language used in *AAE* is geared primarily to high school and college students and adults, and it has a much larger vocabulary than many other encyclopedia sets. Most junior high and elementary school students will have a difficult time comprehending much of the material. In particular, much of the scientific material contained in the set requires some understanding of mathematical and scientific principles. The articles *Fundamental Particles*, *Quantum Mechanics*, and *Relativity* are probably beyond the reach of most high school students and even many adults with no scientific background.

All of the articles are arranged alphabetically word by word in the 20 volumes of text. Each volume is separately paged, and the technique of adding alphanumeric page numbers is used when major revisions are undertaken. For example, the *Computer* article ranges from page 159 through 160h, and the article *Human Body* covers page 296 through 296p. One of the benefits of such a paging system is that an article can be expanded without displacing those surrounding it in the set. By adding material in amounts of approximately one page each, the editors of *AAE* have been able to maintain an almost constant page numbering throughout the work's history. Nearly every article in *AAE* is on the same page number in the 1988 edition as it was in the original edition.

As stated earlier, this encyclopedia was designed primarily to provide quick access to factual information. To meet this goal, most of the articles in *AAE* are much shorter than those in other comparable sets. Over one-half of the articles included in the 1988 edition are less than 500 words. The editors compress *AAE*'s 32,000 entries into under 10,000 pages, compared with 18,000 entries in 14,000 pages for *The World Book Encyclopedia*, 52,000 entries in 27,000 pages for *Americana*, and 65,000 articles in 32,000 pages for *The New Encyclopaedia Britannica*. Of the 10 major sets reviewed by the Board [*RBB* O 15 88], *AAE* contains the third largest number of entries but has the lowest number of pages. It is clear that *AAE* is designed for quick reference and not exhaustive background material. *AAE* is a specific-entry encyclopedia; that is, articles are designed to provide information on specific topics, rather than treating broadly defined subjects. Because of this emphasis, the reader can turn to *AAE* to quickly find brief information on topics as varied as *Cassabanana Vine*; *Frankfort, Kentucky*; *Prions*; *Stealth Bomber*; and *Steinkraus, Bill*. In each case the encyclopedia provides one or two paragraphs describing the basic facts about why the topic is deserving of an entry, without providing lengthy background or historical material.

AAE devotes 35 percent of its space to scientific and technical topics, providing a higher percentage of scientific entries than any other general encyclopedia. The rest of the entries are divided approximately between the humanities (36 percent), the social sciences (14 percent), geographic entries (13 percent), and sports and popular culture (2 percent). The one area where the proportion of coverage is less than in most other sets is geography. The distribution of articles into these broad subject fields changes slightly each year as new articles are added to the set. More new articles seem to be added in the areas of sports, popular culture, and the sciences than in the social sciences or humanities.

In addition, approximately 35 percent of all the entries are biographies. Except for persons of major importance such as George Washington or Abraham Lincoln, the biographical articles tend to be only one or two paragraphs in length and provide a short sketch of the life and contributions of the biographee. From data collected in surveying a random sample of articles from throughout the set, it became apparent that the biographical and scientific articles tended to be shorter on average than those in the other fields. While there are obviously some longer articles on both people and technical topics, the specific nature of the subject matter presented in these areas lends itself to shorter articles. Longer entries tend to deal with geography, history, and the humanities. Articles on the nations of the world are typically several pages in length, as are the articles on the U.S. states and Canadian provinces. Entries on the history of nations or areas of the world (e.g., *Africa, History of*; *Middle East, History of the*; *United States, History of the*) are generally the lengthiest in the set.

In keeping with the intent of providing rapid access to brief information, some articles that were originally written in a longer format have been subdivided into several articles during the revision process. One example of this is the article *Hormones*. Originally appearing as a single article of 4¼ pages, it has now been divided into two articles that together use up the same space: one titled *Hormone, Animal* and the other, *Hormone, Plant*. Apparently the editors feel that this treatment makes access to this material easier. With the exception of the small amount of information that has been added over the past eight years, the same information is provided in the new two articles as in the original single article.

The writing in *AAE* is remarkably free of political, ethnic, or social biases. Potentially controversial subjects such as *Abortion, AIDS, Creationism, Fundamentalism, Homosexuality, Ku Klux Klan, Strategic Defense Initiative*, and all of the articles beginning with the word *Sex* are treated frankly and fairly. The basic facts of each topic are discussed along with the positions of both the proponents and opponents of the current controversy. Each of the articles presents potentially difficult material without glossing over some of the more sensitive issues. *AAE* does not appear to take a stance but to present the facts.

Nonsexist language is used as much as possible throughout the set. Articles on careers such as *Engineering, Library, Medicine, Nursing*, and *Police* avoid the use of gender-specific pronouns entirely and do not imply that these fields are the sole domain of either sex. *AAE* is not quite as current in its use of language to describe racial and ethnic groups, using "Oriental Americans" and "American Indians" to describe Asian Americans and native Americans. Other minority groups are indicated by the most common terms currently in use in the U.S.

In addition to the lack of bias, *AAE* strives to maintain an ethnic and geographic balance. Although the set contains proportionately more information on North American and European subjects than on the rest of the world, it provides a more balanced view of other geographic regions than most encyclopedias. Its coverage of the geography, history, and people of the Middle East, Africa, and Asia appears to be much wider than that of *World Book, Americana*, or even *Britannica*. For instance, there are 72 entries in *AAE* for African peoples, while *Collier's* has 6, *Britannica* has 29, and *World Book*, 6. The editors seem to make an extra effort to include topics and persons significant to the history, politics, and culture of less-developed nations.

While *AAE* received good reviews for its initial edition, the true measure of any work comes in its ability to maintain its excellence over time. Grolier has an active revision process. Since 1985, the editors have added almost 500 articles on new subjects, completely replaced over 200 articles, and made major revisions in almost 700 entries. In addition to these major changes, almost 7,000 articles have received minor updates. These minor updates usually involve an update of statistical information, such as population or sales figures, the addition of new material to tables of events such as award winners or sports records, or the addition of a sentence providing more recent material on a topic of current interest. These figures are impressive and are on a par with or above the levels of revision of other general encyclopedias such as *Americana, Collier's*, or *World Book*. However, Grolier may need to increase its efforts in this area as *AAE* begins its second decade of publication if it wants to maintain its lead in currentness.

One aspect of revision that is often overlooked is the method in which publishers make room for new and expanded articles, since these sets generally do not grow in overall size. If a publisher desires to maintain as close to the same pagination scheme as possible when new material is added and doesn't add a whole new page with an alphanumeric designation, some of the nearby entries must either be shortened or eliminated. In *AAE*, for example, the entry *Bosse, Abraham*, a seventeenth-century French engraver, was shortened and the bibliography removed in order to make room for the article *Bossy, Mike*, the hockey player. *Police* was shortened to expand the article *Poliomyelitis*. When *Weinberger, Caspar Willard* was added, *Weingartner, Felix* was shortened and *Weir* was completely eliminated. This procedure of shortening older material to make room for new events or people tends to skew the work toward more contemporary events. This practice helps the work maintain its currency but does so at the expense of more traditional historical material. The inclusion of material on current events that may have a period of limited interest may cause problems for future editions. Whether *Anderson, John*; *Doors, The*; *Holmes, Larry*; *Jackson, Reggie*; *Pit Bulls*; and *Springsteen, Bruce* will be dropped when their time in the limelight of popular culture is over is a question that only future editors can decide.

According to the publisher, almost 13,000 entries contain bibliographic references to other sources. This figure was actually found to be an underestimate in the sample of articles studied by the Board, which discovered that approximately 57 percent of the articles in the 1988 set contain bibliographies. The number of references cited varied from 1 to 20, with the average article containing a bibliography of four references. Time, however, is beginning to take its toll on the material cited in *AAE*. Of the bibliographies examined, only 27 percent had been updated at any time over the last eight years. By using *AAE* in the online format, the Board was able to identify the number of entries in the bibliographies by year. Of the estimated 20,000 articles that contain bibliographies, 3,515 cite books or articles with publication dates in the 1980s. The majority of the material cited is from the 1970s, with smaller numbers of references to sources from past decades and centuries. The dominance of the 1970s dates back to the original edition, which attempted to provide up-to-date material when it was first published.

Although the dating of the bibliographies may not be critical for many articles in the humanities and social sciences, it can be important for scientific and technical articles. Finding topics such as *Rubidium*, *Oxide Minerals*, or *Immunodeficiency Diseases* with the newest references cited as 1965, 1979, or 1981, respectively, tends to take away some of the credibility of an otherwise excellent work. In a similar manner, no new references have been added since the first edition to most of the articles on the states of the Union, despite the fact that other aspects of these articles have been updated on a regular basis. Even some social-sciences and humanities entries may need some updating. The short article *Client-Centered Therapy* cites only a single work from 1951, and the article *Hinduism* cites nothing newer than 1974. The editors need to speed up the bibliography revision program to ensure that the resources cited in *AAE* are as up-to-date as the entries themselves.

One of the most outstanding features of *AAE* is the quality and quantity of its illustrative material. The publisher reports that over one-third of the page space within the set is composed of illustrations and that 75 percent of these are in color. These data have been verified by the Board, but the illustrations were not found to be evenly distributed. In the Board's survey, 71 percent of the articles contained no illustrations at all. However, the articles without illustrations tended to be the shortest entries on the most specific topics. All but one of the articles of at least 10 paragraphs in length were found to contain illustrations, over two-thirds of which were in color. Some of the longest articles (e.g., *Computer*; *Indians, American*; *Sun*) contain dozens of high-quality drawings and photographs. Most geographic entries (e.g., *Africa, Maryland, Yugoslavia*) provide color maps developed for *AAE* by Rand McNally. The dates of most of the 1,000 maps included in the set were found to be 1979–80. The printing process and coated paper used in *AAE* provide clear reproductions of each of the illustrations. Most of the graphics contained in the set also provide useful additional information not presented in the text and are not simply pretty pictures. Over the past four years, Grolier has added over 350 new color illustrations and revised approximately 50 of the illustrations from the original set. Since society has become more visually oriented through the dominance of other media formats, the excellent illustrations greatly enhance *AAE*'s value.

The final volume contains an alphabetical index to all of the information contained in the set. In addition to entries for all articles and parts of articles, the 200,000 index entries include references to all of the illustrations, tables, maps, and bibliographies. Variations in typeface are used to discriminate between topics that are the subject of a complete article and those contained as parts of another entry, with boldface print used to indicate the main headings. The purpose of the index is to serve as a finding tool, and the only factual information provided by the index is the latitude and longitude of each map entry.

4. OTHER FORMATS. In addition to the 21-volume paper set, *Academic American Encyclopedia* also comes in two electronic formats: online through vendors such as BRS and Dialog and on CD-ROM directly from Grolier. All of the information in the articles, bibliographies, and tables from the paper edition is also available electronically. The advantage of searching an electronic format is that the user can easily retrieve information contained under any combination of keywords or other search factors. The electronic formats essentially become a superindex capable of retrieving any part of the total information contained in *AAE*. Grolier says the online version is updated four times a year so it is more current than the printed version.

Several problems arise in using *AAE* electronically, particularly with the online version. The most obvious difference between the electronic and paper formats is the lack of illustrative material in the former. Since the illustrations constitute one of the best features of the print version and occupy one-third of the entire page space, their loss greatly reduces the value of the electronic versions. While illustrations will probably never be available in the online format, CD-ROM technology has the potential to provide both audio and visual information in addition to the text. Grolier is currently experimenting with the possibility of including such material in future compact-disc editions. If the publisher is able to successfully apply this technology to *AAE*, it will produce the most important advancement in the encyclopedia industry in this century. The Board eagerly awaits the results of these experiments.

However, in addition to the illustration problem, the economics of online searching do not encourage its application to encyclopedias as they are used in libraries. In the online mode, the information is paid for each time it is used. If the database is consulted frequently, the cost of searching for a single year could greatly exceed the cost of the paper set. The information contained in any encyclopedia is generally not unique but is a synthesis of the known information in the field. With its emphasis on short articles, *AAE* takes this concept to an even greater length than most comparable works. However, online searching is most effective for in-depth research in comprehensive databases. While the ability to combine search terms may have some applications for encyclopedias, the excellent index volume of the paper set makes the online version unnecessary for libraries that own the paper set.

CD-ROM technology does eliminate some of the drawbacks of the online format. Since Grolier's *New Electronic Encyclopedia* on CD-ROM is a one-time purchase for a set fee of $395, a library knows in advance the total investment that will be required in its acquisition. There is no subsequent pay-per-use charge. The CD-ROM version also allows users to conduct their own searches without learning the online command language. To many users, the high-tech electronics may actually inspire curiosity about the product and promote its use. The CD-ROM software also allows the user to do some things not possible in the online version, such as examining two different articles simultaneously, retrieving linked articles through keywords within the text, highlighting and saving information of interest to the user, and downloading information to disk. However, until the time comes when the user can retrieve text, audio, and video in one format, the electronic formats will not completely replace the traditional paper format. (*RBB* will publish a fuller review of *The New Electronic Encyclopedia* later this year.)

On the whole, *Academic American Encyclopedia* is one of the best general encyclopedias currently on the market. None of its entries is over 10 years old, it provides a generous number of useful illustrations, the articles are objective and free from bias, and it has relatively up-to-date bibliographies. The concentration on short entries providing basic facts and the high quality of the indexing make the set very easy to use. However, Grolier must maintain a vigorous revision program, so *AAE* will be able to maintain its lead as the most current encyclopedia of its kind. *AAE* remains the only encyclopedia to be published in multiple formats, one of which (CD-ROM) has the potential to change the whole concept of encyclopedias as we know them. If Grolier is successful in this venture, the electronic *AAE* will become the standard against which all others are measured. *AAE* remains an excellent work that is one of the best encyclopedias for senior high school, college, and adult readers.

Compton's Encyclopedia and Fact-Index. 26v. Ed. by Dale Good. Compton's Learning Co., div. of Encyclopaedia Britannica, 1989. bibliog. illus. index. maps. retail $699; $539 to schools and libraries, $510 each for two or more sets (0-85229-494-8).
031 Encyclopedias and dictionaries [OCLC] 87-73073

Compton's Encyclopedia and Fact-Index, first published in 1922 as an eight-volume home and school reference work, had as its original purpose "to inspire ambition, to stimulate the imagination, to provide the inquiring mind with accurate information told in an interesting style, and thus lead into broader fields of knowledge." This edition extends that purpose by providing "a pleasurable and stimulating reading experience for young people." Publication of the 1989 edition completes a long-awaited, radical revision process begun in 1983.

1. AUTHORITY. Editor Good was assisted by an editorial staff of 68, along with 20 editorial advisers, four advisory boards, 62 artists, and approximately 500 contributors. The first volume begins with a list of contributors, their professional credentials, and the articles each contributed to *Compton's*. More than 50 percent of the contributors are new since the 1982 edition; the number of contributors has increased by about 100 since then. Over half the contributors have academic affiliations; others are from research institutes, professional organizations, libraries, and the publishing world. A few, such as Allan Nevins and Wallace Stegner, are widely recognized by the American public. Of the 500 contributors, 135 are listed as "former," "emeritus," "late," or "retired."

Near the beginning of each signed article is a small box containing the contributor's name and credentials. It is difficult to ascertain who wrote the majority of the articles in *Compton's*, however, since most are not signed. Of those that are signed, most are identified as "contributed by," while others are designated "reviewed by" or "reviewed and updated by."

2. SCOPE AND TREATMENT. *Compton's*, consisting of 25 text volumes, each with its unique "Fact-Index," and a one-volume "Master Fact-Index," is designed for use by students in upper elementary grades through high school. Each volume is independently paginated, with the exception of letters of the alphabet that require two volumes. In these instances both volumes are paged consecutively. *Compton's* contains about 5,200 articles in the text and 26,000 capsule articles in the "Fact-Index." In general, the articles are on subjects of interest to young people or on curriculum-related subjects. At the beginning of each volume is a two-page outline of most of the topics covered in that volume. This outline, "Here and There in Volume . . . groups the subjects into nine broad categories such as arts, living things, technology and business, and potpourri. This is followed by an "Exploring Volume . . . section, with color photographs and questions with page references leading to answers in that volume. Entries range from one-fourth page for simple or less significant subjects to many pages for broader or more important ones. *Passionflower*; *Paton, Alan*; and

Peace Corps are each covered in one-fourth page; *Paper* in 4½ pages; *Paris* in 7; *Petroleum* in 15; *Pennsylvania* in 24; and *Painting* in 56. *Compton's* takes more of a broad-entry approach to information than some other sets. For instance, *Compton's* has the long article *Citrus Fruits*, while *World Book* has short articles on each type of citrus fruit.

As in many other encyclopedias, articles are arranged alphabetically letter by letter. This is generally not a problem in the text but may confuse students using the "Fact-Index" where, for example, *A Cappella* comes between *Acanthocephala* and *Acapulco*. Subjects beginning with *Mc* are arranged as if they all began with *Mac*; there is no cross-reference from *Mc* to *Mac* in either the text or "Fact-Index."

Articles on similar topics have similar coverage. For instance, each U.S. state article begins with an introduction and then discusses climate, people, economics, recreation, education, and other topics, followed by a historical sketch. Interspersed are a colored box highlighting statistics, a chronology of notable events, groups of color photographs, a "State Fact Summary" with a bibliography, and an indexed political map. Although most country articles have been rewritten and usually have a similar format, they don't all have the same organization and depth of coverage. Both *Sweden* and *Switzerland* have been rewritten but do not have nearly the appeal of *Spain*.

Cross-references are provided both within the text and at the ends of articles; most lead from broad articles to specific entries. A few *see* references are used as entries in the text, for example, "*Illiteracy* see Literacy and Illiteracy," but most of these are found in the "Fact-Index." With the completion of the revision process begun in 1983, *Compton's* has eliminated from the text all boxed cross-references to the "Fact-Index." The publisher states that this change provided most of the space for the 900 new articles added to the set.

Each volume has its own "Fact-Index" (even if a letter is spread out over two volumes), which indexes that volume and leads the user to related articles found in other volumes as well. In addition to indexing the volume, the "Fact-Index" also provides capsule articles for topics not found in the text. This practice is unique to *Compton's* and *The New Book of Knowledge*. Approximately 40 percent of the entries in the "Fact-Index" are capsule articles. The last volume is the "Master Fact-Index," a compilation of the 25 single-volume "Fact-Indexes." First-level, second-level, and sometimes third-level subheadings are given for larger topics. Illustrations are indexed, but bibliographies are not. One feature of the "Fact-Index" that may slow students down a little is that reference is made only to a letter and page. Thus, students looking for items cited in letters *A*, *C*, *M*, *N*, *P*, and *S*—each in two volumes—must look at the spine label to decide which volume to use.

Shaded boxes outline quick-reference tables in the "Fact-Index." Color-shaded boxes also highlight many of the special lists throughout the text volumes. (The list accompanying *Abbreviations* needs to have the post office abbreviations for states added.) Many longer articles begin with a boxed "Preview," which serves as a table of contents for that article.

3. RANGE, QUALITY, AND CURRENCY OF CONTENTS. Curriculum-related topics are treated well in *Compton's*. Geographic articles make up a large portion of the set. Articles on countries have been rewritten and contain new color photographs, new captions, and updated bibliographies. The article *Union of Soviet Socialist Republics* has been completely revised since the 1988 edition, in which it was listed under *Russia*. It has many beautiful color photographs and statistics updated through 1987. Books in the bibliography are as recent as 1988. Descriptive titles of articles have been eliminated. In earlier editions *Swift, Jonathan* was titled, *SWIFT—Unhappy Genius Who Created Gulliver*. Articles in the revised edition are more factual rather than trying to tell a story. In the 1982 edition *Spain* began, "To the Western European nations of the 16th century, the kingdom of Spain was known as the Mistress of the World and as the Queen of the Sea." The 1989 edition begins, "The country of Spain (known as España to its citizens) has had a greater influence on the rest of the world than that of most countries." *Compton's* still attempts to have interesting leads for its longer entries.

Articles such as *Cat*, *Space Travel*, *Insect*, and *Storytelling* are well written, thorough, and attractively illustrated and will appeal to young people. We criticized *Compton's* in the past for its avoidance of controversial topics of high interest to young people. These topics are now all treated, but some entries still need improvement. *Abortion* devotes only two sentences to why people are anti-abortion or pro-choice, mentions the 1973 Supreme Court decision but does not name *Roe v. Wade*, and recommends only *The Merck Manual* (which will not be found in most school libraries) for further reading.

The articles *Baseball*, *Basketball*, and *Football* emphasize history, rules, and play but don't mention current players. There is an article on Kareem Abdul-Jabbar as well as a capsule in the "Fact-Index," but his name is not mentioned in *Basketball*. The article *Olympic Games* is mostly historical, as are its illustrations. Highlighted boxes listing sports championships are found in the "Fact-Index."

Although *Compton's* is written for North American young people, it has worldwide coverage, especially of biographical and geographic topics. Racial and sexual biases are not evident in photographs or captions; this is a great improvement over previous editions. Some articles are extremely current. There is a four-page article on George Bush, which identifies him as the forty-first president of the U.S. The article includes a photograph of Bush with Dan Quayle following Bush's August 18 acceptance speech. Quayle rates only a capsule entry in the "Fact-Index," but it concludes by stating that he is a vice-presidential candidate. Glasnost and perestroika are mentioned in the article on Gorbachev. This article also mentions the INF treaties he signed with Reagan and the 1988 Moscow summit. Technological advances such as HDTV and superconductivity are discussed. *Compton's* is fairly current in recording the deaths of noted people, for example, Richard Feynman, Robert Heinlein, and Robert Joffrey. However, Louise Nevelson's death in April 1988 is not recorded in the "Fact-Index."

Only the longest articles have bibliographies. Citations refer to books, or occasionally periodicals, and include author, title, publisher, and date. Some bibliographies indicate which books are especially appropriate for children or for young adults and teachers. Many bibliographies are up to date and include titles appropriate for young people; others need work. For instance, the citations in *Camping* are dated. Most of the books cited in *Capitalism* are much too advanced for young readers.

The language of the set is appropriate for its audience without using a controlled vocabulary, and, for the most part, is nonsexist and unbiased. In the "Fact-Index" *Negro* has a *see* reference to *Black Americans* and *Blacks*; and likewise, *Native Americans* to *Indians, American*. Some revised articles still need updating. The table that accompanies *Etiquette* implies that all Protestant clergy, Army officers, ambassadors, and associate justices of the Supreme Court are men.

For the most part, illustrations are excellent and occupy about 30 percent of the space in the *Encyclopedia*. During the six-year revision process, 4,519 four-color and 5,996 two-color and black-and-white illustrations were added. Thus, the number of four-color pictures has more than doubled during this period. In total number of illustrations, *Compton's* compares favorably with other sets. In terms of the proportion of four-color illustrations, *Compton's* (35 percent) does better than *Merit Students* (25 percent) but is still far behind *World Book* (more than 80 percent). While *Compton's* no longer has illustrations that misinform, there are still some dated pictures that are not very attractive for young readers. A variety of color maps—political, population, topographical, agricultural, and industrial—are commonly found in geographic articles. Graphs are attractive and easy to understand.

To get a sense of the amount of change during this six-year revision, we compared almost 100 pages in the *E* volume of the 1982 set with the 1989 set. The following entries were added: *Ellington, Duke*; *Ellis, Havelock*; *Elytis, Odysseus*; *Employment Agency*; *Employment and Unemployment*; *Endangered Species*; and *Enlightenment*. Two former short entries were incorporated into larger articles: "*Elk see Deer*"; "*Emu see Birds, Flightless.*" *Embargo Acts* was changed to the more general *Embargo*. The articles *Emery*, *Employer's Liability*, and *Engraving and Etching* were dropped (though references in the index lead to other articles where information on these topics can be found).

El Salvador (formerly alphabetized under *S*) is now more than twice as long, has a fact box, a better map, and a color photograph. *Emotion* has been shortened, with the section on how to attain emotional maturity eliminated. *Engineering* has been rewritten and has a new bibliography and new illustrations, including female engineers. *England* has some new color photographs and has been partially rewritten. The article *English Language* has been redone and a bibliography added. *English Literature* is basically the same, though the section on literature since World War II has been expanded. There are new color pictures for *Elizabeth I, Elizabeth II,* and *Enamel*. Only six brief entries and the longer articles *Embryology; Emerson, Ralph Waldo;* and *Energy* are largely unchanged, though the bibliography for *Energy* has been updated.

4. PHYSICAL FORMAT. *Compton's* is bound in bright red washable fabric trimmed in black. "Compton's" is stamped in large gold letters on the front cover and also on the spine. Good-quality coated paper is used; illustrations and print do not bleed through. The typeface is simple, large, and crisp, but a slightly different typeface appears to have been used recently when new pages were set. Headings are in boldface and easy to find. Pages are attractively arranged and have 5/8-inch margins on all edges. The arrangement, easy-to-read print, vocabulary, illustrations, and special features make it easy for young people to browse through as well as use for research.

A version of *Compton's* on CD-ROM will be available this fall. It will contain more than 15,000 images, including maps, charts, graphs, and pictures, and articles will be enhanced with color, sound, and animation.

The thoroughly revised *Compton's Encyclopedia* is generally attractive, unbiased, and reliable. *Compton's* staff is to be commended on their excellent revision thus far, and the Board hopes they will continue with significant annual revisions. *Compton's* is recommended for school and public libraries. Although *Compton's* is written for students in grades five through high school, it is also suitable for family use.

First Stop: The Master Index to Subject Encyclopedias. Ed. by Joe Ryan. Oryx, 1989. 1,582p. bibliog. hardcover $195 (0-89774-397-0).
031 Encyclopedias and dictionaries—Indexes ‖ Reference Books—Indexes [CIP] 88-28870

First Stop selectively indexes the articles in 430 subject-oriented reference works. The main title is highly appropriate since reference librarians traditionally recommend that the first step a user should take in researching a topic is to consult a subject encyclopedia in order to obtain a broad overview of the topic. However, the subtitle is somewhat misleading since the work indexes not just subject encyclopedias but also handbooks, dictionaries, yearbooks, annual reviews, and other sources. Among the diverse works covered are the *International Encyclopedia of the Social Sciences*, *Sports: A Reference Guide*, *Europa Year Book*, the various Cambridge histories, and eight years of *Editorial Research Reports*.

The editor, a reference librarian at the University of Vermont, has limited the works indexed to English-language sources, focusing primarily on those in print, with the exception of several standard works such as the *Encyclopaedia of Religion and Ethics*. Over three-fourths of the titles covered were published within the last 10 years. Although a few 1988 yearbooks are cited, for the most part the cut-off date of publication appears to be 1987. Excluded are general encyclopedias, biographical dictionaries, and encyclopedias of associations. Also omitted are sources devoted to single individuals or eras and encyclopedias of legal terms and biblical interpretation. Although the editor indicates that sources pertaining to a single foreign country are not covered, both *The Cambridge Encyclopedia of China* and the *Encyclopedia of China Today* are indexed. Other seeming inconsistencies in types of sources covered raise a number of questions. Why, for example, is *Literary History of Canada* indexed but not *Literary History of the United States*? And why cover *Ancient Writers: Greece and Rome* but not the similar Scribner compilations *American Writers*, *British Writers*, and *European Writers*? In the view of the Board, the most serious omission is the *Encyclopedia of Education* (Macmillan, 1971), which, though now somewhat dated, continues to be a standard work.

In some respects, *First Stop* does for subject-oriented reference sources what the *Biography and Genealogy Master Index* does for biographical sources. However, an important distinction is that *First Stop* indexes the titles it covers selectively rather than comprehensively. Articles chosen for inclusion had to have at least 250 words, an identifiable author, and include bibliographic citations. In addition, most biographical entries were excluded, as were plot summaries and art, film, music, literary, and theater criticism.

The heart of the volume is the alphabetical keyword index. Keywords appear in boldface followed by an alphabetical list of articles that include the term. Although some effort was made to eliminate variant spellings by listing them under the American form of the word (for example, *labour* was changed to *labor*), similar terms (such as *theater* and *theatre*) appear with no cross-references. The problems inherent in all keyword indexes are apparent here. Since no cross-references are provided, the user must think of synonymous, broader, and narrower terms in order to identify relevant articles. The editor acknowledges this problem in his instructions to the user. In some instances, qualifiers have been added to article titles to avoid confusion. For example, an article entitled *Migration* from the *The Audubon Society Encyclopedia of North American Birds* is listed as *Bird Migration* in the keyword index. Following the title of each article is an abbreviated title of the source, the volume number (when appropriate), and the inclusive pagination. The abbreviated titles are arranged alphabetically at the front of the volume in a source list, which provides bibliographic information as well as a small (and generally inadequate) space for libraries to write in their call numbers.

Following the source list is an index that classifies the titles covered by broad subject categories. This index reveals some interesting subject strengths and weaknesses of the volume. For example, the *Engineering* category lists 33 titles, while *Literature* includes 29. There are 17 titles for *Medicine* and 10 for *Art*, 23 for *Political Science* and 2 for *Drama*, 26 for *Psychology* and 6 for *Philosophy*. Obviously, the sciences and social sciences are much more broadly represented than the humanities.

First Stop will be most useful in libraries that own a large percentage of the titles indexed. However, it cannot substitute for the expertise of a knowledgeable and perceptive reference librarian. For instance, this work will not lead the user to the excellent article on land-grant colleges in the *Encyclopedia of Education* or to the historical overview on television commercials in *TV Genres: A Handbook and Reference Guide* (Greenwood, 1985), since neither of these works is indexed. Moreover, there is a danger that librarians relying too heavily on *First Stop* might overlook indexed sources containing pertinent articles that did not meet the editor's indexing criteria, for example, the article entitled *Pets* that treats pet therapy with the elderly in the *Encyclopedia of Aging* or the entry *Lafayette Escadrille* in the *Dictionary of American History*. In addition, by utilizing the subject indexes and cross-references provided within many of these sources, one can locate articles that are not readily identifiable in the keyword index of *First Stop*. For instance, a user of the *Encyclopedia of Bioethics* can easily locate the section on burial practices within the article *Cadavers* by utilizing the subject index or through a cross-reference provided in the text. The average user of *First Stop* probably would not think to look under the keyword *Cadavers* for such information.

While *First Stop* will undoubtedly be a handy ready-reference tool, it should be used with caution due to its unevenness in subject representation, its selectivity, and its keyword approach. In fact, it will be most effective when used not as a "first stop" but rather as a backup when sources that a librarian initially identifies as most appropriate for a particular topic do not yield sufficient information.

Funk & Wagnalls New Encyclopedia. 29v. Ed. by Leon L. Bram and Norma H. Dickey. Funk & Wagnalls, 1988 (c1986). bibliog. illus. index. maps. $140 (0-8343-0072-9).
031 Encyclopedias and dictionaries [OCLC] 72-170933

Funk & Wagnalls first published an encyclopedia in 1912; in 1971 the sixth edition was published under the current title, *Funk & Wagnalls New Encyclopedia* (*F&WNE*), and a continuous revision policy was established. A major substantive revision was published in spring 1983 [*RBB* D 15 83]; since that time, revisions have been made semiannually, and nearly 13,000 pages have had some revision by the fall 1988 printing. Though the size of the set is unchanged, almost 200 new articles have been added, more color illustrations have been included, and articles, maps, and bibliographies have been updated. Because of supermarket sales requirements, the copyright date for this new printing still shows 1986, but there is a note stating that "volumes are published subsequent to copyright dates to contain the latest updated information."

1. AUTHORITY. *F&WNE* has long had a distinguished roster of consultants and writers and this continues; for example, the current article on AIDS (under *Acquired Immune Deficiency Syndrome*) was prepared by Robert Gallo, chief of the Laboratory of Tumor Cell Biology of the National Cancer Institute. Other well-known consultants include Stephen Jay Gould for biology and Leon Edel for American literature. Newly named consultants included among the 73-member list are Frederick I. Ordway, Office of Policy and Evaluation, Department of Energy, for space research and Michael C. Latham, director of the International Nutrition Program at Cornell University, for nutrition. Over 900 contributors of signed articles are listed by their initials and identified. However, the majority of entries are unsigned and written by F&W editorial staff. An almost completely new board of 16 bibliography consultant-contributors is listed. In 1987–88 all contributors were asked to review their credentials listings and update them for current position and publication information; deceased contributors are so identified (e.g., *M. Sl.* "Marc Slonim, Ph.D., late professor emeritus of . . .

2. SCOPE AND TREATMENT. *F&WNE* is designed primarily for home use in the U.S. and Canada, but its coverage is broad so it is not parochial but worldwide in scope. Designed to be read and used from the level of junior high school and up, the editors say, "we envision the typical reader as one who may have little or no background in the subject being consulted." Entries range from brief identifications of a line or two to many pages; the majority are less than one page. The longest noted was for *United States of America* (107 pages); the shortest noted was 1¼ lines for *Alderney*—"most northerly of the Channel Islands (q.v.)." *F&WNE* uses a concept of "networks of core articles supported by short, specific articles"; there is little overlap between articles. Longer articles progress "from the simple to the complex, the general to the specific." Readers thus can choose to read on or stop after the first 800 to 1,500 words of basic information, depending upon their comprehension level. Although some entries contain so much information in a very short space that they take intense concentration (e.g., *Rhyolite* or *Geometric Progression*), most entries are readily understandable, and both students and nonspecialist adults will benefit from reading them.

Topical coverage is greatest for history and geography (about 39 percent); physical and life sciences get the next largest portion (about 23 percent). The 25,000 articles are arranged alphabetically letter by letter, except for inverted phrases (e.g., *Korea, South* comes before *Korean Art and Architecture*), and prepositions, conjunctions, etc., are omitted in the alphabetization so that *Cape of Good Hope* comes between *Cape Girardeau* and *Cape Guardafui*. Identical titles are alphabetized in the order of person, place, thing; terms with more than one meaning are given separate entries and identified (e.g., *Depression, in Economics* and *Depression, Psychiatric Disorder*). Pronunciation is not indicated. Measurements are given first in metric, then in customary measure—e.g., *Amazon River*: "about 6275km (about 3900 mi)." The transliteration from the Chinese generally uses the new pinyin system, with a few exceptions including *Peking*; there is a *see* reference from *Beijing*. The set of 29 volumes has 448 pages in each of volumes 1–28; there are 480 pages in volume 29, which is the index. Since spines are labeled with only five letters to indicate contents, in a number of cases the same five letters end one volume and begin another (e.g., *AMERI* both ends volume 1 and begins volume 2, the actual last and first entries being *American Elk* and *American English*).

Articles on similar topics are handled according to a pattern. Articles on countries progress from their geographic location to cover land and resources, population, education and cultural activity, government, economy, and history; a map (four-color except for smaller countries) is always included along with an index to it. States of the U.S. and provinces of Canada likewise include all of the above and also have a striking two-page, four-color spread showing graphically statistics on population, economy, and climate, along with motto, flag, flower, electoral votes, highest and lowest points, etc.

There are many cross-references in the text, both specific and implied. Terms not used as entries have referrals to the entry term (e.g., "*Abbasids*—see Caliphate"). Within entries a *q.v.* following a word or term indicates a separate entry under that term (e.g., *Accounting and Bookkeeping* has *q.v.*s after mentions of the Securities and Exchange Commission and the Internal Revenue Service). *See* is also used at times within entries. Articles covering overviews of a subject such as *Latin American Art and Architecture* conclude with "For additional information on individual artists, see biographies of those whose names are not followed by dates." *See also* references frequently are used as well; the above article includes one to *Pre-Columbian Art and Architecture*. Bibliographies are referred to by number at the ends of subject entries: "For further information on this topic see the Bibliography in volume 28, section 856" (for *African Literature*); for bibliographies for biographical entries, "See the section Biographies in the Bibliography in volume 28."

The index fills all of volume 29; a two-page guide explains its use. A main heading in boldface capital letters indicates an entry under that term; a heading in Roman capital letters means information can be found on that topic under a different heading. Index entries use both subheadings and sub-subheadings and *see* and *see also* references. References are to volume and page number. The editors urge all users to begin with the index because, even if the term searched is an entry and could be found in the main body of the *Encyclopedia*, further information may be found under less obvious headings. For example, *Homing Pigeon* is an entry found in volume 13, but there is also information about homing pigeons in volume 2 under *Animal Behavior*; the reference is to the specific page in that nine-page entry where mention of the homing pigeon's navigational system is explained. *Biofeedback*, while having its own entry, also has seven subheadings in the index leading to other terms ranging from *Behavior Modification* to *Pain*.

The index was found to be quite accurate. It is not absolutely complete, however, as not all mentions of a topic are indexed. For example, for the Norwegian sculptor Gustav Vigeland, who has no entry of his own, the index refers only to the article *Sculpture* where he is mentioned briefly. Other mentions of him are made in the entries *Oslo* and *Norway*, but these are not indexed. Also, illustrations are not indexed. For example, there are portraits of Knut Hamsun and Sigrid Undset in the article *Norwegian Literature*, but index entries for both persons refer only to their individual entries, which do not include photographs. A print by Rockwell Kent illustrates the entry *Prints and Printmaking*, but there is no mention of it in the index; the only reference is to the article on Kent himself.

3. RANGE AND QUALITY OF CONTENTS. *F&WNE* covers all facets of knowledge and, going beyond a Western-only perspective, it provides good coverage, for example, of African, Asian, and Islamic countries and cultures. It avoids sex-biased language. Articles covering controversial subjects such as *Abortion*, *Capital Punishment*, *Creation*, and *Sex Education* are well written, cover all sides, and are balanced in their coverage. Illustrations likewise are free from racist or sexist stereotypes. *Family*, for example, discusses the many changes in the nuclear family; the illustration shows a black two-parent family. *Bicycle* pictures a U.S. woman winning the first-ever (1984) Tour de France cycle race for women. One of the illustrations for *Festivals and Feasts* shows the African harvest celebration of Kwanzaa.

Country articles have their statistics updated to the mid-1980s, with exchange rates showing figures for 1987. Texts also have been changed to show late political developments or happenings. The entries for the USSR and the U.S. mention the May 1988 meeting of Reagan and Gorbachev; *Panama* discusses the 1988 U.S. grand jury indictment of General Noriega for drug trafficking; *Haiti* includes the January 1988 election of Leslie Manigat as president. *Supreme Court* has an illustration that still shows Justice Powell, but the caption says he resigned and was replaced by Anthony Kennedy in February 1988; there are separate entries for Antonin Scalia and Anthony Kennedy. Among those for whom death dates of 1987 or 1988 were noted were Jascha Heifetz, Louise Nevelson, Robert Joffrey, Alan Paton, Frederick Loewe, and the former archbishop of Canterbury, Arthur Michael Ramsey. South Africans of such disparate persuasions as Bishop Desmond Tutu and P. M. Botha have entries; while neither Mandela has an entry, there is a 1986 photo of Winnie Mandela at a press conference just after her release from a governmental ban on speech to the press. Wole Soyinka now has an entry of his own as well as mention in *African Literature*. Architect I. M. Pei's entry mentions the opening of his Jacob Javits Center in New York City in 1986 and the rebuilding of the Louvre to be completed in 1989. The entry *Paris* includes a color photograph of the main concourse of the Musée d'Orsay, a former railway station opened as a museum of nineteenth-century art in 1986.

Many science articles have been rewritten or updated; this has been a major thrust of the past five years. The use of anabolic steroids and their dangers are listed under *Steroids* and also under *Sports Medicine*; in the bibliography for the latter entry, one of the eight titles included is a book on drug abuse in sports. *Superconductivity* includes several mentions of 1987 discoveries and the 1987 Nobel Prize. *Elephant* mentions the mammal's rumbling sounds below the range of human hearing, which were first observed in the mid-1980s, and *Earthquake* includes a table of devastating quakes through 1985, mentioning those in Mexico and Chile, and has a color illustration of the Mexico City destruction. *Life Span* gives statistics as of 1987 for the average lifespan of persons in industrialized countries (about 75 years). Tables of sports championships have been brought up to date through 1987 in most cases, with 1988 bowl games and superbowl champions for *Football, American*. Computer entries have been updated over the years; new entries this year include *Computer Aided Design/Computer Aided Manufacture* and *Computer Security*. The ozone hole is mentioned in *Antarctica*, and while *hole* is not a subheading under *ozone* in the index, among the nine subheadings listed there are *Air Pollution, Antarctica, Fluorocarbons,* and *Environment*.

One subject not found at all was gun control; the index entry *gun* refers to *Artillery* and specific types such as *Machine Gun* and *Shotgun*. There is no entry *Handgun*, and such entries as *Rifle, Revolver, Pistol,* and *Target Shooting* give good technical and historical descriptions but no reference to gun control. Likewise no mention is made under *Crime, Juvenile Crime, Murder, Manslaughter,* or *Homicide*. No mention was found of the experimental aircraft *Voyager*, which made a nonstop round-the-world flight in 1986. *Oil spill* cannot be found in the index under *oil* or *petroleum*, but the term is a sub-subheading under *pollution*. The issue of hormones in beef cannot be found through the index, but it is mentioned in *Animal Husbandry*, and a 1984 book titled *Modern Meat* in bibliography #609 has the subtitle *Antibiotics, Hormones and the Pharmaceutical Farm*. It is referenced only from the entries *Food Processing and Preservation* and *Food Supply, World*, not from *Meat, Meatpacking Industry,* or *Animal Husbandry*.

Bibliographies are all gathered together in the last half of volume 28. A two-page preface and guide explains the scope and arrangement. Preceding the numbered lists themselves, a general breakdown (#1–24 General Works, #25–48 Philosophy, #49–132 Religion, etc.) followed by a specific topic listing (e.g., #40 Chinese Philosophy, #78 Ecumenical Movement, #324 Adult Education, etc.) serves as a kind of index. The main access to the bibliographies, however, is the references at the ends of articles that refer to them by number; these have about doubled in number since 1983. Subject bibliographies contain from 3 to 30 items; biography lists are shorter, ranging from one (e.g., Saint Thomas Aquinas) to six (e.g., Benjamin Franklin). All entries are for books, and a brief annotation is included for each. Many 1987 and 1988 publication dates were noted. The bibliography consultants are almost all librarians, and the lists are pertinent and well chosen.

Two additional helps are found in volume 28. First is a five-page "How to Use the Library," which includes information about online catalogs and computer-assisted research as well as card catalogs and periodical indexes; following is the three-page "How to Write a Term Paper," which talks about using a word processor as well as outlining the paper, note taking, etc. Volume 1 provides a four-page "Guide to *Funk & Wagnalls New Encyclopedia*," which explains its scope and arrangement. A one-page condensation of this appears in volumes 2–28. All of these promote the use of the index as a starting point for any search. Volume 1 also includes a selected list of abbreviations used in the text, with referral also to the entry *Abbreviations and Acronyms* and to other subjects that include other such charts.

Illustrations are generally effective, are placed in good proximity to the text, and serve to expand and clarify it. The total number of illustrations has dropped slightly over the five-year period, but the number of color illustrations has increased by over 100. Still, almost two-thirds of all illustrations are in black and white, and the set has fewer illustrations than any other general encyclopedia. Many illustrations are bled to the edges or gutter of the page, so rebinding could be a problem. Drawings and diagrams are used as well as photographs and reproductions of paintings, etc. The great majority of maps are by Hammond and of excellent quality. Occasionally the print is very small (e.g., *Norway*), but all are clear. Because of narrow margins, some maps with a two-page spread lose detail in the gutters (e.g., *China, Alaska, West Germany*). In addition to the usual geographic maps, others show climatic regions, growth, landforms, land use, population distribution, vegetation, history, etc.

4. PHYSICAL FORMAT. Volumes are approximately $6^{1}/_{2}$ by $9^{1}/_{2}$ inches, regular book size, neatly bound in gray and blue Kivar with a gold printed spine. The volumes seem sturdy and stood up well to examination. (Trying to photocopy a double-page map could possibly be damaging, however.) Type is small but clear; different sizes and boldness of typeface set off entries and subheadings well. Running heads are provided for each two-page spread. The paper is opaque with only an occasional shadow of show through. It is not coated, however, so illustrations do not have quite as much impact as they could, though most are reproduced clearly. A few particularly attractive examples noted were of *African Art and Architecture*, dew on a young blueberry blossom (*Photography*), a Chinese scroll painting (*Painting*), and a skyline of Manhattan (*New York City*).

5. SUMMARY. *Funk & Wagnalls New Encyclopedia* is unique among encyclopedias in that it is sold in supermarkets (though libraries can order it directly from the publisher). It is not as detailed and scholarly as, for example, *Collier's, The New Encyclopaedia Britannica,* or *The Encyclopedia Americana*, but it does provide good, clear, up-to-date coverage of global events in a readable style for an audience of nonspecialists from junior high school age upward. While designed primarily for home use, it is a suitable purchase for libraries and gives good value for its purchase price.

The Harper Dictionary of Modern Thought. Rev. ed. Ed. by Alan Bullock and others. Harper, 1988. 917p. hardcover $29.95 (0-06-015869-7).

031 Encyclopedias and dictionaries [CIP] 87-45604

Bullock explains in his preface that two facts of modern life create a need for a comprehensive, quick-reference dictionary of thought. First, specialization causes most of us to be ignorant of "whole areas of modern thought," and "most of us never quite give up the attempt, however sporadic, to explore our areas of ignorance." This source seeks to cover the middle ground between standard dictionaries, which are too comprehensive and give overly brief definitions, and encyclopedias, which may be too large to provide handy, quick reference. "It takes key terms from across the whole range of modern thought, sets them within their context and offers short explanatory accounts . . . written by experts, but in language as simple as can be used without *over*-simplification or distortion." "Modern" is defined as twentieth century, and entries draw almost exclusively from Western thought. Contributors were instructed to write for "the non-expert venturing into unfamiliar territory."

This new edition of *The Harper Dictionary* deserves a favorable review like the one given to the first edition by the Board [*RSBR* Je 1 78]. The articles are clear, informative, and concise, and many cross-references help readers see connections among various disciplines. According to the introduction, more than 1,000 entries have been added, and of the 80 percent carried over from the 1977 edition, half have been revised. The largest number of new entries is in the area of contemporary history and politics (e.g., *Thatcherism, Reaganism*). Fields of study that have received greater attention in the 1980s are given fuller treatment. For example, the 1977 edition contained less than 200 words on the topic *feminism*. This edition has over 1,500 words in articles covering *feminism, feminine sexuality, feminist history, feminist theology,* and *feminist criticism*. Biographical entries are not included, but entries for concepts such as Marxism and Reaganism contain some basic information about the people with whom they are associated. The earlier edition of this work listed names of individuals as headings, with cross-references to articles in which they were mentioned. This feature has been dropped, and a reader seeking to identify Lawrence Ferlinghetti, for example, will have to know that the poet would probably be covered in the entry *Beat*.

Editors Bullock and Stephen Trombley are both established authors and editors. The more than 200 contributors are almost all British, and most are connected with academic institutions. Each article is signed. Entries are arranged alphabetically and range from less than 50 to over 900 words. A sample of 90 entries showed that approximately half include bibliographies. These are very brief (several items) and list material as old as 1932 and as recent as 1987. The same sample of entries, loosely classified by field of study, showed representation of over 25 disciplines, including music, medicine, religion, linguistics, computer science, psychology, and philosophy. Readers will find definitions for terms as disparate as *bilateral/cognatic descent, earth shelters, glasnost, sprung rhythm,* and *yuppie*. Many definitions begin by noting the field in which the term is used, and some provide definitions from more than one field. For example, the entry *regulation* is presented in four numbered sections. The first section starts with "In embryology... the second with "In engineering... the third with "In cybernetics... and the last with "In economics... Explicit *see* and *see also* references are provided. In addition, implicit cross-references are given in the text of entries through the use of small capital letters. As a general rule, readers are instructed to seek words and phrases directly, not under "some more comprehensive term."

Anyone considering the purchase of *The Harper Dictionary* should realize that the style in which it is written assumes a solid vocabulary and broad liberal education. As an example, the entry *empathy* states, "Projection (not necessarily voluntary) of the self into the feelings of others or, anthropomorphically, into the 'being' of objects or sets of objects; it implies psychological involvement, at once Keats' pain and joy."

This work does achieve a middle ground between dictionaries and encyclopedias. Without being simplistic, it defines a tremendous number of terms drawn from many fields of study. At $29.95, it is a recommended purchase for libraries serving people who have the necessary background and interest in twentieth-century thought.

The New Electronic Encyclopedia. Rev. ed. [CD-ROM] Grolier, 1988. Updated annually. $395, including compact disc, software diskette, and User's Manual; $100 to owners of Version 1.0. Network versions: up to 8 workstations, $1,795; 9–100 workstations, $3,000.

031 Encyclopedias and dictionaries [BKL]

The New Electronic Encyclopedia is the title of the second CD-ROM edition of Grolier's *Academic American Encyclopedia* (*AAE*). It includes all the text of the 1988 online version of *AAE* on a compact disc along with specialized search software that allows the user to retrieve information contained anywhere within that text. Several new features have been added to this edition. Cross-references have been added to the disc by the editors to create a kind of hypertext stack with the capability of accessing linked articles, accompanied by keyword Boolean searching. These features allow the user to search the CD-ROM *Encyclopedia* in ways that are not possible in either the print or online versions.

1. HARDWARE REQUIREMENTS. This edition of *The New Electronic Encyclopedia* has been developed to run on IBM or IBM-compatible microcomputers. The minimum system requirements include an IBM PC-, XT-, or AT-compatible machine with 512K of memory, a CD-ROM drive with the appropriate controller card, and DOS version 3.0 or higher. A hard disk drive or additional memory will speed up the program but will not provide any additional features. A color monitor can be used to aid the user in accessing the information by highlighting some of the search features, but the system is also very easy to use on a monochrome monitor.

Software may be obtained on either a $5\frac{1}{4}$- or $3\frac{1}{2}$-inch disk, depending upon the needs of the individual microcomputer. The installation process for the program is relatively simple. A single *install* command runs the installation program and prompts the user for relevant information about the hardware being used. Telephone assistance is available through an 800 number for anyone requiring help.

This summer Grolier plans to issue a version of *The New Electronic Encyclopedia* for the Macintosh computer. In the fall, they plan to issue school versions of the *Encyclopedia* for both Macintosh and IBM-compatible systems that will include an online tutorial and practice exercises for students. There will be four subject-specific teacher's guides, one of them on library research skills.

2. PROGRAM CONTENTS. *The New Electronic Encyclopedia* reproduces the text of the 1988 online version of *AAE*, including the bibliographies and fact boxes. This text is very similar to, but not an exact duplicate of, that of the 1988 print edition, which the Board recently reviewed [*RBB* F 15 89]. In some cases the user may find additional material that has been dropped from the print encyclopedia. The CD-ROM and online versions contain 10 million words, compared with 9 million words in the printed set. A comparison of *The New Electronic Encyclopedia* and several recent print editions yields some interesting results. For example, the *Baseball* article on CD-ROM contains an additional paragraph of history when compared with the print article. The fact boxes in the CD-ROM edition often contain more information than those in the print set. For example, the entries for nations of the world all contain such items as currency exchange rate, highest and lowest elevations, major crops, and the name of the head of state that are not in the fact boxes of the print version. The 1989 print version of *AAE*, of course, contains some current information not found on the compact disc. Grolier plans to issue new discs annually, with the next to be published in late 1989 or early 1990.

A significant difference between the CD-ROM and print versions is the lack of illustrations in the compact-disc version. *Academic American Encyclopedia* has been highly praised by the Board for its illustrative material, and a great deal of information in the print edition is provided in the form of photographs, drawings, maps, charts, and graphs. Also, the captions accompanying illustrations in the print version often provide information that is not included in the text of an article and thus is not on the CD version. For example, the *Baseball* entry contains an entire page of diagrams indicating the dimensions of the playing field and the types of equipment used by baseball players, including a caption that explains the use of the equipment and the basic strategies used by a batter. Some of the information that has been added to the fact boxes in the CD-ROM version is intended to make up for information provided visually in the print edition.

3. SEARCH SOFTWARE. Four distinct search modes are provided with *The New Electronic Encyclopedia*. The search mode most analogous to that used in the printed version is the "Browse Titles" mode. In this procedure, the user types in the first few letters or words of a particular topic. The software then displays a menu listing the article titles closest in the alphabet to the search terms. The user may scan forward or backward in the alphabet until an article of interest is found. By hitting the RETURN key, the entry is selected and the text dis-

played on the screen. This procedure is equivalent to opening a volume of the print encyclopedia to a specific portion of the alphabet and then turning the pages until the desired article is located. Beginning searchers will find this mode a very easy means of searching the text.

A more advanced form of searching is provided by the "Browse Word Index" mode. In this procedure, the user types in a term, which results in an alphabetical display similar to the "Browse Titles" display. However, instead of the titles of entries, each matching word used in the *Encyclopedia* is displayed. By selecting a word from this display, all articles containing that word are retrieved. In order to help the user find the most relevant materials on the topic, the software sorts the entries in descending order based upon the number of times the specific search term occurs within the text. The system is designed to retrieve up to 50 entries with any one search. (This default mode can be reset by the librarian so that fewer or more entries can be retrieved.) For example, a word search on the term *railroad* will retrieve the 50 most relevant of the 555 entries containing that word, ranging from the entry *Railroad*, which uses the word 32 times, to *New Mexico*, which mentions *railroad* three times. The user may then select any of the retrieved articles for display. After the user has finished with an article, it is possible to return to the retrieval menu by using the ESCAPE key. In this manner, any or all articles using a specific search term may be retrieved sequentially.

This search mode is roughly the equivalent of using the index of the print encyclopedia to retrieve all articles on the subject of interest, regardless of the volume in which they are contained. In this case, the CD-ROM has two major advantages over the print version. First, the index in the print edition is limited only to those terms selected by the editors. On the CD-ROM, every term in the entire text is indexed. Secondly, the electronic *Encyclopedia* sorts the articles from most relevant to least relevant based on the number of times the term is used; this is impossible to do using the printed index.

The third search mode expands on the "Browse Word Index" by allowing the user to combine terms using Boolean operators. This mode, known as "Word Search," enables users to retrieve articles containing a combination of several different search terms. Up to four distinct concepts may be entered during any single search. The default operation is to connect the terms with *and*, but *or* and *not* may also be used. Both internal and right-side truncation are available. The user may specify which fields are to be searched, such as titles, bibliographies, or full text, and may also specify the relationship between the search terms, such as anywhere in the article, in the same paragraph, within words of each other, or in exact word order. In addition, the user may view the dictionary of all words included in the text for help in selecting search terms.

To retrieve an article using "Word Search," the searcher enters each term on a different line on a menu. For example, in a search for the railroads of Colorado, the user enters the term *railroad* on the first line of the menu and *Colorado* on the next line. The search software then retrieves each of the articles containing all of the terms selected in the desired relationship. While the search time for this mode is longer than that for the other search procedures, it is still quite short. Even on words with a very large number of postings, the longest search time required by the system was 35 seconds. In our test of the software, almost all searches were executed in under 15 seconds.

When the system has identified articles containing the desired search terms, the titles are displayed in descending order from the entry containing the highest number of search terms to those containing the fewest. The user may then select the full text of those entries of interest. The "Word Search" mode combines the advantages of browsing the word index with the power of Boolean search commands. This mode is the closest to that used with the online version.

The fourth and final search mode is unique to the CD-ROM version of the encyclopedia and has the potential to be the most powerful of all search functions. It functions like a hypertext stack, so the user is able to move from article to article within the set by taking advantage of links established on the disc. Certain terms within each article are linked directly to other related entries within the file. All linked terms appear in capital letters within entries, and using the ALT-L key moves the user through the text from link to link. By hitting the RETURN key while the cursor is located on one of the linking words, the search software will retrieve a menu of article titles centered on the linked term. This menu is similar to the one used in the "Browse Titles" search mode. The full text of the linked article may then be displayed as an additional window over the original text. The user may read the text of the linked article, use a link in the new article to retrieve additional material, or return to the original entry using the ESCAPE key. For example, a user interested in the novel *For Whom the Bell Tolls* can follow the link from that entry directly to *Hemingway* and from there may also follow links to the entries *The Sun Also Rises* or *A Farewell to Arms*. The link function allows the user to find related entries that would not be retrieved using the same keywords or Boolean operators.

One problem with the link feature is that the system searches for individual words rather than for phrases. For example, if the cursor is located on the word *bell* in *For Whom the Bell Tolls*, the link function will bring up a menu of articles beginning with the letter *B* rather than the letter *F*. This is explained in the documentation; users must check that the cursor is at the beginning of the linked phrase. Also, some links are blind cross-references. For instance, the link to Felix Mendelssohn does not work because his name was mistakenly entered as *endelssohn*. The cross-references for *Missa Ecce Sacerdos Magnus* and *Pousseur, Henri* also lead nowhere. In the Board's test of the product, no limit was reached on the number of linked articles that could be retrieved and written over the original source entry. Using the link mode is the electronic equivalent of reading the text of several volumes of the print encyclopedia simultaneously.

Another unique feature of this edition of *The New Electronic Encyclopedia* is that the software allows the user to create new links that have not been established by the editors. By using the "bookmark" feature, the user may enter additional links into the software and retrieve material through those links. For example, a user looking for material on binary numbers may wish to know how the binary system is used as a basis for modern computing technology. While *Binary Numbers* is linked to the articles *Number* and *Duodecimal System*, there is no link with the entry *Computer* on the disc. If the user retrieves the article *Binary Numbers* and then the article *Computer*, however, a link may be made between the two by executing the bookmark function. The bookmark is specific to the exact paragraph that was on the screen at the time of its execution, so the user can be very specific in linking lengthy entries, identifying the exact page and paragraph of interest. The bookmark function gives the user the power to decide which entries are relevant to a specific search topic, rather than relying only on search terms or predetermined relationships.

4. DISPLAYING, PRINTING, AND DOWNLOADING RESULTS. Once material of interest is found, it may be displayed, printed, or downloaded to a disk file. The default display treats each successive article as a new window that overwrites any previous screen displays. However, each new window is slightly smaller than those displayed previously, so the user may simultaneously view the currently displayed entry and an index of all of the lower-level windows. The index indicates the title and paragraph number that were displayed when the next window was retrieved. Users may return to any previous windows by hitting the ESCAPE key until all successive windows have been cleared. With this display mode, the total search history is visible at a glance.

In addition to the title and paragraph indexes, many long articles are subdivided into sections. At the bottom of the window, the user may be given options for selecting various parts of the text. Occasionally an outline provides the user with a menu of options for progressing through the text. These outlines are generally the same as the boldface subheadings in the print edition. By selecting one of the options from the outline menu, the user is placed directly into the portion of the text that discusses the chosen topic. In addition to the outline menu, some entries provide similar shortcuts to finding the bibliography or the fact box.

Two other display functions are available in addition to the standard window. A "zoom" feature is provided that will expand any article displayed to the full screen size. This function enlarges the amount of material displayed at any one time and enables the user to read entries more easily. However, with the zoom feature on, the user loses the indexing information for the previously retrieved entries. In general, the zoom function should be used when reading articles but not while searching. In addition, the user can change the size of the windows on the screen to display two different entries simultaneously side by side. While the windows used for this option are small, they allow the user to compare two different pieces of text at the same time.

One of the most popular features of the CD-ROM version of the encyclopedia is that it allows users to print or download all or any part of an entry. By using the "mark" feature, the reader may indicate exactly which portion of the text is to be printed or copied. Several paging and formatting options are available for both printed and downloaded text. Downloaded material may be sent to either a disk file or to a temporary notepad file for recall later during the search session. By combining the mark, bookmark, notepad, and downloading features, a user may retrieve text from several different entries and reformat it on a disk file. This file can then be loaded onto another system such as a word processor or database manager for additional processing.

5. INSTRUCTIONAL MATERIALS. The *User's Guide* that accompanies *The New Electronic Encyclopedia* provides basic instruction in the setup and use of the system. After a brief description of the use of windows and menus, 54 pages of text discuss the various features included in the software. Each feature discussed is accompanied by several clear screen illustrations highlighting specific functions. Many examples are used, and the text is easy to understand. By following the examples in the *Guide*, a novice user can quickly learn the search, display, and print functions. However, the more advanced features of the system, such as link, bookmark, and notepad, are given only brief treatment and could benefit from more detailed explanation.

The on-screen help included in *The New Electronic Encyclopedia* is singularly unhelpful. When the help function is selected, it provides instructions on moving the cursor throughout the text and also some tips on searching. Unfortunately, the help screen is the least readable of all of the screens on the system. The user can learn more about the software by either consulting the *User's Guide* and looking at the examples or by experimenting with some of the option menus on the screen. The help screens need a great deal of work before they can perform the function for which they were designed.

6. OVERALL EVALUATION. *The New Electronic Encyclopedia* is an exciting application of new technology to a traditional reference source. Keyword Boolean searching allows the user to retrieve any single term or combination of terms mentioned anywhere in the text, and cross-references inserted by the editors allow the user to link between related articles. With these two features, the user has more indexing and cross-referencing than could ever be incorporated into the other formats of the encyclopedia. The ability of the user to add new links and to download and print any selected sections also adds to the versatility of the CD-ROM version. However, because much of the information in *Academic American Encyclopedia* is presented visually, the lack of illustrative material detracts from the usefulness of the electronic version.

With *The New Electronic Encyclopedia*, Grolier has moved further toward its goal of providing encyclopedia information in an advanced electronic format. As the technology continues to develop, Grolier should be able to add high-quality music and voice tracks, still pictures, and full-color video. Several electronic products are currently under development that include both audio and visual material, one of them by Grolier and another based on *Compton's Encyclopedia*. When these formats can be incorporated into the text of *The New Electronic Encyclopedia*, Grolier will have pushed encyclopedia publishing into an entirely new dimension.

Raintree Children's Encyclopedia. 11v. 4th ed. Raintree, 1988. 1,023p. illus. indexes. maps. hardcover $180 (0-8172-3050-5); paper $109.45 (0-8172-3052-1); individual paper volumes, $9.95.
031 Children's encyclopedias and dictionaries [CIP] 87-16543

Not nearly as comprehensive as an encyclopedia, this is a series of very short articles arranged in 10 topical volumes (*People, Animals, Plants, The Earth and Beyond, Famous Men and Women, Travel and Communications, The Modern World, Countries and Customs, Arts and Entertainment*, and *Sports and Recreation*), accompanied by an index volume. Each volume is subdivided into 7 to 13 subtopics, with a number of articles under each, not alphabetically arranged. For example, the *Arts and Entertainment* volume has sections on painting, drawing, sculpture, crafts, dance, opera, music, theater, circuses and fairs, and radio, television, and the movies. Subtopics under circuses and fairs are clowns, jugglers, and fairs. Painting includes schools of painting, oil painting, portrait painting, mosaics, and collage, plus a number of other topics. Each section has an introduction, often only a page long. Articles typically run about one-half page each (two to three paragraphs). Each volume has 96 pages. The set is generously illustrated with color pictures on each page: photographs (scenes, people, artifacts), diagrams, cutaways, drawings, and maps. Some processes are traced, for example, sound recording. Entries give a few basic facts but not necessarily an adequate overview. While the style is kept simple, little attempt is made to clarify abstract concepts. The intermediate child, for whom this set is intended, who already knows something about the subject will be unlikely to learn much new from reading many of these articles. Analogies are rarely made. Oversimplification occurs, as in this explanation of *data processing*: "Data is the kind of information that can be put into computers." *Industry* is defined as "different kinds of work that occur in the world." Yet the articles do not begin to reflect the total world of work.

Each volume has an index, but only to entry terms. The set's index is slightly broader in its coverage and provides the only opportunities for cross-referencing topics. A section in the index volume outlines each of the preceding volumes but is identified as "Facts and Figures" rather than "Contents." Ten pages of miscellany follow, covering such subjects as the metric system, dates of modern Olympic Games, presidents, and longest rivers.

The set is very attractive and appealing to page through. It strives to be multiethnic and nonsexist; the scope is broad. While based on a British set, illustrations are drawn from all over the world, and topical coverage does not show a British slant. For instance, in the *Sports and Recreation* volume, lacrosse and baseball are covered along with rugby and cricket. Children will enjoy reading about familiar topics, and readers introduced to something here might be motivated to learn more about it, though there are no bibliographies. But the child who approaches *Raintree Children's Encyclopedia* with something specific to look up may very well be disappointed. Even if the item is included and can be accessed through the index, the coverage is likely to be superficial.

The Board reviewed Raintree's *Let's Discover Library* [RBB F 15 87]. That set is in 15 topically arranged volumes with an index. While some of the volumes cover the same subjects, these are two distinct sets. Children's librarians will want to consider carefully whether the attractive format and breadth of *Raintree Children's Encyclopedia* are enough to justify its purchase and, if purchased, whether it belongs in the reference collection.

Young Students Learning Library. 24v. Weekly Reader Books; dist. by Field Publications, 1988. illus. index. maps. hardcover $253 retail; $199 to schools and libraries.
031 Children's encyclopedias and dictionaries [OCLC] 88-159295

First published in 1972, this set was previously called *Young Students Encyclopedia* [RSBR D 1 78, Jl 15 80]. It attempts to introduce elementary school children "to people, places, and events that have shaped their world."

Each of the 22 slender text volumes has about 125 pages. More than 3,000 alphabetically arranged topics are presented in brief articles, usually from 250 to 600 words. There are occasionally longer articles too; *English Language* and *Evolution* each cover three pages. Articles are unsigned; there is a list of editorial staff at the beginning of volume 1, but no credentials are given for them. Topics chosen for coverage indicate an awareness of the curriculum needs and personal interests of children ages 7 to 13. Balanced coverage is given to physical and natural sciences, technology, history and geography, government, arts and crafts, education, social sciences, fine arts, and sports and games.

Much emphasis is given to places. Included is information about physical features, history, economy, natural resources, and culture. An information box for most nations includes a locater map, flag, capital city, area, population, natural resources, exports, unit of money, and official language. No dates are given for population figures, but they appear to be current. The 50 U.S. states and the Canadian provinces are treated individually. Accompanying each state and province are two informational boxes—one providing a small locater map, flag or emblem, tree, flower, and bird; the other covering such items as capital, area, population, highest point, largest city, motto, and famous people. Detailed maps are provided for states and provinces. Larger countries also have detailed maps; smaller ones have only locater maps that place them on their continent. The entry for each month of the year is accompanied by a boxed listing of "Dates of Special Events in . . . ."

Some updating is evident; for example, the article *Terrorism* concludes with the 1986 bombing of Libya by the U.S.; also noted are the presidential candidacy of Jesse Jackson, the *Challenger* disaster in 1986, and the election of Margaret Thatcher to a third term and the signing of the nuclear arms treaty in 1987. However, because many entries are so brief, they don't go into enough detail to treat some recent events. For instance, Anthony Kennedy's appointment to the Supreme Court is not noted because no list of justices is given, though there is a separate biography of Sandra Day O'Connor. Entries added to the set include *Acid Rain*; *Blume, Judy*; *Compact Disc*; *Dallas*; *Fiber Optics*; *Hydroelectricity*; *Meir, Golda*; *Stress*; *Teresa, Mother*; and *Yiddish Language*.

Cross-references are used frequently. *Also read* leads users to related topics. In some cases, cross-references are classified into groups following *For further information on*. For instance, the entry *Tree* is followed by four categories ("Ecology and Forestry," "Kinds of Trees," "Tree Anatomy and Growth," "Tree Products"), each followed by the names of other articles in the set. The style of writing is clear, appealing, and appropriate for the audience. For instance, the article *Flour Making* begins "Can you imagine what a peanut butter and jelly sandwich would be like without bread?" Objectivity is generally maintained, though many controversial topics like homosexuality and abortion are not treated at all. Under *AIDS* there is a cross-reference to *Virus*, where a brief description is given. The set has no bibliographies.

Almost every volume contains "Learn by Doing" activities. Examples include testing for acids and bases, making a model room, knitting, composing haiku, and determining chance and probability. Such activities are set off at the ends of articles to which they relate. Items in the margins contain bits of human-interest information, curious facts, and other trivia. Instructions for children's games include a couple of card games, checkers, and chess.

There is profuse use of graphics—drawings, photographs, charts, diagrams, reproductions of paintings, and maps. Illustrative material generally ranges in size from $1^3/4$ by 2 inches to a full page. About 70 percent of the 5,000 graphics are in color. There is a balance of sexes and races in the pictures. In volume 22 is a 74-page index, prefaced with clear instructions on its use. Each topic that has its own entry is in boldface type, and illustrations are indexed.

Included in the price of this encyclopedia are a separate atlas and a dictionary. *Young Students World Atlas* has been prepared for Weekly Reader Books by Rand McNally. At the beginning of the 96-page volume is a section including "The Earth in Space," "Mapping the World," "Geographic Features," and "Using the Atlas." Then there are maps for each continent (or in some cases, parts of continents) showing terrain, environment, animals, countries, and cities. There are also text and color photographs for each continent. The volume concludes with a glossary, "World Facts and Comparisons," "Principal Cities of the World," and "Index of Major Places on the Physical-Political Maps." All in all, this is a useful basic atlas for its intended audience.

The 800-page *Young Students Intermediate Dictionary*, the last volume in the set, is a slightly revised version of *The Xerox Intermediate Dictionary* (1974). The *Dictionary* is based on a nationwide search for words that children use in everyday speech and in the classroom. There are useful sections on "How to Use Your Dictionary," "Guide to Pronunciation," and "Latin and Greek Roots." About 34,000 entries, including derived and compound forms, are arranged in two columns. Where there are several meanings for words, these are arranged by frequency of use. Sometimes sample sentences using the words are included. The definitions are clear and accurate. There are geographic entries only for the states, and no biographical entries. The emphasis on contemporary vocabulary is evidenced throughout the volume, for example, the inclusion of such words as *blastoff*, *bummer*, *busted play*, *crack*, *recycle*, and *uptight*. Verb tenses are shown. There are no synonyms and antonyms indicated. The usual stress marks are not used; rather the accented syllable is typeset in small capitals. A pronunciation key is given, though not on every page. Small but clear black-and-white illustrations appear in the outer margins and are identical to those in *The Xerox Intermediate Dictionary*.

The 24 volumes in this set are sturdily and attractively bound, and the whole format is attractive. *Young Students Learning Library* will not replace comprehensive standard encyclopedias for children. It has less than one-third the pages of *The New Book of Knowledge* and less than half those of *Children's Britannica*, for instance. While most of the topics covered in *NBK* can also be found here, the entries are much briefer. More than 16 pages are devoted to *Rhode Island* in *NBK*; the entry in *Young Students* is about $3^1/2$ pages. *Ronald Reagan* gets more than 3 pages in *NBK* and about one-half page in *Young Students*. Entries in *Children's Britannica* are also more lengthy. While considerably smaller than any of the annually revised encyclopedias, *Young Students Learning Library* is an attractive, relatively inexpensive supplementary set for elementary schools and libraries, especially for beginning readers who do not need extensive treatment of topics.

Number One in the U.S.A.: Records and Wins in Sports, Entertainment, Business, and Science with Sources Cited. By Thomas P. Slavens. Scarecrow, 1988. 196p. index. hardcover $20 (0-8108-2140-0).
031'.02 World records [CIP] 88-14823

This compilation by librarian Slavens is divided into four sections (sports, entertainment, business, and science, subdivided by topic) and gives records that were found in magazines and newspapers over the past two years. For example, in the sports section under basketball is the entry "The winningest coach in high school basketball for girls is Thednal Hill of Highland High in Hardy, Arkansas." This is followed by a full citation to the source, *Sporting News*, including page number. The sports records date from 1987, but the other records were set over a wider time span. For example, the leading honey-producing states are given for 1986, the number of doctors disciplined by states for 1985, and the worst nuclear accident is noted as occurring in 1979. Slavens consulted a wide range of popular serials for the records, but most frequently quoted are the *New York Times*, *USA Today*, and his hometown newspaper, the *Ann Arbor Times*. The volume concludes with an index. From the introduction, it appears that this may be an annual publication.

While many sources of sporting records, awards, and "famous firsts" can be found in libraries, *Number One in the U.S.A.* is very browsable. Public and high school libraries may want to consider purchase.

Children's Britannica. 20v. 4th ed. Encyclopaedia Britannica, 1988. illus. index. maps. hardcover $331.86 retail; $299 to schools and libraries (0-85229-206-6).
032 Children's encyclopedias and dictionaries [OCLC] 87-81078

This encyclopedia for children in the middle grades is the fourth edition of a set first published in Great Britain in 1960, but it is being sold here for the first time. The purpose of the set is implicit in the title; that of the revision is "to adapt the encyclopedia for young students living in the technological age of the late 20th century and to do so on a broad, international basis." Articles range from a paragraph (usually longer) to several pages; among the longest are those on the U.S. (18 pages) and U.S. history (21 pages). The scope is truly encyclopedic, with articles on people, geography, natural science, technology, holidays, religion, education, history, anthropology, fine and applied arts, literature, and economics. According to the publisher, there are 4,000 articles and information on 35,000 topics.

The set is in 19 equal volumes (320 pages each); volume 20 is the 639-page "Reference Index" incorporating brief dictionary entries on topics not found in the main body of the set. Typical "Reference Index" entries are *Dionne Quintuplets*, *Mongol Dynasty*, *Pelé*, and *Tasman Sea*. The index volume has six pages of directions. As an example of its organization, looking up *Greek Language* in the index indicates that the main article is found under *Greek* 6:262b and cites additional references in the articles *English Language*, *Etymology*, *European Languages*, *Greece*, *Hebrew Language*, and *Hieroglyph*; a bullet indicates that the reader should also look in the index under *Greek Alphabet*. Part of volume 19 is a 159-page atlas, with political maps of continents and smaller areas (e.g., Central Europe, Northern Africa, Middle America). This world atlas is separately indexed. (Most country articles in the body of the set are accompanied by a simplified map.) Individual political maps of the U.S. states and Canadian provinces follow, with keys to principal cities and towns on each map. Some detail of these maps is lost in the gutter when maps extend across two pages.

Articles are unsigned; the preface states that they have been prepared by "leading authorities" in their fields. The final volume concludes with a list of over 450 writers and advisers, some of which are institutional (e.g., "Ontario Government"; "Netball Association, U.K."; "IBM"). People named are most likely to be from the United Kingdom, followed by those from the U.S.; citizens of Canada, Australia, and several non-English-speaking countries are also cited. Some authorities are listed as being authors, but more have some field of subject expertise noted (e.g., orchestra conductor, law professor, flying instructor, botanist, architect, or librarian). Only a few are well known (e.g., Max Beloff, Ralph McGill, Konrad Lorenz). There is no indication of who contributed to which article or in what way.

A one-page preface introduces the set, followed by a page of instructions on use. Arrangement is alphabetical, letter by letter, with volume number and range ("Aardvark to Argentina," "Philos to Rasp," etc.) on the spine. Because the volumes are of equal length, letters are split, something other sets for this age group avoid. *See also* references are usually internal and parenthetical, with the entry title in caps. Occasionally *see also* references appear at the end of an article. *See* references are also used (e.g., "*Canton* see *Ghangzhou*"). There are no bibliographies. Illustrations, usually black-and-white photographs, are found on most pages. Color photographs, maps, drawings, diagrams, and art reproductions are also used. Credits for illustrations are usually given. Pictures are captioned, and placement is appropriate. The choice of pictures sometimes seems arbitrary rather than thoughtful. For example, why show the portrait of a nineteenth-century New Zealand prime minister, when space is so limited? Many plants and animals are drawn or photographed in monochrome, when a color photograph or drawing—preferably with some indication of relative size—would be more revealing. Opportunities are missed to clarify and expand concepts through illustrations. For example, there is no picture of Stonehenge; the shape of Lake Superior is described but there is no map; the concept of how long ago the Stone Age was—and its duration—could have been clearer with a timeline.

Although *CB* is not considered a continuation of *Britannica Junior*, a comparison of articles occasionally shows similarities. Some articles are obviously based on *Britannica Junior* entries, although the *CB* articles always show some revision.

CB is for younger readers than are *World Book*, *Merit Students*, or *Compton's* and for approximately the same audience as *The New Book of Knowledge*. *CB* is a smaller set, with about 6,700 pages compared with about 10,500 pages in *NBK*. Looking at the coverage of the two, *NBK* has about the same number of articles but takes a broad-entry approach. Articles in *NBK* tend to be longer; there are more illustrations (22,000 versus 6,000 in *CB*), much greater use of color, and more flair shown in layout.

As a comparative sample of coverage, *CB* has separate articles on *Detergent* (one column) and *Soap and Soap-Making* (2½ pages), while *NBK* combines *Detergents and Soap* (three pages). *CB's Detergent* article defines *detergent* as part of "a class of chemicals used for cleansing processes." A typical method of manufacturing is described, followed by a brief explanation of how detergents work. The final two sentences mention that problems can be caused in the water system, so biodegradable detergents are now sold. The article *Soap and Soap-Making* states that *detergent* is the name of a group of cleansers, which includes soap; the term *detergent* tends now to be used for synthetic cleaners. A paragraph describes how soap works. The remainder of the article deals with soap-making history, going back to the Phoenicians. The process of soap-making is described, and four black-and-white pictures show steps on a soap-making assembly line.

NBK states that "Detergents and soaps are substances that make things clean." Soap is made from natural substances, detergent from synthetic. The explanation of how cleaning works is more technical than in *CB* and uses terms like *surfactant* and *hydrophilic*. A three-frame cartoon illustrates the process, albeit on another page. Other uses of soap and detergent are outlined. Pioneer soap-making and modern processes are described; pictures contrast hand-and machine-made products. Almost a page is devoted to environmental concerns, and a river clouded by detergent is shown. The article was reviewed by a university professor, author of *Fatty Acids and Their Industrial Applications*.

Exposition in *CB* is generally clear. The articles seem well focused, with enough detail to explain and not so much as to confound. These qualities make the text useful for younger readers. However, a check of readability, using the Fry Graph, shows an average reading level of ninth grade, probably because the sentences are quite long. Apart from the occasional intrusion of condescension, older readers will be comfortable with the set. Briticisms are not apparent. The balance of coverage is more international than in an American set. The articles *Baseball* and *Cricket*, for instance, are almost equal in length, and there is a separate article for the British game *Rounders*. There are not articles in the body of the set for all U.S. presidents. Ronald Reagan, Abraham Lincoln, and others receive lengthy coverage in the text, but John Quincy Adams, John Buchanan, Jimmy Carter, and others have only capsule entries in the "Reference Index." British prime ministers are treated in the same fashion. The international focus results in more entries from Commonwealth nations, especially places (e.g., English counties), politicians, and history. The article *Police* has sections on law officers in Britain, America, Canada, Australia and New Zealand, and other European countries. The photographs in *Motor Vehicle* show cars from many different countries. However, the broadened scope of the set does not seem skewed or intrusive, and it may be useful for American children to have this exposure. Metric measurements are given, with American/British units in parentheses. Sexism in language has not been avoided, e.g., the term *early man* is often used, and Walt Whitman "glorified the individual man." Three times the generic *man* is used in the article *Wood*, which immediately following *Women's Rights*.

Unlike the British set, there are plans to update *Children's Britannica* every year. A revised printing will be available in the spring of this year.

Children's Britannica is basically sound in scope, accuracy, and readability; however, it does not reflect an imaginative approach to encyclopedia making. Its appearance is drab, and the set does not invite browsing. Nevertheless, this reasonably priced encyclopedia is a valid purchase for elementary school libraries and children's rooms; it is a possible addition to middle/junior high school libraries. Even as contents of juvenile encyclopedias overlap, *CB* adds some subjects not found elsewhere and provides alternative approaches to topics that overlap. Many libraries stagger the purchase and replacement of their juvenile encyclopedias, and *Children's Britannica* could well be added to the schedule.

The Hutchinson Encyclopedia. 8th ed. Century Hutchinson; dist. by David & Charles, 1988. 1,273p. illus. maps. hardcover $39.95 (0-09-172290-X).

032 Encyclopedias and dictionaries [OCLC]

This one-volume general encyclopedia is published in Great Britain. It is arranged in dictionary format and provides current, nontechnical information in over 25,000 entries. It is accurately described as "a companion to world events, history, arts and science." The coverage is broad—a sample page includes a Gainsborough painting, a diagram of a galaxy, and the entries *Galileo, Galla,* and *Gall Bladder.* (Filing is letter by letter, hence *Galla* is before *Gall Bladder.*) The English viewpoint predominates in the text but is not overwhelming. *Airplane* is *aeroplane,* American football players are "kitted out," and New York City is called a town. Information is current through 1987 and early 1988, with the inclusion of the December 1987 signing of the INF Treaty, the Minnesota Twins' victory in the 1987 World Series, the awarding of a 1987 Nobel Prize to Joseph Brodsky, and the death of actor Trevor Howard in January 1988. Internal cross-references are noted with arrows, and pronunciation is given for most entries.

There are numerous tables, diagrams, and black-and-white photographs illustrating the text. Photographs are appropriately placed and labeled. A 32-page world atlas is not indexed, but the color maps are clear and current. (The 1984 name change of Upper Volta to Burkina Faso is included.)

The Hutchinson Encyclopedia compares favorably with other one-volume encyclopedias. The single alphabet is an advantage over *The Random House Encyclopedia*'s (1983, o.p.) "Colorpedia" and "Alphapedia." *The New Columbia Encyclopedia* (1975, o.p.) has longer articles with bibliographies but no photographs and very few pictures or diagrams. *The New American Desk Encyclopedia* (NAL, 1984, paper, $12.95 and $6.95) has shorter entries and in some instances is out-of-date. *The Concise Columbia Encyclopedia* (Columbia, 1983, hardcover $29.95, paper $14.95) is closest in depth, currency, and price to the *Hutchinson* but has no photographs and very few diagrams and tables.

The Hutchinson Encyclopedia, eighth edition, is recommended for purchase by public, high school, and academic libraries as a current complement to other one-volume encyclopedias.

Encyclopedia of Associations: Regional, State, and Local Organizations, 1988–89. 1st ed. 7v. Gale, 1988. indexes. hardcover $400/set, $85/vol. (0-8103-2083-5; ISSN 0894-2846).

061.3025 Associations, institutions, etc.—U.S.—Directories ‖ Societies—U.S.—Directories [OCLC] 76-46129

The *Encyclopedia of Associations,* long a standard source for information about national organizations, now has an additional seven regional volumes to provide coverage of 50,000 local, state, and regional associations. Four of the volumes are now available; the other three will be published by the end of the year. Despite a claim to be "the first comprehensive source" for such information, coverage is far from comprehensive in the sense of covering all organizations within its stated scope: "trade and professional associations, social welfare and public affairs organizations, labor unions, fraternal and patriotic organizations, religious, sports, and hobby groups, and many other types of organizations consisting of voluntary members." Anyone can check his or her home city or town and find many omissions.

A hallmark of the *Encyclopedia of Associations* has been a conscientious effort to base entries on data received directly from associations themselves. This standard has been abandoned in this work, which relies heavily on secondary sources: "local telephone directories; newspapers, magazines, and other periodicals; state and local chambers of commerce; and, most importantly, national organizations.... Questionnaires were mailed selectively." Despite obvious efforts to gather data, it is very difficult to predict which organizations will be included and which will not. Local chapters of the Medical Library Association are included, but not those of the Special Libraries Association or the American Society for Information Science. All the local chapters of Presbyterians for Lesbian/Gay Concerns and of Dignity (the organization for lesbian and gay Roman Catholics) are listed, but not chapters of similar organizations associated with the Episcopal, Methodist, Lutheran, or Seventh Day Adventist churches. Local councils of churches abound in towns, cities, counties, and states, but only five are listed in the volume for the middle Atlantic states.

Full entries include the organization name, acronym, address, telephone number, name and title of chief official, founding date, number of members, size of staff and budget, names of affiliated local groups, general description, information about telecommunication services, publications and affiliated organizations, alternative names, supercessions, mergers, name changes, and meetings. Few entries actually provide this level of information. By far, the great majority are limited to name, acronym, address, telephone number, and sometimes the name of a director.

Entries are arranged alphabetically: first by state, then by city or town, then by association name. The town or city is chosen on the basis of the association's address, causing some associations to be listed where their secretaries happen to live rather than where they actually function. For example, Dignity/New Brunswick (New Jersey) is listed under Bound Brook. Similarly, statewide organizations are listed in whatever town they happen to use for their address.

"The primary value of *Regional, State, and Local Organizations* is as a basic guide to information on specific subjects." "Complete name and subject access . . . is provided." While the first statement may be true, the second is not. Subject entries in the combined "Name and Keyword Index" are based on keywords in association names, plus additional words added by the editors. However, there are no cross-references. Thus, persons looking for lesbian and gay organizations will find several listed under these terms, but no indication is given that even more are listed under *homosexual,* the editor's preferred term. Dignity/New Brunswick is described in its entry as "Gays and lesbians who are members of the Roman Catholic Church," but it has no index entry under *Catholic,* whereas all the local chapters of the Knights of Columbus do have *Catholic* entries.

This first attempt to provide access to regional, state, and local organizations on a national scale is far from perfect, but it is a notable effort worthy of support. Local and state directories do exist for some areas and for some subjects, and some are quite good and will be more comprehensive, but such coverage is spotty at best. Despite its shortfalls, *Regional, State, and Local Organizations* will be the best source of such information for many areas, and libraries needing such information will want to have it.

Traveler's Guide to Museum Exhibitions, 1989: U.S. Edition. Museum Guide Publications, P.O. Box 25369, 1619 31st St. NW, Washington, DC 20007, 1989 (c1988). 157p. illus. index. paper $8.95 (0-923041-00-1; ISSN 1041-0724).

069.5 Museums—U.S.—Directories ‖ Exhibitions—U.S.—Directories [BKL]

This guide "for the art lover who travels and for the traveler who loves art" provides the 1989 exhibition calendars for 110 American museums. Titles and brief annotations for these exhibits are provided. Additional data supplied include museum address, telephone number, admission charges, hours, tours, accessibility for the disabled, and refreshment opportunities. Strengths of the permanent collection and its highlights are also noted. Ninety small reproductions, more than half of them in color, are placed in the outer margins of the pages.

Museums are entered by city name, not state, and there is an index of museums at the back. The Board's only complaints about this handy guide concern omissions and arrangement. Fine museums in popular destinations such as San Antonio, Newark, and Sarasota are missing. No cross-references or indexing by state is provided. Therefore visitors to New York may miss the Brooklyn Museum entered under the name of that borough or neglect making an excursion to Mountainside, New York, to see the Storm King Art Center and sculpture park. Dallas and Fort Worth, Cambridge and Boston, as well as San Francisco and Oakland should be connected by *see also* references.

Despite these drawbacks, libraries serving travelers may want to enter a standing order for this inexpensive annual.

Children's Media Market Place. 3d ed. Ed. by Dolores Blythe Jones. Neal-Schuman, 1988. 397p. bibliog. index. paper $45 (1-55570-007-1).

070.483'2 Children's literature—Publishing—U.S.—Directories I Instructional materials industry—U.S.—Directories I Television programs for children—U.S.—Directories I Children's librarians—U.S.—Directories [BKL] 88-60792

This third edition of *Children's Media Market Place* (*CMMP*), like earlier editions, is a directory of sources for children's materials, including books, software, audiovisuals of all kinds, television and radio programs, and periodicals. The major emphasis is on material for grades K–8, with some reference to material and service for grades 9–12. *CMMP* is designed to answer such queries as, Where can I find materials for handicapped children? Who distributes children's media in Spanish? Where can I buy out-of-print children's books? Who distributes Mr. Rogers TV programs?

The directory is divided into two parts: "Directory of Children's Media Sources" and "Names and Numbers Index to Children's Media Sources." Twenty-four areas of interest are covered in the first part, among them "Publishers" and "Audiovisual Producers & Distributors" (classified by format, subject, and special interest); "Periodicals" (for children, for professionals and parents); "Wholesalers"; "Bookstores"; "Book Clubs"; "Agents for Children's Properties"; "Public Library Coordinators of Children's and Young Adult Services"; "State School Media Officers"; "Federal Grants"; "Calendar of Events"; "Awards"; and "Bibliography of Selection Tools."

The section "Reviewers of Children's Media," which appeared in the 1982 edition, has been dropped. Added are the following: "Software Producers & Distributors," "Antiquarian Booksellers," "Museums," and "State Library Media Associations." Most sections are preceded by a brief note indicating methods of selection and sources of additional information. The "Names and Numbers Index" provides the name, address, telephone number, and the section of the book where listed for all individuals, businesses, periodicals, and organizations mentioned in *CMMP*.

Entries are based on questionnaire responses, telephone calls, and research. The preface indicates that a listing does not constitute a recommendation. Abbreviations and acronyms for organizations are listed following the preface.

Some omissions were noted that may be due in part to lack of response to the questionnaire or inquiry. Although there are omissions, occasional errors, and some already out-of-date information, *Children's Media Market Place* is a convenient and useful guide for librarians, teachers, parents, and others who work with children, especially ages 5 to 13.

Poet's Handbook. By Lincoln B. Young. Fine Arts Press; dist. by Quality Books, 1988. 188p. paper $9.95 (0-911666-33-8).

070.502 Poetry—Marketing [OCLC]

Sandwiched between eight brief essays advising the reader about various aspects of this special publishing market are 137 pages of references to sources that publish poetry. The essays cover topics such as the marketing of poems and the selling of song-poems, etc. The tone in these pieces is straightforward, perhaps even a bit blunt, the sort of thing one might expect to encounter from a weary editor who had just received one too many badly prepared manuscripts.

The bulk of the volume is a list of magazines that publish poetry, poetry book publishers, and greeting card firms that accept poetry submissions. By far the largest of these three segments is the list of magazine publishers, covering 121 pages. Entries in this section contain the name and address of the publication, a one-sentence annotation describing the types of poetry sought, and a statement regarding what sort of payment is made to authors. The listings for book publishers generally contain only a name and address; only 23 of the 145 entries have even a brief annotation. None of the entries for greeting card companies accepting free-lance submissions are annotated. Although sources in England, West Germany, Australia, and New Zealand are contained in the magazine listing, well over 90 percent of the entries are for U.S or Canadian publications. There is no index to the volume.

When compared to works such as *The Poet's Marketplace*, *Poet's Market* [RBB Mr 1 87], or *Directory of Poetry Publishers* [RBB D 15 86], this slim volume fails to impress. Each of the other titles provides much more information about publishing sources, for example, circulation, the number of manuscripts received and percentage acceptance rate, and average response time regarding acceptance or rejection. *Poet's Market* and *Directory of Poetry Publishers* have extensive subject and geographic indexes as well. Overlap among all these sources is high, although given the quixotic nature of little magazines, each contains many unique entries. Competitors of *Poet's Handbook* are from $2 to $10 more expensive to purchase, yet the physical quality of this volume will make the cost of rebinding an almost certain additional expenditure.

For those collections attempting very thorough coverage of the poetry marketplace, *Poet's Handbook* may be a desirable purchase. For most other collections, however, purchase of one or more of its competitors will be a wiser investment.

Microform Market Place, 1988–1989. Ed. by Ellen S. Wasserman. Meckler, 1989. 229p. bibliog. indexes. paper $42.50 (0-88736-282-6; ISSN 0362-0999).

070.5'7 Micropublishing—Directories I Microfilm services—Directories [OCLC] 74-4811

This is the eighth edition of *Microform Market Place* (*MMP*), which first appeared with the 1974–75 edition, is biennial, international in scope, and one of many publications about microforms published by Meckler. *MMP* "provides comprehensive information about micropublishers." It does not provide information on micrographic equipment or supply manufacturers.

MMP comprises six sections: "Directory of Micropublishers"; "Subject Index"; "Geographic Index"; "Discontinued, Acquisitions, Name Changes"; "Organizations"; and "Bibliography of Primary Sources."

The biggest section in *MMP* is the "Directory of Micropublishers," which includes nearly 400 listings, varying in length from two lines to a page and arranged alphabetically. A typical entry includes address, telephone number, microformats offered, principal officer(s), publication programs, and date the organization began micropublishing. Some listings include telex and fax numbers.

The subject and geographic indexes and cross-references in the "Directory of Micropublishers" provide multiple access points to desired information. However, the U.S. Government Printing office is listed under *USG* in the directory section, and ERIC is not listed under *education* in the subject index. Section 4 lists those publishers that appeared in the 1986–87 edition and have since been acquired, changed names, or ceased micropublishing. The "Organizations" section provides information on seven associations concerned with microform standards and education. *MMP* concludes with an annotated bibliography of 47 titles, a core collection of monographs and serials on microforms.

Microform Market Place is the only directory devoted solely to micropublishers. The *International Micrographics Source Book* (Microfilm Publishing, biennial) contains a chapter on micropublishers in addition to information on equipment and services, but *MMP* is a more comprehensive directory of micropublishers. Any library that acquires or services a microforms collection will want this title.

PHILOSOPHY, PSYCHOLOGY, RELIGION

Dictionary of Demons: A Guide to Demons and Demonologists in Occult Lore. By Fred Gettings. Trafalgar Square Publishing; dist. by David & Charles, 1988. 255p. bibliog. illus. tables. hardcover $24.95 (0-943955-05-X).

133.403 Demonology—Dictionaries I Devil—Dictionaries [OCLC] 88-70614

The publisher advertises this work as a who's who of the underworld. It is actually a compendium of historical, biographical, and factual information on demons. A lengthy introduction explaining the historical evolution of demonological traditions precedes the alphabetically arranged entries. Gettings includes pagan, occult, pre-Christian, and Christian evil spirits and devils. He has also added authorities on the occult and the demonic, great literary works on relevant themes, and the authors of these works. Thus one finds entries for Milton, Blake, Dante, Bodin, Blavatsky, and Ouspensky, as well as for Satan, Asmodeus, and Moloch. *See* references connect the name variants.

This book offers extensive coverage of the inhabitants of the underworld in their many forms. It explains the origin of each demon and its representation in different traditions. Many attractive illustrations in color and black and white enhance the presentation. Twenty-five tables and charts demonstrate things like the relationship of demons to zodiac signs, the inhabitants of each level of Dante's *Inferno*, the nature and sources of William Blake's demons, and the symbols used in magical calendars.

The entries vary in length from one line to several pages. There are four pages of "devil phrases" listing such terms as *printer's devil*, *Devil's Island*, and *devil's dozen* (13, of course!). The *Q* section contains 10 pages of quotations, including proverbs and literary excerpts about the devil. Most of the definitions are clear, but a few are confusing. The definitions of *seal* and *sigil* do not adequately clarify the differences between them. The author seems to be writing for those with previous knowledge of occult traditions, but the uninitiated will be able to use this book.

The bibliography at the end of the book lists titles referred to in the body of the text. The entries consist of author, title, and publication year.

Although one occasionally gets lost in the underworld while using the *Dictionary of Demons*, it should be quite useful for students of literature, art, and the occult. It is more scholarly than works such as *Man, Myth, and Magic* [*RBB* My 1 84] and therefore a welcome addition to both public and academic reference collections.

Lives and Letters in American Parapsychology: A Biographical History, 1850–1987. By Arthur S. Berger. McFarland, 1988. 381p. illus. index. hardcover $39.95 (0-89950-345-4).

133.8'092 Psychical research—U.S.—Biography I Psychical research—U.S.—History [CIP] 88-42537

This book outlines the significant events of American parapsychology and provides "the life stories and work of the predominant figures . . . who shaped the events and represent the growth and development of the field." It is divided into five time periods and concludes with brief portraits of contemporary parapsychologists. Each period begins with short introductory comments followed by chronologically arranged highlights of the history of scientific investigation in parapsychology. The emphasis of the book is on the life stories of the men and women who contributed to this investigation. The author, president of the International Institute for the Study of Death, contends that the persons described are "unfamiliar because parapsychology . . . remains largely *terra incognita*" and proposes to bring them life through his biographical portraits. Among the personalities highlighted are Richard Hodgson, Gardner Murphy, and William McDougall and Joseph Banks Rhine, founders of the Parapsychology Laboratory at Duke University. Gertrude Schmeidler and Montague Ullman are revealed largely through their autobiographical notes.

The biographies, each accompanied by a black-and-white photograph, are interesting to read. They contain many quotations from the person's own writings and speeches and are lavishly footnoted. The sketches discuss the formative years of each person's life, reveal his or her motivation, and trace research and publications. Some of the sketches conclude with bibliographies, although there is little consistency in this regard. Preceding the detailed index that cites persons, titles, and topics are 54 pages of "References," endnotes for all works cited, but there is no comprehensive bibliography.

The one-page summaries of the careers of 27 contemporary parapsychologists identify each person's professional affiliation, include a mailing address, give birth date and place, and state educational background, marital status, and number of children.

This book is recommended for large public and academic libraries. Because it serves as a historical overview of American parapsychology and offers fascinating, colorful portraits of the major figures in this field, it will be used by both scholars and general readers. Its scope and format make it more useful for circulation than strictly for reference.

The International Dictionary of Psychology. By Stuart Sutherland. Crossroad/Continuum; dist. by Harper, 1989. 491p. illus. hardcover $49.50 (0-8264-0440-5).

150'.3 Psychology—Dictionaries [CIP] 88-39340

Sutherland is professor of experimental psychology at the University of Sussex (U.K.) and author of several books, as well as numerous journal articles, on psychology. He compiled this book to meet a need he perceived for a real dictionary for psychologists—rather than an encyclopedia, which, he claims, most recent "dictionaries" in the field have been. His purpose is to define those terms likely to be encountered in reading psychological literature; for that reason, terms from related fields like physics, psychiatry, optometry, neurology, anthropology, sociology, and others are included. The aim is to give sufficient information for each term so the reader can grasp both its meaning and significance.

The book's approximately 10,000 entries are arranged alphabetically letter by letter (with numbers ignored, so that *16PFQ* falls between *peyote* and *PGR*). Entries range from less than 5 to more than 120 words, with most entries containing 20 to 50 words. Cross-references, indicated by small capitals, are given liberally in the body of entries as well as in *see* references, e.g., "*family*. (Biology) See TAXONOMY." Pronunciation is not given, and spelling is British. No biographical entries are included. The book contains a few illustrations, almost all of which help to define optical-illusion terms (e.g., *Kanizsa figure*, *Helmholtz square*, *twisted cord illusion*). In an appendix are five different maps of the brain.

Sutherland succeeds in defining a wide range of terms and, for the most part, definitions succeed in fulfilling the book's purpose. However, the choice of words and sentence structure in some entries may hinder readers from a quick understanding. The Board noted editorializing in a few entries, which detracts from what is otherwise a scholarly tone ("*love.* A form of mental illness not yet recognized in any of the standard diagnostic manuals"). As Sutherland admits in his preface, "I have not hesitated to make unconventional comments on some of the more controversial terms or to censure from time to time those who invented them and those who have propagated them."

Several titles can be compared to Sutherland. *Dictionary of Psychology* (2d ed., Dell, 1985) offers fewer and shorter definitions aimed more at the general reader. Reber's *Dictionary of Psychology* (Viking, 1986) offers entries that are in many cases longer and meatier without becoming encyclopedic essays. Wolman's *Dictionary of Behavioral*

Science (Van Nostrand, 1973) also offers some longer entries and contains biographical entries. *The Longman Dictionary of Psychology and Psychiatry* (Longman, 1984), now out of print, covers more terms with its 21,000 entries and has a reputation for clear and concise definitions. Wolman and Reber are first choices for libraries. Sutherland can serve as a supplementary purchase for academic libraries serving psychology students.

Books to Help Children Cope with Separation and Loss: An Annotated Bibliography. v.3. By Joanne E. Bernstein and Masha Kabakow Rudman. Bowker, 1989. 532p. bibliog. indexes. hardcover $39.95 (0-8352-2510-0).

016.1559'3 Separation (Psychology)—Juvenile literature—Bibliography I Loss (Psychology)—Juvenile literature—Bibliography I Bereavement—Psychological aspects—Juvenile literature—Bibliography I Bibliotherapy for children [CIP] 88-7591

Bibliotherapy, as defined by the American Library Association, is "guidance in the solution of personal problems through directed reading." In the third volume of *Books to Help Children Cope with Separation and Loss*, Bernstein and Rudman provide annotations for more than 600 books useful in bibliotherapy. It supplements the second edition published in 1983, which listed books published from 1955 to 1982. (The second edition superseded the first edition published in 1977 [*RSBR* Mr 15 78].)

The newest volume reflects the increase in the number of books available on this topic. The titles included are written for children ages 3 to 16 (the majority of works are for children under 12), with 90 percent of them published between 1983 and 1988. Criteria for the selection of works of fiction and nonfiction are outlined in the introduction. They include publication date, scope and nature of the work, accuracy, emotional impact, and literary worth. Titles are arranged in categories by the primary loss experience dealt with in the work. The number of books in each category varies. For example, the bibliography lists 76 titles on "Serious Illness," 69 on "Death," but only 3 on "Prisons" and 4 on "Losing a Pet." More detailed access can be found through the subject index. For instance, *serious illness* has the subheadings *AIDS*, *Alzheimer's disease*, *cancer*, *drug abuse*, etc.

Each entry includes full bibliographic citation, availability in hardcover or paperback, interest level or intended ages, reading level based on the Fry Readability Graph, and a lengthy annotation. Prices are not given. Annotations are both descriptive and evaluative. Works that contain misinformation, a controversial subject, or a biased point of view are so noted.

In addition to the annotated list, *Books to Help Children Cope* includes the essay "Using Books to Help Children Cope with Separation and Loss" and a bibliography, "Selected Reading for Adult Guides." There are also eight interviews with noted authors, such as Jane Yolen, Cynthia Voigt, and Elaine Landau, who are included in the bibliography. The appendix is a list of organizations, both professional and voluntary, that provide services for children facing a loss or separation. Five indexes complete the volume: author, title, subject, interest level, and reading level.

The Board recommended the first edition of this book to teachers, social workers, ministers, and guidance counselors. It seems likely that volume 3 will appeal to those same groups. Public libraries will want to add this to their shelf of bibliographies.

The Dying Child: An Annotated Bibliography. Comp. by Hazel B. Benson. Greenwood, 1988. 270p. indexes. hardcover $39.95 (0-313-24708-0; ISSN 0147-1082).

016.1559'37 Terminally ill children—Psychology—Bibliography I Children and death—Bibliography I Terminally ill children—Care—Bibliography I Terminally ill children—Family relationships—Bibliography [CIP] 88-11008

This descriptively annotated bibliography of more than 700 entries provides access to the literature on the dying child for researchers, clinicians, students, parents, and others. The majority of the sources (all English-language from around the world) are from the years 1960–87, but a few citations are from earlier years. Articles are drawn from more than 180 popular (e.g., *New York Times*, *Reader's Digest*, *World Health*) and professional journals in the fields of medicine, allied health, education, psychology, and social work. Also included are books, conference reports, government documents, pamphlets, and dissertations (the latter are not annotated).

Entries are grouped according to six major categories: "General Aspects," "The Young Child," "The Adolescent," "The Family," "The Caregivers," and "Physical Care." Each category is divided into five or more subcategories. "General Aspects," for instance, lists bibliographies of children's books and titles on historical views, religious aspects, legal and ethical issues, and grief and mourning. "The Caregivers" includes such groups as the physician, psychologist, nurse, pastoral counselor, and social worker. Hospitals, the home, and hospices are covered in "Physical Care." Each entry provides the complete citation, including, for books and monographs, the presence of a bibliography and, for articles, the number of references.

Appendix A annotates some 25 children's books and indicates age groups. Appendix B lists about 50 audiovisual titles with an indication of their intended audience. Appendix C briefly describes the scope and purpose of such support organizations as the American Cancer Society, Children's Hospice International, Leukemia Society of America, and Ronald McDonald House. Some organizations that seek to grant the wishes of dying or seriously ill children are listed in appendix D. Two organizations that can provide information on the availability of hospice care for pediatric patients and a list of bibliographic tools used in identifying/verifying the citations in this book constitute the last two appendixes. The author index and the "Selective Key Word Subject Index" include entry numbers. The final section lists journal abbreviations. Benson, head of the Ohio State University Pharmacy Library, is the author of another book in Greenwood's Contemporary Problems of Childhood series, *Behavior Modification and the Child* (1979).

The Dying Child will be a useful addition to public and academic libraries serving professional patrons and the general public interested in terminally ill children.

Ecophilosophy: A Field Guide to the Literature. By Donald Edward Davis. R & E Miles, 1989. 137p. index. paper $8.95 (0-936810-18-1).

016.1791 Ecology—Philosophy—Bibliography [BKL] 88-92036

This annotated bibliography lists monographs, periodicals, and organizations that address "the basic ecophilosophical tenet of seeking the unqualified re-unification of humans with nature." Davis has written on environmental themes for journals such as *Environmental Ethics* and has been a consultant for the Foundation on Economic Trends.

Readers who are unfamiliar with the term *ecophilosophy* will want to read passages from the foreword, such as the following: "In its literal sense, 'ecophilosophy' means the love of wisdom of household place, or less literally, the loving pursuit and realization of the wisdom of dwelling in harmony with one's place." "If we ask what ecophilosophy is, we can say that it is the development of a truly ecological philosophy and sensibility."

The main section of *Ecophilosophy* lists over 280 monographs, arranged alphabetically by name of author or editor. Two appendixes list periodicals and organizations to bring the total number of sources to 334. Davis notes that "many of the authors represented in this bibliography would deny any professional or personal relationship to something called 'ecophilosophy'" but reminds the reader that his goal was not to simply assemble texts that "were, per se, ecophilosophical," but to "compile and comment on a body of knowledge that has been, or could been [sic] used to provide a better understanding of humanity's place in the natural world."

Entry elements for monographs include title, imprint, and pagination. The annotations, often over 200 words, are descriptive and critical (e.g., "This initial bibliography falls short of its intended goal, which was to provide crux resource material in an informed search for an environmental ethic"). Most of the works included were published within the last 10 years, although an occasional source from the 1950s or 1960s will be found. Forthcoming books have also been included.

An index, listing entry numbers, provides access to authors, other individuals, and major subject areas. A couple of blind references were noted when a random sample of index entries was checked for accuracy.

Davis is to be commended for undertaking the task of compiling a bibliography for such an extremely interdisciplinary field of study. Readers will find titles ranging in scope from Martin Buber's *I and Thou* to John Muir's *Wilderness Essays* to Joseph Meeker's *The Comedy of Survival: Studies in Literary Ecology*. This is an intriguing work that will be appreciated by anyone studying the relationship between people and planet.

Television & Ethics: A Bibliography. By Thomas W. Cooper and others. G. K. Hall, 1988. 203p. indexes. hardcover $45 (0-8161-8966-8).

174'.97914 Television broadcasting—Moral and ethical aspects—Bibliography I Ethics—Bibliography [CIP] 88-7206

The subject of communications ethics encompasses a wide variety of controversial topics: invasion of privacy, free speech, pornography, effects of violent programming, sensationalism, and source protection and confidentiality. These high-interest concerns are the subject of a bibliography edited by a faculty member in mass communications at Emerson College. In his introduction Cooper writes, "This bibliography is designed to assist readers and researchers interested in the relationships between television and ethics. There are more appropriate bibliographies for readers interested in *either* television *or* ethics, or those interested in mass communication or philosophy, although selected entries from each of those fields are included here. In this bibliography we have selected books, articles, speeches, and theses that treat the ethical dimensions of television *programs* and *practices*." The introduction details the specific concerns of the field and the scope of the literature available.

The work is divided into two sections, "Ethical Contexts" and "Television and Ethics." "Ethical Contexts" offers citations to materials on "Classical Ethics"; "Professional Ethics: Business, Legal, Medical, Governmental, Scientific, and Engineering"; "Communication and Mass Media Ethics"; "Journalism Ethics"; and "Education: Teaching Media Ethics." The second part has chapters dealing with topics like advertising, children and television, television news, politics and government, law and courtroom coverage, and public television.

The editor and consultants have created this work through online searches of *ERIC*, *Psychological Abstracts*, *Sociological Abstracts*, and other databases. Scholars provided suggestions for entries from their course reading lists. Manual searches were made of *Social Sciences Index*, *Humanities Index*, and *Communication Abstracts*. More than 1,000 sources, including journals, dissertations, conference papers, and books, are included. More than one-half were published within the last 10 years. Abstracts that vary in length from a sentence to a short paragraph accompany 473 of the entries. The source of the abstracts is noted by initials. Citations are in standard form, and separate author and subject indexes are included to assist the reader.

This title will provide access to information on and raise awareness about the moral dilemmas that face the mass media. For large libraries, particularly those supporting communication studies courses.

A Dictionary of Quotations from the Bible. Comp. by Margaret Miner and Hugh Rawson. NAL, 1988. 305p. index. hardcover $18.95 (0-453-00631-0).

220.3 Bible—Quotations, maxims, etc. [CIP] 88-21046

Miner and Rawson, compilers of *The International Dictionary of Quotations* (Dutton/Signet), have selected "nearly 3,000" quotations from the Old and New Testaments and Apocrypha for use by writers and speakers who wish to quote from this veritable fount. Most passages are short, not more than a few lines, but longer passages are also included (e.g., up to half a page on the Beatitudes, the Exodus from Egypt, the birth of Jesus). Many quotations are accompanied by explanatory annotations, and although the King James translation with its dated but beautiful language is used most, other more modern versions (e.g., Revised Standard) are occasionally referred to for purposes of clarity.

Quotations are grouped under "more than 400" relatively broad topics, arranged in alphabetical order. Filing is letter by letter rather than word by word, so that *Gods, False* and *God's Glory* precede *God, Silent*. *See* and *see also* references are generously provided. Within explanatory annotations, terms that also serve as subject headings are printed in small capitals. Headings tend to be more generic than specific. Under *Animals* are found quotations dealing with asses, eagles, horses, lions, adders, ants, foxes, etc., but none of these have cross-references, although they do appear in the keyword index.

When a quotation could fall under two or more headings, it is sometimes repeated, or a cross-reference points from a partial quotation to the full version under another heading. Under headings, quotations are arranged as they occur within the traditional order of the biblical books. Each quotation on a page is numbered so that keyword index entries refer to specific quotations, not just page numbers. The compilers have made a special effort to identify relevant quotations on topics of special contemporary interest, such as *Cities*, *Crime*, *Environment*, *Equality*, *Families*, *Government*, *Physical Fitness*, *Science*, and *Sex*.

The keyword index does not index every keyword in a quotation, but only "the most important or memorable word or words." This is appropriate, since its purpose is to point to quotations on subjects as opposed to the location or identification of known or partially known quotations, for which a concordance should be used. The compilers have succeeded in producing a well-designed *Dictionary* that will help users find interesting and useful quotations, which is exactly what they set out to do.

The International Standard Bible Encyclopedia. 4v. Rev. ed. Ed. by Geoffrey W. Bromiley and others. Eerdmans, 1979–88. illus. hardcover $159.95 (0-8028-8160-2).

220.3 Bible—Dictionaries [CIP] 79-12280

The International Standard Bible Encyclopedia (*ISBE*) was first published in 1915 and revised in 1929. This third edition, now complete, is presented as a "thorough updating of both matter and format," although some material from previous editions is preserved. In volume 1, for instance, 97 contributors to previous editions are listed along with 251 new contributors.

The use of the word *Standard* in the title can be misleading. The views presented in *ISBE* reflect no generally accepted or authorized "standard" adopted by biblical scholars or the Christian church, or even a part of it. The standard has been set by the editors and publisher and represents what is often described as the "conservative," "fundamentalist," or "evangelical" branch of Protestantism. The stance is described by the general editor as "reasonable conservativism," claiming this new edition to be "at once more scholarly and more conservative than its predecessor." This is reflected in the choice of contributors. More than a quarter of the approximately 450 current contributors are affiliated with 10 seminaries, colleges, or universities, all but one of which are associated with conservative Christian views. The largest number of contributors, including the general editor and two of the three associate editors, come from Fuller Theological Seminary in Pasadena, California, which describes itself as an "evangelical community" with "evangelical commitment." Major centers of biblical study, such as Union Theological Seminary in New York, are not represented at all; Harvard Divinity School is represented by one retired professor, and Yale by one graduate student. Within this general context, the general editor assures that "freedom has naturally been allowed to individual contributors to express their views on debatable matters."

In keeping with this stance, *Eden* is presented as a specific, historical place: "Most modern scholars dismiss the passage in question as either legend or myth, having no significant basis in historical reality. However, the present writer views the bulk of Genesis as having been transmitted in a readily recognizable tablet form from a very early period of Mesopotamian history; thus this kind of material represents early attempts at the writing of history." This is followed by an attempt to determine its exact location. The article *Archeology of Mesopotamia* states that "In this general vicinity the Garden of Eden was located and civilization began." The flood was likewise a specific historical event: "In faith the Genesis account is accepted as historical, but numerous unanswered questions remain." With respect to the origin of the universe and life itself, "The date of creation is fraught with numerous problems."

The intended audience for *ISBE* is described as "the more advanced student and yet also, the average pastor and Bible student." Some articles assume a high level of sophistication, however. The first sentence on the text of the *Acts of the Apostles* states, "The Byzantine text of the 4th cent. and later is represented in Acts by the uncials HLPS and by the majority of the minuscules." There is no explanation of these symbols, nor a reference to the article on *Text and MSS of the NT*, where they are explained. *ISBE*'s scope is intended to be comprehensive, covering "every name of a person or place mentioned in the Bible . . . all other terms in the Bible that have theological or ethical meaning, and on expressions that would be puzzling or unclear to the average reader; sources of our knowledge about the background of the Bible [e.g., archeology]; the development of some of the doctrines . . . and practices . . . that are based on biblical teachings." Articles range in length from a few lines to as many as 25 pages (*Paul the Apostle*), 30 pages (*Israel*), 34 pages (*Jerusalem*), and 50 pages (*Religions of the Biblical World*). When appropriate, articles begin with information on pronunciation, etymology, associated terms in biblical languages, variant renderings, biblical references, and definitions. Longer articles include an outline and conclude with a bibliography and the authors' names. Sources are cited not only in bibliographies but throughout the text of articles. Bibliographic citations are brief, giving only author, title, and date for books, and author, journal, issue, and pages (but no title) for journal articles. Frequently cited works are abbreviated, and each volume includes a list of abbreviations. Nevertheless, citations are not uniform and can lead to confusion. The article *Acts of the Apostles* includes a reference to "Ephrem, comm. in loc.," but *Ephrem* is not found among the abbreviations in the list "Ancient Authors and Documents." The article *Luke*, however, has a reference to "Ephrem Syrus (ca. 306–373; Comm. on Acts)," and he is mentioned in the article *Commentaries*: "Ephraem Syrus (4th cent.) wrote such a comm." (Note the different spellings: *Ephrem* vs. *Ephraem*.)

The indexes of the previous edition have been eliminated in this revision, which relies instead on cross-references. Practice is not uniform. In some cases, a cross-reference is implicit, shown by putting a term in small capitals. In other cases, the explicit terms *see* or *see also* are used, but they are often used too sparingly. For example, the article *Apocalyptic Literature* has the major section (three pages) "Apocalyptic as Eschatology," but there is no reference to this treatment from the major article *Eschatology*, even though it refers to "Jewish apocalypic eschatology." Nor is there a reference from *Apocalyptic Literature* to *Eschatology*. A good alphabetical subject index would have linked these scattered discussions.

ISBE has many illustrations, including separate pages of attractive colorplates, in each volume. Some illustrations are of poor quality and clarity, for example, some pictures in *Jerusalem*. Volume 1 includes a collection of color maps, while black-and-white maps, plans, and charts are scattered throughout the set.

ISBE succeeds in presenting a comprehensive range of biblical subjects from a conservative Protestant point of view.

The Eerdmans Analytical Concordance to the Revised Standard Version of the Bible. Comp. by Richard E. Whitaker. Eerdmans, 1988. indexes. 1,548p. hardcover $49.95 (0-8028-2403-X).

220.5'20423 Bible—Concordances, English—Revised Standard I Hebrew language—Glossaries, vocabularies, etc. I Greek language, Biblical—Glossaries, vocabularies, etc. I Latin language—Glossaries, vocabularies, etc. [OCLC] 88-19217

Although a number of concordances cover portions of the Revised Standard Version of the Bible, this is the first concordance to the entire RSV, including the Old and New Testaments and the Apocrypha. Heretofore the most exhaustive concordance of the Revised Standard Version was *Nelson's Complete Concordance of the Revised Standard Version Bible*, compiled by John W. Ellison (2d ed., Thomas Nelson, 1984). However, *Nelson's* is not analytical (i.e., it does not indicate what original-language word is being translated in each context), nor does it cover the apocryphal books, which are treated separately in *A Concordance to the Apocrypha/Deuterocanonical Books of the Revised Standard Version* (Eerdmans, 1983). The Apocrypha are also excluded from Bruce and Isobel Metzger's *Oxford Concise Concordance to the Revised Standard Version of the Holy Bible* (Oxford, 1962), which provides highly selective coverage of the Old and New Testaments. The only previous concordance offering analytical coverage of the RSV is Clinton Morrison's *Analytical Concordance to the Revised Standard Version of the New Testament* (Westminster, 1979), which, as the title indicates, is limited to the New Testament. Thus, the publication of *The Eerdmans Analytical Concordance to the Revised Standard Version of the Bible* represents a milestone in biblical scholarship.

This compilation of over 400,000 entries was achieved by a judicious blend of computer technology and the editorial skills of a team of Bible scholars coordinated by Richard E. Whitaker. It has been kept to a reasonable size by the exclusion of certain frequently used words, such as articles, personal pronouns, and common prepositions and conjunctions. The main portion of the concordance is arranged alphabetically, three columns to a page. Headwords, which appear in boldface, are followed by a numbered list of the original Hebrew, Aramaic, Greek, or Latin words from which the term was translated. Beneath the headword the occurrences of the word and its variant forms are cited within a line of context in a columnar arrangement. All forms of a word are treated within the same entry (e.g., *tells*, *telling*, and *told* are included under the heading for *tell*). However, phrases that stem from a single original-language word or for which there is no correspondence between the original-language words and the English translation are listed separately. For example, the phrases *tell a story* and *tell the good news* have separate entries. Within an entry, lines of context that include the concorded term or any of its forms are arranged in the order in which they appear in the Bible with citations to the appropriate book, chapter, and verse appearing to the left of each phrase. A number to the right of each quotation refers to the original-language term that was used in that particular context. Cross-references are provided when words are treated in more than one place. For instance, the phrase *marriage vow* is listed after the entry *vow*, and a cross-reference to *vow* appears at the end of the entry *marriage*.

Following the main section of the concordance are separate sections treating proper names and numbers. The latter, which is arranged numerically, includes fractions and numbers over 20. Concluding the volume are indexes that list the original Hebrew, Aramaic, Greek, and Latin words and indicate the entries in the concordance that cite those words.

Because of the extensive analytical treatment that this work provides, it will be particularly valuable in collections that support the scholarly study of the Bible. However, the concordance's completeness of coverage, its ease of use, and its reasonable price make it a desirable purchase for general users as well.

New Dictionary of Theology. Ed. by Sinclair B. Ferguson and others. Inter-Varsity Press, 1988. 738p. bibliog. hardcover $24.95 (0-8308-1400-0).

230'.03 Theology—Dictionaries [CIP] 87-30975

Though the preface to this work states that "no attempt has been made to exclude or minimize diversity of interpretation" of the biblical basis for theological knowledge and judgment, in fact a more accurate title would have been *New Dictionary of Protestant Theology*.

Within the broad bounds of conservative Protestant theology, the work is well edited, informative, and comprehensive. There is a good mix of biographical and subject articles, ranging in length from half a column to two or three double-columned pages. Each article has a bibliography, and each is signed by one of about 200 contributors. The religious or academic affiliation of each is given at the beginning of the book, and the contributors appear to be largely from Protestant schools of divinity or similar institutions throughout the English-speaking world; in addition, a very few are from German-speaking countries, Africa, and Japan.

Since there are many dictionaries of theology, comparison with at least one contemporary dictionary seems appropriate. In 1969 Alan Richardson edited *The Dictionary of Christian Theology*, a work that has since been completely rewritten and brought up to date by John Bowden and published in 1983 as *The Westminster Dictionary of Christian Theology* [*RBB* D 1 84]. This work, which sells for the same price as the work under review, appears to have a somewhat broader theological outlook; among its contributors one finds many members of Catholic orders indicating that several points of view are presented.

In more specific comparison, let us look at a topic in *The Westminster Dictionary* touching on a subject of recent controversy in the Roman Catholic church: clerical celibacy. The entry *Celibacy* has 2½ columns; by contrast, the work under review has a *see* reference under *Celibacy* to *Sexuality*, where the word *celibacy* is mentioned once, but only in passing. In another example, for the entry *Existentialism*, *Westminster* has 6½ columns, while the *New Dictionary* has only two.

The *New Dictionary*, however, has articles not found in *The Westminster Dictionary*, for example, *Bioethics* and *Black Theology*. It has brief entries on some smaller denominations or organizations, such as the Mennonites and the Salvation Army. Some other groups, such as the Unification Church, are also referred to but not allotted entries of their own.

There are some editorial infelicities. There is no entry for *Orthodoxy*, nor any *see* reference from that word to the entry *Eastern Orthodoxy*, nor any *see also* reference in that article to a related topic, *Russian Orthodoxy*. There is no *see* reference from the word *Catholic* to *Roman Catholic Theology*. (This latter article is signed *J.C.*, but this person is not listed among the contributors, unless he is the same as *J.E.C.*, a London clergyman.)

Libraries already possessing the 1983 *Westminster Dictionary of Christian Theology* or other theological dictionaries may want to add the *New Dictionary of Theology* because it represents a different viewpoint. The theological language makes the *New Dictionary of Theology* appropriate for the educated layperson.

Lives of Famous Christians: A Biographical Dictionary. By Tony Castle. Servant Publications, 1988. 306p. paper $10.95.

270 [B] Christian biography—Dictionaries [OCLC]

This reference work identifies "over 1,500 well-known Christians from the first century to the twentieth." It includes Protestant, Catholic, and Orthodox figures: saints, theologians, statesman, reformers, artists, popes, clerics, and others who had an impact on the history of Christianity. The compiler, the author of *New Book of Christian Quotations* [*RBB* D 15 83] and other works, provides no introduction and does not outline his criteria for inclusion. The expected names are here, but there are omissions, such as Henry VIII and Mary Baker Eddy. There is good coverage of the twentieth century, though no living people are included. The most contemporary figure is Martin Niemöller, founder of the Pastors Emergency League formed to protest Nazi interference in church affairs; Niemöller died in 1984.

Entries are brief, ranging from a sentence or two to just over half a page. Birth and death dates are supplied, along with a brief summary of the person's activities and significance. There are no cross-references, bibliography, or indexing.

Lives of Famous Christians overlaps considerably with *The Oxford Dictionary of the Christian Church*. The review title has better coverage of Americans, of later Catholic saints, and of twentieth-century figures. Elizabeth Seton, Thomas Merton, C. S. Lewis, Dorothy Day, Sojourner Truth, Kathryn Kuhlman, Fulton Sheen, Maximilian Kolbe, Stefan Cardinal Wyszynski, and the recently canonized Rose Phillipine Duchesne are all included in *Lives of Famous Christians* but not in the Oxford book. On the other hand, *The Oxford Dictionary of the Christian Church* is a superior reference work, with longer entries, lists of primary sources, and cross-referencing. Because of its reasonable price and its coverage of contemporary figures, *Lives of Famous Christians* might be considered as a supplemental source.

Twentieth-Century Shapers of American Popular Religion. Ed. by Charles H. Lippy. Greenwood, 1989. 494p. bibliog. index. hardcover $65 (0-313-25356-0).

291'.092 [B] U.S.—Religion—20th century I Religious biography—U.S. [CIP] 88-15487

The title *Twentieth-Century Shapers of American Popular Religion* indicates this text's distinctive temporal and topical scope. The 69 people profiled by 25 contributors, most of them academics, were selected for their influence on audiences that "cut across denominations and faith traditions to include ordinary men and women of every religious affiliation and no affiliation at all." In nearly all cases, successful use of mass media was a key ingredient in their ability to reach these broad audiences. Many of the subjects thrive today; a few, however, find themselves in disgrace following revelation of their sexual peccadilloes (i.e., Jim Bakker and Jimmy Swaggart). The one exception to the twentieth-century time frame is Wovoka, the Paiute who popularized the Ghost Dance that led to the massacre of 300 Sioux at Wounded Knee on December 29, 1890. Several essays treat persons whose careers have been closely linked through common purpose, marriage, or lineage (e.g., Daniel and Philip Berrigan; Bill and Gloria Gaither; Bob Jones, Sr., and his son and grandson).

The range of persons included is a testament to the pluralism of American religious expression. Among the biographees are pretelevision fundamentalist Billy Sunday, ecumenist John Foster Dulles, black leader Malcolm X, Catholic socialist Dorothy Day, apocalyptic prophet Hal Lindsey, contemplative Trappist monk Thomas Merton, novelist Morris L. West, Zen popularizer Alan Watts, positive-thinking proponent Norman Vincent Peale, Reconstructionist rabbi Mordecai Kaplan, and civil rights leader Will D. Campbell. Because the selection criteria are general, one can question the absence of Elijah Muhammad, founder of the Black Muslims; L. Ron Hubbard, creator of Scientology; Paul Wierwille, founder of The Way International; and others.

Each of the profiles follows a four-part format consisting of biographical summary, appraisal of the subject's contribution to popular religion, a survey of secondary literature, and a selected bibliography of primary and secondary works. The entries run from five to eight pages. The result is a collection of insightful essays, each highlighting the most significant formative experiences in its subject's life and analyzing his or her influence on religious institutions and sentiments. A combined topical and personal-name index concludes the book. A separate index to subjects by denomination/sect would have facilitated analysis of trends through the century.

Henry W. Bowden's *Dictionary of American Religious Biography* (Greenwood, 1977) provides capsule biographies of 425 individuals significant in American religion who were deceased by July 1, 1976. Only 20 of these also appear in the title under review. J. Gordon Melton's *Biographical Dictionary of American Cult and Sect Leaders* (Garland, 1986 [*RBB* D 15 86]) concentrates on the founders of religious groups outside the mainstream of American religious expression who died before January 1, 1983. Only six figures from Melton are also in *Twentieth-Century Shapers of American Popular Religion*. This work is a valuable complement to Bowden's and Melton's historical biographical dictionaries and will be useful in academic and public libraries.

Women and Judaism: A Select Annotated Bibliography. By Inger Marie Ruud. Garland, 1988. 232p. indexes. hardcover $45 (0-8240-8689-9).

016.296'088042 Women in Judaism—Bibliography I Women, Jewish—Bibliography [CIP] 87-29109

The preface states that this book's purpose is to provide access to works dealing with aspects of women's lives in Judaism from ancient to modern times. The majority of the entries are about women in Israel and the U.S. The "basis of selection" centers on providing an annotated bibliography of monographs, journal articles, and dissertations in major languages, defined as English, German, French, and the

Scandinavian languages. "Due to language problems, materials in Hebrew are not included."

The majority of the 842 numbered entries were published in the twentieth century, and the author, a librarian at the Royal University Library, Oslo, examined most of the items except for a few monographs and dissertations. A list of the approximately 180 journals that are the sources of many of the entries opens the book. They range from science journals to those in women's studies and religion. The full address and any previous names of the publications are usually noted.

The bibliography is arranged alphabetically by author. Most of the entries have annotations ranging from one sentence to a paragraph, except where the title reveals its contents. No judgment is made on the value of the item. The index is divided into three sections: geographic (by country, but American cities are noted), subject, and author. The latter is useful if the entry had multiple authors as there are no cross-references in the bibliography itself. The long strings of numbers after some headings in the geographic and subject indexes make them cumbersome.

Another work on the same subject is *The Jewish Woman, 1900–1985: A Bibliography* (Biblio Press, 1987), edited by Aviva Cantor and others. This second edition of a work first published in 1979 has approximately 1,800 entries. It includes unpublished papers and has a strong feminist orientation, with some annotations noting "Know the enemy" or "devastating." A sampling of entries in both works showed very little overlap. The work under review contains standard, traditional sources while the Cantor bibliography lists more unconventional sources, such as papers presented at conferences. A comparison also makes clear that Ruud missed a number of important sources, such as articles that appeared in important contemporary periodicals, e.g., *Moment*, or books such as *Jewish Yellow Pages*. Perhaps of greater concern is the fact that the compiler includes writings published in Scandinavian languages but not Hebrew, although there are many entries on Israel. Still, because the Ruud work is fairly well annotated and includes many standard sources, it will be useful in libraries where there is great interest in Jewish studies.

The Facts On File Encyclopedia of World Mythology and Legend. By Anthony S. Mercatante. Facts On File, 1988. 807p. bibliog. illus. indexes. hardcover $95 (0-8160-1049-8).

291.1'3 Mythology—Dictionaries I Folklore—Dictionaries [CIP] 84-21218

Compiled by the author of several other books on mythology, folklore, and religion, this work is designed "to provide an ever-increasing number of readers with a full, comprehensive, ready-reference work on the entire range of world mythology and legend from the ancient Near East to present-day voodoo." The more than 3,200 entries, arranged alphabetically according to the most common English transcriptions, include personal names, place-names, scriptural and literary works, legends and fables, and zoological and botanical symbols and encompass a variety of traditions. One can find entries not only from classical civilization, but also from Egyptian, Babylonian, Norse, and Celtic mythology; Australian, Japanese, Polynesian, and Siberian legends; ancient and medieval epics; Jewish, Muslim, and Hindu sacred texts; Christian hagiography; Aesopean fables; Grimms' fairy tales; and American folklore.

Each entry is assigned a unique number and ranges from two- or three-line definitions to several pages of discussion. The longer entries are generally those devoted to various texts, such as the Bible and the *Aeneid*. Each entry provides a translation of the name, if known; for example, "*Rusalka* (female water spirit)"; "*Rama* (charming)." Dates are provided for historical figures. There are no keys to pronunciation. As the author explains in his preface, "this was found to be impractical in a work that encompasses so many words from various languages." Many of the definitions or discussions include citations to relevant art, music, film, and literature. The entry *Pygmalion* mentions the George Bernard Shaw play of the same name, the musical *My Fair Lady*, and the movie *One Touch of Venus* starring Ava Gardner.

The introduction discusses the differences between myth, legend, fable, folktale, and fairy tale. There is a key to variant spellings and also an extensive, annotated bibliography. Books in the bibliography are arranged according to the culture to which they pertain. Access to the entries is facilitated by two indexes: a cultural and ethnic index, which classifies terms under more than 75 cultural groups, and a general index. The general index helps link the user to terms and concepts (such as *underworld*) that are scattered throughout the text. It also helps the user identify cultural influences. Under *Shakespeare*, for example, is a list of entries in which Shakespeare's work is mentioned. Both indexes refer the user to unique entry number rather than page, a useful timesaving device. A further enhancement to the text are the numerous black-and-white illustrations, chosen from a variety of sources. Though their reference value is slight, the illustrations help to enliven the book.

There are many other books on mythology and legend, as the bibliography provided in this work attests. However, few of these books attempt to be as inclusive as this *Encyclopedia*. Some treat only mythology, others treat only folklore. Gertrude Jobes' *Dictionary of Mythology, Folklore, and Symbols* covers much of the same territory but is not as comprehensive, lacking, for instance, coverage of voodoo and American folklore. The *Funk and Wagnall's Standard Dictionary of Folklore, Mythology, and Legend* has a different emphasis, dealing more with popular culture and less with systems of belief. Because of the way it gathers such a wealth of information into a single source, *The Facts On File Encyclopedia of World Mythology and Legend* is a useful ready-reference tool for most libraries.

SOCIAL SCIENCES

International Directories in Print, 1989–90. 1st ed. Ed. by Julie E. Towell and Charles B. Montney. Gale, 1988. 1,125p. indexes. hardcover $175 (0-8103-2511-X; ISSN 0899-255X).

300 Directories—Directories [OCLC] 89-659513

International Directories in Print includes listings for approximately 5,000 domestic and international directories from over 100 countries, in more than a dozen languages, in the areas of business and finance, agriculture and environment, government and law, science, biography and genealogy, entertainment, public affairs, and medicine. Each listing provides (as fully as possible) bibliographic information, including the publisher's address and telephone number, the directory's scope, language, arrangement, approximate number of pages, frequency of publication, editor, price, ordering information, and if it is available online. To a lesser extent, the entries also indicate whether advertising is accepted, alternate titles, other available formats (e.g., mailing labels, 3-by-5-inch cards), circulation, types of indexing, and other relevant information. Particularly helpful is the indication whether the directory has a distributor in the U.S. Entries are arranged alphabetically under 15 general subject headings, and additional access is provided through three indexes: geographic (by country); detailed subjects (over 3,000 headings); and title/keyword (including former titles, variant titles, foreign-language titles, and discontinued titles). Good cross-referencing is used throughout each of the indexes.

This work is meant to complement the frequently used *Directory of Directories* (to be called *Directories in Print* in its sixth edition). About 500 of the directories listed have a U.S. address, but they are either international in coverage or deal with a foreign country. *International Directories in Print* will be especially helpful in academic and large public libraries, as well as in special libraries whose clienteles are involved in international marketing or research.

Dictionary of Gerontology. By Diana K. Harris. Greenwood, 1988. 201p. bibliog. illus. index. hardcover $37.95 (0-313-25287-4).

016.3052'6 Gerontology—Dictionaries I Gerontology—Bibliography [CIP] 87-25142

This dictionary in the new and rapidly growing field of gerontology serves a twofold purpose: "to further the development of a specialized gerontological terminology; and, because of the multidisciplinary nature of gerontology, to assist students, scholars, researchers, and practitioners in the field in understanding the terminology that is used in the various disciplines that gerontology encompasses."

Entries are in alphabetical order. The definitions range from one to five sentences and are clear, concise, and as jargon-free as possible. As in other Greenwood publications, internal cross-references are noted by asterisks, and *see also* references are given for related terms. The cross-references are well done.

The *Dictionary* includes well-known terms (*pet therapy*, *living will*, *elderhostel*, *empty nest*, *hot flash*, *pigeon drop*); common terms applied to the field of aging (*adaptation*, *cholesterol*, *community*, *introversion*, *social strata*); vocabulary related to medicine and research methods; and specialized theories, studies, terms, and organizations in the field. The author states that the *Dictionary* also serves as a bibliography because, following each definition, from one to four citations to works on the subject are given. Also, when possible, the name of the person who originated the term and the date of its first use are mentioned. Users will find most bibliographic citations helpful; some appear to be contrived and seem to be given only to fulfill the intention to include a citation for each entry. It is doubtful that a citation is needed to clarify such words as *age*, *mean*, and *wisdom*. In many cases, however, citations are likely to provide exactly the clarification intended by the author, who teaches sociology at the University of Tennessee at Knoxville. Monographs, government documents, and journal articles are cited; few citations are to works later than 1986.

Several diagrams and graphs give additional information, and the book concludes with an index to personal names. The *Dictionary of Gerontology* is a good and useful effort that will be helpful in academic and public libraries.

A Guide to Research in Gerontology: Strategies and Resources. By Dorothea R. Zito and George V. Zito. Greenwood, 1988. bibliog. index. hardcover $35.95 (0-313-25904-6).

016.3052'6 Reference books—Gerontology I Gerontology—Bibliography I Gerontology—Information services II Gerontology—Library resources [CIP] 88-17773

The authors of this *Guide* are a gerontological information consultant and an associate professor of sociology, respectively. Both have published articles in their areas of specialty. Here they explain how to design a research strategy, how to evaluate different information sources (primary, secondary, tertiary, and nondocumentary), and the role of various kinds of reference sources (e.g., handbooks, directories, encyclopedias, abstracts) in research. They also explain how to get information from agencies (with a list of appropriate agencies and their addresses), computerized data services, and community resources. The book contains four appendixes that list and annotate reference books, indexes and abstracts, databases, and journals. It concludes with a very brief subject index. A title index would have been a useful addition.

The intended audience for this work includes information specialists and professionals concerned with gerontology in all of its aspects—psychological, social, and medical. Persons trained in any of these disciplines will find the work readable. The use of examples from gerontological experience and literature is especially helpful. *A Guide to Research in Gerontology* will be a desirable addition to libraries serving students and professionals in disciplines concerned with any aspect of gerontology. Large public libraries may also consider purchasing it as a good introduction to information strategy in any discipline.

Violence and Terror in the Mass Media: An Annotated Bibliography. Comp. by Nancy Signorielli and George Gerbner. Greenwood, 1988. 233p. indexes. hardcover $39.95 (0-313-26120-2; ISSN 0742-6895).

303.6 Violence in mass media—Bibliography I Terrorism in mass media—Bibliography I Sex in mass media—Bibliography [CIP] 87-29556

The portrayal of violence and terrorist actions by the mass media as both news and entertainment not only reflects world events but influences them and makes strong impressions on individual personalities and societal consciousness as well. The thirteenth in Greenwood's series of reference works in sociology, this bibliography grew out of a UNESCO international survey of published sources on the subject and a subsequent search of the literature through spring 1987.

The editors have strong expertise in this field. Signorielli is associate professor of communication at the University of Delaware and has authored several works on similar subjects. Gerbner is professor and dean of communications at the University of Pennsylvania and editor of the *Journal of Communication*. Drawing primarily on the literature published in scholarly journals and collected essays, but also including popular journals, some conference papers, U.S. and foreign government publications, and relevant dissertations, the editors have compiled an authoritative survey of the available scholarship. The bibliography is arranged in four main sections: violence and mass media content, violence and mass media effects, terrorism and the mass media, and pornography. The bulk of the 784 numbered entries are in the first two sections, which are general in scope. Only 36 entries focus on pornography and 74 on terrorism. The sections are not completely exclusive, however, and one finds coverage of pornography and terrorism topics in the first two sections if applicable. The entries in each section are arranged alphabetically by author, numbered sequentially, and consist of a complete bibliographic citation and a one-paragraph annotation. Page headers facilitate browsing. One major strength of the bibliography is that the annotations are clearly written, succinctly descriptive of the original work's research with test groups, and evaluative of research results. An author index gives the entry numbers for both primary and joint authors, and the subject index has a mix of entries both specific (*Red Brigades*, *Pope John Paul*, *Iran*, *Achille Lauro*) and general (*overviews*, *longitudinal studies*, *perceptions*, *crime*, *cartoons*, and *newspapers*). Entries are indexed under more than one term for convenient subject access.

Students and researchers with access to strong communications and sociology collections, and especially periodical literature, will find this annotated bibliography useful as a guide to an important area of inquiry.

Population Information in Twentieth Century Census Volumes: 1950–1980. By Suzanne Schulze. Oryx, 1988. 317p. bibliog. maps. tables. hardcover $82 (0-89774-400-4).

304.6'0973 U.S.—Census—Indexes II U.S.—Census, 17th, 1950—Indexes II U.S.—Census, 18th, 1960—Indexes I U.S.—Census, 19th, 1970—Indexes I U.S.—Census, 20th, 1980—Indexes [CIP] 88-17937

Population Information in Twentieth Century Census Volumes: 1950–1980 is the last of three volumes authored by Schulze and published by Oryx. Together with its predecessors, *Population Information in Nineteenth Century Census Volumes* (1983 [*RBB* F 1 85]) and *Population Information in Twentieth Century Census Volumes: 1900–1940* (1985), it provides easy access to population data found in the tables of U.S. census publications. Its purpose is the same as the first two volumes: "to assist anyone searching for information about United States population in reports of the decennial censuses." It is important to note that this book is a guide to printed population statistics only and does not provide assistance in locating agriculture, government, and economic census information.

The "Guide to Volumes" on the inside front and back covers serves as an index. This "chart index" is similar to those in the first two volumes and to what appears on the endpapers of the 1970 and 1980 census reports. The subjects (race, housing, occupations, etc.) are on the vertical, and the census year, volume, and part are on the horizontal. When one has selected a subject and census year, one moves across the table to find a mark for the appropriate volume and part. This information can be used to find the appropriate place in the text. The entire process is clearly explained in "How to Use This Book." Each chapter covers one census and begins with an introduction that includes a map, an explanation and overview of the census, and a list of the major population volumes.

Complete bibliographic information is given for each census part, including Superintendent of Documents, Library of Congress, and Dewey classification numbers and LC card number. For the 1950, 1960, and 1970 censuses the University of Texas census number and Research Publication microfilm number are provided. The *American Statistics Index* abstract number is provided for 1970 and 1980, and the Bureau of Census publication number is part of the 1980 entry. The entry concludes with the table guide, which gives the table number in the census volume. The extensive definitions of the terms used by the Bureau of Census are very helpful in the use of this guide and the Census of Population reports.

The usefulness of this publication to libraries with complete census collections is obvious. These three volumes are the best and most complete index to the 20 decennial censuses published to date. The library with no or an incomplete census collection should also consider purchase of Schulze's books. The amount of information, the consistency in format, and the ease of use will make this set an effective referral and verification reference source. The cost may prohibit smaller libraries from purchasing this set. However, if all three volumes are purchased, the cost is $164, or if any two are purchased, the cost is $123, a savings of 33 percent or 25 percent, respectively.

Just as Henry J. Dubester and his *Catalog of U.S. Census Publications, 1790–1945* (1950) have become synonymous with census research, so too will Schulze and her three census guides. She has made locating, retrieving, and verifying printed population census information a simplified and logical procedure. This volume, and the entire set, is a required acquisition for all research and academic libraries, documents and depository collections, and any library that handles reference questions or ILL requests for census information.

Black Children and American Institutions: An Ecological Review and Resource Guide. By Valora Washington and Velma La Point. Garland, 1989 (c1988). 432p. bibliog. indexes. hardcover $64 (0-8240-8517-5).
305.2'3 Afro-American children—Bibliography ǀ Afro-American children [CIP] 88-16490

This work aims to examine unique elements in black child development, institutional barriers confronting black children, and the contexts (social, economic, political) in which black children exist. Washington is a professor and dean of faculty at Antioch College; La Point is an assistant professor at Howard University.

The first half of the book is a bibliographic essay. Chapters focus on developmental features, education, support (family, public assistance, child welfare), criminal justice, and physical and mental health. Chapter 7 lists advocacy groups for black children under such categories as *Adoption and Foster Care, Child Labor,* and *Research and Professional Organizations*. Seven major organizations are then highlighted (e.g., Children's Defense Fund, National Association of Black Social Workers). The final chapter, "Promoting Black Children: Community Initiatives and Public Action," makes various recommendations, including priorities for all stages of development (e.g., promoting breast-feeding, increasing access to mental health services).

A bibliography, alphabetically arranged by author, completes the book. About a third of the items are starred, indicating they are cited in the text. Sources listed are books, journal articles, conference papers, technical reports, government publications, newspapers, dissertations, and ERIC documents. Concluding the book are two indexes, one by author and name (organizations, agencies), the other by subject. The former indexes both text and bibliography, the latter only the text. Therefore, there is no subject access to half the book.

It would be easier to evaluate this work if the authors described their search process and grounds for inclusion. Items cited were only occasionally published prior to the 1970s; the cutoff date appears to be sometime in 1987. It is unclear why some sources are annotated and others (up to two-thirds) are not, although the starred items (discussed in the text) are more likely to be annotated than others.

This review of the research could be useful to educators, social workers, sociologists, government policy planners, and concerned lay readers. Thus academic, public, school-district professional, and appropriate agency libraries should consider purchase. *Black Children* may be most useful in the circulating collection.

Resources for Middle Childhood: A Source Book. By Deborah Lovitky Sheiman and Maureen Slonim. Garland, 1988. indexes. hardcover $27 (0-8240-7777-6).
305.2'3 Child development ǁ Child development—Bibliography ǀ School children ǁ School children—Bibliography ǁ Socialization [CIP] 88-18046

Designed to "help the parent, teacher, and student of child development gain a better understanding of the growth and needs of the six to 12 year old child," this book includes eight thematic chapters, each with an annotated bibliography. Chapters deal with physical, psychosocial, and cognitive development; play; and children's relationships with family, society, school, and peers. Each chapter summarizes popular thinking and research in five to eight pages, followed by 30 to 50 sources. These are fairly current, with most from the late 1970s and early 1980s and some classics from the 1950s and 1960s (Piaget, Holt, and Erikson, for example). Two- or three-sentence annotations tell how each book might be useful to parents and professionals. About 300 works are included, evenly divided between popular titles (*Making It as a Stepparent*) and more technical ones (*Measurement and Evaluation in the Classroom*).

While the bibliographies are thorough, the text is not always as well done. For example, the chapter "Cognitive Development" mentions gifted children briefly, but source material on the topic follows the "Schooling" chapter, and neither one includes special education at all. Under "Physical Development" we are told that "most children look forward . . . to wearing orthodontic braces," with no source cited. In addition, sources quoted in the text are not always included in the bibliographies. Editing is somewhat sloppy. For example, *semenal, reflexion,* and *complimentary* are misspellings found.

At least two other volumes in this Garland series, Reference Books on Family Issues, have been well reviewed (*Parent and Child* [*RBB* Ag 88] and *Adoption* [*RBB* S 1 87]). They include far more sources and have very useful subject indexes. This volume is not indexed by subject, although it does have author and title indexes. Since the chapters are interrelated ("stress" might be found under school, society, or peers), this is a problem. However, the book can be used topically and will be of interest in professional collections and public libraries.

Women of Color and Southern Women: A Bibliography of Social Science Research, 1975 to 1988. Ed. by Andrea Timberlake and others. Center for Research on Women, Memphis State University, Memphis, TN 38152, 1988. 264p. indexes. paper $15 (0-9621327-0-5).
305.40973 Women—U.S.—Bibliography ǁ Women—Southern States—Bibliography ǁ Women, Black—U.S.—Bibliography ǁ Ethnicity [OCLC] 88-63010

This bibliography is the print version of part of an online database produced by the Center for Research on Women at Memphis State University. The editors' goal for both formats is to "improve understanding about the racial/ethnic and regional diversity among women in the United States." The work integrates the latest social-science research on "women of color and southern women," using an interdisciplinary approach. The citations come from works in progress, dissertations, book chapters, articles, books, and unique publications not often found in other indexes. Five distinct groups (African American, Asian American, Latina, native American, and southern women) are covered under six major headings: *Culture, Education, Employment, Family, Health,* and *Political Activism/Social Movements.*

The 2,683 citations included here represent 56 percent of the citations in the database. Works that treat more than one topic or racial/ethnic group are cross-referenced under all appropriate headings; the book contains 1,866 unique entries. The starting point of 1975 was selected because the mid-1970s saw the beginning of significant research on women from a social-science perspective. Within each topical section, entries are arranged by racial/ethnic group and then alphabetically by author's name. The inclusion of 3 to 12 keywords taken from *A Women's Thesaurus* for each entry helps enhance subject access and partially compensates for the lack of annotations. The author and keyword indexes are accurate, though there are long lists of numbers under some keywords. It is difficult to imagine more access points in a print bibliography than are provided here.

The approach, organization, and usefulness of this work plus the reasonable price make it a must purchase for all libraries supporting research on women in general and minority/southern women in particular. It would not be out of line for any social-science collection.

Women of Color in the United States: A Guide to the Literature. By Bernice Redfern. Garland, 1989 (c1988). 156p. indexes. hardcover $25 (0-8240-5849-6).

016.3054'8 Minority women—U.S.—Bibliography I Afro-American women—Bibliography [OCLC] 88-24614

A resurgence of interest in women of color has resulted in the publication of several bibliographies on the subject. *Women of Color in the United States* is a guide to scholarly books, journal articles, book chapters, and dissertations published since the mid-1970s. The emphasis is on the scholarly, with popular books excluded unless they are highly significant. Medical literature is also excluded.

The work is divided into four chapters: "Afro-American Women," "Asian American Women," "Hispanic American Women," and "Native American Women." Each chapter begins with an overview and characterization of the material available on each group, followed by broad divisions: bibliographies; general works; autobiography, biography, and life histories; education; employment; feminism and women's studies; history and politics; literature and the arts; and social science. The short essays on the literature are a valuable resource on their own since they show what research has been done and what needs to be explored. The author and subject indexes are accurate and helpful in locating works by key authors of the magnitude of Maya Angelou or Zora Neale Hurston, or on such narrow subjects as oral tradition or picture brides.

The recently published *Women of Color and Southern Women: A Bibliography of Social Science Research, 1975 to 1988* [*RBB* My 1 89], edited by Timberlake, covers the same general subject area and time period. Timberlake's work contains more citations than Redfern (2,683 and 636, respectively) and is broader in scope because it also covers southern women. Timberlake covers only social-science research, while Redfern also includes literature and the arts. A comparison of titles reveals some duplication but not enough to recommend one over the other. Because the approaches are different and the prices reasonable ($15 and $25), both works will be essential for collections in women's studies. Redfern would be an excellent sourcebook for researchers in this area, as well as a guide to the literature for graduate and undergraduate students.

Dictionary of Afro-American Slavery. Ed. by Randall M. Miller and John David Smith. Greenwood, 1988. 866p. bibliog. charts. index. maps. hardcover $95 (0-313-23814-6).

305.5'67 Slavery—U.S.—History—Dictionaries I Afro-Americans—Dictionaries and encyclopedias [CIP] 87-37543

Afro-American slavery is a central issue in the American experience. While long a subject of historical inquiry, the last 20 years have seen a burgeoning of scholarship, applying new methods of historical analysis and incorporating research of other disciplines such as anthropology, musicology, and linguistics to study the "peculiar institution." This one-volume reference work seeks to provide a synthesis of the vast scholarly literature and make it accessible to the nonspecialist and general reader. The focus is on slavery in the U.S. from the time of the first English settlements until Reconstruction. The editors are both professors of history who have published several scholarly works on slavery. Smith was also the editor of the two-volume bibliography *Black Slavery in the Americas* (Greenwood, 1982).

The essays, which range from a few paragraphs to over five pages, are arranged alphabetically. Each is signed by one of the over 200 contributors, primarily college professors, who are listed in an appendix with their affiliations. The essays treat both broad subjects, such as the slave trade, abolition, and education, as well as more focused topics like the underground railroad, slavery in specific cities or states (*Philadelphia, PA, Slavery in*), and biographies. Maps, charts and statistical tables are included where appropriate, for example, in the entry *Economics of Slavery*. The articles bring modern findings and debates and controversial opinions into the discussions, and each entry has a bibliography appended. The writing styles vary, but the text is for the most part accessible. Some essays quote the words of slaves or other sources without clear attribution, which might frustrate the reader who would like to follow up on the references. A chronology of events follows the entries.

A fairly detailed subject index provides access to the subjects covered in the *Dictionary*, and some topics are cross-referenced within articles. It is necessary to use the index, as some topics are split or under headings that would not necessarily come to mind; for example, there is the major essay *Slave Trade, Atlantic* but also the entry *Closing of the African Slave Trade*, discussing the efforts at suppression. The two are not linked in the text, only through the index. Terms in an entry that have separate entries are supposed to be cross-referenced with an asterisk, but this is not consistently done. There are also some blind or unclear references. The cross-references are often from a word or phrase in the text that is in a different form from the entry title it refers to, or it is unclear which part of a phrase is the entry word. For instance, "Revolutionary* idealism had led..." apparently refers to the entry *American Revolution, Slavery and the*. Nevertheless, this is a very valuable reference tool, synthesizing a wealth of material on a complex subject. It is an essential addition for academic and public libraries; secondary school libraries should consider it too.

Irish American Material Culture: A Directory of Collections, Sites, and Festivals in the United States and Canada. By Susan K. Eleuterio-Comer. Greenwood, 1988. 107p. bibliog. index. hardcover $35 (0-313-24731-5; ISSN 0743-7528).

305.8'9162 Irish Americans—Material culture—Directories II Irish—Canada—Material culture—Directories [CIP] 88-11038

The raison d'être of this new series is that though ethnic studies "have until recently used conventional methods of historical research" and relied for the most part on sources such as letters, diaries, and oral interviews, researchers "are now seeking to use physical objects as sources of immigrant history. ... These include buildings, photographs, household objects, tools, musical instruments and clothing created, brought, or transformed by members of particular ethnic groups." This series of directories will "locate and describe ethnic material culture and photographic collections in the United States and Canada."

The compiler of the first volume in the series is Eleuterio-Comer, whose degree is in folk culture. She uses the term *Irish-American* to mean immigrants and their descendants from the Republic of Ireland and Northern Ireland who have settled in the U.S. and Canada, as well as the group known as "Scotch-Irish." The introduction explains the waves of Irish emigration and traces the course of "their movement from urban ghettos to seeming assimilation in the suburbs."

The directory's three sections cover collections, sites, and festivals. In each section the arrangement is alphabetical by state or province, and entries are sequentially numbered. "Collections," the largest section, consists of descriptive entries for Irish-American holdings in 90 museums, libraries, historical societies, archives, and centers. Data provided include address, telephone number, administrators, number of staff, hours, accessibility, and policy on loans. Descriptions of holdings from questionnaires returned range from a less than helpful "not catalogued by ethnic group" and the bare "historical photographs; objects not catalogued" to detailed listings of resources and guides to the collection.

The second section presents data on 46 sites of Irish-American significance, most of which were taken from the *National Register of Historic Places*. The third section on festivals is included because they are frequently the most comprehensive sites of both historical and contemporary culture. Each listing includes location, contact person, a description of events, a brief history, annual dates, audience size, and availability of photographs to researchers.

A short bibliography of books and journal articles concentrating on Irish history and material culture completes the volume. There is a name index leading directly to entries. A somewhat idiosyncratic subject index (i.e., *sod from Ireland, door from ship*) pulls the three sections together.

A fault of this otherwise useful tool is the typography, which while satisfactory for the tabular entries is less than felicitous for the text. The valuable introductory essay is compressed with too little space between the lines.

Libraries supporting research in ethnic studies will want to acquire this series.

Western Europe, 1989: A Political and Economic Survey. 1st ed. Europa; dist. by Taylor & Francis, 1989 (c1988). biennial. 545p. bibliog. maps. tables. hardcover $190 (0-946653-47-X; ISSN 0953-6906).

314 Europe—Economic conditions—1945- .—Periodicals I Europe—Politics and government—1945- .—Periodicals II Europe—Social conditions—1945- .—Periodicals [BKL] 89-25775

Western Europe, a new biennial, defines the region not in geographic but in political terms. Thus it covers "all the member countries of the European Communities and the European Free Trade Association." This definition embraces Cyprus, Malta, and Turkey, but not East Germany. Eight signed essays, each 5 to 12 pages, appear at the beginning of the book. These cover the coming integration of Europe, the European macroeconomy, agriculture, industry, energy, socioeconomic trends, the environment, and defense. Future volumes will bear watching to see what becomes of these essays, since the temporal sweep of each far exceeds a single year and substantial revision every two years will be difficult. The profiles of 21 major and 12 smaller countries and territories follow a pattern, divided into the seven broad categories of "Geography," "Recent History and Politics," "Economy," "Social" (issues), "Media," "Transport," and "Tourism." Among the topics covered within these categories are climate, defense, mining, consumer affairs, education, telecommunications, and civil aviation. A selected bibliography of recent books and publications of governments and international organizations concludes each profile. Profiles of some of the small countries (e.g., Andorra, Monaco) omit some categories. Territories (e.g., Denmark's Greenland) are treated as appendixes to the parent countries' profiles.

The "Recent History and Politics" and "Economy" sections of each profile consist of signed essays commissioned for this volume. The 43 contributors are affiliated with corporations and universities in the U.S. and Europe. The political histories are cast as analytical essays and emphasize the period since World War II. The essays on the nations' economies, also emphasizing the post-war years, incorporate statistical tables and short directories of organizations that were inserted by the editors. The statistical data have been drawn from such standard sources as the United Nations and national governments and these sources are cited. Other sections of each profile were prepared by the editors. Some of this information has been borrowed from another publication from the same publisher, the *Europa Year Book* [*RBB* Ap 15 84], which covers the entire world.

The two books differ in structure. Profiles of countries in *Europa* consist of three parts. The first is an essay covering recent history, economics, defense, education, tourism, and social issues. The second is a series of statistical tables drawn principally from the respective national governments. The third is a directory of senior government officials, political organizations, embassies in the capital, churches, newspapers, publishers, radio and television stations, banks, insurance companies, industrial associations, labor organizations, trade fairs, and transportation carriers. Profiles in *Western Europe* include counterpart directories, but they are headed "Major . . . " or "Principal . . . "and are much more selective than the corresponding directories in *Europa*. Unique to *Western Europe* are brief introductions to each of the directories. Overall, *Western Europe* presents social issues more analytically than does *Europa*. *Europa*, on the other hand, presents more extensive statistical data. *Western Europe* joins other *Europa* companions such as *The Middle East and North Africa* [*RBB* Ag 86], *Africa South of the Sahara*, etc.

The differences between *Western Europe* and *Europa* exceed their similarities and are impossible to quantify. Large libraries can cite those differences as justification for having both. Other libraries will have to judge what sort of international coverage they need. If they need information on only the countries of western Europe, then *Western Europe* is an attractive alternative to the more comprehensive and more costly *Europa*.

The Radical Right: A World Directory. Comp. by Ciarán O' Maoláin. Longman; dist. by ABC-Clio, 1987. 500p. index. hardcover $70 (0-87436-514-7).

320.52 Conservatism—Directories [OCLC]

Revolutionary and Dissident Movements: An International Guide. 2d ed. Ed. by Henry W. Degenhardt. Longman; dist. by Gale, 1988. 466p. index. hardcover $140 (0-8103-2056-8).

322.4'2 Government, Resistance to—Societies, etc.—Handbooks, manuals, etc. [CIP] 87-29718

These two directories are part of a series of excellent new publications produced by Keesing's Reference Publications. Notable among these have been *Political Parties of the World* (2d ed., 1984 [*RBB* D 1 85]), *Treaties and Alliances of the World* (4th ed., 1987), *Maritime Organizations* (1985), and *Latin American Political Movements* (1985). The first three were edited by Degenhardt, while the latter title was edited by O'Maoláin, a former associate editor of *Keesing's Record of World Events*.

The Radical Right provides information on approximately 3,000 conservative or far-right groups worldwide. The compiler defines *radical right* in rather broad terms to include right-wing conservative fringe groups, extreme nationalists, right-wing guerrilla groups, and anti-Semitic and racist groups. This broad definition leads to the inclusion of such groups as Accuracy in Media, defined as a right-wing conservative group; the Aryan Nations, defined as a white supremacist organization; the Moral Majority, defined as a Christian fundamentalist group; the Republican Party, defined as a mainstream conservative group; and the Unification Church, defined as an anticommunist religious cult. These are rather strange bedfellows. The directory is arranged alphabetically by country with numerous cross-references. Listings are provided for 83 countries and four colonies or portions of countries (Northern Ireland under *United Kingdom*) where right-wing groups have been active between 1985 and 1987. For each country, after a brief introduction, there is an outline of the origins of far-right activity, followed by the entries for active groups and publications. Information provided includes names, addresses (when available), a description of leaders, comments on political orientations, and a history of the group. The roster of active groups is followed by one of defunct groups, and finally a short list of individuals involved in right-wing activities but not affiliated with any one group in particular.

Of the pages devoted to country listings, 55 percent are taken up by nine countries: the U.S. (80 pages), the U.K. (40), France (37), West Germany (24), Spain, the USSR and Belgium (11 pages each), and Nicaragua and South Africa (10 pages each). The section on the U.S., which consumes approximately 20 percent of the directory, lists 168 active organizations and major publications, followed by 31 defunct groups, and hundreds of minor groups. Only seven unaffiliated individuals are noted. Well-known publications listed include the *National Review*, *Public Interest*, *Soldier of Fortune*, and the *Washington Times*. Although the compiler admits to potential errors in the listings, because of the secretive nature of some of these groups, there can be no doubt that this is the most comprehensive listing of radical-right groups on the world stage. Directories such as *Spectrum* [*RBB* Ja 1 88]) list more right-wing groups in the U.S. but lack the scope and broad international coverage of this directory.

Revolutionary and Dissident Movements is a successor to *Political Dissent: An International Guide* . . . (1983 [*RBB* D 1 84]) and is based on the extensive resources of *Keesing's Record of World Events*. The present directory concerns itself with the activities of movements rather than individual dissidents or political parties (although many of the latter are included). Also excluded are pressure groups that pose no direct threat to the existing order. Rather its focus is on those revolutionary and dissident movements of both Right and Left, currently out of power. An important component of many of them—although not all—is their willingness to use violence, ranging from hostage taking to hijacking, to reach their objectives, usually the overthrow of the existing government.

The directory is organized alphabetically by country. For each of the 167 countries listed, there is a brief paragraph on the political organization of government, followed by a short discussion of recent political history and then detailed listings of various revolutionary and dissident movements including right-wing, left-wing, and separatist groups.

Unlike *The Radical Right*, coverage here is rather equally divided among the various countries with the longest section devoted to the Palestinian movements (19 pages). In contrast, the section on the U.S. is limited to four pages. The work contains detailed histories and recent activities of the Mujaheddin Alliance in Afghanistan, the FNLA in Angola, the Sikh movements in India, SWAPO in Namibia, anti-Sandinista movements in Nicaragua and surrounding countries, and detailed information on the various factions of the PLO. The information is given in two columns of small print and is current through June 1987. There is a selected bibliography (rather too short to be very helpful) and a detailed index.

The information provided in this title is available nowhere else in such a detailed, unified manner. The section on the PLO, for example, is far more detailed than that in the recent *Political Dictionary of the Arab World* (Macmillan, 1987 [*RBB* Ap 1 88]), and the information is generally more complete and more current than that in the recently published *Encyclopedia of Terrorism and Political Violence* (Routledge & Kegan Paul; dist. by Methuen, 1987 [*RBB* Mr 1 88]).

Both of these volumes are sure to have broad appeal to political scientists, politicians, journalists, and librarians. They should prove particularly helpful to collection-development specialists who are frequently bombarded by free publications from some of these organizations yet are unable to determine their actual orientation.

Vital Statistics on American Politics. By Harold W. Stanley and Richard G. Niemi. Congressional Quarterly, 1988. 403p. bibliog. charts. index. tables. hardcover $16.95 (0-87187-472-5); paper $11.95 (0-87187-471-7).

320.973'021 U.S.—Politics and government—Statistics [CIP] 88-3594

The compilers of this compendium, two professors of political science at the University of Rochester, have assembled over 200 tables and figures on key aspects of politics in the U.S. There are chapters not only on such basic features as elections, parties, and the branches of the federal government but also on the mass media, public opinion, interest groups, federalism, and foreign, social, and economic policy. Where the availability of data permits, coverage of long periods is provided for historical perspective.

The introduction discusses several important considerations relating to the interpretation of statistical tables and offers some suggestions for locating further material. An annotated guide to reference sources at the back supplies additional help. It is somewhat irritating to have to consult a separate list that follows to find the publisher and date of publication of the sources cited.

Each chapter is introduced by a couple of pages of explanatory commentary. Sources for the data are indicated at the bottom of the tables or figures. A set of questions concludes each chapter; the introduction notes that a teacher's manual is available with the answers and additional discussion topics.

The following selected list of topics from various chapters may serve to give some sense of the breadth of coverage: public opinion on gun control; percentage of news stories about policy issues; split-ticket voting; number of pages in the *Federal Register*, 1936–86; presidential approval, Gallup Poll, 1938–87; and blacks, Hispanics, and women as percentages of state legislators and state population. The most extensive table gives basic facts about each member of the House in the 100th Congress, including percentage of vote and campaign expenditures in the 1986 election and a selection of voting ratings.

Although conveniently brought together here for students of the political process in the U.S., much of the data derives from readily available and fuller sources such as the *Statistical Abstract of the United States* and other federal government sources, *The Book of the States*, and other Congressional Quarterly publications such as *Vital Statistics on Congress, 1987–88*. In this sense, this compendium cannot be considered an indispensable reference source, but many libraries will find it a valuable and timely addition to reference or circulating collections.

Public Interest Profiles, 1988–1989. By the Foundation for Public Affairs. Congressional Quarterly, 1989 (c1988). biennial. 928p. indexes. hardcover $137.50 (0-87187-461-X).

322.4'025 Pressure groups—U.S.—Directories [CIP] 88-28534

Published biennially since 1977 in a loose-leaf format by the Foundation for Public Affairs, this edition marks a change in publisher and format. Now published by Congressional Quarterly, *Public Interest Profiles* (*PIP*) appears for the first time as a hardbound volume. It continues to be edited by the foundation, a nonprofit research and educational organization that monitors some 2,500 public interest and public policy groups. For this edition, 250 organizations were chosen from the foundation's files for inclusion based on the following criteria: "the extent of the group's influence on national policy, the number of requests received by FPA for background on the organization, the range and quantity of news coverage generated by the group, and the representative nature of the group in its field of interest and activity." With one exception, the groups are all based in the U.S.

Preceding the main text is a 30-page analysis of the ways in which pressure groups work to achieve their goals in the political process. Profiles of the organizations appear next, arranged in 12 sections, such as "Civil/Constitutional Rights," "Community/Grassroots," "Consumer/Health," "Corporate Accountability/Responsibility," "Environmental," "Religious," and "Think Tanks." The organizations are arranged in alphabetical order under the appropriate subject. Among groups included are the Children's Defense Fund, Handgun Control, National Rifle Association, Mexican American Legal Defense and Educational Fund, Eagle Forum, Rainforest Action Network, Accuracy in Media, Center for Law in the Public Interest, American Jewish Congress, and the Brookings Institution. Each organization's profile, which runs from two to five pages, gives the founding year, address and telephone number, number of staff, budget, director (with a paragraph of background on the person), scope (membership and chapter information), statement of purpose, tax status, how the organization operates (legislative monitoring, research, training and technical assistance, congressional testimony, grassroots organizing, etc.), topics of current concern, publications, names of the board of directors, funding sources, and if the group has a PAC. Next in the profile is a section titled "Effectiveness," which presents two to four excerpts from newspapers and journals discussing the organization. An effort was made to obtain both supportive and critical comments. Last is an assessment of the political orientation of the organization, again taken from a printed source. Titles and dates are given for the quoted publications, as are authors when known.

An index of organizations gives access both to those groups profiled and to brief mentions in the text of those and other groups. The names of profiled groups are given in boldface. Unfortunately, it is not possible to tell from the index which page reference refers to the profile and which ones are to brief mentions of these organizations. A personal-name index provides access to listings of board members, people mentioned in the "Effectiveness" quotes, or journalists whose quotations were used in the "Effectiveness" section.

PIP has several strengths. Groups included represent a diverse range of issues and a good balance of opposing agendas. The background information on directors is excellent for tracing connections with other groups. The quotes in the "Effectiveness" sections assist greatly in imparting the personality of the groups. The frequent practice of using quotes that came directly from the organizations themselves in the purpose statements may be the best way to describe them, but may not serve the reader who wants a disinterested description. A point of weakness is the lack of a specific subject index. For instance, the introduction mentions that AIDS is an area of concern, but organizations with such an interest could be located in almost any of the 12 sections.

Libraries already possessing the *Encyclopedia of Associations* (*EA*) may wonder about overlap between these two publications. Only a few groups in *PIP* are not also found in *EA*, and while many of the same categories of information (budget, membership, publications) are provided in both, and though the purpose descriptions in *EA* are sometimes superior, *PIP* succeeds in imparting the flavor and personality of the groups in its multipage profiles that *EA* cannot do in its brief-entry format. Also, public affairs organizations are scattered throughout the many thousands of entries in *EA*. *PIP* is recommended for academic and other libraries where an interest in public affairs organizations is sufficient to justify the rather high cost of this useful tool.

America at the Polls 2: A Handbook of American Presidential Election Statistics, 1968–1984. Comp. by Richard M. Scammon and Alice V. McGillivray. Congressional Quarterly, 1988. 594p. maps. tables. hardcover $84 (0-87187-452-0).

324.973'092 Presidents—U.S.—Election—Statistics [OCLC] 87-33221

Researchers accustomed to using Congressional Quarterly's America Votes series will be on familiar ground with this volume. In similar fashion, it presents county-by-county statistics of U.S. presidential elections from Richard Nixon's victory in 1968 to Ronald Reagan's reelection in 1984. Coeditor Scammon is director of the Election Research Center, Washington, D.C. He edited the first edition of this work (Univ. of Pittsburgh, 1965), which covered elections from 1920 to 1964, and has edited all 17 volumes of *America Votes* (most recently reviewed by the Board [*RBB* Je 15 86]) on which this book is based.

The main section of *America at the Polls 2* consists of chapters for each of the 50 states plus a chapter for the District of Columbia. Each chapter begins with tables showing the statewide popular and electoral vote for each presidential election, 1920 to 1984. Following is a clearly drawn county map of the particular state. Next is a county-by-county table for each of the presidential elections from 1968 to 1984. These tables give county name, population, total vote (Republican, Democratic, other), plurality, and percentages for the Republican and Democratic total and major votes. Data are taken from official state canvass reports as certified by state elections authorities and are presented—without any editorial comment or analysis—on clear, full-page tables. Print size is larger than in the 1965 volume, and more white space has been left between columns. State chapters end with an "Election Notes" section. These notes give "the breakdown of 'other' category voting in each state," and "detail other special aspects of the vote reporting as may be required."

Preceding the state chapters is a section detailing the state vote for presidential elections back to 1920. For each election there is a table giving the electoral vote and total vote (Republican, Democratic, other), plurality, and percentages for the Republican and Democratic total and major vote. Each table is accompanied by the full list of candidates for president and vice president. Some brief explanatory notes are included. For example, "In August 1974 President Nixon resigned and was succeeded by Vice-President Ford." Concluding this volume is a 30-page summary of presidential primary elections by state and candidate for 1968 to 1984.

Presidential Elections since 1789 (4d ed., Congressional Quarterly, 1987) provides statistical information on primaries, conventions, and electoral and popular votes. It includes maps, analysis, information on election laws, and biographical directories of presidential and vice-presidential candidates, but it does not give county-level statistics.

Volumes 8, 10, 12, 14, and 16 of *America Votes* contain the county statistics for the presidential elections covered in *America at the Polls 2*. Libraries with that series should purchase *America at the Polls 2* only if the one-volume convenience seems worth it. Other libraries serving researchers working in history, political science, or sociology will find it useful.

The International Relations Dictionary. 4th ed. By Jack C. Plano and Roy Olton. ABC-Clio, 1988. 446p. index. hardcover $42.95 (0-87436-477-9).

327'.03 International relations—Dictionaries [CIP] 87-26943

The third edition of this work was found useful by the Board [*RBB* D 15 83], and the current work continues in the same vein. The authors are on the faculty of Western Michigan University, and Plano has compiled other dictionaries, in addition to serving as editor for the Clio Dictionaries in Political Science series.

The arrangement of the current work is the same as the earlier edition. Within subject chapters (e.g., "International Law," "Diplomacy"), the 570 numbered entries are arranged alphabetically. Each has a definition paragraph, followed by a paragraph headed *Significance*. This approach enables the historical roots as well as the contemporary importance of the term or phenomenon to be discussed.

The preface notes that the fourth edition has 34 new entries, the definitions and *Significance* paragraphs have been expanded and updated, and a number of national (as distinct from international) political system entries have been deleted. A new alphabetical "Guide to Major Concepts" at the beginning of the book provides quick access. The longer index at the end of the book enables the user to locate entries for concepts, personalities, documents, activities, and nations or regions. Both aids refer the user to the entry number rather than the page. Cross-references at the end of definition paragraphs provide additional access.

The fourth edition of this important work has clear definitions of *Gorbachevism*, *New International Economic Order*, and *New World Information and Communication Order*. While it contains separate entries on the League of Nations and Central Treaty Organization (both of historical interest only), there are no entries on the Islamic Revolution, Iran's role in world terrorism, or the international arms trade, though information on these topics can be found within other entries. Neither South Africa nor the Republic of South Africa are in the index or the "Guide to Major Concepts," although there is the entry *Apartheid*.

Despite these shortcomings, the latest edition of this standard work will again prove useful in academic and large public libraries, in particular for students of international relations.

The Encyclopedia of American Intelligence and Espionage: From the Revolutionary War to the Present. By G. J. A. O'Toole. Facts On File, 1988. 539p. bibliog. illus. index. hardcover $50 (0-8160-1011-0).

327.1'2 Espionage, American—History—Dictionaries l Espionage—U.S.—History—Dictionaries [CIP] 87-30361

O'Toole, a former chief of the CIA's Problem Analysis Bureau and now a professional writer, compiled this work of nearly 700 alphabetically arranged articles from openly available (i.e., unclassified) sources. Some 70 percent of the entries are biographical, including both major figures of American intelligence (e.g., William J. Donovan, the "father of American intelligence"; Allen W. Dulles; and

Ralph Van Deman, the "father of American military intelligence") and persons who have had some affiliation with American intelligence but who are notable for some other pursuit (George Bush, Julia Child, the Reverend William Sloan Coffin, William Somerset Maugham, George Washington, William F. Buckley, Jr., etc.). These entries (varying from a few lines to a page or two) usually provide the biographee's full name, birth and death dates, education, and intelligence and nonintelligence careers. (As a test of currency, a few 1987 death dates were noted.) The sources appended to the biographies include standard biographical and nonbiographical references. Those for Child, for example, are *Who's Who in America* and "Hunt, *Undercover*," which is identified more fully in the bibliography as E. Howard Hunt's *Undercover: Memoirs of an American Secret Agent*; those for Washington include Boatner's *Encyclopedia of the American Revolution* and "*WAMB*" for *Webster's American Military Biographies*—determined first by consulting O'Toole's list of abbreviations and then the bibliography.

The remaining 30 percent of the entries (which also conclude with bibliographic references) consist of articles on (1) American intelligence organizations (*CIA*, the longest article—18 pages—in the volume; *Naval Intelligence*; *Office of Strategic Services*); (2) the role of intelligence in each of the nine major wars of American history (the *Vietnam War* essay of 15 pages is the longest); (3) topics of predominant importance in American intelligence history (*Covert Action*, *Cryptology*, *Overhead Reconnaissance*); and (4) events or incidents in American intelligence history (e.g., *Bay of Pigs Invasion*—12 pages, *Cuban Missile Crisis*, *Pearl Harbor Attack*). In addition, a few terms (*A-2*, *agent*, *black propaganda*, *graymail*) are briefly defined.

The author has made extensive use of cross-references, both within the text and at the end of articles. The text is supplemented by a list of abbreviations and acronyms and a 400-item unannotated English-language bibliography, primarily of twentieth-century books, articles, and government documents, but including a few nineteenth-century and unpublished materials. The book concludes with a detailed index.

For scholars and buffs alike, *The Encyclopedia of American Intelligence and Espionage* will be a most useful addition to collections in academic and public libraries. It is a worthy complement to such titles as Blackstock and Schaf's *Intelligence, Espionage, Counterespionage, and Covert Operations: A Guide to Information Sources* (Gale, 1978), Buranelli and Buranelli's *Spy/Counterspy: An Encyclopedia of Espionage* (McGraw-Hill, 1982), Constantinides' *Intelligence and Espionage: An Analytical Bibliography* (Westview, 1983), and, for the period 1939-80, Smith's extensive compilation, *The Secret Wars: A Guide to Sources in English* (ABC-Clio, 1980).

The Nobel Peace Prize and the Laureates: An Illustrated Biographical History, 1901-1987. By Irwin Abrams. G. K. Hall, 1988. 269p. bibliog. illus. index. tables. hardcover $35 (0-8161-8609-X).

327.1'72 [B] Pacifists—Biography I Nobel prizes—History I Peace—Awards—History [CIP] 88-16313

This dictionary provides biographical information on all individual and organizational winners of the Nobel Peace Prize up through the 1987 laureate, Oscar Arias Sánchez. The author has published widely on the history of the peace movement; the informal, personal tone of this volume contributes to its readability and distinguishes it from the many other recent biographical dictionaries of Nobel Prize winners (most notably H. W. Wilson's *Nobel Prize Winners* [*RBB* Ap 15 88]). The length of the articles is comparable to those in the Wilson volume (which covers all Nobel Prize winners), but the bibliographies at the end of every entry in Abrams' compilation are less complete than those found in *Nobel Prize Winners*. Abrams devotes 40 pages to Alfred Nobel and the establishment of the Peace Prize, the Norwegian Nobel Committee, and Nobel's wishes and the record of the Norwegian Nobel Committee.

The entries on the laureates are grouped by time period: 1901-18, 1919-39, 1940-59, and 1960-87; within each time period entries are arranged chronologically. Black-and-white photographs are provided for all individual winners. Each set of entries is preceded by a three- to four-page discussion of trends and controversies in the nomination and award selection process. Appendixes provide a number of tables analyzing trends in the awards; the text of Alfred Nobel's will; the text of the invitation for nominations; and a chronological list of the laureates.

While most of the information here can be found elsewhere, this book can be recommended for academic and public libraries for its readable biographies.

Peace Organizations Past and Present: A Survey and Directory. By Robert S. Meyer. McFarland, 1988. 266p. bibliog. index. hardcover $24.95 (0-89950-340-3).

327.1'72 Peace—Societies, etc.—Directories [CIP] 88-42515

Peace Resource Book, 1988-1989: A Comprehensive Guide to the Issues, Organizations, and Literature. Ed. by Carl Conetta. Ballinger, 1988. 440p. bibliog. index. paper $14.95 (0-88730-289-0; ISSN 0740-9885).

327.17206 Peace—Societies, etc.—Directories I Antinuclear movement—U.S.—Directories [OCLC] 88-659917

These two very different reference works on peace groups provide hard-to-find information on a subject of increasing interest. The first, *Peace Organizations Past and Present*, begins with a historical essay on efforts for peace throughout history, with emphasis on the League of Nations and the United Nations. Treaties (Anti-Ballistic Missile Treaty of 1972, etc.), regional organizations (European Common Market), and organizations promoting international cooperation (World Health Organization) are briefly mentioned.

The main body of the book is made up of entries for three categories of peace organizations: those using personal approaches in promoting peace, primarily through friendship, pacifism, service, and understanding (e.g., Peace Corps, American Friends Service Committee, World Pen Pals); those using instructional approaches, through research, publishing, and education (Physicians for Social Responsibility, SANE/FREEZE, Union of Concerned Scientists); and those using structural approaches, through world unity, federation, citizenship, and law (Campaign for World Government, Planetary Citizens).

Ninety-two organizations are listed in the book. Each is characterized in detail, with information about its founding, purpose, activities, accomplishments, and publications. In some cases quotations from the group's most important documents are included. The lengthy entries provide for thorough coverage of each group. An additional section on developing future approaches characterizes the peace movement as a whole and suggests future prospects.

Appendixes include an explanation of the author's research method and a copy of his survey, a directory of the organizations included (giving addresses, but not telephone numbers), texts of six documents judged historically important in peace efforts, a bibliography that includes the 1986 edition of *Peace Resource Book*, and an index.

Peace Resource Book, 1988-1989 is described as "a working tool for those who are active in efforts to achieve arms control, disarmament, and world peace—or thinking about how to become more active in such endeavors." Earlier editions of this work were *American Peace Directory, 1984* and *Peace Resource Book, 1986*. This edition has been expanded to include 7,000 peace groups, many of which are local branches. Plans are to continue to update this work every two years. The sponsor of *Peace Resource Book* is the Institute for Defense & Disarmament Studies, which "conducts research and fosters public education on long-term trends in world-wide military forces and on alternative policies for arms control and disarmament."

Part 1 consists of essays on peace issues and strategies. The status quo of the world military system, government arms-control negotiations, and peace movement alternatives are discussed. Part 2 is a directory composed of several sections. The first lists over 300 national peace groups in entries similar in format to those in the *Encyclopedia of Associations*. This list has a broader scope than the Meyer book: it includes groups with less direct involvement in the peace movement. Examples are the American Library Association Peace Information Exchange Task Force; Greenpeace, USA (environmental activities); and Guatemala News and Information Bureau (educates

U.S. public about political issues in Guatemala). The second directory section lists over 100 peace-oriented educational programs at U.S. institutions of higher learning.

The third directory section lists over 7,000 peace groups, including all local chapters of national groups. This list is limited to giving a zip code and sometimes a telephone number. The fourth directory section lists the same 7,000 groups in order by state and zip code, giving complete addresses.

Part 3 of the directory is a bibliography of peace-related literature, which includes over 1,000 items grouped by topic. Complete bibliographic information and a short annotation are given for each item. Included are books, reprints of journal articles, and pamphlets, with prices. The bibliography has an author index, and an address list for publishers and distributors facilitates ordering materials.

Both of these books belong in academic and large public libraries and may also find use in smaller public and high school libraries. Libraries that can afford to purchase only one will find that many of the organizations in Meyer's book can also be found in *Peace Resource Book*, though with much less descriptive information.

Congress A to Z: CQ's Ready Reference Encyclopedia. Congressional Quarterly, 1988. 612p. bibliog. charts. illus. indexes. tables. hardcover $75 (0-87187-447-4).

328.73'003 U.S. Congress—Dictionaries [CIP] 88-20336

With *Congress A to Z*, Congressional Quarterly has created an encyclopedia that describes the role of Congress as both a historical institution and a modern legislative body. It attempts to explain, in brief, nontechnical language, the importance of the legislative branch of government to the history of the U.S. Many of the entries cover the structure of Congress and the parliamentary techniques used in writing, debating, and passing legislation. Entries as long as nine pages ared provided for *House of Representatives*, *Senate*, *Legislative Process*, *Budget Process*, and other broad subject areas. These entries sometimes conclude with bibliographies. Briefer entries are included for individual committees and procedural issues, such as *Amendments*, *Caucuses*, *Executive Session*, and *Motions* of every conceivable type. In addition, the relationship between government and society is explored in articles like *Ethics*; *Reform, Congressional*; and *Television*. Historical entries covering congressional policy and major scandals are also included, from *Reconstruction Era* through *Teapot Dome*, *Watergate Scandal*, and *Iran-Contra Affair*. Brief biographical sketches of important senators and representatives throughout the history of the institution are found within the main alphabetical sequence.

Several appendixes provide information on topics such as congressional leaders, organizational charts, how a bill becomes a law, and a bibliography of additional sources. The book concludes with two indexes, one to members of Congress who are mentioned in articles and one to subjects, and adequate cross-references are also provided within the text. Many black-and-white photographs and charts and drawings are distributed throughout the book.

Another Congressional Quarterly product, *Congressional Quarterly's Guide to Congress* (3d ed., 1982 [RSBR Jl 83]), provides much of the same material as *Congress A to Z*. However, the *Guide to Congress* is written primarily for a college-level readership, whereas *Congress A to Z* would be much more useful for high school students and the general public. Although the *Guide to Congress* contains more material than *Congress A to Z*, the encyclopedic arrangement of the latter makes the information easier to retrieve, and it is more up-to-date. High schools and public libraries should find *Congress A to Z* a useful and popular reference source for information on this branch of the U.S. government.

BUSINESS, ECONOMICS

Business Serials of the U.S. Government. 2d ed. By Priscilla C. Geahigan and Robert F. Rose. American Library Association, 1988. 86p. indexes. paper $11.95 (0-8389-3349-1).

016.330973 U.S.—Economic conditions—Periodicals—Bibliography I U.S.—Government publications—Bibliography [CIP] 88-3428

Government Reference Serials. Comp. by LeRoy C. Schwarzkopf. Libraries Unlimited, 1988. 344p. indexes. hardcover $45 (0-87287-451-6).

015.73'053 U.S.—Government publications—Periodicals—Bibliography I Reference books—Bibliography I Serial publications—U.S.—Bibliography [CIP] 87-37846

These two books offer an interesting view of serial publications produced by the U.S. government. A committee within ALA's Reference and Adult Services division compiled the second edition of *Business Serials*. Schwarzkopf, a respected government documents librarian, compiled *Government Reference Serials*. This latter publication is intended to be a supplement to Schwarzkopf's *Government Reference Books: A Biennial Guide to U.S. Government Publications*, which will no longer include serials.

Business Serials is intended to serve as a ready-reference tool for small or medium-sized academic and public libraries. It contains 183 signed, annotated entries for government publications in business and economics. Each evaluative annotation is from 30 to 250 words. The citation includes title, issuing agency, initial date of publication, frequency, and SuDocs number. Where the item is indexed (e.g., ASI, PAIS) is also given. The arrangement of the work is by broad subject categories such as economic conditions, demographics, and international business. Access is also available through title and subject indexes.

Government Reference Serials is an annotated bibliography of 583 publications. Each citation has full bibliographic information and SuDocs classification number, along with OCLC, ISSN, monthly catalog, and item numbers. Included in the publishing history for each serial is a listing of variant titles and classification numbers. The evaluative annotations are about the same length as those in *Business Serials*. The arrangement is by broad subjects such as education, computers, and biological sciences, each with specific subdivisions. Access is further enhanced through indexes by title, subject, and SuDocs class number.

These two bibliographies have both positive and negative aspects. They both suffer from being issued in static print formats while the environment surrounding government publishing is explosive and changing almost daily. More titles than ever are disappearing or changing formats. Both works also fall short in giving specific criteria for their selection processes. For example, Schwarzkopf does not define what a reference serial is. While most of the titles in *Business Serials* can also be found in *Government Reference Serials*, there are some unique items. For instance, Schwarzkopf has not included the depository serial titles *Public Roads* or the *Annual Report* from the FCC, both of which are in *Business Serials*. *Business Serials*, on the other hand, does not include such important titles as *Current Wage Developments* or the *National Survey of Professional, Administrative, Technical, and Clerical Pay*, both of which would seem to be within its scope. On the positive side, both works have excellent annotations, and the publishing history provided by *Government Reference Serials* fills a void. *Business Serials* achieves its stated goal of serving small or medium-sized libraries, and its price is quite attractive too.

Libraries already subscribing to the *Guide to U.S Government Publications* by Andriot, *PAIS*, or the *Monthly Catalog* already have access to government serials. However, those libraries desiring an annotated list of a select group of serials would benefit from either of these publications.

Almanac of the American People. By Tom and Nancy Biracree. Facts On File, 1988. 336p. index. hardcover $29.95 (0-8160-1821-9).

330.973'0927 U.S.—Economic conditions—1981– —Statistics I U.S.—Social conditions—1980– —Statistics [CIP] 88-3882

Almanac of the American People purports to "not only select the most important facts about everyday life in today's U.S.A., but also to tie these statistics together in a comprehensive narrative. For example, this book not only tells you how many more women are working and why, but also explains the effects their entrance into the work force is having on leisure time, marriage, children, spending patterns, housing trends, and a wide variety of other issues."

Selection of data, organization, and page layout make this an appealing book. Chapter 1 describes ethnicity, health, education, crime, and other aspects of American life. Chapters 2 through 9 deal with residence, money, love life, children, property, fun, and food. Some of the tables on sex are very explicit. The writing style is straightforward and readable. The "average American" is described in such a way that one wants to read on and learn more.

Sources are documented. Most data are from U.S. government publications, but magazine surveys, industry reports, professional organization reports, poll results, and the authors' own compilations are included. Source notes give authority and/or title and sometimes dates; volume number, pages, and usually dates are omitted. There is an index, but its classified arrangement makes it difficult to use, and there are no cross-references.

Information is described as "the most up-to-date and accurate." Most data given are for 1985 and 1986, with a few citations before 1985 and even fewer for 1987. Information here will become dated, and nothing is said about revision plans.

Almanac of the American People is not a substitute for a general statistical yearbook, such as the *World Almanac* or the *Statistical Abstract of the U.S.*, nor does it duplicate to any significant degree the *People's Almanac* [*RSBR* N 1 82]. However, it can be a useful addition to either the circulating or reference collections of public libraries.

Guide to Federal Technical, Trades and Labor Jobs. 1st ed. Ed. by Rod W. Durgin and others. Resource Directories, 3361 Executive Pkwy., Toledo, OH 43606, 1988. 277p. illus. indexes. tables. $69.95 (ISSN 0899-8078).

331.124 U.S.—Officials and employees I Civil service—U.S. [BKL] 88-2175

Excluding the U.S. Postal Service, approximately 950,000 federal employees work in jobs that do not require a college degree. Identifying these jobs and explaining the application process is the purpose of *Guide to Federal Technical, Trades and Labor Jobs*. The *Guide* provides detailed descriptions for Wage Grade (WG) and General Schedule (GS) jobs (in addition to pertinent information on jobs with the postal system), pay scales and benefits, how to locate federal job vacancies, and how to apply for those vacancies. The *Guide* is divided into two major sections; within each section, the job descriptions are organized by their WG or GS numbers, which indicate occupational categories. An alphabetical job-title index at the beginning of each section leads the reader to the full job description. A sample entry with an explanatory key is part of both major sections.

Entries for WG jobs include job description, positions and salary, federal agencies employed by, and job locations. The "Positions and Salaries" section divides the total number of jobs between men and women employed in that capacity, the number of supervisors of each sex, and their average salary. "Employed By" lists the top four federal agencies that employ people in the job described. "Job Locations" gives the number of people employed in Washington, D.C., the U.S. (not including D.C.), and overseas.

Entries for GS positions include the same basic information as the WG jobs. However, these entries also include the type of service, whether competitive or excepted, education and experience requirements, and the type of exam required. Position and salary information and education and experience requirements are listed for each GS level. Generally the jobs described fall into the GS-1 through GS-4 levels.

Other sections include a useful glossary of terms and acronyms, employment indexes that classify WG and GS jobs by occupational group, and appendixes listing the addresses and telephone numbers of Federal Job Information Centers and State Employment Security Offices. The employment indexes are especially helpful for those readers who are looking for a type of job, rather than a specific job. These indexes help them choose a job family and then lead them to a full job description.

The *Guide* is similar in format to the same publisher's *Guide to Federal Jobs* [*RBB* N 15 85], which contains descriptions for professional and technical jobs available to college graduates. Though Krannich's *Complete Guide to Public Employment* covers some of the same information, describing the types of federal jobs available and how to apply for them, the focus of the review title is narrower, making it more useful for patrons seeking blue-collar employment.

Libraries that have found *Guide to Federal Jobs* useful will want to find room on their shelves for this volume, as the works are complementary. The detail provided for each job and the number of jobs included make *Guide to Federal Technical, Trades and Labor Jobs* a worthwhile tool for public libraries.

The Trainer's Resource, 1988: A Comprehensive Guide to Packaged Training Programs. 2v. 6th ed. Ed. by Eugene Fetteroll and others. Human Resource Development Press, 22 Amherst Rd., Amherst, MA 01002, 1988. 594p. paper $49.95 (v.1: 0-87425-063-3; v.2: 0-87425-064-1).

331.25'92 Employees, Training of I Personnel management [BKL]

The National Directory of Corporate Training Programs. 2d ed. By Ray Bard and Susan K. Elliott. Doubleday, 1988. 373p. bibliog. indexes. hardcover $27.50 (0-385-24202-6); paper $14.95 (0-385-24203-4).

331.25'92 Employees, Training of—U.S.—Directories II Corporations—U.S.—Directories [OCLC] 88-298

The Trainer's Resource, 1988 is the sixth edition of an annual listing of currently available packaged-training programs. To be included, a package must use two or more media, be usable on-site by vendors' representatives or in-house leaders, meet a generic training need, and have been available at least a year. Vendors fill out a questionnaire for each package listed, thus providing the user with comparative information. Packages are organized in 20 categories, e.g., "Communication Skills," "Customer Relations," "Performance Appraisal," "Sales Training," "Time Management," and "Wellness and Health"; arrangement is alphabetical by title within category. Sample packages include "Speak Up on Television," "Systematic Listening," "Interviewing Skills," "Interpersonal Managing Skills," "Non-Manipulative Selling," "The Productive Supervisor," "CPA Review," and "Alcohol Server Responsibility." The two-volume 1988 edition has over 500 listings; 265 are new.

There is one entry per page. Items include audience; program description (objectives, topics); delivery system (length of time involved, number of participants accommodated, media used, workbook availability); instructional strategies (methodology, availability of customization); names and addresses of three recent users (sometimes "available on request" replaces the list); date of introduction; and cost (purchase, rental, availability of preview, availability as public seminar, and need for training the presenter).

An introduction discusses the uses of packaged programs and solicits information on items not included, while a foreword explains use. Subject, title, and vendor indexes complete the book.

Most packages are aimed at group presentations—often at least a day long and usually at a high cost. *TR* provides a good opportunity for identifying and screening possible programs, with the information on previews and users offering help in determining value. A feature suggested for future editions would be citations to published critiques or reviews. The most likely purchasers of *The Trainer's Resource* are corporate trainers with large budgets. Corporate libraries, public libraries with strong business sections, and academic libraries supporting human resource development and business curricula will want to consider purchase.

The National Directory of Corporate Training Programs, the second edition of *Breaking In*, has a very different role from *The Trainer's Resource*: it describes 300 companies and the training programs they provide. Entry-level job seekers are the audience. Alphabetically arranged entries briefly describe each company, its training programs, employee qualifications sought, location(s) of positions, salaries and benefits (often data from the 1986–87 College Placement Council Salary Survey, rather than company-specific), and contact information. Data were gathered from questionnaires completed by companies, interviews, and recruitment publications. There is a 31-item bibliography on career planning and job hunting, followed by training-program, industry, and geographic indexes. Several interviews are interspersed throughout the book, reflecting varying participants' (e.g., recruiters, training graduates) views of training programs.

The National Directory of Corporate Training Programs has some value to entry-level job seekers who want to join companies with strong training programs, but the companies are large ones (e.g., PPG, General Mills, Taco Bell) about which information is readily available. Acceptable for large career and job-placement collections.

Dictionary of Finance. By Eitan A. Avneyon. Macmillan, 1988. 486p. illus. hardcover $50 (0-02-916420-6).

332'.03 Finance—Dictionaries [CIP] 87-28326

The *Dictionary of Finance* contains approximately 6,000 terms on all aspects of investment and finance. Economics, accounting, banking, business, the stock market, real estate, management, and insurance are among the fields represented in this work. The author has tried to include both new and traditional subjects. Thus one finds entries for new Wall Street jargon (*junk bonds, index funds*); abbreviations and acronyms of important organizations and concepts (*CPI, SBA, SEC*); and economic theories (*Marxism, neo-classical economics, Keynesian economic theory*). While the compiler is an Israeli economist, both U.S and British usage is given for terms.

The entries are arranged alphabetically, letter by letter. Terms consisting of more than one word are treated as single units. The entries vary in length from one-line definitions to longer paragraphs for complex theories or terms with multiple meanings. *Buy-back* has five definitions; *call* has six. There are ample cross-references and *see* references. Charts and graphs help illustrate concepts when needed, and charming sketches of famous economists accompany the explanations of their theories.

A comparison of the definitions of selected words in the *Dictionary of Finance* with those in two other works, Donald E. Moffat's *Economics Dictionary* (Elsevier, 1976) and David L. Scott's *Wall Street Words* (Houghton, 1988 [*RBB* Mr 1 88]), revealed differences in scope and depth of treatment. In *WSW*, the term *inflation* receives four lines that state only that it is a price increase, with no further explanation. *ED* allots nine short lines and, saying that there are many definitions, calls it a decrease in purchasing power. The *Dictionary of Finance* provides a paragraph with concise explanations of the various factors involved in inflation. *Consumer Price Index* receives three lines in *WSW*, while *ED* provides 1½ pages of history and explanation. The *Dictionary of Finance* offers a clear one-paragraph summary of this term. All three works are comparable in their treatment of *investment*. *Supply-side economics* does not appear in *ED*, but *WSW* provides four lines on this subject. The *Dictionary of Finance* offers a paragraph with a complete explanation.

The broad scope and clear definitions in the *Dictionary of Finance* make it a useful work for all library collections. Both the novice and expert will find the necessary information clearly presented here.

The Financial 1000: A Directory of Who Runs the Leading 1000 U.S. Financial Organizations. Ed. by James E. Marsh and others. Monitor Publishing Co., 104 Fifth Ave., New York, NY 10011, 1988– . annual. 553p. indexes. paper $95 (ISSN 0894-7627).

332 Banks and banking—U.S.—Directories I Insurance—U.S.—Directories I Brokers—U.S.—Directories I Financial institutions—U.S.—Directories 88-646469

This directory is produced by the same company that publishes both the *Congressional Yellow Book* and *Federal Yellow Book*. It also publishes a companion volume to this book called *The Corporate 1000* [*RBB* Jl 87], which covers manufacturers, service businesses, and utilities. The stated goal of *The Financial 1000* is to "help you identify and contact the executives who manage America's leading companies." It is a directory of people who manage or are on the boards of directors of banks, insurance companies, Wall Street firms, and thrifts. Included are both public and private companies.

The main body of the book is alphabetical by the name of the company. Each entry contains an address, stock exchange symbol (when appropriate), and fax and telex numbers. Also included is a one-sentence description of the business and, for public companies, a dollar amount of assets. This asset value is the only statistical data provided in the work. Then follows a list of the officers and managers, usually down to the level of vice president. For example, under *Morgan Stanley Group Inc.*, there is a long list of the managing directors. Some entries also include telephone numbers for individuals. A list of major subsidiaries, divisions, and affiliates follows. Large subsidiaries are listed separately with a note to also see the parent organization: for example, under *Harris Trust and Savings Bank*, one is instructed to also see the complete listing under the parent, *Harris Bankcorp Inc.* The entry concludes with a list of the board of directors and the positions they hold within their own institutions.

There are five indexes to access the information. The first is a master index of every organization listed in the directory. This includes not only parent companies, but subsidiaries, divisions, and affiliates as well. An index by parent organization, its subsidiaries, and divisions follows. Under *State Street Boston Corporation*, for instance, are the names of six subsidiaries. The geographic index lists the firms by the state in which the headquarters is located. There is an index by type of financial service rendered, for example, investment banks, brokerage firms, money management companies. The final index is a list of each individual listed in the directory.

Bits and pieces of the information provided here are available in publications such as the various *Moody's* manuals, *Standard and Poor's Security Dealers of North America*, various banking directories, and annual reports of public companies. However, as a one-stop directory of the important people in the financial industry, *The Financial 1000* is recommended for public and academic libraries having patrons who seek this type of directory information.

American Banker Year Book, 1988. Ed. by William E. Zimmerman. American Banker Inc.; dist. by Gale, 1988. 482p. charts. index. tables. hardcover $95 (0-9618162-1-X).

332.1'02 Banks and banking—Yearbooks [BKL]

This annual, in its second year of publication, "is designed to be a comprehensive reference tool to help financial services executives put their hands on the information they need." It is a compendium of some of the articles, research reports, statistics, and surveys that were published in the journal *American Banker* during 1987.

Arranged in five main sections, access to information is fast and efficient either through the detailed table of contents or the index. There is also a table of contents page at the beginning of each section.

Except for the statistical and directory sections, the other sections are primarily short articles written by the reporters at the journal.

The first section, "Key Trends & Developments," is an overview of the important events in banking during 1987. Among its 10 subheadings are subjects like *Commercial Banking, Technology, Retail Services, Regional Banking, People,* and *Washington.* The next section covers "Dates & Events" and includes top news events and major meetings for 1987 and important dates in 1988. The "Surveys & Special Reports" section includes the narrative and statistics from special reports appearing in the journal during 1987. These include reports on consumers, technology, cash management, and bank failures. "Directories" is a potpourri of names and addresses including lobbyists, congressional committees, governmental regulators, state banking associations, and 60 influential people within the banking profession. There are also addresses, arranged by state, for several hundred banks and thrifts. The last section is an annotated index arranged by subject and date to the most important articles in *American Banker* during 1987. For example, under the subject *Lending—Corporate* is a chronological list of approximately 100 news items and the pages on which they appeared in the journal.

However, the section of most interest to libraries appears in the middle of the book. This section, entitled "Statistics: Historical & Current," is by far the largest, covering almost 180 pages. There are various statistics on commercial banks, nonbanks, thrifts, and international banks. Some of the data to be found include the top banks in assets, deposits, credit-card operations, business loans, executive remuneration, agricultural loans, mortgages, and personnel. All of the data were developed by the staff at *American Banker* and cover at most the years 1986 and 1987. The most current data found include the period up to June 30, 1987.

This book is well written, and the layout is attractive. As mentioned above, all of the material in this annual has already appeared in *American Banker* during 1987. However, this book is an excellent reference guide for its intended audience: banking executives and professionals. Business libraries and others desiring a good overview of banking for 1987 and a one-stop place for 1985 and 1986 banking statistics should consider purchasing this guide.

Barron's Real Estate Handbook. 2d ed. By Jack C. Harris and Jack P. Friedman. Barron's, 1988. 700p. bibliog. illus. indexes. tables. hardcover $19.95 (0-8120-5758-9).
333.33 Real estate business—Handbooks, manuals, etc. ‖ Real estate business—Dictionaries ‖ Business mathematics—Real estate business—Tables [CIP] 88-3345

Barron's Real Estate Handbook combines a glossary of real estate terms with guides for buyers, sellers, professionals, and potential professionals. The authors, from Texas A&M University, have revised the first edition, incorporating changes from the Tax Reform Act of 1986.

Preceding the glossary are several text chapters: a home buyer's guide, a home seller's guide, and information on the investment aspects of real estate. There is also a separate section on related regulations (from the 1890 Sherman Antitrust Act to the present), and a chapter on real estate careers.

The glossary itself contains over 1,500 terms in its 300-plus pages. Beginning with *abandonment* and ending with *zoning ordinance*, the terms cover finance, law, architecture, construction, and associations and organizations. The brief and clear definitions are frequently followed by examples like that under *liability insurance*: "Abel slipped on a broken step . . . in an apartment complex owned by Baker. Baker's *liability insurance* pays Abel for the doctor and hospital fees." There are numbered illustrations made up of tables, diagrams, and drawings of architectural styles. However, these figures are not always on the same page as the terms they illustrate. There are few cross-references.

Following the glossary, there are more than 200 pages of mortgage tables, from the standard (monthly payments and remaining balance) to the less frequently found (premiums for assumable loans and depreciation). Also included are a list of abbreviations, measurement tables, and sample forms and worksheets like a purchase agreement, a loan application, and a settlement statement. The appendix "House Cross Section" suffers from poor printing quality. The bibliography suggests from 1 to 10 sources for each of 80 topics. The index is minimal (three pages).

Of the real estate reference sources published in the last year, *Barron's* is one of the most comprehensive. It has more terms than Thomsett's *Real Estate Dictionary* [*RBB* O 1 88], though there is much overlap. *Barron's* is similar to *Webster's New World Illustrated Encyclopedic Dictionary of Real Estate* [*RBB* Ap 15 88] but has additional information provided in the opening text chapters. *Barron's* is inexpensive and is recommended for public and academic libraries.

The Dictionary of Real Estate Appraisal. 2d ed. American Institute of Real Estate Appraisers, 430 N. Michigan Ave., Chicago, IL 60611-4088, 1989. 366p. bibliog. hardcover $28.50 (0-911780-93-9).
333.33'2 Real property—Valuation—Dictionaries ‖ Real estate business—Dictionaries ‖ Real property—Dictionaries [CIP] 88-26205

The Dictionary of Real Estate Appraisal is, as its title indicates, a compendium of terms related to the valuation of all types of real property. The second edition, comparable in size to the first (1984), contains over 3,000 words and phrases. The fields covered in both editions include accounting, agriculture (*feeder cattle, cow year long*), arbitration, architecture, banking, computer programming, construction, finance, insurance, law, and urban planning. The second edition has dropped some obsolete terms in order to increase the coverage of economic concepts, environmental concerns, legal terms, market analysis, and quantitative techniques. Comparison of random pages, however, showed little readily apparent change. The entry *sagebrush* has been omitted, for instance, while *festival shopping center, income model,* and *radon* have been added. While most of the terms are easily linked to real estate appraisal (*easement appurtenant, shared appreciation mortgage, tie beam*), it is unlikely that a patron or reference librarian would go to this source for definitions of terms such as *hard copy* or *impact printer*.

Concise definitions average three lines each; *see* and *see also* references are given, as are synonyms ("*profitability index* . . . Also called *benefit/cost ratio*"). There is a brief list of symbols and a fairly extensive list of information sources ranging from bibliographies to sources of market data and business operating ratios. This bibliography has been updated since the first edition, especially in regard to listing recent publications of the institute. Unlike many real estate dictionaries, this book has no illustrative drawings.

While *The Dictionary of Real Estate Appraisal* is quite useful for appraisers and real estate professionals and seems to be the standard work for appraisal terminology, libraries with the first edition may not need to buy the second. The need for general real estate terms can also be met with one of the following sources: *Barron's Real Estate Handbook* (2d ed. [*RBB* D 15 88]), *The Language of Real Estate* (3d ed. [*RBB* Ja 15 89]), or *Webster's New World Illustrated Encyclopedic Dictionary of Real Estate* [*RBB* Ap 15 88].

Real Estate Dictionary. Comp. by Michael C. Thomsett. McFarland, 1988. 220p. charts. tables. hardcover $29.95 (0-89950-321-7).
333.33'03 Real estate business—Dictionaries ‖ Mortgage loans—Dictionaries [OCLC] 87-43196

Real Estate Dictionary defines terms from the world of residential and commercial real estate, real estate investments, loans, and related legal issues. Thomsett, author of *Investment and Securities Dictionary* (favorably reviewed by the Board [*RBB* Je 15 87]) has here prepared a glossary for real estate professionals and consumers. It includes over 1,100 words, phrases, agencies, and associations, ranging from loan terms (*buy-down mortgage, rate cap*) to legal terms and acts (*lis pendens, Uniform Partnership Act*) and from insurance phrases (*floater policy, 11 common perils*) to professional associations (*American Land Title Institute, Realtors National Marketing Institute*). The terms are in boldface type and are followed by succinct definitions. These definitions are, for the most part, straightforward, but when jargon is used in a definition, the reader is referred to that term elsewhere in the glossary. This cross-referencing is fairly extensive (for example, the entry *listing* has multiple *see also* references including *exclusive listing*, *multiple listing*, and *open listing*) but occasionally lacking (*11 common perils* is under *11* with no cross-reference from *common* or *perils*). A particular strength of the book is the black-and-white charts, tables, and diagrams that frequently serve to guide the reader through a process, such as figuring the costs and savings of refinancing. The glossary is followed by a series of checklists for home buyers—neighborhood, home inspection, home layout, and mortgage evaluation. There are also factor-type amortization tables (i.e., tables by rate and number of years that provide a factor by which to multiply the loan amount to get the monthly principal and interest payment). The final appendixes are remaining balance tables and 101 commonly used abbreviations (*ACRS*—accelerated cost recovery system, *ZRM*—zero rate mortgage), many of which have entries in the glossary. Thomsett's *Real Estate Dictionary* is a handy source, particularly for consumers, but libraries may want to consider the significant overlap in terms with the more comprehensive *Arnold Encyclopedia of Real Estate* (Warren, 1978, $75). Libraries owning *Webster's New World Illustrated Encyclopedic Dictionary of Real Estate* (3d ed., Prentice-Hall Press [*RBB* Ap 15 88]) will also find considerable overlap. Thomsett takes a more serious approach and is easier to use than another recent publication, *Street Talk in Real Estate*, [*RBB* My 1 88], even though the latter does include more slang terms.

The Language of Real Estate. 3d ed. By John W. Reilly. Longman Financial Services, 1988 (c1989). 467p. illus. paper $26.95 (0-88462-673-3).

346.7304'3 Real property—U.S.—Dictionaries I Real estate business—Law and legislation—U.S.—Dictionaries [CIP] 88-21032

Reilly's *Language of Real Estate* is a dictionary of words and phrases designed for real estate professionals but is also helpful to consumers. The 2,400 entries emphasize architectural and building terms (*muntin*, *punch list*), real estate lingo (*cold call*, *comparables*), legal terms (*muniment of title*, *replevin*, *Uniform Residential Landlord and Tenant Act*), and financial terms (*impound account*, *Keough plan*, *thin capitalization*). Also included are associations (*Building Owners and Managers Association*, *Federal Savings and Loan Insurance Corporation*) and some slang terms (*alligator*, *netting out*, *yuppie*).

Reilly, a real estate attorney, broker, and instructor, added 200 terms to this third edition and revised definitions as needed. The book begins with a subject classification of terms. For example, under *Death* there are 28 related terms listed such as *codicil*, *dower*, and *widow's quarantine*. Then the 450-page glossary begins. The entries are arranged letter by letter and include the definitions, applications of the term involved, and cross-references. Entries vary from one line (*nosing*, *topography*) to several pages (*lease*, *option*) and sometimes include line drawings. The appendixes are a list of abbreviations, a copy of the "Realtor Code of Ethics," and a sample closing problem that describes a transaction and then shows a worksheet and an actual settlement statement.

The Language of Real Estate has more terms than two other similar titles published this year, Thomsett's *Real Estate Dictionary* [*RBB* O 1 88] and *Barron's Real Estate Handbook* [D 15 88], as well as more expansive entries. It is also the only one of the three to have an entry for *radon*. However, *The Language of Real Estate* has fewer "extras" such as mortgage tables or home buyers' checklists. It is a fairly comprehensive specialized dictionary while *Barron's* is a more consumer-oriented handbook, but both are well done and reasonably priced.

International Trade Names Dictionary, 1988–89. 1st ed. Ed. by Donna Wood. Gale, 1988. 366p. hardcover $240 (0-8103-0690-5; ISSN 0899-7586).

929 Business names I Trademarks [BKL] 88-659352

International Trade Names Dictionary, 1988-89: Company Index. 1st ed. Ed. by Donna Wood. Gale, 1988. 350p. hardcover $210 (0-8103-0691-3; ISSN 0899-7594).

929 Business names I Trademarks [BKL] 88-659377

This new Gale publication is a companion to its *Trade Names Dictionary*, which covers U.S. firms. It has information for consumer products worldwide, although only a limited number of countries are covered in this first edition. The first volume is a dictionary of about 40,000 trade names and company names, and the second is a company index. The sources of this information are the 21 publications listed in the front of each volume.

The *Dictionary* volume is a straightforward *A–Z* arrangement, intermixing product and company entries. Each product entry begins with the product or brand name in boldface. The type of product, the name of the company, and the source of this information follow. For instance, under the product name *Abecote* one finds that this is a paint product from African Bitumen Emulsions (PTY.) Ltd., a South African company. The source of this information is *TISA*, which stands for *National Trade-Index of South Africa*. The company entries, in regular typeface, give a complete address. The *Company Index*, the second volume, contains the names and addresses of each company in an alphabetical arrangement. In addition, product names are listed, along with a notation showing what the products are and in what source this information was found. The entry *Clarke Bros. (Liverpool) Ltd.* includes a complete address and the 14 product names represented in volume 1.

This work contains only consumer-oriented products like apparel, beverages, food, hardware, toys, and pharmaceuticals. Only a limited number of countries are covered. As stated in the preface to volume 1, "Among the countries extensively covered in this first edition are: Australia, Canada, Denmark, Japan, Kenya, Singapore, South Africa, Sri Lanka, Trinidad and Tobago, and the United Kingdom." It is also claimed that future editions will include more countries. An interedition supplement called *New International Trade Names* will keep this series current.

This is a very specialized and expensive resource. Libraries having extensive business collections and those who found the series dealing with U.S. trade names useful should consider it. Those libraries serving a clientele who develop and market products overseas or academic libraries with international business students may also want to consider this set.

A Historical Dictionary of American Industrial Language. Ed. by William H. Mulligan. Greenwood, 1988. 332p. bibliog. index. hardcover $55 (0-313-24171-6).

338'.003 U.S.—Industries—History—Dictionaries II English language—U.S.—Etymology—Dictionaries I Americanisms—Dictionaries [CIP] 87-37544

Unique in concept, this *Dictionary* endeavors to survey the language of American industry in the period prior to World War I. Included are more than 3,000 alphabetically arranged terms drawn from industries ranging from bookbinding to woodworking. The greatest number of entries focus on the mining of metals (532), milling (358), coal mining (264), and metal processing (217). Less complete lists are offered for ropemaking (3), tobacco processing (5), upholstery (2), and woodworking (4). The editor chose to exclude terms for transportation and agriculture because of their large and complex vocabulary and because he felt they differed considerably from manufacturing industries. The quantity and quality of the entries, according to the editor, were largely determined by existing research on particular industries. Thus industries that have been little studied are represented incompletely.

Definitions are generally short (1–2 lines). They are limited to identifying the industry or industries in which the term was used, describing the tool or process, and noting its purpose. Exceptions to this pattern are the entries for carpetmaking like *axminster carpet* and *tapestry carpet*, which extend to half a page. *See* and *see also* references and embedded cross-references noted by asterisks are used liberally. The terms are grouped together by industry in an appendix, and there is an extensive list of industry-specific dictionaries, encyclopedias, and handbooks in the bibliography. The index is limited to institutions and people mentioned in the definitions.

The work is a collaborative effort of 20 contributors drawn largely from historic libraries and museums. The editor is the director of the Clarke Historical Library at Central Michigan University, who has written extensively on working-class history and craftsmen.

Because of its unique scope, no comparisons can be made with existing reference works. However, a check of some standard reference works on particular industries, such as *Fairchild's Dictionary of Textiles*, reveals that many of these historic terms are not included. Thus, this new reference work succeeds in recovering the lost vocabulary of one of the most important segments of American society. It should prove invaluable to any student of the history of America's industries and crafts.

International Directory of Company Histories. v.1. Ed. by Thomas Derdak and others. St. James Press, 1988. 758p. index. hardcover $95 (0-912289-10-4).

338.7'4 Corporations—History [BKL]

The publication of this volume marks the introduction of a projected five-volume set by St. James Press. During five years of development the aim of the publisher has been to "ensure that the *International Directory of Company Histories* becomes the 'bible' of its field; as indispensable to business history as *The New Grove* is to music." It is designed for students, job candidates, business people, librarians, historians, and investors wishing to research the "historical development of the world's most important companies." Calling it a *Directory* is a misnomer; it is actually a collection of company histories.

Companies chosen for inclusion have minimum annual sales of $2 billion (U.S. dollars) or are a leading influence in a specific industry or geographic location. They are headquartered in Europe, Japan, Australia, or North America. Company information was gathered from public sources, including annual reports, business magazines, and scholarly journals. The unsigned entries were prepared by a team of writers and researchers whose names appear on the title page. Institutional affiliations or credentials of the writers are not provided.

The five volumes in this set will cover 1,250 companies, arranged alphabetically by a classification scheme related to area of activity, and then by company name. The classification scheme is not based on a standard format (e.g., SIC code) and appears to have been developed for this set. The 250 companies listed in volume 1 are in the activity areas of automotives, advertising, aerospace, airlines, beverages, chemicals, conglomerates, construction, containers, and drugs. Forthcoming volumes will include industries like electronics, food services, hotels, forestry, petroleum, shipbuilding, technology, and utilities. The editor notes that the companies in the volume have not seen or endorsed the entries.

Information preceding each historical essay includes company logo, headquarters address, telephone, type of ownership (public, private, or state controlled), earliest incorporation date, number of employees, sales and market value for fiscal year 1986, and an indication of where the company is listed for public trade of stock shares. Separate entries are given for large subsidiaries (e.g., there are entries for Miles Laboratories and its parent company Bayer).

Essays are usually 2,500 words in length but may be much longer (e.g., Ford Motor Company, 4,500 words). They are designed to trace the history of a company by providing information on key personalities, events, and inventions, all within the context of the social, economic, and political climate of the times. This makes for interesting reading as facts about activities of a company are related to the larger activities of the society in which it operates. For example, the section on Dow Chemical Company discusses the adverse publicity Dow received because of its production of napalm during the Vietnam War. Similarly the entry for Greyhound Corporation explains that the company tried to discourage civilian ridership during World War II because its efforts were devoted to the transportation of workers employed at shipyards and munitions factories. (One Greyhound advertisement of the time was "Don't Travel Unless Your Trip Is Essential.") Less significant details are also included. The entry on Anheuser-Busch mentions that as the company expanded its sales into Texas in the mid-1850s, cowboys reportedly deserted their "beloved red-eye whiskey for the light taste of Budweiser." A list of principal subsidiaries and a brief bibliography of books complete most entries. The most recent bibliographic entry noted was for 1987. Within the text, running heads give activity area and company name. A 40-page index of companies, subsidiaries, and personal names is provided, with boldface used to indicate the presence of a separate entry.

The Encyclopedia of American Business History and Biography: Railroads in the Age of Regulation, from Facts On File, was favorably reviewed by the Board [RBB Ag 88]. The first of a projected 50-volume set, it contains company, biographical, and topical entries that run to 10,000 words. It covers only U.S. companies, while *Company Histories* is international in scope. It also includes entries for companies that are no longer in business, while the work under review does not. A major difference between these sources is that over half the entries in the Facts On File work are biographical. Both sources successfully chronicle business activity within the context of the larger historical period. Both sources are adequately indexed, provide bibliographies, and are reasonably priced. They are significantly different in coverage and should not be considered as competitors. Both are worthy of consideration by libraries serving users who study business history.

The Computer Industry Almanac. 2d ed. By Egil Juliussen and Karen Juliussen. Brady; dist. by Prentice Hall, 1988. various pagings. index. tables. paper $29.95 (0-13-167537-0; ISSN 0893-0791).

338.7'61004 Computer industry—Periodicals [OCLC] 87-658176

The second edition of *The Computer Industry Almanac*, much like its predecessor, is a conglomeration of facts and figures, people, and products from the world of computers. The *Almanac* is divided into 17 chapters, most with numerous sections and subsections, all of which are listed in the table of contents.

At least half of the information contained in the *Almanac* has been reprinted from a variety of other sources, including *Forbes*, *Fortune*, *Inc.*, and standard computer magazines. Much of it is in the form of lists: "200 Best Small Companies in America," "The 100 Leading U.S. Information System Companies," "Top U.S. Electronic Companies in Japan." Where the list includes both noncomputer and computer companies or services, the editors have listed only those from the computer industry. In some cases the 1988 rankings are compared to the 1986 rankings. The rest of the information in the more-than-700-page volume is the work of the editors and their editorial board.

In a review of the first edition of this work [*RBB* S 15 87], the Board particularly noted the following flaws: poor indexing, incomplete information, paucity of original information, and duplication of information already existing in many libraries. The first two of these problems have been partially corrected. The index has been expanded to include all personal and company names. However, the first-edition index had one helpful feature that has since been eliminated—the titles of the various lists (e.g., "The 500 Largest Foreign Companies") were indexed.

Information cited as incomplete in the first edition was in the areas of awards, education, and computer-industry people. The list of people still includes little more than name, position, and company. However, unlike the previous edition, this 1989 *Almanac* does include elsewhere in the work addresses and telephone numbers for the people listed. Other lists cited by the Board as being incomplete, such as "The Top University in Computer Science" and "Award Winning Advertising Campaigns," have been deleted here. Where award-winning products or people are listed, the criteria for the award are also given.

The biggest problem with the *Almanac* continues to be the lack of original information and its duplication of information found in other sources. While the lists may be interesting to computer or trivia mavens, they are of little practical value to the librarian. Company names, personnel, educational programs, organizations, even the history of the computer are readily and easily available in other sources. For the price, *The Computer Industry Almanac* has a lot of bits of information, but not much byte.

Corporate TrendTrac. Ed. by A. Dale Timpe. Gale, 1988–   . bimonthly. indexes. tables. paper $174/six issues (ISSN 1041-1712).

338.8'3 Consolidation and merger of corporations—Periodicals—Indexes—Periodicals [OCLC] 89-646503

News of "merger mania" continues to fill the business press. This new bimonthly indexes 26 business and financial publications for news of changes in corporate ownership. Among the publications indexed are *Crain's Chicago Business, Financial Times* (London), *New York Times, Moody's Investor Services*, and six different editions of the *Wall Street Journal*. Acquiring or initiating companies are listed alphabetically by name in four sections: "Mergers & Acquisitions," "New Stock Exchange Listings & Suspensions," "Company Name Changes," and "Bankruptcies, Liquidations, Reorganizations & Organizational Changes." Each entry gives the location of the company and its SIC code, notes the activity and the company acquired ("merged with . . . ," "acquired minority interest in . . . "), and lists the indexed source(s) that reported this activity with date and page number. There are no cross-references from acquired companies to the main entry for acquiring companies; the company index must be used for this purpose.

Tables at the end of each issue summarize the corporate activity reported in that issue. For instance, one table gives the number of friendly takeovers, hostile takeovers, unsolicited takeovers, etc. Another ranks the transactions by reported dollar value (with R. J. R. Nabisco leading the list). Another shows interaction between industries by listing the SIC codes for both the acquiring and the acquired companies. A similar table shows international interaction. Here it is possible to ascertain the number of U.K. firms that bought U.S. companies, for instance. There are cumulative indexes in each volume by SIC code, by place, and by company name.

So far, three issues of *Corporate TrendTrac* have been published, with a fourth due out in late spring. There appears to be a four- to five-month time lag in the indexing of newspapers and periodicals. Many libraries already have access to these articles through *Business Periodicals Index, Predicasts F&S Index, New York Times Index*, and *Wall Street Journal Index*. The indexing is more current in their print versions, and they are all available online as well. In libraries serving the business community, an index devoted specifically to covering changes in corporate ownership will be welcome, but indexing needs to become more current for this title to be useful.

Major Companies of Europe, 1988. v.1–2. 8th ed. Ed. by R. M. Whiteside and others. Graham & Trotman; dist. by Gale, 1988. annual. indexes. tables. hardcover v.1, $330 (1-85333-036-1; ISSN 0266-934X); v.2, $220 (1-85333-038-8; ISSN 0268-4667).

338.94 Corporations—Europe—Directories I Europe—Industries—Directories I [OCLC]

Anyone needing information about the finances, personnel, structure, products, and profitability of European companies will be interested in these volumes. Part of Graham & Trotman's Major Companies of the World series, *Major Companies of Europe* consists of three volumes. Volume 1, *Major Companies of the Continental European Economic Community*, covers 3,500 "top companies," and volume 2, *Major Companies of the United Kingdom*, lists 1,500 companies. The third volume, not covered in this review, lists nearly 1,400 companies of Western Europe outside the EEC. Information published for each company is "intended to provide a convenient descriptive reference in succinct form which will be useful to businessmen." Other books in this series cover the Far East, the U.S., and the Arab world.

The introduction states that the companies listed have been selected "on the grounds of the size of their sales volume or balance sheet and their importance to the business environment of the country in which they are based." More specific selection criteria are not provided. Information presented is the result of "an extensive and careful research operation" in the 12 EEC nations. Companies are not charged for being listed, and the publishers invite any company to contact them about possible inclusion in future editions. First published in 1982, the set is updated and published each year.

The companies are alphabetically listed in sections arranged by country. Entry elements may include address; telephone, telex, and telefax numbers; executive officers; a description of principal activities; trade names; parent, subsidiary, and associated companies; principal bankers; principal shareholders; number of employees; and financial information. The financial information, given in the currency of the host country, includes sales turnover, dividends, profit before tax, profit after tax, and investment income. The depth of coverage for each company varies considerably. Entry information for Laboratoires de Cosmetologie Yves Rocher includes only address, telephone, six words of activity description, parent company, and sales turnover. In contrast, the information supplied for Andelsbanken Dandebank also includes board of directors, management board, executive staff, profit, dividends per share, share capital, deposits, total assets, and number of employees.

Volume 1 ends with three indexes. The first lists all the companies in alphabetical order regardless of their country of operation, while the second lists them within country of operation (largely replicating the arrangement of the book). The third index lists companies by business activity, subdivided by country. A list of all business activity categories (e.g., *Copper and Copper Alloys; Generators; Property, Real Estate*) appears at the beginning of the volume. Companies with varied activities may be listed in more than one category. There are two similar indexes in volume 2: the first one listing alphabetically all the U.K. companies, the second listing them by business activity. A minor flaw in the indexing is that page numbers occasionally lead the reader to *see* references in the body of the volume instead of directly to the right page (e.g., the volume 1 index entry "*Société JAs Hennessy & Co*—289" leads to "SOCIETE JAS HENNESSY & CO see Hennessy, Société JAs & Co").

In many libraries international business directories may suffice if extensive coverage is not a major concern. *Moody's International Manual* (Moody's Investors Service, 1987) gives more information per company but does not list nearly as many companies. For Denmark, France, Italy, and the U.K., *Moody's* has approximately 70, 130, 75, and 550 listings respectively. The comparable figures for *Major Companies* are 345, 1,300, 500, and 1,500. The same set of figures for *Ward's Business Directory of Major International Companies* [RBB O 15 86] is 200, 1,100, 560, and 1,000. *Ward's* ranks companies by sales and, in tabular format, includes data on SIC codes, net income, assets, employees, and facilities. If rankings are important, *ELC's United Kingdom's 1,000 Largest Companies* (ELC International, 1988) and *Europe's 15,000 Largest Companies* (ELC International, 1988) should also be considered. They provide rankings by sales, profit, and number of employees. Libraries that support business or research activities with a focus on the EEC should consider *Major Companies of Europe*.

Biographical Directory of the Council of Economic Advisers. Ed. by Robert Sobel and Bernard S. Katz. Greenwood, 1988. 301p. bibliog. index. hardcover $49.95 (0-313-22554-0).

338.973'0025 Council of Economic Advisers (U.S.)—Directories I Economists—U.S.—Directories [CIP] 86-14984

As editor Sobel points out in a short, informative introduction to this encyclopedic dictionary, before the first administration of Franklin Roosevelt, economists played a very small role in creating national economic policy. During Roosevelt's administrations, they became increasingly important in formulating governmental policy, and under Harry Truman's first administration, the Employment Act of 1946 mandated the formation of a Council of Economic Advisers (CEA). Succeeding administrations used the council with varying frequency, and the influence of the CEA rose and fell according to the administration.

This book consists of essays on the 45 economists who have served on the CEA, covering their economic and political programs and ideas as well as their lives. Written by knowledgeable, professional economists and other scholars, the essays, which range in length from 2 to 12 pages, attempt to show "who were or are these people, what were their ideas, and how they influenced economic thought and government behavior." The entries are analytical, focusing on the contributions each CEA member made rather than on personality attributes or ideological correctness. Each of the essays begins with the economist's date of birth (and death, if appropriate) and term of office on the CEA. Following every essay is a short bibliography of writings by the subject economist. At the end of the book, a chronological list of CEA members according to administration appears along with an index to all names in the entries.

Only 7 of the 45 people covered here have biographies in *The New Palgrave: A Dictionary of Economics* [*RBB* Ap 1 88], and their entries there are briefer, though their bibliographies are more extensive. This new biographical dictionary is an authoritative and substantive reference source covering federal economic policy since World War II through biographical information on the various economic advisers appointed in this period. University and four-year college libraries should have this in their reference collections, as well as large public libraries and libraries serving government at the state and federal levels.

The Basic Business Library: Core Resources. 2d ed. Ed. by Bernard S. Schlessinger and others. Oryx, 1989. 278p. index. hardcover $38.50 (0-89774-451-9).

016.0276'9 Business libraries ‖ Business—Bibliography ‖ Business libraries—Bibliography ‖ Reference books—Business—Bibliography [CIP] 88-37381

The first edition (1983) of this book was, according to the Board's review [*RBB* Ag 84], a helpful guide to collection development for small academic, public, and business libraries. In this second edition the three-part arrangement has been retained and slightly enlarged. Part 1, "Core List of Printed Business Reference Sources," now identifies 177 (up from 156) basic sources for the small library, providing for each a statement on its authority and scope, followed by a paragraph evaluating its value in libraries. (More than 100 of the core titles are newer editions of those in the 1983 work.) The core list includes serials as well as books. The second part, "The Literature of Business Reference and Business Libraries," is an annotated bibliography of 219 articles and books for librarians. It retains the 109 items for 1976–81 in the first edition and adds the output for 1981–87. Part 3 consists of 10 state-of-the-art essays concerning business reference sources and services. The topics covered are those of the 1983 volume—online databases; U.S. government business information sources; acquisition, collection, and organization of materials in business libraries; an annotated core list of periodicals; reference service; promoting the value of business information service; education for business librarianship—and, new to this edition, an essay on best investment sources. Of the essayists who contributed to the earlier edition, half revised their essays; the other writers are new to this edition. The indexes to each part of the first edition have been replaced by a comprehensive author/title/subject/publisher index to the entire book.

There are several selective and comprehensive guides to the business literature for librarians. Two recent books are Lavin's *Business Information: How to Find It, How to Use It* (Oryx, 1987, $49.50 [*RBB* Je 15 87]) and Strauss' *Handbook of Business Information: A Guide for Librarians, Students, and Researchers* (Libraries Unlimited, 1988, $37.50). Each book annotates more than 700 sources (books, journals, databases, etc.). Both provide in-depth descriptions for some of the sources, with the basic concepts essential for using them effectively explained. These descriptions are often accompanied by sample pages from the sources or a summary table or graph (e.g., sources of federal tax decisions). Strauss appears to be the more comprehensive of the two guides and will be an excellent text for library school courses on business information. Daniells' *Business Information Sources* (rev. ed., 1985 [*RBB* My 1 86]), a standard in many libraries, annotates more than 3,000 business titles. For small libraries, the core list in Schlessinger will be a useful acquisitions and collection-evaluation tool. For larger libraries owning some of the books above, this book's usefulness lies in its unique features—the annotated bibliography on business reference and business librarianship and the essays on business reference sources and services.

Hotel and Restaurant Industries: An Information Sourcebook. By Judith M. Nixon. Oryx, 1988. 240p. indexes. hardcover $38.50 (0-89774-376-8).

016.3384'7647 Hotels, taverns, etc.—Bibliography ‖ Restaurants, lunch rooms, etc.—Bibliography ‖ Food service—Bibliography [CIP] 88-15413

In recent years the hospitality industry has grown dramatically. Oryx Sourcebook Series in Business and Management, number 17, was compiled to assist in collection development in academic libraries that support hotel, restaurant, and food-service programs. The author, a librarian at the Consumer and Family Sciences Library at Purdue University, first recommends and then annotates a core collection of over 100 books and journals, the majority of which were published in the 1980s. The core collection lists books on architecture, law, cookery, sanitation, marketing, and accounting. These same subjects, plus others related to the industry, are used as chapter headings for the rest of the book. In each chapter an additional 5 to 25 books are annotated. It is obvious that the author has made a careful selection, concentrating on the best titles in the field. The specificity of many of the titles is amazing—the history of the linen-supply industry, the most efficient way to clean restrooms, and the problem of theft of stock in bars.

Two appendixes list the addresses and telephone numbers of hospitality associations and of colleges that have hotel, restaurant, and food-service majors. There are also author, title, and subject indexes.

This annotated bibliography is a current, selective list of sources in a fast-growing industry. It will supplement and update Cornell University School of Hotel Administration's *Subject Catalog of the Library* (G. K. Hall, 1979). Certainly a necessary purchase for libraries whose clienteles are involved in the hospitality industry.

Synerjy: A Directory of Renewable Energy. v.15 (summer/fall 1988). Synerjy, P.O. Box 1854, Cathedral Sta., New York, NY 10025, 1974– .semiannual. 71p. paper $45/yr.

016.333794 Renewable energy sources—Bibliography ‖ Renewable energy sources—Directories [BKL]

This bibliography/directory owes its start-up 15 years ago to the energy crisis and the resulting desire to promote alternative sources of energy. Its purpose is to provide "information about practical, nonpolluting alternatives to fossil fuels and nuclear energy." There are references to books, journal articles, conferences, associations, government publications, and manufacturers.

Synerjy is divided into nine subject areas: *Solar Energy, Biomass Fuels, Hydrogen Fuels, Geothermal Energy, Water Power, Wind Power, Electric Energy Utilization, Energy Transfer and Storage,* and *Miscellaneous.* Each area is further subdivided into headings like *Books and Patents, Government Publications, Articles, Manufacturers, Research,* etc. Access to these areas is through a table of contents. There is no index.

Most of the references are to technical or scientific publications. However, there are some citations to popular literature. Most of the government publications cited are from the National Technical Information Service or the Patent Office and include the NTIS number and price or the patent number for easier retrieval. The citations to books and articles are also complete. However, the use of unexplained abbreviations for periodical titles could be troublesome for the inexperienced user. For example, *J Chem Tech Biotech* or *Brown Boveri Rev* could easily have been written out. None of the citations are annotated.

There are several unique and useful aspects of this publication. It is international in scope, including English-language publications from throughout the world. Both the researcher and general user benefit by having patents, articles, books, and government-funded research in one resource. This publication is also unique because of its listings of names and addresses for foreign and U.S. manufacturers, facilities using alternative energy sources, and groups and organizations doing research with these energy sources.

Synerjy is published twice a year, and the summer/fall issue cumulates the citations from the winter/spring issue. (It is possible to subscribe to just the summer/fall issue for $30.) Libraries having a demand for information about alternative or renewable energy sources should consider this source.

The Rating Guide to Franchises. By Dennis L. Foster. Facts On File, 1988. 298p. indexes. hardcover $29.95 (0-8160-1891-X).

381'.13 Franchises (Retail trade) [CIP] 88-3740

Foster, the author of several monographs on franchising and president of a consulting firm, has compiled this guide rating approximately 200 franchises. It surveys each business and provides a critical evaluation to assist readers in making intelligent business decisions.

The monograph is organized alphabetically in 12 sections, e.g., "Automotive Franchises," "Business Services," and then by company name. Each section is introduced by a one-page survey of the particular field. A table of contents allows rapid access to the various subject sections. A seven-page introduction describes the importance of franchises, tells how to use the book, and explains the steps to follow in evaluating a franchise. An alphabetical name index and a cross-reference "Index by Category" in the back of the book are intended to assist readers in locating entries.

Each entry begins with a rating of six subjects: industry experience, financial strength, fees and royalties, franchising experience, training and services, and satisfied franchisees. A single star signifies the lowest, and four stars, the highest rating. Following the company address and telephone number is such information as company history and number of outlets. Next are 7 to 10 sections describing the franchise and franchisees, projected earnings, franchisor's services, initial investment, advertising, contract highlights, litigation, and fees and royalties. These sections can be as short as one line or up to several lines. Concluding is a succinct list entitled "Franchise Highlights," which details for quick reference eight items of information: year operation began, year franchising began, outlets open, initial franchise fee, monthly royalty, advertising fee, training program, and term of franchise contract.

Generally throughout this work, boldface type highlights headings and contributes to easy use of the volume. The exception to this is the "Index by Category," which mixes various typefaces in a confusing manner, making it difficult to distinguish headings from entries.

Because franchises are a popular business topic, there is a plethora of books on the topic. *The Franchise Annual* [*RBB* Ag 87] covers over 3,600 businesses, the GPO's *Franchise Opportunities Handbook* [*RBB* D 15 83], about 1,500, and *The Source Book of Franchise Opportunities* [*RBB* D 15 85], approximately 1,400. Each of these works presents much of the same basic information as *RGF* but without the ratings. Similar in type of information provided but more selective in inclusion of companies is the slightly dated *Dow Jones-Irwin Guide to Franchises* (1982) and *220 Best Franchises to Buy* (1987).

In conclusion, there are several works that cover more franchises, give the same basic information, and have superior indexes. *RGF* is recommended only to public libraries that desire to supplement their collections.

LAW, PUBLIC ADMINISTRATION, SOCIAL PROBLEMS AND SERVICES

Family Law Dictionary: Marriage, Divorce, Children & Living Together. 1st ed. By Robin D. Leonard and Stephen R. Elias. Nolo Press, 1988. 193p. charts. illus. tables. paper $13.95 (0-87337-061-9).

346.015'03 Domestic relations—U.S.—Dictionaries [BKL] 88-60701

This *Dictionary* provides definitions for the layperson of over 500 legal terms and phrases used in the area of family law. Examples of family law issues are marriage, divorce, adoption, support, custody, guardianship, living together, paternity, and abortion. In addition to legal terms, nonlegal but related terms like *extended family* are defined. The authors of the *Dictionary* are both lawyers.

The book is arranged alphabetically and the outside edges of pages are marked to show the beginning of each new letter. Each entry is easy to discern because it appears in slightly larger, boldface type. The definitions of words and phrases vary in length from one sentence to several paragraphs; most entries are a paragraph or two. The authors employ several features to make entries clear. The context in which terms are used is explained, there are boxed examples to illustrate meaning, numerous cross-references to related terms are provided, and charts are sometimes used when concepts that vary from state to state are discussed. However, many entries generalize about state law, and readers may have to consult other sources to find the law for their state.

Black-and-white drawings are interspersed throughout the text, along with some "lesser known international comparisons" included to make the text entertaining. Though intended to be humorous, these features sometimes detract from the book. For instance, next to the definition of *discretion of the judge* is a drawing of a judge using his gavel to hit a person on the head.

This book presents clearer definitions than those found in *Black's Law Dictionary*, which is designed for the law student, lawyer, and judge, and libraries providing legal reference works for the general public will want to consider it.

Encyclopedia of Legal Information Sources. 1st ed. Ed. by Paul Wasserman and others. Gale, 1988. 634p. hardcover $140 (0-8103-0245-4).

016.34973 Law—U.S.—Bibliography l Law—Information services—U.S. [OCLC] 87-25901

The *Encyclopedia of Legal Information Sources* is an extensive subject bibliography designed to meet the needs of both legal professionals and laypersons searching for law books, periodicals, databases, and organizations. Like the other works published by Gale with similar titles, it is not an encyclopedia. It contains over 19,000 citations to 19 types of information sources, including laws, loose-leaf services, reference works, indexes, newsletters, statistics, and audiovisuals. Emphasis is placed upon federal law and national organizations. However, there are excellent sections listing legal sources for each state. Materials written for the layperson are included when high-quality publications exist, but lay publications for specific states, such as *California Marriage and Divorce Law* (Nolo Press, 1987) are not listed. Most materials have been published since 1980. Bibliographic citations include author, title, imprint, and publisher's address, but not price. Organization entries provide name and address, but no telephone number.

Entries are organized alphabetically in over 460 subject categories. Categories are further subdivided by type of source, for example, statutes, textbooks, or periodicals. Examples of categories are *Age Discrimination*, *AIDS*, *Bioethics*, *Veterans*, and *Wildlife*. A detailed outline of contents at the beginning of the book provides an alphabetic list of subject categories and cross-references for easy scanning. There are no title or organizational name indexes. These would be useful additions to future editions.

Prolific Gale editor Wasserman and university law librarians Gary McCann and Patricia Tobin have developed a valuable tool for all libraries providing legal information.

The Executive Branch of the U.S. Government: A Bibliography. Comp. by Robert Goehlert and Hugh Reynolds. Greenwood, 1989. 380p. indexes. hardcover $49.95 (0-313-26568-2; ISSN 0742-6909).

016.35304 U.S.—Executive departments—Bibliography [CIP] 88-24704

This source, part of Greenwood's Bibliographies and Indexes in Law and Political Science series, is designed to help "librarians, students, researchers, and government personnel" locate information about the executive branch. While the primary focus is on cabinet-level departments, some material dealing with subagencies (e.g., FBI, Census Bureau, IRS) will be found here. The listings, all for English-language works and mostly from 1945–85, include research monographs, articles, and dissertations. Government documents have been excluded. The editors tried to limit coverage to scholarly, analytical works that were "commercially available and that could be found in medium to large academic libraries." Goehlert is librarian for economics, political science, and criminal justice at Indiana University, and Reynolds is an evaluator in the U.S. General Accounting Office.

Most citations in this volume were selected from 11 indexes such as *Business Periodicals Index*, *Legal Resources Index*, *U.S. Political Science Documents*, *Writings on American History*, and *Sage Public Administration Abstracts*. Article entries give author, title, journal, pages, and date. Entries for monographs show author, title, and imprint. Annotations are not provided.

The approximately 4,100 citations are arranged in 15 chapters, the first covering general studies, the remaining covering individual departments like Agriculture, Defense, State, and the Postal Service. Numbering is consecutive throughout the volume; entries within each chapter are alphabetical by name of author. Accurate author and subject indexes are included. The subject index has subdivisions, but they are not extensive. It would be helpful if future editions had chapter subdivisions and a more detailed subject index.

Goehlert coauthored another bibliography on one part of the executive branch, *The American Presidency: A Bibliography* [*RBB* D 1 87]. It contains over 7,000 unannotated citations and is arranged by topical chapters (e.g., "The Presidency and the World," "The Selection of Presidents"). *The Executive Branch* doesn't focus on the presidency, so there is little overlap. Of a random sample from the chapter "General Studies" in this book, less than 10 percent were found in *The American Presidency*.

The Executive Branch may be a useful addition to small collections that do not contain the indexes from which it was compiled. However, since many of those indexes are available in electronic form, researchers may prefer to create their own customized bibliographies.

BNA's Directory of State Courts, Judges, and Clerks: A State-by-State Listing. 2d ed. Comp. by Kamla J. King and Judith Springberg. BNA Books, 1988. 446p. index. paper $50 (0-87179-598-1).

347.73'1 Courts—U.S.—States—Directories I Judges—U.S.—States—Directories I Clerks of court—U.S.—States—Directories [CIP] 88-22264

The first edition of *BNA's Directory of State Courts, Judges, and Clerks* (1986) has been revised with a useful addition: charts of the structure of each state's court system. These charts, which were first published by the National Center for State Courts in *State Court Organization, 1987*, include courts of last resort, intermediate appellate courts, general jurisdiction courts, and courts of limited jurisdiction. Each chart indicates routes of appeal, subject matter of jurisdiction, number of authorized judicial officers, and types of trials. The editors mention as a caveat that the directory information is more up-to-date than the charts, so there may be discrepancies between the number of judicial officers in the charts and in the directory listings.

The directory listings, which were verified between February and June 1988, include judges and clerks for the three top levels of the court structure in the 50 states, the District of Columbia, American Samoa, Guam, Puerto Rico, and the Virgin Islands. The courts are arranged by level beginning with the court of last resort. Each entry has the official name of the court; the name, address, and telephone number of the clerk; and the name and title of the judge, the city where the judge has an office, and the telephone number. Judges are listed either with the presiding or chief judge first, alphabetically, or by seniority, depending on what the state court administrators supplied. An appendix lists the state court administrators, their addresses, and telephone numbers. A personal-name index concludes the book.

Compared with the first edition, the editors claim that 85 new courts have been added and 85 percent of the courts reported changes. This is a specialized, comprehensive directory that is a necessary purchase for law libraries and others that require current information regarding state courts, judges, and clerks.

The Public Administration Dictionary. 2d ed. By Ralph C. Chandler and Jack C. Plano. ABC-Clio, 1988. 430p. bibliog. index. hardcover $39.50 (0-87436-498-1); paper $18 (0-87436-499-X).

350'.0003 Public administration—Dictionaries [CIP] 87-32045

This is another in the fine series of Clio Dictionaries in Political Science. The authors, faculty members at Western Michigan University, have edited other titles in the series. The format remains the same: 330 alphabetically arranged entries within seven subject chapters. Chapter headings include "Public Management," "Bureaucracy and Administrative Organization," "Financial Administration," and "Public Law and Regulation." In each entry, after an initial definition paragraph, a second "Significance" paragraph places the concept, theory, theorist, or institution in historical or contemporary perspective.

The editors have added 25 new entries (e.g., *double dipping*, *Circular A-95*) since the first edition in 1982 and revised numerous others. Cross-references and an index add to the book's accessibility. A $7^1/_2$-page bibliography includes 1987 titles.

The Facts On File Dictionary of Public Administration was reviewed by *RBB* [Je 15 86] and found satisfactory. It is a larger book that defines more terms, although usually more briefly. The 5,000 entries often include bibliographic references current through 1984, thus enhancing its usefulness. A comparison of the two works shows that the work under review provides more detailed definitions of such terms as *cooptation*, *privatization*, *line and staff*, *burnout*, and *quasi-legislative*. While the "Significance" paragraphs are especially useful, the succinct definitions in the Facts On File work coupled with the references could suffice for many users.

In summary, *The Public Administration Dictionary* is another quality work that academic, special, and large public libraries will find useful, but libraries owning *The Facts On File Dictionary of Public Administration* may not need the newer work.

The Municipal Year Book, 1988. v.55. ICMA, 1120 G St. NW, Washington, DC 20005, 1988. 459p. bibliog. charts. index. tables. hardcover $69.50 (0-87326-963-2; ISSN 0077-2186).

352.008 Municipal government [OCLC] 34-27121

This is the fifty-fifth edition of the basic reference annual on local government, last reviewed in *RSBR*, December 1, 1981. The format of recent years has been retained: six sections furnish a combination of analytical articles, tabular data, directory information, and bibliographic references. A cumulative index covers the four preceding editions as well as this volume.

The first section consists of five substantial, footnoted articles on selected current issues such as privatization. Both here and in subsequent sections, tables and well-designed graphs supplement the text, and key points are highlighted in boxes. The second section contains four surveys of intergovernmental developments, including two regular features: reviews of federal and of state actions affecting local governments.

The remaining four sections contain important recurring features. Three salary surveys (municipal officials; county officials; police, fire, and refuse collection) make up the third section: the accompanying analyses carefully outline the methodology and limitations of the data. The fourth section contains profiles of individual cities and counties in tabular form arranged by state; data are supplied for a selection of demographic and financial indicators.

The fifth section is in two parts. The first consists of 10 directory listings covering a variety of local government associations, and, by state, lists of the names of seven top municipal officials in all U.S. cities with over 2,500 people and six top county officials for all U.S. counties. These latter two listings also include for each governmental entity a mid-decade population estimate and a telephone number. The second part contains descriptions of 73 organizations providing professional services of importance to local and state governments. The address and telephone number, the executive director, and any major publications are indicated.

The final section provides bibliographic references under 17 headings (basic references, statistical sources, and 15 functional areas). An annotated list of books and reports is followed by a periodicals list and, often, a description of online services. Sources listed date mainly from 1986. The section concludes with a list of publishers' addresses.

Contributors of articles include academics, professional staff of the International City Management Association (ICMA) and other associations, government officials, and specialists from the private sector. Much of the data was obtained through a questionnaire program administered by ICMA.

This yearbook remains a fundamental source for serious students of local government in the U.S.

Free Help from Uncle Sam to Start Your Own Business (Or Expand the One You Have). By William M. Alarid. Puma Publishing Co.; dist. by Quality Books, 1988. 158p. bibliog. index. paper $9.95 (0-940673-37-1).

353.0082'048 Small business—Government policy—U.S.—Handbooks, manuals, etc. [CIP] 88-2411

More than 90 programs of federal support for small business are described in this guide. The descriptions are taken from the *Catalog of Federal Domestic Assistance* and are arranged, like those in the *Catalog*, according to the five-digit federal domestic assistance program number scheme, where the first two digits identify the administering agency. Only some of the *Catalog* descriptors are carried over into this guide—*Federal Agency, Objectives, Types of Assistance, Uses and Use Restrictions, Eligibility Requirements,* and *Information Contacts*—and the information included under a descriptor may not be as extensive as that found in the *Catalog*. *Catalog* information not reprinted in this guide includes application and award process, assistance considerations, examples of funded projects, and criteria for selecting proposals. Following the main body of the guide is a 15-page section containing brief descriptions of a variety of additional federal support and information programs and services. Three appendixes list selected nongovernment business associations, a few "Useful Books," and selected federal agency telephone numbers.

An introductory section defines 15 types of assistance, seven of them financial, and assigns them letter codes *A* through *O*. Then follow lists of program descriptions, letter-coded, under nine broad headings. There is also a subject index at the back of the guide. Included in the front matter is a section of brief anecdotal accounts of more than 20 grants awarded to individuals or firms for particular projects, reprinted from Matthew Lesko's *Getting Yours*.

This inexpensive guide could serve as a convenient alternative source, even in libraries that get the annual *Catalog* and its midyear set of update pages, since the *Catalog* is forbiddingly complex in its arrangement and covers much more than small business. But no plans for updating this guide are disclosed, and those in need of fuller information on the programs covered are not referred to the *Catalog* either in the "Useful Books" list or elsewhere in the book.

Records of the Presidency: Presidential Papers and Libraries from Washington to Reagan. By Frank L. Schick and others. Oryx, 1989. 309p. bibliog. index. hardcover $49.50 (0-89774-277-X).

353.0085'2 Presidents—U.S.—Archives [CIP] 88-28222

This survey of presidential papers and libraries is arranged in four parts. The latter three describe the major types of repositories for presidential papers: the Manuscript Division of the Library of Congress (23 presidents), historical societies and special libraries (7 presidents), and the presidential libraries administered by the National Archives (10 presidents). The first part furnishes background information on the three types of repositories and on federal legislation relating to presidential libraries. Also discussed are guides to presidential records and presidential book collections in the Library of Congress, the White House libraries, and presidential homes.

Brief biographies of each president are provided in the appropriate section in the latter parts of this guide along with abbreviated outlines/indexes of the collections. Following each biography in the second part is a summary of the provenance information found in the Presidents' Papers Index series, issued by the Library of Congress for all the presidents with papers in the Manuscript Division except Van Buren, for whom there is a published *Calendar of the Papers.* The third part reviews the sets of presidential records maintained by historical societies (five presidents) or special libraries (Hayes and Hoover).

The fourth part of this guide describes the eight presidential libraries: the planning of the buildings, the research materials available, and any associated facilities. A chapter is devoted to the two libraries in the planning stage (Nixon and Reagan). An appendix supplies several statistical tables on the presidential libraries. Two further appendixes are directories: of major presidential records collections and of presidential historic sites. A fourth appendix presents an overview of the White House filing system.

A bibliography at the back of the guide cites selected works on the general subject of presidential records and on each president. Schick, the principal compiler, holds a Ph.D. from the University of Michigan and has served as a federal government official. Former president Gerald Ford contributed a foreword.

This informative, up-to-date guide will be a valuable addition to reference collections in academic and public libraries where there is an interest in historical research.

The State and Local Government Political Dictionary. By Jeffrey M. Elliot and Sheikh R. Ali. ABC-Clio, 1988. 325p. index. hardcover $37.50 (0-87436-417-5); paper $17 (0-87436-512-0).

353.9'03 State governments—Dictionaries I Local government—U.S.—Dictionaries I Federal government—U.S.—Dictionaries I Municipal government—U.S.—Dictionaries I Local finance—U.S.—Dictionaries [CIP] 87-18722

This new title in the ABC-Clio Dictionaries in Political Science series is arranged in the same format as previous titles, i.e., with definition and significance paragraphs for each term. The authors (members of the faculty of North Carolina Central University) have a combined total of 20 years of study, research, and teaching of state and local government.

The work is divided into 11 subject chapters, with the 290 entries arranged alphabetically within them. Representative chapter headings are "The Judicial Branch," "Cities and Metropolitan Areas," and "Financing State and Local Government." *See also* references are noted at the end of each entry. Five pages of notes at the end of the volume document direct quotations in the entries and serve as a bibliography. Works cited are current through 1987. A 14-page index provides further access for users.

The entries provide clear explanations that will be helpful for a wide range of users. In some instances, examples of the term or the pros and cons of the topic are explored, thus providing the user with a good perspective beyond a straight definition. However, some of the topics covered are also in another recent ABC-Clio title, *The Public Administration Dictionary,* reviewed above, although the text is unique in each book.

For libraries where users need special access to state and local government terms, this new work will be helpful.

American Governors and Gubernatorial Elections, 1979–1987. Comp. by Marie Marmo Mullaney. Meckler, 1988. 101p. bibliog. tables. hardcover $35 (0-88736-316-4).

353.9'131 Governors—U.S.—Election—Statistics I Elections—U.S.—States—Statistics [CIP] 88-13248

This slim volume supplements a 1979 compilation from the same publisher covering the period 1775–1978, compiled by Roy R. Glashan. In this supplement, each state gets a pair of facing pages containing two brief tables and much white space. The first table lists governors who held office during the period covered and provides birthplace and date, age upon assuming office and the date, party affiliation, major occupations, state residence, and (when appropriate) age at death and the date. The second table supplies information about gubernatorial elections held during the period, giving the dates, the Democratic and Republican vote totals and the percentage of the total vote they represented, other significant vote totals, and the total scattered vote, each with the percentage. An occasional explanatory note is included to elucidate special circumstances. A brief bibliographic note at the end of the book cites sources of further information, including the *Almanac of American Politics*, the latest edition of which provides fuller coverage for the more recent years while not limiting itself to governors.

The parent compilation included excerpts from the governors' speeches and writings; this supplement does not. It will not be an essential purchase for most library collections.

The ABCs of Armageddon: The Language of the Nuclear Age. By Donald J. Colen. World Almanac; dist. by Ballantine, 1988. 208p. bibliog. index. hardcover $16.95 (0-345-35224-6).

355'.0217 Nuclear warfare—Dictionaries [CIP] 87-50913

Disinformation, Bambi, MAD, and *exotic kill mechanism* are some of the more than 250 terms covered in what the author describes as a "primer with a point of view." Definitions have been derived from books and periodicals on the subject of nuclear arms and strategy since Hiroshima. Notes at the end of the book provide documentation for entries. In addition to the notes, there are appended sections with a list of acronyms, a bibliography, and a short index with two sorts of entries: broad concepts, such as *arms control*, and personal names, such as *Weinberger, Caspar*. Entry length ranges from one paragraph to several pages, and italicized words indicate that those terms are also entries. Coverage extends to the December 1987 negotiations on intermediate-range missiles in Europe.

The introduction gives a short history of the arms race, and what the author sees as the insanity of these policies and their "verbal cloud of obfuscation" is the point of view evident throughout the book. This tone enlivens some entries (e.g., "*likely*—A not-very-nuclear sounding word that is as close as an expert will ever get to saying 'maybe'"), but detracts from the work's credibility as a reference source (e.g., referring to McGeorge Bundy, George F. Kennan, Robert S. McNamara, and Gerard Smith as the "Gang of Four").

Some of these terms are briefly defined in the *Department of Defense Dictionary of Military and Associated Terms* (Joint Chiefs of Staff, 1986) and the *Dictionary of Military Terms*, compiled by Trevor Dupuy (Wilson, 1986; [*RBB* Ja 1 87]), but there are two dictionaries that are very similar to this work in their coverage of the language of nuclear confrontation: *The A-Z of Nuclear Jargon* (Routledge & Kegan Paul; dist. by Methuen, 1986) and *The Language of Nuclear War* (Harper/Perennial, 1987), both reviewed in *RBB* [Jl 87]. The latter work is the most extensive and balanced of the three, with 1,200 entries, but only Colen provides source documentation. Libraries with either of the books reviewed last year will likely not need *The ABC's of Armageddon* for definition of terms; however, Colen's lengthy entries, use of source material, and readable style give the book added value.

Encyclopedia of the World's Air Forces. By Michael J. H. Taylor. Facts On File, 1988. 211p. illus. index. tables. hardcover $35 (0-8160-2004-3).

358.4'003 Air forces—Dictionaries [CIP] 88-6970

For the price, this is a worthwhile addition to medium-sized to large libraries. The text, heavily illustrated with attractive color photographs (many of them stock photos), gives a brief description of each country's air force, including its origins, and has a table giving indigenous (official) name, where headquartered, number of major bases, and number of aircraft by kind. Large air forces, naturally, have longer write-ups; entries range from one-half page to six pages. Each entry also includes a small reproduction of the basic insignia and a very small world map with the country marked. These little maps are totally inadequate, barely able to indicate continent. At the end of the volume is a specifications table arranged alphabetically by aircraft, giving version, engines, wingspan, length, maximum take-off weight, maximum speed, service ceiling, range, and "Accommodation/Weapons/Remarks." There is a brief glossary and an index of aircraft. The author is noted as affiliated with the Jane's organization, so it is assumed his information is the best available, though no sources are cited.

Naval and army aviation units, when they exist in a country, are given generally short shrift. Bophuthatswana, Ciskei, Transkei, and Venda (so-called "independent tribal homelands" within South Africa) are accorded independent nation status in this work, and their small air forces, none of which have combat aircraft, are described. While this is a useful work for libraries, one might wish it had a few features found in some of its predecessor works in the field. William Green and John Fricker's *Air Forces of the World* (Macdonald, 1958) has several plates of insignia, including naval variants. *Air Forces of the World* (Simon & Schuster, 1979) by Mark Hewish and others includes maps indicating the major air bases in each country and has as a supplement silhouettes of the aircraft mentioned. If one needs that sort of information, there is always *Jane's All the World's Aircraft* (annual), but better maps and larger insignia would be a help here.

The Facts On File Dictionary of Health Care Management. By Joseph C. Rhea and others. Facts On File, 1988. 692p. bibliog. illus. hardcover $50 (0-8160-1637-2).

362.1'068 Health services administration—Dictionaries [CIP] 87-6831

Here is a fairly comprehensive *Dictionary* for the health-care management field. It covers much more than just definitions of terms and concepts. Also included are biographies of significant individuals, summaries of laws and court decisions, descriptions of periodicals, and information on associations and government agencies relating to health-care administration. Criteria for inclusion were based on the use of terms in several texts on health-care management and their central importance to individuals working in the field. Terms included encompass the following areas: accounting, basic business practices, ethical issues, finances, labor relations, management, personnel, program evaluation, project management, public administration, and public relations.

Most entries range in length from one sentence to one-half page, with some exceptions. For example, the entry *code of ethics* includes the codes for the American Medical Record Association, the American College of Hospital Administrators, and the National Association of Medical Staff Services and goes on for five pages. Several entries are accompanied by illustrations (e.g., *billing journal*) and graphs projecting estimates (e.g., *estimated income*). Although there are entries for journals and associations, no directory information is given. These entries provide only a description. Price information for journals and addresses and telephone numbers of associations will need to be checked in other resources. The *Dictionary* is very generous in its use of *see* references, especially for alternate names and acronyms. *See also* references are also used effectively. For example, the entry *proxy decision-making* includes references to *Baby Doe regulations*; *competency*; *dilemma, ethical*; *ethics committee*; and *paternalism*.

There are two appendixes. Appendix 1 provides a chronology of American health-care management from 1633 to 1987, and appendix 2 is a bibliography of sources consulted in developing the *Dictionary*. Because the subject of health-care management is of concern to many individuals, this *Dictionary* is recommended for medical libraries, academic libraries with programs relating to health care, public administration, or public policy, and large public libraries.

National Continuing Care Directory: Retirement Communities with Nursing Care. 2d ed. Ed. by Ann Trueblood Raper and Anne C. Kalicki. AARP Books; dist. by Little, Brown, 1988. 449p. bibliog. indexes. hardcover $19.95 (0-673-24885-2).

362.1'6 Life care communities—U.S.—Directories I Retirement communities—U.S.—Directories I Aged—Care—U.S. [CIP] 87-28831

Continuing-care or life-care retirement communities have become increasingly popular, as they provide for independent living and include on-site nursing care at a fixed cost set by a life-care contract. The second edition of this *Directory* not only includes information on U.S. centers but also offers guidelines to potential retirees. It was produced by the American Association of Retired Persons in conjunction with the American Association of Homes for the Aging, a nonprofit organization concerned with nonprofit housing, health, and community services for the aged.

The first section reviews continuing-care options and, new to this edition, includes various worksheets and checklists for users to calculate potential expenses and make comparisons easily. The directory section includes 366 one-page descriptions arranged alphabetically by state and then by name. Each entry is divided into four parts. The first part includes the name, address, telephone number, date when opened, description of the buildings, current population, geographic location of the facility with an accompanying outline map, and if there is availability or a waiting list. The second part provides details on housing and services, such as size of living units, entrance fees and monthly fees, and if meals, housekeeping, transportation, and utilities are included in the fees. The third and fourth parts of each entry provide details on assisted living and personal care and nursing care—all inclusive plans. Additional services such as beauty shops, craft programs, libraries, or swimming pools are shown in chart form in the "Special Features Index," which follows the directory section.

There are two indexes: a metropolitan-area index followed by a listing of communities in nonmetropolitan areas, and a subject index that includes mostly the names of each facility. This up-to-date guide, containing many new facilities opened since the first edition was published in 1984 [*RBB* Ap 1 85], will be an essential reference item for most public libraries.

Directory of Residential Centers for Adults with Developmental Disabilities. Oryx, 1989. 396p. indexes. paper $75 (0-89774-533-7).
362.1'968 Developmentally disabled—Institutional care—U.S.—Directories I Group homes for the developmentally disabled—U.S.—Directories [CIP] 88-30451

Until recently, care for people with developmental disabilities took one of two forms: home care with no community assistance or a comprehensive public institution. Today there are a variety of care and treatment centers available. The *Directory of Residential Centers for Adults with Developmental Disabilities* describes over 1,400 facilities nationwide offering the following services: "residential treatment, supervised apartment settings, group homes, outpatient/day treatment programs, inpatient/hospital programs or crisis shelters." It is a descriptive list of programs, not an evaluative guide to choosing a program.

Treatment centers are cataloged alphabetically by state and by city. There are entries for each of the 50 states and the District of Columbia. All entries include address, telephone number, contact person, facility profile, client profile, and details of specific services. The facility profile may contain all or some of the following: year established, accessibility of services, sponsoring agency, programs offered, ownership, sources of referral, and funding sources. A brief description of the purpose and location of the center is included in this section. The client profile outlines the ages served, IQ range, and developmental disabilities treated. Services offered are divided into two sections. The first, "Clinical, Social and Rehabilitative Services," lists the therapeutic approach of the program, the type of service offered (counseling, support, physical or occupational therapy), and the number of professionals employed by the center. The second, "Educational and Vocational Services," lists various life-skill programs. Information about the treatment centers was gathered through questionnaires and telephone interviews. The amount of information provided, therefore, is dependent on the responses given by the centers.

Two indexes provide access to the entries. The first categorizes programs by the disorders they treat—autism, cerebral palsy, chronic mental illness, Down's syndrome, etc. A second index categorizes the programs by the type of service offered, such as group home, residential treatment, or supervised apartment living. Entries in the index give program name, city, and state, not page number.

A foreword by associates at the Center for Residential and Community Services at the University of Minnesota defines developmental disabilities as well as gives a historical overview of their treatment. A brief bibliography at the end of this section suggests further reading. The book's appearance is like other Oryx directories; the typeface used throughout is small.

The *Directory of Residential Centers for Adults with Developmental Disabilities* is a useful guide for public library patrons beginning a search for a treatment center.

Third Opinion: An International Directory of Alternative Therapy Centers for the Treatment and Prevention of Cancer. By John M. Fink. Avery, 1988. 268p. bibliog. indexes. paper $12.95 (0-89529-382-X).
362.1'96994 Cancer—Alternative treatment—Directories [CIP]

Entries in this directory for the consumer are divided into four major sections: "Treatment Centers," the largest section; "Educational Centers," listing places where people can be educated about programs available at various treatment centers; "Support Groups"; and "Information Services," organizations providing information about treatment centers and patient organizations. Under each entry are a discussion of costs and method of payment, background information for many clinics, name of person to contact for more information, treatments offered, and length of treatment. Also included are a glossary of terms and an up-to-date bibliography on the subject of alternative medical treatment for cancer. There are geographic and subject indexes.

The glossary provides definitions of many of the therapeutic treatments mentioned in the text, such as *laetrile, antineoplastons, coffee enemas,* and *Gerovital H3*, that can easily be understood by the layperson. However, there are many terms used to describe treatments not included in the glossary: *zinc, Pingxiaopian Formula, Krebs cycle.* The indexing could be improved by grouping those clinics that are registered charities, those that are nonprofit, and those primarily holistic in their approach to disease. However, the index does an adequate job of identifying most therapeutic treatments.

Coverage of institutions is adequate, giving users an idea of treatments available to them across the U.S. and abroad. Other countries included are Mexico, West Germany, England, Australia, Greece, Switzerland, Scotland, Spain, and the Philippines. The author contacted personnel at all clinics. Programs and individual clinics are not evaluated. Directions such as "Call first; they may move from this address shortly" may help users evaluate services. Librarians should be aware that some of these clinics and treatments are quite controversial, and most are not accepted by the medical establishment. A statement in the introduction promises updated editions, and a "Questionnaire for Patients" is included for users wishing to send comments to the author.

This directory is superior to *The Directory of Holistic Medicine and Alternate Health Care Services in the U.S.* (Health Plus Publishers, 1986 [*RBB* S 15 86]). It does not contain as many entries as that directory, which covers more than just cancer treatment, but it gives more information for the establishments selected for inclusion. Many of the educational or informational organizations included here are also listed in Gale's *Encyclopedia of Associations*, but information on treatment centers is difficult to locate. An excellent discussion of available reference sources on holistic medicine is found in *Medical Reference Services Quarterly* (vol. 7, no. 2, 1988).

This directory may be useful in public libraries getting questions concerning alternative medical practice or holistic medicine.

The Encyclopedia of Suicide. By Glen Evans and Norman L. Farberow. Facts On File, 1988. 434p. bibliog. charts. index. tables. hardcover $40 (0-8160-1397-7).
362.2 Suicide—Dictionaries I Suicide—U.S.—Dictionaries [CIP] 88-11173

Evans, president of the American Association of Journalists and Authors, and Farberow, a psychologist, cofounder and director of the Los Angeles Suicide Prevention Center, and coauthor of several books related to the subject, have produced a comprehensive work on a socially prevalent and disturbing problem. *The Encyclopedia of Suicide* has been patterned after and is intended to be a companion reference to Facts On File's encyclopedias on alcoholism and drug abuse (favorably reviewed by the Board [*RBB* O 15 83, My 15 85]). The authors state this is a "work in progress" to be updated with the results of new research in subsequent editions. The work is directed toward both professionals and laypersons. Following Farberow's extensive introduction giving an overview of suicide as a social, cultural, and historical phenomenon from antiquity to the present, the body of the *Encyclopedia* treats various aspects of the subject. Arranged in A–Z format, over 500 entries explore everything from "psychological concerns to political and legal factors, from socioeconomic aspects to educational and religious considerations" in nontechnical language. Entries range from a few sentences (*humor, loss of* or *insomnia, as suicide clue*) to very extensive discussions (*assisted suicide, Alcoholics Anonymous*, or *homosexuals*), but most are about 700 words.

The entries identify famous suicides (Judas, Socrates, Hitler, Plath, Hemingway); noted authors or researchers on the subject (Freud, Durkheim, Alvarez); historical events involving suicide (Masada, Jonestown, Treblinka); particular groups (adolescents, dentists, farmers, black Americans, Protestants); geographic areas (New York City, South Dakota, India, Africa); names of organizations and agencies (alcoholic treatment center, Hemlock Society, American Association of Suicidology); titles of books and movies (*Romeo and Juliet, The Bell Jar, The Sorrows of Young Werther*); related medical or psychological problems (anorexia nervosa, bulimia, depression), various methods of suicide (firearms, autocide, pills); and numerous miscellaneous subjects (M*A*S*H theme song, Dungeons and Dragons, lithium, the business cycle). There is the entry *Empire State Building*, but curiously not one for the Golden Gate Bridge.

Relevant statistics are found in some entries. References to published works are of two types: either informal internal mentions or more formal bibliographic citations at the end of the entry.

The only weakness of the *Encyclopedia*'s organization is its cross-references, which are of two types: *see* and *see also* references and internal references in capital letters; however, the latter type is not always applied. Cross-references are conspicuously lacking for some obviously related or redundant entries: no direct linkage is made between *notes, suicide* and *suicide notes*, for example, nor between *fallacies about suicide* and *myths concerning suicide*.

Several appendixes provide detailed statistical figures and tables on U.S. suicide rates by race, sex, geographic area, marital status, month of occurrence, and method of suicide. Most of these list the source of the information. An extensive section on sources of information covers U.S. national organizations, associations, and government agencies, but the alphabetical arrangement makes this less than ideally useful. Another section lists suicide prevention centers by state and city, giving name, address, telephone, and hours of availability. Canadian provincial or territorial agencies and selected international and foreign organizations are also covered. Major English-language journals are listed to complete the section on sources of information. The book concludes with an extensive bibliography and a subject index.

Because of its scope, authority, and coherent presentation of the myriad aspects of the subject, *The Encyclopedia of Suicide* will be essential for guidance counselors, public health workers, and for high school, public, and academic libraries.

Crime and the Elderly: An Annotated Bibliography. Comp. by Ron H. Aday. Greenwood, 1988. 118p. indexes. hardcover $35.95 (0-313-25470-2; ISSN 0743-7560).
016.3628'8 Aged—U.S.—Crime against—Bibliography I Aged offenders—U.S.—Bibliography [CIP] 88-30051

This is number 8 in a series of bibliographies on the elderly in America. Three prior volumes in the series have been reviewed in *RBB*: *Elder Neglect and Abuse* [Mr 15 86], *Retirement* [Ap 15 87], and *Federal Public Policy on Aging since 1960* [Ja 15 88]. This one also follows the bibliographic format of the social sciences, with publication date in parentheses following the author's name and the use of initials instead of first names. The minor irritations of this format (difficulty in finding an author solely by initials in a very large catalog) were commented on in the 1988 review cited above. Monograph citations give publisher and city but not address or price; journal citations give pagination, volume, and number but not month (unless there are no volume numbers).

Editor Aday is an authority on two aspects of crime and the elderly: the elderly person as a potential victim of crime and the elderly criminal, especially the aging felon in prison. He is presently associate professor of gerontology at Middle Tennessee State University.

The bibliography is divided into 10 chapters, five covering aspects of crime against the elderly, including abuse and neglect, and five covering the elderly as criminals themselves, including crime patterns, causes of criminality, and a chapter on rehabilitation. There is a third section entitled "Resources and Information," listing crime-prevention programs, state agencies for the elderly, state corrective agencies (usually the State Department of Corrections), and such organizations as the American Geriatrics Society, Legal Services for the Elderly, and the Select Committee on the Aging. Author and subject indexes conclude the volume.

Each of the 361 items in the bibliography is given an annotation averaging about 10 lines. These summary annotations are descriptive rather than critical but are generally helpful. Reflecting the relatively recent interest in this topic, materials listed were published in the 1970s and 1980s.

This work satisfies a need, particularly since works on criminality among the elderly have not previously been gathered into so convenient a format. Like the other numbers in this valuable series, it will find a place in academic, large public, and social-service libraries.

Genocide: A Critical Bibliographic Review. Ed. by Israel W. Charny. Facts On File, 1988. 273p. bibliog. index. hardcover $40 (0-8160-1903-7).
016.3641'51 Genocide—Bibliography [CIP] 87-33215

Intended to stimulate the study of genocide and its prevention, this book contains commentary and bibliography on all its aspects. Editor Charny, executive director of the Institute of the International Conference on the Holocaust and Genocide, Jerusalem, explains in his introduction that efforts to understand, even define, genocide in its broadest sense are new and cross-disciplinary. In order to organize what is now known, he has assembled articles written by scholars in various fields such as history, psychology, sociology, literature, and political science. The carefully selected, critically annotated bibliographies of print and nonprint materials that support these essays should both facilitate and encourage further exploration.

In addition to the introduction, Charny himself has contributed three chapters: "The Study of Genocide," "Intervention and Prevention of Genocide," and "Understanding the Psychology of Genocidal Destructiveness." He describes these and the other 10 chapters as providing "an authoritative, encyclopedia-like statement of the knowledge base in a given field or area of study." Background information about the 10 contributing editors is given in the introduction, but their expertise and concern for their subjects are readily apparent in the text. The Holocaust, the Armenian genocide, and the Cambodian genocide are treated separately. Other chapters cover less-known genocides, history, and philosophical concerns. Three chapters by Samuel Totte, a peace researcher from the University of Arkansas, are devoted to the literature, art, and film of the Holocaust, genocide, and nuclear destruction.

Each contributor was asked to follow uniform guidelines in addressing the topic. The result is that the chapters, while reflecting the different topics and approach of the authors, are clearly organized. The bibliographies are current, extensive, and annotated and arranged to complement the content of the text. A detailed author, subject, and title index is provided to the entire book.

Other recent comprehensive bibliographic works have focused specifically on the Holocaust, for example, David Szonyi's extensive compilation, *The Holocaust: An Annotated Bibliography and Resource Guide* [*RBB* Ag 85], and Abraham and Hersel Edelheit's *Bibli-*

ography on Holocaust Literature [*RBB* My 15 87]. These both include sections dealing with legal aspects and world responses. Charny notes the omission of these concerns in the present book and indicates that a second volume is planned to treat them separately. In this book Charny has appropriately broadened the focus. The Holocaust continues to loom large (the essay here by Alan L. Berger is entitled "The Holocaust: The Ultimate and Archetypal Genocide"), but its implications need to be studied in the even wider context made possible by this excellent text.

Genocide: A Critical Bibliographic Review offers more than a compilation of references. Much can be learned through reading its essays and annotations. It fulfills the editor's intention of providing an authoritative overview of the subject from a variety of perspectives. It will be an excellent starting place for more study. Not surprisingly, its tone throughout is one of sincere concern; it both informs and enlightens the reader.

Intellectual Freedom and Censorship: An Annotated Bibliography. By Frank Hoffmann. Scarecrow, 1989. 244p. indexes. hardcover $27.50 (0-8108-2145-1).

016.3633'1 Censorship—U.S.—Bibliography I Freedom of information—U.S.—Bibliography I Libraries—U.S.—Censorship—Bibliography [CIP] 88-18811

Hoffmann is an associate professor at the School of Library Science, Sam Houston State University. He wrote *Popular Culture and Libraries* (Library Professional Publications, 1984) as well as several music reference publications. He conceived this bibliography as a general introduction to the field of intellectual freedom and censorship, with students in high schools and colleges as its primary audience. Its 900 entries include books, professional journals, the popular newspaper and magazine press, and government reports. Hoffmann has limited citations to items valuable for research, those easily understood by the lay reader, and, for the most part, those readily available in libraries. The scope is further restricted to the U.S. Each citation has complete bibliographic information and is followed by a descriptive annotation ranging from less than 10 words to more than 100. Sources cited cover a wide range of the sociopolitical spectrum.

Hoffmann has organized the citations into five parts: "Theoretical Foundations of Censorship and Intellectual Freedom," "Key Court Cases," "Professions Concerned with Intellectual Freedom," "Pro-Censorship/Anti-Censorship: Representative Individuals and Groups," and "Cases of Censorship in the Mass Media." The beginning of the book has a five-page chronology of "Milestones in the History of Censorship," and each section begins with a one- or two-page introductory essay. Citations were found for such topics as significant court cases, the Pentagon Papers, freedom of access to government information, privatization, the U.S. Commission on Obscenity and Pornography, the Meese Commission, as well as to materials dealing with individual censored items like books, rock music, theater, and television programs. Most of the citations are from the 1970s and 1980s. Separate personal-name and subject indexes give access by author of article cited, author of material censored, people discussed in the annotations, title of material censored, organization, and place.

Medium-size and large libraries may own Ralph McCoy's *Freedom of the Press: An Annotated Bibliography* (Southern Illinois Univ., 1968) and its *Supplement* (1979). That work, with its more than 12,000 citations, is a comprehensive treatment through 1977. Arranged alphabetically by author, it has an index similar in coverage to Hoffmann. Its descriptive annotations run about the same length. Hoffmann's work is more accessible due to its topical organization, limited scope, and more manageable physical size. In addition, it carries citations to many important events that have occurred since McCoy's cutoff date.

The Board recommends Hoffmann's work as an important purchase for all libraries in aiding access to information about intellectual freedom and censorship.

Drug, Alcohol, and Other Addictions: A Directory of Treatment Centers and Prevention Programs Nationwide. Oryx, 1989. 775p. paper $45 (0-89774-416-0).

362.2'9286 Narcotic addicts—Rehabilitation—U.S.—Directories I Alcoholics—Rehabilitation—U.S.—Directories I Drug abuse—Treatment—U.S.—Directories I Alcoholism—Treatment—U.S.—Directories [CIP] 89-2867

This is a comprehensive directory of substance-abuse treatment facilities and programs in the U.S. and its territories. Nearly 18,000 centers and programs involved in the prevention and treatment of alcohol, drug, and behavioral addictions are listed. The entries are from state and local directories of programs, telephone companies' yellow pages, professional journals, and the National Institute of Drug Abuse's NDATUS database. All addresses have been verified through the U.S. Postal Service's "Address Correction Requested" form. Each agency has been contacted by mail and verified in secondary sources whenever possible.

The entries are arranged by state, then by city, and, within city, alphabetically by the name of the center or program. A table of contents directs the user to the pages for each state or territory. A list of abbreviations used and a sample entry explain the format. Each entry includes the name, address, and telephone number of the facility. Sometimes more information is provided. Entries may include any of the following features: name and title of contact person, addictions treated, treatment methods, setting and number of clients, client services offered, number of clients served in 1987, specialty groups served, type of ownership, and principal sources of funding.

Unlike other directories for substance-abuse centers published recently, *Drug, Alcohol, and Other Addictions* offers no evaluation of the programs listed in its pages. No one has visited any of the facilities. There is no introductory material about the nature of addiction. There is, however, a list of questions that those seeking a treatment center would do well to ask. *Rehab: A Comprehensive Guide to Recommended Drug-Alcohol Treatment Centers in the United States* (Harper, 1988) and *The 100 Best Treatment Centers for Alcoholism and Drug Abuse* (Avon, 1988), both reviewed by the Board [*RBB* Mr 15 89], are two inexpensive directories that offer evaluations of a limited number of facilities (164 and 100, respectively). Their more detailed descriptions complement this work.

The size and scope of this work make it very useful for all public library collections. Patrons from Guam to New York City will be able to locate a treatment facility or educational program within a reasonable distance of their homes. The Board hopes the directory will be updated on a regular basis.

The 100 Best Treatment Centers for Alcoholism and Drug Abuse. By Linda Sunshine and John W. Wright. Avon, 1988. 452p. bibliog. index. paper $10.95 (0-380-75489-4).

362.2'9286 Alcoholics—Hospitals—U.S. I Alcoholics—Hospitals—U.S.—Directories [OCLC] 88-16829

Rehab: A Comprehensive Guide to Recommended Drug-Alcohol Treatment Centers in the United States. 1st ed. By Stan Hart. Harper/Perennial, 1988. 513p. index. hardcover $22.95 (0-06-055133-X); paper $10.95 (0-06-096296-8).

362.2'9 Alcoholism—Hospitals—U.S.—Directories [CIP] 88-45033

Both of these books are directories of substance-abuse treatment centers in the U.S. *The 100 Best Treatment Centers* is by two journalists who prepared a similar guide to hospitals (*The Best Hospitals in America* [BKL N 15 84]). The information in their book is based on recommendations from professionals actively working in the chemical-dependency field and on responses to detailed questionnaires sent to almost 200 centers. All centers included in their book have been highly recommended by professionals. The author of *Rehab* is a recovering alcoholic who spent two years traveling around the country evaluating treatment centers. He has personally visited the 164 centers included in his book.

Although the authors of these guides have different perspectives on the subject, the information contained in their books is quite similar, and many of the same treatment facilities appear in both. Sunshine and Wright include an introduction that covers the signs and symptoms of chemical dependency, how to seek help, what to look for in a treatment program, and how to select the best treatment center. They also have appendixes with lists of therapists, organizations offering help for families, selected books, and support groups. Hart's book has a more personal point of view. His introduction explains what he considers to be a good treatment program. Both books have glossaries of terms used in the chemical-dependency field.

The main body of both directories is a list of centers, organized alphabetically by state and city or center name. Each entry consists of an overview of the center's treatment philosophy, statistics, admissions policy, special programs offered, costs and insurance coverage, staff, address, and telephone number. Hart adds personal comments based on his visit and a rating of good, very good, or excellent. He also has briefer entries listing centers for women only and those receiving honorable mentions. *Rehab* concludes with an index that lists the names of the centers by state. *The 100 Best Treatment Centers* has an excellent detailed subject index that lists types of addictions (gambling, cocaine), special groups served (gays, professionals, senior citizens), types of treatment (outpatient, antabuse), and types of admission and payment.

Both of these books will be useful additions to consumer, health, and social-science collections. They will help those faced with substance-abuse problems in the family or workplace to make some difficult decisions. *The 100 Best Treatment Centers* offers a more complete and impartial overview of the chemical-dependency field, while *Rehab* provides the unique perspective of a recovering abuser.

Financial Aid for the Disabled and Their Families, 1988–1989. By Gail Ann Schlachter and R. David Weber. Reference Service Press, 1988. 269p. bibliog. indexes. hardcover $32.50 (0-918276-04-7).

362.4'0482 Handicapped—Scholarships, fellowships, etc.—Directories I Federal aid to handicapped services—Directories I Grants-in-aid—U.S.—Directories [OCLC] 87-63263

One has high expectations of a work by Schlachter, most widely recognized as editor of *RQ*'s reference book reviews, and Weber, teacher and author, who have compiled other financial-aid directories for minorities, women, and military personnel. Again, their combined experience culminates in a well-crafted, easy-to-use, and affordable resource on financial aid for a special segment of the population.

Described are over 500 programs available to disabled applicants or their families, from the high school through postdoctoral levels, covering activities such as education, research, training, career development, public service, special projects, travel, and emergency situations. Where previous funding directories for the disabled and their families are more selective and specialized, and many are dated, this current work broadens the scope to include programs sponsored by federal and state government agencies, professional organizations, foundations, educational associations, and military/veterans organizations. Some entries duplicate those in *Financial Aid for Veterans, Military Personnel, and Their Dependents* [RBB Je 1 88].

Descriptions of programs are divided into six chapters, depending on type of disability or eligibility: general, orthopedic and developmental, hearing, visual, communication, and families of the disabled. This classification is based on PL94-142, the Education for All Handicapped Children Act. Each chapter further arranges entries by type of program assistance: undergraduate scholarships, graduate fellowships, loans, research grants, awards and prizes, and internships. Running heads identify the particular subsections for quick browsing.

Within each subsection, entries appear alphabetically by program title. Numerous *see* references lead to formal titles. Programs offering more than one type of assistance or assistance to multiple groups are listed under all relevant subsections.

Most descriptions are about one-half page. Each profile adheres to a standard format, providing the sponsoring organization's address and telephone number, purpose, eligibility, funding awarded, duration, special features, limitations, number of awards, and application deadline. Current data were collected through the end of 1987 from questionnaires. The authors intend to update the directory biennially, with the 1990–91 directory to be released in late 1989.

A directory of state sources of information on benefits comprises the second major section. State agencies are grouped by type of support and then listed alphabetically by state within each group. Information is brief: state agency name, address, and telephone number only.

A third section, an annotated bibliography of 75 general financial-aid directories, will prove useful to users seeking additional leads and to librarians with collection development responsibility in the area of grantsmanship. Only directories published since 1980 are included, grouped by type of assistance.

Five indexes provide access to the financial-aid programs by title, sponsoring agency, geographic location, subject, and calendar filing date. The program-title and sponsoring-organization indexes employ two-letter codes for each listing to identify "availability" or disability groups (e.g., hearing disabilities) and funding type (e.g., scholarships). The geographic and subject indexes subdivide the listings by availability and funding type. Numerous cross-references suggest broader terms and preferred access points. The calendar index deviates from the other indexes by arranging entries by funding type first and then by availability group. Within each subsection, entries are listed chronologically. Arguably, this overclassification results in more work for an applicant with a deadline seeking assistance from more than one category.

The currency and scope of this directory make it suitable for most libraries, especially high school, academic, and public.

The Encyclopedia of Police Science. Ed. by William G. Bailey. Garland, 1989. 718p. bibliog. illus. index. hardcover $77 (0-8240-6627-8).

363.2'03 Police—U.S.—Dictionaries [CIP] 88-11455

Bailey, criminal justice bibliographer at Sam Houston State University, has produced a long-needed reference work on police operations. *The Encyclopedia of Police Science* is an overview of the various areas of police work today. The 143 entries cover all aspects of police science including detection techniques, administrative issues, psychological and social issues, types of crimes, and other police issues. Biographies of important people in the field and brief histories of various police departments from around the country complete the volume.

Since the *Encyclopedia* is meant to be an introduction to the topics covered, entries are general in scope. They may be as short as two pages (for instance, the biographical sketches). The longest entries—*Police History*, *Police Women*, and *Crime Analysis*—are 14, 12, and 12 pages, respectively. The average length of an entry is four to six pages. The majority of the entries are divided into sections and provide a brief history or definition of the topic. In addition, entries may include step-by-step procedures (e.g., for conducting an arson or homicide investigation); statistical tables such as "Murder of Police Officers" or "Reactions of Police Officers Involved in Shooting"; and reviews of pertinent studies, surveys, or legal cases. Entries are signed by the contributors who include people from all aspects of police work, with the majority being professors of criminal justice, law, or law enforcement. Unsigned entries are the work of the editor. A list of the contributors with their credentials is included in the work. The bibliographies, which conclude each entry, include works almost a century old or as recent as 1987. However, the majority of works cited were published in the 1980s, and the second largest group between 1970 and 1979.

In addition to the lists at the end of each entry, the *Encyclopedia* includes two other bibliographies. One is a "Bibliography of Police History" that includes historically important books, dissertations, and articles. A "Bibliography of Bibliographies" lists 71 works in chronological order by publication date from 1909 through 1986. There are two indexes to the *Encyclopedia*: one of legal cases cited within entries and a general index. Also included in the volume are two sections of black-and-white photographs. Though they are not listed in the table of contents, they are easy to find.

The Encyclopedia of Police Science serves two functions. The first is to introduce the subject to those unfamiliar with it. The second is as a reference guide and bibliographic resource. Though the information on police techniques is too general to be of use to students of police science or criminology, librarians may find it helpful for answering the queries of the general public or high school students. The historical information on police work will be useful for a wide audience.

Guide to State Environmental Programs. Ed. by Deborah Hitchcock Jessup. BNA Books, 1988. 578p. bibliog. paper $40 (0-87179-583-3).

363.7'056 Environmental policy—U.S.—States—Handbooks, manuals, etc. I Environmental law—U.S.—States—Handbooks, manuals, etc. [CIP] 88-6373

Working from direct contact with state regulators, materials furnished by the states, and study of state regulations themselves, Jessup has assembled a guide to programs that relate to air pollution, water quality, industrial siting, waste management, coastal protection, toxic spills, utility transmission line siting, water rights and use, mining activities, and permit fees in all 50 states. The goal of the book, as described in the foreword, is to lead its audience, primarily industry officials, through the maze of regulations that differ from state to state, and to provide "practical information on the hows, whats, and wherefores of state regulatory programs." BNA is a well-known publisher of books and loose-leaf services whose other publications in this area include *Air & Water Pollution Control, Environment Reporter, Hazardous Materials Transportation,* and *Index to Chemical Regulation.*

The *Guide* begins with a 20-page overview of federal laws and regulations (Clean Air Act, Clean Water Act, groundwater protection, Resource Conservation and Recovery Act, superfund spill reporting, and coastal zone protection), tracing their histories, powers, and purposes. The major portion of the book, which follows, is state-by-state profiles, ranging from 7 to 15 pages each, that tell which state offices are involved in environmental regulation (and how they interrelate), provide the address and telephone number for each agency, and give the reader the "flavor" of the state's environmental protection and regulatory effort. (For example, the section on Missouri reports that "the state manages a pragmatic environmental program. It on one hand works cooperatively with the federal government and is quick to assume authority over federal programs. On the other hand, it is not known for adopting more stringent regulations than necessary to solve actual problems.")

A "first suggested contact" agency is given for general inquiries into environmental provisions, and then the different topics mentioned in the first sentence of this review are discussed, along with the appropriate agencies. Much of the practical information contained here will be of value to industries. For example, "New transmission lines 100 kilovolts and over require a certificate of need from the Maine Public Utilities Commission," and "Allegheny County also has specialized requirements, with emphasis on the particulates emissions that it considers of greatest concern." This is followed by a directory of the various divisions, research labs, and regional offices of the Environmental Protection Agency, and the divisions of the Army Corps of Engineers. State economic development agencies are provided next. Last is a directory, by state, of various county or regional offices. For each listing, the address, telephone number, and contact person and title are provided. This final listing has rather uneven coverage from state to state. The Illinois portion, for example, runs four pages and tells where to secure help for bird problems and ask questions about navigable waterways, among other topics, while some states run only one page or are missing altogether. A glossary to help readers decipher acronyms such as *CWA, POTW, ADEM,* and *RCRA* would have been highly useful. Acronyms appear frequently throughout the book but are only defined the first time they are mentioned. The *Guide* contains practical background information—until now unavailable in one source—which is sure to be useful to its audience. Academic libraries supporting environmental studies programs, public libraries serving business and industry, and some special libraries will no doubt find this a valuable acquisition.

Insurance Dictionary. Comp. by Michael C. Thomsett. McFarland, 1989. 243p. charts. hardcover $29.95 (0-89950-391-8).

368'.003 Insurance—Dictionaries I Insurance—Abbreviations—Dictionaries [CIP] 88-7947

Thomsett, an insurance expert and prolific author of business articles and reference books (e.g., *Real Estate Dictionary* [RBB O 1 88]), has compiled a useful new dictionary of insurance terms. It also includes a list of state insurance commissioner addresses, Canadian provincial agency addresses, and a four-page list of insurance abbreviations. A random sampling determined there are about 1,300 entries. Definitions vary in length from a few sentences to a full page. The work is abundantly illustrated with 149 appropriately placed line drawings. Numerous cross-references direct users to related terms or the location of nearby illustrations. While illustrations generally support the definitions, a few (e.g., *modified cash refund annuity*) appear to be incomplete or redundant attempts to duplicate the text and are confusing or unnecessary. In contrast, several definitions (e.g., *loss clause, nominal interest*) contain useful examples of mathematical problems to demonstrate a term. As with most technical dictionaries, no pronunciation or etymological information is supplied.

A number of insurance dictionaries can be compared to Thomsett. The *Dictionary of Insurance* by Davids (Rowman & Allanheld, 1984), with 3,561 terms, and *The Insurance Dictionary* by Ingrisano (Research and Review Service of America, 1978), with 3,296 terms, are the largest. The more recent *Dictionary of Insurance Terms* by Rubin (Barron's, 1987) has 2,500 terms. In examining the language used in these works, it appears that Thomsett is slightly less technical and thus better suited for the general public. Furthermore, the books by Davids and Rubin are in paperback; Thomsett is hardbound. In conclusion, though Thomsett's *Insurance Dictionary* is not the largest dictionary in coverage, it is current and less technical and is recommended for business collections in academic, public, and special libraries.

Directory of American Youth Organizations: A Guide to Over 400 Clubs, Groups, Troops, Teams, Societies, Lodges, and More for Young People. By Judith B. Erickson. Free Spirit Publishing, 123 N. Third St., Ste. 716, Minneapolis, MN 55401, 1988. bibliog. index. 154p. paper $14.95 (0-915793-11-3).

369.4'025 Youth—U.S.—Societies and clubs—Directories [CIP] 88-295

This slender book lists a variety of national nonprofit membership organizations that "serve children and youth of high school age and under" that are "conducted under adult supervision." Each listing includes the organization's name, address, telephone number, contact person, and a short description of the group's activities and purpose. Groups are arranged alphabetically within each of the following categories: hobby and special interest, career education, sports, political, character-building, social welfare, religious, conservation, service, self-help, substance abuse, hereditary and military, ethnic heritage, and agriculture and livestock. Some clusters, such as sports, religious, and political organizations, are further subdivided, allowing rodeo, ice skating, or Catholic groups to be listed together.

Honor societies and school subject clubs are included with hobby and special-interest groups. Here the math honor society Mu Alpha Theta follows Magical Youths International. There is some overlapping of categories: the Greek Orthodox Young Adult League is under "Ethnic Heritage Groups" rather than "Religious Organizations"; the National Catholic Forensic League is under "Religious Organizations," but the National Forensic League is under "Hobbies and Special Interest Groups."

Because there is a name/subject index, however, students will be able to locate most organizations of interest. Under *actors* or *theater* (but not *drama*) are listed the International Thespian Society and Young Actors Guild, and under *stamp collecting* is the Junior Philatelists of America. On the other hand, there is no entry *Latin*, even though the National Junior Classical League is "for high school students studying Latin."

While most listings are appropriate, some organizations are included that do not fit the book's purpose. For example, the JWB, a federation of Jewish community centers, "serves member agencies" (and not youth directly); the U.S. Twirling Association is an association of coaches; Do It Now Foundation "is not a membership organization"; and Woodcraft Rangers "operates only in the Southern California area."

Originally published in 1983, the book has been updated with a list of "changed status" organizations and asterisks marking those that are still believed to be active. Even the new Lutheran Youth Organization, replacing the Luther League as of 1987, is listed. Twenty pages of historical background information about youth organizations and 30 pages of "resources for administrators and leaders" are found at the end of the book. These include awards programs and professional associations (PTA, United Way, Outward Bound) and citations to readings about volunteerism, youth, and model programs (most sources are from 1980–82).

With so much of the book meant for adults, it may seem hard to justify its purchase for young people. However, although nearly all the groups are listed in the far more comprehensive *Encyclopedia of Associations*, here they are organized in a single volume that is attractively printed and inviting. This would be a useful title in elementary, middle school, and high school libraries and in children's collections.

EDUCATION, COMMUNICATION, CUSTOMS

The Facts On File Dictionary of Education. By Jay M. Shafritz and others. Facts On File, 1988. 503p. illus. hardcover $40 (0-8160-1636-4).

370'.321 Education—Dictionaries [CIP] 88-24554

According to the authors' preface, *The Facts On File Dictionary of Education* contains "virtually all of the words, terms, phrases, processes, names, laws, and court cases" pertinent to education, specifically preschool through high school. It includes such recent educational concepts and programs as time-on-task and the Holmes Group, as well as significant historical topics. The authors, experienced administrators and writers in education, note that this field and its language are dynamic. They attempted to make their *Dictionary* as comprehensive as possible but are aware that new terms and concepts constantly arise. In seeking entries, they scanned standard texts from education and related fields, such as accounting, personnel, psychology, economics, and medicine. The breadth and depth of coverage should ensure that this *Dictionary* will become a standard reference source.

The *Dictionary* contains approximately 5,000 alphabetical entries. Definitions are straightforward but do not include pronunciation or etymologies. When more than one interpretation applies to a term, the separate definitions are numbered. Many terms have brief entries, but those that address current concerns are treated in more detail. These often include commentary and interpretation and provide bibliographic references for users seeking more information. For example, *affirmative action* contains references to three recent journal articles and concludes with six cross-references to other terms and legal cases described elsewhere in the *Dictionary*. The entries are alphabetized word by word; this is necessary because there are many phrases beginning with the same word (e.g., *affirmative action groups, affirmative action officer, affirmative action plan, affirmative action program, affirmative order, affirmative recruitment*). Cross-references for acronyms lead to entries under the full form of the term.

Many special features make this work a flexible ready-reference source. These include concise biographical entries for important figures, with pertinent bibliographic citations; brief reviews of court cases and legal decisions, including the full legal citation to the text of the complete case; titles of key journals and subscription addresses; summaries of laws; activities of major organizations and professional associations; and descriptions of standard tests and inventories with publishers' addresses. The 50 black-and-white illustrations include sample forms.

Subject dictionaries, including several published by Facts On File, have in recent years tended to focus on very specific subjects. This new *Dictionary*, however, provides comprehensive, contemporary coverage. Libraries that own Good's *Dictionary of Education* (McGraw-Hill, 1973) will want to retain it because of its scholarly reputation and extensive number of entries (33,000), but, apart from being now quite dated, it lacks the special features that make *The Facts On File Dictionary of Education* particularly appealing. Thorough and sound, the *Dictionary* represents a collaborative effort of informed practitioners in the field and is a welcome addition to reference collections.

World Education Encyclopedia. 3v. Ed. by George Thomas Kurian. Facts On File, 1988. 1,720p. bibliog. charts. index. tables. hardcover $175 (0-87196-748-0).

370'.321 Education—Dictionaries [OCLC] 82-18188

The *World Education Encyclopedia* facilitates the study of comparative education by providing a global survey of the state of education for the closing years of the twentieth century. Far more than an overview, it describes the educational systems of 181 countries authoritatively and in depth.

In his introduction, editor Kurian provides an objective summary of the educational process and its problems. He states that the purpose of this work is to provide information about various educational systems and to compare and analyze them, but not to evaluate, criticize, or judge them. Section 1, "Global Education," includes an interpretation of "World Education and World History" by Patrick Alston. Even broader in scope than Kurian's, this overview forms an effective preface to the detailed material that follows. Readable and relatively brief, it manages to place world education in a context that stretches from prehistoric man to the end of the twentieth century. The remainder of section 1, "Statistical Dimensions of Global Education," provides 10 tables of statistical data for continents, major areas, and groups of countries on such topics as enrollment (by age groups, sex, etc.), teaching staff, and pupil-teacher ratios. These tables are unattributed, but in his preface, Kurian notes that the basic data for individual countries are based on the *UNESCO Statistical Yearbook* (1984).

Sections 2, 3, and 4 contain the detailed descriptions of educational systems. Countries have been grouped into three categories according to the availability of information about them, not their size. Ninety-three are considered major, 33 middle, and 55 minor. Vietnam and Kampuchea, for example, are considered minor because information about them is lacking. Articles are 10 to 20 pages for major countries, about four pages for middle countries, and less than a page for minor countries. Within each group, the descriptions are arranged alphabetically by the name of the country.

The strength of this *Encyclopedia* lies in the consistency with which it presents its data. This results from the use of an "Information Classification Schedule" to organize the information about each country. Thus, although the essays were written by many different hands, comparisons can readily be made between them. Major divisions in the classification are *Basic Data* (e.g., population, literacy rate, public expenditures on education); *History & Background*; *Constitutional & Legal Foundations*; *Educational System—Overview* (textbooks, curriculum, foreign influences); *Preprimary & Primary Education*; *Secondary Education*; *Higher Education*; *Administration, Finance & Educational Research*; *Nonformal Education* (e.g., adult education, open universities); *Teaching Profession*; and *Summary* (general assessment, international programs, need for changes). The major country articles follow the classification scheme carefully, and the information provided is as exhaustive as possible. Each article concludes with an extensive, current bibliography of both English-language and other materials and a glossary of terms and acronyms specific to the country being examined.

This work is an authoritative text. Its 67 contributors include specialists in comparative education from universities around the world. Sharing the virtues of other Facts On File publications that Kurian has edited (the *World Press Encyclopedia* and the *Encyclopedia of the Third World*), it is clearly printed and presented. *Basic Data* sections for each country are conveniently boxed and set in boldface type at the beginning of each article. Diagrams and charts, as well as statistical tables, are generously provided.

Section 5 consists of three appendixes. "Global Education Rankings" is a UNESCO-based statistical record of 16 educational topics such as literacy, male and female enrollment, textbooks, professors, etc. Topics are more specific than those in the global statistics provided in section 1, and tables list individual countries, not just continents. This section is from Kurian's *New Book of World Rankings* (Facts On File, 1984), with revisions anticipating a new edition of that work. The second appendix is a general bibliography of key works on global and regional education. A detailed index to countries, topics, persons, and institutions completes the set.

In concept, Kurian's *Encyclopedia* competes head-on with the *International Handbook of Education Systems* (Wiley, 1983), an entirely satisfactory reference work that also provides consistently organized, documented essays on educational systems. That three-volume set is still in print and costs $81 per volume. It is less extensive, however, in that it covers 70 major countries compared with Kurian's 181 "major, middle and minor." Both address a longstanding need for a reference resource of this nature. UNESCO's extensive *World Survey of Education* (1955–71) was for many years the only compilation, and it has been updated very erratically via the *International Yearbook of Education*. Similar information is also found in another recent reference source for education, *The International Encyclopedia of Education* (Pergamon, 1985), in which detailed descriptions of educational systems are found under country entries. The Pergamon work is an expensive set, however, too exhaustive for many libraries.

Reasonably priced and current, the *World Education Encyclopedia* is now likely to be the popular choice for libraries seeking good coverage of comparative education. Its country essays are detailed, well researched, and thoroughly documented. The supplementary material is suitable and adequate. The *Encyclopedia* achieves its goal of presenting a comprehensive overview of the state of world education as the present century approaches its last decade.

Who's Who in American Education, 1988–1989. 1st ed. Ed. by Jeffrey Franz. National Reference Institute, P.O. Box 627, Owings Mills, MD 21117, 1988. hardcover $69.95 (0-940863-07-3).

370.973 Educators—U.S.—Biography I Education—U.S.—Bio-bibliography [BKL]

A new creation with no connection to earlier biographical dictionaries of educators, *Who's Who in American Education* nevertheless invites comparison with one of the most notable of those dictionaries, *Leaders in Education*. The first edition of *Leaders in Education* was published in 1932; the most recent edition was published by Bowker in 1974. The Board reviewed it favorably as "a reliable, easily used biographical reference work of men and women prominent in the field of education, with emphasis on educational administrators and education professors in many different specialties." Unfortunately, it has not been updated during the past 15 years, leaving a void in education reference literature. Even more unfortunately, this "inaugural edition" of *Who's Who in American Education* does not fill that void.

One can establish this book's scope only by inference after examining its contents. The foreword by editor Franz notes that the National Reference Institute "recently appointed a Board of Advisors comprised of many of the most outstanding leaders of today's educational community. At its initial meeting, the Board concluded that 'it is indeed time to begin honoring the consummate professionals among us.'" The members of this board are not named. Nor can we establish the credibility of Franz's credentials. He is listed in OCLC only as the editor of *Who's Who in American Nursing* (Society of Nursing Professionals, 1984–   ). Neither the Society of Nursing Professionals nor the National Reference Institute appears in standard directories of publishers.

Most of the entrants are teachers and administrators (principals, assistant principals, librarians, superintendents, etc.) working in elementary and secondary education. One finds among them, however, a handful of professors of education and independent consultants. The 10,000 people listed in this edition were selected "upon a variety of factors . . . foremost [of which] is the extent to which an individual is of reference interest." That, in turn, "is based upon professional accomplishment that has significant impact on education and the enhancement of education as a profession." The paragraph describing the criteria that determine this reference interest and impact merits quotation in full: "Elements which determine an individual's significance of accomplishment are assessed through a system of weights assigned to: educational achievement; advancement to positions of responsibility which represent substantial or far-reaching influence on education; contribution to the literature or pool of research knowledge; honors, awards, fellowships or special appointments; demonstrated leadership in professional organizations; and singular achievement within education which is ordinarily considered to be beyond that of the vast majority of contemporaries." Just how each of these is weighted is never explained.

As a test of the effectiveness of the editor's system, the Board looked up recent officers of the American Association of School Librarians. Only one of the 10 persons who have served as executive director or as an officer of AASL since 1985–86 is listed. This is a poor hit rate for a book that purports to identify "those educators who are making a difference in today's society." The front matter does not explain how the information about each individual was collected or whether it was verified by the subject.

As applicable, entries include name, birth date and place, parents' names, children's names, colleges and universities attended with dates of degrees, type of work performed, areas of educational practice, current position, previous positions, military service, membership and offices in professional organizations, honors and awards, certification, publications, research activities, and address. All too often the address is only the person's city and state. The lists of positions lack dates. One cannot tell when a person started the job listed as present position nor the dates earlier jobs were held. Citations to publications rarely include dates, ERIC document numbers, or other useful identifying information. This economy is, of course, widely practiced by publishers of biographical directories. Another economy practiced in this directory will try frequent users' patience: the type is very small. Since each element in each biography is introduced by an abbreviation, it can be a challenge to pick out, say, a person's current position in the block of small type summarizing his or her professional life. These abbreviations as well as acronyms and other abbreviations are explained in a list in the front matter.

An index by 11 specialties is organized by state. The categories are *Administration, Adult Education, Elementary, Gifted/Talented, Library/Media Services, Private/Parochial, Research, Secondary, Special Education, Speech/Language,* and *Supervision*.

It is not clear how the persons included in this book were identified, but it is clear that the selection of people presented is not necessarily that which would have resulted from rigorously applied criteria. The directory lacks credibility, and the Board declines to recommend it.

Encyclopedia of School Administration & Supervision. Ed. by Richard A. Gorton and others. Oryx, 1988. 321p. index. hardcover $74.50 (0-89774-232-X).

371.2'003 School management and organization—U.S.—Dictionaries I School supervision—U.S.—Dictionaries [CIP] 87-34959

Intended for administrators in elementary and secondary schools, the purpose of this single-volume, alphabetically arranged *Encyclopedia* is to provide concise, summary information on a wide range of topics relating to administrative leadership. It covers 300 different topics in such areas as community-school relations, curriculum, legal issues, school facilities, teachers, and tests and measurements. Some entries treat practical topics, for example, corporal punishment, mainstreaming, the school business manager, and teacher absenteeism; others cover more theoretical subjects: administrative theory, human relations, and Theory Z. Entries range from one-half to two pages. They close with cross-references and bibliographies listing one to three current books or journal articles on the topics.

Two hundred scholars and school administrators were selected as contributors to this work, based on their publications and professional expertise. Each entry is signed. Profiles of the contributors are given at the beginning of the book, along with "A Guide to Related Topics" that groups titles of individual articles under broader headings and an alphabetical list of articles. The volume concludes with an index.

This valuable resource should be considered by academic libraries that support teacher-training programs, school library professional collections, and large public libraries.

Survey of Early Childhood Software, 1988. By Warren Buckleitner. High/Scope Press, 600 N. River St., Ypsilanti, MI 48198, 1988. 151p. illus. paper $20 (0-931114-32-2).

371.39445'029 Computer-assisted instruction—Equipment and supplies—Catalogs I Education, Preschool—Computer programs—Catalogs I Education, Primary—Computer programs—Catalogs I Computer software—Catalogs [BKL]

Now in its fourth year, this is a survey of software designed to be appropriate for children aged three to six. It is available in either book or disk form (Apple hardware and Appleworks software required). The survey reviews 286 programs for the Apple, C64, IBM, and Atari computers. The publisher, the High/Scope Educational Research Foundation, has been integrating computer technology into its curriculum at its demonstration school and publishes a monthly computer newsletter called "Key Notes," which introduces new software reviews as well as comments on computer applications in a school setting.

The text begins with an index of computer program titles followed by an explanation of the descriptions used in the annotations. It explains that software is given a percentage rating on user friendliness, educational value, and instructional design based on an evaluator's findings. Keeping the age and proclivities of the young child in mind, the evaluator checks the programs for glitches as well as positive features (for example, locking up when a child presses all the keys), independent menu use, the level of challenge to the user, and the absence of racial or gender bias.

The alphabetical listing of software descriptions follows, with publisher, date and price, suggested age level, hardware needs, and conceptual areas taught. Conceptual areas include language, time, number, spatial relations, and creative projects.

The evaluation process is complete and complex and is explained in a separate chapter. Appendixes list addresses for software producers; software listings by content area giving title, concept, and overall rating; and software arranged by computer brand. A glossary completes the text.

This software bibliography is thorough in coverage. It will be of value to parents, day-care centers offering computer use, primary teachers in elementary schools, and children's librarians.

Peterson's Guide to Independent Secondary Schools, 1988–89. 9th ed. Ed. by Greg Muirhead. Peterson's Guides, 1988. annual. 1,312p. indexes. hardcover $33.95 (0-87866-740-7); paper $18.95 (0-87866-690-7).

373.2 Private schools—Directories [OCLC]

Private Independent Schools, 1988. 41st ed. Bunting and Lyon, Inc., 238 N. Main St., Wallingford, CT 06492, 1988. annual. 745p. hardcover $65 (0-913094-41-2; ISSN 0079-5399).

373.2'22 Private schools—Directories [OCLC] 72-122324

These are two excellent, annually updated guides for parents and libraries that provide information on private schools in the U.S. and Canada and American schools overseas. *Peterson's* lists secondary schools that are "primarily college preparatory . . . and are free of undue religious or political influence," although a number of schools are religiously affiliated. All schools included are accredited by a regional group or approved by a state department of education.

Three different kinds of general listings are given. The general register (20 pages) has state-by-state charts listing 1,380 schools, giving enrollment, number of faculty, sports and advanced placement subjects offered, and whether a full description follows. Short (500-word) profiles of most of the schools were compiled from surveys. These include a brief student profile, faculty and facilities summary, list of subjects offered, graduation requirements, special academic programs, college placement, student life, tuition, athletics, and names of school head and admissions contact. The third section includes alphabetical entries for 340 schools that paid for the inclusion of two-page descriptions. These include more information about each school's history, philosophy, program, student body, student life, and admissions procedure. One or two photographs and several student quotes usually accompany these descriptions.

BOOKLIST's last review [BKL Je 15 82] noted *Peterson's* standardized entries and praised its inexpensive paperback format. Cost is still a strong point, but so are the 30 indexes ("directories") that categorize special features such as type of school (day, boarding, military), "schools reporting a guaranteed tuition plan," "schools with barrier-free campuses," and "schools reporting a community service requirement."

Private Independent Schools (the *Blue Book*) offers similar information for many of the same schools, but arrangement and emphasis are different. Included are 1,181 "private schools that meet our standards of acceptance," from prekindergarten through twelfth grade. Although the standards aren't defined, schools included appear to be highly academic, college prep, and fully accredited.

Schools that did not pay to be included in the book get only a name and address listing. There are 807 schools that paid for short listings (number of students, school history and/or philosophy, tuition, director, and summary of program). Another 333 schools paid for in-depth coverage, which includes geographic highlights, campus facilities, student makeup and activities, academic program, admission policies, tuition, a campus photo, and, notably, faculty credentials. Arrangement is alphabetical by state or country, regardless of the length of entry. Both an alphabetical index at the beginning and comparative charts at the end simplify finding information. Special sections on summer programs, administrators, and placement services for students and faculty are found at the end of the book. While much is unchanged from the last edition, admissions counseling now requires a $50 registration fee (instead of an open invitation to call for advice) in addition to an $800 counseling fee. Service to parents, students, and prospective faculty is a strong feature of this company.

Coverage here overlaps both *Peterson's* and Porter Sargent's *Handbook of Private Schools* [RSBR Jl 1 81] but is not replaceable by either. The *Blue Book* is more selective, although it covers elementary as well as secondary schools. Complete sentences and clearer type make the descriptions more readable, too. In sampling one letter, where the *Blue Book* had full entries for 24 schools, *Peterson's* had only 12 of them. Where *Peterson's* had 18 long entries for another sample, the *Blue Book* had 11. *Peterson's* has wider coverage and is more inclusive of schools serving underachievers and other special needs. Public libraries will want to have both of these newest editions available.

Adult Literacy/Illiteracy in the United States: A Handbook for Reference and Research. By Marie Costa. ABC-Clio, 1988. 167p. bibliog. index. tables. hardcover $34.95 (0-87436-492-2).

374'.012 Literacy—U.S.—Handbooks, manuals, etc. I Literacy—U.S.—Societies, etc.—
Directories [CIP] 87-31696

In 1983 Secretary of Education Terrel H. Bell declared adult illiteracy a national problem and launched an Adult Literacy Initiative. Since then much has been written about the problem and its solutions. This handbook is not a "tool for 'fixing' illiteracy, but for learning about illiteracy and its role in our lives and our society." Written for teachers, students, and volunteers, Costa intends her work to lay a foundation for understanding the problem of illiteracy and to identify the resources "that can lead to greater understanding in the hopes that understanding will lead in turn to effective action."

To this end Costa identifies 23 key figures of the literacy movement and more than 30 groups that played an active role in the movement. Entries for organizations include address and telephone number, brief history, statement of purpose, and publications. As with the biographical sketches, the organizations are arranged alphabetically. Costa also includes a chronology of significant dates and events, beginning in 1647 with the first compulsory school law in Massachusetts to 1990, UNESCO's International Literacy Year.

An annotated bibliography of print and nonprint sources includes price, ISBN, and distributor, if applicable, for ease in ordering any of the recommended titles. Online databases, computer networks, and computer-readable databases are part of the nonprint bibliography, along with video-and audiocassettes and TV programs. Statistical tables illustrating various methods of measuring the literacy rate are included in the "Facts and Data" chapter. This section is meant to be an overview of literacy definitions, measurement methods, and legislation. Entries are brief, intended to raise questions rather than answer them.

The excellent index makes it easy to find the information needed, and within the text, *see* references direct the reader to related topics. A glossary of common terms is extremely useful for the beginning researcher.

Some of the information presented by Costa is available elsewhere. For example, *The Community of the Book* [RBB Jl 87] lists some of the same organizations as Costa, but in most cases with more detailed information. However, the focus is different. *Community of the Book* lists groups that promote books, reading, and literacy. Costa concentrates on those organizations directly involved in the literacy movement. Her unique perspective makes this a useful handbook both for reference librarians and for students researching the problems of illiteracy in the U.S.

Books for Adult New Readers: A Bibliography Developed by Project: LEARN. 4th ed. Rev. by Frances Josephson Pursell. New Readers Press, 1320 Jamesville Rd., Box 131, Syracuse, NY 13210, 1989. 210p. paper $14.95 (0-88336-599-5).

016.374012 Readers for new literates—Bibliography I Libraries and new literates [OCLC]

In the late seventies, the Cleveland Area Metropolitan Library System and Merrick Settlement House joined Project: LEARN in a literacy project. A study determined that only a limited amount of adult interest/low reading-level books were available to adult new readers in Cleveland area public libraries. A local foundation funded the creation of a sample collection and an annotated bibliography of appropriate materials recommended for public library purchase. Now in its fourth revision, this annotated bibliography lists 643 titles for English-speaking adults reading at the seventh-grade level or below. The introduction notes that 64 percent of the titles included are written at the fifth-grade level or below and 95 percent are available in paperback. This edition contains 169 new titles and a new section titled "Computer Learning" that lists materials focusing on the needs of adult learners. The intent was to create a bibliography of titles that would teach basic skills (communication, computation, problem solving, and interpersonal relationships) rather than minute detail. Some of the criteria used to choose titles were short paragraphs and chapters; a book length that was not intimidating; uncrowded pages containing much white space; title and cover with adult appeal; large type; durable format; realistic stories with adult characters; an uncomplicated plot with action, conversation, and a minimum of description; and a reasonable price. While material pertinent to Cleveland and Ohio was among the criteria, the regional focus is minimal.

Fiction is subdivided into the areas of general fiction, mystery and horror, science fiction, and classics and folklore. The nonfiction includes such topics as biography, computers, psychology, religion, government, jobs, community resources, writing and grammar, mathematics, health and safety, homemaking, parenting, and history and travel. Each entry is numbered sequentially and contains an asterisk if the title is new to this edition, author, publisher, date, pagination, price, ISBN, series, a critical annotation, and reading level.

Useful appendixes offer a core collection of about 100 titles; series recommendations and an index to titles in series in the bibliography; a list of books likely to be in the juvenile collections of many libraries that are appropriate for adult new readers; bibliographies on literacy for the librarian and the tutor; a title index; a subject index to nonfiction; and publishers' addresses.

Public libraries should be armed with this title to help combat the growing problem of illiteracy in America.

Resources for Educational Equity: A Guide for Grades Pre-Kindergarten–12. By Merle Froschl and Barbara Sprung. Garland, 1988. 266p. indexes. hardcover $39 (0-8240-0443-4).

016.37019'0973 Educational equalization—U.S. I Educational equalization—U.S.—Bibliography I Textbook bias—U.S. [CIP] 88-16445

In the introduction, the editors state that this "is the most comprehensive and up-to-date compilation of available resources to help teachers locate the materials they need to create equitable curriculum and classroom environments." There is nothing comparable in the field. Materials listed include curriculum guides, teacher packets, student texts and workbooks, audiovisual materials, and periodical articles concerning educational equity. While most of the entries focus on sex equity, stereotyping and bias due to race and disability are also addressed.

Following an introductory essay on the Women's Educational Equity Act (Title IX), chapters are organized thematically. Themes include early childhood, guidance counseling, computers, mathematics, sports, teenage childbearing, and libraries. Each is by a different subject authority (most affiliated with colleges or state education departments) and includes a four- to six-page essay followed by a bibliography of approximately 50 annotated resources, roughly grouped as elementary, secondary, or professional interest. As in others in this series, there are variations in chapter quality and style, some repetition of information and bibliographic entries, and some inconsistencies because all chapters don't specify the same selection criteria. For example, some chapters include only materials that have actually been examined or successfully classroom tested, and some limit materials to those published since 1980. Overall, the bibliographies are thorough and the annotations are helpful. This would be even more useful for collection development if publisher addresses were consistently included and if information on length, in-print status, or cost of items was provided.

Author and subject indexes are included, but minor errors show that proofreading is needed. (Some entries are out of order—*Braille* follows *Career Education*; *The Learning Seed* is listed with the *T*s.) The subject index could be improved with more consistent cross-references, and a title index would be helpful.

Subjects occasionally overlap chapters—guidance and vocational education, libraries and literature—and there are areas that seem forced, such as textbook selection in the chapter on libraries. However, the comprehensiveness of this volume outweighs any minor problems. Highly recommended for curriculum libraries and most professional collections.

The Self-Help Sourcebook: Finding & Forming Mutual Aid Self-Help Groups. 2d ed. Comp. by Edward J. Madara and Abigail Meese. Self-Help Clearinghouse, Saint Clares-Riverside Medical Center, Pocono Rd., Denville, NJ 07834, 1988. 134p. bibliog. index. paper $8 (ISSN 8756-1425).

374.22 Self-help groups—U.S.—Directories [BKL] 87-641482

Self-help is the theory that a group of people facing a common stressful situation can share experiences and information and thereby provide practical assistance and emotional support for each other. Today, over 500,000 mutual-aid self-help groups meet around the country. First published in 1986, this directory of self-help resources offers more than 500 listings for national and model groups as well as over 100 national toll-free help lines. It was compiled by members of the Self-Help Clearinghouse at Saint Clares-Riverside Medical Center in New Jersey.

Describing organizations for a wide variety of life crises including illnesses, addictions, bereavement, parenting, or family concerns, each was selected for inclusion based on these guidelines: the group must be nonprofit, composed of individuals who share a common experience, and run by and for its members. Entries are arranged under headings like *AIDS, Alcoholism, Amputation, Anorexia/Bulimia, Battering, Burn Victim, Caregivers of Aging/Ill, Debt, Foster Parents, Head Injury/Brain Tumor/Coma, Infertility, Mastectomy, Multiple Sclerosis, Parents of Disabled/Ill Children, Phobia, Short/Tall Stature,* and *Skin Disease.* Each entry gives address, telephone number, whether a national or local chapter, date founded, and statement of purpose.

Brief appendixes discuss "Self-Help 'Groups' via Home Computer," "Resources for Rare Disorders," "Resources for Genetic Disorders," and "How-to Ideas for Developing Groups." The nine titles included in the bibliography explore the self-help concept. Toll-free telephone numbers are given for help lines dealing with cleft palate, endometriosis, incontinence, organ donation, runaways, sickle cell, sudden infant death syndrome, and many others. An index assists the user.

While information about some of these groups can be found elsewhere, identification of others is often difficult. This handy paperback is an essential reference source for public libraries, providing easy access to valuable information.

American College Regalia: A Handbook. Comp. by Linda Sparks and Bruce Emerton. Greenwood, 1988. 380p. indexes. hardcover $45 (0-313-26266-7).
378.73 Universities and colleges—U.S.—Insignia—Handbooks, manuals, etc. [CIP] 88-188

Based on responses from 469 institutions, this handbook provides the reader with up to seven pieces of information about the trappings of American four-year colleges and universities with enrollments of 2,500 or more. The entry for each school contains its address and may contain some or all of the following information: nickname, colors, mascot, name of newspaper, name of yearbook, text of the alma mater, and text of the fight song. Because of varying responses from institutions and a variety of copyright restrictions, not all categories of information are included for each institution. (School songs have been particularly affected by the copyright restrictions.) No illustrations of school logos or mascots are included, and no information regarding academic costume is presented here. For coverage of the latter information, one will need additional tools such as Ray Franks' *What's in a Nickname?* (1982) and Hugh Smith's *Academic Dress and Insignia of the World* (1970).

Most of the information is self-explanatory, but the nickname and mascot categories are frequently inconsistent. In the nickname category, for instance, the editors sometimes include the name used for the athletic team rather than the school's actual nickname (e.g., *Eli* for Yale), and in other instances, they just indicate how the school is referred to locally (e.g., *ASU* for Arizona State University). In the mascot category a specific name of the mascot may be listed with no explanation of what it is. One cannot find out from this book, for example, that Shasta, the University of Houston's mascot, is a cougar. In other cases the type of mascot is specified (beaver, lion, etc.) without indication of its name.

Arrangement is alphabetical by state and institution name. Indexes by school name, color, and mascot increase the accessibility of the information. No attempts have been made, however, to do additional cross-referencing in the indexes, which can be problematic for the reader. For example, in the color index, only the first-named color is indexed, and the variety of hues of a color are listed separately—requiring the reader to look under many headings to find the information desired. A case in point: reds are listed under *cardinal, cherry, crimson, garnet, Harvard red, red, scarlet,* and *vermillion*—and possibly *flame.* Similar problems exist with the mascot index. For instance, it is necessary to look under at least nine separate entries for bears as mascots.

As incomplete as some of the entries are in this work, and though it covers less than one-third of all four-year colleges and universities in the U.S., this handbook does pull together a great deal of information that can be difficult to find in other sources. For large collections, this would be a worthwhile purchase; at $45, its value to smaller collections is questionable.

The GIS Guide to Four-Year Colleges, 1989. By the editors of the Guidance Information System. Houghton, 1988. 630p. tables. paper $14.95 (0-395-47348-9; ISSN 0897-8956).
378.73 College, Choice of—U.S. l Universities and colleges—U.S.—Directories [OCLC] 88-6829

With all of the college guides that are available, here's one with an unusual twist. It is based on the Guidance Information System, a widely used college database. While the database is far more comprehensive, students do not have to be familiar with it to enjoy using this new guide to selection. (The computerized version allows students to access two- or four-year schools—the book includes four-year institutions only—based on factors such as location, religious affiliation, public or private status, accreditation, requirements, and availability of scholarships and ROTC that are not indexed in the print version.) Costs are more narrowly defined—the book only specifies "least expensive," "moderately expensive," or "expensive" compared with six subdivisions in the database.

In using the book, just as in the database, users answer questions about characteristics desired in a school (setting, size, sex, type, cost, and selectivity). Then they scan the state-by-state "Express Access" list to find the colleges that have those characteristics. A "scanning card" provided with the book to check the coded list will probably disappear in libraries, but simply reading through the list works, too.

Following the "Express Access" lists are alphabetically arranged profiles of over 1,500 colleges. A sample profile and a thorough list of terms and abbreviations are provided. Each entry begins with complete address and telephone number, founding date, type of school (fine arts college, university, etc.), religious affiliation, and whether the school is coed or not. Tuition, other costs, percentage of students receiving financial aid, number of students, calendar plan, selectivity (mean SAT, freshman profile), number of faculty, and ratio of students to faculty are also listed. (Tuition figures that were received too late to be incorporated into entries are updated at the end of the book.) Admissions requirements and deadlines, financial-aid sources, residential life, sports, major programs, and special programs (honors, independent study, sign-language services, ROTC) are summarized.

Entries range from one-sixth to two-thirds of a page, depending on the number of programs included. One-paragraph "student comments on campus character" are listed for the most popular 285 schools. For example, "students take their studies very seriously. . . . for fun, students go to the Student Union to eat or bowl or play pool." Or, "life outside the classroom is important, too. A lively, intellectual ferment is encouraged in hundreds of political, social, cultural, and recreational events and scientific symposia every week—more than many campuses could offer in an entire semester." These subjective comments enliven the entries and give a kind of *Insiders' Guide to the Colleges* flavor. Unique also are 22 "bests" lists: "Most Athletic Student Body," "Most Underappreciated Public University," "Best Science Facilities," "Best School for the Quiet Student," and "Friendliest Students." Prepared by high school guidance counselors, these lists of 15 schools each are sprinkled throughout the book (and appear in the table of contents) and will spark additional interest in categories that aren't usually discussed in college guides.

A thorough "Majors Directory," taking up nearly 200 pages, is grouped by broad discipline with subdivisions. For example, *Agriculture and Natural Resources* includes *Agricultural Business, Agricultural Economics, Agricultural Journalism, Animal Science, Ornamental Horticulture, Poultry Science*, and many more. Schools are listed alphabetically within each category.

While one may question the need for yet another college guide, this one is concise (with clear though tiny print), easy to use, affordable, reputable, and appears certain to be updated yearly. Even though most students probably won't depend totally on the "Express Access" list as a way of eliminating schools—choosing a college is too complicated to be encompassed in six characteristics—*The GIS Guide* contains enough distinct features to recommend it to public and high school libraries.

Peterson's Guide to Certificate Programs at American Colleges and Universities. Ed. by George J. Lopos and others. Peterson's Guides, 1988. 343p. indexes. paper $35.95 (0-87866-741-5).

378.73025 Universities and colleges—U.S.—Directories I Vocational education—U.S.—Directories I Continuing education—U.S.—Directories [OCLC] 88-43018

This *Guide* was developed by Peterson's in conjunction with the National University Continuing Education Association, a group of colleges and universities that are major providers of continuing higher education for adult part-time learners. Recognizing that a growing number of these students pursue programs that lead to a certificate, NUCEA convened a group of experts from universities, accrediting agencies, and government to plan a publication to help students meet their educational objectives "whether they are seeking to advance in their career, acquire new skills and knowledge, or qualify for certification in their field." It was edited by Lopos, associate dean of continuing education at the University of Iowa; Margaret Holt, associate professor in the College of Education at the University of Georgia; and two members of the Peterson's staff.

A brief "About Certificate Programs" section lists six criteria used to determine the programs to be included in the *Guide*: each program must be officially approved by the institution offering it, be designed to meet the needs of a defined audience, be available independent of a degree program, include an evaluation of student learning, not discriminate against any qualified student, and culminate in the award of a certificate signed by the institution's chief academic officer.

Over 1,400 programs, representing 260 schools, are presented in alphabetical order by state, then by institution, and finally by program classification. Programs are classified by the National Center for Education Statistics' Classification of Instructional Programs (CIP) taxonomy. Examples of CIP categories are criminal justice, general marketing, music, and real estate. Students seeking programs in a specific subject area start by checking the CIP display to identify the relevant classification. Next, the "Index by Program Classification" is consulted to identify the appropriate institutions. Since this source does not list programs for every CIP category (although over 200 are covered), the index provides *see* references to more general categories (e.g., "*alcohol/drug abuse specialty*—see entries under mental health/human services"). An alphabetical index by institution name is also included.

Each entry includes information about program content, format, evaluation criteria, enrollment requirements, cost, student services, and contact person. Entries also indicate whether a program confers academic credit and is endorsed by any professional organizations. Good use of boldface type and ample white space between sections make entries very easy to read.

Peterson's Guide to Certificate Programs will be a useful addition to any collection serving adult learners.

Peterson's Higher Education Directory, 1988. Ed. by Kim R. Kaye and others. Peterson's Guides, 1988. 1,057p. indexes. paper $34.95 (0-87866-644-3; ISSN 0896-2944).

378.73 Universities and colleges—U.S.—Directories [OCLC]

Over 3,500 U.S. institutions of postsecondary education that meet accreditation standards recognized by the U.S. Department of Education or the Council on Postsecondary Education are profiled in this *Directory*. The profiles are arranged alphabetically by institution name and are divided into the following sections: name, address, and telephone number; county and congressional district; Federal Interagency Committee on Education (FICE) number and the "entity" number used in the Higher Education General Information Survey; levels of degree offerings; date of foundation, calendar system, and type of control; type of student body, campus setting, total enrollment, and tuition and fees; accreditation (general and specialized); research facilities and affiliations (including computer facilities); roster of administrative officers (classified into 59 categories) with direct telephone numbers; and major academic units (schools, colleges, divisions) and unit heads, with telephone numbers. Three indexes are found at the back of the *Directory*: names of administrative officers and academic unit heads listed in the profiles; accrediting bodies, with institutions listed alphabetically under subject headings; and alphabetical lists of institutions by state.

An introduction supplies background information and definitions and is followed by two pages of pie charts giving summary statistics on characteristics such as institutional type and total enrollment levels. Six appendixes list, respectively, U.S. Department of Education offices concerned with higher education, state higher education agencies, recognized accreditation bodies, higher education associations, consortia, and members of select higher education associations.

This *Directory* is very similar in purpose and kinds of data provided to *The HEP Higher Education Directory, 1988* [*RBB* Je 1 88]. Peterson's *Directory* does provide information on a few topics not covered by the HEP publication, such as library resources, computer and research facilities, and institutional membership of higher education associations. And Peterson's *Directory* is only slightly higher in price. Both these books are comparable to the *Colleges and Universities* volume of the *Education Directory* issued irregularly by the U.S. government; however, the last two editions of the government directory (1983–84 and 1985–86) no longer included the lists of principal administrative officers found in the two commercially published titles.

The Broadcast Communications Dictionary. 3d ed. Ed. by Lincoln Diamant. Greenwood, 1989. 255p. bibliog. hardcover $35 (0-313-26502-X).

384.54'014 Broadcasting—Dictionaries [CIP] 88-25093

This is the first new edition of *The Broadcast Communications Dictionary* since 1978. The first edition was published in 1974 [*RSBR* Je 1 76]. Designed for "both beginning and experienced communications personnel," it contains more than 5,000 of the most frequently used technical, common, and slang words (about 1,000 more than the previous edition) from every area of contemporary electronic communication. For instance, *cobalt-energized*, *costumes*, and *couch potato* are defined using 3 to 20 words. Broadcast communication terms from English-speaking countries around the world are included, and cross-references are made to equivalent British terminology.

Terms defined are drawn from the areas of "cable television; . . . television programming and production; network and station operations; broadcast equipment and engineering; audio and videotape recording; performing talent; agency and client advertising procedures; media usage; research; defense, government, trade, and allied groups."

BCD entries consist of brief definitions, and cross-references are given liberally. There are a few illustrative quotations. Definitions are readable, accurate, and remarkably current. There are a few biographical entries (*Henson, Jim*) and entries for companies (*Teledata*). Some entries have a date to indicate the introduction of the word or product. Arrangement is alphabetical, letter by letter, and acronyms are alphabetized as words. The book concludes with a bibliography that lists titles as current as 1988. The editor is a broadcasting professional who has also taught at the college level.

BCD is recommended for academic libraries serving broadcast communications curricula. Public libraries serving people interested in broadcasting may also want to consider purchase. Because of the rapid expansion of the broadcast communication vocabulary, libraries owning either the first or second edition of *The Broadcast Communication Dictionary* will want to update with the current edition.

Passport to World Band Radio. 1988 ed. Ed. by Lawrence Magne and others. International Broadcasting Services, Ltd.; dist. by Quality Books, 1987. 399p. paper $14.95 (0-914941-15-1).

384.54'5 Radio, Short wave—Amateurs' manuals I Radio stations, Short wave—Directories [CIP] 87-22739

This is a consumer's guide to radio receivers plus a directory to shortwave radio broadcasting around the world. The first section, "How to Tune in the World," has entertaining feature articles on Latin American music, Jackie Gleason as a radio buff, Middle East English-language broadcasts, and world-band broadcasting from China, Russia, Ghana, and Canada.

The buyer's guide to world-band radio section rates receivers and lists them in various categories (portables, tabletop, and special categories, including a section on antennas). The appraisals can be very brief or rather detailed, but generally include list price, advantages, disadvantages, and an overall conclusion.

For libraries, other features will be more appealing. Foremost among them is a table of radio stations broadcasting on world band listed by country and accompanied by information on frequencies and languages. We find, for instance, that Radio Tirana in Albania broadcasts in Spanish on 11985 KHz. Another table records the number of hours broadcast and hours jammed within each country. The largest section of the volume is "Worldscan: The Blue Pages," a chart arranged by frequency, noting which countries and stations broadcast on that frequency. This chart has a world time table (Greenwich time) for each station, listing the hours broadcast by that station. Symbols indicate the language of the broadcast, whether it is jammed, and if it is seasonal. Alternate frequency, days (if not daily), transmitter power, network, and target zones (intended audience) are other elements indicated. Four lexicons follow and conclude the volume: English, French, Spanish, and German. They explain abbreviations used and have several in-depth definitions of terms. This is, however, not the easiest book to use. The definitions are scattered in the book—not, alas, at the beginning where a novice needs this information.

Though a specialized work, this title is affordable for most public libraries. Libraries with shortwave radio buffs among their users will want to consider purchasing it.

The Historical Encyclopedia of Costumes. By Albert Racinet. Facts On File, 1988. 320p. illus. index. hardcover $40 (0-8160-1976-2).

391'.009 Costume—History [CIP] 88-11186

In late-nineteenth-century Europe "it was essential for the cultivated person to have an interest in and a knowledge of the history of dress." Paintings, novels, and plays with exotic, oriental, and historical themes were popular; tableaux vivants and costume balls were in vogue, and historical accuracy in costume was increasingly required. Auguste Racinet, a French illustrator, took advantage of new reprographic techniques to produce and annotate plates that cover dress "dans tous les temps et chez tous les peuples." Racinet's *Le Costume Historique* (6v.) was published in Paris in 1888.

This classic work (Sheehy BF86) has been translated into English and reorganized, edited, and redesigned by experts from London's Victoria and Albert Museum and the Courtauld Institute of Art. The result is a handsome oversize volume with full-color reproductions of Racinet's original lithographs on every other page with facing pages of text describing the costumes and their backgrounds. Racinet's main organization of four sections has been kept; each section is subdivided into specific regions, countries, and empires. The introduction to each section provided by the editors explains the scope of the coverage and the historical sources for the illustrations and comments on Racinet's reliability as well as on his prejudices.

Section 1, "The Ancient World," depicts men and women of high and low station from the Egypt of 1200 B.C. to the fall of Rome around A.D. 400. Included are illustrations of Amazons, as if they actually existed. The title of section 2, "19th Century Antique Civilizations," was used by Racinet to mean non-European groups: peoples of the Middle and Far East, Australia, the Pacific Islands, American Indians, and Africans. Section 3, "Europe from Byzantium to the 1800s," is organized by country and social class. Section 4, "Traditional Costumes of the 1880s," ranges from peasant costumes worn for festivals to worker's dress to formal wear for the fashionable.

The value of Racinet's work lies in the comprehensiveness and detail of his 2,000 lithographs. The wonderful, strongly nineteenth-century-flavored illustrations with their ethnocentric viewpoint put into a twentieth-century perspective by the editors provide the benefit of a period work with readable text.

Though fascinating, neither Racinet's text nor plates can be considered reliable or scholarly. He doesn't cite sources. The reader cannot always tell which part of the text is translation from the original and which is supplied by editors. Inconsistencies abound in the index. Some place-names are included and many others not. Cross-references are spotty.

Despite these flaws, librarians serving students or professionals in the art, fashion, or design fields will be pleased to be able to acquire this charming book for such a reasonable price.

Festivals U.S.A. By Kathleen Thompson Hill. Wiley, 1988. 242p. index. paper $12.95 (0-471-62636-8).

394.2'6973 Festivals—U.S. [CIP] 87-3479

Festivals U.S.A. lists the nation's best 1,000 festivals as identified by the author. Designed as a travel guide, this directory is organized geographically by region and then by state and by month. Festival entries include the date and location of the festival, a description of the event, foods served, notation of free admission when applicable, type of accommodations and restaurants (but no specific names), and contact name, address, and telephone number for additional information. At least one festival is misplaced because the contact office is in a different state from where the festival is actually held.

A glossary assists users by defining local terminology and jargon, for example, *Acadian, buck dancing, pig pickin'*, and *spotza*. A subject index provides excellent access to festivals featuring antiques, bicycle races, sand sculpture, strawberries, and other activities. There is no direct access by the name of the event such as the Frogtown Frolic or Heritage Days.

This is a helpful reference tool at a time when the popularity of festivals as sources of entertainment has increased. With a different orientation for the weekend traveler or vacation planner, this book is a welcome supplement to Gale's *Festivals Sourcebook* [*RBB* Ja 15 85], which lists more than 4,000 festivals.

LANGUAGE

The Oxford English Dictionary: On Compact Disc. Version 4.10 [1 disc]. Oxford, 1988 (c1987). $950 + $15 shipping & handling (0-944674-01-1).

421.3 English language—Dictionaries ‖ English language—Etymology [BKL]

The Oxford English Dictionary: On Compact Disc is based on the 12-volume edition of the *OED*, which was published in 1933 by Oxford University Press. That edition was a reprint, with corrections and additions, of the 10-volume *New English Dictionary on Historical Principles*, compiled under the editorship of James A. H. Murray and published between 1884 and 1928. The compact-disc version of the *OED* does not contain the entries in the *Supplement and Bibliography* volume, published as volume 13 of the 1933 edition, nor the four-volume *Supplement* to the *OED*, published from 1972 to 1986, which superseded it.

The 4.10 version of the *OED on CD* consists of a single compact disc, two floppy diskettes containing the software for running the *OED* program, and a 106-page *User's Guide*. As the introduction to the *User's Guide* makes clear, the *OED on CD* is not intended to replace the printed work for conventional lookups, since reading lengthy entries on the screen can be tedious. The value of the compact-disc version lies in its enabling the user to access material within the dictionary's entries in very sophisticated ways. (For example, a user could search for words derived from the Latin word *cor*, for words of Turkish origin, for words that have usages specific to Australia or New Zealand, for terms pertaining to medicine, for obsolete words meaning "inebriated," or for quotations from Jane Austen's *Persuasion*.) In addition, it provides the capability of saving or printing the data gathered.

According to the *User's Guide*, the *OED on CD* can be operated on "an IBM PC, XT or AT (or compatibles) with a minimum of 640K of memory." The *OED* disc may be used on any compact-disc drive that runs under Microsoft CD-ROM extensions. In addition, it will run on some older models of drives manufactured by Sony, Hitachi, and Philips. Although the program utilizes color, it will work on either a monochrome or color monitor. For most efficient and effective use, the *OED on CD* should be run on a system that has an EGA (enhanced graphics adapter) interface that converts special characters (such as accent marks and ligatures) so they display just as they appear in the printed *OED*. For this review, the Board used a system that did not have the EGA interface; therefore, special characters were replaced with codes that had to be interpreted by accessing additional screens, further complicating the search process. Queries of the *OED on CD* database originate on the basic search screen, which lists menu options horizontally across the top of the screen. Among these options are the eight searchable fields: four involving the treatment of the word itself and four pertaining to the illustrative quotations. Since the terminology used for these eight fields does not always correspond to the printed *OED*, even veteran users of the dictionary may have initial difficulty developing an appropriate query. The first four searchable fields on the menu are (1) "lemma," which searches the main word listings, including both the headword and any subordinate words (such as compounds or derivatives) treated within the entry; (2) "etym" (etymology), which searches the sections of *OED* articles pertaining to the form history of a word and its roots in other languages; (3) "sense," which searches the actual definitions of words; and (4) "label," which searches all parts of an entry except the illustrative quotations for terms "used to classify a word or meaning in the *OED*," such as abbreviations that indicate parts of speech, geographic designations, or topical usage (e.g., *Mil* for military, *OFris* for Old Frisian, *vb* for verb, and *Obs* for obsolete). The remaining four search functions on the menu screen allow the user to search the illustrative quotations by date or a range of dates from 1150 to 1928 (with a maximum range of 20 years), by author, by title of the quoted work (including books, journals, and newspapers), and by words in the text of the quotation.

At the bottom of the search screen is a window that lists frequently used function keys and briefly notes their uses. This information varies according to the option selected. It should be noted that some of the function keys work only in relation to the search screen, while others work only with the display screen. Still others work with both screens but perform different functions with each. In addition, some function keys duplicate options provided in the menu bar.

Since the printed *OED* was compiled and published over a course of many years, a number of inconsistencies appear among the entries. This is particularly true for the citations to authors and their works that accompany the illustrative quotations and also for the abbreviations used to categorize words. Therefore, prior to searching the label field, the quotation author field, or the quotation work field, it is generally best to review the indexes for those fields in order to identify any variations in spelling, punctuation, or spacing that would affect the precision of the search. (Although the *User's Guide* mentions that capitalization can also sometimes affect the outcome of a search, we did not encounter an example of this problem during our sample searches.) To access an index list before formulating a query, the user highlights the appropriate field on the menu bar in the search screen and presses the ENTER key. Once the designated field appears in the query box, the user presses ENTER again, which results in opening up the index list. The user can then either scroll through the list a line or a page at a time or type in one or more letters to access a specific part of the list. For example, a search for variants of *South Africa(n)* in the label index identified five different designators: *s afr*, *s africa*, *s african*, *south africa*, and *south african*. Similarly, a search for labels pertaining to mythology found *classical mythol*, *gr mythol*, *myth*, *mythol*, and *mythology*. In addition, a search of the quotation author index revealed two variants of *Wordsworth* (*wordsw* and *wordsworth*), while a search in the quotation work index revealed two variants of the *New York Times* (*n.y. times* and *new york times*). Obviously some of these variants could be located only by browsing the complete file rather than looking at just one part of the alphabetical sequence. By highlighting appropriate terms in the index list and then pressing ENTER, the user can select the terms to be used in the search without having to type them again in the query statement. The index lists also indicate the number of occurrences of each term and the number of entries in which the term appears. They do not, however, identify what an abbreviation stands for; therefore, the user must refer to the printed *OED* for that kind of explanation.

Each of the eight searchable fields has an "index specifier," an abbreviation used in searching the dictionary for that index. For example, *qa* is the index specifier for the quotation author field, while *la* is the specifier for the label field. Phrasing the query statement requires designating the appropriate index specifier for each field to be searched, followed by an equal (=) sign, and then the term(s) to be searched. A search can include a number of terms from the same field. For example, the search *se=literature and art* will locate any entries with both of those terms in the definition field. All fields can be searched separately or in combination with one another through the use of the Boolean operators *and*, *or*, and *andnot* or symbols that stand for these operators. For example, a search for a quotation by Keats containing the word *joy* would be phrased *qa=keats and qt=joy*.

After typing the query statement, the user presses F10 to initiate the search. Once the search is underway, a window opens on the right of the query screen and displays a report of the total number of occurrences that match the query. If more than one index is being searched, separate postings appear for each. (In the *Keats/joy* example, the report showed "QA=1531" and "QT=1307.") The actual entries that match both parts of the query then begin to display in a box on the left of the screen. Arranged alphabetically by the headword *lemma*, these listings also note the part(s) of speech and the number of occurrences within the entry. (This figure can be misleading since a match of *Keats* and *joy* together in one entry posts as two occurrences: one occurrence of each search term.) A section at the top of the entry-list box indicates when the search is completed, provides the total number of entries that match the query, and notes whether or not the entry list is complete. Frequently searches are noted as completed long before all entries are actually available for viewing.

The user can begin to display individual entries from the list even when a search is still in progress by scrolling to the entry desired and pressing ENTER. The main portion of the display screen that then appears consists of the entry itself, which follows the basic arrangement of the printed *OED*. At this juncture, the advantage of having a color monitor becomes immediately apparent since the various sections of an entry display in different colors, thus making it easy to distinguish among the different parts of an article, such as the etymology, definitions, and illustrative quotations. The occurrence—that part of an entry that matches the query—is highlighted for easy identification. In the case of entries that take multiple screens to display, if the occurrence does not appear on the first screen, the user can press the plus (+) key to go directly to it. Conversely, the minus (-) key can be used to move to previous occurrences within an entry.

A menu bar at the top of the display screen provides options for going to the previous or next entry, displaying the entry list, or viewing the codes for special characters such as accent marks, phonetic symbols, or Old English characters that display correctly only on monitors supported by an EGA interface. (For example, non-EGA monitors display the word *counter-claim* as "cou AEsdd AFnter-claim." By viewing the codes option, the user can ascertain that "AEsdd AF" indicates a double stress dot.) Among the other options are "take-note," which moves the user to a screen with a notepad area for recording and saving notes about that particular entry, and "map," which provides an outline of longer entries, showing the structure of the entry's sense fields and indicating with an arrow when an occurrence appears in one of these fields. In addition, an "output" option provides the ability to print out or store the information in an entry. Choosing this option results in the display of a submenu that offers the user the choice of printing (or sending to a disk) the entire screen being displayed, the entire entry (up to 10 screens), specific lines within the entry, or the list of all entries that matched the inquiry. The latter option prints out the query statement followed by a list of the entries formatted in three columns but arranged alphabetically from left to right across the page.

When exiting a search, the user can elect to save a query so that it can be used later or combined with other queries. The system provides for the storage of eight separate user profiles. A maximum of 32 queries and their results can be saved in each user profile. This feature would be most appropriate for frequent users of the system who are engaged in ongoing scholarly projects. User-profile screens can be used to modify certain aspects of the *OED on CD* to meet the needs of the individual researcher. For example, the user can indicate that queries should always be saved, or in systems with EGA-supported monitors, the user can alter the color displays by varying the amounts of red, green, or blue used in any portion of the search and display panels.

A very detailed hierarchy of help screens is available throughout the system. Although these screens provide basic information, they are concisely worded and do not contain sufficient detail to answer many of the questions that arise during the search process. Consequently, the user must undertake a very careful and thorough review of the *User's Guide* in order to become familiar enough with the system to feel comfortable and confident in using it. The *User's Guide* that accompanies the 4.10 version is much improved over the one designed for use with the earlier 3.8 version. However, some areas could use more careful editing and additional clarification. For example, the *Guide* initially indicates that all search terms should be placed in quotation marks, but the accompanying example does not use quotation marks. These instructions are clarified on a later page, which notes that quotation marks must be used around multiple-word search terms but are not required for one-word search terms. (They were required in the two-disc 3.8 version, however.) On another page of the *User's Guide*, the instructions indicate that to search a range of dates "a hyphen or space must separate the dates specified." Yet, in experimenting with several queries that included ranges of dates, the Board found that only dates separated by a hyphen worked; those separated by a space would not search. The main deficiency of the *User's Guide*, however, is the lack of an index. A detailed index covering all sections of the *Guide*, including the appendixes and the glossary, would greatly reduce user frustration in attempting to master the system.

A major problem with the *OED on CD* is that searches involving a term or terms with numerous matches take a long time to complete. The search *et=ofris*, for example, to find all the words in the dictionary that derive from Old Frisian, displayed the search status as completed approximately five minutes after the query was initiated; however, the entry list was still not complete after an additional 20 minutes. Searches that include a range of dates are particularly slow. After a wait of 15 minutes, a search for *qa="blake w" and qd=1783-1800* was still in process, and only two entries were available for display. (These observations are based on use of the CD-ROM on an IBM PS/2 Model 30. It is possible that such searches would be processed more quickly on a different system.)

The 4.10 version of the *OED on CD* is a complicated, sophisticated system that requires patience and perseverance to search with precision and effectiveness. However, it allows users to retrieve parts of the dictionary entries that cannot be looked up in the printed version. The types of information it accesses will be most useful to linguists, philologists, lexicographers, and other scholars of the English language, and therefore it will be most appropriate for large academic or research libraries. Serious users will require a setting where they can work with the dictionary for long periods of time without worrying about being interrupted. Reference librarians may also find the *OED on CD* useful for identifying elusive quotations not located in standard quotation dictionaries. However, since the quotations selected for the *OED* are chosen for their representativeness and not their quotability, it is difficult to predict how often a CD-ROM search would succeed when standard printed sources have failed.

Potential buyers of the *OED on CD* should be aware that Oxford University Press is publishing a second edition of the *Oxford English Dictionary* in March 1989, with a prepublication price of $1,995. This 20-volume edition will integrate all printed volumes of the *OED* into one alphabet and will also incorporate approximately 5,000 new words and meanings that have come into use since the *Supplement* was completed. Oxford is also planning to make the database for the *OED*, which is continually being updated, available online and will produce a CD-ROM version of the second edition in 1991.

The Barnhart Dictionary of Etymology. Ed. by Robert K. Barnhart. Wilson, 1988. 1,284p. bibliog. hardcover $59 (0-8242-0745-9).

422'.03 English language—Etymology—Dictionaries [CIP] 87-27994

Based on current scholarship, tracing origins and usage back as far as Middle English, and reporting on some of the newest words in the language, *The Barnhart Dictionary of Etymology* covers the core of American English vocabulary in use today. The Barnhart name is well known in the dictionary field. Editor Robert K. Barnhart served as coeditor with his father, Clarence, of *The World Book Dictionary*, *The Barnhart Dictionary of New English since 1963*, and *The Second Barnhart Dictionary of New English*. In addition, he is the editor of the *Hammond Barnhart Dictionary of Science* (reissued as *The American Heritage Dictionary of Science*). Several eminent language scholars in the U.S. (Ralph DeGorog and Einar Haugen, among others) assisted in the preparation of the *Dictionary*, which has as its purpose "to make examples of the development of English an understandable subject for those with no specialized knowledge of language study."

The Barnhart Dictionary of Etymology contains some 30,000 entries. Each entry includes spelling variations, pronunciation (when not self-evident, as in *cornucopia*, *daub*, *forensic*, and *monomial*), part of speech, a short definition, date of first recorded use in English (with original spelling), and information on the language(s) from which the word evolved. Many times the circumstances of the first known usage in English are noted. The entry *monotony* is a good example: "n. tiresome sameness, tedium. 1706, in Pope's *Letters*; borrowed, perhaps through French *monotonie* (1671), from Greek *monotonía*, from *monótonos* monotonous, of one tone (*mono-* one + *tónos* TONE)." A departure from other etymological dictionaries is evident here—the only abbreviations found are for the parts of speech. Languages are spelled out in full, and use of other lexicographical devices is avoided. Small caps (as in "TONE") indicate a cross-reference to another entry. Some entries continue by commenting on the word's history, fleshing out its meaning and origin for the reader. For example, *humane*: "In the early 1700's, this word became restricted in use to the meaning kind, merciful. See the note under HUMAN. For about 250 years *human* and *humane* shared the meaning "of or belonging to man," but in the 1700's the meanings differentiated with the spellings and the separate pronunciations so that *human* with its stress on the first syllable, retained the original sense and *humane* with its stress on the last syllable, became restricted to the sense of merciful, kind. The process of a differentiation of meaning, however, was gradual, beginning about 1500." The *Dictionary* includes scientific and technical terms (*echovirus, mutagen*), regional vocabulary (*lagniappe, hoosier*), product names (*nylon, Xerox*), slang (*nerd, jeepers-creepers*), as well as words of recent origin (*yuppie, Medicare*). Words that originated in the U.S. or are now commonly used only in the U.S. are labeled as American English.

The *Dictionary* also includes a short history of the English language, a glossary of language names and linguistic terms, and a glossary of pre-1600 literary works cited in entries (for example, "*Apology Made by Him, The* an autobiographical work by Sir Thomas More (1533), written in defense of himself, also known as *Apologie of Syr Thomas More, Knyght*").

This is the first scholarly etymological dictionary to appear since 1966, when *A Comprehensive Etymological Dictionary of the English Language* (by Ernest Klein), *The Oxford Dictionary of English Etymology* (edited by C. T. Onion), and *Origins: A Short Etymological Dictionary of Modern English*, 4th edition (by Eric Partridge) were published. Onion, with 38,000 entries, is highly regarded for its completeness and reliability. Klein is noted for its larger number of entries (45,000) and its coverage of scientific terms and names from mythology. Partridge, while not as thorough as the other two (25,000 entries), has a more inviting style of presentation for the general reader, treats cognate words together under one entry (which allows the reader to more conveniently see word relationships), and has separate sections covering prefixes and suffixes. Each of these books has unique strengths and scopes that will continue to earn them a place on reference shelves for some time to come.

When compared to them, however, *The Barnhart Dictionary of Etymology* offers some unique features as well as a fresh perspective. First is its focus on the core words used in contemporary American English and its designation of words of American origin. Second is its reliance on current American scholarship, which in some cases disputes earlier conclusions. Third is its combination of readability with scholarship—the expansion of its entries with interesting and enlightening facts and the elimination of abbreviations and other shorthand. This combination makes for a sum that is truly greater than its parts, resulting in a reasonably priced work of exceptional quality and attractiveness that will no doubt be the preferred choice of most patrons. Recommended for high school, public, and academic libraries.

Book of Roots: A Full Study of Our Families of Words. By Duane Beeler. Union Representative, 430 S. Michigan Ave., Chicago, IL 60605, 1988. 256p. paper $15.95 (0-918515-00-9).

422'.03 English language—Roots—Dictionaries I English language—Word formation—Dictionaries [OCLC] 88-198405

The Roots of English: A Reader's Handbook of Word Origins. 1st ed. By Robert Claiborne. Times Books, Aug. 1989. 338p. hardcover $18.95 (0-8129-1716-2).

422'.03 English language—Roots [BKL]

These two books both list roots from which English words have evolved but serve different purposes. The author of *Book of Roots* is a labor educator who previously published *Learning Our Language: The Root Concept* (1986). Beeler's purpose in writing *Book of Roots* was to focus on the vital role that recognition of word roots plays in vocabulary building. Following some introductory material briefly tracing the history of the English language, the main body of the book begins with an alphabetical listing of close to 100 prefixes from Latin, Greek, and Anglo-Saxon, their meanings, and selected words containing them ("*bi-*: two, twice—*biennial, bigamy, bilingual, bifocal*"). Next is a similar list of 125 or so suffixes ("*-arian*: person who (n)—*grammarian, antiquarian, librarian*"). A group of simplified major roots follows, with about 200 main entries ("*fort*: strong—*forte, fortitude, comfort, effort, reinforce*"). Following this is a section with about 100 entries, titled "Roots with Selected Derivatives" ("*ject*: throw—*abject, adjective, conjecture, deject, eject, . . .project, . . .trajectory, ejaculate*"). The next portion, titled "Major Roots," accounts for more than two-thirds of the book's pages and covers more than 500 root meanings. All are from Latin, with a few exceptions from Greek. Each entry gives the major root, one or more Latin words, the number of English derivatives, and then lists several English derivatives. (For example, "*cul, col*: colo, cultum—*cultivate, till, care for, 18; cultivate, culture, agriculture, horticulture, colony, colonial*.") Each English derivative is then defined, and a further list of its derivatives given ("*cultivate*: to till and prepare the soil—*cultivable, cultivatable, cultivation, cultivator*"). Last is a list of about 500 minor roots, defined as those often having only one core word and few prefixes ("*pont*: bridge—*pontiff, pontificate, pontoon*"). The Board questions the purpose and need for the "Selected Derivatives" and "Simplified Roots" sections. All the entries found in "Selected Derivatives" were also found in "Simplified Roots," and almost all the entries in "Simplified Roots" were located in the "Major Roots" section. The various sections with their separate alphabetical arrangements can be confusing and hamper the use of the book.

Several titles designed to help improve one's vocabulary incorporate the root approach, for instance, *101 Ways to Improve Your Vocabulary* (Arco, 1983) and *Words Come in Families* (Hart, 1977), neither of which contains as many roots as Beeler's book. *Book of Roots* has several strong points: the number of roots covered, the great number of English derivatives listed and defined, its attractive design, and its reasonable cost. Students and others interested in language study will find it helpful; it is recommended for school and public libraries.

Claiborne, author of *The Roots of English*, has written several books on language, including *Our Marvelous Native Tongue: The Life and Times of the English Language* (1983). His new book goes back a step farther in time than Beeler's by identifying Indo-European roots for English words. His purpose is not vocabulary building, since the connection between the Indo-European root and the English word is usually not obvious, but to entertain the word buff. After a lengthy introduction about the languages that served as sources for modern English, a table shows consonant shifts in major Indo-European languages. For instance, the shift from *P* in Indo-European to *F* in Germanic explains how the words *pyre* and *fire* are related. In the main part of the book, Claiborne groups more than 6,000 common words under their Indo-European root sources. Each entry lists the Germanic, Latin, or Greek descendants of the root. Claiborne doesn't try to include comprehensive lists of derived English words; he gives a few examples and assumes that the reader will be able to supply related words. (For example, "*BHLIG-*, L [Latin] *fligere, flict-*, to strike. If you're AFFLICTed, you're 'struck' by something that someone or something has INFLICTed on you; in a CONFLICT, people are 'striking with' one another, literally or figuratively.") Some entries are quite discursive, for example, the debate as to whether the word *lox* (salmon) derived from *laks*. There is also a modest selection of roots from Germanic and Latin that have contributed to our vocabulary. These are in the main alphabetical sequence but are in brackets. The book concludes with an index of English words and their roots. This entertaining book will be enjoyed by language lovers in public and academic libraries but, like *Book of Roots*, will probably be better placed in the circulating collection.

Morris Dictionary of Word and Phrase Origins. 2d ed. By William and Mary Morris. Harper, 1988. 669p. index. hardcover $25 (0-06-015862-X).

422'.03 English language—Etymology—Dictionaries I English language—Terms and phrases [CIP] 87-45651

The Morrises are well-known lexicographers whose previous publications include *The Harper Dictionary of Contemporary Usage* (2d ed., 1985 [RBB N 1 86]) and *The American Heritage Dictionary of the English Language* (1969 [RSBR F 1 72]). For more than 30 years they have also written a daily syndicated newspaper column, "Words, Wit, and Wisdom." This book is a revision of a book with the same title published in 1977 [RSBR O 15 78], which was itself a revision of their *Dictionary of Word and Phrase Origins*, published in three volumes between 1962 and 1971. This new edition includes an introduction by Isaac Asimov.

The authors state that they wrote this book in order to trace the histories of the more interesting words and phrases in the language, to enlighten and entertain the reader in a casual manner, but also to back up their statements with solid scholarship. From *barrel of monkeys* to *wild and woolly West*, they succeed in imparting, in an informal and casual style, the histories behind the words and phrases whose origins many times cannot be determined. Readers will enjoy the histories so much they may find it hard to set the book aside. As for the scholarship, the Board repeats what it noted in reviewing the first edition: "statements are usually undocumented, sometimes admittedly unverified, and often inexact. Phrases such as 'we suspect,' 'probably originated in,' and 'but that's only a guess' can be found in the entries. In spite of this vagueness, many of the etymologies and phrase origins agree in essence with material presented in a more scholarly fashion with proper citations in other sources." The physical format matches that of the first edition, with the entries arranged alphabetically, letter by letter. Pronunciation is given for those words that are not self-evident (*debilitate*, *segue*). Discussion following each entry varies in length from a sentence to more than a page. A 39-page index provides access to all terms discussed in the body of each entry.

Although information from the publisher claims that 25 percent of the material is new to the second edition, a sampling of entries indicates that a little more than 10 percent are new to this edition. No revision of first edition entries was found. Entries new to this edition include many names (*Abraham, Adam, Laura, Mildred*), a few new additions to the language (*greenmail*), plus many words and phrases that have been in the language for quite some time (*duck, ours but to do or die, snakeoil*).

This dictionary is similar in concept to the late John Ciardi's three books: *A Browser's Dictionary and Native's Guide to the Unknown American Language* (1980 [RSBR Ap 15 81]), *A Second Browser's Dictionary . . .* (1983 [RBB Ja 15 84]), and *Good Words to You* (1987). Although neither the Morrises' nor Ciardi's works are a substitute for scholarly etymological works, they offer something not found in sufficient quantity elsewhere—accessibility for the everyday reader interested in words. Both do that in a delightful way. Neither work is a substitute for the other. Coverage of words and phrases does not overlap significantly, and oftentimes the comments on the same entries offer differing information. The Morrises' work has the added advantage of its index, which gives much greater access to the words and phrases. While this second edition is not a necessary purchase for libraries having the first, libraries without a circulating copy should consider purchasing it for reference and making the older copy available for checkout to the word lovers who will relish reading it from cover to cover.

Common Allusions and Foreign Terms. Rev. ed. By Helen Boese. Simplicity Press; dist. by Quality, 1988. 158p. bibliog. paper $9.95.

422'.4 English language—Foreign words and phrases—Dictionaries I Allusions—Dictionaries [CIP] 88-11333

This dictionary contains 2,000 common allusions and foreign phrases that most Americans are expected to know, conveniently brought together in one book. The author compiled it after experiencing a need for such a book while teaching college English to adults at an air force base. Terms for inclusion were chosen from widely read magazines.

Information covered includes plots, authors, characters, literary terms, fairy tales, children's stories and games, nursery rhymes, foreign words and expressions (especially Latin and French), quotations, proverbs, idioms, historical figures, artists, and musicians. For each listing a simple explanation is given: "*Friendly Persuasion*—Stories (1945) by Jessamyn West about Quaker life in Indiana"; "*Déjà vu*—Fr., the strange feeling that what is happening now has happened before."

A list of sources for more extensive research on allusions and culture in general appears at the end of the book. It includes some 70 works, such as *Benét's Reader's Encyclopedia*, *Brewer's Dictionary of Phrase and Fable*, many Oxford companions, and standard reference books on literature, mythology, the Bible, quotations, idioms, foreign terms, music, art, ballet, and history.

The book is based on an interesting premise and is competently done. It might be a good book to own for a young person or a student of English as a second language. It could be useful in a junior high or high school library. Other libraries would be better served by the traditional reference books that give more extensive coverage of these subjects.

Childcraft Dictionary. World Book, 1989. 900p. illus. tables. hardcover $25 (0-7166-1489-8).

423 English language—Dictionaries, Juvenile [OCLC] 88-50694

This is a completely new elementary school dictionary. (World Book published a *Childcraft Dictionary* in 1982 that was a version of the *Macmillan Dictionary for Children*. This new *Childcraft Dictionary* is not based on any other dictionary.) It will be easy for children aged 8–11 to use because of the large boldface print of entry words, clear illustrations, and readable definitions that deliberately do not include the word being defined. A "How to Use Your Dictionary" section explains the alphabetical order, guide words (in pairs at the top outside edges of every spread), and the parts of entries: variant spellings and multiple definitions, parts of speech, word division and pronunciation keys, and often sample sentences. Homophones, synonyms, antonyms, plural and adjective forms, and idioms are all shown in boldface type. The inclusion of so many idioms (for instance, under *music*, "face the music" and "music to one's ears") is a unique feature of this *Dictionary*. "Language Facts" and "Word History" features are provided for some entry words to make history, usage, and definitions clear and to add interest. For instance, the boxed "Language Fact" for *ain't* states it "is a word most people agree is wrong to use." The pronunciation key is given on the bottom of each left-hand page.

Words are up to date, with *AIDS*, *byte*, and *VCR* included, and meanings from computer science for *program* and *disk*. There are also some unexpected entries, such as specific dog breeds (e.g., *Bedlington terrier*, *Lakeland terrier*, and *Brussels griffon*). Many entries are for plants and animals. Holidays of most major religions and ethnic groups are included (e.g., *Kwanza, Rosh Hashanah*), except *Ramadan*. There are few biographical and no geographic entries in the body of the *Dictionary*. Among the abbreviations defined are *Ms.* and *UNICEF*. The interests of children have been taken into account when building the word list. Defined, for instance, are *Frisbee, origami*, and *skateboard*. There is some inconsistency in words chosen for inclusion. For instance, there is the entry *Lincoln's Birthday* but no *Washington's Birthday*.

Large color illustrations are given for about 10 percent of the entries (two-thirds of these are drawings or charts, one-third are photographs), so that every two-page spread has about three illustrations. A "Letter History" section is found at the beginning of each letter, showing its Roman, Egyptian, and Middle Eastern origins. Vocabulary self-tests for grades 3–6 are found at the end of the *Dictionary*, along with word and name stories and such useful tables as state and national capitals, presidents of the U.S., and metric conversion.

This book is also published with 16 pages of student exercises and a library binding as *The World Book Student Dictionary*. While the *Childcraft Dictionary* is no longer based on the *Macmillan Dictionary for Children*, both contain many of the same features and their pages resemble each other in design. They have approximately the same number of entries. *Webster's Elementary Dictionary* is more difficult to use and will be useful for older elementary children. *Webster's* does not consistently include sample sentences and has far more words on each page. While the *Childcraft Dictionary* won't replace any of the standard dictionaries, it is current, attractive, and useful, and will be a good addition to elementary school and public libraries.

The Lincoln Writing Dictionary for Children. HBJ, 1988. 901p. illus. hardcover $17.95 (0-15-152394-0).

423 English language—Dictionaries, Juvenile [OCLC] 88-11167

Students use a dictionary to look up definitions, pronunciation, usage, etymologies, and parts of speech of words, and this new *Dictionary* for children adequately fills most of these needs. In addition, it is a dictionary meant for reading, specifically created by Harcourt Brace Jovanovich to restore "lost" features of older dictionaries not usually found today. Included are 4,000 quotations from the works of over 500 writers and "600 short essays on the art and craft of writing."

A browser will find plenty of writing help (*irony, opening lines, fragments*) in the appealing essays and enjoy word histories for selected entries, both in highlighted boxes. Many definitions are enhanced by illustrations: Raphael's painting of St. George slaying the dragon illustrates *dragon*, and a photograph of a Calder work illustrates *mobile*. The pictures are excellent—a combination of color and black-and-white photographs, drawings, and paintings—and the pages are laid out clearly and attractively, with pronunciation keys running repeatedly in the corner of every five right-hand pages.

Most definitions are clear and accurate, and each entry includes syllabication, pronunciation(s), part of speech, and other forms of the word (plurals, tenses). Many also include subentries, references, and example sentences. Although students usually appreciate example sentences, these are often literary quotations, not necessarily illustrative or even meaningful. The sentence under *meander* reads "*Meandering* mountain streams watered the lush green grass and the air was warm without being hot (Walter Farley)." Many of the very fine authors whose works are quoted won't be familiar to young readers (Philip Roth, D. H. Lawrence, Joan Didion, Joseph Wambaugh), nor need they be recommended at this level.

There are entries for about 300 personal names (authors, political leaders, etc.) and about 300 geographic entries. Ho Chi Minh, Nehru, and Emily Dickinson are listed, but not Duvalier, Tutankhamen, or Perón. Most "editors' opinions" on usage are backed up by citing other sources (*New York Times*) or experts (Roy Copperud). Occasional errors exist, such as pronunciation keys out of sequence and the wrong page reference from *Negro* to *black*.

However, it is not clear for what age group this *Dictionary* was compiled. The publisher states it is for grades 2 to 6. With 35,000 entry words, it is comparable in size to other dictionaries for this age such as the *Macmillan Dictionary for Children* (30,000 words), *Scott, Foresman Beginning Dictionary* (28,000 words), and *The American Heritage Children's Dictionary* (36,000 words). However, the essays on writing and the quotations from literary figures would seem to appeal more to middle school students and up. Comparable dictionaries for middle school students contain many more words. For instance, Macmillan's *Dictionary for Students* has 90,000 words, and *Webster's Intermediate Dictionary* includes over 60,000 words. Thus, for this age group there are many omissions. *VCR, Ms., Yuppie*, and *fast food* are listed, but not found are *bizarre, ion, flout, flaunt, genealogy, minicomputer, yang, zap*, or *Torah*. Synonyms are not included, nor are obsolete meanings of words (*jet, dear*), and etymologies are not given for all entries.

Elementary school libraries will want to consider this handsome *Dictionary* for students in the upper elementary grades. The juvenile title and appearance may limit its usefulness for older students. Nonetheless, junior and senior high schools and public libraries may want to purchase this *Dictionary* for its unusual readability and admirable emphasis on good writing through essays and literary examples. It would be great to have on hand in every language-arts classroom.

Webster's New World Dictionary of American English. 3d ed. Ed. by Victoria Neufeldt and David B. Guralnik. Simon & Schuster; dist. by Prentice Hall Trade Sales, 1988. 1,600p. illus. thumb-indexed hardcover $17.95 (0-13-947169-3).

423 English language—Dictionaries I Americanisms—Dictionaries [OCLC] 88-1712

First published in 1953 and updated biennially, *Webster's New World Dictionary* (see *RSBR* [Mr 15 74] for a review of the second edition) has earned over the years a reputation for its authority, reliability, clarity, and frequent updating, as evidenced by its adoption by the *New York Times*, the Associated Press, and United Press International. Preparation began in 1980 on this new edition (at the time the *Dictionary* was acquired by Simon & Schuster from the publisher William Collins Sons who had acquired it in 1974 from the World Publishing Company) in order to keep pace with the vast changes occurring in the language. While the *Dictionary*'s purpose remains that of serving the student and other users of today's language, some changes have occurred since the second edition. Guralnik, editor in chief since the first edition, retired in 1985 while the *Dictionary* was still in revision and was replaced by Neufeldt, who had been senior editor since 1984. Neufeldt's credentials include a Ph.D. in linguistics and 10 years' experience as a lexicographer. Several of the permanent editorial staff of the *Dictionary* (still headquartered in Cleveland, Ohio, despite the shifts in ownership) have changed as have many of the more than 50 consultants and contributing editors (whose credentials are given). A major factor that delayed the appearance of the third edition was the complexities encountered in the creation of a new and flexible electronic database. The publisher states that this database will now enable much greater ease in updating and in producing spin-offs (the high school dictionary, speller-divider books, etc.).

In its more than 170,000 entries, *Webster's New World Dictionary* often supplies etymologies, gives definitions in historical order (oldest meaning first), clearly indicates pronunciations and parts of speech, identifies more than 11,000 Americanisms by a star preceding the entry, provides spelling variations, gives plural forms when formed irregularly, indicates capitalization, and supplies usage labels. The editors have provided short made-up phrases in many entries to illustrate meanings. Synonyms and their shades of meaning are found for some words. Antonyms are found less often. Some words have usage notes. A brief pronunciation key is found in the lower corner of each right-hand page, while the full key is provided inside the front cover. Illustrations, though sparse (a total of 750), are well drawn and generally add to the understanding of the entry (e.g., *fleur de lis, gable, golf club, insulator, minaret, parallel bars*). A few of the illustrations are maps (*Everglades, Oregon Trail*). Also found in the main alphabetical sequence are foreign terms and phrases, indicated by italics (*fin de siecle, Erin go bragh, Weltschmerz*), biographical and geographic entries (*Edison, Thomas; O'Keeffe, Georgia; Ozark Mountains; Andhra Pradesh*), literary and biblical references (*Divine Comedy, Falstaff, Lord's Prayer*), and abbreviations and acronyms (*IHS, Msgr, PABA*).

The second edition was noted for its strength in etymologies, Americanisms, slang, colloquialisms, and phrases. This is true for the third edition also. Definitions are clear, and the illustrative phrases are generally helpful, though short. Entries have increased by some 12,000, and while underscoring the *Dictionary*'s continued emphasis on the English language as it is used in the U.S., they reflect changes and additions to the language as well as some shifts in editorial philosophy. New words include *cellular phone, couch potato, diskette, glasnost, parawing, poison pill, Star Wars*, and *Walkman*. Not found were *SDI* or *Reaganomics*. Included for the first time are the Anglo-Saxon four-letter swear words (labeled *vulgar*), as well as racial and ethnic slurs (labeled *slang*). The *Dictionary* continues to describe the language as it is used but to provide usage labels or comments (for example, "*irregardless*—REGARDLESS: a nonstandard or humorous usage," and "*disinterested*—*1* not influenced by personal interest or selfish motives; impartial; unbiased 2 uninterested; indifferent: although objected to by some, this usage is a revival of an obsolete meaning").

A striking difference noticed when first comparing the third to the second edition is the improved readability of the typeface. It now equals that of *The American Heritage Dictionary*, second college edition, which has set the standard in the collegiate-dictionary field in this area. The illustrations, somewhat decreased in number, have been redrawn or new work substituted. One new feature is the inclusion of hairline syllabification marks to indicate where words should preferably not break for line-end hyphenation (for example, "mul l ti • plex" and "mum l my"). Another is the revision of plant and animal entries so that the complete taxonomy can be traced (for example, the entry *dogtooth violet* gives the genus name *Erythronium* and tells that it is in the lily family; the entry *lily* gives the family name Lilaceae and indicates it is in the order of monocotyledonous plants, and so on). Metric equivalents are now provided in parentheses following U.S. customary measures. Biographical entries appear up-to-date (Georgia O'Keeffe's 1986 and Andy Warhol's 1987 deaths are noted). Population figures are, for the most part, from 1980. The first of the two prefatory essays has been replaced, but the second on etymology remains the same. Appendixes include a chart of the Indo-European family of languages, advice on editorial style, and signs and symbols used in various fields. Eliminated since the second edition are listings of colleges and universities and a separate table of weights and measures (one on measures is incorporated into the main text).

Other desk dictionaries comparable to *Webster's New World Dictionary* are *The American Heritage Dictionary*, second college edition [RSBR Ag 83], *The Random House College Dictionary* (rev. ed., 1984), *Webster's Ninth New Collegiate Dictionary* (1986), and *Webster's II New Riverside University Dictionary* [RBB Je 15 85]. While all five have a similar number of entries, each has its distinguishing features. *American Heritage* has a great number of photo-illustrations, clear and inviting typeface, and a very accessible style in its introductory guide to the English language. *Webster's Ninth* in some cases offers a clearer, more precise definition than do its competitors. In addition, it is unique in that it dates the first use in the language for many words. *Webster's II New Riverside* offers detailed word histories for more than 300 entries and has very good usage notes, although its coverage is weaker in slang and disapproved terms. *Random House*, while suffering in comparison from less clarity in its typeface and in some of its definitions, offers the most illustrations (with the exception of *American Heritage*). *Webster's New World* is strong in Americanisms, typeface readability, and ease of comprehension of its definitions. Surprisingly, it lacks a table of spelling-sound correspondences, something found in the other titles. *Webster's Ninth* is the most descriptive and *American Heritage* the most prescriptive in usage guidelines, with *Webster's New World* falling midway between.

This new edition of *Webster's New World Dictionary* will strengthen its position in the competitive desk-dictionary market. It maintains its reputation for authority and ease of use in an attractive and reasonably priced package. It speaks to the needs of today's dictionary users and is highly recommended to high school, public, and academic libraries.

Bernstein's Reverse Dictionary. 2d ed. By Theodore M. Bernstein; rev. by David Grambs. Times Books, 1988. 351p. index. tables. hardcover $19.95 (0-8129-1593-3).

423'.1 English language—Synonyms and antonyms ll English language—Dictionaries [CIP] 87-40596

When you know there is a word for what you want to express, but you cannot remember it, look up the definition in *Bernstein's Reverse Dictionary*. First published in 1975, it has had 2,500 words added, including many relating to sports. Bernstein's original introduction has been retained, as well as his aim to provide a guide to precision in language. The alphabetically arranged definitions are brief. There are no pronunciations, abbreviations, or etymologies. Words may appear in more than one place; for example, *oxymoron* is listed under both "contradictory terms combined in one phrase" and "figure of speech in which contradictory terms are combined." The user can look under either *contradictory* or *figure of speech* to find the term. A comparison of the two editions shows some slight revision, but primarily the addition of new words. Both editions have tables of words: medical specialists, U.S. state nicknames, phobias and manias, and creature terms (words for animal groups, male, female, and young). The book concludes with an index of words defined.

Since words chosen tend not to be ones used daily, there are discoveries to be made. *Hendiadys* are "nouns linked by a conjunction to express the same thought as a noun with a modifier." A *slype* is a narrow passage; *ejecta* is matter cast out, as by a volcano; a married native American is a *sannup*; *satyagraha* means passive resistance; *galligaskins* were loose, wide pants.

Bernstein's Reverse Dictionary works as a thesaurus to some extent (e.g., *predilection* is listed under both *bias* and *impartiality*) and as an aid to memory. Users will not always find what they seek because the definition looked up may not correspond to the wording chosen by the editors. *Bernstein's* should be considered for purchase by secondary school, public, and academic libraries, and the first edition can be transferred to the circulating collection where it can be used by browsers entranced by words.

Concise Dictionary of Acronyms and Initialisms. By Stuart W. Miller. Facts On File, 1988. 175p. hardcover $22.95 (0-8160-1577-5).

423'.1 Abbreviations, English—Dictionaries l Acronyms [OCLC] 87-9140

Miller, a librarian, has compiled a dictionary of acronyms, initialisms, and abbreviations designed to meet the everyday needs of the general public, covering those terms likely to be found in newspapers, newsmagazines, crossword puzzles, or other ordinary reading. In addition, some terminology from librarianship and the publishing world has been included for the convenience of librarians. Motivated by discussion with librarians who felt the need for a less comprehensive work than Gale's *Acronyms, Initialisms & Abbreviations Dictionary*—with its more than 400,000 entries—Miller's goal was to produce a publication of manageable size, reasonable cost, and basic usefulness for ready-reference situations. The dictionary has close to 3,000 entries.

Arrangement is alphabetical, letter by letter, with punctuation and spacing ignored. The terms are presented in all caps, lower case, or a combination, depending on common usage. Some of the entries have been annotated for better comprehension: "*GLF*—Gay Liberation Front (one of the first militant homosexual rights' groups of the late 1960s; defunct)"; "*GMC*—General Motors Corporation (used like a brand name for its trucks)." Almost all of the terms are of American, British, or Canadian origin. Although a wide range of terms are included, some areas stand out: government agencies (*FDA, FCO, DOT*), organizations (*PTL, FOE, MPAA*), companies (*IBM, HoJo, BMW*), places (*Ger., IN, ROK*), airport and ticket coding (*P, LAX, DET*), politics and international relations, (*Comintern, NCPAC, PLO*), health (*GI, GRAS, q.i.d.*), and Latin (*cf., q.e.d., PM*). Some terms of recent origin found were *AIDS, SWAPO, YUPPIE, JR* (from the TV series "Dallas"), *HBO*, and *WYSIWYG*. A few expected terms not found were *AZT* (AIDS drug), *UKC* (United Kennel Club, although *AKC* is included), and *SADD* (Students Against Drunk Driving, although *MADD* shows up). The entry "*AFC*—American Friends' Committee (Quaker relief organization)" should be *AFSC*, American Friends Service Committee. With those exceptions, the dictionary is accurate and covers a variety of the acronyms, initialisms, and abbreviations likely to be needed by the general adult reader. High school students will also find it useful. The library and publishing acronyms are not numerous; they will be familiar to most librarians (*FEDLINK, BPI, BRS, SLA*). The annotations are the unique strength of this book, as they will be helpful to anyone who does not have a background in the term's field.

The way entries that begin with a number are filed may be a barrier to finding them. For example, *4-F* is filed between *F* and *F (Plan)*; *3Rs* is filed between *R* and *Ra*. Filing all entries that begin with numbers together would have made access to them easier. Although no other dictionary of acronyms directed to the needs of the general reader exists, this work can be compared with DeSola's *Abbreviations Dictionary* (7th ed., 1985, $47.50). It has 180,000 entries, thus providing much more extensive coverage of various disciplines, languages, and countries. None of the entries are annotated, however. Libraries seeking a title they can hand to the general reader or an added title for convenient ready-reference purposes will find the *Concise Dictionary* a good choice. Recommended for public and school libraries; academic libraries owning the Gale work may want a copy too for the ease of use.

A Dictionary of American Idioms. 2d ed. Rev. by Adam Makkai. Barron's 1988 (c1987). 398p. paper $11.95 (0-8120-3899-1).

423'.1 English language—U.S.—Dictionaries ‖ Americanisms—Dictionaries ‖ English language—Terms and phrases—Dictionaries [CIP] 84-9247

First published in 1975, the *Dictionary of American Idioms* has been revised and updated by Adam Makkai, a professor of linguistics at the University of Illinois at Chicago and executive director of the Linguistic Society of Canada and the United States. Idioms from citizen's band radio jargon, computer technology, the drug culture, and hippie slang are among those added to the new edition, which treats over 5,000 of the most frequently used American idioms. Some expressions no longer in popular use have been dropped.

An idiom is defined in the introduction as "the assigning of a new meaning to a group of words which already have their own meaning." Three types of idioms are included: lexemic idioms, which correlate with familiar parts of speech (e.g., the noun *scandal sheet*); phrase idioms (e.g., *strike it rich*); and proverbial idioms (e.g., *it never rains but it pours*).

The *Dictionary* contains four types of entries, arranged letter by letter. Main entries include full explanations of an idiom. Run-on entries are appended to main entries and treat idioms derived from the main entry (e.g., the entry *trail blazer* is appended to the entry *blaze a trail*). Cross-reference entries direct the user from a less-used form of an idiom to the more common form under which the explanation is given (e.g., from *catch at a straw* to *grasp at straws*). Index entries list all entries that include the index word when it is not the first word of the idiom (e.g., "*step*—See in step, out of step, take steps").

The "Guide to the Parts of an Entry" explains, in the order in which they appear, the 14 elements that may be included in an entry. While some idioms require more detailed treatment than others, all include definition(s), an illustrative sentence that includes the idiom, and a paraphrase that gives the meaning of the illustrative sentence in nonidiomatic language. Other points of information included in some entries are stylistic labels (e.g., *vulgar, literary*), usage notes, and etymology.

The meanings of some of the idioms are so obvious that one wonders about the need to include them (e.g., *run away* or *run off, measure up, make sense*). On the other hand, some idioms in fairly common use are missing (e.g., *bag lady, dry run, shooting gallery*). The type used in the *Dictionary* is somewhat smaller than the type found in most modern dictionaries.

This *Dictionary* is intended for "anybody who wants to make his English more fluent, more idiomatic." It is quite similar to *NTC's American Idioms Dictionary* [*RBB* O 1 87]. That book is slightly larger; both titles include some unique entries. Students and nonnative speakers of English are among the groups who should find these idiom dictionaries especially useful. High school and most public libraries will want at least one of them for their collections.

The Facts On File Dictionary of Troublesome Words. Rev. ed. By Bill Bryson. Facts On File, 1988. 192p. bibliog. hardcover $17.95 (0-8160-1933-9).

428'.003 English language—Usage—Dictionaries ‖ English language—Rhetoric [CIP] 87-33046

The Dictionary of Confusable Words. By Laurence Urdang. Facts On File, 1988. 391p. index. hardcover $29.95 (0-8160-1650-X).

423'.1 English language—Synonyms and antonyms—Dictionaries ‖ English language—Usage—Dictionaries [OCLC] 88-45090

Handbooks and dictionaries of usage have long been a means through which English stylists have vented their frustrations with those who are less careful than they ought in writing or speaking. They offer sage advice about troublesome words and constructions and often provide entertaining insights into the continuing debate over the proper use of the language. Bill Bryson's *Facts On File Dictionary of Troublesome Words* (*DTW*) and Laurence Urdang's *Dictionary of Confusable Words* (*DCW*) are among the latest entries in this long list of usage guides.

Bryson's work, which first appeared in 1984 and was reviewed by the Board [*RBB* N 15 84], is more traditional in its approach than Urdang. *DTW* represents words or constructions that Bryson, an American copyeditor for the London *Times* and former teacher of English, has found to be stumbling blocks for writers, including some of the confusable words found in Urdang. Entries in *DTW* outline briefly the problem of usage created by a word or phrase or explain the differences in meaning between words often confused with each other. Bryson frequently draws examples of linguistic blunders from sources well known for excellent writing and careful editing, such as the *Manchester Guardian* and the *New York Times*. Bryson writes clearly, often using humor to emphasize his point. For example, to illustrate his disapproval of the practice of omitting initial articles from sentences, he concludes his entry *articles, omitted* with "Inevitable result is stilted sentences. Reader is apt to find it annoying. Writer who does it persistently should have his typewriter taken away."

The work is alphabetically arranged, with internal cross-references from second- or third-listed terms back to the appropriate entry word. This revised edition has been reset in a clearer type and has grown from 173 to 192 pages. The number of main entries is approximately 15 percent greater. The volume concludes with a bibliography of usage and style guides, an appendix on punctuation, and a glossary of grammatical terms.

Urdang's *Dictionary of Confusable Words* is more difficult to categorize than *DTW*. To be sure, it is a usage book, with many clear discussions on the appropriate use of words such as *compliment* versus *complement* and *which* versus *that*. Urdang has produced a work of broader scope, however. He has attempted to provide users with a source that makes clear the differences among the major elements of various classes of terms. For example, in one entry Urdang discusses how a speedometer differs from a mileometer, an odometer, or a tachometer. Elsewhere he compares the QWERTY keyboard with the Dvorak keyboard and discourses briefly on the history of typewriting.

Urdang, a longtime compiler of dictionaries and encyclopedias, observes in his introduction that people often "mix up more or less ordinary things." While there are dictionaries and encyclopedias aplenty to define or explain individual terms, few if any provide his contrastive approach. In selecting terms, Urdang has consciously excluded terms he considers either too abstruse for most laymen (e.g., *general* vs. *special theory of relativity*) or so straightforward that a simple dictionary lookup would provide sufficient information (e.g., *biography* vs. *autobiography*). Given his purpose, it is of little surprise that the resulting work is eclectic. It is, nevertheless, an entertaining volume filled with useful information about words and word groups. Arrangement is alphabetical in the text by first word in a grouping. A 63-page index provides cross-reference access to other terms in the text, supplemented very selectively with subject analysis. As a cross-reference guide, the index appears to be complete, but as a subject guide it is in need of improvement. For example, while Urdang provides nearly a page-long explanation under the heading *Julian calendar/Gregorian calendar*, one will search in vain in the index for an entry under *calendar*. Similarly, while there are rather extensive entries under both *italic/roman* and *serif/sans serif*, there are no index entries under more general class terms such as *typography* or *letters*. Works of this type are inevitably idiosyncratic; none can claim completeness. In terms of their general reference value, Bryson's *Dictionary of Troublesome Words* will prove more useful since it focuses more clearly on terminology and constructions encountered in daily writing tasks. Urdang's *Dictionary of Confusable Words* will be more of a browser's tool, interesting to read and occasionally useful for answering more arcane terminological questions (how often does one need to know the difference between *kakemono* and *makimono*?). Purchase of either of these works should be considered only as supplementary to more standard works such as Fowler's *Dictionary of Modern English Usage*, Partridge's *Usage and Abusage*, etc.

A Dictionary of Contrasting Pairs. By Adrian Room. Routledge, 1989 (c1988). 295p. bibliog. illus. hardcover $35 (0-415-00217-6).

423'.1 English language—Synonyms and antonyms—Dictionaries [CIP] 87-20509

This work consists of more than 1,000 alphabetically arranged entries that describe contrasting concepts or, in some cases, two terms that are in other ways associated with each other. Entries range from a short paragraph to a full column and may include examples of usage. Many of these pairs are very common words, and definitions are obvious (e.g., *fact/fiction, large/small, Atlantic/Pacific, audio/visual*). Other terms are from science and medicine, law, business, heraldry, and other fields, although no basis is given for selection. Some entries will be of interest to the browser, such as the difference between lateral and vertical thinking, or the etymology of *spear* and *distaff* sides of a family. Many entries do not contrast but are linked in some other way; the following examples also indicate the decidedly British orientation of the book: *Access/VISA* (British credit cards), *Rugby League/Rugby Union, Celtic/Rangers* (Scottish soccer teams), and *Canterbury/York*. Other entries seem to be chosen for topical interest (e.g., *Sandinistas/Contras*).

Appendix material provides information on contrasting prefixes and suffixes and gender differentiation. *See* references are provided within the text of some entries and are also given for the second word in a pair, if that word is sought in the alphabetical arrangement of entries. Illustrations and diagrams, when given, are clear and informative. Room has authored a number of dictionaries and gazetteers, but it is difficult to justify the existence of this one. Most of these distinctions are easily understood, and those that are not can be found in standard dictionaries and encyclopedias.

Roget's II: The New Thesaurus. Rev. ed. By the editors of The American Heritage Dictionary. Houghton, 1988. 1,135p. hardcover $12.95 (0-395-48317-4); paper $3.95 (0-395-48318-2).

423'.1 English language—Synonyms and antonyms [CIP] 88-8842

The name *Roget* is in the public domain and has been used by many publishers for their thesauruses. The original *Roget's Thesaurus of English Words and Phrases* had a classified subject arrangement with an index; *Roget's II* is in dictionary form. The editors of *Roget's II* (who are also the editors of *The American Heritage Dictionary*) state in the preface that its purpose is to provide "rapid access to synonyms, which are grouped by precise meanings, . . .[with] thousands of near-synonyms, near-antonyms, and antonyms." Additionally, they point out that the thesaurus defines all entry words, thus making it "self-contained," with synonyms "exhaustively listed."

When *RSBR* reviewed the first edition of this work [Je 1 81], the Board pointed out its unique format. In addition to main entries, it has secondary entries that refer to main entries for full lists of synonyms. For example, at *eschew* the reader is referred to *avoid*, where nine synonyms are listed (one of them *eschew*), along with four idiomatic synonyms. This is done to eliminate the need for redundant listings, but it makes the thesaurus more complicated for the novice to use and makes access less rapid.

This thesaurus is intended to stand on its own, with no need for the user to resort to a dictionary. Although the editors are to be commended for their addition of definitions for all main entries, the definitions are not always useful. Many include the word to be defined as part of the definition (e.g., *aspirant* is defined as "one who aspires"), and definitions often disregard multiple meanings (e.g., *reference* is defined only in terms of character references; *tonality* is defined only in terms of music; and the definition of *uproot* does not consider the displacement of people, nor does it deal with the obvious gardening definitions). The limited definitions are reflected in the range of synonyms given. *Distraught*, a secondary entry, is defined as "afflicted with or exhibiting irrationality and mental unsoundness," and one is referred to *insane*, where several dozen synonyms are listed. However, *distraught* has another meaning of "anxious" or "worried."

In their attempt to define main entries, the editors often include illustrative quotes to "provide guidance in usage." These quotes sometimes exhibit overt sexism (*meddle* uses illustrative quotes such as "tried to keep her mother-in-law from meddling" and "a meddling mother who can't let her daughter lead a life of her own") and stereotyped imagery (*effeminate* is illustrated with "a perverted schoolmaster who corrupted and effeminated his charges"). It is interesting to note that the definitions and illustrative quotes do not seem to come from *The American Heritage Dictionary*, even though the editors are the same.

Roget's II does not, as the preface indicates, list synonyms "exhaustively"; in fact, the number of synonyms listed for main entries is usually much less than that found in other alphabetically arranged thesauruses like *Webster's Collegiate Thesaurus* (Merriam-Webster, 1976), *The Doubleday Roget's Thesaurus in Dictionary Form* (1977), *Webster's New World Thesaurus* (Simon & Schuster, 1985), or *The Random House Thesaurus: College Edition* (1984). This is a result of the editors deliberately avoiding large groupings of words with only vaguely related meanings. In aiming for precision, the result is shorter lists of synonyms. The first edition of this work did not include antonyms. This revised edition has antonyms and near-antonyms; this appears to be the extent of the revision. Despite the editors' claim that "thousands of near-synonyms and near-antonyms" are included, a random sampling from the approximately 17,000 main entries indicates that less than 5 percent are accompanied by these helpful listings.

It is not clear what the audience for this thesaurus is. The preface does not specify one, and the book sometimes has oversimplified definitions (indicating a focus on secondary school students) but often provides highly sophisticated illustrative quotes (indicating a focus on postsecondary audiences). Overall, the focus seems to be on the latter group.

Roget's II does contain some main entries not found in other thesauruses (e.g., *horsing around, la-di-da, zaftig*), and some users may appreciate the precision with which synonyms are given. This book will be useful for those who speak English as a second language or those with limited vocabularies who cannot judge the connotations of words. These readers might be better served, however, by a dictionary of synonyms and antonyms, such as *Webster's New Dictionary of Synonyms* (Merriam-Webster, 1984), that gives explanations of various shades of meaning of words along with definitions and examples. Many writers will still prefer one of the alphabetically arranged thesauruses that provide long lists of synonyms and leave it up to the writer to judge their appropriateness.

The Thesaurus of Slang: 150,000 Uncensored Contemporary Slang Terms, Common Idioms, and Colloquialisms Arranged for Quick and Easy Reference. By Esther Lewin and Albert E. Lewin. Facts On File, 1988. 435p. bibliog. hardcover $40 (0-8160-1742-5).

427 English language—Slang—Dictionaries I English language—Synonyms and antonyms—Dictionaries [CIP] 88-6985

The Thesaurus of Slang "translates" 12,500 standard English words into 150,000 slang equivalents. The selection of standard words was determined by asking "which formal English word was the one most likely to occur to a reader searching for a slang synonym." If no suitable standard equivalent could be found, an entry was made under the slang term itself. The slang terms have been drawn from a wide variety of sources and reflect "the slang commonly used in America today." Many recent slang words and expressions are included, especially those used by young people, technical writers, and politicians. Racial epithets and slang words for sex and drugs are well represented. Selection was not influenced by any attempt to determine which recent words and expressions may become relatively permanent American English.

Entries are arranged alphabetically under the standard English words and indicate part of speech. The most current and widely used slang equivalents are usually listed first. Slang terms are arranged in numbered groups if there is more than one slang sense for the formal word (e.g., the first group of slang equivalents for *distill* includes terms such as *put in a nutshell* and *boil down*, while the second group includes *moonshine* and *cook*). *See* references often direct the user to a broader selection of slang synonyms, and *see also* references identify collateral meanings of the word. The book concludes with a bibliography of sources used to compile it.

The compilers point out in the preface that the *Thesaurus* does not define slang words (except to clarify the meanings of a few obscure slang terms) and is not, accordingly, intended to take the place of a slang dictionary. As a source for finding words and phrases that often express concepts more vividly than formal language, the *Thesaurus* will be a useful addition to high school, public, and academic library collections and a suitable replacement for Berry and Van den Bark's *Thesaurus of American Slang*, which has been out of print for some years.

Webster's New World Guide to Current American Usage. By Bernice Randall. Simon & Schuster, 1988. 420p. bibliog. hardcover $16.95 (0-13-947821-3).

428'.00973 English language—U.S.—Usage—Dictionaries I English language—Usage—Dictionaries I Americanisms—Dictionaries [CIP] 87-36698

Though ostensibly another handbook of modern American usage of the English language, this work is a far cry from the clear-cut, somewhat pedantic, and always didactic work of Fowler (1926) and its later adaptation to American usage by Margaret Nicholson (1957). (See "Guides to English Usage," [*RBB* N 1 86] for more information on usage manuals.) These works and the similar works of Craigie, Evans, Partridge, Copperud, and others are primarily alphabetical in their listing and succinct in their presentation. The present work, on the contrary, is confusing in its arrangement and discursive in its presentation.

Though there are plenty of entries for such problematic expressions as *hung/hanged* and such neologisms as *hopefully*, many of the alphabetically arranged entries are not words or concepts but complete, sometimes humorous, sentences (e.g., *Russian is written in the Acrylic alphabet*, with a cross-reference from *malapropisms*). These sentences, used as entries or headings, are often ungrammatical or full of slang, and they sometimes run to two or more lines. The text that follows them consists of long discussions, replete with examples, of British and American usage of nouns, verbs, commas, slang words, jargon, sentence structure, and the like. These entries are often four or five pages.

For example, a typical entry is *Ice cream your kids today with Rocky Road*. This entry runs to eight pages and includes a discussion of nouns as verbs, with 16 examples of nouns taken from parts of the body and used as verbs (*to face odds, to muscle in, to shoulder the blame,* etc.); it also has a discussion of verbs as nouns (*a ride, a swim,* etc.); adjectives as nouns (*an antique, a primitive, a movie extra*); nouns as adjectives (*tax laws, a fun hobby*); verbs as adjectives (*travel agent, slide rule*); adjectives as verbs (*We true the tires on your car*); and two more pages on "other kinds of functional shift."

The whole work serves, therefore, as a light-hearted survey of English philology as reflected in American speech and writing and is for those who are not in any great hurry to find out whether one should write "a lady's man," "a ladies' man," or "a ladies man" (found under *Saying goodbye may be hard*, with a cross-reference from *plurals*). There is no index to the book, and the above example is not listed in the alphabetical sequence, even though a good many such expressions *are* listed and cross-referenced to the composite entries.

The quick reference value of the work, without an index, is dubious. Even so, for the serious student of language willing to spend some time browsing, this book is useful. In the back matter, it has a list of works from which excerpts have been taken as examples; these writings are easy to correlate with the text, even though not precisely identified by footnote numbers, as is usual in scholarly writing. The book should be classed as a reference work by reason of its alphabetical format, its occasional ready answer, and the scholarly research involved in its composition. But it will hardly replace any of the more recent commentaries and dictionaries of modern American usage as a source of quick reference for a patron who wants to know the difference between *majority* and *plurality* for a political candidate, or whether or not to pronounce the *h* in *honorarium*.

English Language and Orientation Programs in the United States. 9th ed. Ed. by James E. O'Driscoll. Institute of International Education, 809 United Nations Plaza, New York, NY 10017, 1988. 214p. indexes. paper $21.95 (0-87206-161-2).

428.24 English language—Study and teaching—U.S.—Directories I English language—Study and teaching—Foreign speakers—Directories I Education—U.S.—Directories [BKL]

This directory, first published in 1964, provides a listing of programs "designed to meet the preacademic training needs of persons intending to pursue academic study in the United States." Although intended for this audience, programs listed may be suitable for business people, professionals, and other international visitors. It does not include programs geared to the survival-skill needs of refugees or recent immigrants, nor does it include information for English-as-a-second-language (ESL) teacher training. Editor O'Driscoll is manager of the Institute of International Education Office of English and Special Services.

This ninth edition includes 79 new programs that did not appear in the previous (1984) edition, and 94 programs that are no longer in existence have been dropped. Program information was gathered by sending questionnaires to ESL directors and foreign student advisers, in addition to using catalogs. The bulk of information is in the section "Intensive English as a Second Language Programs." Entries are arranged by state and alphabetically by sponsor within state sections. Each entry begins with a number that is keyed to the two indexes: sponsoring organization and beginning date of program. The beginning-date index enables the user to determine that, for example, Santa Barbara City College offers a program that starts in February and runs for 18 weeks. Two additional chapters, "English as a Second Language Courses at Postsecondary Level" and "English as a Second Language Courses at Secondary Level," list programs for foreign students already enrolled at U.S. colleges and for foreign secondary school students. Entry elements in all three chapters include address, telephone number, and term length, plus information on cost, accreditation, faculty, eligibility, credit, housing, class size, and tests. Appendixes reprint various standards and guidelines. There are numerous advertisements for sponsoring institutions.

This source is well organized and moderately priced. Any library serving the audience for which it is designed should give it serious consideration.

SCIENCE

Encyclopedia of Physical Science and Technology. 15v. Ed. by Robert A. Meyers. Academic Press, 1987–88. bibliog. illus. index. tables. hardcover $2,500 (v.1–5: 0-12-226898-9; v.6–10: 0-12-226899-7; v.11–14: 0-12-226900-4; v.15: 0-12-226915-2).

503'.21 Science—Dictionaries I Engineering—Dictionaries I Technology—Dictionaries [CIP] 86-1118

The *Encyclopedia of Physical Science and Technology* (*EPST*) is a comprehensive encyclopedia covering the physical sciences, engineering, and mathematics. Subjects treated include chemistry, physics, astronomy, geology, meteorology, minerology, and computer science. It is complete in 15 volumes and consists of approximately 550 articles in 11,000 pages. Some representative articles are *Acoustical Measurement, Air Pollution Control, Boolean Algebra, Computer Speech, Engineering Seismology, Food Colors, Fuzzy Systems and Sets, Lasers, Mathematical Logic, Naval Architecture, Nuclear Safeguards, Petroleum Geology, Photochemistry, Space Technology,* and *Volcanology*. Volume 15 is the subject index containing 45,000 entries. According to the publisher, there are 4,200 entries in the glossaries that accompany articles, 6,000 figures, 2,000 tables, and 4,000 titles listed in the bibliographies. The idea of compiling an encyclopedia of this size was initiated in 1983 with the encouragement of a distinguished group of scientists who later became the executive advisory board: S. Chandrasekhar, University of Chicago; Linus Pauling, Linus Pauling Institute of Science and Medicine; Vladimir Prelog, Swiss Federal Institute of Technology; Abdus Salam, International Centre for Theoretical Physics; Glenn T. Seaborg, University of California, Berkeley; Kai Siegbahn, Uppsala University; and Edward Teller, University of California. In addition, 50 scholars served on the editorial advisory board, and 649 contributors wrote the articles. The contributors represent U.S. and foreign universities and research laboratories.

EPST is intended for undergraduate science and technology majors, graduate students, researchers, university faculty, practicing scientists and engineers in industry and research institutes, and anyone who works in fields closely allied to science, engineering, or mathematics. It is not intended for high school use, though advanced students with a knowledge of chemistry, physics, and calculus might find it useful. It is a technical work intended for those in research at the college level or above.

EPST is arranged in alphabetical, word-by-word order by broad topic. A table of contents in each volume lists the articles within that volume. All of the articles are signed and are in the same format: table of contents for the article, glossary of terms that pertain to the subject in question, definition, detailed discussion, and bibliography of books and articles, current to 1985. Following some articles are cross-references. For example, following the article *Mossbauer Spectroscopy* is the reference "*Motors, Electric* see Electric Machines, Drives." It is interesting to note that this is the only place "Motors, Electric" appears; it is not in either of the indexes.

The index volume consists of a relational index and a subject index. The relational index brings to the attention of the reader pertinent related articles by grouping their titles together. It is in reality a *see also* index. Having this access in one place may have some advantages, but the unsuspecting user who accesses the *Encyclopedia* without using the index may miss this access point. The subject index is very detailed and arranged with specific *see* references. The index volume also lists all contributors with their affiliations and the titles of the articles they wrote.

How does *EPST* compare with other multivolume encyclopedias, and is there a need for such a reference work? There is only one other encyclopedia that it can be compared to: *McGraw-Hill Encyclopedia of Science and Technology* (*MHEST*). These two encyclopedias are quite different as a result of their intended purposes and audiences. *EPST* is more limited in scope, more detailed in individual article coverage, and intended for a more advanced audience. *MHEST* is broader in coverage (life sciences as well as physical sciences and technology), briefer in coverage of individual topics, and intended for a more general audience.

A comparison of articles reveals the differences in coverage of *EPST* and *MHEST*. *Absorption* in *EPST* covers 25 pages, only 9 in *MHEST*; *Acetylene* takes 36 pages in *EPST*, one-half page in *MHEST*. In every case where the same subject appears in both encyclopedias, the coverage in *EPST* for a corresponding topic is far more comprehensive. The average length of articles in *EPST* is 20 pages, while *MHEST* has many entries of only a few sentences. With more than 7,000 entries, *MHEST* treats both narrow and broad topics. *EPST*, on the other hand, is a broad-entry encyclopedia and is intended to give detailed, comprehensive coverage of fewer topics with the articles approaching a treatise-like presentation, including historical facts as well as current knowledge. Because of its specific-entry format, *MHEST* often allows the reader to go directly to an entry without accessing the index. *EPST* requires one to use the index to locate information on a subtopic unless there is enough familiarity with the topic to know in which article the information may be found. *MHEST* has far more illustrations than *EPST*. *EPST* contains many more charts, graphs, formulas, and diagrams, which is to be expected in detailed technical articles.

EPST has more current bibliographic entries than *MHEST*. In the article *Analytical Chemistry*, *EPST* has 10 citations to books, with the oldest from 1979 and the latest from 1985. *MHEST* has 4 books listed, with the oldest 1963, and the latest 1982. One book listed in *MHEST* is a 1975, fourth edition of a McGraw-Hill imprint that is listed in *EPST* in the 1985, fifth edition. Although bibliographies are not the major reason for using an encyclopedia, they are very important in guiding the reader to more detailed information, with currency an important criterion in determining which items should be included. The *Encyclopedia of Physical Science and Technology* has a definite place in academic and special libraries. While it is expensive when compared with subject encyclopedias of a comparable size, it is comprehensive, current, easy to use, and authoritative, and it exceeds all of its goals of providing a scholarly encyclopedia covering the physical sciences, mathematics, and engineering. It is highly recommended for large public libraries with a science-technology division, academic libraries, and special libraries with an interest in science and engineering.

The Encyclopedic Dictionary of Science. Ed. by Candida Hunt. Facts On File, 1988. 256p. illus. index. hardcover $29.95 (0-8160-2021-3).

503'21 Science—Dictionaries [CIP] 88-16396

The *Encyclopedic Dictionary of Science* "explains and defines some 7,000 terms and concepts...that...span the most up-to-date knowledge in all areas of science, including astronomy, biology, chemistry, geology, medicine, physics, technology, [and] science history." Some social-science topics are also covered. The intended audience includes high school students and general readers. It was compiled in Britain by contributing consultants "selected for their skill in writing popular science as well as their knowledge of the subject matter"; they include a television consultant, a lecturer in astronomy, and a physical-science editor. Each has written other works on his or her specialty.

"Fully developed, 'encyclopedic'-type entries...expansive in content and explanatory in nature" are claimed by the publisher, but the length of entries varies from two words to $1\frac{1}{2}$ columns. Articles start with a definition, sometimes followed by further explanation or a brief history. The 850 brief biographical entries are more retrospective than contemporary; most living people listed are Nobel Prize winners. The publisher claims the book is "as readable as it is informative." The definitions tend to be readable, but the expanded entries are sometimes more technical. Arrangement is alphabetical with embedded cross-references to related articles and page references to illustrations. There are no bibliographies.

An outstanding feature of the work is the 50 pages of full-color illustrations, including specially commissioned artwork on more than 150 subjects. Some of the subjects illustrated are animal evolution, plate tectonics, magnetism and electricity, Nobel Prizes in science, and the periodic table. The illustrations are especially well designed to clarify complex information for lay consumption. They are not necessarily found with related articles in the alphabetical sequence.

Because of its generally readable definitions, attractive illustrations, and reasonable price, high school and public libraries needing a popular dictionary of science will want to consider purchasing this slender work. Other libraries owning more comprehensive science dictionaries and encyclopedias (*Hammond Barnhart Dictionary of Science* [RBB Mr 1 87] or *Van Nostrand's Scientific Encyclopedia* [RBB My 1 89]) may wish to purchase it for the illustrations alone.

McGraw-Hill Dictionary of Scientific and Technical Terms. 4th ed. Ed. by Sybil P. Parker. McGraw-Hill, 1989. 2,137p. illus. hardcover $95 (0-07-045270-9).

503'.21 Science—Dictionaries I Technology—Dictionaries [CIP] 88-13490

The fourth edition of the *McGraw-Hill Dictionary of Scientific and Technical Terms* continues to provide definitions for scientific and technical terminology for the professional community as well as the general reader, a purpose established in 1974 with the first edition. It has grown in pages (over 300 more than in the third edition) and in number of terms (7,600 new to this edition), for a total of 100,100. It is well designed; the print is easy to read and the 3,000 black-and-white photographs and drawings have been slightly enhanced for better clarity. The large volume is thumb indexed for easier use. Editor Parker, 28 consulting editors, and 9 contributing editors also produced the third edition.

The most important change in this edition over the previous one is the addition of pronunciation for all terms. This is very welcome since few science and technology dictionaries give pronunciation. The definitions are brief but clear, with each having a code that indicates to which of the 102 subject or scope fields it belongs. If a term has more than one definition, each is numbered and a different scope field is given if necessary. Entries also include synonyms, acronyms, and abbreviations, when appropriate. There is little change in the individual definitions from the third edition. The entry *superconductivity* does not note that some ceramics are superconductors at temperatures higher than absolute zero. It is disheartening to discover that neither *AIDS* nor *acquired immune deficiency syndrome* has an entry. The *Dictionary* does include medical terms for other sexually transmitted diseases. Appendixes include such expected information as the International System or SI conversion tables, the Greek alphabet, the periodic table of the elements, mathematical notation, schematic electronic symbols, and the classification of living organisms. The last appendix is a biographical dictionary of over 1,200 noted historical and contemporary scientists giving name, birth and death dates, nationality, and field of interest. Two tables that were in the third edition have been dropped—specialized abbreviations and international graphics symbols.

The *McGraw-Hill Dictionary of Scientific and Technical Terms* is still one of the best and most comprehensive dictionaries available for general readers. It is recommended for high school, public, and academic libraries.

The New Illustrated Science and Invention Encyclopedia. 27v. Rev. ed. H. S. Stuttman, Inc.; dist. by Marshall Cavendish Corp., 1988. illus. index. hardcover $399.95 (0-86307-491-X).

503'.21 Science—Dictionaries I Engineering—Dictionaries [CIP] 85-30973

This is an ambitious set of 27 alphabetically arranged volumes focusing on about 1,000 topics in the sciences. Each volume in the main part of the set (1–23) covers approximately 40 subjects. Coverage ranges from one to eight pages for each topic. Volume 24 includes science biographies, volume 25 features inventions, and volume 26 is the glossary and index to the set. *Careers in Science* is the last volume. The first edition (published under the title *How It Works*, 1977) was only 20 volumes and was recommended in the *Senior High Catalog*, where it was noted for its strong illustrations. Although color photographs and other illustrations appear on every page, still making the set extremely attractive, there is little else that makes it unique. The appearance of the set (the slender volumes and the heavy reliance on illustrations) makes it seem geared to low-level readers, but the reading level is not easy. While the set does treat all areas of science, coverage still seems better for technology, and the previous title of *How It Works* seems more descriptive of the contents.

Comparisons with general encyclopedias show that most articles here are longer and more technical. For example, *Power Plant* includes many types of power within a single article, with cross-references to *Hydroelectric* and *Nuclear*. Some entries, such as *Supernova*, will be confusing to the student. Although the reader is told needlessly that our galaxy is the Milky Way, no explanation is given for "spiral" or "elliptical" galaxies. Technical terms are not always explained in context, and many are not included in the glossary.

Special sections are found in some articles to highlight unusual information. "Frontiers of Science" sections describe new theories and discoveries, such as the disappearance of dinosaurs under *Paleontology* and UFOs under *Piezoelectricity*. "Fact Files" usually include three or four interesting facts about a topic. While these features may be interesting, the information is often not related to the article itself. More organization is needed throughout; President Reagan's "laser defense system" is mentioned in *Laser Surgery*. Most articles conclude with cross-references, but they are not always adequate. For instance, the article *Telephone* mentions cellular telephones but does not have a cross-reference to the article *Cellular Radio*, nor are cellular telephones listed in the index. The index includes only major topics, not people or organizations mentioned within an entry. A more thorough index would add significantly to the usefulness of this set.

Material from the *Inventions* volume repeats whole phrases from related articles in the main part of the set and isn't really necessary, since many articles begin with a historical view. For example, *Gunpowder* in volume 25 is very similar to the information in *Explosives*. About 125 "great scientists" are featured in the biography volume, including economists Marx and Keynes. The *Careers* volume includes descriptions, duties, and expected growth for many science professions. Some ordinary ones are missing—astronaut, pharmacologist, and dietitian. Far more information, including salaries, is found in encyclopedias and the *Occupational Outlook Handbook*.

Found in the index volume is a list of editors and contributors, but articles are not signed. No sources or additional references are suggested; bibliographies would have been helpful for articles on semi-scientific topics such as *Pyramid Power*. Not found anywhere are some current subjects, including Chernobyl, surrogate mothers, test-tube babies, and the latest advances in superconductivity.

Keeping up with a science yearbook will probably give comparable coverage for many subjects. McGraw-Hill's *Encyclopedia of Science and Technology* [RBB S 15 87] is much more thorough but is aimed at an even higher reading level and is much more expensive. *The New Book of Popular Science* (Grolier, 1988 [RBB F 1 85]) has longer articles and is thematically arranged, with each of its six volumes devoted to several sciences (i.e., astronomy, earth sciences, physical sciences). It is also heavily illustrated, lists selected readings, and is much less expensive than the set reviewed here. However, some subjects such as Teflon (polytetrafluoroethylene) and spectroscopy get only a paragraph each in the Grolier set, compared to four pages here. Other topics, such as speech, tachometer, and stroboscope, are not included in *The New Book of Popular Science*.

Vocational-technical collections and public libraries may want to consider *The New Illustrated Science and Invention Encyclopedia* for its illustrations and its practical "how things work" approach, but libraries owning one of the science encyclopedias mentioned above

Information Sources in Science and Technology. By C. D. Hurt. Libraries Unlimited, 1988. indexes. hardcover $29.50 (0-87287-581-4); paper $21.50 (0-87287-582-2).
016.5 Reference books—Science—Bibliography I Reference books—Technology—Bibliography I Science—Bibliography I Technology—Bibliography [CIP] 88-22977

This volume in the Library Science Text series is a guide to the diverse literature of science and technology. It is intended to be a revision of the third edition of Malinowsky's *Science and Engineering Literature* (Libraries Unlimited, 1980) and offers comprehensive coverage of the sources available in these fields. The author, director of the Graduate Library School at the University of Arizona, begins with a rambling attempt to explain the differences between science and technology and how these differences affect the literature. He then proceeds to the main body of the work, an annotated guide to more than 2,000 reference sources.

The book's first two chapters cover the history of science, treating each discipline individually, and multidisciplinary sources of information—guides to the literature, abstracts, encyclopedias, directories, government documents, theses and dissertations, etc. The following chapters cover individual disciplines such as astronomy, zoology, mathematics, and transportation engineering. Each chapter is divided by subdisciplines and by type of reference work. The form divisions are similar in each chapter, making the work easy to use. The arrangement of the book is similar to that of Malinowsky. The author emphasizes current in-print and online sources and supplies concise, critical annotations defining their scope, special features, and intended audience. The chapters on engineering literature are the most greatly expanded over the previous volume.

This is an extremely useful text. The continuously changing, vast quantity of material that librarians who work in this area must use presents a challenge. This guide will help novices, professionals, patrons, and students learn to use the literature in their discipline effectively and will be a helpful selection tool. *Information Sources in Science and Technology* is a necessary purchase for scientific and technical collections.

Science and Technology Annual Reference Review, 1989. Ed. by H. Robert Malinowsky. Oryx, 1989. 236p. indexes. hardcover $45 (0-89774-487-X; ISSN 1041-2557).
016 Science—Indexes—Periodicals I Technology—Indexes—Periodicals I Reference books—Science—Book reviews—Periodicals I Reference books—Technology—Book reviews—Periodicals I Reference books—Science—Indexes—Periodicals [OCLC] 88-2564

Malinowsky, past president of the Special Libraries Association and author of several reference works, has edited another useful collection-development tool. STARR is the first volume in a projected annual survey of science and technology reference literature for academic, public, high school, and special libraries. Seventy-two librarians, many subject experts, wrote the reviews of 602 reference books. The editor took on the mind-boggling task of writing nearly 30 percent of the reviews.

Arranged by discipline, chapters cover fields like agriculture, astronomy, chemistry, computer science, mathematics, medicine, and technology. Materials surveyed include handbooks, abstracts, dictionaries, examination review sources, how-to books, textbooks, treatises, etc. Reviews vary from a quarter- to half-page in length, and complete bibliographic information is provided for each book. With a couple of exceptions, material is from 1986–88 and is in English. Four excellent indexes (title, name, subject, type of library) allow users easy access to specific reviews. The type-of-library index will be especially useful in high school and public libraries for finding appropriate materials.

As stated in the introduction, ideally each review should include a description of the book, comparison with similar titles, a critique, and a recommendation. A random sampling determined that most reviews are strong on all of these points with the exception of comparison with similar titles.

There are numerous sources that review science and technology publications (e.g., *Science Books and Films*, *NYPL New Technical Books*, and *Technical Book Review Index*). They are either specialized in scope, do not designate reference items, or are infrequent in publication. The latest edition of *American Reference Book Annual* (1988) reviews 376 science and technology reference works, while STARR covers 602. STARR is a well-designed work in format and coverage that will be extremely useful in academic, public, high school, and special libraries for collection development.

Van Nostrand's Scientific Encyclopedia. 2v. 7th ed. Ed. by Douglas M. Considine and Glenn D. Considine. Van Nostrand, 1989. 3,180p. charts. illus. index. tables. hardcover $195 (0-442-21750-1).
503'.21 Science—Dictionaries I Engineering—Dictionaries [CIP] 88-10601

For 51 years *Van Nostrand's Scientific Encyclopedia* has provided libraries and individuals with a compact source for scientific information. For many years it was known as the best one-volume desk encyclopedia for the sciences. Beginning with the sixth edition, it has been published in two volumes. It covers animal life, biosciences, chemistry, earth and atmospheric science, mathematics and information science, medicine, anatomy, physiology, physics, plant science, and space and planetary science. There is some coverage of technical or engineering subjects in the areas of energy sources, power technology, and materials and engineering sciences. It is difficult to separate pure science from technology, and Van Nostrand has handled the problem quite well by being selective on technological subjects but still including subjects that one would expect to find like biomass and waste, nuclear energy, solar energy, wind power, laser technology, and microelectronics.

The physical makeup of this hefty (in weight) *Encyclopedia* is well done. It is printed in a two-column format with a typeface that is pleasant to the eye. There are over 3,000 black-and-white illustrations. Some entries include bibliographies, and new to this edition is a 100-page subject index. However, *see also* entries have been retained within the body of the *Encyclopedia*.

With the overwhelming amount of scientific information to be covered, the editors had to strive for conciseness in each of the 6,773 alphabetically arranged entries, more than 800 of which are new or revised. They used two techniques—"crisp organization of topical matter and customizing that information to a wide-spectrum audience." In addition, the longer articles are "of a tutorial nature." The first few paragraphs orient the user to the topic, followed by more detailed discussions that become more complex toward the end of the article. If at all possible, the writers have presented the topics from a practical viewpoint and in an interesting manner. The illustrations and 500 tables help carry out the editorial guidelines.

Scanning the *Encyclopedia* reveals that most subjects are covered well. Such current topics as *AIDS*, *gene mapping*, *fractal geometry*, *superconductivity*, *lasers*, *microchips*, and *quarks* are adequately defined and discussed. Over 250 scientists, engineers, and educators have contributed their expertise in writing these articles. Unfortunately, there is no explanation of what determined which articles are signed and which are not. For example, *AIDS*, *Airplane*, and *Electric Circuits* are long articles that are not signed, while *Electric Clock* (four paragraphs), *Epidemiology* (one paragraph), and *Flare Stars* (two paragraphs) are signed.

The black-and-white illustrations are adequate, especially the diagrams and line drawings. However, some leave much to the imagination, such as the illustration for the development of basidium and the formation of spores in mushrooms. Photographs vary in clarity. Some are too dark to show what was intended, such as one of a tomato with fungus blight.

As in any encyclopedia, bibliographies are important, especially for topics that must be covered concisely. Many of the entries here have brief bibliographies of scholarly articles, books, reports, and dissertations. The articles are fairly current, with many listings for 1987. Bibliographies, however, vary in regard to citing the latest edition of books. For instance, *Elementary Fluid Mechanics*, fifth edition

(1976), is cited, but a sixth edition was published in 1982. *Mortimer's Chemistry*, fourth edition (1979), is listed though the sixth edition (1986) is available. Finally, the alphabetical arrangement needs some explanation by the editors. *Pluto* took a couple of attempts to locate. It follows the entry for *Plutonium Fuel* only because it has *(Planet)* in regular typeface following the word *Pluto* in boldface. Parenthetical words usually are used in cases where there are two or more entries that are spelled the same but have different meanings, but there is only one *Pluto* in this *Encyclopedia*. Users will need to consult the index in cases like this.

In spite of these idiosyncrasies, *Van Nostrand's Scientific Encyclopedia* continues to be a recommended work for high school, public, college, and university libraries. The entries are accurate, appropriately written for the audiences intended, and current. This *Encyclopedia* has gone through six revisions in half a century and continues to be an authoritative desk encyclopedia.

McGraw-Hill has just published a second edition of its *Concise Encyclopedia of Science and Technology*. It is broader in scope, has fewer pages, and is less expensive ($110). Libraries wanting to purchase a new science desk encyclopedia may want to wait for a comparative review.

Science Experiments Index for Young People. By Mary Anne Pilger. Libraries Unlimited, 1988. 239p. hardcover $35 (0-87287-671-3); computer-disk version $30 (available for Apple, MacIntosh, or IBM).

507'.8 Science—Experiments—Juvenile literature—Indexes [CIP] 88-13870

Science Experiments on File: Experiments, Demonstrations and Projects for School and Home. Ed. by Katherine Bruce and others. Facts On File, 1989. various pagings. illus. index. loose-leaf $145 (0-8160-1888-X).

507'.8 Science—Experiments I Science—Laboratory manuals [CIP] 88-3883

Although both these titles deal with science experiments, they differ in purpose, scope, and format. *Science Experiments Index for Young People* (*SEIYP*) is a subject index to science experiments and activities found in 694 elementary and intermediate books and is available in print and computer formats. *Science Experiments on File* is a large notebook containing 84 science experiments, demonstrations, and projects written by science teachers.

SEIYP, prepared by an elementary school library media specialist, is arranged by subject. The subject headings are followed by a two- to eight-word phrase describing the experiment, a book number, and page numbers within the book. The key, with bibliographic citations for all book numbers, is found in the "Books Indexed" section, where the books are arranged by book number, not by title. Though the books were published from 1941 to 1988, 42 percent were published in the 1980s and 36 percent in the 1970s. Grade, difficulty, or reading levels are not given for the experiments or the books. Although this book is fairly easy to use, the lack of cross-references as well as some inconsistencies in subject headings detract from its usefulness. Many experiments are listed more than once to compensate for the lack of cross-references. For instance, an experiment might be found under *Pollution—Air* and *Air Pollution*. An experiment listed under *Levers* might also be found under *Simple Machines—Levers*. There are four listings under *Musical Instruments—Piano* and five under *Piano*, but none is duplicated. *Seismograph* has three entries, while *Earthquakes* has seven with only one of those also found under *Seismograph*.

SEIYP is also available in Apple, Macintosh, and IBM computer-disk formats. The Board examined the version designed to be used as database files for Appleworks. It consists of five double-sided disks with three data files on a side. Each file contains subject entries for an average of 25 titles arranged by book number. The information for each experiment in the database is the same as in the print version. The last disk contains the bibliography of books indexed, again with the same information as the print version. One great asset of the computer format is that the last disk also contains a database of cross-references: "*Bubbles* see also Soap Bubbles," as well as "*Seismograph* see also Earthquakes." The documentation is straightforward and includes the list of books indexed in number order. The introduction instructs the user to make backup copies of all disks and use them to personalize the files. The user can delete any titles not owned by the library, add other titles, and add a field for local call numbers. The resulting files and cross-references may be merged and alphabetized depending on the capacity of the library's computer. Copies of the resulting customized index can be printed and used in the library.

SEIYP bears some similarity to *Science Fair Project Index, 1973–1980* [RBB F 1 84] and its 1960–72 predecessor. These earlier works, intended for use by students in grades 5 through 12, index 300 titles, contain many cross-references, have much more detailed subject headings, and give the last name of the author and a simplified title instead of just a book number. They also index selected periodicals. Many titles listed in *SEIYP* are also found in *Science Fair Project Index*. Although *SEIYP* is more up to date, the Board anticipates that *Science Fair Project Index* will be updated in the future.

Science Experiments Index for Young People is recommended for purchase by public and school libraries. However, libraries that regularly purchase *Science Fair Project Index* may want to consider this new title an optional purchase.

Science Experiments on File serves two purposes. The first is "to provide a resource for students, grades 6–12, of every level of science ability and expertise, from which they can obtain challenging, inexpensive, *fun* science experiments to do independently at home or in the school lab." The second is "to offer a forum through which a group of master teachers—selected by the National Science Foundation to receive Presidential Awards for Excellence in Science Teaching—can share a concrete product of their experience with other science teachers across the country." The format is similar to other On File publications.

Following a discussion of safety precautions, the 84 experiments are grouped into four categories: earth science, biology, physical science/chemistry, and physics. For each experiment the author gives an introduction, time and materials needed, safety precautions, step-by-step procedure, and analysis. The author's findings are given in a separate section rather than with the experiment so that students will draw their own conclusions and then compare them with the published analysis. Line drawings and charts accompany many of the experiments. There are several appendixes that index the experiments by grade level, supervision requirements, setting (home or school), and number of participants, and lists of experiments that can be completed in less than an hour and of sources of materials and equipment. *Science Experiments on File* concludes with a subject index. There are no cross-references in the index. The experiments are simple but innovative and well documented. The only drawback to the volume is that some of the experiments are divided in awkward spots, such as in the middle of the procedure section, to ensure that all the information fits conveniently into the page requirements.

Science Experiments on File is highly recommended for public and school libraries. It may even be useful in academic libraries.

The Timetables of Science: A Chronology of the Most Important People and Events in the History of Science. By Alexander Hellemans and Bryan Bunch. Simon & Schuster, 1988. 656p. indexes. hardcover $29.95 (0-671-62130-0).

509 Science—History—Chronology—Tables [CIP] 88-23920

The Timetables of Science is the third book in Simon & Schuster's Timetable series, with the other titles covering history and American history. It is arranged in a columnar format beginning with 2,400,000 B.C.—"Hominids in Africa manufacture stone tools"—and ends with events happening as late as May 1988. In the early years, only the headings *Astronomy, Life Science, Mathematics,* and *Technology* are used. These are expanded through the years as science itself expands, until the later years have *Anthropology/Archaeology, Astronomy and Space, Biology, Chemistry, Earth Science, Mathematics, Medicine, Physics,* and *Technology* as headings. There is also a *General* heading used throughout to identify important world-history events to place all other events in perspective.

The chronology is divided into nine sections from "Science Before There Were Scientists: 2,400,000–599 B.C." to "Science after World War II: 1946–1988." In addition to events, many of the entries are tied to either the birth or death of a prominent scientist or engineer, thus adding an important biographical facet. Also, numerous entries are made for notable publications that describe a particular event or discovery. The entries are brief and listed in columns under the appropriate subject heading within each year or span of years. Some 100 essays are dispersed throughout the book, covering such topics as "The Calendar," "Classic Volcanoes," "1543: A Great Year in Publishing," "The Velocity of Light," "When Was the Industrial Revolution?" "The Theory of Evolution," and "God Is Left-Handed."

This is a fascinating book to browse through. The information presented is varied, accurate, and scholarly, yet entertaining and inviting. For example, animal crackers went on sale in 1902, contraceptives were introduced in Egypt around 2000 B.C., the first Atlantic telegraphic cable was laid in 1858, and chemists reported over 400,000 new chemical compounds in 1988. There is both a name index and a subject index to help in locating a specific event, person, or discovery. Ellis Mount and Barbara List's *Milestones in Science and Technology* [*RBB* Ap 1 88] contains the same kind of information, but it is arranged by subject, not chronological order. High school, public, and academic libraries will find this an excellent reference work at a very affordable price.

Comparative World Data: A Statistical Handbook for Social Science. By Georg P. Müller. Johns Hopkins, 1989 (c1988). 495p. bibliog. hardcover $49.95; $87 with diskettes (0-8108-3734-0).

519.5 Statistics [CIP] 88-45391

Comparative World Data is a compendium of statistical data for 128 nations of the world, providing social, economic, and demographic information for each country. It then uses this data to rank the country globally through the use of percentiles and to compare one country with "sister" or "partner" countries. Thus, through the use of statistical data and variables, *Comparative World Data* provides analyses of international rank orders, international exchange relations, and reactions induced by the world system. Compiler Müller is a researcher at the University of Zurich.

Data are provided only for nations that were independent at some time between 1960 and 1980 and that had a population of at least one million people. Coverage is primarily for three specific years (1970, 1975, 1980), with some exceptions.

The country profiles are arranged alphabetically by country in chapter 4, which makes up the largest part of the book. Each profile contains 51 variables, providing information on such traditional topics as population, income per capita, infant mortality rate, student enrollment ratio, military expenditures, gross national product, and gross domestic product. Also included are variables that are often difficult to locate: for example, the degree of civil liberties and political rights; the number of riots, political strikes, and protest demonstrations; the share of Nobel Prize winners; and import and export partners.

Chapters 1–3 provide in-depth information on the use of *Comparative World Data*, explain how the data were compiled, and explain and identify the variables and statistical correlations. Chapter 3 describes in detail each of the 51 variables; each description includes definition, computational procedure, statistical overview, scaling, quality of data, availability, and sources used, which range from books to machine-readable data files. A person with little or no statistical training will find the introductory chapters difficult reading. The appendix includes the list of footnotes, the list of countries (with *see* references to name changes), and a brief description of the organization of the computer-disk version.

Since coverage ends with 1980, *Comparative World Data* is not a useful source for current data. *Europa Year Book, Statesman's Year-Book*, and the United Nations' *Demographic Yearbook* are better and more up-to-date sources for basic social, economic, political, and demographic data. The use of abbreviations, codes, and symbols throughout the country profiles and the lack of column headings make the retrieval and interpretation of data difficult and frustrating. One finds oneself constantly going back and forth between the introductory chapters and the country-profile chapter. Country-abbreviation headings are found at the top of each page for ease in locating the desired country. However, their meanings are not always immediately apparent: for example, KORSO (South Korea), ELSA (El Salvador), CENTRA (Central African Republic).

Despite some layout and format deficiencies, *Comparative World Data* is a good source of retrospective data for 1970–80, some of which are difficult to locate. It also highlights relationships that would otherwise be hard to see. Libraries that collect in the areas of international business and economics or foreign relations and large academic or public libraries will want to consider this title for selection.

The Guinness Book of Astronomy. 3d ed. By Patrick Moore. Guinness; dist. by Sterling, 1988. 288p. illus. index. maps. hardcover $19.95 (0-85112-375-9).

520 Astronomy [CIP]

The Guinness Book of Astronomy, edited by the prolific astronomy writer Moore, lacks a preface to inform as to its purpose. The book is arranged in five sections. The first and largest, "The Solar System," has chapters on planets, meteors, comets, etc. A typical chapter, "The Moon," has a data box listing facts such as distance from the earth, revolution period, diameter, and volume. This is followed by "firsts," such as "first telescopic map of the Moon" and "first attempted lunar probe." Lists of lunar craters, seas, eclipses, mountains, and other features follow. The article is illustrated with black-and-white photographs and drawings. The next section gives similar types of information for different types of stars. Section 3 is a star catalog arranged alphabetically by constellation and illustrated with star charts. Brief sections are devoted to telescopes and observatories, the history of astronomy (basically a chronology), and brief biographies of astronomers. An insert of color photographs shows an eclipse, the surface of Mars, etc. The book concludes with a brief glossary and an uneven index.

The jacket claims that "this book has become accepted as a standard reference book not only for amateurs, but also for professionals." In places, the book does appear to be written for the specialist. Star charts are detailed, as are the maps and tables of satellites—including those discovered or first photographed by *Voyager 2*. In contrast, the oversimplified writing style may offend even the nonspecialist. The tendency to start paragraphs with superlatives does not make for interesting reading. Another disadvantage to the emphasis on superlatives is that in such a rapidly changing discipline, "the largest," "the brightest," etc., are not likely to be accurate for very long.

Although five other astronomers read and commented upon the work, there are no signed articles. The British viewpoint may limit the work's usefulness slightly in American libraries; for instance, all 22 known meteorite falls in the British Isles are listed, while only 11 meteorite falls are listed for the rest of the world.

Libraries owning *The International Encyclopedia of Astronomy* edited by Patrick Moore [*RBB* Mr 1 88] may wish to consider *The Guinness Book of Astronomy* for its inclusion of the *Voyager 2* findings and its detailed charts. In no case is the latter a substitute for the former with its signed, well-written, alphabetically arranged articles.

The Cambridge Atlas of Astronomy. 2d ed. Ed. by Jean Audouze and Guy Israël. Cambridge, 1988. 432p. bibliog. charts. illus. index. tables. hardcover $90 (0-521-36360-8).

523 Astronomy—Charts, diagrams, etc. [OCLC] 84-73453

The first edition (1985) of *The Cambridge Atlas of Astronomy* was praised in *RBB* [Ap 15 86] as current, informative, readable, balanced, and scholarly, with superb photographs and other illustrations—a must for astronomy collections and appropriate for college students and adults. This work, a translation of *Le Grand Atlas de L'Astronomie*, was prepared by a team of 44 European astronomers, most of whom were associated with the Centre National de Recherche

Scientifique, Cambridge University, and the Royal Greenwich Observatory.

Inspection of the 1988 edition reveals that much of the *Atlas* is little changed. To the original authors/translators, two translators have been added. With the same number of pages, most of them unchanged in text and/or illustrative matter, the work still contains 350 color photographs, 420 black-and-white photographs, and 350 color diagrams. The book concludes with the same three sky maps; a revised, updated (to 1988) bibliography for further reading; the same glossary; and a subject index that fails to reflect, for example, that the principal essay on Halley's comet includes four, not two, pages. The new material includes results from recent space missions such as the *Voyager 2* encounter with Uranus, the *Giotto* mission to Halley's comet, and a series of Russian spacecraft used to explore Venus and its atmosphere. To be sure, in the interest of accuracy and currency, a few tables have been changed (e.g., satellites of the planets), as have some text and photographs (the balloon and scientific platform *Vega*).

The *Atlas* continues to be divided into five major sections—"The Sun," "The Solar System," "The Stars and the Galaxy," "The Extra-Galactic Domain," and "The Scientific Perspective"—each of which is subdivided. The introduction is new.

For those academic and large public libraries that did not buy the first edition, the second edition of *The Cambridge Atlas of Astronomy* will be a wise purchase. Those with the 1985 edition may feel that they can settle for updating through encyclopedia yearbooks or the journal literature.

The Facts On File Dictionary of Biology. Rev. ed. Ed. by Elizabeth Tootill. Facts On File, 1988. 326p. illus. hardcover $19.95 (0-8160-1865-0).

574'.03 Biology—Dictionaries [OCLC] 88-45476

The Facts On File Dictionary of Chemistry. Rev. ed. Ed. by John Daintith. Facts On File, 1988. 249p. illus. hardcover $19.95 (0-8160-1866-9).

540'.3 Chemistry—Dictionaries [OCLC] 88-45477

Facts On File has issued new editions of these dictionaries, first published in 1981. They are edited by British scientists Tootill (biology) and Daintith (chemistry), assisted by panels of 15 to 21 contributors, many with advanced degrees. Both books are designed to be used by high school and undergraduate students, teachers, and practitioners. They have an alphabetical arrangement with entries emphasized in boldface type in a double-column format on each page. As with many technical dictionaries, pronunciation guides and etymological information are omitted. Entries vary in length from one sentence to half a page. There are numerous cross-references. Each book has about 40 line drawings appropriately placed to illustrate complex definitions. A comparison and random sampling of the illustrations and entries in the first and second editions of both books showed that most of the original text has been retained with only slight revision. The major difference between the editions is that the revised ones have been expanded. A random sampling of *The Facts On File Dictionary of Biology* showed that there is an increase in the number of entries. According to the publisher, this has been concentrated in the areas of genetics and molecular biology and includes such new terms as *AIDS, endonuclease, fingerprinting,* and *retrovirus.* A multitude of dictionaries exist in this area. *Henderson's Dictionary of Biological Terms* (Longman, 1979) has 22,000 entries and provides etymological information and an outstanding classification chart of the plant and animal kingdoms. The *Student Dictionary of Biology* (Van Nostrand, 1973) covers 8,000 terms and has pronunciation guides. *Barnes & Noble Thesaurus of Biology* (1983) has 2,500 definitions and 500 color illustrations. It is organized by subject, and access is provided by an index. In contrast *FFDB* has over 3,000 entries.

The Facts On File Dictionary of Chemistry has approximately 300 new entries and is significantly easier to read because of larger print. A short list has been added of all abbreviations and their meanings. Many entries make extensive use of these abbreviations, so this addition is extremely valuable. As in the first edition, there are several appendixes listing chemical elements, physical constants, elementary particles, the Greek alphabet, and the periodic table. Access to the appendixes is aided by a table of contents positioned at the beginning of the appendix section. Unfortunately, there is no table of contents at the front of the volume to alert the user to the location of these special sections. There are several reference books that can be compared to *FFDC*. The comprehensive Miall's *New Dictionary of Chemistry* (Wiley, 1968) is a standard work that has become dated. The more recent *Van Nostrand Reinhold Encyclopedia of Chemistry* (Van Nostrand, 1984) has approximately 1,300 entries with long, detailed definitions. Even larger is the *Condensed Chemical Dictionary* (Van Nostrand, 1981) with more than 10,000 entries. *FFDC*, with 2,500 entries, is not the largest or most detailed chemical dictionary. However, its succinct definitions are up-to-date.

Both these books have been reprinted from the British editions with no revision of spelling for American audiences. Thus, for instance, in *FFDB* there is no *see* reference for *esophagus* telling the reader to see *oesophagus*. However, in general these inexpensive dictionaries will be useful in high school, college, and public libraries to complement the more scholarly dictionaries. Facts On File is also releasing revised editions of *The Facts On File Dictionary of Mathematics* and *The Facts On File Dictionary of Physics.*

Earth Science on File. By Diagram Visual Information Ltd. Facts On File, 1989 (c1988). various pagings. illus. index. maps. loose-leaf $145 (0-8160-1625-9).

550'.7 Earth sciences—Study and teaching—Audio-visual aids II Astronomy—Study and teaching—Audio-visual aids [CIP] 88-21322

Earth Science on File is another addition to Facts On File's On File series, a collection of reproducible maps, charts, and graphs on various topics. Some previous titles in the series include *Life Science on File* [*RBB* O 1 86] and *American Historical Images on File* [*RBB* Ap 1 89]; also see *Science Experiments on File* [*RBB* Je 1 89].

The purpose of *Earth Science on File* is threefold: to serve as a guide to the earth and universe; as a reference source of maps, charts, and images for photocopying; and as a source for tests and examinations. It groups drawings for subjects such as geology, astronomy, meteorology, oceanography, evolution, and energy into seven chapters ("Earth and Space," "The Restless Rocks," "Air and Oceans," "Shaping the Surface," "Earth History," "Resources," and "Maps, Tables and Scales"). The table of contents and index provide adequate access to the illustrations, but cross-references are inconsistent and used sparingly. For example, under *ocean floor* there is a *see also* for *sea floor*, and under *rocks—metamorphic* there is a *see* reference for *metamorphic rocks.* However, there are no *see also* references from *rocks—igneous* to *igneous rocks* or from *stars* to *constellations.* If one wants to find illustrations of drumlins and eskers, one has to know to look under *glacial deposits.*

The 300 black-and-white charts, diagrams, maps, and figures treat topics like the evidence for continental drift, weather map symbols, and the formation of deltas. The title and legend are printed in the margin, which enables teachers to use the figures for testing purposes by covering the margins when making multiple copies for student use. Facts On File grants permission to the purchaser "to reproduce in any form...all materials...for non-profit educational or private use."

The quality of the drawings is good. The spacing, use of shading, and different line thicknesses and lettering result in easy-to-read and -use figures and illustrations. They are not adequate for scholarly publications, but they are a good resource for the elementary and secondary school science teacher.

Public libraries and school libraries will want to consider this reasonably priced source. Academic libraries that support an education curriculum or have an educational resource or media center also may want to purchase *Earth Science on File.*

The Facts On File Dictionary of Marine Science. By Barbara Charton. Facts On File, 1988. 325p. illus. hardcover $22.95 (0-8160-1031-5).

551.46'003 Oceanography—Dictionaries [OCLC] 82-15715

This *Dictionary* provides clear definitions of nearly 2,000 terms and covers its subject comprehensively: seas, rivers, currents, marine plants and animals, seabirds, persons and vessels involved in marine exploration or experiments, reefs, waves, tides, sea ridges and troughs, islands, and more. Definitions range from a few lines (*bight, baleen, cnidoblast, Cocos Islands*) to more than a page (*plate tectonics*). Entries are quite up-to-date and present information on new developments as in, for example, the entries *Alvin (research vessel)* and *submersibles* that refer to exploration of the sunken *Titanic*. No pronunciations are given. Arrangement is two columns to the page with alphabetization word by word.

There are many cross-references, and *see* is used to mean both *see* and *see also* ("*tsunami*...See waves," and "*currents*...See Antarctic Current, Ekman Spiral," etc.). A few *see* references, however, are unclear. For example, one following the entry *mid-ocean ridges* says "See individual plates"; there is no entry *individual plates*. What is referred to are entries under the individual plate names mentioned in the definition, but *individual plates* is printed in italics as are other entries referred to, so it looks as if it should be a direct entry. This happens rather frequently, and while it becomes clear with use, it can be frustrating to the first-time user. Only one *see* reference was found leading to nothing: *explorers and explorations*, after its nearly one-page entry, says "See history," under which there is no entry. In a few other cases the term referred to is not exactly right but close enough that it is easily found: for example, *Gambia Abyssal Plain* refers also to *abyssal plain*, while the entry term is *abyssal floor*; and *macrobenthos* refers to *benthos*, but the entry is *benthic organisms*. The liberal use of *see* references, however, provides much information to the user, and problems are rare.

The approximately 75 black-and-white illustrations further enhance the volume's usefulness. Four appendixes provide further help: a descriptive geologic time scale, a chronology of significant events in marine history, a taxonomic classification, and a brief listing of agencies involved in marine science research projects.

Two earlier dictionaries that can be compared with this work are Donald G. Groves' *Ocean World Encyclopedia* (McGraw-Hill, 1980), which contains some 400 entries, and David F. Tver's *Ocean and Marine Dictionary* (Cornell Maritime Press, 1979), which includes some 8,000 entries, all of them very short. Groves more closely approximates *FOF* in its varying lengths of articles but contains less than one-fourth the number of entries. Comparing definitions of several terms: *currents*: *FOF* $1^{1}/_{3}$ columns, Groves $1^{3}/_{4}$ pages including a diagram, *El Niño*: *FOF* 1 column, Groves no entry, Tver $3^{1}/_{4}$ lines; *kelp*: *FOF* $1^{1}/_{2}$ columns including a drawing, Groves 7 lines, Tver 12 lines.

Compiled by an academic science librarian who has also taught science, with a biology professor as scientific adviser, *The Facts On File Dictionary of Marine Science* expands and updates other dictionaries in the field. It is quite comprehensive and authoritative and provides clear definitions for science students, interested laypersons, and professionals. It should be useful in high school libraries as well as in public, academic, and special oceanographic and marine engineering and biology libraries.

The Macmillan Illustrated Encyclopedia of Dinosaurs and Prehistoric Animals: A Visual Who's Who of Prehistoric Life. By Dougal Dixon and others. Macmillan, 1988. 312p. bibliog. illus. index. hardcover $39.95 (0-02-580191-0).

566 Vertebrates, Fossil [CIP] 88-1800

In this handsome book, vertebrate history is recorded since the Cambrian period, portraying—according to the publisher—over 600 species. Despite being singled out in the title, dinosaurs make up less than one-quarter of the book. Mammals receive even greater emphasis, with less space devoted to other vertebrate classes.

Arrangement is by evolutionary sequence from jawless fishes through mammals. Mammal-like reptiles are discussed after birds, even though mammal-like reptiles were extinct before birds appeared. This could be a little confusing to the lay reader, but a chart is provided to clarify the matter. Within each chapter, animals are arranged in families. After a brief discussion of the family, a typical entry for an animal includes the time when it lived (e.g., late Eocene), locality, and size. Several paragraphs are devoted to the animal's physical appearance, what it ate, how it differed from other members of the family, and how it compares with animals living today. An introduction briefly describes plate tectonics, fossilization, and evolution.

The basis of distinction between mammals and mammal-like reptiles is not clear from a lay viewpoint. Some animals are pictured as furred and described as warmblooded, yet classified as reptiles. To a layperson trained to think of reptiles as coldblooded and of mammals as the only furred animals, further explanation is in order. *Mammal Evolution* by Savage and Long (Facts On File, 1986) handles this very well.

This book is high in visual appeal, with attractive pages, evolutionary charts, and four-color illustrations that promote interest and understanding on nearly every other facing page. The foreword tells how paleontologists and artists worked together to create the color illustrations, most of which show the animal only, with little or no portrayal of its environment. The arrangement and writing style are more conducive to browsing and reading than to quick reference, but an extensive index renders the work useful for reference also. Dixon is well known for his *After Man: A Zoology of the Future* (St. Martin's, 1983).

The glossary at the back of the book is useful, though it does not include all of the technical terms used in the text. There is also a bibliography, an international list of museums of natural history, and a classification of vertebrates.

High school, public, and academic libraries needing an attractive, readable, general work on prehistoric animals will want to consider purchasing this book. While the writing level of the text is too advanced for young children, libraries that serve them may want to consider purchase for the appealing illustrations.

Encyclopedia of Human Evolution and Prehistory. Ed. by Ian Tattersall and others. Garland, 1988. 603p. illus. hardcover $87.50 (0-8240-9375-5).

573.2'03 Human evolution—Dictionaries I Man, Prehistoric—Dictionaries [CIP] 87-23761

"Up to now no comprehensive encyclopedia dealing with the evolution of humankind has been available," justifiably claim the editors, researchers at New York's American Museum of Natural History. Defining human evolution in its broadest sense, the *Encyclopedia* presents material from various viewpoints, including systematics, genetics, primatology, primate paleontology, and paleolithic archaeology. This authoritative work is balanced in its comprehensiveness and even in its detail and will likely become the standard reference work on the subject.

Forty contributors, leading authorities in their specialties, wrote the individual entries. Because contributors were given editorial freedom to present the major points of view on a topic, as well as to develop their own interpretation, the book reflects a variety of opinions within the field of paleoanthropology. The editors state that the contributions were "written to be accessible to those with no prior knowledge of the subject, yet they contain sufficient detail to be of value as a resource to both students and professionals." The work will appeal most to college-level readers or scholars, however, because of subject matter and vocabulary level. It will not be generally comprehensible to younger students or casually interested laypersons.

Arranged in A–Z format, the *Encyclopedia* has over 1,200 topical headings, half of which are cross-references ("*Painting, Cave* see Paleolithic Image"; "*Tell* see Archaeological Sites"). A "Detailed List of All Articles by Topic" appears as a classified outline at the beginning of the book. The entries vary in length from a single paragraph to multipage articles. Each entry is signed by its contributor. The list of contributors and their affiliations appears at the front of the book. "All but the shortest entries are accompanied by suggestions for further reading. These reference lists are not exhaustive bibliographies but are pointers to (primarily) recent and easily accessible works." Each entry has, at the end, *see also* references to related entries in the

Encyclopedia. Most entries have from three to five references, but many longer articles have more—as many as 25, 70, or even 90 *see also* references. Because internal referencing is so thorough, the lack of a back-of-the-book index is hardly noticeable.

The contents of the book range widely, providing identifications and definitions for concepts (*Diet, Hunter-Gatherers, Immunological Distance, Sexual Dimorphism, Speech*); scientific methods (*Stratigraphy, Geochronometry, Multivariate Analysis*); geologic processes (*Plate Tectonics, Glaciation, Sea-Level Change*); places (*Near East, Kenya, Lascaux, Piltdown*); primate populations (*Catarrhini, Monkey, Australopithecus, Neanderthals*); paleocultures (*Acheulian, Aurignacian, Solutrean*); numerous fossil finds or anatomical features (*Fontechevade, Swartkrans, Teeth*); tool types and ages (*Burin, Scraper, Stone-Tool Making, Mesolithic*); and short biographies of people, mostly deceased, such as J. Desmond Clark, Charles Darwin, Louis and Mary Leakey (but not Richard), and Sherwood Washburn.

The *Encyclopedia* is heavily illustrated with a variety of black-and-white photographs, line drawings, diagrams of scenes, graphs, timelines, and maps. Evolutionary trees are commonly presented at important junctures in the text. The illustrations are clear and coordinate well with the accompanying text.

The *Encyclopedia of Human Evolution and Prehistory* is a comprehensive and authoritative source, filling a unique niche, that will be essential to academic libraries and will be an important resource for large public libraries as well as any place there is an interest in anthropology and archaeology.

Anti-Evolution: An Annotated Bibliography. By Tom McIver. McFarland, 1988. 385p. indexes. hardcover $39.95 (0-89950-313-5).
016.575 Evolution—Controversial literature—Bibliography l Creationism—Bibliography [CIP] 88-42683

McIver, "a medical librarian living in Santa Monica, California" (according to the publisher's flyer), has compiled an annotated bibliography of books and pamphlets that oppose the theory of evolution. Journal articles, films, videos, and other visual media are excluded. Most items represent the Christian creationist view, but other beliefs are included—theosophy, Hinduism, and Erich von Däniken and other UFO devotees. Each work is given a brief bibliographic citation. Unfortunately, pagination is omitted. Smaller works are characterized as "booklet" or "pamphlet," terms that are not defined. Almost all works are in English, and most were published in the twentieth century in the U.S.

Annotations, ranging in length from a few lines to a column, aim at characterizing, rather than critically evaluating, the claims of the work. In most cases, brief biographical data are given about authors. Relations among works are noted by using boldface references to authors listed elsewhere in the bibliography. Works not seen by the compiler are described on the basis of secondary sources, which are cited in the annotation.

Compilation of the work was partially supported by the National Center for Science Education, "which publishes the *Creation/Evolution Newsletter* and monitors creationist activity in conjunction with its efforts to promote and defend the integrity of science education." Important sources for the compilation were the antievolution/creationist collection of the Institute for Creation Research, "creationist meetings and conferences [and] creationist journals and periodical literature."

This is a subject bibliography, yet access to the works by subject is poor. The main arrangement is designed for known-item searches or browsing, since the 1,852 entries are arranged by author. The compiler states that "one of the most important aims of this collection is to differentiate between the diverse types and forms of anti-evolutionist and creationist theories and doctrines." The compiler's annotations do this on a micro level, but a subject classification is essential to display the diversity of the literature as a whole. Instead, we must settle for a mediocre subject index that features too many single-concept headings with too many undifferentiated entries. Headings like *Great Britain* are almost meaningless by themselves. They need topical, contextual subheadings. The grouping of entries by date does not help much; it does not tell the searcher what aspect of "Great Britain" is related to a particular entry. Undifferentiated entries under types of authors (e.g., *biologists*) and religious denominations (e.g., *Seventh-Day Adventist*) create similar problems. Straightforward name and title indexes are also provided.

Despite this flaw, this is a useful compilation that should find a home in collections for the study of religion, popular culture, and science. The compiler is urged to rethink the presentation of his material when he prepares a second edition.

World Nature Encyclopedia. 24v. [plus paperbound cumulative index]. Raintree, 1989. illus. indexes. maps. hardcover $363.75 (0-8172-3325-3).
574.5 Ecology—Natural history [OCLC]

A beautiful collection of separate monographs dealing with the natural history of 24 areas of the world, this set has much not found elsewhere. The 24 volumes include *The Antarctic and Patagonia, Australia, Central America, India, The Mediterranean, Mountains of Europe, New Guinea, Southeast Asia*, and a cumulative index. The areas are divided biogeographically, ignoring political or other usual groupings. Because of this, the same country may be treated in more than one volume. For instance, *Northeastern America* includes the U.S. and Canada to the Mississippi, and *Atlantic Ocean* treats the north Atlantic area, including the northeastern U.S. Information focuses on the plants, animals, and climate of each region, along with the effects of people on the environment. For instance, *The Amazon* treats the destruction of the rain forests of Brazil and the exploitation of the Indians. Over 1,300 attractive, large color photographs and 700 drawings, charts, and maps illustrate the text. Binding, type, and layout are all well done.

The set was originally published in Italy in 1985. It has a world, rather than an American, view, with equal emphasis given to all regions. Each volume has a name on the title page; it is not clear if this person is the translator or editor or the author of this material. No credentials are given for these writers. Overall, the text is clearly written and appropriate for grades six and up. No sources are provided for anything but artwork, even when specific authors are quoted, and there are no bibliographies.

Within each volume, organization is similar but not identical. Volumes are not arranged alphabetically, and each can be used independently of the others. Each book opens with an introduction describing the area covered, and most titles have a chapter on its history and geography, chapters on specific areas within the given region, and then chapters on plants and animals found within the area. For example, *Equatorial Africa* includes "The Equatorial Forest," "The Rulers of the Canopy," "Chimpanzees and Gorillas," "Ungulates," "Zoological Discoveries of the Twentieth Century," "Predators," "Winged Inhabitants of the Tropics" (birds and bats), and "Army Ants." *Waters of Africa* includes sections on mountains, marshes, lakes, and rivers; *The Pacific Ocean* is subdivided by name of island group (New Zealand, New Caledonia, Easter Island). Each book has a helpful "Guide to Areas of Natural Interest" that describes the special features and locations of national and state parks and reserves, indicating their locations on a map, and concludes with a glossary and an index. The glossaries include some terms in common (*plateau, nocturnal, herbivore, ecology*) and others peculiar to the region. For example, *Deserts of America* includes *fault, butte,* and *influorescence; Atlantic Ocean* has *spermaceti* and *zooplankton;* and *Sahara* includes *torpor* and *opisthoglyph.* Although definitions are clearly written (as is most of the text), there are far too few of them. The statement that gazelles' "main food source is asfu" is not explained anywhere. Words such as *caldera, cauliflory,* and *karoo,* which are defined in the text, are not repeated in the glossaries and do not appear in the indexes.

Overall, indexes are fair to poor and are the major problem with this set. Arrangement of the indexes is letter by letter, so that *seal* precedes *sea lamprey* and is separated from *seal hunting*. In the cumulative index, the form of entries is somewhat inconsistent, with *manta rays* and *rays* both listed but referring to different volumes. The index entry *areas of natural interest* lists all of the areas included in each volume, but there is no cross-reference from *national parks* or *parks*. Photographs are not indexed, although this would seem natural in such a well-illustrated set, making it useless for the typical "I need a picture of a snow leopard" assignment. Photographs are not always illustrative of accompanying text. A geological description of the Ethiopian plateau is accompanied by a photo of a vervet monkey and drawings of antelope heads (*Waters of Africa*), and the ring-tailed lemur is pictured four pages before it appears in the text (*Southern Africa*). Some minor editing errors also exist. There are a few fragments and some misspellings ("Bacterian camel").

Despite these flaws, there is no comparable work. *The Living Earth* (Grolier, 1975) is much shorter and is grouped by biomes rather than geographic region. *Grzimek's Animal Life Encyclopedia* (Van Nostrand, 1972–75) includes more information about animal habits and behavior but not about the interrelationships with people or geography. Time-Life's series on rivers covers about the same material for the Amazon and Nile, but Raintree's includes the rest of the world. *World Nature Encyclopedia* will be a useful purchase in school and public libraries where patrons anxiously await *Audubon* and *Natural History*.

Dictionary of Genetics & Cell Biology. By Norman Maclean. New York Univ.; dist. by Columbia, 1988 (c1987). 422p. illus. tables. hardcover $60 (0-8147-5438-4).

575.1'03 Genetics—Dictionaries l Cytology—Dictionaries [CIP] 87-28153

The fields of genetics and cell biology have experienced rapid growth in the past few years resulting in new terminology and words from other fields given new, specialized meanings. For the researcher, the precise meaning of a term in the fields of genetics and cell biology is quite important. Someone reading an article on genetics may encounter a general term such as *housekeeping* and wonder what its relationship is to genetics. Maclean, of Southampton University, compiled this dictionary with the help of nine contributing authors. He wrote the definitions of over 80 percent of the entries. His intention was to not just define the terms but to "explain what certain words mean and what their relationship is to other terms in the same field." He admits that there could be separate dictionaries for genetics and cell biology but points out that a large number of the terms are used and have the same meanings in both fields.

The entries are in alphabetical order, letter by letter, disregarding numerals used as prefixes. British spelling is used with no cross-references to, for instance, *oestrogen* from *estrogen*. Words appearing in small capitals within a definition are defined elsewhere in the dictionary. *See also* references are included for information on related topics. The definitions tend to be technical and range from 10 to more than 500 words. The few black-and-white illustrations are very helpful and appear in close proximity to the definitions they explain. There are five appendixes at the beginning of the volume covering common and Latin names of some key organisms, chromosome numbers in various species, DNA content of haploid genomes, the Greek alphabet, and the classification of living organisms.

This dictionary is a welcome addition to science collections. It is intended primarily for researchers but will also be of use to scientists and students outside the fields of genetics and cell biology. Even though libraries may have general biology dictionaries, they will find this dictionary useful for its terminology specific to genetics and cell biology. Academic and special libraries will benefit most from this book.

The Marshall Cavendish Illustrated Encyclopedia of Plants and Earth Sciences. 10v. Ed. by David M. Moore. Marshall Cavendish Corp., 1988. bibliog. illus. index. hardcover $299.95 (0-86307-901-6).

580'.3 Botany—Dictionaries l Botany, Economic—Dictionaries l Crops—Dictionaries l Angiosperms—Dictionaries l Earth sciences—Dictionaries [CIP] 87-23927

Here is a beautiful work that provides a comprehensive introduction to the related subjects of plant biology, ecology, and geology. The *Encyclopedia* is made up of a "Dictionary of Plants" in volumes 1–3, a guide to "Flowering Plant Families" in volumes 3–5, "Plant Ecology" in volumes 6–7, and "Earth Sciences" in volumes 8–9. Volume 10 includes the indexes, glossary, and bibliography. There are more than 120 specialist contributors listed in the front of volume 1, and the initials of specific contributors are provided at the end of major entries. The contributors are primarily British or European with just a scattering of North American authors. However, the scope of the *Encyclopedia* is worldwide.

The "Dictionary of Plants" contains over 2,200 entries, arranged alphabetically by genus or, for groups of plants, by popular names. Emphasis is placed on species of economic or ornamental importance; all important crop species are included. Each entry contains information on geographic distribution, characteristics, economic uses (if any), cultivation (if any), and a listing of the major families with approximate number of species. Numerous excellent color photographs are used to portray the species or their economic uses. This section includes 21 special feature articles on important plant groups such as algae or products such as alkaloids. The feature articles, which may be several pages long, provide greater detail and include diagrams and charts of reference information (such as common alkaloids, their main sources and pharmaceutical characteristics). The section "Flowering Plant Families" is arranged by botanical and evolutionary classification of families and orders. The classification used is summarized on two pages following the section introduction. For each family or order, there is a listing of common names, a general description, and information on distribution, diagnostic features, classification, and economic uses. Each entry also includes an outline map of the world that graphically shows distribution, with summary data on number of genera and species, and economic uses. These entries include clear drawings of leaves, stems, roots, and flowering parts of representative species.

The "Plant Ecology" sections of the *Encyclopedia* are mostly essays on topics such as taxonomy, paleobotany, evolution, soils, and the effect of man on the environment. Similarly the "Earth Sciences" sections cover the earth and other planets, geologic processes such as earthquakes, the ocean floor, and geologic history of the earth and man. The section on economic geology also includes brief entries for several minerals and elements. In both the "Plant Ecology" and "Earth Sciences" sections, beautiful color photographs and diagrams are used judiciously to illustrate points in the text. A feature missing from these longer articles is specific bibliographic references for further reading. Instead, only more general references are provided in the bibliography in volume 10.

A major strength of this *Encyclopedia* is the number of access points available. First, cross-references for entries are used throughout. Terms with entries of their own elsewhere are noted with asterisks. The comprehensive alphabetical index in volume 10 includes more than 5,000 entries, with major entries noted in boldface type. For ease of use, both volume and page numbers are given. The thematic index, also in volume 10, is divided into 14 subject areas—e.g., *Families of Conifers*, *Crop Plants*, *Prominent Figures*, *Natural Vegetation Zones*, *Prehistoric Animals*, and *Minerals*. This index brings together similar entries that appear in different sections of the *Encyclopedia* and is a good place to start for readers interested in broader topics. The bibliography in this volume is divided into seven topical sections (e.g., *Ecology and Biogeography*, *Flora and General Botanical Works*, *Trees and Shrubs*, *The Solar System*, and *Earth Sciences*). The majority of entries cited are from the 1970s and early 1980s.

Although much of the information here can be found in other encyclopedias and botanical reference books, this attractive set is recommended as a handy resource that will be of greatest use in high school and public libraries, especially for background information for student term papers. Users of academic libraries may also find valuable the "Dictionary of Plants" and "Flowering Plant Families" sections, along with the handsome photographs and drawings.

Atlas of Wintering North American Birds: An Analysis of Christmas Bird Count Data. By Terry Root. Univ. of Chicago, 1989 (c1988). 312p. bibliog. index. tables. hardcover $60 (0-226-72539-1); paper $35 (0-226-72540-5).

598.297 Bird populations—North America—Geographical distribution I Birds—North America—Wintering—Geographical distribution [CIP] 88-8591

Thousands of people have participated in Christmas bird counts, an annual event sponsored by the National Audubon Society since 1900. Data from these counts remained largely inaccessible over the years because of the sheer bulk of the information. Now Root, a professor at the University of Michigan, utilizing a previously computerized data bank of the 1963–72 counts, has produced the first large-scale biogeographic account of birds wintering in the 48 contiguous United States and southern Canada. Using sophisticated computer techniques, she has analyzed distribution and abundance data on more than 500 birds in both traditional contour maps and maps that simulate three dimensions.

The main portion of the *Atlas* consists of black-and-white maps and brief textual descriptions of the distribution and abundance patterns of most of the birds, listed (in Latin) in the order used in the American Ornithologists' Union *Check-List of North American Birds* (1983). Maps (with no accompanying text) with possible problems of interpretation are placed in appendix B. Appendix A, "Species List," indicates by common name which maps are in the main text, which are in appendix B, and why certain species were excluded altogether—usually because too few sites were recorded. The maps are enriched by 11 transparent overlays—in a pocket pasted inside the back cover—that show state and provincial borders, one-degree latitude/longitude blocks, elevation, vegetation, average minimum January temperature and mean winter ocean-surface temperature, average length of the frost-free period, mean annual precipitation, general humidity, national wildlife refuges, and count locations. Following appendix B is an extensive unannotated bibliography of journal articles, books, and government documents (U.S. and Canadian) from 1917 to date and an index of both common and scientific names.

The pioneering nature of the *Atlas of Wintering North American Birds* and a plea for additional research studies with Christmas bird-count data are cited at least three times in this volume. This *Atlas* will clearly be a valuable addition to the ornithological collections of academic and large public libraries.

MEDICINE, HEALTH

Product and Process: An Index to the Way Things Work. By Robert Finnegan. Scarecrow, 1988. 238p. hardcover $25 (0-8108-2113-3).

016.6 Technology—Indexes I Manufacturing processes—Indexes [CIP] 88-6691

This work is an index to selected one-volume sources of information on science and technology. The author's preface states that the book was developed as a response to requests from students preparing reports for a technical writing course for information about simple objects or processes. To serve this purpose, the index should refer the users to sources that are up-to-date and complete. This work cites 19 sources published between 1967 and 1986. However, most date from the 1970s. In checking the catalog of a large public library system, we found that many of the sources used were in the juvenile collection. These facts do not seem to fit the author's purpose.

The index itself is well organized. The topics are arranged alphabetically using Library of Congress subject headings. There are ample *see* and *see also* references. The citations consist of abbreviations of the source titles and page numbers. At the beginning of the book, one finds user instructions and a key to the title codes. It is very easy to use.

The title *Product and Process: An Index to the Way Things Work* implies industry and technology, but a perusal of the index turns up items such as *altruism, bathing suits, malocclusion, popes—election*, and *puns and punning*. In checking the sources cited for the quality of information, one finds great variation. The brief article *Tides* in *The Way Things Work Book of Nature* covers the essentials in a rather technical explanation, while the material on *Umbrellas* in *Everyday Inventions* says a great deal about the history and customs relating to use, but nothing about construction or design. In most cases a student could find the same or better information in a good encyclopedia article.

This index is of limited usefulness. A library would have to own most of the sources cited to make it worthwhile. Even then, the age of the sources, the varying quality of the information they contain, and the fact that this information is readily available in updated form in general or technical encyclopedias serve as recommendations against purchase.

Key to High-Tech: A User-Friendly Guide to the New Technology. By Robert J. Cone. Galcon Press, P.O. Box 17835, Rochester, NY 14621, 1987. 153p. index. paper $10.95 (0-943075-17-3).

600 High technology [OCLC] 87-81270

Seventeen major high-tech topics (such as *Artificial Intelligence, Chip, Cryogenics, Fiber Optics, Genetic Engineering, Robots, Strategic Defense Initiative,* and *Supercomputers*) are described by the author. The topics were selected by a "careful survey of media coverage of technology, in addition to extensive discussions with members of the scientific and commercial communities." The book intends to be a general guide, not the ultimate authority on any of the topics. Engineering details and operational minutiae are omitted as "not likely to help the intelligent 'outsider'" or reader.

For each topical entry, a three- to five-page basic description of the technology, its applications, and background is given. Text is written for the layperson. There are no illustrations or bibliographic citations for further reading. Terms defined more fully in other entries are indicated by a plus sign. A table of contents outlines the 17 topics covered in section 1. Section 2 discusses binary numbers and digital signals as two aspects of most other technologies, and section 3 briefly discusses 12 additional topics that "contribute to . . . the operation" of the major technologies described in section 1. These include *CAD, CAM, CRT, Holography,* and *Communications Satellites*. A subject index provides "bare bones" access to the terms and topics.

The layperson's approach to the topics presented by *Key to High-Tech* makes it more suitable for general collections and casual reading than as a scholarly reference work, and therefore it is appropriate for public, high school, and community college libraries.

Allied Health Education Directory, 1988. 16th ed. Ed. by William R. Burrows and Hannah L. Hedrick. American Medical Association, 535 N. Dearborn St., Chicago, IL 60610, 1988. 313p. tables. paper $27.95 (0-89970-312-7; ISSN 0194-3766).

610.7 Paramedical education—U.S.—Directories I Health occupation schools I Health education—U.S.—Directories II Medical education—U.S.—Directories [OCLC] 79-644041

This directory provides information on educational programs in allied health occupations and on the accreditation process used by the American Medical Association Committee on Allied Health Education and Accreditation (CAHEA). The book is arranged in five sections. The first, "Allied Health Education and Accreditation," provides the history of AMA support for allied health education, describes the responsibilities of CAHEA, and presents an overview of the accreditation system.

The second section, "Occupational Descriptions and Program Listings," will be useful for individuals seeking career information. It contains information on 26 allied health specialties, such as cytotechnology, surgical technology, and medical illustration, taught in 1,600 institutions around the country. Arranged alphabetically by occupation, each entry provides the following information: history of the occupation, job description, employment characteristics, and general information about educational programs, including length and curriculum. Also provided are a list of informational sources for accreditation, careers, certification, licensure, or registration. Following this is a list of accredited educational programs for the occupation in alphabetical order by state. Entries for specific programs include institution address, telephone number, director, class size, beginning date, length of program, tuition, degree/certificate awarded, date of next accreditation review, and affiliated institutions.

The third section lists, in alphabetical order by state and city, the 1,600 institutions that sponsor the allied health educational programs and tells which programs are offered, so the reader can consult the appropriate part of section 2. The fourth section contains two research reports from the AMA, one that assesses the reliability and standards for allied health educational programs and the second that reports on characteristics of graduates, employment opportunities, and the effects of the prospective payment system on allied health education. The final section contains four appendixes with a variety of information such as acronyms, a glossary, and statistics.

Barron's Futures in Health: A Complete Career Guidance Handbook for Prospective Allied Health Professionals is broader in scope, including career data for podiatrists, pharmacists, physical therapists, chiropractors, art therapists, and nursing home administrators. But *Barron's* gives only names and addresses for schools, while the *Directory* includes detailed data on accredited institutions. Libraries serving patrons interested in health careers will need this *Directory*.

Health Resource Builder: Free and Inexpensive Materials for Librarians and Teachers. Comp. by Carol Smallwood. McFarland, 1988. 251p. index. paper $15.95 (0-89950-359-4).

610'.72073 Health—Information services—U.S.—Directories I Health—Bibliography [CIP] 88-42639

Health Resource Builder will be useful for librarians, teachers, and health educators seeking current sources of information about physical health, mental health, or safety. It lists organizations that publish free or low-cost materials. Though not comprehensive, it is an excellent supplement to encyclopedias, periodicals, and books or a starting point for building information files.

The book is organized alphabetically by more than 200 subjects, including names of specific diseases and topics such as aging, child safety seats, grief, and medical ethics. There are no *see* or *see also* references in the text, but they do appear in the index. Some conditions like PKU are listed only by their abbreviations with no indication of their full names. The entries are numbered consecutively and consist of the name, address, and telephone number of the organization and a brief description of the type of material available. Titles of specific publications are not generally given. A separate section classifies organizations by type of item available (e.g., audiovisuals, databases, indexes).

Three appendixes provide important information. Appendix A lists the addresses and telephone numbers of state and regional offices of public agencies under headings like *Medicaid* and *EPA Radiation Representatives*. Appendix B is a "National Health Observances Calendar," which will be useful for planning programs, displays, and other activities. Appendix C contains telephone numbers for hotlines and federal offices equipped with telecommunications devices for the deaf. The book concludes with a detailed name/subject index.

Health Resource Builder is a valuable resource for anyone involved in health education. Librarians concerned with information and referral and vertical-file maintenance will find this a most useful tool. It is a recommended addition for all public, health-science, and education collections.

Encyclopedia of Good Health. 6v. Ed. by Mario Orlandi and Donald Prue. Facts On File, 1989 (c1988). illus. indexes. hardcover $89.95/set, $18.95/vol. (0-8160-1665-8).

613.043'3 Youth—Health and hygiene [BKL]

This set is designed for browsing and leisure reading by young adults rather than for serious research. It reads like long "Dear Abby" pamphlets, full of common sense, good advice, and frank, clear examples. The six slender volumes run about 125 pages each, with many topics complete in a single page or two-page spread. Volume titles are *Nutrition*, *Exercise*, *Stress and Mental Health*, *Maintaining Good Health*, *Substance Abuse*, and *Human Sexuality*. Included is information on eye and hair care, CPR, and first aid (*Good Health*); aerobic and nonaerobic exercise (*Exercise*); the difference between stress and stressors (*Stress*); and menstruation, birth control, and STDs (*Sexuality*). Each volume is independent, but there are some references in the text to related subjects in other volumes. This is important since there is no overall index to the set. For example, in a discussion of "runner's high" in *Substance Abuse*, readers are told to "see *Exercise*." There are cross-references within each book as well; for instance, in *Nutrition* from "Complex Carbohydrates" to "What's a Calorie?"

Each volume's introduction, "How to Use This Book," explains how the information is important to junior high students and how the series is arranged. While the set is intended for junior high, many of the illustrations show older teens and the text includes lots of older references (getting a driver's license, studying all night for exams). Older students will be put off by the "junior high" references throughout; younger teens may not relate to some of the examples because they aren't relevant yet.

On the plus side, the mostly black-and-white illustrations in the set show a nice mix of boys and girls (and the text is deliberately nonsexist), as well as portraying a variety of ethnic groups. The two series editors are psychologists with "wellness" specialties. The volume authors are free-lance health writers. Writing is clear, with question-and-answer format, abundant charts, diagrams, illustrations (mostly appropriate), self-quizzes, and personal examples. Each volume contains associations to contact for further information, a glossary, and an adequate index; there are no bibliographies.

Sexuality may be the most helpful volume; all of the important facts are given (though some prior knowledge is expected), plus some less-usual information (how to use a tampon, for example). Abortion, premarital sex, homosexuality, and masturbation are all mentioned as possible conflict items with religious groups.

Scattered throughout are some primitive drawings (*Sexuality*), questionable statements (e.g., "Women's magazines usually can't print bad news about smoking, since the publishers need the money that advertisers pay," in *Substance Abuse*), and upper-middle-class assumptions (e.g., "tell yourself you can go to the record store after you take a walk," in *Stress*). However, the appealing format invites browsing, and even reluctant readers may pick up the volumes and painlessly absorb some useful information.

Despite the title, this is not an encyclopedia and will find more use outside the reference collection. It should be considered for grades 6–12 in schools and public libraries.

Women's Health Perspectives: An Annual Review. v.1. Ed. by Carol J. Leppa and Connie Miller. Oryx, 1988. 238p. bibliog. index. hardcover $45 (0-89774-452-7).

613'.0424 Women—Health and hygiene [CIP] 88-19676

This bibliography is the result of a growing interest in women's health issues and the expanding literature that accompanies it. It attempts to organize and analyze the literature to provide a synthesis and critical review of research. The scope of this subject has broadened from reproductive health to all aspects of health and health-care delivery as they relate to women. This includes the sociocultural and economic patterns that produce health problems and the physical and psychological aspects involved in well-being.

The compilers aim to evaluate information services in the area of women's health and to provide a means of identifying areas that need further study. They have limited the sources included to those that are women-centered or feminist: areas affecting women exclusively or affecting women differently. Where the amount of material is overwhelming, as in reproductive-health areas, they have chosen representative or review articles or developed a theme as a focus within the subject area.

The 13 chapters contain more than 450 critically annotated citations and 300 additional bibliographic citations. Each chapter is compiled by a female health professional. Most are registered nurses who hold university faculty appointments. The subjects covered include access to health information, mental health, body image, alcohol and drugs, sexuality, the menstrual cycle, the health of older women, and women as health-care providers. The chapters begin with a critical essay that furnishes an overview and historical perspective on the topic. This is followed by a list of references cited in the essay and the annotated bibliography on that topic. The lengthy annotations summarize the work and offer the compiler's critical appraisal. The compilers have chosen works of both historic importance and current research on their topics. In the chapter "Women and Mental Health," for instance, one finds Simone de Beauvoir's *Second Sex* (1952) and J. B. Miller's *Toward a New Psychology of Women* (1986).

The final three chapters are topical bibliographies on women and abuse, cancer, and osteoporosis. Each has a brief introductory essay and an unannotated bibliography. These subjects will be fully treated in later volumes of this series.

Women's Health Perspectives is a unique work. It combines a female point of view with an interdisciplinary approach to an important subject area. It also provides an overview of research on topics of interest to both health-care professionals and the general public. Librarians in health science, social science, women's studies, and public libraries will find this a welcome addition to their collections. They will want to add subsequent volumes as they appear.

Spas, 1988: The International Spa Guide. 1st ed. Ed. by Joseph H. Bain and Eli Dror. B.D.I.T., Inc., P.O. Box 7708, Flushing, NY 11352, 1987. 294p. illus. maps. paper $14.95 (0-9618612-0-7).
613.122'025 Health resorts, watering-places, etc.—Directories [BKL]

Ancient civilizations believed in the therapeutic benefits provided by bathing in mineral waters and hot springs. Today, the definition of *spa* has come to mean health resorts, a variety of fitness and weight-loss programs, pampering, and beauty treatments, as well as treatment centers that employ drugs and other techniques to fight the aging process. The introduction suggests, "When selecting a spa that offers medical benefits, it is recommended to check with your physician."

This guide contains information on more than 200 spas in 30 countries, including the U.S. Information was garnered from national tourist offices, individual spas and hotels, travel agents, and tour operators and advertisers.

Spas are classified according to the programs they offer: 1) medical programs and treatments; 2) thermal, mineral, hot springs, thalassotherapy; 3) beauty, cosmetic, aesthetic treatments, pampering; 4) fitness, exercise, and diet programs. Star symbols are employed to describe each spa or spa hotel from five stars (deluxe) to two stars (tourist category).

Each country's section begins with an outline map showing the location of the spas in relation to major cities and a paragraph or two about the country's spas. Each spa is described in turn, e.g., Atami, Beppu, and Hakone in Japan. The hotels are listed under each spa, with brief descriptions and tabular information on the number and type of rooms, transportation, rates, facilities, programs, and treatments and medical supervision provided. Black-and-white photographs are scattered through the book. Appendixes include spa travel agents and tour operators and a glossary.

Two other spa guides were recently reviewed in BOOKLIST [N 1 88]. *The Spa Book* is limited to American spas and lists more of them; *The Best Spas* is also international in scope and more extensive in coverage. Each book has some unique listings. Public libraries and academic libraries supporting hotel curricula may want to consider *Spas, 1988*.

The Columbia Encyclopedia of Nutrition. Comp. by Myron Winick and others. Putnam, 1988 (c1987). 349p. index. tables. hardcover $19.95 (0-399-13298-8).
613.2'03 Nutrition—Dictionaries [CIP] 87-10782

The purpose of this work is to present the latest clinical data on nutrition, emphasizing topics of concern in disease prevention and promotion of well-being. Sponsored by the Institute of Human Nutrition of Columbia University's College of Physicians and Surgeons, the book has four compiler-editors (one physician, three scientists), with acknowledgment of seven others. There are over 100 alphabetically arranged articles, ranging from a page or less to nine or more pages on *Infection, Pregnancy, Workplace, Obesity,* and *Exercise*. Many entries refer to specific aspects of food (e.g., *Sulfur, Vitamin D, Fiber, Taurine*). Others are physical irregularities and their relation to diet (e.g., *Allergy, Hypertension, Diabetes, Stress, Anorexia Nervosa*). Some are prescriptive (e.g., *Breast Feeding, Food Balancing, Reducing Diets*). Specific foodstuffs are rarely entries.

Presentation is geared to the lay reader, and the style is conversational. Articles do not assume prior knowledge and attempt to give clear (if condensed) explanations. The article *Junk Food* suggests that occasional consumption of empty calories is acceptable and that many fast foods have nutritional value, although they should be balanced with lower calorie foods. *Kelp* states that these supplements are potentially dangerous; *Aspartame* says that the sweetener appears to be safe for most. The *Food Balancing* entry says that the idea of basic food groups has proven impractical and instead calls for varied foods with high nutrient density. There are occasional references to specific studies and publications, but no bibliographies. Topics may be discussed in more than one article (e.g., *Cholesterol* and *Arteriosclerosis*); cross-references and an index facilitate use.

The book includes some recipes and menus; among the many tables and lists are naturally occurring nutrients, average cholesterol readings, drugs that affect nutrients, fiber content of selected foods, effect of processing methods, and potassium sources. There are no illustrations. The subject is vital, the text readable and authoritative, the coverage relevant to most readers' interests, and the cost reasonable. *The Columbia Encyclopedia of Nutrition* is recommended for secondary school, public, health science, and academic libraries.

Disease Prevention/Health Promotion: The Facts. Bull Pub. Co., 1988. 341p. bibliog. charts. tables. paper $24.95 (0-915950-89-8).
614.4'4 Public health—U.S.—Handbooks, manuals, etc. ‖ Public health—U.S.—Statistics ‖ Medicine, Preventive—U.S.—Handbooks, manuals, etc. ‖ Medicine, Preventive—U.S.—Statistics ‖ Health promotion—U.S.—Handbooks, manuals, etc. [CIP] 87-32013

This is a compilation of facts and statistics prepared by the Office of Disease Prevention and Health Promotion, U.S. Public Health Service, Department of Health and Human Services. The emphasis is on facts that can support those involved in disease prevention and health promotion such as educators, writers, program planners, and policy makers.

The outline of the book is based on the "1990 Health Objectives for the Nation," published by the Office of Disease Prevention and Health Promotion. The chapters are divided into seven main sections: "Health Promotion" with chapters on smoking, alcohol and drugs, nutrition, fitness, and stress; "Health Protection" with chapters on toxic agents, occupational health, accidents and injuries, dental health, and infectious diseases; "Preventive Health" with chapters on high blood pressure, family planning, pregnancy and infant care, immunization, and sexually transmitted diseases; "Age Groups"; "Minority Populations"; "Diseases"; and "Settings," covering prevention in the workplace and clinical settings. Each chapter begins with an introductory section providing background information on the topic along with statistics and facts. The 15 chapters in the first three sections are further organized under prevalence, public and professional awareness, service delivery, and significant trends. "Age Groups" and "Minority Groups" have sections on demographic, socioeconomic, and risk factor data and significant trends. The diseases chapters have sections on incidence and prevalence, risk factor prevalence, and interventions. Several chapters also include tables and graphs. Besides this detailed arrangement, keywords in boldface are given to the left of the facts to aid in their location. However, this does not make up for the lack of an index, which is a serious obstacle for users of this information, who will need to browse to locate the appropriate statistic or fact.

Facts are coded with letters signifying the sources of the information, and each chapter concludes with a list of references. Many of the references are government documents, and some are unpublished reports. Another shortcoming of the book is that most references do not include page numbers.

The facts and statistics contained in this book have significant reference value. So, even with the serious shortcomings of the lack of an index and incomplete references, this book is recommended for academic and large public libraries.

AIDS: Political, Social, International Aspects. [quarterly issue of Contemporary Social Issues.] Comp. by Joan Nordquist. Reference and Research Services, 511 Lincoln St., Santa Cruz, CA 95060, 1988. 72p. paper $15 (0-937855-19-7; ISSN 0887-3569).

016.6169792 Acquired immune deficiency syndrome—Bibliography [BKL]

AIDS Bibliography for 1981–1986. Comp. by Nancy C. Weissberg. Whitston, 1988. 643p. index. hardcover $55 (0-87875-356-7; ISSN 0895-9331).

016.6169792 Acquired immune deficiency syndrome—Bibliography [BKL]

The number of books and periodical articles on AIDS is increasing at a rapid rate. There are few publications that can be bought at the newsstand that do not have an AIDS-related article. Added to these general publications are scientific and technical journals reporting research, viewpoints of the gay and lesbian communities in their national publications, and government documents. For anyone doing AIDS bibliographic research, the amount of material is overwhelming.

AIDS: Political, Social, International Aspects and *AIDS Bibliography for 1981–1986* are two new bibliographies that are quite different. The first is a pamphlet that is part of the Contemporary Social Issues series ($40/year). It is purposely small so current information could be published quickly. Over 700 entries are included, with most from 1987 but several from 1986 and 1988. There are 14 separate sections, each covering some aspect of AIDS as it relates to issues such as the law, the workplace, minorities, women, children, and drugs. Within sections, entries are arranged alphabetically by author with books, pamphlets, and documents in one list and articles in another. The last four chapters list bibliographies, other resources, organizations, and periodicals. There is neither an author index nor any annotations. In scope, this work would appear to be similar to Tyckoson's annual *AIDS Bibliography* (Oryx, 1985–   [*RBB* D 1 85]). However, when part 1 of his *AIDS Bibliography, 1988*, listing about 550 1987 publications, was compared with the title under review, little overlap was found. Public and high school libraries may prefer the Oryx bibliography because of its helpful annotations, but libraries wanting comprehensive coverage will want Nordquist's list too, especially since it includes books and pamphlets.

The *AIDS Bibliography for 1981–1986* is an impressive compilation of some 4,000 citations for the years 1981–86. The bulk of the references are to periodical articles, with only 43 to books, government publications, and monographs. The periodical articles are listed twice with full citations: once alphabetically by article title and once by subject. The subject headings are well constructed, using a controlled thesaurus of terms and phrases covering all aspects of AIDS

from the technical to the general. There is also an author index. There are no annotations. From the list of 917 journals indexed, it is clear that comprehensiveness was intended. There is international coverage with journals from all areas of the world; controversial coverage with such journals as the *Militant*; gay and lesbian literature with such titles as the *Advocate, Gay Community News, Lesbian Contradictions*, and *I Know You Know*; and popular literature represented with such titles as *Woman's Day* and *People*. This, by far, is one of the best bibliographies available on AIDS. According to the preface, it is to be updated on an annual basis.

While several other AIDS bibliographies are available (see "Reference Materials for or about Gays and Lesbians" [*RBB* Je 1 88] for a more complete list), both of these bibliographies can be recommended for their relatively recent coverage.

Alternative Therapies, Unproven Methods, and Health Fraud: A Selected Annotated Bibliography. By Micaela Sullivan-Fowler and others. American Medical Association, 1988. 47p. bibliog. paper $20 retail, $16 to libraries and schools (0-89970-319-4).

016.6155 Alternative medicine—Bibliography I Quacks and quackery—Bibliography [CIP] 88-14511

This brief bibliography of 117 book and journal articles was compiled by the AMA's Division of Library and Information Management. The book's introduction defines alternative therapies as unproven alternatives to generally recognized surgical, radiological, pharmaceutical, or nutritional therapies. The compilers have been selective, but the works cited here should satisfy medical staff and laypersons. There are 2 to 12 bibliographic citations provided for each of the 18 topics included. Citations are complete, and the brief annotations serve as an additional selection aid. Also included is a list of books for further reading and names of associations to contact for further information.

Topics are arranged alphabetically, including diseases (*Arthritis, Cancer*) and treatments (*Cellular Therapy, Hair Analysis*). Each topical entry begins with a carefully worded brief description that serves as a warning to those interested in alternative therapies. Two sentences taken from the discussion of AIDS serve to give the flavor of these brief introductions: "Some argue that since the medical community has not yet found a cure for AIDS, individuals should not be faulted for attempting to find their own cures. Unfortunately, while some of the therapies might have a palliative effect, generally they are unproven or fraudulent."

This bibliography is limited to readings stating the case against alternative treatments. It should be added to most public and academic libraries, especially those owning such titles as *Third Opinion* by John M. Fink [*RBB* D 15 88] or *The Directory of Holistic Medicine and Alternate Health Care Services in the U.S.* [*RBB* S 15 86], which advocate alternative therapies.

Health Media Review Index, 1984–86: A Guide to Reviews and Descriptions of Commercially Available Nonprint Material for the Medical, Mental, Allied Health, Human Service, and Related Counseling Professions. Ed. by Deborah J. McCalpin. Scarecrow, 1988. 751p. hardcover $59.50 (0-8108-2172-9).

016.61 Health—Audio-visual aids—Indexes I Health education—Audio-visual aids—Indexes I Public health—Audio-visual aids—Indexes I Nursing—Audio-visual aids—Indexes [CIP] 88-18452

This guide updates the original edition published in 1985 [*RBB* O 15 85]. Its purpose is to index and provide abstracts of reviews of over 3,000 audiovisual productions and computer-software programs. The editors relied upon reviews in approximately 110 health-related journals and reviewing sources from 1984 through 1986 to identify items commercially available in the U.S., Canada, and England.

The two editors of the original volume serve as contributing editors here, and all three editors are librarians. They have created an update that is similar in format to its predecessor, though with improvements.

The first section of the work lists titles by subject. The National Library of Medicine's medical subject headings are used, and there are many cross-references to lead users to the correct terms. Improvements in this section include the listing of computer-software programs in italics and the use of "(PA)" to indicate the material is intended for a professional audience only.

The use of "(PA)" is also carried over to the main alphabetical title section of the book. In this section complete bibliographic information is provided for each entry, along with an objective description of content, award(s) won, a rating supplied by the editor, where reviewed, excerpt from an original review, and the subject headings used in indexing the title.

An awards section lists organizations sponsoring nonprint media festivals, along with basic data on the organization and a list of winning titles. The distributor section lists the names of more than 1,000 distributors whose titles appear in the *Index*.

The updated *Index* continues to be a valuable resource for libraries supporting health professionals and those interested in medical and health-related topics.

Psychological and Medical Aspects of Induced Abortion: A Selective, Annotated Bibliography, 1970–1986. Comp. by Eugenia B. Winter. Greenwood, 1988. 162p. indexes. hardcover $37.95 (0-313-26100-8; ISSN 0742-6941).
016.6188'8 Abortion—Bibliography I Abortion—Psychological aspects—Bibliography [CIP] 88-194

This bibliography lists 500 classic or representational books and articles on the psychological and medical aspects of abortion. Some audiovisual materials have also been included. The articles chosen are in English, although some are translations into English, and tend to be from health-science journals. The preface includes a two-page review of the literature, and the introduction provides definitions of the 10 major subject divisions of the bibliography, which include "Abortion Clinics," "Abortion Decision," "Abortion Techniques," "Counseling," "Morbidity and Mortality," "Abortion Effects on Subsequent Pregnancy," "Psychological Effects," and "Psychosocial Aspects." Each entry is numbered, and where a book has a bibliography it is noted. Brief descriptive annotations for each item are provided by the compiler, a librarian at California State University, Bakersfield.

There are author, title, and subject indexes. Cross-references in the subject index could be improved: they were created for those with some knowledge of the field; others may find it difficult to orient themselves to the technical language. For instance, under *abortifacients*, the reader is told to "*See also* specific names of abortifacients."

This bibliography supplements Muldoon's *Abortion: An Annotated Indexed Bibliography* (E. Mellen, 1980), which provides broader coverage but fewer annotations, and Gale's annual *Bibliography of Bioethics*, which includes abortion in the topics covered. It will be useful in academic and health-science libraries.

The American Medical Association Guide to Prescription and Over-the-Counter Drugs. Ed. by Charles B. Clayman. Random, 1988. 576p. charts. illus. index. $25 (0-394-56949-0).
615'.1 Drugs—Handbooks, manuals, etc. I Drugs, Non-prescription—Handbooks, manuals, etc. [CIP] 87-43202

This handbook for the layperson covers the most common prescription and over-the-counter medications. Originally developed by a British publishing firm, it is the second volume in the AMA Home Health Library, following *The American Medical Association Family Medical Guide*. The book uses clear nontechnical language and attractive graphics to facilitate locating information quickly and easily. Much of the information comes from the *AMA Drug Evaluations* (6th ed.); inclusion of drugs and detail of descriptions is based on data on medical use from the *National Drug and Therapeutic Index*.

The book is divided into five sections. Section 1, "Understanding and Using Drugs," covers such topics as the classification of drugs, mechanisms of action, methods of administration, and the proper use and storage of medications. The second section, "Drug Finder Index," is an identification guide with color photographs of over 500 brand-name tablets and capsules plus an index of approximately 5,000 generic and brand-name drugs. The color guide includes an easy-to-follow flowchart. Section 3 deals with major drug groups, arranged by either human body systems or major diseases. Each of these groups is described with information on uses, actions, effects, and risks. Many entries include accompanying illustrations on their mode of action and charts providing comparisons and summary information. Common drugs mentioned in this section are highlighted within a box, and these are then discussed individually in greater detail in section 4, "The A–Z of Drugs," covering 320 of the common generic kind. Each one-page entry includes brand names; combined preparations, if any; information for users on dosage, storage, and missed dosage; overdose action; possible adverse effects; interactions; special precautions for pregnancy, the aged, or driving; and information on prolonged use. The top right-hand corner of each entry provides quick reference information, including the reference to the discussion of the drug group in section 3, an overdose and dependence danger rating (high, medium, low), whether a prescription is required, and whether the drug is available in a generic form. Following "The A–Z of Drugs" are sections on vitamins and minerals, drugs of abuse, and food additives.

The last section of the book contains a glossary of terms and a general index to information contained in sections 1 and 3. Entries in the index that are also in the glossary are designated with the letter *g*. The index does not list drug names; brand names for drugs must be looked up in section 2, "Drug Finder Index," to find the generic names used in the A–Z section. The last three pages of the book contain a drug-poisoning emergency guide and essential first aid information.

United States Pharmacopeia Drug Information for the Consumer [RBB S 15 87] provides greater detail and more entries but does not contain pictures of tablets and capsules. The book under review provides a more graphic approach, with many illustrations, and several more points of access. The prices of the two books are the same. Because of the great need for consumer drug information, many libraries will want to have both books. *The AMA Guide* is also recommended as a very useful reference source for the home.

Orphan Drugs. Rev. ed. By Kenneth Anderson and Lois Anderson. Body Press, 360 N. La Cienega Blvd., Los Angeles, CA 90048, 1988 (c1987). 253p. bibliog. index. paper $14.95 (0-89586-643-9).
615'.1 Chemotherapy I Orphan drugs I Drug trade—Directories [CIP] 87-35933

This work provides for the layperson and physician basic information on drugs that have been licensed or tested in other countries but are not yet generally available in the U.S. In most cases this is because they lack FDA approval, can't be patented, or lack a sponsoring manufacturer. Useful information is provided in the introduction on finding physicians overseas and obtaining the drugs through a U.S. physician or directly from the manufacturers. Kenneth Anderson, coauthor of the book, is a former editor of *Today's Health*, a popular consumer health magazine published by the American Medical Association.

Approximately 1,500 generic and brand-name drugs are described. Entries are arranged alphabetically by generic name and include for each drug a list of brand names, actions of the drug, disorders it is used for, precautions, dosage and administration, and manufacturer and country. Addresses of the approximately 200 manufacturers, arranged alphabetically, are included in the "Sources Directory" following the drug entries.

The major point of access, unless the generic name of a drug is already known, is the "Symptoms Directory," which precedes the drug entries. Unfortunately there appears to be little control of headings in this index, and cross-references are nonexistent. For example, there are different page numbers appearing for *anticancer drugs* and *cancer*, for *headache* and *migraine*, and for *insomnia* and *sleep disorders*, just three of many examples. Very specific headings such as *ear cancer* are lost unless the user reads through the entire index, because of the lack of cross-references. Surprisingly this index includes no heading for AIDS or acquired immune deficiency syndrome, although there are the entries *immune response* and *immunosuppressive therapy*. The index at the end of the volume provides access to the entries by brand names and generic-name synonyms. The book also contains a bibliography of recent articles and books on orphan drugs.

Because of the unique information provided by this guide (since these drugs aren't listed in the standard drug handbooks), it is recommended for most public and academic libraries. However, as noted, librarians should be cautioned of the less-than-adequate access by symptoms or diseases.

The Illustrated Dictionary of Natural Health. Comp. by Nevill and Susan Drury. Sterling, 1989. 304p. bibliog. illus. paper $12.95 (0-8069-6924-5).

615.535 Naturopathy [OCLC]

This *Dictionary* attempts to provide a comprehensive reference source for the many popular alternative health therapies. The book is divided into three parts: "Healing Plants," "Alternative Health Therapies," and "Diet, Nutrition and Body Function." Each of these parts has two alphabetical sections. The first section lists and defines each subject term. The second lists conditions that may be treated using the modalities listed in the first. The 1,500 entries are brief, ranging from a sentence to a few short paragraphs. One can find *aura, Bircher-Brenner System, Brazilian foot massage, past-lives therapy, spirulina,* and various herbs here. There are *see* and *see also* references and attractive illustrations to complement the entries. The authors, Australian writers on health and other topics, cite many American and European therapies.

Although this book provides an overview of the alternative health field, the entries in all areas are too brief to provide complete understanding of these eclectic subjects. The section on plants is only partially illustrated, which limits its usefulness. A good herbal like *The CRC Handbook of Medicinal Herbs* (CRC, 1985) will offer better information on botanical medicine, and *The New Holistic Health Handbook* (Stephen Greene, 1985), along with Dana Ullman's *Homeopathy: Medicine for the 21st Century* (North Atlantic, 1988), provide more comprehensive coverage of alternative therapies. *The Illustrated Dictionary of Natural Health* does have a good bibliography for further research, although some sources are dated; for example, the 1978 edition of *The Holistic Health Handbook* is cited rather than the revised 1985 edition.

This attractive book will be useful as a supplemental source or as a circulating addition to health collections in public libraries.

Holistic Resources Directory, 1988/89. 1st ed. Ed. by Susan James. Holistic Resources; dist. by Quality Books, 1988. 262p. index. paper $25.

615.89 Holism—Directories [BKL]

The purpose of this *Directory* is to promote communication and networking among the thousands of individuals, retail stores, health clinics, resorts, and others involved in holistic activities, activities defined as those concerned with "fundamentals of unity." Included is a heterogeneous assortment of over 8,000 services grouped according to 138 subjects that are listed in a table at the front of the book. These categories include *Accounting, Astrology, Clothing, Crafts, Hypnosis, Rebirthing, Regression and Past Life Recall,* and *UFO and Extraterrestrial Contact.* Under each subject heading, entries are listed alphabetically, intermixing publishers, periodicals, organizations, retailers, and individual practitioners. Entries include address, telephone number, and, for many, a brief explanation of services. While many of the services listed have a New Age cast, the range of interests represented is very wide. For instance, under *Spiritual Resources* are listed several Trappist monasteries and a Druid fellowship. The book concludes with a cross-reference section that is an index to all names in the *Directory*.

The number of different services included here make this a companion volume to *The Directory of Holistic Medicine and Alternate Health Care Services in the U.S.* [*RBB* S 15 86], which is narrower in scope, listing holistic practitioners. Both directories are useful for those seeking alternatives to traditional health care and, in the case of the James work, life-styles. Public libraries will make a decision on purchasing *Holistic Resources Directory* based on the interests of their readers.

Peace of Mind during Pregnancy: An A–Z Guide to the Substances That Could Affect Your Unborn Baby. By Christine Kelley-Buchanan. Facts On File, 1988. 367p. charts. index. hardcover $24.95 (0-8160-1907-X).

616.043 Fetus—Effects of chemicals on l Teratogenic agents l Abnormalities, Human—Etiology l Pregnancy [OCLC] 88-45295

This guide was written by the former coordinator of the California Teratogen Registry, which studies environmental causes of birth defects, who also taught continuing education classes in teratology to health-care professionals. It is designed to provide parents-to-be with information on many different kinds of substances and activities that may affect the unborn baby. Nearly 200 agents are discussed, including those found in the home, workplace, and general environment.

The main section of this book is arranged alphabetically, usually by the generic name of a drug. However, the agents or activities that are not drugs appear under their common names, for instance, *Air Travel, Alcohol, Exercise, Measles,* and *Microwaves.* In some cases, a number of drugs belonging to the same medical classification are grouped together for discussion. For example, there is the alphabetical entry *Antacids* in the main section of the text; the subject index lists each generic name in the group and refers to the *Antacids* section.

The entries on substances or activities are uniform. Each begins with an overview of the agent's name or names, its U.S. Food and Drug Administration Risk Category, and an estimated risk summary that identifies the time during pregnancy, if any, when the risk occurs. There is also a graph for each entry indicating the "time and degree of risk for the term of pregnancy." Following this information is a narrative summary about the agent. This summary varies from a couple of paragraphs to several pages with a list of bibliographic references. These references are to health professional journals. The author's experience in this area is very evident in these sections. She addresses issues that concern many expectant parents. For instance, in the section *Air Travel* she discusses altitude, cabin noise, vibration, jet lag, and airport security machines. In some sections there is a personal narrative by an expectant parent that helps illustrate the concern about a particular agent or substance. Some sections also provide "natural remedies" where safe alternatives to medication are explained. The author points out that these "remedies" have not been medically proven. After the main section of this text is an alphabetical list, by state, of information centers that may provide additional information. A glossary and subject index complete the book.

The material provided in this book is not a substitute for professional health care but rather a resource to aid in making informed decisions. It will be valuable in all libraries serving expectant parents.

AIDS Information Resources Directory. 1st ed. Ed. by Trish A. Halleron and Janet I. Pisaneschi. AmFAR, 1515 Broadway, 36th Flr., New York, NY 10036-8901, 1988. 192p. indexes. paper $10 (0-9620363-0-7; ISSN 0897-9693).

616.97'92 Acquired immune deficiency syndrome—Directories [BKL]

The American Foundation for AIDS Research (AmFAR), the publisher of this directory, is one of the major nongovernmental funding agencies for AIDS research and also a key agency for the distribution of educational materials on AIDS and safer sex. It has done a remarkable job in pulling together a wealth of resources on all aspects of AIDS. Over 1,100 educational and informational materials are listed, the majority brochures, pamphlets, and posters, but also including cards and inserts, public-service campaigns, curricula and instructional programs, books and manuals, videotapes and films, and multicomponent programs. With the help of several corporate sponsors, this resource directory is available at a very reasonable price.

It is divided into four major chapters with four indexes. Chapter 1, the largest and most important, is "A Guide to Selected AIDS Educational Materials." A panel of 34 experts reviewed each item. The materials are arranged by "primary target audience" such as the black community, drug users, gay and bisexual men, the Latino community, college students, and sexually active adults. Each entry includes a bibliographic description, including a note on the language of the item, an abstract, and in some cases a comment from the reviewer. Almost all entries have prices. The only thing lacking is any indication of personal authors, editors, or compilers. Chapter 2 is a list of producers and distributors. It is arranged alphabetically by name of company and gives address, telephone number, and items listed in chapter 1 that are available from that company. Chapter 3 contains late entries and materials still being developed. Chapter 4 is a collection of resources and services that were not reviewed, including periodicals, databases, and publications produced by various federal and state agencies. This chapter also lists 16 national resource organizations and 53 state AIDS agencies and hotlines.

The four indexes are alphabetical listings of (1) titles with a product-type indication, (2) organizations and agencies, (3) titles sorted by type of material, and (4) titles available in languages other than English. Unfortunately, the indexes are computer produced and contain blind page referrals and titles filed under articles. For example, in the index of titles available in other languages is an entry referring to a blank page. Computerized indexing is a great tool, but indexes still need a certain amount of editing.

This is an excellent resource for pamphlets, brochures, and posters. The reviewers have done a commendable job of evaluating the entries. The work does fairly well in listing videos and films but does a poor job in listing commercially published books and directories. The subject coverage is very good, including all areas where AIDS is a concern. This publication will complement Malinowsky and Perry's *AIDS Information Sourcebook* [*RBB* Je 15 88], which contains information on a wider range of topics. Its directory of organizations and facilities includes detailed information about each, including a list of publications. Its bibliography does not include many brochures, pamphlets, and posters, but it does contain many more books, a selected list of articles, and a chronology.

Libraries will want both titles, since between them they will have a fairly comprehensive list of currently available materials and information on organizations that pertain to AIDS. The *AIDS Information Sourcebook* will be published annually; the second edition of the *AIDS Information Resources Directory* is scheduled for June 1989.

How to Find Information about AIDS. By Virginia A. Lingle and M. Sandra Wood. Haworth, 1988. 130p. bibliog. indexes. hardcover $12.95 (0-86656-752-6).
616.97'92 AIDS (Disease)—Information services—Directories l AIDS (Disease)—Bibliography [CIP] 88-758

This is a current guide to organizations and resources that provide information on AIDS. The authors, both reference librarians at the Milton S. Hershey Medical Center, have developed a work for health professionals, researchers, and the general public.

The book is arranged in seven chapters, each covering a different type of resource. The first lists, in alphabetical order, more than 125 organizations that deal with AIDS. The authors describe the range of services available from the organizations, in particular testing, counseling, legal aid, newsletters, and educational materials. They concentrate on national groups and make references to existing directories and resources that identify local groups. The type of service provided is only noted when it is unique or representative of a range of possible services. The next chapter on state health departments begins with a description of the services they may provide. Departments are listed by state with address and telephone number.

Chapter 3 lists groups that fund or conduct AIDS research. The research institutions are listed alphabetically by name with a brief description. The grant funding sources are listed alphabetically by name of organization. A section entitled "Other Federal Sources of Information" lists agencies that coordinate services for AIDS patients nationwide. Chapter 4 lists telephone hot-lines, many of which have toll-free numbers.

Chapter 5 provides information concerning online databases, electronic bulletin boards, and a computer-assisted instructional program (CAI). Thirteen databases are presented with references to others that may be of interest. Each entry contains a brief summary of its content, producer and availability (i.e., database vendor), coverage, size, update frequency, and print counterpart. The one CAI program, designed for health professionals, is available for an IBM personal computer. The database vendors' addresses and telephone numbers are listed at the end of the chapter. The bulletin boards and messaging systems are listed with their telephone numbers.

Chapter 6 is a current bibliography of print sources that refers primarily to the professional health sciences literature. It is subdivided by formats such as indexes and abstracts, bibliographies and alerting services, and reference sources and monographs. The final chapter contains an alphabetical listing of audiovisual producers who have programs on AIDS. The entries include the producer's address, telephone number, and a list of titles with their running times. *How to Find Information about AIDS* has a general title, name, organization, and institution index. There is also a separate geographic index.

This book is similar to the *AIDS Information Sourcebook* by Malinowsky and Perry [*RBB* Je 15 88]. Both titles were compiled by librarians, but there is a different emphasis. The *Sourcebook* is a guide to educational resources for the general public; the title under review is designed for the health professional as well as the general public. For example, the latter title has a whole chapter on grant sources. The directory of organizations in each title has a bit of a different emphasis. *How to Find...* emphasizes national organizations while the *Sourcebook* includes local groups. The bibliographies of print sources in each reflect the emphasis on different audiences; the *Sourcebook* contains more popular journal articles. The *Sourcebook* has a chronology of the AIDS epidemic while *How to Find...* has information about online sources. Both titles are well developed, current, although not comprehensive, reference tools. The differences in audience emphasis may be a determining factor for libraries, though some libraries may need both.

TECHNOLOGY, MANAGEMENT

Dictionary of Engineering Acronyms and Abbreviations. By Harald Keller and Uwe Erb. Neal-Schuman, 1989. 312p. hardcover $75 (1-55570-028-4).
620'.00148 Engineering—Acronyms l Engineering—Abbreviations [CIP] 88-28840

Acronyms, abbreviations, and initialisms are found in all literatures, whether recipes or chemical formulas or engineering terms. When pressed for time, researchers will abbreviate if it will enable them to write more quickly, especially if the terms are difficult to spell. If a researcher's paper is published, then the abbreviations used set a precedent for future authors.

Dictionaries such as *Acronyms, Initialisms and Abbreviations Dictionary* (*AIAD*; Gale, 1988) cover all disciplines, and others like *Elec-*

tronics and Computer Acronyms (Butterworth, 1988) cover a narrow field. All general dictionaries that define words also contain some acronyms, abbreviations, and initialisms. In engineering, the overlap in terminology among fields has created a need for a comprehensive dictionary of acronyms. This work attempts to fill this need by listing more than 30,000 terms from 40 engineering fields. There is a great deal of overlap with *AIAD*, but having just engineering terms in one dictionary is a great help to researchers. Since in some cases there are many meanings for each acronym, engineers will not have to sort through long lists of acronyms from other disciplines. This *Dictionary* is based on a database created by searching for acronyms, abbreviations, and initialisms in engineering reference books, encyclopedias, and textbooks and then supplementing them with terms found in current periodicals.

This is a very impressive volume, covering everything from *NV* for *Nevada, new version,* and *nonvolatile* to *ZPCK* for *carbobenzyloxyphenylalanyl chloromethylketone.* Compiled by two Canadian engineers, it has especially good coverage of Canadian acronyms, though many English-speaking nations are represented. Since it is based on a database, it should be easy to update on a regular basis, an important consideration because these terms are coined continually.

This is an essential purchase for the academic or special library that serves engineering and technology researchers.

Dictionary of Building. By Randall McMullan. Nichols Publishing, 1988. 262p. illus. hardcover $44.50 (0-89397-319-X).
690'.03 Building—Dictionaries I Building—Great Britain—Dictionaries [CIP] 88-12598

Dictionary of Energy. 2d ed. Ed. by Malcolm Slesser. Nichols Publishing, 1988. 300p. illus. hardcover $49.50 (0-89397-320-3).
621.042'03 Power resources—Dictionaries I Power (Mechanics)—Dictionaries [CIP] 88-12563

Oil and Gas Dictionary. Ed. by Paul Stevens. Nichols Publishing, 1988. 270p. tables. hardcover $78.50 (0-89397-325-4).
333.8'23 Petroleum industry and trade—Dictionaries I Gas industry—Dictionaries [CIP] 88-19626

These three dictionaries originated in Great Britain. *Dictionary of Building* and *Oil and Gas Dictionary* are being issued in the U.S. for the first time; *Dictionary of Energy* is the second edition of a title originally published in 1982 [*RBB* Ja 15 84]. The intended audiences for these works are laypersons, students, and subject specialists. All are arranged in double-column pages and are abundantly illustrated with appropriate line drawings and tables in the text or appended. *Dictionary of Energy* and *Oil and Gas Dictionary* were edited by subject specialists assisted by contributing scholars, and entries in *Energy* are signed by the contributors. *Dictionary of Building* was authored by a distinguished construction physicist. Though compiled in Britain, there are cross-references when needed from British terms to American ones. A random sampling determined approximate entry numbers for each work as 5,750 for *Building,* 1,980 for *Oil and Gas,* and 2,350 for *Energy.* Most entries in *Building* are only a few sentences. Entries in *Energy* are usually about a paragraph, and *Oil and Gas* has some definitions that exceed two pages. All of the books contain ample *see* and *see also* references, using boldface words or asterisks.

Dictionary of Building compares favorably to similar single-volume subject references—e.g., *Architectural and Building Trades Dictionary* by Putnam (Van Nostrand, 1983) and *Illustrated Encyclopedic Dictionary of Building and Construction Terms* by Brooks (Prentice-Hall, 1976). It has fewer entries than the latter book but more than the former and has fewer illustrations than both.

Oil and Gas Dictionary has a 24-page chronology of significant oil and gas events in history and an appended 33-page list of statistical tables. It is somewhat similar to *Oil Terms* by Crook (International Publication Service, 1976), which has 27 pages of statistical tables appended as well as a short bibliography. *Oil Terms* is intended for the engineering specialist and does not duplicate many of the terms in the work under review. *Oil Terms* is more suited for technical libraries and *Oil and Gas Dictionary* for general libraries.

A comparison of the first and second editions of *Dictionary of Energy* determined that there have been significant additions to the text. Unfortunately, a number of address errors were noted for professional organizations in the second edition (e.g., American Nuclear Society and ASHRAE have moved, and ASTM has an incorrect street name). *Energy* compares favorably to the standard work, *Energy Dictionary* by Hunt (Van Nostrand, 1979), which is substantially larger, though dated, and does not contain definitions of recent terms like *acid rain* or *Chernobyl.*

These three well-designed works are current, comparable, and complementary in coverage. We recommend them to academic and public libraries needing dictionaries on these topics.

The Illustrated Dictionary of Electronics. 4th ed. By Rufus P. Turner and Stan Gibilisco. TAB, 1988. 648p. illus. index. tables. hardcover $36.95 (0-8306-0900-8); paper $23.95 (0-8306-2900-9).
621.381'03 Electronics—Dictionaries [CIP] 88-2252

When one sees the word *Illustrated* in the title of a dictionary, it is only natural to think that a large number of the entries have illustrations to help define the terms. Unfortunately, illustrations are not the strong point of this *Illustrated Dictionary.* There are only some 500 illustrations for the more than 22,000 entries. Crisp and clear schematics make up the majority of the illustrations. The rest are, for the most part, poor and in some cases, such as the one for *slide switch,* so dark that the item could not be identified if it stood alone. Also, there is no consistency in what is illustrated. There is an illustration for *male plug* with its definition making reference to a "female plug," but no illustration of a female plug. The definitions are very brief, most only three or four lines. Italicized terms are defined elsewhere in the dictionary. *See, also see,* and *compare* are used freely and frequently to guide the user to related terms. The format is very pleasing with double columns, beginning and ending terms at the top of each page, and good choices of type fonts. The appendix includes a list of schematic symbols and several tables of data including resistor color codes, mathematical functions, and electronics abbreviations.

All in all, this is a good electronics dictionary, in spite of the relative lack of illustrations. It is comprehensive, readable, and accurate, though less scholarly than the *IEEE Standard Dictionary of Electrical and Electronics Terms* (Wiley, 1984). School, public, and college libraries will find it very reasonably priced and authoritative.

McGraw-Hill Encyclopedia of Electronics and Computers. 2d ed. Ed. by Sybil P. Parker. McGraw-Hill, 1988. 1,047p. bibliog. illus. index. hardcover $75 (0-07-045499-X).
621.381 Electronics—Dictionaries I Computers—Dictionaries [CIP] 87-37592

McGraw-Hill Encyclopedia of the Geological Sciences. 2d ed. Ed. by Sybil P. Parker. McGraw-Hill, 1988. 722p. bibliog. illus. index. hardcover $72.50 (0-07-045500-7).
551'.03 Geology—Dictionaries [CIP] 87-35357

The *McGraw-Hill Encyclopedia of Electronics and Computers* (*MEEC*) and the *McGraw-Hill Encyclopedia of the Geological Sciences* (*MEGS*) are extracts from the sixth edition of the *McGraw-Hill Encyclopedia of Science and Technology* [*RBB* S 15 87] and several accompanying yearbooks. Each volume contains 520 articles arranged alphabetically. A list of contributors at the beginning of each work shows the writers' affiliations and ranks. All articles are signed and many have short bibliographies. The length of articles varies from a paragraph to several pages. Most entries have appropriately placed illustrations, photographs, or tables. There are abundant *see* and *see also* references scattered throughout the articles. Both works have detailed indexes. The books are designed to reach an educated audience: writers, teachers, scientists, students, and laypersons. As indicated in our review of the *McGraw-Hill Encyclopedia of Science and Technology,* the mathematics and reading level do not make these works appropriate for elementary or junior high school levels, and they will be difficult going for many high school students. A random sampling and comparison of articles in *MEEC* and *MEGS* with the *McGraw-Hill Encyclopedia of Science and Technology* showed very few changes in the articles from the sixth edition, mainly new locations for equations, illustrations, etc., and the use of black and gray in illustrations instead of various colors.

The second edition of *MEEC* has 45 new and 120 completely revised articles compared with the first edition, which was based on the fifth edition of the *McGraw-Hill Encyclopedia of Science and Technology*. Some new subjects included are *Artificial Intelligence, Junction Diode, Radar, Computer-Aided Engineering*, and *Negative-Resistance Circuits*. As with any work that is not comprehensive, there are some interesting subjects excluded; for example, *modem* is not listed in the index or cross-referenced under the subject *Modulation*. To find a discussion on this term, users would have to be familiar enough with the subject to look under *Demodulator*. The second edition of *MEGS* has 40 new articles, and 235 other articles have been revised or rewritten when compared with the first edition.

There are a number of works similar to *MEEC* and *MEGS*. Two very good comparable volumes are the *Encyclopedia of Computers and Electronics* (Rand McNally, 1983) and *The Cambridge Encyclopedia of Earth Sciences* (1981). Both of these works are slightly dated compared with the titles under review. *The Cambridge Encyclopedia of Earth Sciences* has longer essay-type articles that make access to some information more difficult. It has the advantage of having color illustrations. Both volumes are less expensive than *MEEC* and *MEGS*.

It should be emphasized that *MEEC* and *MEGS* largely duplicate articles found in the *McGraw-Hill Encyclopedia of Science and Technology*. Thus librarians will have to consider currency, expense, and possible duplication of material in deciding whether to add these spin-offs to their collections. We recommend them to academic and public libraries that can afford them and need to duplicate information found in the parent set.

Gardener's Index for 1987. By Joy L. McCann. CompuDex Press, P.O. Box 27041, Kansas City, MO 64110, 1988. 155p. index. paper $12 (0-945621-01-9; ISSN 0897-5175).

635.05 Gardening—Periodicals—Indexes I Horticulture—Periodicals—Indexes [BKL]

The *Gardener's Index* provides detailed access to articles that appeared in six major gardening and horticultural magazines over the past year. Magazines indexed are *American Horticulturist, Flower and Garden, Garden, Horticulture, National Gardening*, and *Rodale's Organic Gardening*. This is the second year this index has been published. It is intended for the home gardener and tends to use the common names of plants rather than scientific names.

The index is divided into three sections. Part 1, "Subject Guide," is an index to major articles under broad subject headings. The section begins with a list of the subject headings used. Citations are in a column format with columns for subject, source (abbreviated), month and beginning page, article title with a one- or two-sentence annotation, and author. Full names of the magazines are given at the bottom of each page. Part 2, "Subject Index," includes entries for more specific topics: plant varieties or species, insects and pests, gardening techniques, etc., as well as material in each magazine's letters section and columns. If an article uses a scientific name, a *see* reference is made to the common name. Some plant names are inverted so that all varieties of a plant (elms, for example) appear together in the index. Books reviewed or described in new book columns or in articles are listed under the heading *books* in the index. Similarly all food-related articles are indexed only under *recipes*. Letter notations are included after page numbers to signify, for example, if the item is an article, includes cultural requirements, provides a description, has an illustration or photograph, or is a letter. The entries in the subject index include only the subject of the article, a very brief descriptive phrase, the abbreviation of the journal, month, pages, and the letter notations. The bottom of each page includes the full titles of the indexed magazines as well as a listing of the letter notations. Part 3, "Name Index," includes the authors of articles, columns, books reviewed, and reader's letters, as well as the names of gardeners and experts quoted in articles.

Each entry in this section includes the name, abbreviated title of the journal, month, and page.

Although all of these magazines are indexed elsewhere (two in the *Readers' Guide*, two different titles in *Magazine Index*, and three in *Biological and Agricultural Index*), no one index covers them all or provides the level of detail this index provides. The *Gardener's Index* is recommended for most public libraries and other collections that support horticultural and gardening programs.

The Completely Illustrated Atlas of Reptiles and Amphibians for the Terrarium. By Fritz Jürgen Obst and others. TFH Publications, 1988. 830p. illus. index. hardcover $100 (0-86622-958-2).

639.39 Amphibians I Reptiles I Terrariums [BKL]

Dr. Burgess's Atlas of Marine Aquarium Fishes. By Warren E. Burgess and others. TFH Publications, 1988. 736p. illus. index. hardcover $59.95 (0-86622-896-9).

639.34 Aquarium fishes—Pictorial works I Aquarium fishes—Identification [BKL]

TFH Publications is well known for its guides to aquariums, fishes, reptiles, amphibians, etc., and these two new efforts add additional luster to the line. *The Completely Illustrated Atlas of Reptiles and Amphibians for the Terrarium* is a remarkable achievement. An alphabetically arranged encyclopedia, this work covers thousands of species as well as hundreds of topics like removing ticks (see *Acariasis*) and explaining the operation of the *Vocal Sac*. The encyclopedia is illustrated with 2,000 beautiful color photographs, and the individual entries are clearly written. For example, the pictures of the "poison arrow frogs" (*Dendrobates*) are magnificent, and the accompanying article is informative. The "Guidelines for Use of Live Amphibians and Reptiles in Field Research" remind potential collectors of the number of these animals that are near extinction and must be left in their natural habitat. The encyclopedia concludes with a list of common names with their scientific-name counterparts. (The entries in the encyclopedia are by scientific names with cross-references from the common ones.) A novice will have difficulty since the entries are set up in such a way that a user must know exactly what he or she is looking for. For example, if a reptile or amphibian is suspected of having a parasite, one must know the infestation is by ticks in order to learn what to do about it.

Although comprehensive and colorful, the price of this book is fairly high for small budgets. Some less costly alternatives, such as *The Encyclopedia of Reptiles and Amphibians* by Tim Halliday [BKL Je 1 86] and *The Care of Reptiles and Amphibians in Captivity* by Christopher Mattison [BKL Je 15 87], are also less comprehensive. This encyclopedia is recommended for those libraries where collecting and keeping reptiles and amphibians is a popular hobby among patrons.

Dr. Burgess and Dr. Axelrod have become "the" names in aquarium books. Their latest effort, *Atlas of Marine Aquarium Fishes*, is the saltwater equivalent of *Dr. Axelrod's Atlas of Freshwater Fishes* and *Dr. Axelrod's Mini-Atlas of Freshwater Aquarium Fishes* [BKL D 1 87]. This work was designed so an aquarium enthusiast could identify a fish by its picture and have basic information on food, habitat, and disposition. About 560 colorplates and over 4,000 photographs make this work a delight to peruse. The "Aquaristic Section" is an introductory guide to the maintenance of marine fishes, but the work is primarily an identification guide, not a how-to book on setting up a saltwater aquarium. It includes species of fish found only in public aquariums and warns about species not suitable to keep in captivity at any level. The "Systematic List of the Families of Fishes of the World" explains the arrangement of the *Atlas*. The book concludes with lists of scientific and common names and their equivalents, which also serve as indexes to the pictures in the *Atlas*. The final page is a conversion table of weights and measures.

Very few works devoted to marine aquariums are available, and most are written by either Dr. Axelrod or Dr. Burgess, who seem to take turns having their names appear first in different works. Because of the quality of the pictures and information, this work would be a good purchase for libraries where there is a demand for information on saltwater fishes or a need to identify species.

Domestic Technology: A Chronology of Developments. By Nell Du Vall. G. K. Hall, 1988. 535p. bibliog. index. hardcover $35 (0-8161-8913-7).

640'.9 Home economics—History I Domestic engineering—History [CIP] 88-21110

As librarian M. E. L. Jacob (writing under the pseudonym of Nell Du Vall) states in the preface, most histories focus on major events, leaving to the imagination what daily life in earlier times was like. Since little is known about the activities of ordinary people, she decided to try to shed light on the past by "finding out what tools and techniques were available at that time and how they might have been used." Drawing on an impressive array of sources (including such varied books as *Woman's Work: The Housewife, Past & Present*; *Ancient Engineers*; *Clean and Decent*; *Eureka! An Illustrated History of Inventions from the Wheel to the Computer*; *Encyclopedia of Medical History*; *Famous First Facts*; *Food in History*; *Fashion in Costume, 1200-1980*; *Old Farm Tools and Machinery*; and numerous journal and newspaper articles), Jacob has compiled a narrative and chronology that describe the introduction of various items of everyday use.

Beginning with the introduction of fire, circa 500,000 B.C., and running through the 1987 introduction of a new computer by Compaq, the book covers events throughout the world. Jacob admits that the emphasis tends to be on the English-speaking world, as all of her sources are in English. More than half of the events cited have occurred since the 1860s. Although one may question the inclusion of some items (the fact that Nabisco baked more than 60 million Ritz Crackers per day in 1987, the opening of T. J. Cinnamons Bakery in 1985, and the marketing of Jell-O Pudding Pops in 1979), the compiler's eye for detail is balanced by other more significant facts presented (for example, the development in 1986 of a tobacco strain that kills insects, the approval of aspartame for use in soft drinks in 1983, and the birth of the first test-tube baby in 1978).

The narrative portion of the book is organized by topic: food origins and production, food preservation and processing, cooking, clothing, cleaning, water and waste disposal, heating and housing, lighting, tools, and health and children. Each topic is broken down into several subtopics, each of which is accompanied by a chronology listing the major events discussed. The narrative conveys some fascinating and hard-to-find information. For example, the snacks section in the chapter on food preservation and processing discusses the forerunner of modern snack foods (Saratoga Chips, devised in 1853), goes on to outline the history of peanut butter, and then mentions Vegemite, described by the compiler as "that salty, dark brown substance that could easily be mistaken by the unwary for axle grease....Vegemite is made from a yeast slurry, a brewery waste product, combined with water, salt, onion, and celery flavorings and concentrated into a stiff dark brown spread....A little goes a long way."

The narrative chapters are followed by a master chronology that combines all the chapter chronologies. Each item mentioned in the chronology has a code that refers to one of the sources in the bibliography consulted for this information. This is followed by an index to the master chronology and by the bibliography. Using the index, one can find references to the appropriate year in the chronology, not to the narrative chapters. So the reader can look up *Vegemite*, find references to 1908 and 1926, then go to the chronology and learn "Fred Walker & Company began the manufacture and sale of Vegemite" and "Kraft bought an interest in Fred Walker & Company, manufacturer of Vegemite." What cannot be accessed, unfortunately, is the discussion in the narrative on Vegemite. One must go to the table of contents and guess at the appropriate section in which it is discussed.

While *Domestic Technology* encompasses a wealth of information and has no rivals for its detailed scope, much of its richness can be uncovered only by detective work. As a book to sit down and read chapter by chapter, it is a welcome addition for students, historians, and trivia buffs and fulfills its purpose well. As a reference tool, it is flawed by its lack of adequate indexing. Recommended with this reservation as a supplemental source for school, public, and academic libraries.

Arrow's Complete Guide to Mail Order Foods. 1st ed. Ed. by N. J. Kocs. Arrow Clearinghouse, P.O. Box 341-CC, Ardmore, PA, 19003, 1987. 157p. indexes. paper $19.95 (0-944894-07-0).

641'.029 Food—Catalogs [OCLC] 87-71024

This guide is a directory to "nearly 700 food-by-mail companies." There are 12 chapters, each devoted to a particular kind of food: "Meat and Poultry," "Cheese," and "Ethnic Foods," to name a few. The compiler gathered her information by collecting catalogs and brochures. Each entry includes company name, address, telephone number (if available), and a list of the kinds of foods offered. There are indexes of company names and of products.

The well-known names in mail-order food are here: Swiss Colony, Harry and David, Omaha Steaks. According to the preface, the guide includes "not only large, established firms, but also the tiny, one-person producers selling their own homemade or homegrown products." Some examples are the firm in Blackduck, Minnesota, that sells wild rice, and several New England producers of maple syrup. No such distinction is made in the entries; some indication of the size of each company would have been helpful. Also helpful would be a note indicating whether the company offers a catalog, or only a brochure, and the cost of that catalog or brochure, if any.

Companies appear under one main food category, no matter how many kinds of foods they provide. Balducci's, for instance, is listed under "Meat and Poultry," though they also sell mustards, chocolates, vinegars, nuts, and other foods. Short of browsing, the only link between Balducci's and these other products is the index, which is not always specific enough; the index terms *mustards* and *chocolates*, for instance, yield long lists of page numbers without subdivision—although it should be noted that other terms, such as *breads* and *mushrooms*, are helpfully subdivided by kind. An index linking specific products with specific company names would improve access to the varieties of foods many of these companies offer. The compiler might also consider assigning an entry number to each company; strings of page numbers in the index are not helpful, because one must then scan the pages to find the desired information.

There are other directories that list mail-order food companies. *The Great Book of Catalogs* (Pinkerton Marketing, 1981) lists only 132 food companies but provides more information than *Arrow's*, including information on when a company was founded and whether a catalog is available. The older *Catalog of American Catalogs* (Random House, 1976) lists only 64 companies but provides even more information. For "Mrs. DeWildt," who sells mainly Indonesian and Dutch foods, for instance, *Arrow's* gives only name, address, telephone number, and a list of foods. The *Catalog of American Catalogs* gives a history of the company and also notes that Mrs. DeWildt provides all the ingredients for a Rijstaffel dinner. The *Directory of Mail Order Catalogs* (Grey House Publishing, 1984) lists nearly 400 mail-order food companies and indicates whether catalogs are available but has minimal information about the products. The entry for Mrs. DeWildt, for instance, lists only honey and apple syrup.

No directory is as current or as inclusive as *Arrow's*. More information about the individual companies would make future editions of this guide even more useful. Recommended for public libraries with strong consumer collections.

The Cook's Book of Useful Information. By John C. Lawrence. Golden West; dist. by Quality, 1988. 176p. paper $5 (0-914846-38-8).

641.5'03 Cookery—Dictionaries [CIP] 88-25072

During his years as a cook, Lawrence was "often frustrated by not finding information he needed in his work" so he "set about to compile a book that cooks of all kinds would find useful." The first section, "Terms Used in Preparing and Processing Foods," gives one- to two-line definitions of such words as *caramelize*, *eviscerate*, *parch*, *sharpen*, and *uncork*. Although the definitions are accurate, they are often too brief to be of much practical help. The second section, "Dictionary of Cooking Terms," is arranged alphabetically and includes foreign words (followed by an abbreviation signifying language of origin). Here again, although the definitions are accurate, they are often not useful; for instance, "*cow*—a four-footed bovine. The word cow refers to both the meat and milk animal." There is no internal consistency between definitions (*XXXX sugar* is defined as "confectioner's sugar," but the definition for *confectioner's sugar* suggests that it can also be called "dessert sugar" or "powdered sugar"). No pronunciations are given.

The third section, "Spices, Herbs and Edible Flowers and Wild Plants," gives instructions on how items are used (e.g., "*apple blossoms* . . . may be fried then dusted with sugar and served as a dessert or used as a garnish"). The weights and measurements section includes charts that give dry and liquid measure equivalences, British and American comparisons for measures, a formula to convert Fahrenheit to Celsius, a substitutions table, etc. The last section, "Helpful Hints," tells, for example, how to soften brown sugar and determine if an egg is fresh.

Most libraries will have other sources for this information. For definitions, a library reference collection should have the *New Larousse Gastronomique* (Crown, 1988). For the peripheral material in Lawrence's dictionary, *The Cook's Book of Essential Information* (Sumner House, 1987) or a selection of cookbooks (e.g., *Better Homes and Gardens*, *The Joy of Cooking*, etc.) will be quite adequate.

Cooking A to Z. By Jane Horn and others. Ortho Books, P.O. Box 5047, San Ramon, CA 94583, 1988. 640p. illus. index. hardcover $32.95 (0-89721-147-2).

641.5 Cookery—Dictionaries [OCLC] 87-072103

Rarely does one find a reference book that—when it isn't being used for its substantial information content—can serve as a coffee-table enhancer. *Cooking A to Z* is such a treasure. Beautifully illustrated, well organized in an alphabetical format, and thoroughly indexed, this resource includes more than 600 user-friendly recipes (from mashed potatoes to oyster loaf) and nearly 500 entries that either define cooking terms (from *dry-heat cooking* to *trussing*), describe and illustrate cooking techniques (i.e., how to flute a pie crust, various cutting techniques, how to grill), offer information about specific ingredients (i.e., black beans, what each cut of meat is good for and where it comes from, arugula), or provide consumer and maintenance information about kitchen equipment (from kitchen knives to mixers, microwave ovens, and waffle irons). Entries range from a few sentences (*shuck, to*; *giblets*; *rancidity*) to 5 pages for *chocolate* and 10 for *shellfish*. Recipes usually appear as part of another entry, for instance, to illustrate an entry for an ingredient or a cooking technique. Additionally, the margins are filled with helpful and interesting tips (such as how to cook with vinegar, stages of sugar syrup, and how to dry chile peppers), as well as *see also* references to recipes and information related to the main entries. The recipes are easy to follow, and most do not require inordinate time to prepare. Beautiful four-color photographs appear on almost every page.

Compiled in consultation with the California Culinary Academy and written by two free-lance food writers (each with several other cookbooks in publication), the only drawback to this volume might be its 9½-by-11½-inch, 6-pound size. Use it in the kitchen with a cookbook holder, curl up on the couch for a pleasant browse, or refer to it in the library's reference department. This will be a welcome addition to any library's cookbook collection and will be especially useful as a reference work.

The Guide to Cooking Schools, 1989. 1st ed. Shaw Associates, 625 Biltmore Way, Ste. 1406, Coral Gables, FL 33134, 1988. 300p. indexes. paper $14.95 (0-945834-01-2; ISSN 1040-2616).

641.5'07 Cooking schools—Directories I Cookery—Study and teaching—Directories [BKL] 88-92516

Whether you are interested in training as a professional chef or in turning out the perfect bouillabaisse for family and friends, *The Guide to Cooking Schools* can direct you to the right program. It contains detailed information on cooking classes, travel programs, and culinary-arts schools in the U.S., Canada, and abroad.

Arranged alphabetically by school name, the first section of the *Guide* lists 218 programs for cooks of all ages and experience levels. After a brief description of the program, facilities, and teaching methods, each entry includes information on student requirements, class schedules, culinary specialties, faculty credentials, tuition, and tourist attractions in the surrounding area. Some of the entries are followed by an unattributed quotation, presumably from a satisfied student, about the program. The second section of the *Guide*, also arranged alphabetically, contains information on seven culinary organizations. These entries include information on the purpose of the organization, membership requirements and services, and annual dues. All of these organizations are located in the U.S.

Seven appendixes complete the *Guide*. A geographic index arranges the entries by state and country; the specialty index does the same for types of cuisine. There are also indexes that list the tour and travel programs, professional programs, children's courses, programs affiliated with inns, hotels, and resorts, and those affiliated with restaurants.

The names and addresses of culinary-arts programs accredited by the American Culinary Federation Educational Institute are listed in a separate index. Also listed are schools accredited by the National Association of Trade and Technical Schools that offer culinary-arts training and those junior or community colleges or vocational schools that offer cooking programs. The three lists are arranged by state.

Though the *Guide* is arranged by course name, it is sometimes difficult to know exactly where to look. For example, is *Nell Benedict Cooking Class* entered under *N* or *B*? The final index eliminates this confusion by listing proper names, last name first, and citing the correct page number.

The Guide to Cooking Schools is an easy-to-use directory that pulls together information not readily obtained elsewhere. Public librarians with an interested clientele will find it a worthwhile purchase. The needs of secondary school librarians could be satisfied with volumes such as *American Community, Technical and Junior Colleges: A Guide*, which provide more in-depth coverage of those programs. Though likely to be outdated quickly, the low cost of *The Guide to Cooking Schools* makes its purchase a valid one.

The American Regional Cookery Index. Comp. by Rhonda H. Kleiman. Neal-Schuman, 1989. 221p. hardcover $49.95 (1-55570-029-2).

016.6415973 Cookery, American—Indexes [CIP] 88-27823

This is a subject index to 25 in-print English-language cookbooks whose primary contents are "hard-to-find recipes of a regional nature" from every part of the U.S. Over 10,000 subject headings are keyed to a specific recipe in one of the fully analyzed cookbooks, which, according to the author, are not indexed elsewhere. Sixteen other cookbooks are referred to as "General Books of Interest" but are not analytically treated. Cross-references are amply provided to complement the subject headings, which include specific names of well-known dishes (*Enchilada, Bouillabaisse, Chutney*); types of dishes (*Pot Roast, Salad Dressing, Soup*); major ingredients (*Bear Meat, Huckleberry, Huckleberries; Zucchini*); preparations (*Au Gratin; Parmigiana; Spice, Spiced, Spicy*); and ethnic groups, states, or regions (*Basque Cookery, Zuni Indian Cookery, Maryland Cookery, Southern Cookery*).

Recipe names are not used as access points, except where the dish has a well-known name. Within subject areas, recipe names are given in English (if possible), with alternate names indicated in parentheses after the English name. Also indicated in parentheses after recipes are any necessary clarifications regarding their ethnic origin, region, state, or major ingredients, as well as variations appearing on the same page. Often, when a state or region is used as a subject access point, it is followed by a list of "Books of Interest," which will be helpful in locating additional relevant recipes.

The original potential list of 50 cookbooks to index was compiled from an examination of the collections of the Brooklyn and New York Public libraries and bookstores, from titles suggested by librarians, and from reviews in cookery magazines. This list was then cut down to 25, based upon the recommendations of cooking and food-information professionals. Excluded are cookbooks that deal with special diets, vegetarian and health foods, appliance cookery, and large-scale cookery. Included are books by such notable authors as James Beard and

Paul Prudhomme, plus a balanced collection representing resources from specific geographic regions and ethnic groups.

Kleiman's *Index* provides an excellent companion to the more general coverage of regional cookery found in *Garland Recipe Index* [*RBB* S 15 84], and it has much more detailed subject access than Axford's *English Language Cookbooks, 1600–1973* (Gale, 1976). As a companion to the author's earlier *International Cookery Index* [*RBB* S 1 87], this will be a very valuable tool for librarians whose collections include the cookbooks indexed and whose patrons are interested in regional cuisine. It will be especially helpful in communities where there are dining clubs in which a different dining motif is chosen for each meeting, in large cosmopolitan communities, and in academic institutions whose curricula include hotel or restaurant management.

Condo Vacations: The Complete Guide. By Pamela Lanier. Lanier Publishing, dist. by Ten Speed, 1989. 416p. illus. index. paper $12.95 (0-89815-301-8).

647'.94 Resorts—U.S.—Directories l Resorts—Directories l Condominiums—U.S.—Directories l Condominiums—Directories [CIP] 89-300028

Vacation Condominiums for Rent. 1st ed. By Frank Walsh and others. MarLor Press; dist. by Contemporary, 1989. 199p. paper $10.95 (0-943400-37-6).

643.2 Condominiums—U.S. l U.S.—Description and travel—1981– —Guidebooks [BKL]

Vacationers tired of cookie-cutter designed hotel rooms will want to check out these useful guides to condominium rentals. Arrangement in both is alphabetical by state, city, and property name. Information on the individual properties includes address, telephone number, available unit sizes, and amenities available either in the unit (TV, linens, etc.) or at or near the property (restaurant, swimming pool, athletic club, fishing, skiing, etc.). Price ranges are given, but readers are warned to check prices before making reservations.

Condo Vacations lists over 1,200 properties in 42 states plus Puerto Rico and the Virgin Islands; *Vacation Condominiums* lists more than 500 properties in 41 states. There are condominiums in the latter book that aren't duplicated in the former. *Condo Vacations* has maps for each state showing resort locations and a few black-and-white photographs. It also has narrative descriptions of each resort that are helpful though not evaluative; some sound like tourist-board recommendations ("Beautiful sunsets and a white sandy beach for bathing and long moonlit walks").

Libraries needing only one directory of this sort will choose the more comprehensive *Condo Vacations*. In communities where there is a big demand for this information, libraries may want to purchase both of these inexpensive travel resources.

National Directory of Retirement Facilities. 2d ed. Oryx, 1988. 878p. index. hardcover $175 (0-89774-450-0).

646.7'9 Retirement, Places of—U.S.—Directories l Retirement communities—U.S.—Directories l Life care communities—U.S.—Directories [CIP] 88-19628

The much improved second edition of *National Directory of Retirement Facilities* increases its coverage from 12,000 to 18,000 for-profit and nonprofit "residential alternatives," including personal/boarding care, congregate/semi-independent living, independent living, life care, and multiple-care facilities. Facilities that provide only nursing care are not listed.

The information (compiled from "state licensing agencies, associations formed around the needs of older Americans, membership directories of religious, fraternal, and/or maternal agencies" and Dialog's "Electronic Yellow Pages") was, for the most part, verified by questionnaires sent to each listed facility, or through telephone interviews.

Arranged by state and city, then by facility, each listing includes address, telephone number, contact person or director, type of facility, capacity, and a facility profile. To varying degrees, the profiles provide information concerning a facility's average monthly fees, ownership (an asterisk following the name of an owner indicates an owner of more than one facility), services (i.e., nursing, transportation, indoor pools, etc.), affiliation (religious, fraternal, professional society, or other affiliation), entrance age requirements, and 100-word comments about the facility, for which the entrants have paid a fee. No critical evaluations of the facilities are provided, and users are cautioned that a listing in the directory "should not take the place of an on-site inspection." New to this edition (and especially helpful) is the indication of a facility's affiliation, as well as whether the average monthly fees are government subsidized. In its review of the first edition [*RBB* Jl 86], the Board had noted the need for this information.

An index by facility name enhances access to this already well-organized and extremely useful resource. Recommended especially for public and academic libraries, this extensive *Directory* will be invaluable for people contemplating retirement, as well as for the adult children of aging parents. *The National Continuing Care Directory* [*RBB* F 1 88] gives more detailed information on 366 retirement communities that offer nursing care.

Marketsearch: International Directory of Published Market Research. 12th ed. Ed. by Kathleen Mann. Arlington Management Publications Ltd.; dist. by Marketsearch, P.O. Box 5228, Evanston, IL 60204, 1988. annual. 648p. paper $215/year (0-906616-09-3).

016.65883 Marketing research—Bibliography [BKL]

Marketsearch, compiled by a British publisher in association with the British Overseas Trade Board, and now in its twelfth annual edition, is a directory of some 18,000 foreign and U.S. market-research studies published in 1983 or later. Nearly 700 publishers are included; while most are British or American, many other countries are represented, among them Switzerland, France, Germany, Japan, Chile, Brazil, and Malaysia. Entries are arranged in numerical order using the British Standard Industrial Classification scheme "as augmented and expanded by the publishers." Classifications with many entries are then subordered in two ways: if the number covers a variety of separate products, these are listed alphabetically; if it covers only one product or service, listings are arranged geographically, beginning with worldwide surveys and working down through groups of countries to single countries in alphabetical order. Listings are condensed into two lines and provide SIC number, title, usually the number of pages, countries covered, date, source, price, and often a brief descriptive phrase. Symbols are used to indicate country, frequency, source, and language if not English. Two examples of entries for code 2180, *Fruit and Vegetable Products* follow: "*Potato Markets*, EEC, W, A-4, R, Production, price, market information" and "*Potatoes*, 280pp, USA, 1983, P-12, $700." The first covers European Economic Community countries, and is a weekly publication of Agra Europe with price available on request; it covers production, price, and market information. The second was published by Packaged Facts in 1983 and costs $700; no description is given.

Access to the SIC numbers by which the entries are arranged is provided by a detailed alphabetical index in part 1 of the volume; part 2 is the main directory of studies; part 3 is a list of reports by publisher (new to this edition), and part 4 is the source index with publishers' names and addresses. Parts 3 and 4 are both arranged by the publishers' code numbers. While these are basically alphabetical, they are not absolutely so; one cannot easily assure that a publisher is either included or excluded (e.g., Easton Consultants, Inc., is *A-19* and Pure Data Holdings is *D-35*; there are no cross-references from the *E* or *P* listings). *Marketsearch* is updated for its subscribers with a supplement in midyear and also with a hot-line service that requires a telephone call to the U.K. Entries are verified annually by the publishers of the reports.

Comparing this to *Findex* (also annual, with an update [*RBB* Mr 1 88]), *Marketsearch* includes both more reports—nearly 18,000, compared with some 11,000—and more publishers—670 rather than 500. The arrangement is quite different, as *Findex* is arranged by subject in chapters with many subheadings; *Findex* also provides longer summaries containing more detail. There is overlap, but each provides a considerable number of unique titles. Using video games as an example, *Marketsearch* includes them in SIC 3659, *Video Games and*

Recorders, and includes 59 reports in all; of 11 entries identified as specifically relevant to video games, only 2 were in *Findex*. The index to *Findex* identified 14 specific entries (not all in the same chapter) for video games, of which 7 are in *Marketsearch*, but as they are listed under different SIC codes, most are not easily found by subject. Of the 5 publishers of the *Marketsearch* reports, 4 are also included in *Findex*; of the 12 publishers of the *Findex* listings, 11 are in *Marketsearch*. Even where the same publisher is included in both, however, different reports may be found.

These differences pose problems for libraries having to choose between these sources. Large academic and public libraries or special libraries that need comprehensive coverage of market research will need both titles. Others will have to determine whether they want *Marketsearch*, which has more entries with not quite as many access points or as much description (and a somewhat more British orientation and slightly lower price), or *Findex*, with fewer entries but a bit more accessibility and more detailed descriptions. Both titles are for libraries with specialized business collections only, however, as prices for the reports listed can be astronomical.

Bricker's Short-Term Executive Programs. Ed. by Christopher Billy and Donna Lee Healy. Peterson's Guides, 1988. 169p. indexes. hardcover $95 (0-87866-687-7; ISSN 1040-7618).

658.4'007 Executives, Training of—Directories I Management—Study and teaching—Directories II Business education—Directories [BKL] 88-2824

Moving Up: University Executive Seminars to Keep Your Career on Target. Ed. by Christopher M. Billy and Donna Lee Healy. Peterson's Guides, 1988. 175p. indexes. paper $16.95 (0-87866-826-8).

658'.007 Management—Study and teaching (Higher)—U.S.—Directories I Executives—Training of—U.S.—Directories [CIP] 88-39734

Bricker's Short-Term Executive Programs (*STEP*), published for the first time as a companion volume to the nineteenth annual edition of *Bricker's International Directory* (*BID*) [RBB Je 1 88], is arranged almost exactly the same way as *BID* and serves the same corporate audience. Both directories selectively describe intensive managerial training or continuing-education programs for mid- to upper-level executives. The main difference between them lies in the length of the programs covered: *BID* covers programs lasting at least five days, and *STEP* describes highly focused programs two to four days in length.

Most programs are university based, conducted in English, open to the public, not limited to any one organization or industry, and have been offered at least once before. Programs selected for inclusion must "treat either general management in broad terms . . .or some important functional area such as finance, marketing, operations, or strategy." Program listings are arranged by subject and then alphabetically by institution. Section labels appear at the bottom of each page, but their placement on the inner margins and smaller type size reduce their effectiveness for browsing.

STEP describes 140 programs offered by 37 institutions (29 U.S., 4 Canadian, 2 British, 2 European). Each one-page description in tabular format gives the following information: program name and inauguration date, academic department sponsor, program duration, cost, location and 1989 dates, profile of typical participants, subject-matter focus, methods of instruction, faculty, facilities, and official contact. Like *BID*, an additional section at the end of the book provides concise, informative descriptions of each institution. Four appendixes provide access to programs by institution, functional area, calendar starting date, and geographic location.

Large libraries that purchased *BID* for its usefulness as a continuing-education directory for an elite clientele may want to consider *STEP* for its supplementary coverage of similar, but shorter, executive training programs.

An alternative purchase is Peterson's *Moving Up*, which is almost exactly the same book as *STEP*. At a greatly reduced price, *Moving Up* will appeal to a much larger group of public, academic, and special libraries that cannot afford *STEP* in hardcover. The differences in content are minor. *Moving Up* covers 130 programs or "seminars" offered by 33 U.S. and Canadian institutions. Programs are arranged alphabetically by institution, not by subject. The program descriptions are slightly pared down from *STEP*: they lack actual course dates and descriptions of the faculty, and profiles of participants are briefer; other than that, they are identical descriptions. *Moving Up* also provides brief institutional descriptions, and its appendixes give access by geographic location, subject, and university or institute.

Moving Up credits Ray Watson, director emeritus of Duke University's Fuqua School of Business, as consulting editor, as does *STEP*'s promotional literature. Curiously, neither publication mentions the other title, although *STEP* identifies related publications in the Bricker line. This omission will prove misleading to libraries that in good faith purchase both titles.

Training and Development Organizations Directory. 4th ed. Ed. by Janice McLean. Gale, 1988. 684p. indexes. hardcover $270 (0-8103-4348-7; ISSN 0278-5749).

658.007 Management—Study and teaching—U.S.—Directories I Executives—Training of—U.S.—Directories [BKL] 81-643973

The fourth edition of *Training and Development Organizations Directory* is considerably expanded from the second edition, reviewed favorably in *RSBR* [D 15 81]; the third edition (not reviewed) was published in 1983. There are now 2,312 numbered entries arranged alphabetically by the name of the firm. Organizations included provide seminars and courses that may be open to the public, courses connected with institutes at universities, or special seminars custom-designed to meet a particular company's specific needs. All entries provide address, telephone number, founding date, number of staff with names of principals, indication of the type of courses and their audiences, and a brief description of the courses or training; some also provide fee information, indicate if they have preproduced training programs, or if more detailed brochures are available. Information is provided by the organizations themselves in answer to a questionnaire; many entries have been updated from previous editions, while some firms were deleted because they did not respond to an update request. The publisher states that new firms make up more than 50 percent of the entries.

The organizations run the full gamut from the World Modeling Association, which offers training both in administering a modeling school or agency and workshops for models themselves, to the Foreign Service Institute of the U.S. Department of State, Tank Industry Consultants (seminars on building and maintaining water storage tanks), Aaron Cohen Associates (spatial planning of libraries, offices, and educational facilities), and the Back School of Atlanta (programs for physical therapists and industrial safety engineers on back injury prevention and wellness). Programs and their descriptions will be helpful to individuals looking for personal growth or those opening new businesses, as well as to companies both large and small seeking help in training personnel. This edition makes a point of identifying organizations that have preproduced video or computer training programs and indexes them under the heading *Packaged Training Programs*.

The arrangement and format are more pleasing and helpful than in earlier editions; while the type is smaller, the entries are clearly set off and easy to read. Previous editions were arranged geographically; a new geographic index now provides that access, and the subject index also mentions the city and state or Canadian province where the firm is based. A personal-name index includes all names of principals as well as independent trainers. The main index is by subject, ranging from *Ability Testing* and *Absenteeism* to *Leadership*, *Writing Skills*, and *Yoga*. A six-page thesaurus of terms used provides detailed help in finding the appropriate heading. *See* and *see also* references appear in the subject index as well as in the thesaurus. Organizations may be indexed under several headings; for example, *Nonverbal Communication* has a *see also* reference to *Body Awareness*; there are 13 entries under *Body Awareness* and 25 under *Nonverbal Communication*, with 5 entries indexed under both terms.

This *Directory*, in its specific focus on training, is both broader and narrower than other directories. Comparing *TDOD* with *Dun's Consultants Directory* (Dun & Bradstreet, 1988) and *Consultants and*

Consulting Organizations Directory (8th ed., Gale, 1988), there were 61 entries listed under the letter *F* in *TDOD*, over 850 in *Dun's*, and over 450 in *CCOD*. Of the 61 in *TDOD*, 10 were also in *Dun's* and 30 in *CCOD*; 6 entries were in all 3. In almost every case the descriptions in *TDOD* were longer (always in the case of *Dun's*) and always more focused on the training activities of the organization. There is a very high degree of overlap with *The Trainer's Resource* [*RBB* D 15 88], which describes packaged training programs in greater detail.

With the increasing emphasis on continuing education, personal growth, and the need for companies to train their employees in new techniques, this expanded fourth edition of *Training and Development Organizations Directory* continues to be a helpful source for special libraries and large academic and public libraries serving both a general and business clientele.

Training Directory for Business and Industry, 1989–90: A Tool for Successful Employee Development. Gale, 1989. 659p. indexes. paper $59.95 (0-8103-2232-3).

658.007 Management—Study and teaching—Directories I Executives—Training of—Directories I Personnel management—Directories [BKL]

Global competition, corporate restructuring, and continuing deregulation of many U.S. industries are key market forces underlining the need for employee retraining and greater business productivity. Like the *Training and Development Organizations Directory* [*RBB* F 1 89] and the *Seminars Directory* [*RBB* Mr 1 89], also published by Gale, this executive sourcebook facilitates the corporate manager's or human resource development officer's task of identifying appropriate training programs nationwide.

The *Training Directory* describes 1,600 training organizations, institutions, university-related programs, consulting firms, and individual trainers. The "Company Profiles" section provides, in one alphabetical listing, descriptions for each program: address and telephone number, founding date, staff size, principal executives, course emphasis, typical client or target audience, brief description of the course or training, availability of preproduced or packaged training (videotapes or computer-based training modules), fees, and if any additional information, such as a brochure, is available. Program descriptions clearly indicate whether the format is classroom-based for group training, preproduced and packaged, or custom-designed for the client company.

How the *Directory* was compiled and by whom is not clearly described. Apparently, information for the "Company Profiles" was provided by the responding organizations, for the book cautions that they varied considerably in the length of information supplied, and that, therefore, relative size or importance of the training program may not be deduced from the length of its listing.

There are two indexes. The "Training Specialties Yellow Pages" provides subject access to the program listings. Several hundred subject terms are used; listings include address and telephone number. The use of boldface for subject headings and the placement of headings at the top left of each verso page makes browsing easy. Typical subject headings are *Ability Testing, Alcohol Use and Abuse, Annual Report Preparation, Computer Security, Fund Raising, Hazardous Waste Management, Job Analysis and Description, Manufacturing Management, Quality Circles,* and *Work Simplification.* Those programs that are preproduced are indexed under the subject heading *Packaged Training Programs.* Cross-references facilitate browsing ("*Compensation* see also Wage and Salary Administration"). Organizations may be listed under several subjects.

Unfortunately, while program descriptions indicate course emphases, these do not always match the subject terms. So, while the introduction boasts that the *Training Directory* includes outdoor adventurer training programs, such as those offered by Outward Bound USA, Executive Adventure Inc., and Executive Ventures Group, there are no subject headings matching the course emphases given, nor are these companies listed under broader subjects like *Leadership, Management Development, Physical Fitness,* or *Team Building.*

The second index, "Training White Pages," lists programs geographically by state and city (Canadian provinces and cities follow U.S. entries). Each listing provides address, telephone number, and a list of training specialties (the subject headings used in the yellow-pages section). Although Outward Bound USA lists nine training specialties, it is indexed under none of them. The different type size for this and the other two adventure companies suggests they were last-minute additions to the *Directory*.

The *Training Directory for Business and Industry* has an attractive layout and is reasonably well organized. It will be most useful to large corporate, academic, and public libraries that serve business clientele. For the price, it is a better value than either of the other two Gale training directories we have reviewed recently, at least for those libraries that can only afford one. Because local and regional workshops and training programs will appeal more to cost-conscious managers, this *Directory*'s geographic index is a major advantage over the *Seminars Directory*. As Gale invites comments and suggestions regarding this publication, may we suggest that their three directories be combined into one or, at most, two products with name, subject, and location access?

The Guide to Background Investigations, 1988. By National Employment Screening Services. Source Publications, 8801 S. Yale Ave., Tulsa, OK 74137, 1988. 630p. paper $95 (0-941233-16-2; ISSN 0897-3156).

658.311'2 Employee selection I Personnel management [BKL] 88-554

This guide was published in order to provide employers and others involved in background investigations with a tool to help them tap into the information available in public records on their employees and job applicants. First published in 1987 with the title *National Employment Screening Directory* [*RBB* Jl 87], coverage has been expanded in this edition. The publisher claims extensive updating of information since last year's publication. It is planned that the guide will be revised every six months. For those interested in this more frequent updating, an annual subscription is available (at $124.95) for two issues.

Following an introductory section that provides tips on the value and use of records in making investigations, the guide contains three major sections: "State Records Directory," "Federal Courts Directory," and "Educational Records Directory." The first, arranged alphabetically by state, covers the various data that can be obtained from state records and details how to go about requesting it. For each state, an introductory paragraph discusses any statutory or other limitations on access to records and then provides a state hot-line number to call for further information. The names, addresses, and telephone numbers of the state agencies dealing with driving records, worker's compensation records, vital statistics (birth, marriage, and divorce), and criminal records are then listed, with each followed by a profile of what information will be released by telephone or by mail request, to whom, at what fee, and for what purposes. This is followed by names, addresses, and telephone numbers for each county courthouse office dealing with criminal records and a summary of its policies and procedures regarding release of information. The section for each state ends with a city-county cross-reference, so researchers can find out which county to contact when they know only the city of the person being investigated. In the previous edition, this information was arranged by type of record, rather than by state.

The second section, new to the 1988 edition, is a directory of federal courts, prefaced by a brief description of the federal courts system and of civil, criminal, and bankruptcy cases. State by state, the address and telephone number for each district federal court and bankruptcy court are given, along with policies and procedures regarding records and counties under its jurisdiction. Section 3 covers over 3,500 colleges, universities, and trade and technical schools. Each entry in this listing, alphabetical by institution, supplies the address and telephone number for the office that handles student records and, new to this edition, policies and procedures concerning release of information.

Over the past few years, the practice of background checking has mushroomed, with several major firms reporting significant increases in requests for their services. Their fees can run from close to $100 to over $200 per individual, depending on the occupation of the person being checked, so *The Guide to Background Investigations* may well prove to be an attractive alternative for employers. The addresses and telephone numbers supplied can be obtained fairly easily from other library reference materials. However, the information concerning the policies and practices of agencies in regard to releasing their records is not to be found in any other published source. Medium-sized to large public libraries offering services to the business community will find this a valuable addition to the collection.

Seminars Directory. 1st ed. Gale, 1988. 973p. indexes. hardcover $125 (0-8103-2842-9).

658.312'4 Seminars—Directories I Congresses and conventions—Directories I Workshops—Directories [OCLC]

In today's increasingly competitive marketplace, businesses that recognize continuing education as a cost-effective way of improving their employees' efficiency and productivity may need help in choosing appropriate training programs. Based on a database maintained by Seminar Clearinghouse International and available in print for the first time, *Seminars Directory* describes 9,512 "national and regional public seminars, workshops, and training programs sponsored by for-profit companies, universities, and associations." The offerings of about 2,000 vendors or seminar sponsors are listed, and they purportedly represent programs of interest to "all levels of the workforce: senior or executive management, middle management, supervisory management, professional/technical staff, and secretarial/clerical employees."

The *Directory* is divided into 31 broad subject chapters. Very detailed contents pages at the front of the book outline what is contained within each chapter. Subjects range from "Administration," "Communications," "Customer Service/Relations," "Engineering," and "Finance" to "Law," "Manufacturing," "Office Automation," "Purchasing," "Safety/Security," and "Sales." Similar seminars are grouped together in sections within each chapter. For example, the chapter "Human Resources Management" has the sections *Coaching/ Counseling*, *Compensation and Benefits*, *Human Resources Law*, *Industrial Relations*, *Interviewing/Selection*, *Job Analysis/Design*, *Performance Appraisal*, and *Personal Growth*. Scope notes indicate that the *Human Resources Law* section "includes affirmative action, comparable worth, drug testing, equal employment opportunities, and sexual harassment." Within each section, seminars are listed alphabetically by title. Information on each seminar was provided by the vendor. Each numbered entry may include vendor name, address, telephone number (toll-free if available), a description of the topic covered, length, cost, location, remarks, and rarely an evaluation (if more than 10 evaluators responded). A random survey of 14 pages, covering more than 175 entries in seven different subject areas, failed to find any evaluations. The only evaluations found were located in the areas of "Administration," "Executive Development," and "Management." Listings do not indicate actual seminar dates or any seasonality of programs. Length and costs vary widely, from Harvard's 12-week Program for Management Development at $24,450 to Careertrack's one-day Power Communication Skills for Women at $49, but most seminars last two days and fall in the $500–$900 range.

Access to the seminars is provided by title and vendor indexes at the back of the book. Notably, there is no geographic index. The limitations of title indexing are obvious, so most users will consult the contents pages or browse subject sections directly. A detailed "List of Subjects Covered" at the front of the book provides, in one alphabetical sequence, all chapter and section headings, as well as additional subject terms. *See* references guide one to subject headings used (*Retirement* see: Compensation and Benefits, p.359). The lack of subject or keyword indexing allows for some anomalies. For example, the "List of Subjects Covered" indicates that seminars on *WordPerfect* and *Wordstar* may be found in the "Software" section but omits similar entries in "Office Automation." Similar courses on writing user documentation are found in "Communications" and "Computers," with no cross-references linking them.

This book is aimed at the same corporate market as another title from Gale, *Training and Development Organizations Directory* (4th ed. [*RBB* F 1 88]). The latter book is arranged by vendor rather than course and includes slightly more vendors. Entries describe courses offered by vendors but usually don't give specific course titles or fees. The work has detailed subject and geographic indexes. A comparison of the two books showed that only about 10 percent of the vendors were found in both. Since the amount of overlap is so low, public and academic libraries needing comprehensive coverage of the continuing-education field will want to consider buying both. Gale would perform a real service by merging these databases, eliminating the duplication, and publishing one comprehensive directory with indexes by keyword and geographic location.

FINE ARTS, DECORATIVE ARTS

Images of Blacks in American Culture: A Reference Guide to Information Sources. Ed. by Jessie Carney Smith. Greenwood, 1988. 390p. bibliog. illus. index. hardcover $49.95 (0-313-24844-3).

700 Afro-Americans in art I Arts, American [CIP] 87-24964

The 10 essays here explore the images of blacks in historical and contemporary American culture. Negative and stereotypical images of blacks have been deeply embedded in our art, music, literature, film, theater, and other forms of expression. On the other hand, as the preface states, black artists and others have also celebrated "images of strength, beauty, and achievement." Reflecting the complexity of the relationship between the races, these two elements are often intertwined. This reference work explores these images, both positive and negative, and their historical development and impact on both black and American culture. For example, the chapter on instrumental music and song treats not only the negative, insulting aspects of the minstrel show but also the considerable contributions of Scott Joplin to American music. The authors, composer T. J. Anderson and reference librarian Lois Fields Anderson, extend their discussion to images in modern black music and cover the range from jazz and blues to art music.

Contributors are all academics or librarians with a special interest and background in the topic and are listed with biographical information in an appendix. Chapters cover topics in art, musical stage, instrumental music and song, literary criticism, children's books, and film and television. There are general chapters on images of the black female and on male images in popular culture. Toys, games, and dolls as cultural products are discussed. The final chapter on black Americana treats a neglected area in scholarship, that of artifacts and other memorabilia. Jessie Carney Smith, university librarian at Fisk University, has lectured and written widely on black American collectibles. She attempts here to examine the relationship of "images of Black

Americans as depicted in printed works and other areas of artistic creativity and those presented in various forms of memorabilia." This chapter has appended extensive lists of sources of materials and further information on galleries, libraries, collections of artifacts, clubs, exhibitions, and sales as well as a bibliography on collecting. All of the other chapters are also documented with notes and bibliographies. There are 21 black-and-white illustrations.

There is a certain amount of duplication in the chapters in documenting the development of images that appear in different forms of expression, although that certainly points to the strength and pervasiveness of those images. An author, title, and subject index assists the reader in finding all references to a topic such as images of women, references to minstrel shows, and citations to authors. Some topics, such as images of blacks in film and television, have certainly been more exhaustively studied elsewhere, as the 14-page bibliography attests, but it is useful to have all of this material pulled together.

This work grew out of a lecture-exhibit series, "Images in Black Artifacts: Negative and Positive," funded at Fisk University by the Tennessee Humanities Council. Its unique qualities are the discussions and sources for studying and understanding those artifacts as well as the provision of a historical perspective on the images. Recommended for academic and public libraries.

The New Encyclopedia of Science Fiction. Ed. by James Gunn. Viking, 1988. 524p. illus. hardcover $24.95 (0-670-81041-X).
700 Science fiction—Dictionaries [OCLC] 87-40637

This is the fourth book published in this decade that provides biographical and critical information on science-fiction authors. In addition, this work contains topical essays.

David Cowart and Thomas L. Wymer's two-volume *Twentieth-Century Science Fiction Writers* (Gale, 1981), an installment in Gale's Dictionary of Literary Biography series, treats 91 American authors. The alphabetically arranged, lengthy essays analyze the interplay between the authors' lives and works.

E. F. Bleiler's *Science Fiction Writers* [*RSBR* Ap 15 83] includes among its 76 subjects the genre's nineteenth-century pioneers (e.g., Mary Shelley, Edgar Allan Poe) from both the U.S. and Europe as well as contemporary writers. Its scholarly essays, longer than those in *Twentieth-Century Science Fiction Writers*, also explore the life and works of these authors, assessing their overall contribution to science fiction. The work takes a historical approach, arranging the essays chronologically in historical groups. Approximately half of the 91 authors treated in *Twentieth-Century Science Fiction Writers* are also treated in *Science Fiction Writers*. Most of the authors unique to *Science Fiction Writers* date from the nineteenth century, and those unique to *Twentieth-Century Science Fiction Writers* belong to the second echelon of American sf authors of this century.

The second edition of Curtis C. Smith's *Twentieth-Century Science-Fiction Writers* [*RBB* Mr 15 87] is the broadest in biographical coverage, with 551 English-language authors, 38 foreign-language authors, and five major fantasy writers. With a few exceptions made for the field's trailblazers, all are twentieth-century figures. Entries follow a standard format, opening with a succinct who's who sort of biographical summary. Entries also include an optional comment by the author on his own work and a short signed article assessing the author's contribution.

The book under review here, Gunn's *New Encyclopedia of Science Fiction*, is significantly different from the other three, which are strictly biocritical works. Gunn recognizes that science fiction has affected film at least as much if not more than the novel or the short story. In addition to articles on 529 writers and illustrators, his book includes articles on over 250 sf films and TV shows and 96 topical "essay" articles. Topics of these one- to three-page articles include biology, the business of science fiction, comic books, computers, evolution, Germany, lost worlds, monster movies, nuclear promise or threat, small presses, time travel, and women. The topical articles tend to take a historical perspective, tracing the development of the topic from its origins through recent times. Articles on authors, films, and topics are arranged in a single alphabet. Of the 720 authors and movie producers treated in Smith and Gunn, 360 are treated in both, 191 in Gunn only, and 196 in Smith only. Author articles in Gunn vary. Some on minor figures in the genre (e.g., Miles Breuer, Marge Piercy, Frank R. Stockton) are as brief as three sentences, while others (e.g., Samuel R. Delany, Robert Heinlein, Jerry Pournelle) run nearly a full page and are accompanied by one of the volume's 200 black-and-white photographs. The articles identify birth and death dates, nationality, and genre of the author before summarizing the career and contributions. The longer articles identify the key plot elements in major works and trace the author's ideas from their genesis in early works through their development in later ones. Articles on authors conclude with bibliographies of works not cited in the articles. Citations consist only of title and date. Articles on films and television shows list credits, describe plot, and judge their artistic merits and contribution to the art form.

Articles include liberal *see also* references represented by a term's appearance within the text in small caps or at the conclusion of an essay article. *See* references are used to refer from less-known names to those better known, the latter usually authors' pseudonyms. A small insert section of colorplates reproduces science-fiction illustrations.

Gunn, former president of the Science Fiction Writers of America and the Science Fiction Research Association, winner of the Hugo and Pilgrim awards, and author of *Alternate Worlds: The Illustrated History of Science Fiction*, has assembled an impressive group of 107 contributors, some academics, others active contributors to science fiction as editors, authors, or publishers. Names on this distinguished list include E. F. Bleiler, Arthur C. Clarke, Hugo Award winner Philip José Farmer, and longtime award-winning sf author Jack Williamson. The list of authors states their credentials and doubles as a key to the signature initials concluding each article.

Much of this book is unique. It alone treats the audiovisual manifestations of science fiction, creations that have reached far wider audiences than even the best sf novels and short stories. The distinguished authors have produced succinct, readable analyses of the people and works that have advanced the field from a subgenre of the novel to a flourishing field worthy of study in its own right, to say nothing of enjoyment for its own sake. Even libraries that have all three of the other works discussed above need this book, both for its unique contributions and its quality where it overlaps.

Plain Talk about Art. By N. E. Lahti. York Books, P.O. Box 40-1112, Brooklyn, NY 11240-1112, 1988. 157p. bibliog. $9.95 (0-9620147-0-2).
703 Art—Dictionaries [BKL] 88-50220

This slender book is intended for the layperson studying visual art who desires quick dictionary-style information. It has approximately 900 entries presented in a succinct style that vary in length from a single sentence to several pages. Entries are arranged alphabetically, and a contents page directs users to other sections of the book: a color vocabulary section and a bibliography. The author's emphasis is on Western art, but many entries present a synopsis of art in non-Western countries, e.g., *Chinese Art*. In addition, the range of historical coverage includes art styles and schools from early (*Etruscan Art*) to present times (*Performance Art*), art terms, and artistic techniques. Entries for art movements usually contain the names of some representative artists and their birth dates. There are no separate entries for artists. The section on color vocabulary is designed to introduce the user to the various nuances of these specialized terms. The work has ample and accurate cross-references. As in many technical dictionaries, pronunciation is not given. It does give dates for art movements and English translations for foreign-language terms, e.g., *Guerrilla Girls (1980s)* and *November Group, The (die Novembergruppe)*. There are no illustrations. A three-page bibliography with many recent publications concludes the book. Unfortunately, the bibliography is arranged in a haphazard manner that follows no logical format.

With a plethora of reference material available on art, why should a library consider this book for its collection? Many of the standard multivolume reference sources on art were published in the 1960s and

1970s, e.g., *Encyclopedia of World Art* (McGraw-Hill, 1960), *McGraw-Hill Dictionary of Art* (1969), *Phaidon Encyclopedia of Art* (1971), and the *Praeger Encyclopedia of Art* (1971). Even the single-volume works based upon these multivolume sets are dated, e.g., *Dictionary of 20th Century Art* (McGraw-Hill, 1974) and the *Phaidon Encyclopedia of Art and Artists* (1978). These single-volume works do have the advantage of having several times the number of entries and more detailed definitions. In contrast, *Plain Talk* is succinct in style and offers information on recent terms and movements. This inexpensive paperback is recommended for academic and public library collections.

The Oxford Dictionary of Art. Ed. by Ian Chilvers and Harold Osborne. Oxford, 1988. 548p. hardcover $39.95 (0-19-866133-9).

703'.21 Art—Dictionaries [OCLC] 88-5138

The Oxford Dictionary of Art is an alphabetically arranged compendium intended for the layperson and student. Based upon three standard reference works, *The Oxford Companion to Art* [RSBR S 1 71], *The Oxford Companion to Twentieth-Century Art*, and (to a lesser extent) *The Oxford Companion to the Decorative Arts* [RSBR Je 15 76], it is not a substitute for any or all of them. The late Osborne, editor of the companions, is listed as coeditor, but the editing of the *Dictionary* was done by Chilvers, author of *A–Z of Art and Artists*, with Dennis Farr of the Courtauld Institute Galleries in London as consultant.

Arranged in the familiar two-columns-per-page Oxford format are approximately 3,000 entries, of which 300 are topics new to the *Dictionary*. Almost all entries from the companions have been rewritten more briefly with updated information, if necessary. The *Dictionary* treats Western art from ancient times to the present, excluding architecture and oriental art, except when there is relevance to other topics. Art terms, movements, museums, and biographies are included, but entries for individual countries (found in the companions) are not. Biographical entries include artists, dealers, patrons, scholars, and collectors. Architects are excluded unless they have importance in other visual arts (e.g., Robert Adam, Brunelleschi).

Unlike the companions, the *Dictionary* has neither illustrations nor bibliography, although in biographical entries titles of books and publication dates are sometimes cited in the text. Pronunciation is also omitted, a disadvantage in a handbook for laypersons unfamiliar with the art world. On the positive side, the generous use of asterisks in the text leads the reader to related topics with their own entries. Unfortunately, the gutter margins are so narrow that text will be lost at the first rebinding.

The Oxford Dictionary of Art will have its greatest use in libraries that do not own the parent companions. It will also be helpful in large libraries for ready reference, although the experienced art librarian will probably prefer the appropriate companion because of greater detail.

Contemporary Artists. 3d ed. Ed. by Colin Naylor. St. James Press, 1989. 1,059p. bibliog. indexes. hardcover $120 (0-912289-96-1).

709'.2 Art, Modern—20th century—Biography I Artists—Biography [BKL]

A new edition of this authoritative biobibliography is a welcome publishing event. The panel of advisers' guidelines for selection of biographees are unchanged: they "should have worked as professional artists for at least five years, have exhibited their work in several individual exhibitions at important galleries, and have been included in large-scale museum survey shows—and be represented in the permanent collections of major museums throughout the world. . . . young—and perhaps lesser-known—artists . . . should have already attracted serious critical attention in the current art media. The inclusion of deceased artists is dependent upon the continuing influence of their work on current art activity." For this edition "no artist deceased prior to 1960 has been included." This accounts for most of the 149 artists dropped, since the cutoff date in the previous edition was the beginning of World War II. Thirty new entrants were added for a total of 849 biographees from around the world.

A typical entry contains detailed biographical data, including schools attended, teaching posts held, and honors received. Listings of one-person and group exhibitions, collections that include the artist's work, and books and articles by and about the artist follow. Most entries include a statement by the artist on his or her work and a signed critical essay by one of 121 contributors. A black-and-white illustration of a representative work is often included.

A list of the artists included precedes the entries. Advisers and contributors are identified at the end of the volume with a list of the essays each contributed.

A comparison of the third with the second (1983) edition shows that updating has been extensive but uneven. Some artists' statements appear for the first time, and new illustrations have been chosen. Most readily and uniformly accomplished was extending the lists of individual and group exhibitions, even through 1988 in many cases (LeWitt, Manzu, Marden, Moore); however, Georgia O'Keeffe's much-heralded retrospective, which opened in Washington, D.C., in November 1987, is omitted. Unfortunately the bibliographies about the artists' work are in many cases unchanged. For example, there are no citations after 1981 for Jennifer Bartlett although her breakthrough shows in the 1980s received much attention. The major catalog *David Hockney: A Retrospective* is omitted although the show is listed.

Users can learn a good deal from the essays, a feature that distinguishes this series from other biographical dictionaries. They discuss the philosophy and unique characteristics of the artists and offer thoughtful assessments of their achievements. The ideal would be to provide essays for all biographees and to review them for each edition. There are essays for 22 of 30 new entrants, but some artists important enough to be included in the two latest editions (e.g., Anselm Kiefer) have no essay. In terms of currency, the essay on Frank Stella—unchanged from the first (1977) edition—does not reflect his recent three-dimensional projective works. It would be useful if essays were dated as well as signed, because change is so frequently a characteristic of contemporary art.

The publisher has responded to criticisms of paper and format by using heavier glossy stock that allows cleaner, sharper reproductions of illustrations and ends the bleed through of print prevalent in the second edition. A larger page size allows for the much-needed running heads missing before. Some high school libraries, as well as most academic and public libraries, will want the new edition of *Contemporary Artists*. Many librarians will choose to retain earlier editions for the dropped artists' entries.

Dictionary of Contemporary American Artists. 5th ed. By Paul Cummings. St. Martin's, 1988. 738p. bibliog. illus. hardcover $65 (0-312-00232-7).

709'.2 [B] Artists—U.S.—Biography I Art, Modern—20th century—U.S. [CIP] 82-7337

The fifth edition of the *Dictionary of Contemporary American Artists* extends the coverage of the previous 1982 edition through May 1987. (The Board reviewed the third edition [RSBR D 15 77].) Alphabetically arranged on double-column pages, the 900 entries present information on U.S. painters, printmakers, and sculptors, including 87 new artists but dropping 127 from the fourth edition. More selective but with longer entries than *Who's Who in American Art*, the *Dictionary* treats established artists who met the editorial criteria of having works in major collections and exhibitions, success as teachers, or critical recognition. Although the majority of entries are for living, currently active artists, the work includes deceased artists as far back as Charles Demuth (died 1935) and William Glackens (died 1938).

Entries are limited to professional information: dates, place of birth and death, art schools attended, awards, teaching positions, address, dealer's name, exhibitions, and sources of further information, including the Archives of American Art. Entries refer to works on the artists in the book's bibliography. Abbreviations are used throughout, and many users will need the 28-page "Key to Museums and Installations" that precedes the entries. The key identifies the city in which museums and art schools are located, but colleges, universities, and business organizations are unfortunately almost always cited without location. A black-and-white reproduction of a representative work accompanies 149 of the entries (compared to 115 entries in the 1982 edition). Small but reasonably clear, the majority of reproductions are one column in width. An alphabetical list at the beginning of the book indicates those artists whose work is illustrated.

Preceding the entries are a list of artists classified by medium (painter, printmaker, assemblagist, mosaicist, etc.), providing pronunciation for more than 100 names, and a directory of commercial galleries in North America and Europe representing each artist. Two bibliographies follow the entries: the first cites sources of further information on specific artists, and the second lists books providing general background on American art.

This book could have benefitted from more careful proofreading. In the illustrations index, the entries for William Brice and Joel Fisher are misfiled. In the biographical section, there is occasional lack of agreement between the spelling of a name used as a running head and the name appearing in the entry, e.g., *Cinni, Peter* versus *Chinni, Peter*. The *Dictionary of Contemporary American Artists* retains its usefulness in general and art reference collections for professional information about established American artists.

The Traveler's Guide to American Gardens. Rev. ed. Ed. by Mary Helen Ray and Robert P. Nicholls. Univ. of North Carolina, 1988. 375p. illus. index. maps. hardcover $22.50 (0-8078-1787-2); paper $9.95 (0-8078-4214-1).

712'.5 Gardens—U.S.—Guide-books I U.S.—Description and travel—1981— Guide-books [CIP] 87-40539

Previously published in 1982 as *Guide to Historic and Significant Gardens of America*, this revised edition includes more than 1,000 U.S. gardens open to the public. Gardens are considered to include several historical sites, parks, and squares. According to the authors, gardens were included based on longevity (that they have been in existence for 75 years or more), nonprofit status, historical significance, or inclusion of unusual features or designs. For-profit commercial gardens have been excluded. However, mention of these gardens is noted at the end of each state's chapter as other places of interest.

Entries are arranged into state chapters and then alphabetically by city or town. Each chapter begins with a brief discussion on the state's topography, climate, demography, history, scenery, and culture. Each chapter also includes an outline map pointing out the general location of the gardens. The entries are very brief and include address, hours when open, fee (if any), telephone number, and short description. These descriptions note when and how the garden became established and any special features or services (such as nature walks). Entries may also include a rating of one star (superior) or two stars (must see). Over 40 pen-and-ink drawings are included to illustrate special features of some of the gardens. Photographs would have been much better, as the illustrations are often unclear and add little value to the book. There is one index to the names of places and gardens covered.

Gardens of North America and Hawaii: A Traveler's Guide, by Irene and Walter Jacob (Timber Press, 1985 [BKL Je 15 86]), is very similar to this book. It includes much of the same information with identical geographic arrangement and similar descriptions. It also includes a rating system of one to four stars, plus symbols for the type of gardens and plants included (e.g., herb garden, bonsai). Canadian gardens are also covered. Libraries that already own the more comprehensive Jacob guide can probably pass on the Ray and Nicholls guide. Libraries will also want to acquire excellent regional guides such as *Great Public Gardens of the Eastern United States* by Doris Stone (Pantheon, 1982), which provide much more detail on each garden discussed. Otherwise, *The Traveler's Guide to American Gardens* is recommended as a current directory source, primarily for public libraries.

Encyclopedia of Architecture: Design, Engineering & Construction. v.1. Ed. by Joseph A. Wilkes and Robert T. Packard. Wiley, 1988. 749p. bibliog. illus. tables. hardcover $200/vol., $180/vol. on subscription (0-471-80747-8); $850/5-vol. set prepaid (0-471-63351-8).

720'.3 Architecture—Dictionaries [CIP] 87-25222

Although the Board hesitates to review one volume of a five-volume set, the *Encyclopedia of Architecture: Design, Engineering & Construction* should be brought to the attention of reference librarians. The *Encyclopedia*, an alphabetically arranged compendium of subject and biographical entries, is unusually wide ranging in coverage. Sponsored by the American Institute of Architects, the work includes not only the expected articles on individuals, firms, categories of buildings (*Airports, Amusement Parks, Banks, Bus Maintenance Facilities*), and techniques and materials (*Ceramic Tile, Brick Masonry, Acoustic Insulation and Materials*), but also topics not readily found in architecture reference books (*Bonds and Sureties, Air Quality, Behavior and Architecture*). The emphasis of the set is on architectural processes and building technology, but historic and artistic topics are treated as well. Articles like *Acoustics, Chromium Plating*, and *Concrete Forming* use technical language and probably will be of greatest interest to the practicing architect or builder, but the articles *Architectural Press, Architectural Styles*, and *Careers in Architecture* will appeal to a wide readership.

Clearly written by 82 practicing architects, architecture faculty members, and architectural historians, the signed articles in volume 1 (covering *Aalto, Alvar* to *Concrete—General Principles*) emphasize nineteenth- and twentieth-century Western architecture, with the Orient and Africa receiving minimal attention. There are no entries for individual structures or national schools. Entries average five to eight double-column pages with several running to 25 or more. *See* and *see also* references direct the reader to the preferred form of entry and to related articles. The preferred form of entry will occasionally be questioned by users. (Why *Architectural Woodwork* rather than *Woodwork, Architectural*, when a comparable entry, *Competitions, Architectural Design*, is inverted?) Similarly, the choice of architects included (and excluded) may be questioned. (Why is Alberti here when Borromini, Bramante, and Brunelleschi are not? Why include Mario Botta when Gordon Bunshaft, designer of Lever House and recipient of the 1988 Pritzker Architecture Prize, is omitted?) However, these are minor concerns when the overall worth of the volume is considered. The *Macmillan Encyclopedia of Architects* [RBB S 1 83] provides biographical information on architects not found in this work.

Crisp black-and-white line drawings, photographs, diagrams, and tables generously support every entry. The publisher states the completed set will have more than 3,000 illustrations and 500 tables. Only the *Color in Architecture* article has colored illustrations, and those are of good quality. A bibliography of English-language books and journal articles is appended to each entry.

The lack of an index in the first volume of the *Encyclopedia* is a deterrent to efficient and thorough use because smaller topics are buried in articles. The publisher states that there will be an overall index to the entire work at the end of volume 5, to be published in late 1989, but in the meantime it will be missed. Another concern is the "Conversion Factors, Abbreviations, and Unit Symbols" section that precedes the text of volume 1. The abbreviations *SI units*, *ASTM*, and *CIPM* are used in notes and captions without explanation. The Board hopes that this section will appear in each volume of the work to save readers from having to refer repeatedly to volume 1.

The *Encyclopedia of Architecture* is (thus far) an incomparable reference work. If succeeding volumes reach the same level, it will become a standard reference source. Its coverage of construction technology makes the work valuable both in art and architecture and technology collections. Although the price is high, reference librarians should seriously consider acquiring the *Encyclopedia* for readers with an interest in architectural design and construction.

Architecture and Women: A Bibliography Documenting Women Architects, Landscape Architects, Designers, Architectural Critics and Writers and Women in Related Fields Working in the United States. By Lamia Doumato. Garland, 1988. 269p. index. hardcover $40 (0-8240-4105-4).

016.72'088042 Architecture and women—U.S.—Bibliography [CIP] 88-17698

Doumato, a librarian at the National Gallery of Art in Washington, D.C., and author of other titles in the arts, has compiled a selective bibliography of women who have made significant contributions to architecture. Alphabetically arranged by surname from Diana Agrest to Florence Yoch, 128 architects, landscape architects, interior designers, architectural critics, writers on gardens and landscapes, housing reformers, and planners are included. While the title is limited to coverage of women who have worked in the U.S., it does include those who were not born or trained here. The author states in her introduction that "the primary motivation for compiling this volume was to encourage research on the history of women in architecture. The intention was not to solve any polemic discussions concerning the roles of women nor to assert in any way their superiority to their male colleagues nor to bemoan the difficulties encountered by women in the field."

The first section documents women in architecture in general. Entries for individual women that follow typically include their names as most often cited, birth and death dates as appropriate, locations for archival materials and manuscripts, their publications, secondary works, and exhibition catalogs and reviews. Book reviews are usually omitted unless the compiler felt they established a new theory.

Citation dates range from the nineteenth century through 1987. The author notes that "monographs; dissertations and M.A. theses; essays; articles and interviews in journals and other serial publications; exhibition catalogs and reviews; selective newspaper coverage; conference proceedings; chapters in anthologies; manuscripts; and archival sources are listed."

One minor flaw should be noted. Inserted in the center of the book are 20 unnumbered pages containing illustrations of a title page and various buildings and plans. There are no notations appearing either in the text or index indicating the existence of these illustrations. They might have been either better placed by the appropriate entry or otherwise left out.

As no comprehensive predecessor to this bibliography exists, large public and academic libraries supporting architecture or women's studies programs will want to consider purchase.

A Dictionary of Ancient Near Eastern Architecture. By Gwendolyn Leick. Routledge, 1988. 261p. illus. index. hardcover $49.95 (0-415-00240-0).

722'.5 Architecture, Ancient—Middle East—Dictionaries l Architecture—Middle East—Dictionaries l Middle East—Antiquities—Dictionaries [CIP] 87-23375

Compiled by Leick, a lecturer at U.K. universities, *A Dictionary of Ancient Near Eastern Architecture* is a glossary of 252 alphabetically arranged terms covering architecture from the Neolithic era to Ptolemaic Egypt. The concise, well-written definitions are supported by clear black-and-white photographs, line drawings, and site plans. The entries include architectural structures, details, and sites; geographic locations; and "national" schools. No architects are listed because (with the exception of *Imhotep*) they are unknown. Cross-references lead to appropriate entries.

Straightforward in presentation of information, the *Dictionary* is intended for the student or beginner in the field. Pronunciations are not indicated, a disadvantage because some of the entries will not be found even in unabridged English-language dictionaries. More than four-fifths of the entries include citations to French- and German-language or out-of-print materials that may not be available in many libraries.

Preceding the main part of the *Dictionary* are a list of illustrations and five black-and-white outline maps showing Asia Minor, Egyptian, Persian, Mesopotamian, and Syro-Palestinian sites. The work concludes with a list of entries and a subject index with references to both entries and illustrations.

Despite its price, *A Dictionary of Ancient Near Eastern Architecture* merits serious consideration in libraries whose readers are interested in ancient architecture. There is apparently no comparable English-language reference source, and histories of ancient architecture do not consistently define terms and identify sites fully. The work is recommended for academic and large public library reference collections.

Old-House Dictionary: An Illustrated Guide to American Domestic Architecture (1600–1940). By Steven J. Phillips. American Source Books; dist. by Quality Books, 1989. 239p. bibliog. illus. index. paper $16.95 (0-9621333-6-1).

728.0973 Architecture, Domestic—U.S.—Dictionaries [BKL] 88-83158

This alphabetically arranged glossary of terms relating to U.S. domestic architecture from the start of the seventeenth century to World War II should prove to be a much-used reference source. Straightforward in presentation, the work briefly and clearly defines both design and construction terms, citing synonyms. More than half of the 750 definitions are crisply illustrated with black-and-white line drawings, often with component parts and details labeled. If necessary, there are references to illustrations elsewhere in the *Dictionary*. Running heads indicate the first and last entries on each page.

A 14-page cross-reference section helps users who cannot remember the name of an architectural element or feature. Under 17 broad headings (*Framing, Arches, Masonry*, etc.), the reader is directed to the appropriate entries in the main part of the *Dictionary*. A concluding bibliography cites more than 150 English-language sources, many with a one-sentence descriptive annotation. Arranged by type (glossaries and pictorial guides, historic preservation, pattern books, etc.), the sources range in date from 1703 to the present.

Apparently unique in focusing exclusively on U.S. domestic architecture, the *Old-House Dictionary* is recommended for public libraries serving readers involved in historic preservation or remodeling an old house. The *Dictionary* will also be helpful in academic libraries serving architecture and architectural history students. Although the work will receive heavy use in many reference collections, unfortunately it is available only in paperback with narrow gutter margins that will allow no more than one rebinding.

Walter Breen's Complete Encyclopedia of U.S. and Colonial Coins. By Walter Breen. Doubleday, 1988. 754p. bibliog. indexes. hardcover $75 (0-385-14207-2).

737.4973 Coins, American [CIP] 79-6855

This impressive encyclopedia took 10 years to produce and includes every major and minor American coin from the first brass Bermuda shillings of 1616 to modern-day coins in circulation. It is the only book that is this comprehensive, with over 7,800 entries, including rarities and variations. It is divided into eight parts: "Early American Coins," "Federal Minor Coinages," "Federal Silver and Sandwich-Metal Coinages," "Federal Gold Coinages," "Commemorative Coinages," "United States Provisional Branch Mint at San Francisco (1851–53)," "Private, Pioneer, and Territorial Gold Coins," and "Other Authorized Local Issues." Within each section the coins are listed chronologically. To locate a coin, one determines the section it belongs in and then proceeds chronologically, reading text and viewing illustrations. The introduction for each coin gives mint, designer, physical specifications, authorizing acts, and grading standards. Other information that may be included is historical circumstances of issue, quantity minted, and level of rarity. Not every coin is priced. The author indicates that prices vary so much that listing one may be a disservice. However, some coins do include an auction price.

This book is for the serious coin collector. The information is as complete as possible. All coins are not illustrated, but the reproductions are excellent for those that are. The source of every illustration is given, with full bibliographic information on the sources at the end of the text in a section called "Bibliography, Abbreviations, Typographic Conventions." Also included are a glossary and two indexes, one to names and one to subjects.

Breen is considered the foremost U.S. coin historian and is the author of two other coin encyclopedias: *Walter Breen's Encyclopedia of United States and Colonial Proof Coins, 1722–1977* and *The Encyclopedia of United States Silver and Gold Commemorative Coins, 1892–1954*. This is an essential purchase for large public libraries, a valuable reference source for academic and special libraries, and highly recommended for coin collectors.

Pictorial Price Guide to American Antiques: And Objects Made for the American Market. 1988–89 ed. By Dorothy Hammond. Dutton, 1988. 224p. illus. index. paper $14.95 (0-525-48382-9).

745.1 Antiques—Prices [OCLC]

This guide to the more popular antique items made for the American market is now in its ninth edition, and its strength as a reference source remains the number of items (5,000) included in it and the fact that a black-and-white photograph accompanies each entry. Most items included are described briefly (identification, size, color, condition), and the selling price realized at an auction is noted, along with the name of the auction house, date of sale, and state in which it took place. Descriptions are brief but serve to indicate to experienced auctiongoers items of merit and their condition. Users without experience might not realize the importance of condition, and the guide's brief introduction does little to inform them of what to look for when examining an item for purchase. The descriptions printed here appear to have been taken from printed auction catalogs; while some houses are acknowledged in the introduction, there is no list of catalogs used. The author is a columnist for *Colonial Homes* magazine.

The guide is divided into 12 small sections and a large section entitled "Miscellaneous." Items included represent a small part of the marketplace for American antiques. The sections are "Banks," "Ceramics," "Clocks," "Furniture," "Glass," "Kitchen Items," "Lighting," "Metals," "Shaker Items," "Textiles and Painting," "Tools," and "Toys/Games/Dolls." Two of these sections—"Ceramics" and "Glass"—have a glossary defining terms associated with these popular items. Both glossaries are too brief to be helpful, and some definitions are misleading. For example, the explanation given for what has become a generic term—*delft*—limits production of these earthenware products to the Netherlands. This will confuse some users since several of the delft items included in the ceramics section are correctly identified as English. Items such as lacy glass or important pressed glass patterns are not discussed. The section "Textiles and Prints" (called "Textiles and Paintings" in the table of contents) is one of the weakest in the guide. There are four similar prints (all Audubons) identified and three unimportant paintings. This is very limited coverage of the year's auction record for this important category of antique. Not one native American textile is included in the textile section; there are no English printed fabrics included; and of the five oriental rugs pictured, three are not properly identified.

The "Miscellaneous" section consists of illustrations of different items grouped together. Here, users will discover some items not included elsewhere, but most of these items (furniture, stoneware, lighting) are like those pictured in other sections. They are here because they are in a group photograph with items from different categories and, therefore, would not fit in any one of the preceding sections. This arrangement makes it difficult to survey prices for a particular category of antique. Including this section did enable the compilers to make maximum use of illustrated auction catalogs, and a good index enables users to locate items no matter where they are placed in the guide.

It is regrettable that the publisher did not continue a similar guide published a decade ago: *Americana at Auction: A Pictorial Record of More Than 700 American Antiques Sold by Twenty Auction Houses* (Dutton, 1978), by Samuel Pennington and others. This guide had excellent illustrations and served as a first-rate introduction to trends in the marketplace. The guide under review could be improved if there was better editing, if coverage was limited to quality antiques and no attempt was made to cover the collectibles market, if illustrations showed more detail, and if an initial chapter devoted more space to trends in the market. Both *The Kovels' Antiques & Collectibles Price List* [RSBR My 1 76] and *Warman's Antiques and Their Prices* [RBB O 1 87] are not limited to American items, cover more antiques, and have fewer photographs. The *Pictorial Price Guide's* chief value is the large number of items pictured, thereby making it useful for those needing to identify antiques. Recommended for libraries needing to maintain a large collection of price guides for antiques.

Fairchild's Dictionary of Fashion. 2d ed. By Charlotte Mankey Calasibetta. Fairchild, 1988. 749p. illus. hardcover $50 (0-87005-635-2).

746.92'03 Fashion—Dictionaries I Costume—Dictionaries [BKL] 88-80198

The second edition of *Fairchild's Dictionary of Fashion* has been significantly revised and updated; it draws upon the considerable resources of *Women's Wear Daily*, *W*, and the Fairchild Costume Library. As in the first edition [RSBR My 1 76], most of the text consists of over 10,000 alphabetical entries for organizations (*Chambre Syndicale des Paruriers*); persons (*Vreeland, Diana Dalzial*); slang terms, so labeled (*specs, shades, long johns*); trademarks (*Viyella*); clothing; hair styles; jewelry; and fabrics.

Entries are clearly explained. If a term has more than one meaning, the most common is given first. If the look of a garment, for example, has changed through the years, definitions are chronological. Pronunciation is supplied inconsistently: "*challis* (shall-e)"; "*cuir* (queer)"; "*Inverness* (in-ver-ness)"; but not for *glissade, orhna,* or *vambrace*.

Within the alphabetical arrangement are 96 categories (*Heels, Glasses, Cuffs, Shoulders*) under which groups of these items are defined and displayed. Terms in each category are also listed in their alphabetical places with a *see* reference to the category. Running heads keep the user from becoming confused by subalphabets; the format is clean and clear. Numerous main-entry *see* references, small caps, and *see* and *see also* references within and at the end of entries also help bring the material together.

Particularly effective are the numerous black-and-white drawings that illustrate terms. Sixteen full-color pages containing 50 illustrations of costume from ancient Egypt to 1988 America are cross-referenced to entries, but the entries do not refer readers to the pictures.

The appendix contains 171 brief biographical entries (approximately four per page) for fashion designers—from retired Lilly Daché and deceased Jean Patou to currently active Issey Miyake and Kenzo—followed by black-and-white portraits of 64 of these designers. The final section consists of looks (mostly created after 1975) by 49 designers. Most, but not all, of the fashion photos here indicate year.

This authoritative, well-designed *Dictionary* will be an essential purchase for any library serving fashion students, designers, and the industry.

Who's Who in Fashion. 2d ed. By Anne Stegemeyer. Fairchild, 1988. 243p. bibliog. illus. index. hardcover $15.50 (0-87005-574-7).

746.9'2 [B] Costume designers—Biography [OCLC] 87-82511

The compiler selected 208 people for inclusion in this thoroughly revised edition of *Who's Who in Fashion*. Chosen for inclusion are "designers with an established track record...greats and near greats of the past...influential individuals in related fields, and a selection of the many newcomers who promise to become the establishment of the future." Information came from questionnaires, personal interviews, and the resources of the *Women's Wear Daily* Library.

The entries, which range from a few paragraphs to three pages, begin with date and place of birth (and death, if appropriate) and fashion awards. The well-written, readable sketches cover the background, education, philosophy, career, and hallmarks of the biographees. Many of the entries are accompanied by black-and-white photographs of the designers and most by photographs and/or sketches of their work.

This edition presents all the entries (except for seven people in fields allied to the fashion industry) in one alphabet, an improvement over the first edition with its three sections (50 "Names to Know," 47 "Foreign Designers," and 86 "American Designers"). Information on "real" names has been dropped, e.g., "*Klein, Anne* (born Hannah Golofski)." Sixteen pages of colorplates of fashions have been added. Unfortunately, they are not included in the otherwise useful and accurate index. Students will appreciate the three-page bibliography, which the author notes was "compiled to help the reader in the study of fashion."

Though there is some overlap with the biographies in *Fairchild's*

Dictionary of Fashion [*RBB* D 15 88], most public and academic libraries will want to acquire this attractive and authoritative biographical dictionary. Libraries that own the 1980 edition may want to retain it for the dropped entries.

The New Quilting & Patchwork Dictionary. By Rhoda Ochser Goldberg. Crown, 1989 (c1988). 280p. illus. index. paper $12.95 (0-517-56965-5).

746.9'7 Quilting ∎ Patchwork ∎ Quilting—Patterns ∎ Patchwork—Patterns [OCLC] 88-3836

This source contains a wealth of information for the quilter. The author, former president of the Suffolk County (N.Y.) Chapter of the Embroiderers' Guild of America, has written similar books on knitting and crocheting.

The book is arranged in seven sections. First the basics of quilting are described and illustrated with black-and-white photographs and line drawings. The author explains how to plan and produce a quilt, alphabetically lists tools and accessories, discusses how to build a quilting frame, reviews types of fabrics and estimating yardage, and explains how to enlarge and reduce patterns. Linear and equivalent metric measurements are given along with an illustration of the basic pattern categories.

The second section is the dictionary, which explains and illustrates different quilting techniques. This section contains many clear and easy-to-follow drawings and directions. The entry *Amish Quilting*, six pages in length, provides drawings and photographs of typical Amish patterns. In contrast, the entry *Paper Liners* is two sentences. Other entries include *English Piecing, Hawaiian Quilting, Painted Quilt Blocks, Prestuffed Quilting,* and *Trapunto*.

The third section of the book is the longest; it alphabetically arranges over 600 drawings of patchwork patterns on graph paper. The author includes a color legend for each pattern to help determine shades of fabric. The patterns and color legends will be very useful in planning a full-size quilt pattern. An individual merely interested in the identification of quilt patterns should consult *The Quilt I.D. Book* [*RBB* Ag 87], which identifies more than 4,000 patterns.

Other sections of Goldberg's book include photographs of selected quilt patterns, template patterns, instructions on finishing techniques, illustrations of border patterns, and an alphabetical index of patchwork patterns. This well-illustrated and easy-to-understand source will be useful to both experienced and novice quilters.

Who's Who in Interior Design. 1988–89 ed. Barons Who's Who, 412 N. Coast Hwy., Laguna Beach, CA 92651, 1988. 365p. hardcover $125.50 (0-9620943-0-7; ISSN 0897-5914).

747.025 Interior decorators—Directories [OCLC] 88-70478

This new biographical dictionary contains entries for over 2,300 persons involved in both contract and residential interior design in the U.S.; also included are selected interior-design editors and educators. The introduction states that the volume "offers researchers, scientists, analysts, business executives, and the nation's media a concise directory of the individuals most responsible for the design profession's 'leading edge' of innovation. Concurrently, the text presents design clients—both residential and commercial—with a detailed selection of America's most talented interior design professionals."

The front matter contains a sample biography, a list of abbreviations, and a description of the qualifications for admission and the review process. Candidates for inclusion were sought from mailings to directors of interior-design firms, "names made available by interior design magazines and associations," research in appropriate journals, and recommendations made by the volume's board of trustees. The seven-person board includes the presidents of the International Society of Interior Designers and the Institute of Business Designers, the chief editor of *Interior Design Magazine*, and two educators. Candidates were invited to submit biographical data and career information. Staff prepared entries for those who did not respond (indicated by an asterisk at the end of the entry). Biographees selected for inclusion received a prepublication proof for verification.

Following the name and descriptive tag (e.g., "commercial and office interior designer," "interior design educator"), information is presented in who's who–type format. Personal data elements are date and place of birth, parents, marriage, children, education, political and religious affiliations, avocations, and home and office addresses. Professional data elements are career positions, career-related activities, awards, memberships, published design projects, and major projects. The index arranges biographees geographically by state and city and indicates area of specialization for each entry. Most of the designers practice in the most populous states, with several states having only one to three persons listed.

The main drawback the Board finds with this first edition is the absence of some prominent designers. A spot check of 41 of the personal names of designers included in *Interior Design*'s "100 Interior Giants of 1988" (an annual listing) produced only eight hits: six entries were full and two had been supplied by the directory's staff and included career data only. The *New York Times* of April 27, 1989, reporting on the 1989 Kips Bay Decorator Show House, states that it "presents work of 15 designers" and that "the list of participants is impressive." The 13 designers mentioned by name in the article are not in *WWID*.

The publisher's announced plans for future editions include expanded geographic coverage, adding Britain, France, and Canada. Two American groups, the International Society of Interior Designers and the Institute of Business Designers, have also made their lists available. The famous designer Mario Buatta has also been added to the board of trustees.

Information on interior designers and their work is difficult to locate. Therefore, despite limitations in coverage, the first edition of *Who's Who in Interior Design* may be useful in public and special libraries serving prospective clients and researchers.

Concise Encyclopedia of Interior Design. 2d ed. By A. Allen Dizik. Van Nostrand, 1988. 220p. bibliog. illus. tables. $36.95 hardcover (0-442-22109-6).

747'.03 Decoration and ornament—Dictionaries ∎ Interior decoration—Dictionaries [CIP] 88-5560

The first edition of this book, published in 1976, was titled *Encyclopedia of Interior Design and Decoration*. However, *Concise Encyclopedia of Interior Design* more accurately describes this alphabetical listing of terminology. The author is a fellow of the American Society of Interior Designers.

Principles of interior design are discussed here, as are such subjects as furniture periods, draperies, fabrics, wallpaper, floor coverings, color, and lighting. In addition, allied disciplines such as fine art, architecture, antiques, and construction are covered.

Most entries are one sentence or a short paragraph in length with several up to a few pages. Useful charts offer information conveniently arranged. They detail periods of Oriental style, describe major periods and styles of European and American furniture design, and tell how to calculate wallpaper rollage. Illustrations are limited to black-and-white drawings of architectural symbols and furniture arrangements. More illustrations would have been helpful.

Numerous flaws and inaccuracies hinder the quality of this work. Internal cross-references lead the user to entries with varied headings or dead ends. For example, the entry *Gauguin, Paul* contains a cross-reference to *Nabis*. When one looks up *Nabis*, one finds, "*Nabis*: See modern art." *Bungalow* contains a blind reference to *Verandah*.

Shortcomings in the text coexist with the editing errors. *Nave* is defined as "The central part of a church, running lengthwise from the narthex to the chancel, and flanked by aisles," but *narthex* and *chancel* are not defined. The entry *Marbling* mentions this technique only in relation to bookbinding and not as a method of painting on furniture and walls. *Modern Interior Design* notes "Designers who left an indelible mark on modern furniture design were:" and then goes on to list the names of 25 individuals. One would expect that individuals "who left an indelible mark" would also have entries in this title; however, 11 of the 25 do not. This also occurs in the article *Modern Architecture*. Buckminster Fuller's death date is not noted although he died in 1983. While the author claims that 800 new entries have been added to this edition, numerous contemporary styles (high tech, postmodern), design groups (Memphis), and architects (Helmut Jahn) are not included.

This title uses a popular approach geared toward the novice. Martin Pegler's *Dictionary of Interior Design* (Crown, 1966), with 3,500 entries and 2,500 illustrations, offers a more comprehensive treatment of the field. Reprinted in 1983 by Fairchild with a changed format and a reduction in the number of illustrations, it remains a more scholarly treatment.

The preface of the review title states that "Home owners, interior designers, students, and teachers will find the book to be an essential reference work." However, public and academic libraries will continue to be better served by Pegler's *Dictionary of Interior Design*.

Comic Books and Strips: An Information Sourcebook. By Randall W. Scott. Oryx, 1988. 152p. indexes. paper $30 (0-89774-389-X).

016.7415 Comic books, strips, etc.—U.S.—Bibliography I Comic books, strips, etc.—U.S.—History and criticism [CIP] 88-22377

Since 1970, when popular culture in this country began to be studied seriously, the literature on comic books and strips has proliferated. This bibliography "collects, organizes, and annotates the most important information sources in the comics area: books, periodicals, and library collections." ("Most important" is defined as "makes a contribution to the field.") The list excludes individual periodical articles—an indexing project in itself—and limits its scope to comic strips and comic books, thereby excluding related areas like cartooning and animation.

Most of the 1,033 entries are English-language materials, and both the primary sources appearing as reprints and the secondary sources are usually less than 20 years old. Each entry is numbered consecutively and is followed by a brief, largely descriptive, annotation. The book is divided into five principal sections. "Core Library Collection," consisting of "the 100 most important titles...for college-level research," begins the bibliography. It is followed by a longer, less selective list of books meeting the general criteria of the sourcebook's compiler. The third chapter focuses on books that reprint comics, including a few translations of foreign comic strips into English. Scott then lists and annotates 53 periodicals and journals, most of which are specialty publications and not indexed in any source. Finally, he notes and describes 43 library collections related to comics in the U.S., Canada, Australia, and England.

Separate indexes for authors, titles, and subjects cite entries by citation number. While the indexes are generally accurate, they are incomplete. The subject index, for example, refers readers to entries dealing with *Mad Magazine*, "Peanuts," "Terry and the Pirates," and women comics creators, but it neglects to cite all entries in the bibliography on these topics.

Comic Books and Strips succeeds in bringing together a variety of significant primary and secondary sources of information on comics and comic strips. Although the book is expensive for its size, large public and academic libraries and other libraries with popular-culture collections will find this easy-to-use and well-designed sourcebook a very useful reference tool. Libraries developing collections in the area can rely on this as an authoritative selection source.

Embroidery and Needlepoint: An Information Sourcebook. By Sandra K. Copeland. Oryx, 1989. 150p. indexes. paper $46.50 (0-89774-442-X).

016.74644 Embroidery—Bibliography I Canvas embroidery—Bibliography [CIP] 88-19691

Embroidery and Needlepoint has been created by librarian and needleworking enthusiast Copeland to assist fellow needleworkers in identifying desired pattern books and enlarging their own personal needlecraft libraries. Listing over 1,600 books and periodicals, this bibliography emphasizes books published between 1950 and 1986, with the majority of titles from the 1970s. There are many newer embroidery and needlepoint books listed in *Books in Print* that are not included here. Many books from foreign countries are listed, since a person does not need to read the language in order to use the patterns.

Each entry includes complete bibliographic information, price, and a brief annotation. Books are arranged alphabetically by author within general subject categories such as "Openwork," "Crewel Embroidery," and "Bargello." Separate sections list periodicals and a core library collection. The core library list is not very useful for collection development purposes, since many of the books are out of print.

Author, title, and subject indexes are provided at the end of the bibliography. The subject index provides excellent access to materials by country and by type of needlework. The general subject arrangement of the bibliography is enhanced by subject index entries for terms like *children's stories*, *plants*, or *left-handed*. People looking for a specific pattern such as Mickey Mouse or pansy will have to figure out the broader subject heading. An aid for most public library reference collections, this title will provide better access to established circulating collections and serve as a guide to collection development for a popular subject, especially if a library is willing to search for out-of-print books.

Native American Basketry: An Annotated Bibliography. Comp. by Frank W. Porter. Greenwood, 1988. 249p. indexes. hardcover $39.95 (0-313-25363-3; ISSN 0193-6867).

016.74641'2 Indians of North America—Basket making—Bibliography 87-37570

Porter, author of several books on North American Indians, intends this bibliography to be a comprehensive listing of books, journal articles, dissertations, theses, museum pamphlets, and selected newspaper articles on Indian basketry. Over 1,100 entries are organized by major cultural areas of North America: Northeast, Southeast, Great Lakes, Plains, Great Basin, Southwest, California, Northwest, Plateau, Subarctic, and Arctic. The short annotations are 1 to 15 sentences in length and describe the subject matter, geographic area, and special features of each source. A few entries appear in more than one section because of the broad coverage of their text. Preceding the geographic divisions is a short list, not annotated, of general sources.

The introduction presents a fascinating history of native American basket making from the late 1800s, including the socioeconomic reasons for its decline in the 1920s. Porter states that there has been a recent revival of interest in Indian basketry, not only by collectors, but also archaeologists, ethnographers, and historians. Approximately one-fourth of the items listed are books; two-thirds are journals. Several entries predate 1900, with one from 1866. Although the entries date from every decade of the twentieth century, the majority come from the 1970s and 1980s. The journals include such popular titles as *Arizona Highways*, *Sunset*, and *Hobbies* and lesser-known publications like *American Indian Basketry*, *American Indian Art Magazine*, *School Arts*, and *University of California Publications in American Archaeology and Ethnology*. Topics covered include techniques, collections, social significance, and ethnic traditions of Indian baskets. Some annotations, such as the explanations of the dance basket and the Navajo wedding basket, are a treat to read. The book concludes with two indexes, author and subject, which are keyed to each entry in the bibliography. The subject index lists basket types—*coiled*, *plaited*, *root runner*, *twined*, and *wicker*—under *basketry types*, but there are no separate entries listed under *coiled*, *plaited*, etc. Likewise, individual names of basket makers and their tribes are listed under *basket makers*, but there are no separate entries under these names. Indian tribes are also listed in the subject index.

Native American Basketry will be useful to students, researchers, collectors, curators, and artists. It is recommended for purchase by academic, large public, and some special libraries.

Looking at Prints, Drawings and Watercolours: A Guide to Technical Terms. By Paul Goldman. British Museum Publications and J. Paul Getty Museum; dist. by J. Paul Getty Book Distribution Center, P.O. Box 2112, Santa Monica, CA 90406, 1989 (c1988). 64p. bibliog. illus. paper $8.95 (0-89236-148-4).

760'.03 Art—Dictionaries [CIP] 88-13241

With the aim of aiding gallery-goers, Goldman, a member of the Department of Prints and Drawings at the British Museum, brings together in this slim paperback almost 100 terms used by curators and art historians to describe traditional collections of prints, drawings, and watercolors. He defines and explains techniques (*cliché verre, squaring, metalpoint*); processes (*etching, oleography*); materials (*gum arabic, inks, fixatives*); and tools (*roulette, stylus, presses*). Distinctions among terms (*colour prints* and *coloured prints; ascribed to* and *attributed to*) are made clear. One is told how to distinguish between drypoint and etching and between an etching and an engraving. Goldman does not merely define terms. His entry *fabricated chalks (pastels)*, for example, discusses how pastels are made, their qualities, how artists use them, the paper needed, their origin in sixteenth-century Italy, and the famous artists who have employed them since then. The work's British origins intrude in spelling (*colour*) and in burying American terms such as *serigraph* and *silk screen* under *screenprinting*. Most of the terms are illustrated by color or black-and-white reproductions of prints, drawings, and watercolors from the collections of the British Museum and the J. Paul Getty Museum. As expected, thorough documentation is supplied in the captions.

An effective cross-reference network is employed. A bibliography of technical and historical books is provided at the end of the book in addition to the references at the end of some entries.

Large libraries will undoubtedly own a comprehensive dictionary of art terms, but Goldman's *Looking at Prints, Drawings and Watercolours* is attractive, readable, and authoritative, as well as a bargain. Libraries serving students and gallery-goers should consider it.

Contemporary Photographers. 2d ed. Ed. by Colin Naylor. St. James Press, 1988. 1,145p. bibliog. illus. hardcover $120 (0-912289-79-1).
770'.92'2 [B] Photographers—Biography ‖ Photography, Artistic [BKL]

This is an updated and expanded version of the 1982 first edition. Now published by St. James Press and edited solely by Colin Naylor, *Contemporary Photographers* retains the same scope and format. "The choice of 750 entrants is intended to reflect the best and most prominent of contemporary photographers; photographers from earlier generations whose reputations are essentially contemporary; and photographers from the inter-war years and after who continue to be important influences." Selection was made by a 20-member board of advisers, many of whom participated in the first edition. They include distinguished photographers and critics (for example, Cornell Capa, Beaumont Newhall, Aaron Scharf).

The alphabetically arranged entries begin with a biographical sketch covering date and place of birth, marriage and family, education, photographic studies and teachers, positions held, honors and awards, agent's name and address, and entrant's address or date and place of death. Next are listings of places and dates where individual and selected group exhibitions have been held, museums with major holdings of works, publications by the photographers, and major publications about them. This is followed, for living photographers, by comments by them on their own work or on the current state of photography and by a signed essay written by one of 175 contributors. The essays vary widely in style and content, from delightful personal reminiscenses to incisive critical analyses. Most entries (some 700) are accompanied by a black-and-white photograph, ranging in size from a full to one-quarter page. Living photographers were asked to choose the photo from their work for inclusion.

The first edition, with its 650 entries, was noted for its inclusion of a number of photographers from beyond North America and Western Europe. Several of the 100 additional entries in this new edition are in this category (for example, Tamás Féner from Hungary, Abbas from Iran), giving continued emphasis to wide geographic coverage. A spot check shows that entries from the first edition have been brought up to date in terms of publications and exhibits. The critical essays and the photographers' statements remain the same. Photographs included have in many cases changed (no doubt due to the choice living photographers were given to select their entries). The entire text has been reset, resulting in greater clarity and readability. The quality of the reproductions is generally very good—equal to or superior to that of the first edition.

Since the first edition of *Contemporary Photographers*, a similar work has appeared: *The Macmillan Biographical Encyclopedia of Photographic Artists and Innovators*, compiled by Turner Browne and Elaine Partnow (Macmillan, 1983 [*RBB* O 1 84]. The two works complement rather than duplicate one another. The Macmillan encyclopedia includes more people (2,000-plus) and encompasses the entire span of photographic history. Its criteria for inclusion are broader, covering lesser-known photographic innovators, scientists who contributed to the development of processes, and artists who work in a photographic style. Entries are shorter; although they include similar biographical, publication, exhibit, and museum collection information, they lack the photographers' comments and critical essays. Only 144 photographs are offered, contained in a separate section.

The second edition of *Contemporary Photographers* upholds the publication's reputation for accuracy and broad coverage. Recommended for academic, museum, and large public libraries, although libraries owning the first edition may have to weigh cost against the value of new information in making their purchase decision.

Wide Screen Movies: A History and Filmography of Wide Gauge Filmmaking. By Robert E. Carr and R. M. Hayes. McFarland, 1988. 502p. filmography. index. hardcover $39.95 (0-89950-242-3).
778.5'3 Wide screen processes (Cinematography)—History [CIP] 86-43093

Slightly more than one-half of this combined film history-filmography is devoted to an examination of wide-screen film, describing its evolution from the end of the nineteenth century to the present. Among the processes covered are cinemascope, cinerama, 70mm film, and a variety of sound technologies such as Digital Sound, Quadraphonic Sound, and Feelarama. The 3-D film process is not included except as it relates to wide-screen filmmaking.

Illustrations include a variety of black-and-white reproductions of film posters, stills from movies utilizing wide-screen technologies, and charts and diagrams clarifying the various techniques described. Because the discussion is sometimes technical, readers will need some background in the theory and technology of filmmaking. Although the emphasis is on American films, foreign films are included, and a special feature of this section of the book is its coverage of Soviet films using wide-screen technology. Each of the chapters is followed by an unannotated list of films made by processes described in the chapter; the film company and the year of release are noted for each.

Boldface entries in these lists also appear in the informative 206-page descriptive filmography that makes up the last half of the book. For each of the more than 200 alphabetically arranged films included here, full casts and technical support staff are provided along with basic information such as date and country of release, running time, and film process used. The authors state that many of the Russian films included in the filmography "have previously been unknown outside of the USSR," and that this filmography is the "first-ever, first-anywhere documentation of Soviet 70mm films."

A 35-page index to the narrative half of this reference source provides the reader with access to names of people associated with some aspect of wide-screen films and to the many film processes described in the book. Unfortunately, there is no index to the information in the filmography portion of *Wide Screen Movies*—a feature that would have made the book much more useful for the researcher.

Because of the specialized coverage of this reference source and the sometimes technical information in the narrative portion of the book, *Wide Screen Movies* would be most appropriate in large public libraries, university and college libraries supporting film studies, and all film libraries. Some of these libraries might also consider the option of having a circulating copy instead of or in addition to a copy in their noncirculating reference collections.

MUSIC

Music Directory Canada '88. 4th ed. CM Books, 20 Holly St., #101, Toronto, ON, Canada M4S 2E6, 1988. annual. 607p. bibliog. discography. paper $24.95 (ISSN 0820-0416).

780'.25 Music—Canada—Directories [OCLC] 84-646941

This useful directory has grown substantially since its inception in 1983. The new edition contains 140 more entries than the third, and several new sections, including "Music Consultants," "Music Merchandising," "Financial Services," and "Selected Discography of Canadian Artists." Sections that should prove especially useful to reference librarians are listings of music libraries, subject periodicals, music publishers, and a selected list of books on Canadian music and musicians. Musicians of all types—rock groups, popular singers, performers of classical music—will use those sections concerned with contracts and booking, promoters, audio and video suppliers, and rehearsal studios. For purposes of ready reference, the listing of associations, awards, award winners, and scheduled musical events is highly useful. The section "Artist Contacts" gives the name of Canadian artists, followed by type of music performed, management and booking information, music publisher, and record company.

Sections do not include introductory statements explaining selection criteria or contain statistical information such as attendance or revenue. Coverage of Canada's copyright legislation is not included, but there is a listing of lawyers and also the section "Performing and Mechanical Rights Societies." Dance groups are not included. Annual budgets of festivals, orchestras, or opera companies are not listed. However, fees for music schools and universities are given. Some entries are out of date or incomplete. For example, the opera schedule given for L'Opéra de Montréal does not include fall 1988 productions. Productions are not given for the Canadian Opera Company or the Vancouver Opera Association, the other two important Canadian opera associations. Unfortunately, the directory is not indexed.

The directory is devoted solely to Canadian musical life. For this reason, directories published in the U.S. that contain some information for Canada, for example, *Musical America* [*RBB* Ag 87] and *Music Industry Directory* (7th ed., 1983, Marquis), serve to supplement the extensive coverage given in *MDC '88*. For instance, *Musical America* contains information for Canadian dance companies. It is a good source for photographs, schedules of important events, and selected artists associated with large agencies and management companies. However, most of this information concerns U.S. musical events and performers. *MDC '88* has advertisements but no photographs.

This directory continues to be an important source of information for Canada's music industry and certainly contains far more information on music than the important *Corpus Almanac and Canadian Sourcebook* (Corpus Information Sources, 1965–   . For statistics on the industry, users can turn to *Canada Yearbook* (Statistics Canada, 1905–   . Libraries serving those interested in the Canadian music scene will want to purchase *Music Directory Canada*.

The Norton/Grove Concise Encyclopedia of Music. Ed. by Stanley Sadie. Norton, 1988. 850p. illus. hardcover $40 (0-393-02620-5).

780.321 Music—Dictionaries I Music—Bio-bibliography [OCLC]

The word *concise* is the key to this one-volume encyclopedia edited by Sadie, who also edited *The New Grove Dictionary of Music and Musicians* (1980). However, in the preface he writes that *The Norton/Grove* "should not be regarded as a concise version of the 20-volume *New Grove*." He continues that it was "conceived and written for a different readership...a broad sweep of music-lovers and students." However, he believes that it will also be used by *The New Grove*'s readership for quick or updated information.

The volume is called *The Norton/Grove* because it has the same editor and *The New Grove* was used as the main source of information. An attempt was made to retain the authority of *The New Grove*, with the articles written by specialists but edited by the editor and his assistants, so there would be a uniformity of style.

The entries are in dictionary form with letter-by-letter alphabetization. British terminology is prominent, transliteration follows *The New Grove*, and *see also* references are italicized. The contents include all areas of music—composers, instruments, terminology, performers, and other topics that relate to any aspect of music. There are also over 1,000 entries under names or nicknames of individual works of music, a feature *The New Grove* does not have.

Examples of the broad range of topics are *Billings, William*; *Biggs, E. Power*; *carillon*; *duplet*; *foxtrot*; *Heiligmesse*; *Herman, Woody*; *jive*; *piccolo*; *Syracuse Symphony Orchestra*; *rosin*; and *Wolf Trap Farm Park*. There is a definite emphasis on classical music, although there are the entries *Beatles*, *punk rock*, and *reggae*. For major composers a list of significant works and their completion dates is given. There are some illustrations such as the Bach family tree, early instruments, the diagram of a modern symphony orchestra, and music examples. Although the editor says that *The New Grove* was used only as a source, some phrases and sentences are the same in both works.

Compared with *The New Harvard Dictionary of Music* (1986) and *The New Oxford Companion to Music* (1983), the following differences were noted. The articles are not signed as are those in the two-volume *New Oxford Companion*. Both *The New Oxford Companion* and *The New Harvard* have bibliographies for longer entries; *The Norton/Grove* has none. In a random check of a variety of entries, *The Norton/Grove* is more complete but has shorter entries. It is also more current with facts such as the appointment of Michael Tilson Thomas as the conductor of the London Symphony Orchestra in 1988.

With over 10,000 entries and in the tradition of *The New Grove*, *The Norton/Grove* is certainly an important item for any reference collection. Its modest price makes it particularly attractive for small libraries, and in larger libraries it will complement *The New Oxford Companion*, *The New Harvard*, and even *The New Grove*.

Music Reference and Research Materials: An Annotated Bibliography. 4th ed. By Vincent H. Duckles and Michael A. Keller. Schirmer, 1988. 714p. indexes. hardcover $34.95 (0-02-870390-1).

016.78 Music—Bibliography I Music—History and criticism—Bibliography I Bibliography—Bibliography—Music [CIP] 88-18530

Music Reference and Research Materials is to the music library what Sheehy is to the general reference library. The fourth edition continues in much expanded form the high standards established in previous editions. (The third edition was reviewed by the Board [*RSBR* D 1 74].) Commonly referred to by music librarians and researchers simply as Duckles, the work is arguably the best single guide to reference sources in the field of music. Begun by the noted musicologist-bibliographer-librarian Duckles, the fourth edition became a joint undertaking with Keller, his successor at the University of California-Berkeley, who completed the work after Duckles' death.

Like the earlier editions, Duckles is an annotated bibliography of numbered entries arranged alphabetically by author within broad categories (dictionaries and encyclopedias, bibliographies of music, catalogs of music libraries, discographies, etc.), which in turn are subdivided into narrower subjects. There are more than 3,200 entries compared with over 1,900 in the last edition. Materials published through 1986 are included. An entry may be listed in more than one section when its content is relevant.

Coverage is international and includes Asian materials. Non-Roman titles are transliterated. The clearly written annotations are descriptive with occasional critical comment, and a citation to a review is given for a minority of entries. As in previous editions, biographies as such are excluded, although biographical dictionaries and bibliographies of music by and writings about the music of individual composers are included. The fourth edition reflects current interest with a "Women in Music" section and inclusion of computer-based reference sources. Duckles concludes with indexes totaling 160 pages. Separate indexes treat personal names (authors, editors, reviewers), subjects, and titles.

Music Reference and Research Materials is highly recommended for all reference collections where users are seriously interested in music; it will receive repeated use from both librarians and researchers. The fourth edition is a necessary acquisition because of the quantity of new material added since the last edition. Major libraries may wish to keep earlier editions for information on materials that have been dropped. For its content and price, Duckles is a "first purchase" item for many public and academic libraries.

Blacks in Classical Music: A Bibliographical Guide to Composers, Performers, and Ensembles. Comp. by John Gray. Greenwood, 1988. indexes. hardcover $39.95 (0-313-26056-7; ISSN 0736-7740).

016.78'043 Musicians, Black—Bibliography I Afro-American musicians—Bibliography [CIP] 87-37567

Blacks in Classical Music is an index of biographical information on approximately 300 black composers, performers, conductors, symphony orchestras, and opera companies. The compiler, using Standifer and Reeder's 1972 *Source Book of African and Afro-American Materials for Music Educators* as a starting point, lists materials in periodicals, dissertations, and reference books from the 1700s to the 1980s, with the great majority from the twentieth century. An attempt has been made to list European, African, and Western Hemisphere materials comprehensively, except for items from *Music Index* after the 1979-80 cumulation. Materials on Paul Robeson and Marian Anderson are deliberately limited (because of recent bibliographies on each), and reviews of eight major opera and concert singers are represented selectively.

Two criteria for inclusion of musicians are cited: identification "at some point as a person of color" and activity in Western or "Westernderived 'art music.'" Non-U.S. musicians have their country of birth noted.

The final sections list pertinent reference books (periodical indexes, biographical dictionaries, bibliographies of books and recordings) and major centers for research in black music. Alphabetical indexes of artists and authors conclude the work.

Other indexes to biographical information about black performers cover Afro-American music (e.g., gospel, jazz). While a few well-known singers such as Marian Anderson and Leontyne Price are found in books like Skowronski's *Black Music in America: A Bibliography* (Scarecrow, 1981 [*RSBR* F 1 83]), the strength of this new book is the number of black composers and performers of classical music included. Library patrons with a particular artist's name in mind will be able to find many of the citations here by using *Music Index, Readers' Guide,* and *New York Times Index.* Many of the people listed in *Blacks in Classical Music* are not well known, however, so the book will prove useful to those looking for the names of blacks in the field, as well as a timesaver for those looking for information on a specific person.

Film, Television and Stage Music on Phonographic Records: A Discography. By Steve Harris. McFarland, 1988. 445p. bibliog. index. hardcover $49.95 (0-89950-251-2).

016.7899'12283 Motion picture music—Discography II Television music—Discography I Musical revues, comedies, etc.—Discography [CIP] 87-42509

This discography "concentrates on original and adapted music composed specifically" for theatrical films, television productions, and stage musicals in the U.S. and Britain. The more than 11,000 entries are arranged by production title in three sections ("Film Music," "Television Music," and "Stage Music"), with subsections under each listing related records (pure dialogue records, themes inspired by productions, themes actually written for a different medium, and miscellaneous unverified or erroneous listings). The discography generally provides the following information for each record in a highly abbreviated fashion, which can be tedious to read: production title, date, music quantity (e.g., score, excerpts, etc.), country of pressing, record format, record label, and number. Performer credits are not usually given. Composer credits generally are included only for main record listings, not for related music. A composer index completes access to the recordings.

Recommended as a reference and collection development tool for music libraries and libraries with very strong record collections, this discography will be particularly useful in colleges with courses in music composition for film and television.

The Literature of American Music in Books and Folk Music Collections: A Fully Annotated Bibliography: Supplement I. By David Horn and Richard Jackson. Scarecrow, 1988. 570p. indexes. hardcover $49.50 (0-8108-1997-X).

016.781773 Music—U.S.—History and criticism—Bibliography [CIP] 87-9630

Horn's *Supplement* virtually doubles the coverage of a valuable reference source that first appeared in 1977 [*RSBR* D 15 77]: the basic volume included 1,888 annotated entries for books about American music plus 808 unannotated titles added at the end. The *Supplement* includes somewhat over 2,100 additional titles published through 1980. Horn retains the same classified arrangement used in the original volume and continues to list both scholarly and popular titles. The subtitle *A Fully Annotated Bibliography* is misleading insofar as over half of the titles appear with no commentary at all, grouped at the end of sections or at the end of the book. On the other hand, the annotations do deserve mention, since those for the remaining half are characteristically thoughtful in their evaluations and, in their highly personal style, engaging to read—often more so than the books in question. Furthermore, with some possible exceptions, the titles chosen for inclusion without annotation seem likely to be the less important ones.

For this *Supplement*, Horn, music librarian at the University of Exeter in England, has called on the assistance of Jackson, American music specialist at the New York Public Library at Lincoln Center. The relative coverage of topics has changed somewhat, suggesting a varying emphasis over the decade, whether of the field or of its literature. The modest coverage of American art music has become even smaller, for instance; black music is also down a bit, although perhaps now extensively dispersed in the coverage of popular music, which is virtually doubled to now include a separate category on rock and related topics. One wishes that the indexes in the *Supplement*, separate by subject, name, and title, had been merged as they were in the 1977 set and that both volumes might have been cumulatively indexed here. This *Supplement*, along with the basic 1977 volume, will nevertheless be useful in academic and public libraries that serve a musical audience of almost any kind.

Music: A Guide to the Reference Literature. By William S. Brockman. Libraries Unlimited, 1988 (c1987). 254p. indexes. hardcover $38.50 (0-87287-526-1).

016.78 Music—Bibliography I Reference books—Music—Bibliography [CIP] 87-26462

Brockman's bibliography is a selective annotated list of 559 reference sources on music. Excluded are works not issued separately—for example, lists published in journals. The book will likely be helpful less as a daily reference source than as an acquisitions tool for filling gaps in the reference collection, or as a possible textbook for music bibliography courses built around sources rather than services. It is arranged by type of work: general guides, dictionaries, biographical sets, bibliographies, discographies, etc. Thus reference sources relating to topics like jazz, opera, and folksong are scattered according to format, although they can be extracted using the general subject index.

The book inevitably evokes comparison with standard sources such as Vincent Duckles' *Music Reference and Research Materials* (3d ed., 1974 [*RSBR* D 1 74]), a new edition of which is scheduled to appear this fall, and Guy Marco's *Information on Music* (3 vol., 1975-84). The compiler states that his work "does not attempt to compete" with them, but instead "is offered as a summary guide." For example, international and retrospective coverage is not as complete. At the same time, he does venture into a number of highly specialized areas (e.g., detailed contents listings for five bibliographical series) and includes a good many items that would seem appropriate only to musicology research collections. A few of his ideas seem slightly odd (for instance, the impact of Sonneck's 1905 American music bibliography on current interest in the field), but most of the lengthy annotations are useful in guiding the reader.

The strength of Brockman's work lies in its currency; it appears to be reasonably comprehensive up into mid-1987. This is further reflected in two supplementary lists, the first of which cites 105 major music periodicals, the second, 172 associations, research centers, and other organizations. This book should be especially useful for those libraries seeking to update their music reference collections.

The Music Locator, 1988. 4th ed. Resource Publications, 1988. 1,193p. paper $110 (0-89390-111-3).

016.783'02 Church music—Bibliography [OCLC] 88-3180

The Recording Locator, 1988. Rev. ed. Resource Publications, 1988 (c1987). 1,047p. annual, with three quarterly supplements. paper $160 (0-89390-115-6).

011.38 Gospel music—Discography I Church music—Discography [BKL]

Resource Publications has produced two indexes to Christian music to serve wholly different purposes. *The Music Locator* is a huge, sewn paperback that lists over 114,000 songs in sheet music and songbooks. Designed for use by music dealers, musicians, publishers, and researchers, the work identifies composer, publisher, theme, and style, so that appropriate music may be selected for services. Instructions for use are quite clear; the "Quick Guide to the Music Locator" is followed by "How to Find a Song" and "Planning Music." A complete list of abbreviations is also included.

All of the music is listed at least three times: by title, composer, and category. The alphabetical title index is by far the most thorough and includes composer/arranger, publisher code, copyright year, songbook number, if any, and notes about arrangement. Notes indicate whether a piece is scored for piano, brass, mixed chorus of four parts, or other type of arrangement. Much of the music is for four voices or organ. A user looking for handbell music for "Angels We Have Heard on High" will find five songbook entries, with four different arrangements.

Also included with each entry is a style code (marking the piece as folk, gospel, contemporary, rock, traditional, or children's) and one of 52 category codes supplied by the publishers. Categories indicate the theme, season, or liturgical use of a work (e.g., to be used in advent, at baptisms, or with psalms), and helpful cross-references are given for related categories. For example, for *Confirmation* the user is also directed to *Holy Spirit and Pentecost*, *Baptism*, and *Thanksgiving and Praise*.

Works may also be located using the composer or category indexes. Someone looking for gospel wedding music will find 26 titles to chose from and can refer to each title for specifics. The computer-produced alphabetical arrangement creates one of the only problems; *Saint Saens* is listed separately from *St. Saens*, and over 200 entries for "Amazing Grace" are separate from "Amazing Grace! How Sweet the Sound" and from "Amazing Grace, How Sweet the Sound." Separate lists of songbooks and publisher codes and addresses are found at the end, along with an appendix of copyright information.

The Music Locator is current enough so Amy Grant's 1987 arrangements are listed. Other contemporary composers include Dion, Stephen Schwartz, and Joni Mitchell. The classification of "Rock," which is new to this edition, includes Twila Paris and Keith Green. This update is twice the size of the last (1984) edition. Omitted is the section on liturgical planning, but the book is otherwise much improved. Print is still small, but margins are slightly larger than before. A first-line index would be helpful, as would a selection statement. Inexplicably, some secular music, such as "Frosty the Snowman" and Bob Marley's "I Shot the Sheriff," is included even though not part of an indexed songbook. Still, this work is extremely useful and should be part of most church, music, and large public library collections.

The Recording Locator, however, serves a much narrower purpose. It includes over 100,000 recorded religious song titles and seems primarily for retail use. The largest section of the book is the song list, which alphabetically lists titles and then the names of artists who recorded them, along with the album title and publisher code. Someone looking for Mahalia Jackson singing "I Believe" would find it on three separate albums. The "Artist Listing" then presents titles of individual songs on the album.

Finally there are album, accompaniment tape, music video, and publisher lists. The "Quick Guide to the Recording Locator" makes abbreviations and arrangement clear. All recording formats are included—LP, single 45, compact disc, 8-track, and cassette—and entries note whether each is currently available. Many titles are out of print, so far more are included here than in *Schwann*.

As in the *The Music Locator*, the alphabetical arrangement causes some problems. "Wedding Song (The)" and "Wedding Song, The" are far apart in the lists. Another problem is the lack of a first-line index, practically essential for looking up songs. Currency may be a problem, too. "Kyrie Eleison" is listed, but not for the rock group that recorded it in 1986. While this work is notable for its listing of album tracks and its quarterly supplements, it is not a replacement for *Schwann* and will be of interest primarily to religious music retailers and researchers.

The Schirmer Guide to Schools of Music and Conservatories throughout the World. By Nancy Uscher. Schirmer, 1988. 635p. indexes. hardcover $60 (0-02-873030-5).

780'.7 Conservatories of music—Directories [CIP] 88-1518

The Schirmer Guide to Schools of Music and Conservatories is a straightforward work whose coverage of hard-to-find foreign institutions will be a major selling point, although it also offers comprehensive U.S. coverage.

Arranged alphabetically by U.S. states and foreign countries, the body of the *Guide* lists more than 750 institutions offering professional musical training, with mailing address, telephone number, chief administrator, and accreditation. After a brief statement of the school's purpose, entries include academic information (number of students and faculty, entrance requirements, degree requirements, and areas of specialization available); facilities (concert halls, practice rooms, concert series, library); performance groups; costs (as of the 1986–87 school year); and financial aid. To be included in the *Guide*, U.S. institutions generally must offer at least a master's degree or have more than 10 full-time faculty members above the rank of instructor. Outside of the U.S. and Canada only schools that emphasize musical performance are entered. Foreign universities that offer music as an academic discipline are omitted.

Three alphabetical indexes complete the *Guide*. The first lists schools by name, with city and country; the second and third index schools under areas of study (e.g., accompanying, Afro-American music, choral conducting) and instruments taught.

The Schirmer Guide is a directory that will be used by music and school librarians to help prospective undergraduate music students choose a suitable school. It will also assist undergraduate students considering graduate study. As with all directories, its information will become out-of-date as time passes, and reference librarians will have to decide whether its use will justify the price. Less comprehensive information for the U.S. can be found in the *Music Industry Directory* (7th ed., 1983), the annual *Performing Arts Directory*, and the biennial *Directory of Music Faculties in Colleges and Universities, U.S. and Canada*, but librarians building strong music reference collections will find *The Schirmer Guide* of value.

The Concise Baker's Biographical Dictionary of Musicians. By Nicolas Slonimsky. Schirmer, 1988. 1,407p. hardcover $35 (0-02-872411-9).

780'.92 [B] Music—Bio-bibliography I Musicians—Biography—Dictionaries [OCLC] 87-32328

Slonimsky has been associated with *Baker's Biographical Dictionary of Musicians* since the supplement to the fourth edition in 1949. The current work is an abridgment of the seventh edition (1984) and was conceived as "a music dictionary for quick reference, giving prominence to great figures of music but eliminating the secondary entries." There are neither additions to nor updating of the seventh edition's text; however, a five-page necrology lists name, city, and death date for musicians included in the seventh edition who have died since its publication.

For many, there is no better authority than Slonimsky to be entrusted with the task of selecting names to be retained or dropped. However, in the preface, he is not much help in identifying criteria for inclusion: "The problem in the present abridged edition is to separate true artists of the people from imitators and crown followers." So out go Gerry Mulligan, Linda Ronstadt, Roy Orbison, Giovanni Martinelli, and Patrice Munsel, while surviving the cut are George Harrison, Miles Davis, and Placido Domingo. Contemporary pop music is heavily cut, but this is not surprising given Slonimsky's classical orientation and the difficulty of assessing lasting contributions in an increasingly trendy industry.

The problems with this concise edition are not ones of selection but of format and the shortening of entry information. This work's outside dimensions, sturdy binding, paper, and printing are identical to that of the seventh edition, but the number of pages has been reduced from 2,577 to 1,407. Although shorter, *The Concise Baker's* is hardly a desk edition in the style, for example, of the concise Oxford dictionaries.

The method of text deletion is a more serious problem. In addition to the exclusion of "secondary" musicians, abridgment was accomplished by shortening the "Works" and "Writings" sections of entries that included them and dropping all bibliographies (e.g., 4½ pages of the Mozart article). The cutting of some composers' listings of works is a highly questionable method of text deletion. The works of major composers remain intact from the full edition, but others have had them trimmed at seemingly arbitrary points. For example, Elisabeth Lutyens, an important English composer, has an entry in the seventh edition that includes works under sections for stage, orchestra, chamber music, piano, and vocal, while in the concise edition, only the first two listings (stage and orchestra) are retained. Another example is Boris Blacker, whose works are minus the last four genres in the seventh edition. Slonimsky's preface is as anecdotal and entertaining as ever, but it is difficult to come up with a justification for this edition for libraries, as presently formatted and edited. Much has been lost, the editing of some composers' lists of works gives erroneous impressions of careers, and, at a weight of six pounds, it is abridged but not compact. While the reasonable price may make it attractive for home use, libraries will want the full seventh edition, still available from Macmillan for $95.

Encyclopedia of Pop, Rock & Soul. Rev. ed. By Irwin Stambler. St. Martin's, 1989. 881p. bibliog. illus. hardcover $35 (0-312-02573-4).

784.5'0092 Popular music—Dictionaries I Popular music—Bio-bibliography I Rock music—Dictionaries I Rock music—Bio-bibliography I Soul music—Dictionaries [CIP] 88-29860

Encyclopedia of Rock. Rev. ed. By Phil Hardy and Dave Laing. Schirmer, 1989 (c1988). 480p. illus. hardcover $40 (0-02-919562-4).

781.66'0092 Rock music—Dictionaries I Rock music—Bio-bibliography [BKL]

The Harmony Illustrated Encyclopedia of Rock. 6th ed. By Pete Frame and others. Harmony; dist. by Crown, 1988. 208p. discography. illus. paper $14.95 (0-517-57164-1).

784.5'4 Rock music—Dictionaries [CIP] 88-21473

These three encyclopedias of rock overlap in their coverage of performers, but each has unique features. Libraries wishing to update their coverage of popular music should consider purchasing one or more of them for reference and/or circulating collections.

The revision of *The Encyclopedia of Pop, Rock & Soul* updates the 1974 edition [*RSBR* Jl 15 75]. The dictionary arrangement of the first edition is unchanged, as is the inclusion of three updated appendixes showing platinum- and gold-record awards, Grammy awards, and Oscar music nominations and winners. The first edition included topical entries (e.g., *acid rock, disco, reggae*) and entries for popular musicals (*Cabaret, Hair, Man of La Mancha*) in addition to entries for performers, but they have been dropped from the new edition. Those minor deletions notwithstanding, it is surprising to find that with a decade and a half of new performers to include, the revised edition contains fewer entries than the original one. Among the better-known performers dropped are America, Joan Baez, Glen Campbell, Vicki Carr, and Judy Collins. New to this edition are Abba, Joan Armatrading, George Benson, Blondie, Bon Jovi, Irene Cara, Cher, and Jimmy Cliff. For the most part, entries common to both editions have been updated but not substantially rewritten. The more than 450 articles tend to be lengthy; the one on Bob Dylan, for instance, is 3½ pages. There are no special articles as found in the first edition; the bibliography of popular news articles highlighting individual artists has been updated. There are inserts with more than 90 black-and-white photographs of performers. This edition, like its predecessor, would be improved by the addition of running headers, as entries often span more than one page.

An expanded edition of the 1976 publication of the same name, the *Encyclopedia of Rock* includes entries for solo artists, bands, musical styles, and important people, places, and historic events associated with rock. With more than 1,500 entries, many of the performers deleted from the *Encyclopedia of Pop, Rock & Soul* still can be found here. Corresponding entries in this book are generally shorter than those in the *Encyclopedia of Pop, Rock & Soul*. The layout (with both black-and-white and color photographs interspersed throughout the text, running headers, and a much clearer typeface) makes the *Encyclopedia of Rock* easier to use and more pleasing to the eye than the *Encyclopedia of Pop, Rock & Soul*. Unlike the latter, the *Encyclopedia of Rock* has no bibliography.

Visually, *The Harmony Illustrated Encyclopedia of Rock* resembles the *Encyclopedia of Rock*. The layout is excellent with color photographs throughout the text. However, there are fewer entries (there are "over 700" full-length entries plus, in the appendix, brief notes on some 500 additional artists). Compiled in Britain, a special feature of *The Harmony Illustrated Encyclopedia* is mention of both U.S. and U.K. gold and platinum albums in entries for performers. Some of the British performers included are unknown in the U.S. *The Harmony Illustrated Encyclopedia* has two unique features: discographies for all entries, with an effort made to indicate the label on which individual albums currently appear; and 12 "family trees" that visually delineate the changing personnel of interrelated performing groups.

Find That Tune: An Index to Rock, Folk-Rock, Disco & Soul in Collections. v.2. Ed. by Sue Sharma and William Gargan. Neal-Schuman, 1989. 387p. hardcover $49.95 (1-55570-019-5).

781.66'124 Rock music—Indexes I Disco music—Indexes [BKL]

Find That Tune [*RBB* D 1 84] was originally published to the acclaim of musicians and librarians who recognized that previously published tools for locating sheet music of popular genres had inadequately covered rock music. The first volume indexed 203 collections of sheet music; volume 2 indexes an additional 202 collections. While volume 1 covered music from 1950 to 1981, volume 2 extends that coverage to 1985. *Find That Tune* emphasizes collections of rock, folk-rock, disco, and soul music.

The organization of the second volume is unchanged from that of the first. Of the five sections, part 1 lists collections indexed alphabetically by title; part 2 lists individual songs alphabetically by title, including with each entry "information on composers and lyricists, performers, publishers, and copyright dates" and numeric references to the collections in which the tunes may be found; part 3 is a first-line index, with reference to the title index; part 4 is an alphabetical listing of composers and lyricists, with titles of songs indexed under each artist; and part 5 is a listing of individual performers and groups, with titles of songs again indexed under each artist. (The editors state that "as a result of suggestions from reviewers of Volume 1, a greater effort was made to identify multiple performers for each song.") While easy to use, the organizing principle that gives users references from parts 3, 4, and 5 to part 2 rather than part 1 requires that users consult at least two and sometimes 3 indexes to locate a collection of sheet music containing the particular tune of their interest. This minor drawback aside, *Find That Tune*, volume 2, is highly recommended for libraries with collections of popular sheet music, regardless of whether they own the previous volume.

Opera Annual: U.S. 1984–85. Jerome S. Ozer, 1988. 642p. illus. index. hardcover $48 (0-89198-132-2; ISSN 0899-3645).
782.1073 Opera—U.S. [BKL]

Opera Annual: U.S. 1984–85 is to be the first volume of an annual series reproducing newspaper reviews of performances by major U.S. opera companies. The 1984–85 season was chosen because it was the first in which the now ubiquitous surtitles (slide projections of the English translation of the libretto) came into general use in the U.S.

Reviews in the *Annual* are arranged alphabetically by opera title. Works include light operas (*The Student Prince, Sweeney Todd, A Little Night Music*) formerly not presented by "serious" U.S. companies. The language of the title is apparently the one commonly used in the U.S., although *Il Barbiere di Siviglia* and *La Fanciulla del West* are less used by Americans than *Barber of Seville* and *Girl of the Golden West*.

Following each title are signed reviews of performances by 37 U.S. opera companies. Popular operas such as *Madama Butterfly* and *La Traviata* are represented by reviews of productions by seven or eight companies. Each review is accompanied by a facsimile of the program listing cast, conductor, director, and major production designers and by at least one black-and-white photograph showing stage settings or singers in costume, although occasionally a less informative portrait of a composer or designer is substituted. (*The Rake's Progress* review strangely omits any picture of the striking settings and costumes by David Hockney, providing only a photograph of the designer.)

Reviews are presented in full or in generous excerpts. When there were only one or two reviews, the full text is quoted. If there were multiple reviews of the same production, "review essays" were created to avoid excessive repetition, with editorial bridging indicated by the use of italic type. A 22-page index of all personal names mentioned in the facsimile programs and reviews concludes the *Annual*.

Despite minor typographical errors, the *Opera Annual* is an opera-loving browser's delight, but it will not be indispensable in libraries owning newspapers from major cities. Comprehensive reviews of U.S. operatic productions are also found in *Opera News*. Nevertheless, *Opera Annual* will be useful in music reference collections, especially if future volumes can be published in a more timely fashion.

Catalog of the American Musical. By Tommy Krasker and Robert Kimball. National Institute for Music Theater, John F. Kennedy Center for the Performing Arts, Washington, DC 20566, 1988. 442p. index. hardcover $60 (0-9618575-0-1).
782.81 Musical revue, comedy, etc.—U.S. [BKL] 87-61421

Preservation of materials, regardless of format, is among the most urgent problems facing the library community today. This catalog describes itself as the first phase of a national effort to locate and rescue original performance materials of the American musical theater. This initial volume surveys 75 book musicals of Irving Berlin, George and Ira Gershwin, Cole Porter, and Richard Rodgers and Lorenz Hart, documenting the location and completeness of all original piano-vocal scores, lyrics and libretti, and orchestra scores and parts. Thanks to funding from the National Endowment for the Arts and other sources, the search for research materials was undertaken in a variety of 18 repositories in Washington, D.C. (Library of Congress); the New York area (e.g., New York Public Library, Rodgers and Hammerstein Theatre Library, Shubert Archives, and an astonishing find at the Warner Brothers Music warehouse in Secaucus, N.J.); Amherst (Amherst College Library); New Haven (Yale University Library); and Los Angeles (the private collection of Ira Gershwin).

Following a one-page career profile of the songwriter, information on each musical (in chronological arrangement by its first New York run) is presented in a uniform format. There is basic information about the show itself: title in the original New York run, music and lyric credits, type of show (musical comedy, operetta, etc.), number of acts, opening date and length of the original New York production, producer, director, choreographer, musical director/conductor, a synopsis of the story, comments on such matters as an outstanding cast member or the show's reception, location of original materials, rental status, music publisher, and organizations to contact for further information.

Then follows detailed information on each song written or intended for a show's Broadway run or composed later for road companies, film versions, or revivals; information includes the composer and lyricist; the orchestrator; the location of the composer's manuscript, sheet music, most complete music, most complete lyric, original orchestra score, and original orchestra parts; and notes (alternate titles, historical footnotes, etc.). The appendix lists abbreviations; addresses of rental agents, authors' estates, and repositories of scripts and musical manuscripts; and addresses for inquiries about nonbook musical works by these songwriters. The volume concludes with an index of the more than 1,600 songs listed in the catalog.

This thoroughly researched catalog sets a very high standard for compilers of subsequent volumes on American musicals and can be recommended to public and academic libraries collecting in the area of American musical theater.

Gänzl's Book of the Musical Theatre. By Kurt Gänzl and Andrew Lamb. Schirmer, 1989. 1,353p. discography. illus. indexes. hardcover $75 (0-02-871941-7).
782.81 Musical revues, comedies, etc.—Stories, plots, etc. I Operas—Stories, plots, etc. [CIP] 88-18588

Musical theater in this work encompasses the operetta, comic opera, musical comedy, and what is now simply known as the musical. The book is patterned after *The Definitive Kobbé's Opera Book* [RBB Ja 15 88], as entries of four to six pages include a listing of significant stage and film productions, a cast of characters, and a synopsis of each act. Within the synopsis are references to each song in the production. A distinctive feature is *Gänzl's* international coverage. Arrangement is in five parts, by country, with shows given in chronological order. The 69 selections for Great Britain range from *The Beggar's Opera* (1782) to *The Phantom of the Opera* (1987). France's 53 entries extend to *Les Misérables* (1980). The U.S.' 95 selections begin with *Robin Hood* (1890) and conclude with *La Cage aux Folles* (1983). Part 4 covers Austria, Germany, and Hungary's 74 musical productions from 1865 to 1964. Seven shows are listed for Spain, with the latest, *Luisa Fernanda*, produced in 1932. According to the authors, these are the countries "where the light of musical theatre has grown and blossomed." Each of the five parts is prefaced by an introductory essay on the history of musical theater in that country or countries.

Opera has an established repertoire, but the authors of a guide to musical theater must make selections from thousands of productions, and new shows are staged every year. The productions chosen for inclusion in this work had to meet at least one of three rather disparate criteria: (1) shows that theatergoers would most likely encounter on current stages, (2) productions that have historical significance, or (3) shows that are the authors' favorites, including those that "deserve" a reappearance on the modern stage. This makes for an odd, albeit appealing, mix of the popular and the obscure.

The book concludes with a selective discography of long-playing recordings, presented in the same order as the shows. Entries include original cast recordings and film soundtracks, both in the original language and in translations, as well as "the most interesting and accessible of other recordings." For example, *Jesus Christ Superstar* (1971) includes the concept album, Broadway cast recording, film soundtrack, original cast recordings from 10 other countries, and the Spanish and Swedish revival cast recordings done in the mid-1980s. There is an index of production titles, authors, composers, and lyricists, as well as an index for song titles. The 32 pages of black-and-white photographs are well chosen.

What *Kobbé's* does for opera, *Gänzl's* now provides for a selection of 300 pieces from the repertoire of the light musical theater. Its historical and international coverage gives breadth, rather than comprehensiveness (e.g., no American musicals are listed for the past five years). There are many books that survey the history of musical theater for particular countries and traditions, including Gänzl's recent *British Musical Theatre* (Oxford, 1987), but a broadly based synopsis treatment is a valuable addition to library collections.

The Great Song Thesaurus. 2d ed. By Roger Lax and Frederick Smith. Oxford, 1989. 774p. indexes. hardcover $75 (0-19-505408-3).

784.5'0016 Popular music—Indexes [CIP] 88-31267

The original edition of *The Great Song Thesaurus* [RBB My 15 85] contained information on about 10,000 songs well known in the English-speaking world. The second edition adds information on an additional 1,000 songs that enjoyed popularity between 1980 and 1987. The second edition also adds a new index, "Lyric Key Lines," to the indexes included in the original work. This index enables the user to ascertain the title of a song by looking under the best-known lines of the text. Thus, one can determine that the title of the song that begins with the words "Way down upon the Swanee River" is "Old Folks at Home."

This new index should prove particularly useful in view of the fact that the main section of the book is arranged by song title. Each entry in this section includes the names of the lyricist and composer, the year of composition, the names of musicals or films in which the song was featured, the names of performers associated with the song, and other significant or interesting points of information.

The second-longest section, "The Greatest Hits," provides a chronological listing of notable songs and top hits from 1529 ("A Mighty Fortress Is Our God") through 1986. Notes on historical events and significant developments in music place the songs in their historical contexts. Shorter sections provide listings of award-winning songs, "Themes, Trademarks, and Signatures," and plagiarisms and adaptations.

In addition to the new "Lyric Key Lines" index, the "Song Titles" section is indexed by lyricist and composer (although the entries do not distinguish one from the other) as well as by subject, keyword, and category. The index entitled "American and British Theatre, Film, Radio, and Television" lists under the names of musicals, films, and radio and television programs the titles of songs that owe their popularity to these sources.

The review of the first edition of *The Great Song Thesaurus* characterized it as "an invaluable source for any library with a popular music collection" and stated that it would "also be extremely useful in general reference collections." In view of the work's expanded coverage, wealth of information, and multiple types of access, the original recommendation can be strongly endorsed.

Who Wrote That Song? By Dick Jacobs. Betterway, 1988. 415p. illus. index. hardcover $29.95 (1-55870-108-7); paper $17.95 (1-55870-100-1).

784.5'00973 Popular music—U.S.—Bibliography [CIP] 88-19351

Who Wrote That Song? is a guide to the works of over 5,000 songwriters and lyricists, listing more than 11,000 songs. The work is in three main sections: "The Songs," "The Songwriters," and "The Award Winners." Each entry in "The Songs" identifies the name of the composer and/or lyricist, gives the names of artists who introduced or popularized the song and any Broadway shows or films in which it was used, and lists performers on "cover records" ("a competing record made of the same song after the original record of the song has been issued") and revival recordings. Entries in "The Songwriters" list all the songs credited to the composer or lyricist. If a song is credited to more than one person (e.g., Lennon and McCartney), it is listed under both names. "The Award Winners" lists winners of Academy Awards, NARAS (Grammy) Awards, and Songwriters Hall of Fame Awards.

While the songs listed are mainly popular ones from the twentieth century, a few well-known classical works that have been recorded in a popular style (e.g., Deodato's jazz version of "Also Sprach Zarathustra," the theme music for the movie *2001: A Space Odyssey*) are included. *Who Wrote That Song?* has reminiscences and photographs from the author's 40 years as an arranger, producer, and director in the music industry interspersed with entries. A trivia quiz (whose answers may be found within the book) is included at the end of the book. *Who Wrote That Song?* would have been more useful as a reference tool had a discography (at least covering original performances) been included.

There are many song indexes covering show tunes or movie music or songs in collections. (See "Song Indexes" [RBB D 1 86] for a list of these titles.) However, because of its broad coverage of all types of American popular music, *Who Wrote That Song?* will be a welcome addition to many public and academic library collections.

Heat Wave: The Motown Fact Book. By David Bianco. Pierian Press, 1988. 524p. illus. indexes. hardcover $49.50 (0-87650-204-4).

784.53 Music, Popular (Songs, etc.)—U.S.—Discography ‖ Afro-American musicians ‖ Sound recording industry—U.S. [BKL] 86-60558

"Designed as a basic reference source on Motown's recording history" from its humble Detroit beginnings in 1959 through 1986, this fact book lists 5,500 recordings released by Motown records in the U.S. and the U.K. It also includes about 6,700 references to Motown artists who performed on the records listed in the discographies and over 8,500 references to songs and record titles.

With black-and-white photographs of musical artists and record logos decorating many pages, this massive collection of data is divided into eight sections. The first chapter consists of short biographical profiles of Motown record performers, excluding jazz and country-and-western musicians. Each entry includes a complete Motown discography and, for those performers who also recorded on non-Motown labels, an incomplete listing of their other records. For some of the major artists listed—such as Stevie Wonder—a short bibliography of books and articles also appears. Ending this first section is an annotated bibliography of nine books that have been published on Motown and its music.

A 20-page chronology and a list of Motown Record Corporation labels precede the main body of the book: separate, detailed discographies for the U.S. and the U.K. Each is organized chronologically by label, and each record entry is given an identifying code number. Information in each entry includes label and record number, date of release, title and artist(s), and whether the record is also available on compact disc or cassette. A personal- and group-name index, a song- and record-title index, a date index, and a record-number index are provided for both discographies and give the reader broad access to the information in the book. *Heat Wave* concludes with an appendix listing "Motown-Related Detroit Labels" and records put out by these labels.

Although other rock-music reference sources provide more complete biographical information on some of the Motown artists represented here, this book contains the most complete discographies of Motown music in print. It is an invaluable source of information that gives readers a fair idea of the depth and breadth of Motown's influence on the evolution of rock and popular music during the past 30 years. It is an essential purchase for large and most medium-size public libraries and many university and four-year college libraries. It should also be considered for community college and high school libraries that aim for comprehensive coverage of rock music or black studies.

National Anthems of the World. 7th ed. Ed. by W. L. Reed and M. J. Bristow. Blandford Press; dist. by Sterling, 1988 (c1987). 513p. hardcover $70 (0-7137-1962-1).

784.71 National songs [BKL]

Scholar Reed and musician Bristow have compiled another edition of the useful *National Anthems of the World*. Many embassies, governments, scholars, and educational institutions have assisted the editors in compiling an accurate and current collection of songs. One may question why a new edition is necessary when the last appeared in 1985 and no new nations have emerged since then. Twenty-five of the national anthems in this monograph have undergone significant changes: new lyrics, vocal scores added to music, added languages (e.g., Tamil words for the Sri Lankan anthem), and corrected and revised anthems and translations. The appended list of national days has also seen considerable changes in holidays and dates. In addition, there have been numerous subtle changes: new footnotes, composers' names added, and a rearrangement of verse lines.

Arranged alphabetically by country, this work presents the national anthems of 172 nations. A two-page table of contents assists the user in locating the appropriate anthem. Each anthem has the musical score arranged for piano, the original foreign-language lyrics, and brief notes on the composers and history of the composition. For anthems in a non-Latin alphabet, e.g., Chinese or Japanese, a transliterated phonetic version is substituted to enable the work to be sung by persons unfamiliar with the original language. In this new edition, English translations within the score have been removed and placed at the end of the anthem. The only exception to this is when English is an alternative language for a country, e.g., Irish Republic or South Africa. Then the English words are printed along with the non-English vocal score. Also, at the end of each anthem, words to additional verses or choruses are provided in the original language and English. Reed and T. M. Cartledge are responsible for adapting or arranging almost one-quarter of the musical scores to the piano. An appended four-page list of national days organized alphabetically by country concludes the book. A comparison with the sixth edition noted substantial changes in holidays and dates. Between editions of this source, users would be wise to consult more current lists of national days.

The only work comparable to NAW is National Anthems by Nettl (1967). Organized geographically, the first-line index and general index are helpful in locating the appropriate anthem. This dated work is superior to NAW in providing history, musical affiliation, cultural significance, and bibliographic information. Unfortunately, it is also mainly text and would present difficulties for use by a performer. In libraries with calls for information for school projects, e.g., International Brotherhood Day or other international programs where songs would be useful, the NAW is the most current and complete reference source available. Highly recommended for public and academic libraries.

The New Grove Dictionary of Jazz. 2v. Ed. by Barry Kernfeld. Grove's Dictionaries of Music, 1988. 1,401p. bibliog. illus. hardcover $350 (0-935859-39-X).

785.42'03 Jazz music—Dictionaries l Jazz music—Bio-bibliography [CIP] 87-25452

The Grove name has long been associated with the finest in music scholarship. Titles such as *The New Grove Dictionary of Music and Musicians* [RSBR My 15 82], *The New Grove Dictionary of Musical Instruments* [RBB Je 1 85], and *The New Grove Dictionary of American Music* [RBB F 15 87] have become the definitive reference sources for classical music researchers. With the publication of *The New Grove Dictionary of Jazz*, the Grove brain trust has created a similar work on this musical genre. This two-volume set is the first comprehensive, scholarly reference work on jazz and should become to the literature of jazz what the other sets have become to the literature of classical music. The *Dictionary* is an academic study of jazz. Editor Kernfeld is a former Cornell University music instructor and jazz contributor to *The New Grove Dictionary of American Music* and *The New Harvard Dictionary of Music*. Most of the 250 contributors are academics and represent 25 nations. Because it is a product of the academic community rather than of the musicians themselves, it tends to present a more critical review of the field. The editor has made a special effort to follow the international jazz scene, with almost 20 percent of the entries covering jazz musicians, groups, or institutions in Europe, Australia, Japan, Latin America, and the Caribbean.

The most basic question in developing a work such as this is determining a definition of the scope of the field. The editor decided to limit the scope of the work to primarily mainstream and progressive jazz and to exclude all related musical genres. This decision was made because he "believes that a view of jazz that incorporates vaudeville, ragtime, blues, gospel music, country music, pop, folk music, rhythm-and-blues, rock-and-roll, soul music, hard rock, funk, salsa . . . obscures the musical characteristics that distinguish these genres from one another and from jazz." This rather limited definition of the field may have been necessary in order to restrict the project to a manageable size. However, it has also resulted in the exclusion of some material that many readers will expect to find in such a work. While there is the lengthy article *Blues*, *Funk* receives only a brief definition, and there are no entries for salsa, soul, or gospel music. There is no article on rock and roll, only five paragraphs on the relationship between rock and jazz buried within the general *Jazz* entry. There are also some surprising decisions on the inclusion of biographies. Scott Joplin is excluded (pure ragtime), while Eubie Blake is included ("his playing demonstrates the interconnections between brass-band, ragtime, and jazz"). James Brown is out (all soul?), while Ray Charles is in ("he established himself as a testifying rock-and-roll preacher, a smooth, sophisticated popular singer, a big band leader, and a swinging bop pianist"). George Gershwin is omitted although Hoagy Carmichael is included.

Jazz has a long history of influencing other musical genres. It is not easy to dictate that a given performer, piece, or style does or does not belong to a category called *jazz*. However, if the definition of the editor is accepted, the reader will find a tremendous collection of information here. The alphabetically arranged entries cover all aspects of jazz, including theory, instrumentation, performers, composers, bands, films, and institutions associated with this music. Entries range in length from short definitions of musical terms (*Doit, Extended Chord, Shout*) to short entries on people and bands (*Christian, Buddy*; *Jackson, Willis "Gator"*; *Torme, Mel*) to extensive entries on broad topics or major performers (*Bands*; *Davis, Miles*; *Improvisation*; *Parker, Charlie*; *Recording*; and *Jazz* itself). Longer entries are divided into several sections to help the reader find the desired information. Each article begins with a brief definition of the scope of the topic, followed by a numbered list of subheadings used in the entry. For example, the entry *Notation* is subdivided into (1) *Introduction*, (2) *Notation for performance*, (3) *Notation for teaching and learning*, (4) *Notation for transcription*, and (5) *Notational symbols*. This is the same procedure that has been used for lengthy entries in the other Grove dictionaries. Cross-references (*see* and *see also*) are used both within articles and at the end of entries. These are adequate and compensate for the lack of an index.

Some of the entries included in *The New Grove Dictionary of Jazz* are extracted directly from *The New Grove Dictionary of Music and Musicians* and *The New Grove Dictionary of American Music*. Since both of those works included jazz, the editor originally intended to take as many as one-quarter of the entries from them. However, with the continuous expansion of the work during its compilation, the publisher claims 90 percent of the material contained in *The New Grove Dictionary of Jazz* is new. A comparison of the three sets by the Board tends to verify this.

Of the over 4,500 entries in the *Dictionary*, more than 3,000 are biographies, most for performers, but also for composers, arrangers, record producers, writers, editors, and discographers. Entries for musical groups are generally found under the name of the band leader, with cross-references from the group name if it is different from that of its leader. Only the musical aspects of an individual or group are discussed; very little personal information is included, unless it has a direct relationship to the individual's career, musical development, or influence on jazz. For each biographical entry, both a discography and a bibliography are provided. The discography includes selected recordings that represent the most distinctive works associated with the musician. When possible, recordings include the work of the musician as both a soloist and a sideman. Individual tracks on selected recordings are occasionally highlighted if they were composed by the subject or if they are especially useful in demonstrating the artist's unique style. The bibliographies provide references to both books and journal articles, the dates of which vary widely, depending heavily on the time period in which the artist achieved the greatest popularity. However, many entries cite sources from the 1980s, with some as recent as 1987.

In addition to biographies, the *Dictionary* includes over 200 articles relating to the theory of jazz. Some, such as *Arrangement, Beat*, and

Transcription, are lengthy surveys that provide extensive overviews of the topic. Shorter entries (several paragraphs in length) are provided for specific musical terms. Both of these types of entries include references to specific recordings that demonstrate the features being discussed. Examples of musical scores are also often provided within the text. Lengthy bibliographies are included for most entries.

Each musical instrument commonly used in the performance of jazz has received an entry in the *Dictionary*. These articles include basic information derived from *The New Grove Dictionary of Musical Instruments*. However, the emphasis is on the use of the instrument in jazz, which may be significantly different from its use in other musical genres. Some entries for families of instruments, such as *Electronic Keyboards* or *Percussion*, also serve as an index to the entries on specific instruments within the family. Each instrument entry includes references to specific recordings demonstrating its use as well as a bibliography of sources. Because of the importance of recorded music to the history and development of jazz, entries are also provided for more than 350 recording studios. In most cases, these tend to be short, describing the history of the company and its most prominent releases. Bibliographies and discographies are included when appropriate. The 71-page article on nightclubs provides an international list of prominent clubs from the past and present. The address and location of each club are provided along with a list of highlights from past performances. This guide serves as a record of those clubs that have since closed and as a jazz fan's vacation guide to those that are still in operation. Two appendixes to the main body of the work include an extensive jazz bibliography and a list of contributors.

In addition to the textual material, 220 black-and-white photographs are included in *The New Grove Dictionary of Jazz*. Most of these portray individual performers or groups. Line drawings are also used throughout the work, particularly to illustrate the entries on musical instruments. While only approximately 5 percent of all entries contain illustrations, they are a useful supplement to the text.

Although the *Dictionary* does an admirable job of describing the world of jazz, music is an aural medium and the set's printed format can only partially reflect this. While the scores included in the text are helpful, these transcriptions can never capture all of the nuances of the music. The discographies will be useful to lead readers to appropriate recordings in libraries that have large collections. However, audio technology has developed to such a point that it would be possible to prepare some type of recording cross-referenced to the entries in the set. Although the acquisition of copyright clearance might prevent the inclusion of some music, there should be enough available material to compile a set of examples from the diverse genre of jazz. Perhaps the success of ventures such as the Library of Congress and Smithsonian jazz collections will inspire the editor to consider the production of a set of recordings that can be used along with this *Dictionary*. While libraries would not be able to house the recordings with the *Dictionary*, readers could be referred to another part of the library for them.

The New Grove Dictionary of Jazz provides a scholarly study of jazz and should become the standard encyclopedia in the field. While some readers may disagree with the editor's definition of jazz, none can argue with the quality of the coverage within this scope. The mere publication of an academic treatment of this genre makes a statement as to the integration of jazz into the mainstream of the music community. The Board encourages the publisher to continue to branch out from its traditional focus and to produce similar works for other nonclassical genres such as blues, country, folk, and rock. If they possess the quality of scholarship included in *The New Grove Dictionary of Jazz*, they should all be hits.

CD Review Digest Annual, Volume 1, 1983–1987: The Guide to Reviews of All Music on Compact Disc. [bound in 2 parts.] Ed. by Janet Grimes. Peri Press, P.O. Box 348, Voorheesville, NY 12186-0348, 1988. 864p. indexes. hardcover $135 (0-9617844-0-7; ISSN 0893-5173).

789.913 Compact discs—Reviews I Sound recordings—Reviews [BKL] 87-450

The bibliographic control of sound recordings and their reviews, spotty at best, would appear at first glance to be even more uneven because of periodic changes in the preferred medium of commercial presentation—78 RPM discs before 1949, then LPs, then stereo, later cassettes, now compact discs (CDs), tomorrow (perhaps) digital tapes. Librarians may be bewildered by the obsolescence of the media, along with their requisite hardware. They can take some consolation in the fact that new media often breed new bibliographies. The LP era, for instance, gave birth to the *Schwann* catalog in 1949, a few years later to cataloging for card distribution purposes at the Library of Congress, not to mention the "Index of Record Reviews" (now called "Index to CD and Record Reviews") in the Music Library Association's journal, *Notes*.

Volume 1 of the present work (*CDRD*) cumulates citations to reviews for the years 1983–87, when the compact-disc format gradually emerged. It is scheduled to appear quarterly, and the 1988 cumulation is due to be published this month. The cumulation is divided by genre, with 4,990 entries in volume 1, part 1, for classical music, and 2,629 for jazz and popular music, 296 for soundtrack and show music, and 130 for videodiscs in part 2. Five indexes at the end—by show composer, record-label number, reviewer, title, and performer—are a special virtue of *CDRD*, although the title index apparently covers only the jazz and popular section.

A decision on acquisition of *CDRD* might be measured in terms of the overlap of coverage with reviews in the "Index" in *Notes*. Several differences—very important to some users, probably not at all to others—may be noted. (1) The "Index" concentrates on classical music. (2) It indexes 19 journals, compared with 39 in volume 1 of *CDRD* (expanded to 42 in volume 2), of which 14 are common to both. (3) The "Index," which now enters recordings by label number, has only one index, by composer. (4) *CDRD* provides a more direct evaluation through brief selected quotations, whereas the "Index" uses symbols that summarize the overall evaluation, derived from *Book Review Digest* symbols (+ for a favorable review, - for a negative review, etc.). (5) *CDRD* covers many more titles and cites somewhat more reviews. The first quarterly issue of volume 2 of *CDRD* covers 2,452 discs, whereas the quarterly "Index" lists usually cover only about 400—the latter presumably having been selected as ones most likely to be considered for library collections. Finally, *CDRD* lists only reviews of CDs, while some items listed in the "Index" are available only on LP.

A direct comparison of coverage is hampered by the compilers' decisions on when to cite the work—ideally in both instances the earliest date when the major reviews are all likely to be accounted for. Three examples suggest the problems and the overlap. Yo-Yo Ma's Dvořák cello concerto (CBS 42206) is cited in the "Index" (December 1987) with four pluses, a minus, and one square; *CDRD* (v.1, no.1641; also v.2, no.473) cites seven reviews, two with enthusiastic quotations, the rest with citations only. One review in the "Index" is not in *CDRD*, three in *CDRD* are not in the "Index," three are in both. Handel's *Aci* (Harmonia Mundi, HMC 901253-54), cited with six reviews in the "Index" (December 1988), gets only one in *CDRD* (v.2, no.598)—at least so far. On the other hand, the Seattle performance of Prokofiev's *Romeo and Juliet* (Delos 3050) has four reviews in *CDRD* (v.2, no.981), but none (so far) in the "Index." Another competitor is *Stevenson Compact Disc Review Guide* (Joseph N. Stevenson, P.O. Box 53286, Indianapolis, IN 46253-0286, bimonthly and cumulative, $32/year), its fifteenth issue (v.4, no.5), dated January 1989. It is intended mainly for use in record shops and is comparable to the "Index" in size, if not in quality.

As for reviews of popular music, here *CDRD* stands all alone, with no major competitors since the demise of the *Annual Index to Popular Music Reviews* before the CD era. This coverage must be seen as its most attractive feature for libraries. To be sure, *CDRD* is not without flaws. The graphic design is ill-conceived for reference use. The preface to volume 1 notes that "works intended for a wide-spread audience, including classics, are listed in the second section": it is here that one finds some of the Placido Domingo entries. The entry practices in *CDRD* are derived basically from *Schwann*. The advantages, of pragmatic utility, are often offset by the inconsistencies that result from a lack of authority work: the entry *King's College Choir* appears in volume 1, *Choir of King's College, Cambridge* in volume 2.

In sum, *CDRD* and the "Index to CD and Record Reviews" are essentially complementary. The fact that they cover much the same material but overlap less than fully testifies to the vastness of the recording industry and its reviewing sources. *CDRD* should be of particular value in libraries that do not subscribe to *Notes*, that have extensive demand for reviews of popular music, or that seek completeness of coverage of current evaluative discography.

The History of Rock and Roll: A Selective Discography. By Mirek Kocandrle. G. K. Hall, 1988. 297p. index. hardcover $40 (0-8161-8956-0).

789.9'12454 Rock music—Discography [CIP] 88-21200

This discography covers the history of rock very broadly, beginning with ragtime and including virtually every form of popular music except jazz. Styles covered chronologically to show the evolution of rock include "Boogie-Woogie," "Classical Blues," "Cajun and Zydeco," "Gospel," "Doo-Wop," "Country Music," "Rockabilly and Rock 'n Roll," "Chicano Music," "Folk Music," "Soul Music," "British Pop," "Disco," "Punk," "New Wave," "Heavy Metal," "Rapping," "Reggae Music," and "New Age Music." Due to the encyclopedic scope of this discography, the coverage of individual artists/groups is selective—the author rated recordings from A to F and then included all records worthy of grades of B and better (with a few exceptions for very popular recordings or for cases where there was only one record in print for a particular artist or group). As an example of the book's selectivity, about 400 recordings are listed under "Motown," while *Heat Wave*, the discography of Motown [*RBB* Ja 1 88], lists about 5,500. Asterisks draw attention to recordings of "exceptional artistic quality" or "recordings essential to a comprehensive collection." These ratings are somewhat idiosyncratic, reflecting the compiler's opinions. For instance, almost all of Michael Jackson's recordings are starred, while none of Bob Marley's are.

The more than 12,000 recordings are arranged under the broad headings listed above, and under more detailed subheadings as appropriate, and then by artist. Within the entry for an individual artist or group, singles are listed before the listings for LPs (both arranged in chronological order). Record labels and year of pressing are given, but unfortunately record numbers are not. The author asserts that this information can be found from any reputable record dealer, but he would have saved collectors and dealers valuable time if he had included the record numbers in this discography. The lack of annotations is also regretted. The book concludes with an index to performers.

Dean Tudor's *Popular Music: An Annotated Guide to Recordings* [*RBB* D 1 84] lists 6,200 popular LPs, including jazz. Record numbers are given, and annotations make the book useful for libraries as a buying guide. Many of the records listed in *The History of Rock and Roll* are out-of-print, and with its historical approach, it is intended for the scholar and collector. This discography will be a useful addition to most public and academic libraries with popular-music collections.

PERFORMING ARTS, RECREATION

Disability Drama in Television and Film. By Lauri E. Klobas. McFarland, 1988. 477p. bibliog. index. hardcover $39.95 (0-89950-309-8).

791.4'0880816 Handicapped in television I Handicapped in motion pictures I Handicapped—Public opinion I Stereotype (Psychology) [CIP] 88-13296

The influential television and motion-picture industries are often criticized for failing to portray real-life events and human problems with any degree of depth, sophistication, or sensitivity. *Disability Drama in Television and Film* documents nearly 400 productions in which a disability is portrayed. Yet, in most of these, judging by the author's searing comments, not only have the media not presented the disability accurately, but also they have stereotypically restricted the disabled characters' range of emotions as well as their actions. It is Klobas' view that in the media's sensationalist but superficial fashion, "explorations of real problems are sidestepped while soaring 'miracles' or stories of courage prevail."

Drawing upon 11 years of personal observation, the author allows that "this work does not purport to be an analysis of *every* piece about disability, nor does it stake a claim at having researched all the 'important' pieces. It is a collection of films and programs that came to my attention in one way or another." Motion-picture entries date from Chaplin's *City Lights* (1931) through 1986. Episodes of television series account for a large number of the entries (for example, "Bonanza," 10 entries; "Fantasy Island," 7; "Little House," 12).

A table of contents indicates that eight chapters cover disabilities such as blindness, deafness, amputation, wheelchair use, developmental disability, and small stature. Each chapter begins with a two- to four-page introduction to the disability, noting its special characteristics, aid devices, and the stereotypes of media portrayal (such as the blind "reading" others' faces with their hands).

Television and film entries are generally arranged within each chapter chronologically. The author suggests this arrangement illustrates what might have influenced subsequent writers. Each descriptive entry lists the title of the film (and production company) or television program (and network), episode title, date of release or airing, and major credits (producers, directors, writers). A brief plot summary is given along with a selection of dialogue as illustration of the disability; the author's critical analysis follows.

Although the disabled characters are noted by sex, race, and type of disability (and, in some cases, age), the actors representing them are not identified in the credits. While this omission isolates the responsibility of the creative personnel for media portrayals of the disabled, it also fails to credit the performance of the actors, such as Mickey Rooney who played Bill, a developmentally disabled man, in the Emmy-award-winning "Bill," Patty Duke who won an Academy Award as Helen Keller in *The Miracle Worker*, Jon Voight who won an Oscar for his portrayal of a paraplegic in *Coming Home*, or even Marlee Matlin, a deaf actress who won an Oscar in *Children of a Lesser God*.

An appendix for additional listings of productions on the disabled is divided into three separate sections for television series episodes, feature films, and what the author calls "the regulars," that is, series in which a disabled character was featured or had a recurring role, such as "Ironside," "Longstreet," or "Bronk" ("Special assignment cop Alex Bronkov's daughter was Ellen, a young woman in a wheelchair"). A brief list of references cites television and movie fact books for further research. The index lists names (writers, producers, etc.) and titles (italics for movies, boldface for series).

Disability Drama is a specialized resource, a sometime companion to other television series and motion-picture fact books. Because it omits information on actors, which is usually of key interest to most students and the public, it is limited in its appeal and, thus, best suited for large communications collections or special collections on the disabled.

The American Film Institute Catalog of Motion Pictures Produced in the United States: Feature Films, 1911–1920. 2v. Ed. by Patricia King Hanson and Alan Gevinson. Univ. of California, 1989 (c1988). 1,557p. bibliog. indexes. hardcover $110 (0-520-06301-5).

016.79143'75 Motion pictures—U.S.—Catalogs [CIP] 88-40245

This third installment of *The American Film Institute Catalog* covers the earliest period yet. Previous two-volume installments have covered feature films produced in the U.S. for the periods 1921–30 (1971) and 1961–70 [*RSBR* F 15 77]. The "teens volume," as AFI Director Jean Firstenberg calls it in the preface, records the era during which the film industry began to mature with the industry's settlement in Hollywood, the establishment of the studios, the development of the star system, and the rise of the feature-length film.

The structure of this two-volume set is similar to that of the previously published installments. The main volume consists of profiles of 5,189 films, arranged alphabetically by title. Entries include production company, distributor, release date, number of reels, credits for creative personnel, cast credits, genre, a plot summary, subject descriptors, and citations to reviews. Plot summaries simply relate the incidents of films; they do not evaluate their merit. Notes in some entries explain the sources for the information, since many of the films survive not on celluloid but only in printed records. Other notes point out matters about a film that are not self-evident from the entry, such as "the actor listed as Rudolpho De Valintine later became known as Rudolph Valentino." Subject terms applied to the films are of two types. Those in roman type are "major" headings and those in italics are "minor" headings (i.e., subjects less central to a film).

As with the other installments of the *AFI Catalog*, the second volume consists of indexes to the first volume. In a departure from previous practice, corporate and personal names have been placed in separate indexes. Three other indexes are unique to the teens volume: a list of film titles by year of release, a genre index, and a geographic index. In these latter two indexes, film titles are listed chronologically within genre or place headings. The geographic index identifies films shot "wholly or partially on location" outside a studio. The U.S. section is organized by state and city, followed by listings for other countries.

Other indexes common to the entire *AFI Catalog* series are the literary- and dramatic-source index and the subject index. The subject index observes the major/minor distinction by printing film titles in either roman or italic. As needed, the name, subject, and source indexes employ *see* and *see also* references.

A comparison of the personal-name index with John T. Weaver's *Twenty Years of Silents, 1908–1928* (Scarecrow, 1971) raises questions that cannot easily be answered. Weaver provides a list of credits for those who acted in, directed, and produced silent films but does not further explain its scope. A list of film titles follows each person's name. To cite one typical example, Weaver credits Mary Pickford with seven films in 1913, only two of which appear in the *AFI Catalog*. Why? Perhaps these other five films fall short of the four-reel minimum for inclusion in the *AFI Catalog*. None of the 1913 Pickford films unique to Weaver's list appear in the tenth volume of *The Motion Picture Guide* [*RBB* Ag 87] either. In the absence of a clear explanation of Weaver's scope, one ought to give the benefit of the doubt to the *AFI Catalog*, a product of prodigious scholarship drawing on primary and contemporary secondary sources. AFI plans eventually to publish a volume on the short films of the era, which may account for films that only Weaver lists.

Even if it has missed a few feature films of this early era, from which only 10 to 20 percent of films are extant, the teens volume of the *AFI Catalog* is unquestionably the most complete record of the age when Lon Chaney, Charlie Chaplin, Evelyn Nesbit, D. W. Griffith, Cecil B. DeMille, Mack Sennett, and others created a new American industry. The silent-films volume of *The Motion Picture Guide* describes only about 3,500 films, many of them from the decades flanking the teens and a fair number of them produced and released in other countries. Because of its greater depth of coverage and because it rests on a firm foundation of scholarship, this newest installment of the *AFI Catalog* is an especially welcome addition to film reference literature.

Annual Index to Motion Picture Credits, 1987. Ed. by Byerly Woodward. Academy of Motion Picture Arts and Sciences, 8949 Wilshire Blvd., Beverly Hills, CA 90211-1972, 1988. 374p. hardcover $80; $60 on subscription (0-942102-08-8; ISSN 0163-5123).

791.43'05 Motion pictures—U.S.—Periodicals [OCLC] 79-644761

In order to be eligible to win an Academy Award, a feature film must "open in a commercial motion picture theater in the Los Angeles area for a consecutive run of not less than a week." For 53 years, the Academy of Motion Picture Arts and Sciences has published an annual compilation of information on such films, if basic information (title, distributor, acting and technical credits) can be verified from "two or more reliable sources." Through 1978 it was called *The Screen Achievements Records Bulletin*.

The 1987 edition of this previously reviewed work [*RSBR* S 15 80] consists of listings for 379 films, incorporating over 15,000 individual credits. Organized alphabetically by film title, the entries contain the following information: studio name, dates of completion and release, running time, ratings (*PG*, *R*, etc.), technical credits, acting cast with characters played, and song listings. A short appendix includes 17 films "for which only the releasing company could be verified."

Following the main body of the book are several alphabetical listings of actors, art directors, cinematographers, costume designers, directors, film editors, makeup coordinators, music writers and performers, producers, sound directors, and screenwriters, each with their credits; also included is a listing of releasing companies with films released. The book concludes with two comprehensive indexes: one bringing together all the individuals in the volume with their credits and the other listing all the films appearing in the annual volumes between 1976 and 1987.

The *Annual Index to Motion Picture Credits* continues to be the most reliable and complete source of information about film credits for motion pictures competing for the Academy Awards every year. The annual update volumes of *The Motion Picture Guide* include plot summaries, but the listings of the technical crews are incomplete. For instance, dubbing and sound mixers and second-unit directors are usually listed in the *Annual Index* and not in other film annuals. Film libraries, large public libraries, and academic libraries supporting film studies should have each annual edition.

American Film Studios: An Historical Encyclopedia. By Gene Fernett. McFarland, 1988. 295p. bibliog. illus. index. hardcover $35 (0-89950-250-4).

384'.8 Motion picture studios—U.S.—History—Dictionaries [CIP] 88-42514

The American filmmaking industry began at the Thomas Edison Studio in West Orange, New Jersey. Before film studios gravitated westward to California, production companies emerged all over the country. This book, which was researched from yearbooks, almanacs, and histories of the motion-picture industry, details the successes and catastrophes of 66 film studios of varying sizes and specialties. The late author, who published other books on films and the film industry, also worked as a director, producer, and scriptwriter.

Alphabetically arranged from *Actophone* to *The Whartons*, each article discusses films made by the studio, its stars, competition, and problems in the business of filmmaking. Entries range from 1 to 14 pages and average 4 pages. Among the studios discussed are many that one would expect to find (Fox, MGM, Walt Disney Studio, and Universal) as well as many lesser-known firms (Hawthorn, First National, Selig Polyscope, and Crystal Studios). The tone of the writing is chatty, and entries lack bibliographies.

Fernett notes the difficulties involved in covering all American film studios and explains that less significant ones have been omitted. Black-and-white photographs are found on almost every page. He apologizes for the use of some substandard photographs and illustrations but felt their inclusion was necessary to ensure a thorough historical depiction. Current trends in film studios are very briefly noted in the afterword. The book concludes with a one-page bibliography and an index that notes photographs with boldface numbers.

This book conveniently compiles information about early film studios. Though not a scholarly work, large public and academic libraries supporting a film-studies curriculum will want to consider purchase.

The International Film Industry: A Historical Dictionary. By Anthony Slide. Greenwood, 1989. 423p. bibliog. index. hardcover $55 (0-313-25635-7).

384'.8 Motion picture industry—Dictionaries [CIP] 88-25103

Slide's latest contribution to film literature focuses on world cinema exclusive of the U.S. Thus, it complements his earlier compilation, *The American Film Industry: A Historical Dictionary* [RBB D 1 86]. *The International Film Industry* includes more than 650 entries pertaining to such aspects of filmmaking as studios, production companies, movie theaters, film awards, cinematographic techniques, and organizations. In addition, a number of articles deal with topics treated in films (*cricket, white man's burden*), locales (*Paris, Antarctica*), and film genres (*spaghetti westerns, commedia brillante*). Wisely, the compiler has chosen not to provide entries for individuals or film titles since they are covered extensively in other sources, such as *The International Dictionary of Films and Filmmakers* [RBB Ag 88]. Particularly useful are the articles on individual countries, which provide historical overviews of the film industry in each country, discuss prominent directors and their films, and note motion pictures that used the country as a location. Some articles, such as those on film archives and stock footage libraries, even include directories, and those on extant organizations provide their current address. Most of the entries conclude with a list of bibliographic references.

Articles, arranged alphabetically letter by letter (e.g., *film societies* comes after *films à clef*), range in length from one or two sentences to over 12 pages for *United Kingdom*. (The compiler admits in his introduction that "the largest amount of space is devoted to British cinema.") Although the articles are unsigned, a list of six special contributors and the countries for which they were responsible appears near the front of the volume. Apparently, the remaining articles were written by Slide, who has authored numerous publications on film and other forms of popular entertainment. Some articles are remarkably current. For example, the entry *Monty Python* mentions the 1988 release *A Fish Called Wanda*, while the entry *Carlton Communications* refers to an article published in September 1988.

See references are provided as appropriate throughout the *Dictionary*, and asterisks are used following terms in the text that have their own entries. Additional access is provided by the index, which includes entries for each article header and selectively covers the names of individuals and companies treated within the articles.

This valuable compendium supplements the information in such sources as the annual *International Film Guide* and Roger Manvell's now somewhat-dated *International Encyclopedia of Film* (Crown, 1972). It will be a useful addition to all libraries that support the study of cinema history.

The BFI Companion to the Western. Ed. by Edward Buscombe. Atheneum, 1988. 432p. bibliog. illus. hardcover $60 (0-689-11962-3).

791.43'09 Western films—U.S.—Dictionaries and encyclopedias I Western films—U.S.—History and criticism I Motion picture producers and directors—U.S.—Biography—Dictionaries I West (U.S.)—Dictionaries and encyclopedias [CIP] 88-10402

In his elegantly written and informative foreword to this encyclopedia, renowned film critic Richard Schickel writes that the western movie has depended on "first-hand knowledge and living memory for its vitality"—both of which are gone today. "Now," for our visions of the West, he sadly concludes, "we must look them up in reference books."

Whether or not Schickel's pessimism is warranted, this book—put together by the British Film Institute—celebrates with color and style the rich history of the western in American culture. The encyclopedia aims to present "a panoramic history of the cinematic western" and to describe its cultural significance.

Black-and-white and color photographs, drawings, paintings, and maps related to the text ornament almost every page of the book. Organized into five primary sections, *The BFI Companion* begins with a narrative history of the western from the beginning of the twentieth century to the present. It is followed by an alphabetical dictionary—a potpourri of people and terms important in the evolution of the western. Included are historical and literary figures (*Grey, Zane*; *Holliday, Doc*); genres (*Humour, Drama*); actions common to many westerns (*Baths, Violence, Dragged by a Horse*); plot devices (*Feud, Revenge*); and occupations (*Gunfighter, Banker, Doctor, Sheriff*).

The third part of the book, titled "A Select Guide to the Western Film," is an alphabetical listing of 300 western films the editors deem important. For each entry, there is a summary of the plot and the film's significance. This is followed by basic information (date of release, running time, distributor, and credits). Researchers needing a comprehensive guide to westerns will need to consult *Western Movies: A TV and Video Guide to 4,200 Genre Films* [RBB My 1 87]. The next section treats people—actors, directors, producers, and writers. Each entry analyzes briefly the contributions made by the person and gives a chronological list of the western films he or she helped make.

The encyclopedia concludes with an alphabetical list of all television westerns, the only part of the book that aims for completeness. The program entries include dates, number of episodes, running time, and credits, along with a two- or three-sentence description of the program.

An appendix contains a chart of comparative career dates for 25 western stars and a set of statistical tables on westerns, only one of which has been updated through 1987. There is no index to the book's contents, which is unfortunate because of the vast amount of interconnected information spread throughout the book.

With its attractive graphics and its informative text, *The BFI Companion* is a noteworthy book on the western. But the lack of an index is a major weakness for readers using the work as a reference book. This is a must for film libraries and an appropriate selection for public and academic libraries where books on the cinema are in demand; some libraries may want to consider this encyclopedia for their circulating collections in addition to or in place of a reference copy.

Blacks in American Films and Television: An Encyclopedia. By Donald Bogle. Garland, 1988. 510p. bibliog. illus. index. hardcover $60 (0-8240-8715-1).

791.43'08996073 Afro-Americans in motion pictures I Afro-American entertainers—Biography—Dictionaries I Afro-Americans in the motion picture industry—U.S. I Afro-Americans in the television industry—U.S. [CIP] 87-29241

This encyclopedia selectively critiques both black films and blacks in film and television. Bogle, the author of the prize-winning *Toms, Coons, Mulattoes, Mammies, & Bucks: An Interpretative History of Blacks in Films* and *Brown Sugar: Eighty Years of Black Female Superstars*, developed the encyclopedia from research he did while working on a PBS production of the latter title. Reviewing films and television series, he recorded credits and his own impressions of how blacks were portrayed. Bogle informs us that his intention was to produce a reference work that would give credits for black films and television programs, and at the same time examine the body of work of key performers in historical context.

Divided into three major sections—"Movies," "Television: TV Series and TV Movies, Mini-Series, Specials," and "Profiles" (the biographical entries)—the encyclopedia is arranged alphabetically by the name of the movie or TV program in the first two sections, and by the name of the actor, actress, or director in the third. The "Movies" and "Television" sections begin with a historical essay tracing the development of the portrayal of blacks in each medium. In each entry, the name of the movie or TV program is followed by credits: director, stars, producers, etc. A one- to eight-paragraph plot summary and critique follow. Many of the articles are accompanied by movie stills or posters. The profiles include birth and death dates for individuals with a brief chronology of their careers and accomplishments. Many of the profiles also include photographs. The biographical profiles are selective, including only those individuals known for television and film work, not for a different medium, such as Louis Armstrong, who appeared in films but was better known as a musician. The index is a name-title guide, and there is a brief bibliography.

The encyclopedia is written from a very specific point of view. The author refrains from condemning stars like Stepin Fetchit, reminding the reader of the times in which he worked, but is highly critical of "male interracial bonding" as seen in the movie *The Defiant Ones*. Not everyone will agree with his opinions. The selection of certain movies or TV programs may also draw criticism. For example, he mentions that film star Nichelle Nichols costarred in the television program "Star Trek" but does not have a separate entry for this program, which had one of the first interracial kisses seen on American television.

As a movie and television encyclopedia, this work is interesting on several levels. One, it is an attempt to examine the evolution and even revolution of blacks in films and television. The analysis shows how blacks were portrayed and how at least one black writer responded to the portrayal. As a reference book, it is useful as a traditional finding aid for names, credits, and plot summaries. As a document on black performers, it is challenging and perhaps controversial.

Other reference books on blacks in film treat the subject more narrowly: Sampson's *Blacks in Black and White: A Source Book on Black Films*, for instance, lists only films with all-black casts. For both the breadth of its scope and the level of its treatment, *Blacks in American Films and Television* is recommended for academic, public, and high school libraries.

British Film Actors' Credits, 1895–1987. By Scott Palmer. McFarland, 1988. 917p. hardcover $55 (0-89950-316-0).
791.43'028 Motion picture actors and actresses—Great Britain—Credits I Motion picture actors and actresses—Great Britain—Biography—Dictionaries I Motion pictures—Great Britain—Catalogs [CIP] 87-31098

Nearly 5,000 performers are listed in this extensive work, which includes film actors from Great Britain and other traditionally British areas such as Ireland, Australia, Canada, South Africa, etc. Foreign-born performers who made films in Great Britain are also included.

The book is divided into two sections: "The Sound Era, 1929–1987" and the shorter "Silent Era, 1895–1928." Actors whose careers spanned both eras are listed in the sound-era category; those in the silent-era section made no films after 1928.

The author has attempted exhaustive coverage of his subject. His criterion for inclusion was a performer's having made at least three films. In about 40 cases, however, a performer who appeared in only two films is included when the film was an important one or the actor played a key role.

Entries are alphabetical by performers' names; birth and death dates are given, when known. Next is a brief characterization of the performer, as for Lesley Ann Down: "Lovely dark-haired leading lady of films and television, popular on the 'Upstairs Downstairs' series (1971–1975)"; and for Sir Alec Guinness: "Distinguished, versatile actor of stage (from 1933), screen and television, outstanding in any type of role; also a master of disguise. Also in Hollywood. Autobiography, *Blessings in Disguise* (1985). Father of Matthew Guinness." The characterization is followed by a chronological listing of the performer's films with the date of each. Over 250,000 films are included, some of them made-for-TV movies. There is no film-title index.

The author, who is managing director of the California Performing Arts Centre, includes several special lists in his book: actors with honorary titles, performers who have appeared in 100 or more films, and those who have won American or British Academy Awards.

A comparison of this book, *The Film Encyclopedia* (Crowell, 1979), and *The Oxford Companion to Film* (Oxford, 1976) revealed (as might be expected) that many lesser-known performers in *British Film Actors' Credits* do not appear in the other two publications. Of three groups of 40 entries each in *British Film Actors' Credits*, seven, six, and eight were found in *The Film Encyclopedia*, and only four, two, and one in *The Oxford Companion to Film*. Moreover, listings of films are complete in *British Film Actors' Credits*, and only a sampling of films is given in the other two publications.

This reference work has a place in academic, large public, and other libraries that need sources giving thorough coverage of British film history.

Child and Youth Actors: Filmographies of Their Entire Careers, 1914–1985. By David Dye. McFarland, 1988. 310p. bibliog. illus. index. hardcover $24.95 (0-89950-247-4).
791.43'028 Motion picture actors and actresses—Biography—Dictionaries I Children as actors—Biography—Dictionaries I Motion pictures—Catalogs [CIP] 87-46441

This filmography lists 550 major and minor child and teenage actors who performed between 1914 and 1985. The large majority of the entries are American, and most of the films and stage productions listed are also American. To be eligible for this list, the performer must have had at least two credits in general-release movies, made-for-TV movies, TV series, or a stage production. However, there are a few actors included who have just one credit in their filmography.

The volume begins with an informative four-page introduction providing a historical overview of the changing world of child actors, emphasizing the effect of Jackie Coogan's film successes and the later influence of television. Actors and selected for inclusion appear alphabetically, and each entry is numbered consecutively. Cross-references lead readers from real names to professional names. Relying on his personal screening of films and on research in teen and horror magazines, Dye records for each entry the place and date of birth (if available), a chronological listing of every TV, film, and stage appearance, along with studio name, character played, and brief information on TV series the person performed in. Although Dye admits being unable to substantiate enough facts to make all entries complete, he does try to provide information on the career of the actor, not only as a child, but also as an adult. Small black-and-white pictures of some of those listed appear throughout the book. A short bibliography and a very complete and helpful index of movies, plays, and TV movies and series conclude the book.

Though one could quibble about some child actors omitted—for example, Barry Gordon of *A Thousand Clowns*—this is a unique source of information addressing a category of performer not previously covered in a reference book. Two especially useful features of the volume are the listings of all the actors and in "Our Gang/Little Rascals" and the "Mickey Mouse Club" and the frequent notes regarding circumstances relating to the launching of acting careers, special performances, and untimely deaths of those listed.

This is a valuable reference book for some medium-size and all large public libraries and four-year college and university libraries supporting a film arts program.

Cinema Sequels and Remakes, 1903–1987. By Robert A. Nowlan and Gwendolyn Wright Nowlan. McFarland, 1989. 954p. illus. index. hardcover $75 (0-89950-314-4).
791.43'75 Motion picture sequels I Motion picture remakes [CIP] 88-42650

Many good stories have inspired several attempts by moviemakers to do them justice; by the same token, many films have inspired sequels. This impressive new reference book covers films, silent and sound, from the genres of drama, adventure, romance, comedy, and thriller, that have at least one English-language sound remake or sequel.

Cinema Sequels is arranged alphabetically by the title of the primary film, with *see* references from later film titles to the original one. Thus, all related films are discussed in one entry. Many films have been repeatedly remade, such as *Romeo and Juliet*, *Three Musketeers*, and *A Christmas Carol*, with seven versions each. The film *Here Comes Mr. Jordan* has been remade as *Angel on My Shoulder*, *Down to Earth*, and *Heaven Can Wait*. Sequels are also numerous: witness the four *Rocky* movies, four *Superman* movies, and five *Pink Panther* movies.

Entries for each film include studio, country, release date, cast, and credits. The work (novel, play, etc.) that served as the basis for the movie is identified, and the story is summarized. The remakes are then described, compared, and criticized. The authors, professors of mathematics and library science at Southern Connecticut State University, have high standards for movies and do not hesitate to criticize. For instance, in discussing the *Porky's* series: "How can one adequately describe the stupidity of these three movies?" The entries are of varying lengths, based on the importance of each in the opinion of the authors.

The book's extensive index (over 100 pages) lists actors, directors, and others involved in film production; titles of books, plays, and stories upon which films are based; and titles of songs from films.

Cinema Sequels and Remakes is well written, lively, and entertaining. Black-and-white movie stills add appeal. While most libraries will have other books of film plots and criticism, this book is unique in that it describes all versions of a film together. Of interest to students of film, movie buffs, and general readers, this book would be welcome in any public, high school, or academic library.

Handbook of American Film Genres. Ed. by Wes D. Gehring. Greenwood, 1988. 405p. bibliog. indexes. hardcover $55 (0-313-24715-3).

791.43'75 Motion pictures—U.S.—Handbooks, manuals, etc. I Film genres [CIP] 87-31784

Handbook of American Film Genres does for motion pictures what Brian G. Rose and Robert Alley's *TV Genres: A Handbook and Reference Guide* (Greenwood, 1985 [*RBB* Jl 86]) does for television programs. It provides scholarly introductory overviews of various types of films, lists significant examples of each genre, and recommends sources to consult for additional information.

The 18 genres treated in this guide are organized into five broad categories: action/adventure, comedy, the fantastic, songs and soaps, and nontraditional. Each of these categories is divided into chapters devoted to more specific genres. For example, the comedy section includes chapters on screwball, populist, parody, clown, and black humor films. All of the comedy essays were written by the editor, the author of numerous books on film comedy and comedians, while the remaining 13 chapters were contributed by other film scholars. Averaging about 20 pages each, the chapters follow an established format. The first and longest section of each essay gives a historical and analytical overview of the genre. Appearing next is a "Bibliographical Overview," a review of the literature on the genre. This section is followed by a "Bibliographical Checklist" of recommended readings, including books, periodical articles, chapters in books, and theses. Concluding each essay is a chronologically arranged, highly selective filmography, citing from 10 to 15 major examples of the genre with brief lists of credits.

The index, which is arranged letter by letter rather than word by word, includes entries for individuals, film titles, publications discussed or mentioned in the historical and bibliographic essays, and for films listed in the filmographies. It does not include individuals or companies mentioned in the credits, nor does it cover the works cited in the bibliographic checklists. The latter omission is unfortunate since a number of works cited in the checklists are not mentioned in the bibliographic overviews. Both the index and the text suffer from a lack of careful proofreading, although most of the errors noted will not prevent the user from locating the desired information. For example, *Bicycle Thief* is listed in both the text and index as *Bicycle Thieves*; *Repo Man* is listed in the filmography as *Repro Man*.

As the title indicates, this work emphasizes films produced in the U.S. However, it does not exclude foreign films; in fact, the essay on the art film is devoted almost entirely to European contributions to this genre.

One of the strengths of this guide is its coverage of more genres than such standard studies as Stuart M. Kaminsky's *American Film Genres* (2d ed., Nelson-Hall, 1985), Thomas Schatz' *Hollywood Genres* (Temple Univ., 1981), and Barry Grant's *Film Genre Reader* (Univ. of Texas, 1986). Unfortunately, certain areas have been omitted. The editor acknowledges this in the preface, noting that "disaster films, sports movies, and erotic films" are additional genres that could have been included. Other examples of genres not covered are the historical epic, mystery/suspense films, and detective films. An additional problem is that some types of films are given short shrift due to unevenness in the breadth of the categories selected. For example, an entire chapter, "The World War II Combat Film," is devoted to war movies produced from 1942 to 1945, while all other war movies are covered in much less depth in the chapter on adventure films.

In spite of its shortcomings, *Handbook of American Film Genres* makes a valuable contribution to film scholarship, and it will be a useful acquisition for libraries that support serious film study.

Native Americans on Film and Video. v.2. By Elizabeth Weatherford and Emelia Seubert. Museum of the American Indian, Broadway at 155th St., New York, NY 10032, 1988. 112p. paper $7 (0-934490-44-9).

791.43'09 Indians in motion pictures [OCLC] 81-85266

Supplementing the first volume published in 1981, this filmography lists films and videotapes created since 1980 about Inuit and Indian peoples of North, Central, and South America. The authors are curators of the Film and Video Center of the Museum of the American Indian in New York.

From *Abnaki: The Native People of Maine* to *Yupiit Yuraryarait/A Dancing People*, descriptions are provided for approximately 200 documentaries, animations, and short features. Selection for inclusion was made "on the basis of the quality of the productions' research, filming, and editing, and on the uniqueness of their approach or subject matter, including profiles of native groups about whom few films have been available." Many films were created by native American independent producers, native media centers, or tribal communities working in cooperation with independent media makers.

Well-written annotations detail and analyze the content of each title. These films and videotapes reflect varied viewpoints, styles, and production values. References are made to other films by the filmmaker in this volume and in volume 1. A typical entry also includes release date, running time, production credits, formats available, languages (either spoken in the work or in which the production is available), and distributors for sales or rentals. Age recommendations are not included, but generally these titles are for adult audiences. The authors do recommend viewing films before using them in a program.

Very briefly noted in a two-page chapter titled "Currents" are several areas of concerns of these film producers, including how the native perspective began to be reflected in filmmaking, and funding and assistance available for developing education materials.

While individual films are listed alphabetically, films contained in series are listed under the series title. Both the subject index and index of tribes and regions will quickly aid in selection of a film or videotape. A list of distributors for both sales and rentals covers both volumes.

This title will be useful for public libraries and academic libraries supporting American Indian or anthropology studies.

Revenge of the Creature Features Movie Guide: An A to Z Encyclopedia to the Cinema of the Fantastic; or, Is There a Mad Doctor in the House? 3d ed. By John Stanley. Creatures at Large Press, P.O. Box 687, Pacifica, CA 94044, 1988. 420p. illus. hardcover $40 (0-940064-05-7); paper $11.95 (0-940064-04-9).

791.43'09 Fantastic films—Plots, themes, etc. [CIP] 87-91426

Inspired by the editor's stint as host of a popular San Francisco TV program that highlighted horror and fantasy films, this third edition of the *Revenge of the Creature Features Movie Guide* includes slightly less than 4,000 annotated film entries covering a wide variety of science-fiction, horror, suspense, mystery, and offbeat movies. (The second edition was published by Warner Books, but this edition—as well as the first edition—was published by the author himself.)

The book begins with a 23-page introduction providing the volume's history and isolated comments on specific films, genres, and trends. The main body is an alphabetized film listing consisting of year of release, main actors, director, producer, and a note indicating whether the film is available on video. The book's scope is subjective and eclectic, with coverage extending from Abbot and Costello films,

James Bond films, the baseball film *The Natural* (because it is "an allegory of battle between good and evil forces"), *The Manchurian Candidate*, and *The Wizard of Oz* to the Draculas, Frankensteins, aliens, vampires, and monsters of filmdom. Decorating almost every page are black-and-white movie or animation stills.

The annotations are succinctly written and usually very positive or campily negative. Unfortunately, there are no indexes that might help readers access information by film genre, names of people, or subject. There is also no notation of a film's running time.

Film reference standards such as *Halliwell's Film Guide* and *The Encyclopedia of Film* do not include many of the less-known, unusual movies found here. The multivolume *Motion Picture Guide* contains most of them, but with the relatively cheap paperback price and the wide public appeal of the subject matter, *Revenge of the Creature Features Movie Guide* is a useful reference for most public libraries and for academic collections supporting film arts programs.

Black Dance: An Annotated Bibliography. By Alice J. Adamczyk. Garland, 1989. 213p. illus. index. hardcover $30 (0-8240-8808-5).

016.7933'2 Blacks—Dancing—Bibliography [CIP] 88-29217

Africans brought their social, ceremonial, and religious dances with them to the Americas. Over the years black dance has taken varied forms and has remained a significant part of black culture. This bibliography represents an attempt to compile published material documenting black dance in the Western Hemisphere. *Black Dance* includes material on dance in North America, Latin America, the West Indies, and, to a lesser extent, Europe. Some citations are to material in French, Spanish, Portuguese, or German. Most materials are in the New York Public Library's Schomberg Center for Research in Black Culture, Dance Collection, or General Research Division.

The bibliography is composed of nearly 1,400 citations to books, articles, reviews, and dissertations. Journals indexed range from the *Village Voice* and *Ebony* to the *University of Pennsylvania Museum Journal* and *Journal of American Folklore*. Entries are listed in alphabetical order by author or main entry, and most have brief annotations. There is a subject index that includes names of individuals (*Baker, Josephine; Dunham, Katherine; Hines, Gregory*), dance groups (*Dance Theatre of Harlem, Alvin Ailey American Dance Theater*), types of dance (*break dancing, cakewalk, jitterbug, religious dancing*), and other topics (*Savoy Ballroom, Television, Critics and Criticism, Negro Ensemble Company Dance and Music Festival*). The index is generally well done, although some omissions were noted by the Board. Nine illustrations of historical interest enliven the text.

Black Dance is a unique work that leads to a great deal of material, some of it of a specialized nature. The book is appropriate for college and university libraries supporting programs in dance or black culture and for public libraries with large performing-arts collections.

Comedy on Record: The Complete Critical Discography. By Ronald L. Smith. Garland, 1988. 728p. hardcover $55 (0-8240-8461-6).

016.7927'028 Comedians—U.S.—Discography I Comedians—U.S.—Biography—Dictionaries I American wit and humor—Discography I Sound recordings—U.S.—Catalogs [CIP] 87-35969

Laughter on Record: A Comedy Discography. By Warren Debenham. Scarecrow, 1988. 369p. illus. index. hardcover $35 (0-8108-2094-3).

016.7922'3 Wit and humor—Discography I Comedians—Discography [CIP] 87-35938

While these two discographies ostensibly cover the same turf, the unique features of each complement those of the other. Both cover LPs only, with *Laughter on Record* including more British releases. Both are arranged by comedian, with neither providing a separate title index. Both provide record labels and numbers, where available, and indicate if a record has been rereleased under the same or a different title.

Comedy on Record provides biographical information on the artist(s) and critical information on the individual recordings, including ratings by the compiler (one to five stars) and, in some cases, excerpts from selected cuts. Some entries conclude with "Collector's Notes," which discuss the value of rare pressings or locate specific routines recorded in compilations of the work of many comics. Listings of recordings known mainly by title (with cross-references to artists), compilation albums, Grammy Award winners, and winners of the Recording Industry Auditors of America (RIAA) Gold Awards are included in supplementary pages. Since the entry for an individual comic may continue for several pages, this work would have been improved by the addition of headers indicating the entries on each page.

Laughter on Record is a more straightforward discography, providing no biographical and meager critical information (some entries include a description of the genre, e.g., "Scottish comedy," "Religious drama," "Off-key singing"). Additional access is provided by a topical subject index. A directory of record companies and sources of out-of-print records (in 12 states and the District of Columbia) is included, along with a few black-and-white photographs of comedians.

Comparison of these two discographies based upon quantity of recordings listed is hampered by their differing treatment of rereleases and compilations. *Laughter on Record* has over 4,300 entries, but this number includes separate entries for rereleases and cuts or sides of compilations. *Comedy on Record* has an estimated 1,800 entries, not including rereleases or compilations. An examination of entries by selected artists indicates that each discography includes some artists or individual recordings not included in the other. For large collections, or collections with strong interests in the performing arts.

Media Review Digest, 1987: The Only Complete Guide to Reviews of Non-Book Media. Ed. by Lesley O. Regan. Pierian Press, 1988. annual. 852p. indexes. hardcover $245 (0-87650-231-1).

016.79143 Moving-pictures—Reviews—Bibliography I Audio-visual materials—Reviews—Bibliography I Visual education—Bibliography [BKL] 73-172772

Media Review Digest, 1987 (*MRD*) retains the excellent format, scope, and special features identified by the Board in its favorable review of the 1980 annual [My 1 82]. Although the volume has grown to 852 pages, few changes have been made. *MRD* presents approximately 40,000 citations and cross-references to reviews found in 132 periodicals and services. These reviews cover films, videocassettes and videodiscs, filmstrips, educational and spoken-word records and tapes, slides, transparencies, illustrations, globes, charts, media kits, games, and other media forms. The most significant improvements found in the 1987 annual are the inclusion of a large number of videocassettes and videodiscs and the deletion of the classified subject index.

The educational and entertainment media are subdivided into four sections: "Film and Video" (443 pages); "Filmstrips" (56 pages); "Audio" (formerly called "Record and Tape Section," 40 pages); and "Miscellaneous" (12 pages). Information given for films, videos, and filmstrips includes title or series title, brief description of theme or content, country of origin, producer, distributor, release date, running time, if it is sound or silent and black and white or color, and price. Subject headings and audience levels are provided, followed by citations to reviews. Review ratings (+, +-, -, and *) indicate the general nature of each review, with "*" denoting a descriptive but not evaluative review. Also provided are the rating codes given by the Motion Picture Association of America. In some cases, 25-word quotations from selected reviews are provided. *MRD* recognizes that not all reviews appear in traditional review columns and therefore indexes "discussions contained in full-length articles, commentary on recent film festivals . . .and many other of the less formal and less structured features." Most of the reviews cited appear to be from 1986. Some of the reviews are for media cited in earlier *MRD* volumes. In such cases the year of the *MRD* volume is given in parentheses following the title. Extensive use is made of cross-references to foreign-language titles and series titles.

The extremely helpful introduction explains the volume's scope and arrangement and discusses subject cataloging, audience levels, review ratings, and sources. It also explains the special features and indexes, includes a list of periodical abbreviations, and provides complete information for each of the periodicals and services indexed (i.e., address, subscription rate, frequency of publication, and brief commentary). The special features section lists a variety of film awards and devotes 49 pages to "Mediagraphies," defined as "articles about films that cannot be thought of as reviews of one specific film" and "interviews with or articles about directors, producers, actors/actresses, as well as articles dealing with three or more films, discussions of genre or period, or any particular aspect of filmmaking." Following the four indexes (general subject index, alphabetical subject index, geographic index, and reviewer index) is a directory of addresses for producers and distributors whose media are included in this volume.

The 1982 review stated that "reviews of feature films are well covered. However, in order to improve its usefulness to teachers, more extensive coverage of reviews of filmstrips, records, and tapes is needed." The continued emphasis on films and videos does not seem inappropriate since these are the media most used by teachers, especially now that videos are so readily accessible and easy to use.

Media Review Digest, 1987 is highly recommended for use in large public, academic, and performing-arts libraries. It will be useful in very large school libraries or district selection centers, but its high annual cost puts it out of reach for most school budgets. The publisher reports that the 1988 volume will be published in February.

Dramatists Sourcebook: Complete Opportunities for Playwrights, Translators, Composers, Lyricists and Librettists. 1988–89 ed. Ed. by Gillian Richards and Ray Sweatman. Theatre Communications Group, 1988. 261p. bibliog. index. paper $11.95 (0-9304522-87-9; ISSN 0733-1606).

792 Playwriting—Handbooks, manuals, etc. ▮ Theaters—U.S.—Directories [OCLC]

This is the eighth annual *Dramatists Sourcebook* published by Theatre Communications Group, a national organization for nonprofit professional theater. It is primarily a directory of performance and publication sources for creators of new dramatic works. The largest section is devoted to script submission information for 245 theaters and includes notes on each theater's facilities, interests, special programs, production consideration (e.g., limits on size of casts), deadlines, and response time. Other sections cover playwriting contests, publication sources, and conferences, festivals, and workshops intended for playwrights and the development of their work. Contact people and telephone numbers are given for most entries.

This book departs from the directory format in its prologue, which provides tips from experts on manuscript preparation and submission (excerpted from TCG's *In Their Own Words*, 1988), and in "Roundtable," a 22-page discussion among nearly two dozen composers, lyricists, librettists, and theater-arts administrators on the topic "Modern Theatre is Music-Theatre." The work concludes with a listing of 42 agencies that handle playwrights, organizations that serve theater professionals, state arts councils, and sources of funding (e.g., fellowships, grants, and residencies).

The appendixes consist of a bibliography, a calendar (September 1988–August 1989) of submission deadlines, special-interests categories (e.g., *Asian-American Theatre, Experimental Theatre*), and an alphabetical arrangement of names of theaters, programs, agents, etc. A geographic index would be a useful addition to future editions.

The format of the work has changed little since the 1982–83 edition. A listing of college and university programs in playwriting last appeared in 1983–84, and a section on media sources (e.g., television and radio) was dropped in 1984–85. This year's edition has the new category *One-Acts* in the special-interests index. The numbers of entries and pages have gradually increased over the years; the 1982–83 *Sourcebook* included approximately 400 entries and 184 pages; the 1988–89 edition has 765 entries and 261 pages. The appearance of this title on an annual basis is especially important because of the need for current information in this field, as theaters open and close, organizations form and disband, and contact individuals move on to other opportunities. The "Plays and Playwrights" section of TCG's monthly magazine, *American Theatre*, serves to update information in *Dramatists Sourcebook*.

Authoritative information from TCG's membership and an easily read format continue to make *Dramatists Sourcebook* a valuable and inexpensive guide for librarians and students, as well as writers and other theater professionals. It complements *The Dramatist's Bible* [*RBB* Ja 1 87], which covers England and Canada as well as the U.S. Mollie Meserve's *Playwright's Companion, 1988: A Submission Guide to Theatres & Contests in the U.S.A.* (Feedback Theatrebooks, 1988) is a comparable work that has appeared in four annual editions. Over 1,000 listings are organized under the categories *Theatres, Contests, Special Programs, Publishers,* and *Agents*.

The Cambridge Guide to World Theatre. Ed. by Martin Banham. Cambridge, 1989 (c1988). 1,104p. bibliog. illus. index. hardcover $49.50 (0-521-26595-9).

792'.0321 Theater—Dictionaries [CIP] 88-25804

This new reference work offers a comprehensive view of the history and present practice of theater in all parts of the world. Besides detailed articles on countries that have well-known traditions in theater (such as England, France, Germany, Italy, Japan, and the U.S.), *The Cambridge Guide* includes articles on theater in Nigeria, Peru, El Salvador, Malawi, Kampuchea, and Iceland. Giving a broad interpretation to the word *theater*, the *The Cambridge Guide* also includes popular entertainment, with such articles as *Animals as Performers, Juggler, Mime, Fireworks,* and *Marionette*. Long articles on subjects like folk drama, ancient Greek drama, and Shakespearean performances are very helpful to the scholars, students, and general readers to whom the book is directed. Other topics covered include dramatic theory, criticism, censorship, copyright, lighting, sound, design, and theater buildings. There are many entries for actors, directors, playwrights, and designers. When relevant, radio, TV, dance, music, opera, and film are mentioned.

The Cambridge Guide is arranged alphabetically. Boldface type within an entry identifies a person or subject that has its own entry in the book. *See* references are also used. Articles are signed with the initials of one of the more than 110 contributors. Editor Banham is a professor of drama and theater at the University of Leeds. Members of the editorial advisory board come from Britain and North America. Excellent bibliographies are included at the end of articles on countries and broad topics like *Medieval Drama in Europe*. A general bibliography lists 10 important theater reference books.

It is to be expected that *The Cambridge Guide* will be compared to *The Oxford Companion to the Theatre*, a standard work that editor Phyllis Hartnoll has shepherded through four editions, the most recent in 1983. *The Cambridge Guide*, with its world view and wider, more inclusive definition of theater, does offer new and/or expanded information compared with *Oxford*. The majority of topics in *The Cambridge Guide* are also covered in *Oxford*, however. *The Cambridge Guide* has over 500 black-and-white illustrations throughout the book; *Oxford* has 96 pages of plates grouped together at different points. All of these illustrations are helpful and attractive. *Oxford* does not have bibliographies with articles but has a 15-page bibliography at the end of the book. Both *The Cambridge Guide* and *The Oxford Companion* and their publishers have authority and reputation sufficient to make them desirable in all serious collections.

The Cambridge Guide to World Theatre is an exciting new reference work. It would be a welcome addition to any public, academic, or high school library.

The Facts On File Dictionary of the Theatre. Ed. by Willam Packard and others. Facts On File, 1989 (c1988). 556p. hardcover $29.95 (0-8160-1841-3).

792'.03 Theater—Dictionaries ▮ Drama—Bio-bibliography [CIP] 88-28379

The Facts On File Dictionary of the Theatre (*FOF*) provides little competition to the long-established *Oxford Companion to the Theatre* (now in its fourth edition, 1983) or the new *Cambridge Guide to World Theatre* [*RBB* Je 1 89]. *FOF* emphasizes European and American theater; the Oxford and especially the Cambridge title have a worldwide scope. The latter two books have lengthy articles on theater in various countries of the world. Topics treated in all three sources have briefer coverage in *FOF*. In a sample of entries compared by the Board, only one entry (*Callow, Simon*) from *FOF* was not also found in *The Oxford Companion*; it was found in *The Cambridge Guide*. A few entries in the sample did update entries found in *The Oxford Companion*. *FOF* does include entries for individual plays (with date of first performance and capsule summary), which *The Oxford Companion* and *Cambridge Guide* do not. *FOF* has no bibliography or illustrations; *The Oxford Companion* and *The Cambridge Guide* contain both.

This is not a necessary purchase for libraries already owning one of the other two works mentioned above. It is only about half the size of each but costs more than half as much. Libraries not owning *The Oxford Companion* or *The Cambridge Guide* should purchase one of them before considering purchase of *The Facts On File Dictionary of the Theatre*.

The Book of Card Games. By Peter Arnold. Christopher Holm; dist. by Hippocrene, 1989 (c1988). 279p. illus. indexes. paper $14.95 (0-7470-0003-4).
795.4 Cards I Games [BKL]

The Book of Card Games is a good introduction to many of the most popular card games played in social settings. Author Arnold has written a number of other books on games and cards and is an authority in this area. The introduction states that over 150 games are explained, but the table of contents lists only 77 games, the difference being variations on games (e.g., vingt-et-un and blackjack).

The book is intended as a beginner's guide and takes the reader through the play. A standard formula is used for each game: number of players, how many sets of cards are used and their point rankings, how dealing is done, what "the play" involves, and explanations of sample hands involving a number of players. Entries range from half a page for *Old Maid* and *Go Fish* to more than 20 for *Bridge*. The author states that by following this guide, players will be able to run through a game and get the rudiments sorted out. We tested this by trying to learn how to play poker according to the explanations set out in the book and did not fare too badly.

There are two indexes at the back of the book: a general index that lists the 150 games and a classified index that lists games by number of players (from one to five or more), gambling games, and six children's games. If the reader wants to learn how to play chemin de fer, it isn't in the table of contents but is found in the general index as a variant of baccarat. Almost every game is illustrated with drawings of cards in the appropriate red and black colors. A two-page glossary at the beginning of the book provides the basics of card-game terminology: *cut*, *flush*, *trick*, etc.

A very handy reference, especially for public libraries where this kind of information is often required.

Interactive Fiction and Adventure Games for Microcomputers, 1988: An Annotated Directory. By Patrick R. Dewey. Meckler, 1988. 189p. bibliog. illus. index. paper $39.50 (0-88736-170-6).
016.7948'2 Computer adventure games—Software—Bibliography [CIP] 87-16473

Dewey's work is an annotated directory of one type of computer software game. Interactive fiction (also known as adventure games) is heavily dependent on reading and lets the reader play a role in the story. Arranged alphabetically by name of the game, entries identify producer, cost, appropriate hardware (for example, Apple or Atari), level of difficulty, use of graphics and text, and a description of the plot or action. These descriptions vary from objective plot summaries to subjective analysis of the quality and significance of the game.

In his introduction, public librarian Dewey identifies interactive fiction as a new type of literature and seeks recognition by educators and librarians of this format. Although he never identifies his intended purpose for creating the directory, it could be used as a selection guide for individuals or librarians developing collections in this area.

Game topics focus on mystery (*Suspect*), adventure (*Indiana Jones*), and science fiction (*Star Trek*). However, other topics are interspersed, such as Shakespeare's *Macbeth* and *Ticket to Paris*, a French-language travel quiz. Games are available for Commodore, Apple, IBM, Atari, and Amiga.

Illustrations of program graphics are supplied for some entries, and producer and title indexes supply additional access points. The volume ends with six useful appendixes, including "Solution Books," "Game Magazines," "Sources of Software," and "Making Your Own Adventure" (authoring software).

This unique reference tool will be of value to public and school libraries with microcomputer facilities or clientele who use libraries as a source of evaluative information on computer software.

Sports Talk: A Dictionary of Sports Metaphors. By Robert A. Palmatier and Harold L. Ray. Greenwood, 1989. 227p. bibliog. index. hardcover $39.95 (0-313-26426-0).
796'.014 English language—Terms and phrases I Sports—Terminology I Metaphor [CIP] 88-24646

When we hear the expressions "play ball," "gentlemen, start your engines," and "post time," we know that something is about to begin. In addition to the same meaning, these expressions have other things in common. Their origins are sports related (baseball, auto racing, and horse racing, respectively); they can be used in a nonsports context; and they are all found in *Sports Talk: A Dictionary of Sports Metaphors*.

Sports Talk is an alphabetical, letter-by-letter listing of over 1,700 words, phrases, and expressions that have their origin in sports, games, or recreation and that have now become a part of our everyday language. A typical entry includes the metaphor, an illustration of its correct use, the definition of the popular meaning, the date of its earliest verified use (when possible), the sport from which it originated, and the date of its earliest use as a sports term (when possible). Lettered codes are used to refer to 22 reference sources that also identify the metaphor, and, whenever appropriate, cross-references are provided to similar or opposite entries in the dictionary. These *see also* and *compare to* references are useful and frequent. The dictionary concludes with a classification of the metaphors by the sport or game of origin. More than 100 sports and games, from *Acrobatics* to *Yo-Yo*, are listed, with some *see* references.

Sports Talk, like many sources that trace the origin of a phrase or word, is not always able to identify the definitive source. For example, the expression "sudden death" is attributed to gambling, but the authors indicate that there might be a connection to cockfighting or dog fighting. Another example is "the whole nine yards." Football is given as the source; however, the authors suspect another origin, since 10 yards are needed for a first down. This does not make the work any less authoritative, just inconclusive at times.

The obvious and primary purpose of *Sports Talk* is that of reference, but it can also be read straight through by anyone with an interest in sports and etymology. Libraries with sports collections and those wanting to add to their linguistics and etymological dictionaries will want this title. It will complement such works as *A Dictionary of Americanisms*, *New Dictionary of American Slang* [RBB D 15 86], *The Dictionary of Clichés*, and *The Dickson Dictionary of Baseball* [RBB Mr 15 89], which provides some of the same type of information for just one sport.

Guinness Sports Record Book, 1988–89. Ed. by David A. Boehm. Sterling, 1988. 256p. illus. index. hardcover $16.95 (0-8069-6811-7); paper $10.95 (0-8069-6810-9).
796.0212 Sports—Records [OCLC] 82-642136

Guinness Sports Record Book, 1988–89 is similar in format to various other Guinness record books. It includes an assortment of universally recognized sports—such as soccer, jai-alai, baseball, tennis, swimming, skiing, and golf—as well as less popular sports: joggling (juggling while running), orienteering, snowshoe racing, and trampolining. Eight pages are devoted to games and pastimes, among them chess, contract bridge, marbles, Scrabble, backgammon, poker, billiards, and video games.

A one-page introduction explains how categories are determined and what procedures persons should follow when submitting record-breaking attempts to the Guinness editorial offices. Following a discussion of general sports records, individual sports are presented alphabetically. While sports such as marathons, karate, and lacrosse receive only one page each, as many as 15 pages are devoted to major sports. The section on baseball discusses home runs, individual batting, base running, pitching, fielding, and World Series records, as well as unique records, youngest and oldest players, most stolen bases, fewest strikeouts, most strikeouts in an inning, longest major league career, records for managers, attendance, and baseball memorabilia and even "most rehirings as manager of same major league team." Brief historical coverage is given to several sports. The section on swimming discusses the history of the sport, world titles, Olympic records, swimming in the movies, swimming world records for men and women, long-distance swimming, youngest and oldest swimmers, underwater swimming, and the largest pools.

In most cases, when records are listed they give only the all-time record holders for those events. A complete list of winners, by year, is provided for other types of sports: the U.S. Open, U.S. Women's Open, British Open, and U.S. Amateur golf tournaments; the Indianapolis 500; Le Mans; Wimbledon; Kentucky Derby; Super Bowl; and heavyweight boxing championships. Interspersed with the records are explanations, such as the "Grand Slam" of tennis. Although Olympic records are given in their respective sports, the short section devoted entirely to the Olympics consists mostly of photographs. Black-and-white action photographs are found on nearly every page of the book. Sports from all over the world are included, but the emphasis seems to be on sports in the U.S. Although soccer is a more universal sport than American football, only four pages are devoted to soccer while nine are given to football. A detailed index lists not just the sports but also specific categories in each sport.

Guinness Sports Record Book, 1988–89 will be popular in public libraries and school libraries. However, it is an annual publication and most libraries won't need to purchase each new edition.

The Sports Address Book. Ed. by Scott Callis. Simon & Schuster, 1988. 249p. paper $6.95 (0-671-64771-7).

796.07 Sports—Directories I Sports camps—Directories [OCLC]

Anyone who has ever struggled to locate a sports-related address will welcome the paperback *Sports Address Book*. With 5,000 addresses for players, teams, leagues, conferences, organizations, publications, and other media, this work brings together an incredible amount of information. The compiler acknowledges some omissions, but advises contacting a publication or organization for the missing address. The addresses for individuals usually are the mailing address of an agent, business, or team. Callis, out of respect for an individual's privacy, did not include telephone numbers. Suggestions on how to be sure to receive a response and things to avoid such as asking for more than one autograph are included in the introduction.

The directory is divided into two parts: "Directory of Individual Sports" and "General Directory." The specific sports section covers everything from the NBA and NFL to jai-alai and Frisbee, arranged in alphabetical order. Addresses given for major sports include leagues, teams, publications, camps, and individuals. For lesser-known sports, only organizations and publications are listed. International organizations and sports are included, as well as famous retired players such as Joe DiMaggio. Not every player or coach is listed; missing are Billy Tubbs, Oklahoma basketball coach; Shawon Dunston, Chicago Cubs shortstop; Kevin McHale, Boston Celtics forward; and Olympian Jackie Joyner-Kersee. The "General Directory" lists sports organizations for the disabled, international Olympic committees, sporting goods manufacturers, halls of fame, media, sports medicine clinics, and agents and attorneys. Although some of this information can be found in sources ranging from telephone directories to the *Encyclopedia of Associations*, it is helpful to have it all in one place. Although written mainly for the sports fan, this reasonably priced source will be a boon to reference librarians and has the potential to become essential in public, academic, and school libraries.

Biographical Dictionary of American Sports: Outdoor Sports. Ed. by David L. Porter. Greenwood, 1988. 728p. index. hardcover $75 (0-313-26260-8).

796'.092 [B] Athletes—U.S.—Biography—Dictionaries I Sports—U.S.—History I Sports promoters—U.S.—Biography—Dictionaries [CIP] 87-31780

This *Dictionary* is a companion to two 1987 volumes, *Biographical Dictionary of American Sports: Baseball* and *Biographical Dictionary of American Sports: Football* [RBB N 15 87], in a planned four-volume set. Topics included here are auto racing, communications and media, golf, horse racing, lacrosse, skiing, soccer, speed skating, tennis, and track and field. Howard Cosell, Joe Garagiola, Ring Lardner, and Grantland Rice are examples of the persons listed in the "Communications and Media" section. Several topics are included in a "Miscellaneous" section: administration, bicycling, bobsledding, equestrian sports, field hockey, polo, rodeo, rowing, softball, and yachting. Administrators include Avery Brundage, James E. Sullivan, and Peter Ueberroth. The 200- to 900-word entries include both personal and career information. Most of the facts are up-to-date through 1987. Each entry is signed and has a bibliography; however, few items more recent than 1984 are listed. The bibliographies include both books and periodical articles by and about the subject.

Of the 519 people listed in this volume, only 74 are women. The entries are balanced between living and deceased persons. Approximately half of those living are still active in their sport; the other half are retired. For a person to be included in this volume, he or she must have been "born or spent childhood years in the United States, ...made exceptional career accomplishments in an amateur and/or professional outdoor sport, ...[and] made an important impact on a major outdoor sport." Other considerations include belonging to a sports hall of fame, winning major athletic honors, and representing the U.S. in international competition such as the Olympic Games.

In addition to a list of contributors with their credentials, there are several appendixes similar to those in the two earlier volumes. One especially interesting section gives biographical sketches for 55 race horses. Other appendixes include "Alphabetical Listing of Entries with Sport," which in effect is an index to the section in which the person's name appears, but without page numbers; "Entries by Place of Birth"; and "Women Athletes by Sport."

Biographical Dictionary of American Sports: Outdoor Sports, with its variety of appendixes, is fascinating reading and an excellent sports reference source. This volume is highly recommended for public and academic libraries and also for large high school collections.

The Pro Football Bio-Bibliography. By Myron J. Smith. Locust Hill Press, 1989. 288p. bibliog. paper $25 (0-933951-23-X).

016.796332'64 Football—U.S.—Bio-bibliography [CIP] 88-37741

Convinced that the most interesting way to look at a sport is through the biographies of its players, Smith compiled *The Pro Football Bio-Bibliography* to "draw attention to many of the thousands of titles available on various pro football figures." Approximately 6,600 citations are provided for more than 1,400 players from the 1920s through 1988. Items listed include books, periodical articles, and league and team publications but exclude newspaper articles. While most of the entries are for players, the bibliography also includes broadcasters, coaches, executives, and referees.

The biographees are listed alphabetically with nicknames, position(s), team affiliations, and years played with those teams. If the person held a nonplaying position such as broadcaster, that is sometimes noted. Members of the Pro Football Hall of Fame are identified by asterisks. Following this biographical data, citations are listed alphabetically by author with full bibliographic information. There are no annotations.

The number of citations varies from a single entry each for *Matt Bahr* and *Chuck Long* to 121 entries for *Joe Namath*. The criterion for inclusion was not a person's significance but rather how much literature was available. The increasing popularity of professional football, the expansion of franchises, and the proliferation of media coverage are evident in the large number of players included from the 1970s and

1980s compared with earlier years. In many cases the media coverage reflects the personality, not just the quality, of the player; for example, *George Blanda*, who played for 26 years, has 24 citations, while *Brian Bosworth*, who has played professionally for just two years, has 10 citations.

The introduction lists abbreviations used for player functions and leagues, including the Canadian Football League; U.S. cities that have had NFL teams; and citations for important reference works. Preceding the biographical entries is a "List of Journals Cited." These 167 journals include sports periodicals (*Sports Illustrated, Inside Sports, Athletic Journal*); general periodicals (*Time, New Yorker*); and some unexpected titles (*Family Circle, Literary Digest, Weight Watchers*). While some of the citations in this bibliography are also in *Biography Index*, Smith indexes many journals not found there.

This book is fascinating even for persons mildly interested in professional football. Though its focus is narrow, *The Pro Football Bio-Bibliography* should save time for those researching the topic. It is recommended for purchase, especially by public libraries.

LITERATURE

Critical Survey of Literary Theory: Authors. 4v. Ed. by Frank N. Magill. Salem Press, 1988 (c1987). 1,833p. bibliog. index. hardcover $300 (0-89356-390-0).
801'.95 Literature—Philosophy ‖ Literature—History and criticism ‖ Criticism—Bio-bibliography ‖ Critics—Biography—Dictionaries [CIP] 88-11424

Surveying the work of over 250 critics and theorists, this set is another offspring in the ever-expanding family of literature reference sources edited by Frank N. Magill. Its format will be familiar to librarians who have worked with other sets in the Critical Survey series. Arrangement is alphabetical by author. Each article is divided into standard sections: dates and locations of birth and death; "Principal Criticism"; "Other Literary Forms"; "Influence"; "Biography"; "Theory and Criticism"; "Other Major Works"; and "Bibliography," listing secondary sources. Though they only skim the surface of each critic's life and work, the discussions are not overly simplified. Average length is about six pages. The various contributors, most of whom have academic affiliations, are listed at the beginning of volume 1. All of the articles are signed.

As in the other Critical Survey sets, the final volume contains essays that consider the genre from a historical, geographic, and national perspective. The 12 essays address such subjects as "Classical Greek and Roman Literary Theory," "Literary Theory in the Age of Victoria," and "Japanese Literary Theory." The essays are followed by a glossary containing 147 entries, from *absurdism* to *Yale School*. The index provides access to writers, titles, terms, schools or types of criticism, and nationalities.

The scope of this set is one of its strengths. Coverage ranges from ancient theorists to many living writers. Non-Western traditions—Chinese, Japanese, and African—are represented. Many of the writers included are known primarily as critics, but others better known for other works, such as Leo Tolstoy and Henry James, are discussed here as literary theorists. The variety of theories is enormous, ranging from the classic work of Aristotle to the pioneering feminist criticism of Sandra M. Gilbert and Susan Gubar.

Obviously, by including so much material and fitting it all into the same standardized format, Magill sacrifices some depth of coverage. However, the goals of this set are the same as the rest of the Critical Survey series: to provide convenient introductions to writers and their work. Many students will require no more; for others, *Critical Survey of Literary Theory* will provide a springboard to further study. Five volumes of Gale's Dictionary of Literary Biography (volumes 59, 63, 64, 67, and 71) are devoted to nineteenth- and twentieth-century American critics. The only other comparable reference set is *The Art of the Critic*, part of the Chelsea House Library of Literary Criticism edited by Harold Bloom; this 11-volume set compiles critical texts instead of providing summaries. Though it may not be as much of a priority as other sets in the Critical Survey series, *Critical Survey of Literary Theory* is recommended for libraries that need information on literary critics. It can help round out the literature reference collections of libraries that do not need or want to provide access to the primary texts.

MLA Directory of Periodicals: A Guide to Journals and Serials in Languages and Literatures: Periodicals Published in the United States and Canada. 1988–89 ed. Comp. by Eileen M. Mackesy and Dee Ella Spears. Modern Language Association, 1988. 300p. indexes. paper $30 (0-87352-472-1).
805'.025 Language and languages—Periodicals—Directories ‖ Literature—Periodicals—Directories ‖ Periodicals—Directories [BKL]

This is the abridged, paperbound version of the biennial *MLA Directory of Periodicals* [*RSBR* Jl 1 80], first published in 1979. The complete clothbound volume contains listings for 3,146 journals and series in languages and literatures. Of these, 1,170 published in the U.S. and Canada are listed in the paperbound volume.

The entries in the *Directory* are current as of January 22, 1988, and are preceded by an asterisk if they have been verified and updated since the last hardcover edition. While journals and series are included if they publish on the subjects of language, literature, and folklore, it is obvious that the subjects are interpreted broadly. For example, the *Journal of Abnormal Psychology*, the *Journal of Chinese Philosophy*, *Russian Review*, and *Human Development* are all included.

The volume is arranged alphabetically by title with a sequence number used as a reference from the indexes. Entries are identical to those in the hardcover edition: basic information (editors, address, date of first publication, etc.); subscription information (frequency, microform availability, subscription price); advertising information (acceptance and rates); editorial description (scope, if abstracts are printed, if there is an anonymous submission policy); and submission requirements (restrictions on contributors, length of articles, copyright ownership, time before publication decision, time between decision and publication, articles submitted per year, articles published per year). There are four indexes in the volume: editorial, languages published (other than English, French, German, Italian, and Spanish), sponsoring organization, and subject.

The 1988–89 hardcover and paper editions are the first to include information on blind submission policy. An index of such titles is promised for the next edition. Basic and subscription information for most of the journals may also be found in *The Serials Directory* or *Ulrich's International Periodicals Directory*. (Telephone numbers are sometimes included in *Ulrich's* and *The Serials Directory* but not in the *MLA Directory*.) The editorial description and submissions requirements covered in detail in the *MLA Directory* are vital information needed by the scholar and researcher.

Large academic libraries will still want the complete hardcover edition. Smaller academic libraries and public libraries with a clientele that publishes in U.S. and Canadian humanities journals will find this reasonably priced paperback edition a necessary purchase.

The Writer's Directory, 1988–90. 8th ed. St. James Press, 1988. 1,045p. index. hardcover $95 (0-912289-87-2).

808 Authors, American—Directories I Authors, English—Directories [OCLC]

The eighth edition of this biennial reference work lists more than 16,000 living writers who write in English. The publisher claims that about 1,000 names are new to this edition. The work includes a long list of abbreviations, a "yellow pages" index by writing categories, and the directory, which is alphabetical by the author's last name.

The writing categories are divided into creative writing (e.g., novels, short stories, mysteries, romance, westerns, science fiction, children's fiction, plays, poetry, songs); nonfiction (every subject from administration to zoology); and a miscellaneous category (autobiographies, biographies, documentaries, reportage, humor, and translations).

Each entry in the directory contains the writer's name, pseudonyms, citizenship, birth date, writing categories, current and past appointments, bibliography of writings, and address. The length of the entries varies from a few lines (*Aaron, Chester*) to almost a page (*Cartland, Barbara*). One can always question why some writers like Stephen Ambrose (biographer of Richard Nixon and Dwight Eisenhower) were omitted, as were Marion Chesney (regency fiction), Morgan Lewellyn (*Lion of Ireland, The Horse Goddess, The Bard,* and *Grania*), Jude Deveraux (romance writer), and Terry Brooks (fantasy).

The major weakness of this work is the dearth of information about each author and the fact that some entries are outdated. It is not going to replace tools such as Gale's *Contemporary Authors* (*CA*), which covers almost 90,000 authors, including deceased and foreign writers. A sample of authors from *The Writer's Directory* checked against the cumulative index to *CA* found that almost 90 percent were found there. The advantage of *The Writer's Directory* ought to be currency of information, since it is updated every two years and *CA* is not. However, it continues to list authors who are noted in *CA* as deceased, it gives out-of-date addresses for some writers, and bibliographies are not always up-to-date. The writing categories do provide a useful means of finding authors in particular genres, which makes this a helpful starting point in reader service.

The Writer's Directory is recommended where its predecessors have been useful, but many libraries will continue to rely on *Contemporary Authors*.

Market Guide for Young Writers, 1988–89. 2d ed. By Kathy Henderson. Shoe Tree Press; dist. by Talman Co., 150 Fifth Ave., Rm. 514, New York, NY 10011, 1988. 171p. paper $12.95 (0-936915-10-2).

808.025 Authorship—Handbooks, manuals, etc. I Authorship—Competitions—Periodicals I Publishers and publishing—U.S.—Directories I Children as authors—Periodicals [BKL] 87-62596

Meant to be a juvenile version of *Writer's Market*, the purpose of this little volume is to "provide young writers the opportunity to reach beyond their circle of friends, family and teachers...and to realize the power contained in learning to communicate effectively." It mimics *WM* in its organization of market listings (address, frequency of publication, audience, length and type of submissions accepted, specific features, payment), manuscript guidelines, and even the "Editor Close Up" sections with articles by magazine editors. It goes further in its appeal to youngsters with a "Young Writers in Print" section (interviews focusing on eight who have won contests or been published), hints on preparing manuscripts (typed and double spaced), and answers to questions often asked (Will a magazine steal my idea?). It concludes with a bibliography, glossary, and index. Better organization of this information would help considerably. Interview sections might be arranged *after* the contests, which need not be separate from other markets. (Some, like *Cricket*, are "contests," the prize for which is publication.) The subject index could use a cross-reference from *letter* to the entries *cover letter* and *query letter*.

Surprisingly, this listing of about 100 American and Canadian markets (37 new to this edition) does not duplicate all those listed in *WM* under the headings *Children* and *Teen/Youth,* and there are many different contests listed, nearly half of which require an entry fee. Many periodicals here are not necessarily just for students but will accept young writers (*Poetry Review, Sports Parade*). *Writer's Market,* however, is a better bet all around for libraries, since it includes *Pennywhistle Press, Pennypower, Young Author's Magazine, Young American,* and a number of religious magazines, such as *Touch, Shofar,* and *Pockets,* which all welcome youth submissions but aren't listed here. This is the kind of book that parents will buy for their kids; public libraries might consider it for the children's collection rather than duplicating the more expensive *WM*.

Children's Writer's & Illustrator's Market, 1989. Ed. by Connie Wright Eidenier. Writer's Digest, 1989. 179p. bibliog. illus. indexes. paper $14.95 (0-89879-342-4; ISSN 0897-9790).

808.068 Children's literature—Authorship [OCLC]

With an eye to the burgeoning market for children's literature, Writer's Digest has compiled "a market directory listing the needs of the children's book and magazine industry." Divided into three basic segments, it is designed to help the writer get work published.

General information about the business end of submitting manuscripts is very practical, beginning with an overview of today's market. Marketing, packing and mailing manuscripts, pricing and contracts, business records, taxes, and author's rights are covered in this segment.

The second segment offers information on 102 book publishers, 63 magazine publishers, and 28 publishers looking for work by young authors and illustrators, as well as contests and awards for students and professional writers. Information is given in standard *Writer's Market* style for both writers and illustrators.

The last section lists resources for the author: agents and writers' organizations, workshops, a glossary of publishing and contractual terms, and Newbery and Caldecott winners. There are three indexes: age level for books and for magazines and a general index. A bibliography of related books and a form to record manuscript submissions complete the work.

This book does overlap to some extent with *Writer's Market*. *Writers' Digest* and *The Writer* are two periodicals that offer occasional articles and publisher listings for authors of works for children. However, this book's concentration on the children's market will be useful in public libraries, academic libraries that support curricula in illustration, writing, and education, and in school-district professional libraries as well. Since it is so practical, authors will want a copy for their personal libraries.

Fiction Writers Guidelines: Over 200 Periodical Editors' Instructions Reproduced. Comp. by Judy Mandell. McFarland, 1988. 316p. index. paper $20.95 (0-89950-249-0).

808.3 Fiction—Authorship [CIP] 88-45206

Fiction Writers Guidelines (*FWG*) is a compilation of guidelines for 231 magazines that publish fiction. In addition, comments from 15 editors of publications that do not have written guidelines but accept free-lance contributions are included. A companion volume, *Magazine Writers Nonfiction Guidelines,* was previously listed in *RBB* [Ap 1 87].

Although the book includes titles typically found on the newsstand, such as *Playboy* and *Redbook,* notable literary magazines like *Partisan Review, The Paris Review,* and *The Antioch Review* are also represented. *Jack and Jill, Humpty Dumpty's Magazine,* and *Cricket* are among the well-known magazines for children in the compilation. *FWG* is arranged alphabetically by title, and the writer's guidelines are photoreproduced. The index includes subject headings like *black female, Canadian magazines,* and *poetry*.

To a large extent, *FWG* duplicates two other standard reference sources that provide much the same information: *Writer's Market* and *International Directory of Little Magazines and Small Presses*. *Writer's Market* is a standard reference tool in most public and academic libraries, is more comprehensive in terms of number of journals covered, and is about the same price. However, since *Fiction Writers Guidelines* actually reproduces the magazines' guidelines for writers, it occasionally provides more detailed information.

The Catholic Novel: An Annotated Bibliography. By Albert J. Menendez. Garland, 1988. 323p. indexes. hardcover $40 (0-8240-8534-5).

016.80883'9382 Christian fiction—Catholic authors—Bibliography I Christian fiction—Catholic authors—Stories, plots, etc. I Bibliography—Best books—Fiction [CIP] 88-1718

This annotated bibliography of representative Catholic novels, from popular works to serious literature, lists books ranging in date from the 1820s to 1987. The introduction to this latest title in the Garland Reference Library of the Humanities briefly treats the history of the Catholic novel, primarily emphasizing Catholic fiction in America. The author traces the genre from early polemical novels, "heavy on doctrine and dogma," to modern writers of Catholic novels such as Andrew Greeley or Mary Gordon. He offers this definition of the Catholic novel: "one which reflects the values, culture and conflicts of the Roman Catholic faith and its community." The scope of the bibliography includes authors such as Franz Werfel, who was Jewish but told the story of Lourdes in *The Song of Bernadette*, but not Flannery O'Connor, a Catholic whose novels draw on the fundamentalist Protestant culture of the South. Novels critical of Catholicism are included, but not slanderous "anti-Catholic" fiction. English and American works predominate, but there are representations from many nations in translation. The author states that he has not included novels dealing with biblical and early apostolic times as these deserve a separate volume. Children's works also do not appear to be included.

The first three sections include close to 500 critical works, lists of books and articles on religious novels in general, Catholic novels, and criticism of individual authors. More than 1,700 novels are listed, alphabetically by author. Brief bibliographic citations are followed in most cases by annotations. The bibliographic work does not appear to be exacting: there is no mention of what criteria were used to select editions, some authors' names have typos, and translations are not identified, nor original language indicated. A title index is appended, as well as a subject index that can lead the reader to items in such subgenres as murder mysteries, historical novels, or specific topics such as Fatima or mixed marriages. Menendez provides a separate list of his choices for the 100 best Catholic novels.

There are other bibliographic sources for Catholic novels and fiction, but none so recent or focused. McCabe's *Critical Guide to Catholic Reference Books* (Libraries Unlimited, 1981) lists under *Fiction—Bibliography* only Stephen J. Brown's *Novels and Tales by Catholic Writers: A Catalogue*. This work, compiled by a Jesuit and published (in several editions—the latest is the eighth revised) by the Central Catholic Library in Dublin, served as a source for the work under review. Also including novels is the standard source published by the Catholic Library Association, *Guide to Catholic Literature, 1888–1977* (now combined with *Catholic Periodical Index* to form *Catholic Periodical and Literature Index*). Both of these sources are more comprehensive, including Catholic writing of all types, and novelists who may have been Catholic (such as Joel Chandler Harris, a convert) but whose works do not fit a definition of a "Catholic novel."

Unique in scope, *The Catholic Novel* will be useful to those interested in religious or Catholic fiction and as a readers' adviser.

Fantasy Literature for Children and Young Adults: An Annotated Bibliography. 3d ed. By Ruth Nadelman Lynn. Bowker, 1989. 771p. indexes. hardcover $39.95 (0-8352-2347-7).

016.80883'876 Children's literature—Bibliography I Young adult literature—Bibliography I Fantastic literature—Bibliography I Bibliography—Best books—Children's literature I Bibliography—Best books—Young adult literature [CIP] 88-8162

This is an annotated bibliography of 3,300 fantasy novels and story collections. (The second edition was published as *Fantasy for Children [RBB O 15 84]*.) It is intended for children and young adults, students of young adult literature, and authors doing research on literature for young people grades 3 through 12. Now in its third revision, the work has seen many improvements: 1,600 books have been added to the 1,700 books from the last edition in part 1, the annotated bibliography. The scope now includes books for young adults—those students in grades 8 through 12. Part 1 lists novels and story collections published in English in the U.S. between 1900 and 1988. Out-of-print books continue to appear in the bibliography, which is an asset since many of these works still are found in libraries. The titles are arranged in 10 sections by type of fantasy—animal, ghost, time travel, etc.—and then alphabetically by author. Each book has a one-sentence annotation that gives the gist of the story. This is followed by citations to reviews of the book. Several new professional reviewing sources have been added to this edition. All books in the volume are reviewed in at least 2 of the 17 reviewing sources cited. Symbols to designate the quality of the works have been placed in the left margin. A grade of "Outstanding" means the work has been recommended in five or more professional review sources. Symbols also indicate the appropriate audience for each book, and grade levels are given. Sequels to books continue to be noted in the main annotation. Part 2 is the research guide, the bibliography of secondary sources for adults. It is divided into four chapters: "Reference and Bibliography," "History and Criticism," "Teaching Resources," and "Author Studies." The third chapter is new to this edition. The previous edition treated only 75 writers in the "Author Studies" section; this has been expanded to 600 here. Title and subject indexes also are new; they join the author and illustrator index of the previous editions. Series titles and historical periods, such as *Middle Ages* and *World War II*, are included in the subject index.

A "Guide to Use" instructs the user in the cross-reference system used and the symbols included in each annotation. The introduction is extremely useful, and the reader should take the time to read it before using the book. Fantasy is defined and classified, and its use with children is discussed.

This work is a valuable resource that should be on the shelf of every librarian who works with children, available to teachers, and in the hands of those who study literature for young people. The third edition is the best one yet.

The Gothic's Gothic: Study Aids to the Tradition of the Tale of Terror. By Benjamin Franklin Fisher. Garland, 1988. 485p. indexes. hardcover $67 (0-8240-8784-4).

016.80883'872 Gothic revival (Literature)—Bibliography I Horror tales—Bibliography [CIP] 88-18059

The Gothic's Gothic is an annotated bibliography of secondary sources useful to the study of Gothicism in British and American literature. Coverage extends from the first Gothic novel, *The Castle of Otranto* (1764), by Horace Walpole, to Stephen King. Sources published later than 1977 are not included, as the author believes that the annual bibliography in the journal *Gothic* makes "inessential many references to post-1978 items." Unfortunately, this chronological boundary has precluded any mention of recent bibliographic aids, such as Frederick S. Frank's *Guide to the Gothic: An Annotated Bibliography of Criticism* (Scarecrow, 1984) and Robert Donald Spector's *The English Gothic: A Bibliographic Guide to Writers from Horace Walpole to Mary Shelley* (Greenwood, 1984).

The book is divided into two parts, the first listing authors chronologically by "the time when his or her works began to attract attention." Under each author, items are given in alphabetical order by critics' names. Author coverage includes 64 British writers, 37 Americans, 1 Canadian (Margaret Atwood), and 7 Germans who provided early influence on other Gothics. In addition, there are sections for "miscellaneous" British, American, and foreign Gothics. There are a total of 1,818 entries in part 1.

Part 2 is arranged by 28 subject headings and covers topics that have evolved from or have been linked with Gothicism (e.g., Gothic drama, comic Gothic). There are 796 entries in part 2, with no overlap with part 1. The three indexes are keyed to entry number: author-artist-subject, title (for works mentioned in at least two entries), and critic.

Annotations are somewhat shorter than appear in Frank's *Guide to* the Gothic and are sometimes cryptic and unclear (e.g., an early article on *Jane Eyre* "leaves behind shoddy models from Minerva Press"). Comparisons with Frank indicate similarities in coverage, organization, and format. *Guide to the Gothic*'s 1,193 author entries include 57 British, 18 American, 12 French, and 7 German writers, and there are 515 entries under the 21 topical sections. Frank has 42 entries for Bram Stoker (*Dracula*), and Fisher includes 15, with 5 of those not duplicated in the other work. On the other hand, Fisher is particularly strong in Poe sources, including 282, compared with 123 in Frank.

Generally, *The Gothic's Gothic* casts a wider net in identifying Gothic elements in literature. Fisher includes material on writers not normally associated with Gothicism (e.g., Thackeray and Edith Wharton). He has also extensively mined doctoral dissertations, early literary periodicals, biographies, memoirs, and letters.

The Gothic's Gothic is a major bibliography of pre-1978 sources important to the critical study of Gothicism, an area of rich tradition and ongoing vitality. For large libraries, it is a necessary companion to Frank's *Guide to the Gothic* and other bibliographies. Smaller libraries, however, may well question the need for acquiring another bibliographic guide on the subject.

Index to Literary Criticism for Young Adults. By Nancy E. Shields. Scarecrow, 1988. 410p. hardcover $32.50 (0-8108-2112-5). 016.809'89283 Young adult literature—History and criticism—Indexes I Young adult literature—Bio-bibliography—Indexes I Authors—Biography—Dictionaries—Indexes [CIP] 87-37

Index to Literary Criticism for Young Adults indexes 4,000 authors found in the Gale series *Contemporary Literary Criticism, Twentieth Century Literary Criticism, Nineteenth Century Literary Criticism,* and *Literary Criticism from 1400 to 1800*. Scribner's *American Writers* and *British Writers* and H. W. Wilson's *Twentieth Century Authors* and its *First Supplement* are also covered. The authors included range from Leo Tolstoy to Lily Tomlin, John Steinbeck to Bruce Springsteen, and Willa Cather to Robert Cormier.

The authors are listed in alphabetical order with the titles of reference books indented below each name, followed by volume, and sometimes page, numbers. Easily interpreted condensed titles are given instead of the abbreviations used by the publishers in their indexes. Complete citations for the reference works are listed in the introduction. The print, although easy to read, appears to be a dot-matrix computer typeface instead of something more appealing.

Cross-references are given in the index, and if two authors have the same name, their birth years and nationalities have been included to avoid confusion. Titles of the authors' works are not listed. An ideal index would include titles, but producing it would be a massive undertaking.

An introductory statement that "many of today's researchers have limited time and inadequate skills to cope with the intricacies of finding the proper reference book" may offend school library media specialists who work closely with students to teach them how to use reference sources. This index, which at first seems helpful, may, in fact, become just another unnecessary step for students.

Since this is an index to literary criticism, one wonders why the author chose to include the two Wilson publications that present mostly biographical information and very little criticism. Why, if the author included *Twentieth Century Authors*, did she not also include other volumes in the series such as *World Authors, 1950–1970*? Junior and senior high school students, although they need critical information, more often look for biographical material on authors. The other Wilson titles and even Gale's *Contemporary Authors* fill this need, but are not mentioned in this index. Librarians familiar with *Contemporary Authors* realize that it occasionally includes good critical material and author interviews. Finally, all the Gale titles include comprehensive indexes that cover all the other series. The only contribution this book makes, therefore, is the addition of the Wilson and Scribner titles. In addition, since Gale publishes volumes in each of its series every year, this index will soon be outdated.

It is also not clear why the words *For Young Adults* appear in the title. The reference works cited are used by all age groups, and they appear to have been indexed comprehensively, not just for those authors of interest to teens. Although Richard Peck, Stephen King, Judy Blume, and Lois Duncan are included, young adult authors are not the focus of the reference books listed. Other authors popular with young people are not included—Pierre Boulle, Mary Higgins Clark, and Shel Silverstein, ostensibly because they are not in the indexed sources. The words *young adult* do not appear anywhere in the introduction.

This index might be considered as an optional purchase by school and public libraries, but its benefits are limited. The introduction and Scarecrow's press release promote its time-saving value; however, its limited scope makes it a low-priority purchase for this audience.

More than 100: Women Science Fiction Writers. By Sharon K. Yntema. Crossing Press, 22-D Roache Rd., Box 207, Freedom, CA 95019, 1988. 193p. bibliog. hardcover $44.95 (0-89594-301-8). 016.8093'876 Science fiction—Women authors—Bio-bibliography I Science fiction—Stories, plots, etc. [CIP] 88-3600

This work is a biobibliography covering 104 female science-fiction writers who work with feminist or lesbian themes and characters. Arranged alphabetically by last name, the entries include a brief biographical summary concentrating on birth and death dates, education, parental status, classification of writing, and achievements, or, for new writers, plot lines. Following this is a list of secondary sources (including book reviews for well-known authors) and works written by the author. The work concludes with eight appendixes: "170 Additional Names of Women Science Fiction and Fantasy Authors with Titles and Dates of Their Books," "Authors of Science Fiction and Fantasy for Children and Young Adults," "When Were They Born?," "Where Were They Born?," "Which Authors Are No Longer Alive?," " Who Are Their Literary Agents?," "Recommended Science Fiction Books By Women," and "Other Resources."

One questions the need for this work since all but 17 of the authors mentioned can be found in one of five major sources: *Contemporary Authors* (Gale), *Encyclopedia of Science Fiction* (Grenada, 1979), *Science Fictionary* (Seaview Books, 1980), *Science Fiction Writers* (Scribner, 1982), and *Twentieth-Century Science-Fiction Writers* (2d ed., St. James, 1986). Though the editor has elected to focus on feminist and lesbian writers, works, and themes, that fact is not reflected in the title. The 170 authors who write in the more traditional form are relegated to the first appendix mentioned above. The editor has not explained where she got the information: from the authors? secondary sources? etc. She decided to forego a consistent format so she could see "each woman as a unique entity." This means some entries contain information that others do not. For example, Yntema includes non-science-fiction works for Dorothy Bryant and Celia Holland, but not for Margaret Atwood. Birth dates are not given for Jean Auel and Margaret Atwood.

The bibliographies cite only author, title, and date; publishers and place of publication would have been helpful. Checking some of the authors in the latest *Books in Print*, one finds that the bibliographies are far from complete. For example, three titles of Marion Zimmer Bradley, *The Catch Trap* (1984), *The Colors of Space* (1983), and *Experiment Perilous* (1983), are omitted. Four of C. J. Cherryh's works and six of Anne McCaffrey's works are not listed.

The editor sometimes does not give adequate explanations. For example, in explaining the plot of Vonda McIntyre's work, *The Entropy Effect*, she uses the phrase "the character of Sulu, an Asian woman." If one is not familiar with *Star Trek* or has not read the work, one would not understand that Sulu was an Asian man transformed into a woman, as were all the male crew members except one. In the entry for Melanie Rawn in appendix A ("170 Additional Names"), the statement is made that "rights to all three bought in 1987," but by whom and for what purpose is not explained.

With a price of $44.95, this slender book is a disappointment. Works of better caliber like *The Feminine Eye: Science Fiction and the Women Who Wrote It* (Ungar, 1982) and *Urania's Daughters: A Checklist of Women Science Fiction Writers, 1692–1982* (Starmont House, 1983) are better choices for libraries.

Olderr's Fiction Index, 1987. By Steven Olderr. St. James Press, 1988. 331p. hardcover $50 (0-912289-85-6).

016.8088 English fiction—20th century—Indexes I Fiction—20th century—Indexes I Young adult literature—20th century—Indexes [OCLC]

With the publication of this title, St. James Press launches a new series, Olderr's Annual Indexes. *Olderr's Fiction Index*, as well as *Olderr's Young Adult Fiction Index*, will be annual publications. Olderr is a former librarian and author of *Mystery Index* [*RBB* Ja 15 88]. He states in his preface that "this book is intended to be the missing source for library and research work with fiction."

This first edition analyzes 1,739 works of fiction published in 1987 and reviewed in BOOKLIST, *Library Journal*, and/or *Publishers Weekly*. A single alphabetical list provides several access points to each title. Main entries are by author and include title, publisher, number of pages, and ISBN. Variants, such as trade paperback editions and British imprints, are included. Each title is assigned up to nine subject, national origin, setting, genre, stylistic, and chronological headings, based upon the Library of Congress thesaurus. There are some very specific classifications: *Prisoners and Prison—Czechoslovakia*, *Jews in Sweden*. These headings are followed by the names of one or two principal characters. Finally, every main entry includes citations to reviews in the three journals, along with a rating system of one to four stars to indicate the tone of each review.

In addition to the main entries, the main alphabetical sequence provides entries for years in which the novels are set, subjects, characters, series titles, added authors, U.S. titles, and U.K. titles. There is also the heading *YA Accessible*, based on the recommendations in B OOKLIST. All of these entries give just author and title; the reader must go to the main entry for full information. Appended to the index is a list of the "Best Books of 1987," by which Olderr means those books that have received "four stars in at least one review." There is also a directory of publishers and distributors.

Naturally, Olderr could not read all of the titles analyzed in the index. He relied instead on "descriptive information offered by publishers and reviewers." In some cases, subject headings are misleading. The novel *Blackbird* by Tony Cartano can be classified as French fiction because it was originally published in France; but one questions calling *Travels with Dubinsky and Clive*, by David Gurewich, Russian fiction just because part of it is set in Russia, and there is no reason at all to classify as French fiction *The Flood* by Carol Ascher. Some of the headings, such as *Women, Family Life*, and *Social Alienation*, could apply to many titles and seem arbitrarily assigned. *Tempting Fate* by Laurie Alberts is not set in *Alaska—Rural*, but in a fishing town. There are several errors. *Poverty* is given as a subject heading for *Tempting Fate*, but there is no entry *Poverty* in the index. Lucius Shepard is called "Sucius." More serious in terms of access, Carol Ascher is entered under "Archer," and Candace Flynt under "Flynn." Finally, the four-star rating system is flawed by its arbitrary nature. The system is Olderr's own, based on his interpretation of the reviews. Examining the reviews themselves does not help clarify the difference between, for instance, ***- and ***+.

Wilson's *Fiction Catalog* is the most obvious alternative to *Olderr's Fiction Index*. The 1987 and 1988 supplements to the eleventh edition of *Fiction Catalog* include approximately 500 1987 titles. Whereas *Fiction Catalog* is selective, Olderr analyzes every title reviewed in the library press. The annotations and review excerpts in *Fiction Catalog* are a less arbitrary way of rating a book and help provide a more complete picture of it. On the other hand, even though they sometimes betray an incomplete understanding of the book's contents, Olderr's headings offer a depth of access that *Fiction Catalog* does not. Most librarians won't need to identify titles on *Sri Lankans in Canada*, but those that work with large fiction collections may find *Olderr's* a godsend for answering such pesky questions as "I'm looking for a novel and I don't remember the title, but one of the characters is called Allie and it has something to do with fishing." *Fiction Catalog* will suffice as a finding aid for libraries with smaller fiction collections and remains the first choice as a collection-development tool.

Ottemiller's Index to Plays in Collections: An Author and Title Index to Plays Appearing in Collections Published between 1900 and 1985. 7th ed. By Billie M. Connor and Helene G. Mochedlover. Scarecrow, 1988. 564p. index. hardcover $42.50 (0-8108-2081-1).

016.80882 Drama—Bibliography—Indexes [CIP] 87-34160

This seventh edition of *Ottemiller's Index* covers play collections published between 1900 and 1985, extending the coverage of the previous edition by 10 years. The scope of the index has been expanded to include books published anywhere in the English-speaking world. There has been an increase from the previous edition of over 600 authors, for a total of 2,555. Contemporary playwrights added include Harvey Fierstein, Tina Howe, and David Mamet. An additional 251 collections have been analyzed, for a total of 1,350. The criteria for selection remain unchanged from previous editions: in general, only collections of standard full-length plays in the English language or English translation are included, with collections of children's plays, one-act plays, radio and television plays, and holiday and anniversary plays excluded. However, a play in one of the above excluded categories or a play not translated into English is cited in *Ottemiller's* if it is included in an indexed collection.

The main arrangement continues to be by author, with lists of plays and the collections in which they appear. A "List of Collections Analyzed and Key to Symbols" and a title index complete this indispensable tool for reference, referral, and collection development. Highly recommended for public, academic, and high school libraries.

500 Plays: Plot Outlines and Production Notes. Ed. by Theodore Shank. Drama Book Publishers, 1988. 450p. index. paper $24.95.

808.82 Drama—Stories, plots, etc. [OCLC]

This work is a reprint of a book already on many library shelves. The editor, a playwright and director as well as the author of several other books on the theater, states in his introduction that "when originally published in 1963 we hoped that the book would lead to broader repertoires in theatres around the country which often seemed to be interested primarily in the latest Broadway comedies. We hoped to do this by introducing directors to good plays which they did not know about but which they might be induced to read with a view to possible production."

The book analyzes 528 plays in 11 chapters by nationality, such as Greek drama or American drama. Arrangement within the chapters is chronological. Entries were written by various contributors but are unsigned. Each entry includes a brief plot synopsis and production notes on the numbers and kinds of characters, sets, costumes, and potential problems. These notes can be quite specific regarding the requirements of a play. For example, the notes for J. M. Barrie's *What Every Woman Knows* inform us that the play calls for costumes that are "middle class and fashionable early 20th century," and that "success depends on the ability of the actress who plays Maggie to capture the charm of Barrie's style." Each entry concludes with information on royalties, translations, agents, and recommended texts. There is an author/title index.

The only information revised from the 1963 edition is a directory of agents and publishers, listing a total of six U.S. and British firms. Everything else is a reprint, including the information about agents and texts and the use of such terminology as "Boy: 5–10 (Negro)," which belongs to a different era. The most recent British play in the book is *The Dream of Peter Mann* by Bernard Kops (1960). Contemporary American theater is represented by Lillian Hellman and William Inge. It may be true, as Shank says in his introduction, that theater companies have been clamoring for a reprint because their old copies of *500 Plays* have disintegrated, and some libraries may also need to replace their copies. A completely revised and updated edition would be more useful. Similar titles, such as Evert Sprinchorn's *Twentieth Century Plays* (1966) and Joseph Shipley's *Guide to Great Plays* (1956), are also out of date. There is a need for a work that reflects the tastes and developments in theater over the last 20 or 30 years. Libraries that have gotten along without *500 Plays* since 1963 can skip this reprint, especially at its rather steep price.

The Directory of Humor Magazines and Humor Organizations in America (and Canada). 2d ed. Ed. by Glenn C. Ellenbogen. Wry-Bred Press, P.O. Box 1454, Madison Square Sta., New York, NY 10159, 1989. 186p. illus. indexes. hardcover $27.95 (0-9606190-7-0).

808.87'05 Wit and humor—Periodicals—Directories I Wit and humor—Societies, etc.—Directories I American periodicals—Directories I Canadian periodicals—Directories [BKL] 88-51217

The first edition of this specialized *Directory* appeared in 1985 and contained 65 titles; this edition lists 44 periodicals. Thirteen from the first edition are not included because they have "gone out of business" or did not respond to questionnaires. One of the titles not responding to a questionnaire is the important *Mark Twain Journal*; five other titles are still listed in *Ulrich's International Periodicals Directory*. The editor is the author of *Oral Sadism and the Vegetarian Personality* (Ballantine, 1987) and edits the *Journal of Polymorphous Perversity*, described here as "a humorous and satirical journal of psychology, psychiatry, mental health, medicine, social science, and education."

Among the titles included are *Mad* (circulation 2 million) and the little-known title *Phoebe* (circulation 110). Periodicals are listed under the name of the associations that publish them or under their titles. Entries for associations include number of members and dues. Periodical descriptions include page size, average number of pages per issue, production (typeset, photocopied, etc.), binding (saddle stitched, etc.). Also included are publisher, editor, beginning date, frequency, issues per volume, subscription period, subscription and advertising rates, a description of editorial policy and content, and author information. A one- or two-page representative article or excerpt serves to give the flavor of each journal. An interview with Judy Tenuta and jokes from Jay Leno and Bob Hope make this a more enjoyable directory to browse than most.

The *Directory*'s index includes all journal titles, associations, and personal names. Included also is an index by 47 subject categories (e.g., *Business Humor, Education Humor*). The appendix has two tables, one ranking journals according to circulation, the other summarizing information for authors.

The *Encyclopedia of Associations* lists many more associations interested in humor and comedy. Almost all of the periodicals listed here can be found in *Ulrich's*, though with less detailed information. It would be helpful if future editions of the *Directory* included humor magazines produced by college and university students. Libraries serving comedy writers will want to consider purchase.

Dictionary of Literary Biography Yearbook, 1987. Ed. by J. M. Brook. Gale, 1988. 474p. illus. index. hardcover $98 (0-8103-1835-0; ISSN 0731-7867).

810'.9 American literature—20th century—Bio-bibliography I English literature—20th century—Bio-bibliography I Authors, American—20th century—Biography I Authors, English—20th century—Biography I American literature—20th century—History and criticism—Dictionaries [OCLC] 82-645187

Contemporary Literary Criticism Yearbook, 1987. Ed. by Sharon K. Hall. Gale, 1988. 539p. illus. indexes. hardcover $97 (0-8103-4424-6; ISSN 0091-3421).

809'.04 Literature, Modern—20th century—History and criticism—Periodicals [OCLC] 76-38938

As its title implies, *Dictionary of Literary Biography Yearbook* updates and supplements the entries in *Dictionary of Literary Biography*, a continuing series, 79 volumes of which have been published through 1988. The 1987 *Yearbook* contains 10 new biographies, nine of which treat living authors (including Garrison Keillor and Elie Wiesel). Updated entries are provided for five authors previously covered in the parent series (among them Ernest Hemingway and Eudora Welty). James Baldwin, Richard Ellmann, and Frederick A. Pottle, all of whom died during 1987, are the subjects of lengthy obituaries.

The above material occupies 197 of the *Yearbook*'s 413 pages of text. The remainder of the volume consists of surveys of the year's achievements in the novel, short story, poetry, drama, and literary biography, and a potpourri of contributed articles and essays on literary topics, some of which ("Small Presses," "The Practice of Biography," and "Literary Research Archives") appear in each edition of the *Yearbook*. Included for the first time in the 1987 *Yearbook* are essays on book reviewing in America and new literary periodicals, both of which will be continued in subsequent yearbooks.

In addition to these recurring features, the *Yearbook* contains an article by George Kline of Bryn Mawr College on Joseph Brodsky, winner of the 1987 Nobel Prize in Literature, and a translation of his Nobel lecture. Among the other special articles is an essay by Kenneth Lohf of Columbia University on Butler Library's holdings of the papers of prominent American publishers and literary agents and an article by Kimberly Rae Chambers of the University of Virginia on *Callaloo*, a journal of Afro-American and African arts and letters.

The concluding sections of the *Yearbook* include a list of literary awards and honors for 1987, a selective checklist of the year's books on literary history and biography, a necrology, and a list of contributors with their affiliations (but not their positions). Although 13 of the 47 persons listed in the necrology section are the subjects of articles in *DLB* or the yearbooks, this fact is not noted in the necrology listings. It can, however, be ascertained from the cumulative index at the end of the volume. This index covers 67 volumes of *DLB* and the eight yearbooks published to date. (Death dates have been added in the index entries, however, for only five of the 13 persons noted above who died in 1987.)

In serving both as an updating mechanism for *DLB* and an annual survey of significant events and developments in the field of literature, the *Yearbook* performs two related but somewhat different functions. While there is no question of the value of the annual survey articles and the essays on special topics, not every library that subscribes to *DLB* requires this material, some of which is available in other sources (e.g., information about literary awards). Some of the essays might more appropriately be published in journals and will be lost in reference collections. There seems to be enough material for two separate publications, one devoted to an annual survey of literary events and developments and the other to updating and supplementing the entries in *Dictionary of Literary Biography*.

Contemporary Literary Criticism Yearbook, 1987 is the third published to date and is volume number 50 in the *CLC* series. Serving to update the other volumes in *Contemporary Literary Criticism*, it is more like the volumes in that series and contains less peripheral material than the *DLB Yearbook*. It overlaps slightly with the *DLB Yearbook* with survey articles on the year in fiction, drama, and poetry (though they are written by different authors) and a necrology and a list of literary prizes that are somewhat similar. There are no other essays of the type found in the *DLB Yearbook*. The remainder of the book consists of lengthy excerpts from published criticism for 15 authors new to this series, 15 authors who won prizes in 1987 (among them Joseph Brodsky), and 12 authors who died in 1987 (including James Baldwin and Richard Ellmann) in the standard *CLC* format. The last section of the book provides excerpts of criticism for six recent literary biographies. Cross-references are given to other volumes in Gale series when appropriate. The book concludes with a cumulative author index to all the volumes in the series, a cumulative index to authors by nationality, and a title index to this volume.

Both of these volumes can be recommended to libraries that subscribe to the two series.

The Nobel Prize Winners: Literature. 3v. Ed. by Frank N. Magill. Salem Press, 1988 (c1987). 1,042p. bibliog. illus. index. hardcover $210 (0-89356-541-5).

809'.04 [B] Authors—20th century—Biography I Nobel prizes I Literature, Modern—20th century—History and criticism I Literature, Modern—20th century—Bibliography [CIP] 88-6469

This three-volume set is the first in a "projected series which will cover the Nobel laureates in all award areas." Arranged chronologically, the articles average 3,500 words, synopsizing the prizewinners' lives and works and discussing both current and contemporary views of the laureates' worthiness. While most of the authors covered are included in another Magill series (*Critical Survey of Poetry, Critical Survey of Drama, Critical Survey of Long Fiction, Critical Survey of*

Short Fiction), the articles here are new ones written by different contributors. Though much of the biographical and bibliographic information in the articles is the same, *Nobel Prize Winners* entries have special sections on the presentation of the award, the Nobel lecture, and the critical reception of the prizewinner. There are photographs of the laureates (which are not found in the other series), and bibliographies of primary and secondary source material conclude each entry.

Supplementary material includes a historical overview of the Nobel Prize in Literature, concentrating upon the guidelines under which the Swedish Academy accepts nominations, deliberates, and chooses the Nobel Prize winner. Trends (or the accusation thereof) in the awarding of the prize are analyzed. A timeline charting the recipients with country/language and genre is also included. An author/title/cursory subject index provides access to the articles by book titles in the original language and in translation and also indexes recipients by country.

While this compilation provides more in-depth coverage of the prizewinners in literature than does either the Schlessingers' *Who's Who of Nobel Prize Winners* (Oryx, 1986, $35; [*RBB* My 15 87]) or H. W. Wilson's *Nobel Prize Winners* (1987, $90; [*RBB* Ap 15 88]), both of which cover Nobel Prize winners in all areas of awards, the hefty price of this set should be considered by libraries before a purchase decision is made. Garland has announced a six-volume set of biographies of Nobel Prize winners to be published in 1989, giving libraries yet another series to consider.

The Drama Dictionary. By Terry Hodgson. New Amsterdam Books, 1988. 432p. illus. hardcover $35 (0-941533-40-9).

809.2 Drama—Dictionaries [BKL]

Aimed at students, theatergoers, and performers, as well as lay readers, this new *Dictionary* provides definitions of about 1,300 practical, critical, and theoretical terms used in the theater. Terms relating to cinematography are also included. The *Dictionary* does not attempt to provide exhaustive information about dramatists, plays, theater companies, and theater buildings; as the author notes, these subjects are better covered in *The Oxford Companion to the Theatre* and *The Concise Oxford Companion to the Theatre*.

The *Dictionary* is arranged alphabetically; definitions are generally short, and cross-referencing is done by asterisks and *see* references. The reader must cover broader topics by following up the cross-references; there are few long narrative articles covering broad subjects. Many definitions include citations to important—and in many cases definitive—works on the topic in question. Thirty-one line drawings, mainly on historical subjects and stagecraft, enhance the text. Hodgson is a lecturer in literature and drama at the University of Sussex in England. The *Dictionary* has a British emphasis.

Drama A to Z: A Handbook by Jack Vaughn [*RSBR* N 1 79] is similar to *The Drama Dictionary*. It defines only 500 terms, however, and fewer of them are of a technical nature.

The Drama Dictionary provides definitions for a large group of terms not brought together elsewhere. It is a wise purchase for many high school and public libraries and for nearly all academic libraries.

Critical Survey of Mystery and Detective Fiction. 4v. Ed. by Frank N. Magill. Salem Press, 1989 (c1988). bibliog. indexes. hardcover $300 (0-89356-486-9).

809.3'872 Detective and mystery stories—History and criticism I Detective and mystery stories—Bio-bibliography I Detective and mystery stories—Stories, plots, etc. I Authors—Biography [CIP] 88-28566

Another in the reliable Salem Press Critical Survey series, *Critical Survey of Mystery and Detective Fiction* provides coverage of 270 writers, ranging from Ann Radcliffe, author of *The Mysteries of Udolpho* (1794), to such contemporary writers as Sara Paretsky and Stephen King. Though the emphasis is on British and American authors, coverage is worldwide. The genre has been broadly defined to include espionage, police procedural, psychological thriller, hardboiled detective, and gothic romance. In addition, there are entries for numerous writers like Balzac and Faulkner not generally thought of in terms of mystery and detective fiction. These writers are discussed only in relation to the genre; for a complete picture of their work, one must consult other sources.

The convenient Critical Survey format is familiar to many librarians. Articles appear in alphabetical order by author's last name. Each article begins with a brief ready-reference summary of birthplace and date, death date, types of plot (e.g., master sleuth or police procedural), applicable pseudonyms, principal series, and a short description of principal series characters. Biocritical information is arranged under "Contribution," "Biography," and "Analysis." Bibliographic information is arranged under "Principal Mystery and Detective Fiction" and "Other Major Works." There is also a short list of secondary sources. Essays are approximately 2,500 words, clearly written and accessible to high school students but not overly simplified. The contributors, most of whom are affiliated with smaller universities, are listed at the front of volume 1. Volume 4 contains a glossary and several useful indexes: type of plot, character, and a general index of authors, titles, and terms.

There are several reference sources that cover mystery and detective fiction. Some, such as Steven Olderr's *Mystery Index* and Allen J. Hubin's *Crime Fiction, 1749–1980*, cover many more writers but are simply indexes, providing minimal biographical and no critical information. John Reilly's *Twentieth Century Crime and Mystery Writers* [*RSBR* Je 1 81] provides for more than 500 writers a brief biography, bibliography, and signed critical essay. About two-thirds of the authors in *Critical Survey* are also covered, albeit more briefly, in Reilly. Missing from Reilly, though, are current popular authors such as William Buckley, Ken Follett, and Elmore Leonard. Libraries needing up-to-date reference material in this area will find *Critical Survey of Mystery and Detective Fiction* a useful, accessible tool.

Horror: A Connoisseur's Guide to Literature and Film. By Leonard Wolf. Facts On File, 1989. 262p. bibliog. illus. index. hardcover $27.95 (0-8160-1274-1).

809.3'872 Horror tales—History and criticism I Horror tales—Bibliography I Horror films—History and criticism I Horror films—Bibliography [CIP] 88-11126

"The law of horror literature," writes Leonard Wolf, "is that there is always something to be afraid of, whether it exists or not." In this unique annotated guide to selected horror films and literature, Wolf vividly describes the root of this fear as it appears in 400 novels, short stories, poems, and movies. His criteria for inclusion are very subjective and quite vague ("historical spread," "thematic variety," and "fun"), and his sharply written, opinionated annotations read like considered reviews.

The introduction explains the complexity and importance of horror literature throughout history and shows how this multifaceted genre not only taps the darkest of human emotions but also reflects the myths, archetypes, and symbols of various societies. Wolf also discusses how horror stories embellish plot rather than develop characters, thus differentiating the genre from the literature of tragedy.

The main body of the book is an alphabetical listing by title of all the entries, regardless of form. Each literature entry includes title, author, publisher, place of publication, date of publication, country of origin, and literature form (novel, short story, or poem). Each film entry notes film title, date of release, color or black and white, country where the film was made, running time, technical credits, and major actors (with names of characters they play). Black-and-white stills are provided for many movies. A very complete and helpful bibliography (unannotated) of sources and an index mostly of names conclude the book.

Libraries may already own other sources that treat this topic in more detail. *The Encyclopedia of Horror Movies* [*RBB* Jl 87], for instance, covers 1,300 films compared with the 200 or so in this book. *Supernatural Fiction Writers: Fantasy and Horror* [*RBB* Ja 1 86] provides criticism of 148 writers of this genre. But because of the informative and sprightly written annotations and the public appeal of the subject matter, this book will be of interest to a much broader group of people than specialists in (or "connoisseurs" of) horror film and literature. It should be considered by public libraries and most four-year college and university libraries. It will also be useful in community college libraries supporting programs in film study or courses on fantasy and horror literature.

Science Fiction & Fantasy Book Review Annual, 1988. Ed. by Robert A. Collins and Robert Latham. Meckler, 1988. annual. 486p. index. hardcover $65 (0-88736-249-4; ISSN 1040-192X).

809.3'876 Science fiction—Book reviews | Fantastic fiction—Book reviews [BKL] 88-2780

The publication of the first *Science Fiction & Fantasy Book Review Annual* is an exciting event to devotees of the genre. The editors' aim is to provide "critics, teachers, researchers, librarians, students and fans with a comprehensive critical overview of the genres of science fiction, fantasy and horror in 1987." Beginning with five essays, "Author of the Year," "The Year in Fantasy," "The Year in Horror Literature," "The Year in Science Fiction," and "The Year's Research & Criticism," the tone of the work is set with biography, analyses, and overviews. The remainder of the work covers "Award Winners in 1987," "Reviews of 1987 Books: I. Fiction, II. Young Adult Fiction, and III. Non-Fiction," and a title index. The five beginning chapters are written by recognized experts in the field and consist of an insightful biography of one of the major writers, Orson Scott Card; analytical and perceptive chapters on the trends seen in science fiction, fantasy, and horror; and a thorough examination of the more scholarly titles on these genres. Some chapters end with lists of recommended reading. The reviews section, which makes up the largest part of the book, contains more than 600 reviews by 100 reviewers. Reprint titles and non-English-language works are largely excluded, as well as works that are the results of "packaging." Although concentrating on "significant" works, this book manages to cover the majority of titles published in 1987. The reviews, arranged alphabetically by author's last name, provide basic plot summaries and critical appraisal. Although one may not agree with their point of view, at least these reviewers are not afraid to take a stand. For example, the reviewer of Jack Chalker's *Labyrinth of Dreams* does not hesitate to complain about the poor execution of the plot and the unusually sloppy style from this mainstay of the genre. Interestingly, the reviewer of the second volume in the series is much kinder to Chalker. The division of the reviews into fiction, young adult fiction, and nonfiction (primarily scholarly works) enables users to pinpoint exactly those reviews they care to read. The title index is accurate and helpful in that the titles referred to in the essays are indexed, as well as the ones reviewed. In the next edition, an author index covering the essays and three review sections would be equally helpful. The awards section, which covers not only the Hugo and Nebula awards, but also the World Fantasy awards, Campbell Memorial Award, Sturgeon Memorial Award, British SF Association awards, etc., will be a blessing to librarians and fans who have difficulty locating the lesser-known award winners.

On every level, *Science Fiction & Fantasy Book Review Annual* is an outstanding reference work. It is a must purchase for libraries that have a need for sources in this area. The 1989 edition should be eagerly anticipated.

Authors & Artists for Young Adults. v.1. Ed. by Agnes Garrett and Helga P. McCue. Gale, 1989– . semiannual. 258p. bibliog. illus. hardcover $49.95 (0-8103-2763-5; ISSN 1040-5682).

809.892'83 Young adult literature—Bio-bibliography | Young adults—Books and reading [BKL] 89-641100

At first glance this might appear to be a series that would be easy to pass up. After all, popular authors and artists for young adults, especially notable ones like Lloyd Alexander, Frank Bonham, Stephen King, George Lucas, and Katherine Paterson, have all been written about in other, more comprehensive works such as *Something about the Author*, *Something about the Author: Autobiography Series*, *Contemporary Authors*, and *Current Biography*. However, the quantity of information, especially from personal interviews and letters, coupled with a very readable style make this series unique for this age group. Students looking for biographical information will find plenty about an author's life, influences, and writing habits; librarians looking for interesting booktalk or display ideas will find it hard to put down.

This first volume features 18 "creative artists—the people behind the books, movies, television programs, plays, lyrics, cartoon and animated features" that young adults "most enjoy." Since there are no other criteria, one wonders why William Kennedy, Joan Aiken, Sam Shepard, and Andrew Lloyd Weber were selected for this first volume, which also includes Hila Colman, James Herriot, Gary Larson, Madeleine L'Engle, Toni Morrison, Farley Mowat, Francine Pascal, Richard Peck, and Daniel Manus Pinkwater. Among others planned for future volumes are Judy Blume, Agatha Christie, Jim Davis, Bob Dylan, Cathy Guisewite, Victor Hugo, Norma Fox Mazer, and Gene Roddenberry. Two volumes a year are planned, with about 20 people featured in each.

In addition to personal information, the unsigned articles include complete lists of authors' works, awards, works in progress, and "Sidelights," six-page or longer biographies with many direct quotes. Frank, thought-provoking comments include Richard Peck's "puberty is the same gulag we all once did time in," as well as Morrison's "critics generally don't associate black people with ideas. They see marginal people." Each entry concludes with a bibliography of books, articles, and films for further information.

Awards listed include more than just the National Book Award and Newbery Medal; titles are noted if they were listed as "School Library Journal Best Books" or "New York Public Library Books for the Teen Age." Also unique are the lists of adaptations of works. It's useful to know if movies, television programs, or cassettes have been made of novels or short stories, and these lists, like those of authors' works, appear complete through 1988 with the release of *Willow* and the publication of *Quinn's Book*. Black-and-white photographs of the authors, still photos from film or stage productions, and book and magazine covers add to the attractive appearance of this volume.

While this series may not be essential except in large literature collections, it does "bridge the gap between Gale's *Something about the Author*, designed for children, and *Contemporary Authors*, intended for adults" and gives more information about the biographees than do such other sources. It could be even better with a little more selectivity in the choice of authors and artists.

European Writers: The Twentieth Century. v.8–9. Ed. by George Stade. Scribner, 1989. 1,177p. bibliog. hardcover $75/vol. (v.8: 0-684-18923-2; v.9: 0-684-18924-0).

809'.894 European literature—History and criticism—Addresses, essays, lectures [CIP] 83-16333

These are the first two volumes of the planned six-volume survey of the twentieth century in Scribner's European Writers series. Earlier volumes in the series covered *The Middle Ages and the Renaissance* (v.1–2), *The Age of Reason and the Enlightenment* (v.3–4), and *The Romantic Century* (v.5–7). Two more volumes of *European Authors: The Twentieth Century* will be published this fall, and the final two volumes in the fall of 1990. An index volume will complete the series, and "supplementary volumes may be added at some time in the future."

Like other volumes in the European Writers series, *The Twentieth Century* is a companion to Scribner's British Writers and American Writers and follows the same format. For each author there is a fairly long (around 15,000 words) critical essay, followed by a selected bibliography of primary and secondary source material in the original language and in English. The essays were written by academics whose institutional affiliations are listed in the front of each volume. Volume 8 also provides an introduction and a "Chronology of the Twentieth Century," supplying the dates of significant events (actually beginning with the *Communist Manifesto* in 1848) and also the years of birth of important authors.

Each volume covers 22 authors, arranged by date of birth. The earliest author is Sigmund Freud (born 1856), the latest author in volumes 8 and 9 is Franz Kafka (born 1883). According to the preface, the most recent writer in the series will be Milan Kundera (born 1929). Libraries will have to rely on such resources as *Contemporary Authors*, *Contemporary Literary Criticism*, *Contemporary Novelists*, and *World Authors, 1975–1980* for coverage of younger writers. The main criteria for inclusion in the Scribner set were "whether the writer under consideration was someone that American readers were likely to look up, and whether American readers were likely to look the writer up in twenty years." The essays combine biography with critical evaluation, tracing each writer's artistic development and the evolution of his or her reputation. Though providing more in-depth analysis than other surveys, such as the Magill Critical Survey series, the Scribner essays should be accessible to most educated readers.

All of the writers contained in *European Writers: The Twentieth Century*, volumes 8 and 9, appear in Ungar's *Encyclopedia of World Literature in the Twentieth Century*, which is adequate for general reference purposes. The essays in the Scribner volumes are longer, more detailed, and more analytical. Despite reviews quoted in the promotional literature, these volumes may be too advanced for many high school students. But large public libraries and libraries serving undergraduates will find them useful additions, especially where other volumes in the European Writers series are owned.

Seniorplots: A Book Talk Guide for Use with Readers Ages 15–18. By John T. Gillespie and Corinne J. Naden. Bowker, 1989. 386p. indexes. hardcover $29.95 (0-8352-2513-5).
809'.89283 Young adult literature—Stories, plots, etc. I High school libraries—Book lists I Young adults—Books and reading I Teenagers—Books and reading I Book talks [CIP] 88-27333

For use with readers ages 15 through 18, *Seniorplots* is a companion to *Juniorplots* (1967), *More Juniorplots* (1977), and *Juniorplots 3* (1987 [*RBB* Je 1 88]), which were intended to be used with readers ages 12 through 16. In his introduction, "A Brief Guide to Booktalking," Gillespie provides helpful tips on the preparation and delivery of booktalks and recommends other excellent guides to booktalking.

Although most of the 80 titles included are contemporary fiction, other genres are also represented: drama, biography, and nonfiction. All titles were recommended in standard bibliographies and/or reviewing sources and range from short and easy to read (John MacLean's *Mac*, Gary Paulsen's *Hatchet*, and M. E. Kerr's *Night Kites*) to more challenging (Toni Morrison's *Beloved*, Pat Conroy's *Prince of Tides*, Charles Dickens' *Hard Times*, and Stephen Hawking's *Brief History of Time*).

The titles are grouped under 12 themes like "Growing Up," "Challenging Adult Novels," "Fantasy," "Sports in Fact and Fiction," and "Guidance and Health." Within each theme the titles are arranged alphabetically by author and are quite diverse as exemplified by the "Fantasy" selections: *Magic Kingdom for Sale—Sold!*, by Terry Brooks; *Lost Horizon*, by James Hilton; *The Tricksters*, by Margaret Mahy; *Nightpool*, by Shirley Rousseau Murphy; and *Cat's Cradle*, by Kurt Vonnegut.

Each entry includes title, publisher, copyright date, and price, followed by a short paragraph highlighting the author's literary career, a two-to three-page plot summary, and a brief discussion of thematic material. For each title a section called "Book Talk Material" suggests passages especially suitable for retelling or reading aloud. Approximately 8 to 10 titles with similar themes are identified for each entry, followed by listings of book reviews and sources of biographical information about the author.

The author and title indexes list all titles discussed and summarized, identified by asterisks, as well as those titles only cited in the text or in the "Additional Selections" sections. The subject index lists only those titles fully discussed and summarized in *Seniorplots*.

Seniorplots, like its companion volumes, is "not intended as a substitute for reading the books," nor is it "meant to be a work of literary criticism or a listing of the best books for young adults." For librarians and teachers, however, it will be of great assistance in preparing booktalks and selecting books and is highly recommended for any library serving young adults, teachers, and students of young adult literature. Since many of the titles were originally written for adults, this volume may also be used by librarians preparing booktalks for adult groups.

Imaginary People: A Who's Who of Modern Fictional Characters. By David Pringle. World Almanac; dist. by St. Martin's, 1988 (c1987). 518p. bibliog. illus. hardcover $24.95 (0-88687-364-9).
809'.927 Characters and characteristics in literature—Dictionaries [CIP] 88-60375

This delightful book contains entries of varying lengths that identify more than 1,300 modern fictional characters, mainly from the English-speaking world. Covering roughly the period of the modern novel, from Daniel Defoe to the present, the characters have appeared in novels, short stories, poetry, plays, films, television, operas, ballets, radio, pop songs, and comic strips. Many nonhumans, such as Winnie-the-Pooh, Krazy Kat, Lassie, Tweety bird, and R2D2 are included.

The author's criterion for inclusion is that the fictional character has "lived" beyond its initial appearance, remaining popular because of repeated appearances in various works or adaptations to other media. Pringle says that "we continue to meet versions of them throughout our lives. . . .[they] form part of the furniture of our minds."

The author is a British librarian and writer in the area of science fiction. Although he has done an excellent job of combing U.S. works and popular culture, an American probably would not have omitted Ziggy, Paul Bunyan, or Evangeline.

The characters are arranged in alphabetical order. Surnames precede forenames, generally speaking, but the characters are listed by the best-known form of their names. Entries take such varied forms as *Prufrock, J. Alfred*; *Minnie Mouse*; *Figaro*; *Dracula, Count*; and *She-Who-Must-Be-Obeyed*. Many cross-references help users locate the character they seek. In some cases, several characters are all described under the best known of their group, i.e., "*Tiggy-Winkle, Mrs.*, see under Peter Rabbit."

Each entry includes a brief outline of the character's creation and "career" in various sequels, adaptations in other media, etc. In a few cases the author mentions that a character is based on a person who really lived, such as Willie Stark in *All the King's Men*, by Robert Penn Warren, who was inspired by Huey Long, governor of Louisiana. Most characters are truly fictional, however. *Imaginary People* differs from similar works that identify characters in the length and detail of each entry and in the specifically mentioned period of time and geographic area it covers.

The book is enlivened by over 60 black-and-white illustrations of characters. The author includes an impressive bibliography of the principal sources he consulted.

Imaginary People makes interesting reading and will locate a wide variety of literary and cultural references. It would be a welcome addition to a library of any size or level, from academic to middle school.

Dictionary of Literary Themes and Motifs. 2v. Ed. by Jean-Charles Seigneuret. Greenwood, 1988. 1,507p. bibliog. indexes. hardcover $195 (0-313-22943-0).
809'.933 Literature, Comparative—Themes, motives—Dictionaries [CIP] 87-12004

This ambitious *Dictionary* must be considered a pioneering work, at least for students of literature not fluent in German, for heretofore, the only reference work offering similar coverage has been Elisabeth Frenzel's *Motive der Weltliteratur: ein Lexikon dictungsgeschichtlicher Längsschnitte* (1976), which provides A–Z treatment of significant literary motifs. This new *Dictionary* offers more comprehensive treatment by 98 scholars of nearly three times as many topics as Frenzel covers.

A problem of definition vexes the field, compounded first by the efforts of scholars working in various languages and traditions to differentiate themes from motifs, and second by the need to translate these efforts into other languages without sacrificing a nuance or distorting meaning. In the *Dictionary*'s introduction, François Jost, professor of comparative literature and French at the University of Illinois, delineates the subtle distinction between the two concepts. Both prudent reference librarians and users of these volumes will read the introduction carefully, for an understanding of this essay will enhance their reading of the 143 that follow. In selecting those 143 topics, the editors chose to "follow Frenzel's examples, . . .to limit [coverage] to concrete and abstract common nouns." Acknowledging that "there are at least as many potential themes and motifs in literature as angels on the head of a pin," the editors established as "criteria for selection...relevance to a broad and prominent body of literary works,...significance for the evolution of cultural history, and...vitality as measured by the interest shown by presently active researchers." Some topics (e.g., *Bear, Lion, Philately, Mountaineering*), although of lesser magnitude than most, have been included "as examples of a broad range of narrower themes that could not...be covered" extensively. Perhaps this is also why the admittedly short-lived and relatively minor theme *Hippie* has been included. Most themes, such as *Apocalypse, Clothing, Dragons, Fool, Incubus and Succubus, Love Triangle, Nihilism, Pride, Seduction, Tragicomic Hero*, and *Utopia*, enjoy greater universality and stature in world literature.

The *Dictionary* arranges its articles alphabetically. A "Cross-Index" following the final article in the second volume lists "key words for terms used in entry titles as well as alternate or subsidiary terms" and refers to the term used as an entry. For example, this index leads from *Bridge* to *Afterlife*; from *Contemplation* to *Retreat*; from *Space* to *Science, Time, Travel*; and from *Vagabond* to *Picaresque*. Since most themes and motifs are inherently broad, this index is indispensable, but it would have been even more useful had it been integrated into the table of contents.

The authors approach their subjects from a variety of perspectives, some incorporating psychoanalysis, linguistics, theology, anthropology, and other disciplines. They generally cite and frequently quote seminal secondary works analyzing or defining a theme. Most develop their topics historically, often from ancient times. Most of the examples of a theme's use or development derive from the canon of Western literature. Within this body of literature, the authors demonstrate broad knowledge. Each of the signed articles concludes with *see also* references to other articles and a brief bibliography, generally limited to about five items, most of which are in English.

A general index follows the "Cross-Index." It lists authors cited in the articles; individual works cited are listed under each author. This index is a veritable who's who of the greats of Western literature.

The *Dictionary of Literary Themes and Motifs* offers insightful, scholarly expositions of the development of many enduring themes, both major and a selection of minor (and sometimes relatively ephemeral) ones recurring in world literature. The Board recommends it for every collection whose users conduct analytical studies of literature.

American Women Writers: A Critical Reference Guide from Colonial Times to the Present. Abridged ed. Ed. by Langdon Lynne Faust. Ungar; dist. by Harper, 1988. 899p. index. hardcover $59.50 (0-8044-3157-4).

810'.9 American literature—Women authors—History and criticism I American literature—Women authors—Bio-bibliography I Women authors, American—Biography—Dictionaries [CIP] 87-19204

This one-volume reader's edition is a reprint of a two-volume paperback edition published in 1983 [*RBB* Ag 84]. No changes appear to have been made; the 1987 death date of Clare Booth Luce hasn't been added, for instance. The 1983 edition abridged the original four-volume set with the same title published to great acclaim from 1979 to 1982 [*RSBR* Jl 1 81]; it is still in print. Approximately 40 percent of the original set's 1,000 original articles are included in the abridgements, although most of them have been condensed. The editors have attempted to retain the variety of the original set by including in those articles selected writers from all genres of literature, from essayists to novelists and movie, radio, and television scriptwriters. Nonetheless, some of the omissions are startling: Maya Angelou, Susan B. Anthony, Zelda Fitzgerald, and Emma Goldman are among the writers omitted from the abridged editions. Some articles were revised or had their bibliographies updated, and 10 new articles were added to the abridgements.

Due to its minimal updating, this edition is not recommended for libraries owning the original four-volume set; those owning the 1983 two-volume abridged edition will find that nothing new has been added here.

America as Story: Historical Fiction for Secondary Schools. By Elizabeth F. Howard. American Library Association, 1988. 137p. index. paper $15 (0-8389-0492-0).

016.813'081 Historical fiction, American—Bibliography I Young adult fiction, American—Bibliography I U.S.—History—Juvenile fiction—Bibliography I Bibliography—Best books—Young adult fiction I Bibliography—Best books—Historical fiction [CIP] 88-3453

As many recent surveys suggest, knowledge of American history and geography by American high school students is generally inadequate. A number of reasons have been suggested for this deficiency, ranging from poor-quality textbooks to a general lack of interest among students. To help rectify this, Howard, a library science professor at West Virginia University, has compiled this list of recommended historical fiction for secondary schools. Teaching history through historical fiction is a technique widely utilized in colleges, but far less commonly in secondary schools.

Howard includes some 154 adult and young adult titles by 126 authors in her list, drawn from a variety of sources including the Wilson *Junior* and *Senior High School Catalogs*, lists from the National Council for the Social Studies, bibliographies such as Lillian Shapiro's *Fiction for Youth* (2d ed., 1986), and reviews in *School Library Journal* and *Horn Book Magazine*. She also sought the opinions of a number of consultants ranging from social studies teachers to history professors.

Her selections are conveniently divided into seven chronological chapters ranging from the colonial period to the present. Coverage is balanced, with the greatest number of selections in the chapters on westward expansion and the Civil War. Entries average a page in length and include title, author, date, number of pages, a short synopsis of the book, brief comments on its ideas, a suggested list of reports or related activities, and reading levels noted by bracketed numbers indicating a recommendation for upper-level students (grades 11–12), grades 9–10, and grades 6–8.

Compared with Lynda Adamson's *Reference Guide to Historical Fiction for Children and Young Adults* [*RBB* F 15 88], Howard focuses only on American history and generally on titles suitable for secondary schools. Unlike Adamson, she provides no information about the author and makes no mention of other titles by the same author that students might want to read. Some of her suggestions, particularly in the later chapters, seem more appropriate to college-level courses or advanced high school literature courses rather than as supplementary readings for high school history courses. Gore Vidal's *Burr*, John Steinbeck's *Grapes of Wrath*, Robert Penn Warren's *All the King's Men*, and Tim O'Brien's *Going after Cacciato* are frequently used as supplementary readings for college history courses. Other titles, because of their length (Kenneth Robert's *Oliver Wiswell*, 836 pages), seem unlikely to be read by any but the most enterprising students.

However, despite these shortcomings, and ignoring the author's comment that, "of course, the textbook will continue to be the foundation for teaching American history," this new guide will be welcomed by all who are involved in the teaching of secondary school history and social studies.

American Playwrights since 1945: A Guide to Scholarship, Criticism, and Performance. Ed. by Philip C. Kolin. Greenwood, 1989. 595p. bibliog. indexes. hardcover $85 (0-313-25543-1).

016.812'54 American drama—20th century—Bibliography I Dramatists, American—20th century—Biography—Indexes II Theater—U.S.—History—20th century—Bibliography I American drama—20th century—History and criticism—Bibliography [CIP] 88-10245

This survey is described in the preface as "the first scholarly, in-depth study of the state of research on and history of performances of forty American playwrights." Each of the essays was written by a different contributor. The contributors' credentials appear at the end of the book; most of them are professors of English or theater. Though naturally varying in style, the essays all follow the same format, and all contain a summation and distillation of opinion, rather than the contributors' own assessments. The essays discuss six major areas of research. "Assessment and Reputation" focuses on critical reception.

"Primary Bibliography" lists published and unpublished plays, as well as the playwright's other works. "Production History" documents performances. "Survey of Secondary Sources" identifies major bibliographies, biographies, critical studies, and analyses of major plays. "Future Research Opportunities" is a boon to graduate students seeking thesis topics, noting, for example, that there is a "pressing need" for an Albee biography and also for an exploration of the relationship between Albee's dramatic structure and Stephen Sondheim's musicals. Finally, there is a checklist of the secondary sources cited throughout the essay. The book concludes with two indexes; one for names and another for play and screenplay titles.

Though geared toward researchers, the essays can be appreciated by anyone with an interest in contemporary American theater. The production histories are especially informative. Reading these, one can glean the names of critics, actors, directors, and theater companies, both regional and New York–based, that have contributed as much to theater as the playwrights themselves. The production histories discuss screen adaptations of plays as well as stage versions. They also discuss original screenplays, so that mention is made of two recent David Mamet films, *House of Games* and *Things Change*. The 40 dramatists were chosen because they are "representative, influential playwrights whose works have unquestionably shaped the course of American theatre since World War II." Coverage is wide enough to include writers ranging from the well-known Sam Shepard to the more obscure Jack Gelber and Romulus Linney, from acknowledged masters like Arthur Miller and Tennessee Williams to emerging authors like Marsha Norman, from the Brooklyn Jewish perspective of Neil Simon to the black feminist aesthetic of Ntozake Shange. There is always room for argument about who should be in a work of this sort, but on the whole the editor's choices seem sound.

As reflected in the lists of secondary titles, information on many of these writers is available in other reference sources, especially *Contemporary Dramatists*, *Dictionary of Literary Biography* (v.7), and *Twentieth Century American Dramatists*. *American Playwrights since 1945* differs from other sources because it is a guide to scholarship and reputation rather than a biocritical tool. Its greatest value lies in identifying writing on younger playwrights on whom research has just begun. Recommended for academic libraries and for large public libraries serving serious theatergoers.

The Bibliography of Contemporary American Fiction, 1945–1988: An Annotated Checklist. By William McPheron and Jocelyn Sheppard. Meckler, 1989. 190p. indexes. hardcover $39.50 (0-88736-167-6).

016.813'54 American fiction—20th century—History and criticism—Bibliography I Bibliography—Bibliography—American fiction [CIP] 88-13522

As stated in the preface, this checklist "records and describes bibliographical accounts of contemporary American fiction writers." It lists bibliographies for writers of adult fiction whose reputations have been established since 1945 and is meant to be complete through 1986, with some 1987 and 1988 publications. McPheron is affiliated with Stanford University, and Sheppard with the State University of New York at Buffalo.

The book is divided into two sections, "Multi-Author Studies" and "Single Author Studies." The multiauthor section lists 53 sources, with emphasis on current reference tools such as *Contemporary Authors* and volumes from Gale's *Dictionary of Literary Biography*. Entries are organized alphabetically by main entry and each gives publisher and date of publication and a brief annotation. Annotations are mainly descriptive but do contain some evaluative comment.

The single-author section lists more than 550 bibliographies for approximately 125 writers. Arrangement is alphabetical by writer. Under each writer, entries appear chronologically, allowing the researcher to trace the historical development of the bibliographic work done on individual writers. Eudora Welty is the writer with the greatest number of entries; 16 studies are listed under her name. These include journal articles and the semiannual *Eudora Welty Newsletter* as well as monographs. Entries for other writers include bibliographies appended to unpublished doctoral dissertations. Most of the studies were examined firsthand; those that were not are indicated by an asterisk. As in the multiauthor section, entries supply author or editor, title, publishing information, and a brief annotation. A subject index and an author index complete the book. The subject index refers to authors who are the subjects of studies; the author index refers to authors of studies. There is no title index.

The compilers have attempted to cover a broad range of authors. There are literary and commercial writers, writers of science fiction and mysteries, and regional, ethnic, and small-press writers. Gaps can be explained by a dearth of bibliographic research. For instance, only a single Latino author, Rudolfo Anaya, appears in the single-author section, though three studies of Latino literature appear in the multiauthor section. As the compilers state in their preface, one of the aims of the book is "to highlight the need for additional bibliographical research in the field." Accessible and well arranged, this checklist should prove useful in research libraries.

Handbook of American Popular Literature. Ed. by M. Thomas Inge. Greenwood, 1988. 408p. bibliog. index. hardcover $55 (0-313-25405-2).

016.81'09 American literature—History and criticism—Bibliography I Popular literature—U.S.—History and criticism—Bibliography I U.S.—Popular culture—Bibliography I Books and reading—U.S.—History—Bibliography [CIP] 87-32294

Designed "to provide access to the body of existing commentary and scholarship on several of the main forms of popular literature of the past and present," this work contains 15 bibliographic essays covering such topics as "Comic Books," "Detective and Mystery Novels," "Gothic Novels," "Pulps and Dime Novels," "Verse and Popular Poetry," and "Young Adult Fiction." Ten of the essays were first published in *Handbook of American Popular Culture* (Greenwood, 1978), also edited by Inge. They have been substantially revised for this new work.

Each essay follows the same general format. A brief introduction is followed by a survey of the development of the form, a critical guide to available reference sources, a discussion of research centers and major collections of primary and secondary materials, an evaluative overview of histories and critical works, and a bibliography listing books, articles, and periodicals that support research in the field. The essays average 25 pages. Differences in style and emphasis can be explained by the fact that the essays were written by different contributors, whose credentials are supplied at the end of the book. A stronger editorial hand could have eliminated some of the inconsistencies that are inevitable when a variety of authors make independent contributions to a work. For instance, the essay "Children's Literature" mentions teen paperback series, but the essay "Young Adult Literature" does not. The latter essay cites *Interracial Books for Children Bulletin* in its bibliography, but the former does not. The book concludes with a name index.

On the whole, the essays are informative and analytical. The bibliographies range from two pages for the children's series "Big Little Books" to 11 pages for "Detective and Mystery Novels" and contain material published as early as 1856 as well as material published in 1987, so coverage for the purposes of scholarly research is broad. Only secondary materials are listed in the bibliographies, an important difference between the *Handbook of American Popular Literature* and other popular literature guides. Betty Rosenberg's *Genreflecting* [RBB My 15 87], for instance, covers several of the same literary forms and lists secondary source material. But it also contains extensive lists of the most popular and important authors and titles within the various genres. For this reason, *Genreflecting* is more helpful than *Handbook of American Popular Literature* as a reader's advisory and fiction collection-development tool. For those academic and large public libraries that support research in American popular culture, on the other hand, *Handbook of American Popular Literature* is a useful source. Libraries owning the *Handbook of American Popular Culture* should consider adding this new work because of the extensive revisions.

Vietnam War Literature: An Annotated Bibliography of Imaginative Works about Americans Fighting in Vietnam. 2d ed. By John Newman. Scarecrow, 1988. 285p. indexes. hardcover $27.50 (0-8108-2155-9).

016.81'08 American literature—20th century—Bibliography I Vietnamese Conflict, 1961-1975—Literary collections—Bibliography I American literature—20th century—Stories, plots, etc. I Vietnamese Conflict, 1961-1975—Literature and the conflict [CIP] 88-15747

This work is the second edition of a bibliography first published in 1982 [*RBB* N 1 83]. As noted in the foreword, "since 1982, hundreds more works on Vietnam have been published or reprinted." The 1982 edition listed 226 items; there are more than 700 entries in the new edition, including a few imprints from early 1988.

Based on the Vietnam War Literature Collection at Colorado State University, *Vietnam War Literature* contains entries for novels, short stories, poetry, drama, and such miscellaneous works as cartoon collections and sketchbooks. "The essential goal," states the compiler, "has been to present works that describe the Vietnam War as it was experienced firsthand by relatively few people and watched on television by a great many." All works are in English. All are set in Vietnam, in other war settings such as Cambodia, or in imaginary countries meant to represent Vietnam during the war or they contain flashbacks in which the Vietnamese segment is substantial. Works by Vietnamese are included if they meet the above criteria. Excluded are works of nonfiction, "fantastic postwar adventures," protest literature unless it is set in Vietnam, and any works that could not actually be read by the compiler. An effort was made to include all items regardless of quality; selections range from *Vietnam Vixens* and *Sex Slaves of the Viet Cong* to Larry Heinemann's *Paco's Story*, which won the 1987 National Book Award.

The bibliography is divided into five sections: novels, short stories, poetry, drama, and miscellaneous. Within these sections, arrangement is by year of publication, and then by author's last name. Entries include author, title, essential publishing information, and, for monographs, number of pages and Library of Congress card number. Annotations are evaluative as well as descriptive and are written in a lively style.

An author index and a title index facilitate access to the listed works. There are some inconsistencies in the indexing. In addition, the Board noted cross-referencing errors within the text. However, these are minor errors that should not impede access.

Given the recent and continuous growth of literature about the Vietnam War, the second edition of *Vietnam War Literature* is an important contribution. It is recommended for academic and large public libraries and for any library where interest in the Vietnam War is strong.

We Shall Be Heard: An Index to Speeches by American Women, 1978 to 1985. By Beverley Manning. Scarecrow, 1988. 620p. bibliog. indexes. hardcover $62.50 (0-8108-2122-2).

016.815'54 Speeches, addresses, etc., American—Women authors—Indexes I Women—U.S.—History—20th century—Sources—Indexes I Women orators—U.S.—Indexes [CIP] 88-6644

This is an update to Manning's 1980 book, *Index to American Women Speakers, 1828–1978* [*RSBR* My 1 82]. The subtitle, *An Index to Speeches by American Women, 1978 to 1985*, implies the speeches were given during this time period. However, a number of the books indexed were published before 1978, and some include speeches given over a century ago. Thus there are references to speeches by Lucretia Mott and Elizabeth Cady Stanton, among others.

The new volume has the same format: bibliography (entitled more accurately "List of Books Indexed" in the earlier volume) and author, title, and subject indexes. A list of the periodicals indexed would have been a useful addition to the bibliography. *Vital Speeches*, *Horn Book*, *Women Studies Quarterly*, *Ms.*, *Signs*, and *School and Society* are among those cited. State and federal documents and conference and symposium proceedings are also indexed.

The author index is the main part of the book and lists the speeches under the names of the women who gave them. The coverage is broad but with a few notable exclusions. Gloria Steinem, Ella Grasso, Betty Ford, and Rosalynn Carter are among the approximately 2,500 women included; Nancy Reagan and Barbara Bush are not. The subject and title indexes refer back to the author index. The subject index uses Library of Congress subject headings; some speeches are entered under more than one heading. As might be expected, there are numerous speeches under the subjects *feminism*, *sex discrimination*, and *women*. However, there are also the headings *cable television*, *flood control*, and *income tax*.

The title index may be useful for some speeches, but since congressional hearings were included (the author states that every woman member of Congress from 1975 to 1985 is represented), there are over 12 pages for the title "Statement" and more than six for "Testimony."

Its price may prevent acquisition of *We Shall Be Heard* by small libraries. In addition, libraries that do not have the congressional publications that are heavily indexed will find it less useful. With the above criticisms noted, this is a valuable contribution to the field of women's studies and should be considered for purchase by academic and large public libraries.

Black Writers: A Selection of Sketches from Contemporary Authors. Ed. by Linda Metzger. Gale, 1989. 619p. hardcover $75 (0-8103-2772-4).

810.9'896 Authors, Black—Biography I Afro-American authors—Biography [BKL]

Part of the Gale literary reference family, *Black Writers* is a biobibliographic guide to over 400 twentieth-century black writers. Approximately 75 percent of the writers are American, the rest coming mainly from African and Caribbean nations. There are entries for novelists, poets, and playwrights and also for journalists, essayists, civil rights activists, political and religious leaders, educators, entertainers, historians, and psychologists. Criteria for inclusion are not supplied, except to say that they are "broad." Arthur Ashe, who has written an autobiography and a book on tennis as well as the recently published *Hard Road to Glory*, does not appear, nor does Gail Lumet Buckley, author of the well-received *The Hornes: An American Family*. Ashe and Buckley may have been excluded because of relatively limited output, but it is hard to understand the omission of Angela Jackson.

The format of *Black Writers* will be familiar to librarians who have worked with Gale's *Contemporary Authors*. The table of contents provides brief summaries of each author's significance. Entries are arranged alphabetically and include biographical information: address; career summary; memberships and awards; a list of writings and works in progress; "Sidelights," a signed biographical sketch often containing comments by the writers themselves; and a list of secondary sources. Entries vary in length from half a column on a double-column page to 10 or 12 columns for such writers as James Baldwin, Toni Morrison, and Richard Wright. Editing is not as tight as one might wish. The entry on Booker T. Washington has him working as a houseboy in 1970. There is no index.

Librarians will want to know whether they should buy *Black Writers* if they subscribe to *Contemporary Authors*. Entries for James Baldwin, Toni Cade Bambara, Ed Bullins, Ralph Ellison, Ernest Gaines, and Sonya Sanchez are identical to entries found in *Contemporary Authors New Revision Series*, volume 24. However, entries for writers appearing earlier in *Contemporary Authors*, such as Maya Angelou (volume 19), have been updated, and entries for some authors, such as Gwendolyn Brooks (volume 1), have been substantially revised. *Black Writers* contains entries for some older authors, such as Charles W. Chesnutt, Paul Lawrence Dunbar, and James Madison Bell, not found in *Contemporary Authors* but who can be found in other Gale sets, most notably *Dictionary of Literary Biography*. Libraries that maintain standing orders for *Contemporary Authors* may not need to add this volume, but it is extremely convenient to have information pulled from the cumbersome parent set into a single source. For those libraries that cannot afford *Contemporary Authors*, *Black Writers* is a boon.

Contemporary Black American Playwrights and Their Plays: A Biographical Directory and Dramatic Index. By Bernard L. Peterson. Greenwood, 1988. 625p. bibliog. indexes. hardcover $75 (0-313-25190-8).

812'.54 Afro-American dramatists—20th century—Biography—Dictionaries I American drama—Afro-American authors—Bio-bibliography—Dictionaries I American drama—20th century—Bio-bibliography—Dictionaries I Afro-American theater—Directories [CIP] 87-17814

This work is a biographical directory of more than 700 contemporary black American playwrights, dramatists, screenwriters, and originators of theatrical and dramatic works. Only writers who have been active since 1950 are included. Entries are listed alphabetically by name and provide basic biographical information on family, education, and professional history. Information on the original works of each person is divided into two sections: a selection of "representative" plays or films and a section on "other" works. Plays or films in the representative category appear to be those for which the author was able to obtain the greatest amount of information. However, a plot summary and production history is usually provided for each work, regardless of its classification. Two appendixes provide a list of additional black playwrights for whom no biographical information is available as well as a directory of unpublished manuscripts by black playwrights which are contained in two specific New York City archives. A bibliography of additional information sources on black drama is provided along with a directory of libraries with significant holdings in this field. The book concludes with title and general indexes.

Most of the source material for this book was personally collected by the author over the last 20 years. Of the more than 700 people listed, two-thirds were located by the author, but only about 200 authors personally verified the information in their own entries. Most of the material in this collection does not seem to be available in other standard reference sources. Fewer than 10 percent of the people included in this work are also covered by Macmillan's *Contemporary Playwrights*, and slightly less than one-third are included in Gale's *Contemporary Authors* and its derivatives.

This work provides a wealth of information on obscure and overlooked American playwrights as well as some famous ones; it will be a welcome addition for collections specializing in the theater arts.

An Encyclopedia of British Women Writers. Ed. by Paul Schlueter and June Schlueter. Garland, 1988. 516p. bibliog. index. hardcover $75 (0-8240-8449-7).

820'.9 English literature—Women authors—Dictionaries I Women authors, English—Biography—Dictionaries I English literature—Women authors—Bibliography [CIP] 88-21393

Intended at first as a companion to *American Women Writers* [RSBR Jl 1 81] and its two-volume abridgment [RBB Ag 84], this work contains information on approximately 400 British women writers. A change in focus as the work progressed is alluded to in the preface but never explained. Since *American Women Writers* has entries for 1,000 writers, one wonders how many would be covered in *An Encyclopedia of British Women Writers* if it had been published as originally planned.

The signed articles, written by over 100 contributors (whose credentials are not supplied), range in length from under one page to almost three pages. Arrangement is alphabetical. Each article begins with a short fact summary regarding birth, death, parentage, and marriage and ends with a list of works by and about the author in question. Where applicable, the bibliographies include references to information in standard reference sources, such as *Dictionary of National Biography, Contemporary Literary Criticism,* and *British Authors of the Nineteenth Century*. The index provides access to subjects, professions, and genres, as well as to the writers themselves, and also contains cross-references for variant names and pseudonyms.

Chronological coverage ranges from Marie de France, who was born around 1160 and wrote for the court of Henry II and Eleanor of Aquitaine, to Fay Weldon, Margaret Drabble, and P. D. James. Popular authors such as Agatha Christie and Barbara Cartland are included along with "classic" writers like Eliot and Woolf. Ngaio Marsh, Katherine Mansfield, and other Commonwealth writers appear because "a major portion of their lives and careers was spent in Great Britain." There are diarists, translators, and religious mystics as well as poets, playwrights, and novelists. For earlier writers, in particular, the term *writer* is broadly defined. There are articles on Margery Kempe, an illiterate who dictated her autobiography in the fourteenth century; Anne Askew, whose output consists of the record of her examinations for heresy in the sixteenth century; and Elizabeth Clinton, who wrote a tract on breast-feeding in 1622.

For those who can name only Aphra Behn as a woman writer who predates the eighteenth century, the book is a revelation. A random sample of 37 articles reveals that seven of the women under discussion were born before 1700. Browsing is the only way to identify which women wrote in which eras; a chronological index would have been useful.

The articles themselves are fascinating. One reads again and again of women trying to maintain a balance between the customary roles of dutiful daughter, wife, and mother and finding, in Virginia Woolf's phrase, "a room of one's own." A few nonconformists stand out. Charlotte Cibber Charke, for example, daughter of the infamous eighteenth-century poet laureate Colley Cibber, spent part of her life dressed as a man and nearly succeeded in marrying an heiress; she is remembered for her frank autobiography, as well as several stories and plays.

Information on many of these writers is available in other sources (e.g., over a third of them can be found in *Dictionary of National Biography*). However, it is useful to put even writers of the stature of Jane Austen and the Brontës into the context provided by this book. We are used to thinking that novel writing by British women began with Austen, but this *Encyclopedia* shows that Austen had numerous popular and successful contemporaries, whose works she probably read. If not only the relatively well-known Fanny Burney, Maria Edgeworth, and Ann Radcliffe, but the obscure Jane West, Charlotte Turner Smith, and Sophia Lee never matched Austen's achievements, their careers help us see that Austen was not an anomaly. Especially because of the light it sheds on lesser-known writers, *An Encyclopedia of British Women Writers* is a good addition to the literary reference shelf.

Modern Irish Literature. Comp. by Denis Lane and Carol McCrory Lane. Ungar; dist. by Harper, 1988. 736p. bibliog. index. hardcover $95 (0-8044-3144-2).

820'.9 English literature—Irish authors—History and criticism I English literature—20th century—History and criticism I Ireland in literature [CIP] 87-5090

This new addition to the Library of Literary Criticism covers 87 writers ranging in time from George Moore (1852–1933) to Paul Muldoon (1951–   ). Plays, poetry, the novel, and the short story are all well represented; Conor Cruise O'Brien, best known as an essayist, is also included. As in other titles in the series, a section for a writer contains a selection of excerpts of critical commentary from periodicals, newspapers, or books, arranged in chronological order of publication, with the earliest dating from the turn of the century.

The compilers are members of the City University of New York faculty. Denis Lane, coeditor of another volume in the series (*Modern British Literature*, volume 5), is associate professor of English at John Jay College; Carol McCrory Lane, who compiled the drama selections, is associate professor of theater arts at Borough of Manhattan Community College.

Joyce, Yeats, and Shaw receive the most extensive coverage. Nearly half of the writers are also covered to some extent in *Modern British Literature*, and six are also included in *Major Modern Dramatists*, another title in the series. Some excerpts in this volume are found in one or the other of the above sets, and several excerpts are repeated in all three. This volume does contain ample selections of unique excerpts on writers found in both other sets (e.g., Beckett, O'Casey, Synge); in the *Modern British Literature* set (e.g., Austin Clarke, Frank O'Connor, Liam O'Flaherty); and in its supplements (e.g., Flann O'Brien, Patrick Kavanagh, Seamus Heaney). Among the writers covered only by this volume are Douglas Hyde, Daniel Corkery,

John Montague, and Julia O'Faolain. Only one writer whose reputation is based primarily on work in Irish rather than English is included: Pádraic Oíac Conaire. The omission of the Blasket writers, Máirtí O' Cadhain, and important poets writing in Irish could be questioned, especially since writers not immediately thought of as Irish, such as Louis MacNeice and Iris Murdoch, are included.

Primary bibliographies of each writer, in chronological order, are found in a separate section at the back; a few key secondary sources (bibliography, biography, criticism) may also be noted. Also found at the back is an index to the critics who are excerpted. Two books drawn on at least 10 times each for excerpts are *Modern Irish Fiction* by Benedict Kiely and *After the Irish Renaissance* by Robert Hogan. Nearly 100 periodicals were tapped for excerpts; U.S., British, and Irish sources are all well represented. More than 15 selections were taken from the U.S. review, *Irish Literary Supplement* (1982–   ). Only large library collections will have holdings that in any way approach the range of literary periodicals sampled for this volume.

These 300- to 400-word excerpts represent a fascinating record of a writer's initial reception and evolving reputation and afford a variety of insights into the writer's distinctive qualities and principal achievements. This volume will be a useful addition to public and academic library collections where there is an interest in the Irish literary scene.

The Quotable Shakespeare: A Topical Dictionary. Comp. by Charles DeLoach. McFarland, 1988. 544p. indexes. hardcover $39.95 (0-89950-303-9).

822.3'3 Shakespeare, William—Dictionaries, indexes, etc. I Shakespeare, William—Quotations [CIP] 87-35362

The author of this new reference book describes it as "a work of love that took several years to construct." That it is indeed a work of love is evident from the painstaking analysis DeLoach has made of Shakespeare's writings. The author, a journalist, states that other collections of quotations from Shakespeare may "contain a very heavy volume of selections that have to do with plot, scene description or characterization." DeLoach's book, on the other hand, includes quotations that "contain not only a philosophical axiom, a general truth or a fundamental principle, but also had to be immediately clear in meaning and capable of inspiring or delighting the reader." *The Quotable Shakespeare* contains 6,516 quotations listed under some 1,000 alphabetically arranged topics. Each entry is numbered and includes the name of the character (for quotations from the plays), the quotation itself, the play, and the act, scene, and line as they appear in *The Riverside Shakespeare* (Houghton, 1974). Quotations from poetry are identified by line or sonnet number. Definitions of unfamiliar words or archaic spellings and explanations of usage are given following quotations, at the author's discretion. For example, the phrase "Bell, book, and candle" appears in a quotation under the topic *Bells*, and a note identifies these words as "symbols of Church excommunication." The table of contents lists all the topics used, so that they may be rapidly scanned and easily located on the correct page.

In the title index, each play title is followed by the entry numbers for quotations from it. *The Sonnets* are treated as one listing in this index. The character index lists characters in alphabetical order with a coded abbreviation for the play in which each appears, the topic of the quote, and the entry number of the quote. A typical listing is "*Guildenstern* (*Hamlet*) on ambition 187; on argument 259; on dreams 1537; on fortune 2264; on the substance of ambition 5434." It is possible to study a certain character or to locate a quotation when nothing more than the character associated with it can be remembered.

The topical index furnishes assistance for further developing topics. It serves as a partial keyword index and expands on the information given in the table of contents. A sample entry from this index is "*Manners* 3650–3655; effect of distress on 762, of fasting on 1425; of the executioner 1773; as a cover for sin 5183; *see also* Behavior, Breeding, Conduct, Court, Courtesy, Custom, Etiquette."

There are many reference works on Shakespeare and his work. Stevenson's *Home Book of Shakespeare Quotations*, for instance, contains many more quotations but often cites them very briefly, while DeLoach quotes long passages that put the topic in context. Stevenson contains a separate concordance but does not index the quotations by play title or by character. While it does not take the place of a concordance, the unique features of *The Quotable Shakespeare* make it an appropriate addition to public, high school, and academic libraries.

Contemporary Dramatists. 4th ed. Ed. by D. L. Kirkpatrick and James Vinson. St. James Press, 1988. 785p. bibliog. index. $85 (0-912289-62-7).

822'.914 Dramatists, American—20th century—Bio-bibliography I Dramatists, English—20th century—Bio-bibliography [BKL]

Both the first and second editions of this title received favorable reviews here [*RSBR* O 15 74, Ap 15 79]; the third edition was not reviewed by the Board. In this fourth edition, *Contemporary Dramatists* provides entries for over 360 living English-language writers for the stage, providing biographical information, a full bibliography of their plays and other writings and theatrical activities, frequently a personal comment by the dramatist, and always a signed critical essay on his or her work; there may also be details of other published bibliographies and critical studies and locations of manuscript collections.

Entries range in length from a page to over four pages. Five supplemental sections provide briefer entries, bibliographic only, for screenwriters, radio writers, television writers, musical librettists, and theater groups. There are introductory essays for each of these sections, discussing the genre and some of the writers. If entrants are also well known as stage dramatists there is a *see* reference to the main entry, e.g., under television writers, "*Hare, David.* See his dictionary entry." An appendix includes seven playwrights who have "died since the 1950's but whose reputations are essentially contemporary"; this section remains unchanged from earlier editions. All other sections have grown: the main dictionary expanded by 41 net entries, adding over 70 dramatists while deleting some 30 others; all supplemental sections likewise have net gains. Among the new entrants are Harvey Fierstein, Wendy Kesselman, Bryony Lavery, and Femi Osofisan; those deleted include Lillian Hellman, Christopher Isherwood, and Archibald MacLeish. While the majority of dramatists are British, American, or Canadian, writers from Nigeria, Jamaica, Australia, and Ghana are among those noted. Other entries have been updated, both in biographical details and in additions to the bibliographies. Many 1987 dates were noted and some 1988 ones, for example, the screenplay for Hanif Kureishi's *Sammy and Rosie Get Laid*. Some critiques remain identical to the prior edition, some are slightly changed, and some have been totally rewritten by new authors. For example, both Robertson Davies and Keith Dewhurst have totally new critiques by new authors. In addition, Dewhurst has written a new personal comment for his entry, which has been updated to show that he was writer in residence at the West Australian Academy of Performing Arts in Perth in 1984, had two new plays dated 1982 and 1984, a new screenplay in 1985, TV plays in 1983, 1986, and 1987, and a novel in 1986.

One of the strong points of *Contemporary Dramatists* continued in this edition is its comprehensive title index including all stage, screen, radio, and TV plays cited in the main entries, supplements, and appendix. The citation refers to the entry name with date of first production or publication; if the entry is in one of the supplemental sections, the number of that section is given. This index remains complete and accurate and is an excellent source for finding an author and date if only the title of a play is known.

Entrants are chosen by a distinguished board of advisers and contributors (e.g., Alan Strachan, Herbert Blau); contributors' credentials with a listing of their essays are included after the index. A number of contributors are new to this volume; others have contributed to all four editions. The format has been changed to two columns to the page; legibility is excellent, although the print is small.

Contemporary Dramatists continues to provide biographical, bibliographic, and critical information on playwrights, many of whom are not found in other sources. While some of these writers are in *Contemporary Authors* (Gale, 1962–   ) or *National Playwrights Directory* (2d ed., Gale, 1982), neither of these provides criticism, and the latter includes only Americans. *Contemporary Dramatists*, fourth edition, will again provide public and academic libraries with a convenient source for the purpose of identifying dramatists and the titles and dates of their plays.

A Reader's Guide to the Classic British Mystery. By Susan Oleksiw. G. K. Hall, 1988. 585p. maps. hardcover $29.95 (0-8161-8787-8).

823'.0872 Detective and mystery stories, English—Stories, plots, etc. I Detective and mystery stories, English—Bibliography I Bibliography—Best books—Detective and mystery stories I English fiction—20th century—Stories, plots, etc. I English fiction—20th century—Bibliography [CIP] 88-1735

Guides to mystery fiction frequently evolve from the compiler's own enthusiasm for mysteries, and this one is no exception. Oleksiw, a free-lance writer, states in her preface that *A Reader's Guide to the Classic British Mystery* began with notes and lists kept by her and her mystery-loving husband.

One hundred twenty-one authors are alphabetically listed here, and, under each, titles published through 1985 are arranged chronologically by series character to enable readers "to follow the biography of their favorite characters." There is an element of subjectivity in this arrangement, as Oleksiw admits, because not all the novels are chronologically precise.

"Classic British mystery" is not defined. Oleksiw's interpretation is broad enough to include police procedurals, romances, and thrillers as well as novels of detection; also included are non-British practitioners, such as Martha Grimes, whose books are set in Britain. All of the more than 1,440 novels and novellas are annotated in a way that describes the premise of the mystery without revealing any clues. Each entry includes publisher and date for both British and American editions. There is no information, however, on the authors themselves. Even a minimum of biographical matter, such as birth and death dates, would be useful. Preceding the annotated section is an alphabetical list of authors and their characters. Following the annotations is an alphabetical list of characters and their creators. There are also a list of characters by occupation; titles grouped by period of the story (2000 B.C. to 1959 A.D.); titles grouped by locations outside England; titles grouped by setting, such as *Bank* and *Boardinghouse*; and a "Miscellaneous Information" section listing titles under areas of technical knowledge, such as botany and archaeology, that play a part in the mystery. The author's selection of the 100 greatest British mysteries and maps locating areas associated with different authors are also included. The volume concludes with useful explanations, including charts, of the British police and class systems.

Inevitably, there is some overlap between *A Reader's Guide to the Classic British Mystery* and other guides. Steven Olderr's *Mystery Index* and Allen J. Hubin's *Crime Fiction, 1749–1980* are more comprehensive but are not annotated. The access they provide to British mysteries is limited to mysteries set in England, listed in their geographic location indexes. Melvyn Barnes' *Murder in Print* provides narrative descriptions of the titles it includes but offers no way to find mysteries that are strictly British. Because of its focus on British mysteries and its annotations, *A Reader's Guide to the Classic British Mystery* is recommended as both a collection-development and reader's-advisory tool for libraries that serve avid mystery readers.

GEOGRAPHY

Dictionary of Concepts in Physical Geography. By Thomas P. Huber and others. Greenwood, 1988. 291p. bibliog. index. hardcover $49.95 (0-313-25369-2; ISSN 0730-3335).

910'.02 Physical geography—Dictionaries [CIP] 87-29582

This source is the fifth in the Reference Sources for the Social Sciences and Humanities series, which also includes *Dictionary of Concepts in Human Geography* (1983) and *Dictionary of Concepts in History* (1986). "Dictionaries in this series uniformly present brief, substantive discussions of the etymological development and contemporary use of the significant concepts in a discipline." They are distinguished from other dictionaries by their heavy emphasis on bibliographic information.

Readers of this *Dictionary* will find about 100 alphabetically arranged entries selected by the authors with the intention of presenting those concepts "deemed most important by our colleagues." Huber and coauthor Robert P. Larkin are in the geography department at the University of Colorado, Colorado Springs; coauthor Gary L. Peters is a geography professor at California State University, Long Beach. Designed for serious students and professionals in geography and related fields, this volume places individual concepts "within the proper historical research context."

Each entry begins with one to three brief definitions of a concept. Then follows an essay, averaging 1,000 words, describing the historical growth of the term and citing original research on the concept. The bibliography at the end of each entry lists the books, journals, and state and federal agency documents mentioned in the essay, sometimes with brief annotations. Citations are not restricted to highly specialized geography sources. The entries *cloud* and *beach* make reference to *The Oxford English Dictionary*. In the text of entries, small capital letters are used for internal cross-references. Each essay concludes with a "Sources of Additional Information" section.

A subject index, with *see* and *see also* references, lists terms, people, groups, and places. Several entries were found to lead the reader to a *see* reference in the text. For example, the index entry *hail* lists page 113 where the reader will find "*hail*. See thunderstorm." The volume also includes an appendix that classifies the concepts into related groups.

A related source, *Encyclopaedic Dictionary of Physical Geography* (Basil Blackwell, 1985), was reviewed by the Board in the June 15, 1986, issue. It contains over 2,000 entries compared with about 100 in the volume under review. It also has many charts and pictures, while this newer book has none. Three-quarters of a random sample of entries from the review title were also found in the *Encyclopaedic Dictionary of Physical Geography*. However, the *Dictionary of Concepts in Physical Geography* will be a worthwhile purchase in academic libraries where students and professionals require the etymological background of major terms and the tremendous amount of bibliographic information the dictionary includes.

Place-Names of the World: A Dictionary of Their Origins and Backgrounds. Rev. ed. By Adrian Room. Angus & Robertson Publishers; dist. by Salem House, 1988 (c1987). 259p. bibliog. paper $12.95 (0-207-15539-9).

910'.3 Names, Geographical I Gazetters I Geography—Dictionaries [OCLC]

Place-Names of the World provides explanations for more than 1,000 place-names and covers most of the world's countries and their capitals; many cities, towns, and political or administrative divisions (including all U.S. states and Soviet republics); and a wide variety of geographic features. Because of the availability of other works treating English place-names, their inclusion is limited here primarily to the names of the countries of the British Isles and their capitals and island groups in the surrounding waters. Names that are self-explanatory (e.g., *Great Lakes*) are usually omitted.

Names are entered under the form most familiar to English-speaking persons rather than in their native version (e.g., *Vienna* rather than *Wien*), but multiple entries linked by cross-references are usually made for places that are, or have been, widely known by more than one name (e.g., *Rhodesia* and *Zimbabwe*). More liberal use of cross-references would have been helpful. Although *Peking*, *Peiping*, and *Beijing* are variant spellings for the capital of China, there are no references from the latter two forms to *Peking*, the form under which the meaning of the name is given.

Each entry includes a brief geographic identification that pinpoints the location and helps avoid confusion between places with similar names (e.g., *Mauritania* and *Mauritius*). Pronunciations are not indicated. Inclusion of pronunciations for some of the less familiar names would have been desirable.

The entries are preceded by an informative introduction that provides a historical overview of the development of place-names and discusses the relatively new science of toponymy (place-name study). The compiler, author of many books about names and their origins, points out that comparatively few place-names have been adequately and satisfactorily explained and that the meanings of some of the most familiar names (e.g., *London, Berlin, Moscow*) have not been definitively established, hence the need to include the qualifiers *probably*, *possibly*, and *perhaps* in conjunction with many of the derivations.

Other prefatory sections include a short "Language Guide," which identifies some of the languages mentioned in the entries (e.g., Amharic and Ligurian), and "Elements of Non-English Place-Names," which tells, for example, that *-burg* means "fortified town" in German and *mont* means "mount(ain)" in French. This section can be used to ascertain the approximate meanings of many names not included among the entries, e.g., *Belmont*, which combines the French element *bel* ("beautiful") with *mont*. A bibliography of 56 titles follows the entries. The selection emphasizes both works that are worldwide in scope and those dealing with the names of specific English-speaking countries.

Place-Names of the World is especially suitable for school and public libraries desiring an up-to-date but relatively inexpensive source of information on the subject. Academic libraries not owning more detailed sources may also wish to consider purchase.

Directory of Treasure Hunting, Prospecting, and Related Organizations: An International Directory of Over 640 Treasure Hunting, Prospecting, Adventure, and Related Organizations. 1st ed. By John H. Reed. Research and Discovery Publications, P.O. Box 314, Gibson, LA 70356-0314, 1988 (c1987). 191p. bibliog. index. paper $10.95 (0-940519-00-3).

910.453'025 Treasure-trove—Directories I Prospecting—Directories [BKL] 86-63262

Reed has produced a directory he hopes will promote friendships among treasure hunters. His stated purpose is to identify both active and defunct clubs organized to encourage this activity, including those interested in metal detecting and prospecting. Care has been taken to include all major name changes for a given club. Entries for the more than 700 clubs consist of founding date, name of founder, number of members, scheduled meetings, and special activities, though many entries are incomplete. The titles of newsletters are included when possible; unfortunately, these publications are not listed alphabetically in a separate index. Most of the newsletter titles identified are not listed in the third edition of Gale's *Newsletters Directory*. Clubs are grouped by state, and there are a few listings for clubs located in Canada, the U.K., and other countries.

Books and periodicals dealing with topics of interest to treasure hunters were perused by the compiler to create this list. The titles of all materials surveyed are given in a separate list, and there is an index to all clubs included in the directory. Appendixes list inactive clubs and associations of clubs concerned with treasure hunting. This directory is unique. Neither Bernard Klein's *Guide to American Directories* (11th ed., B. Klein Publications, 1982) nor the fifth edition of Gale's *Directory of Directories* contains entries for this type of book. The publication appears to have been reproduced from a typescript. However, the various elements of an entry are well spaced, and copy is easy to read. This is obviously a labor of love for the author. Public libraries where there is interest in this topic may wish to consider this inexpensive directory.

Women into the Unknown: A Sourcebook on Women Explorers and Travelers. By Marion Tinling. Greenwood, 1989. 356p. bibliog. index. maps. hardcover $55 (0-313-25328-5).

910'.88042 Explorers, Women—Biography [CIP] 88-18677

Tinling, who wrote *Women Remembered: A Guide to Landmarks of Women's History in the United States* [RBB D 15 86], has compiled five-to-six-page biographies of 42 women explorers. The women were selected if they "went into unknown territory, sought new information, and brought back fresh ideas." Not included because of space limitations were mountaineers, sea voyagers, air and space travelers, undersea explorers, and round-the-world travelers.

The women chosen for inclusion range from the Viennese housewife Ida Pfeiffer (1797–1858) who visited Iceland, Brazil, and China when she was over 45, to Christina Dodwell, born in 1951 to English parents, who has traveled extensively in New Guinea, Africa, and China. A few of the travelers are well known—Margaret Bourke-White, Freya Stark, and Elspeth Huxley. Many of the biographies include quotations from the works of the women, and each entry concludes with a detailed bibliography of works by and about the traveler. The book concludes with a subject index and a lengthy selected bibliography of books of exploration and travel written by women.

The description of the fortitude and determination of the women is fascinating. However, for those women still living, Tinling leaves the reader in suspense by not suggesting what the traveler is doing now. Another minor criticism is the inclusion of maps that do not always include cities or regions where the women traveled.

There are no comparable volumes to *Women into the Unknown*. Olds' *Women of the Four Winds* (Houghton, 1985) includes only four women (all in *Women into the Unknown*), and a few are also listed in *The International Dictionary of Women's Biography* and *The Discoverers: An Encyclopedia of Explorers and Exploration* (McGraw-Hill, 1980).

This is an excellent source for high school, academic, or public libraries with a readership interested in women who have succeeded in a predominantly male endeavor. A quotation from the American explorer Harriet Chalmers Adams (1875–1937) sums up their experience: "I've never found my sex a hinderment; never faced a difficulty which a woman, as well as a man, could not surmount."

Place Names of Africa, 1935–1986: A Political Gazetteer. By Eugene C. Kirchherr. Scarecrow, 1988 (c1987). 136p. bibliog. maps. hardcover $17.50 (0-8108-2061-7).

911'.6 Africa—Politics and government—1945-1960 I Africa—Politics and government—1960- I Africa—Gazetteers [CIP] 87-20765

This work by Kirchherr (Department of Geography, Western Michigan University) is "a completely revised, enlarged, and updated edition" of his earlier monographs, the last edition of which appeared under the title *Abyssinia to Zimbabwe: A Guide to the Political Units of Africa in the Period 1947-1978* (3d ed., Ohio University Center of International Studies, 1979). *Place Names* lists, with numerous cross-references, more than 300 former and current names of the principal African territories, nations, and adjacent islands.

Part 1, "General Introduction," briefly discusses the need for and preparation of this political gazetteer and the more than 20 black-and-white maps appropriately placed throughout the book. Part 2, the heart of the volume, is the gazetteer, the alphabetical listing of place-names based on their usual spelling in English-language publications and maps. Variant forms of the names, particularly French spellings, are also included. These place-names appear in the left-hand column of the gazetteer pages, with explanatory notes and comments printed in the right-hand column.

A section of supplementary notes and maps (part 3) provides additional information on certain regions and states (e.g., French colonial federations in West and Equatorial Africa; former Italian colonial territories of Africa, 1935–52; and former British territories of Central and Southern Africa). The fourth part is a highly selective bibliography of authoritative books, periodicals, yearbooks, and general reference works; gazetteers and other sources on geographic names; and special sources such as the area handbook/country studies series prepared for the Department of the Army.

Place Names of Africa, 1935–1986 is a reliable quick-reference guide for the specialist and occasional user needing to know either previous or present names of African territories or states. This political gazetteer is highly recommended for academic and large public libraries where there is an interest in Africa.

The Penguin Atlas of North American History to 1870. By Colin McEvedy. Penguin, 1988. 112p. index. paper $6.95 (0-14-051128-8).

911.7 North America—Historical geography—Maps [BKL]

What this book demonstrates is that a good historical atlas of North America cannot be squeezed into an 8½-by-7-inch format. The base map, used in 47 of 57 depictions here, cuts off most of northern Canada and all of Alaska. The southern boundary of the map follows a line cutting through the middle of Honduras and the West Indies. While admitting that this is a "very small-scale map for a very big continent," the author offers as his defense that it covers "99 percent of the population and 99 percent of the action in the North American area in historical time."

The period covered ranges from 20,000 B.C. to 1870, with a 1987 "postscript." The maps themselves, done in white (for land masses) and blue (for water), with occasional shadings to denote colonial empires, are a rather uninspired lot and noticeably incomplete. For example, the voyages of Columbus are depicted on three maps labeled "A.D. 1492," "A.D. 1500," and "A.D. 1513." The first of these, for 1492, also attempts to illustrate indigenous inhabitants at the time of first European penetration, although no land masses or tribes are identified. In fact, the only places noted on this map are Watling and Samana Cay. (Watling Island for many years was thought to be the first land mass sited by Columbus, while more recent research has suggested that it was probably Samana Cay.) The map for 1500 depicts Columbus' second voyage in 1493–94 and the Cabot expedition of 1497. Columbus' third voyage in 1498 is ignored because it cannot be accommodated on the base map. Columbus' fourth voyage is depicted on the base map for 1513, but incompletely since Columbus sailed south along the coast of Panama and Columbia while the base map used here cuts off at Honduras. There is no mention of Balboa because his voyage cannot be accommodated on the base map. Similarly, the explorations of Frobisher, Drake, and Hawkins could not be depicted for the same reason.

There is no table of contents or list of maps; longitude and latitude are not indicated, nor is the scale of the base map. The only exceptions to the standard base map are a map showing the results of the U.S. presidential election of 1860 and a series of nine small maps depicting U.S. Civil War battles, although in no great detail. The book is rather evenly divided between text and maps. The former is rather pedestrian fare, which, as the author admits, could be "found in any standard history." The only index is to the text rather than the maps.

What one is left with is a series of repetitious maps that in many cases are ill-suited to the subjects they describe. Better fare can be found in most standard American history texts. Libraries will continue to rely on standard historical atlases like the *Atlas of American History* (Scribner, 1985).

Historical Atlas of the United States. Ed. by Wilbur E. Garrett and others. National Geographic Society, 1988. 289p. bibliog. illus. index. hardcover $59.95 (0-87044-747-5).

911'.73 U.S.—Historical geography—Maps [CIP] 88-675398

This magnificent new *Atlas* is a fitting commemorative volume for the one-hundredth anniversary of the National Geographic Society. It encourages browsing and will delight laypersons as well as the most discriminating professional geographer. Its 287 oversize pages (12 by 18 inches) are full of maps, timelines, historical charts, and new and historic photographs that provide a visual panorama of every aspect of American life from hot dog stands to house types. All told there are 380 maps (most in color) done on four varying scales ranging from 1 inch to 300 miles to 1 inch to 900 miles, 450 photographs, 80 graphs, and 140,000 words of text.

The book is divided into six thematic chapters: "The Land," "People," "Boundaries," "Economy," "Networks," and "Communities." Interspersed among these thematic chapters are five chronological chapters highlighting changes from 1400 to 1988. A timeline runs across the bottom of the pages in these chapters, noting representative events, from the significant (the purchase of Alaska) to the merely odd (the discovery of the Cardiff Giant, a nineteenth-century hoax). Since many of the thematic chapters also treat their subjects chronologically, the intermixture of the thematic and chronological chapters is sometimes confusing. It might have been better to put them in two separate sections.

The first thematic chapter, "The Land," focuses on the geology, climate, and natural heritage of the U.S., with interesting maps and charts on such current problems as environmental stress, hazardous-waste sites, and water-table declines.

The next chapter, "People," traces the entrance of people into the Americas from prehistoric times to the most recent immigration. There are gorgeous color depictions of such major Indian civilizations as the Mound Builders and a timeline depicting the expansion of Indian culture from 12,000 B.C. to A.D. 1400. The two-page spread "Indian World at Contact" depicts Indian house types from wigwams to log houses. African immigration is shown by a map of the triangular trade, a chart of internal slave movements between 1810 and 1860, and several historic photographs.

Other highlights from chapter 2 include a chart showing routes to freedom for slaves in 1860, a fascinating chart of segregation by state law in 1949, and a map plotting civil rights occurrences between 1945 and 1972. There is a section on recent immigrants, including Asians and Hispanics. Other two-page spreads chronicle the aging of America, the distribution of religions, internal migration patterns, and the lot of contemporary native Americans.

The third chapter, "Boundaries," describes the breakdown of continental barriers over the centuries, territorial growth, and westward expansion. Maps depict railroad expansion and federal land grants, and charts show the most frequently used names for counties (Washington) and acreage claimed under the Homestead Act.

The "Economy" chapter describes colonial agriculture in 1760 in a beautiful chart with products identified by appropriate symbols (from cattle to wood). Two pages describe barn styles from New England to New Mexico, and two more give contemporary projections on water use and groundwater reservoirs. The section on industry includes a cutaway reconstruction of an 1830 textile mill; a full-page depiction of the 60-acre Highland Park, Michigan, plant where Model Ts were made; and a humorous look at fins on Cadillacs from 1948 to 1964. More current is a chart on the location of domestic automobile plants in 1986 and a sketch of the North Carolina Research Triangle.

The chapter "Networks" begins with Indian trails in colonial Georgia and ends with a rather alarming depiction of the air corridors over New York at 4:30 p.m. on a Thursday. Other forms of transportation—canals, railroads, and highways—are also covered. Publishing, education, the distribution of dialects, the postal service, electrification, and mass communication are treated in this chapter.

The last chapter, "Communities," includes maps and charts plotting the growth of Boston, Chicago, and Los Angeles as representative cities; a section on utopias, including New Harmony, Indiana, and Sun City, Arizona; and a look at changes in the small town of Macon, Missouri.

The bibliography includes copious notes on all maps, charts, and photographs and lists sources and consultants for each section. The sources are an excellent guide for those seeking additional information on aspects highlighted in the *Atlas*. There is an index to the maps and text, with illustrations highlighted in boldface type. Since the arrangement of the *Atlas* results in the same topic being treated in several different sections of the book, use of the index will be essential. The *Atlas* is accompanied by an overlay that depicts the U.S. at the four scales used in the *Atlas* and a plastic magnifier. Libraries will need to manufacture a pocket to hold these items.

Wilbur E. Garrett from the National Geographic Society served as senior editor of the project, with principal consultants including two noted geographers: D. W. Meinig of Syracuse University and Sam Hilliard of Louisiana State University. Historian Michael Kammen was the primary historical consultant.

This *Atlas* is largely a work of historical geography and does not replace standard historical atlases like the *Atlas of American History* (rev. ed., Scribner, 1978). In sum, the *Historical Atlas of the United States* is characterized by the high-quality maps, photographs, charts, and graphs that have made the society's *National Geographic Magazine* an important part of the American scene for the past century. In honor of its centennial, the society is donating 35,000 copies of this *Atlas* to U.S. high schools. School librarians will certainly welcome this gesture. Academic and public libraries will want to purchase copies.

Desk Reference World Atlas. Rand McNally, 1988 (c1987). 528p. illus. tables. hardcover $17.95 (0-528-83287-5).

912 Atlases [BKL] 87-42819

This atlas was deliberately designed as a companion volume to the standard desk dictionary, which it resembles in size and shape. The atlas section consists of 200 pages of maps supplemented by 17 pages furnishing legends, a full-color survey of world flags, and a U.S. mileage chart. An index of over 25,000 place-names supplies alphanumeric grid references to the maps. Between these two sections is a 200-page section of tables, charts, and facts containing ready-reference information of various kinds.

The atlas proper is divided into seven parts. The first contains six double-page thematic maps of the world. The second and third parts, double-page environmental maps of the continents and an 18-page set of metropolitan maps of the world, are reduced-size versions of sets found in Rand McNally's *Goode's World Atlas*. There are two sections of historical maps: of the world (33 pages) and the U.S. (15 pages). The main 89-page section of world political maps contains reduced-size versions of Rand McNally "Cosmopolitan" maps, including individual maps of the states and Canadian provinces. Contiguous countries, states, and provinces appear in contrasting solid colors. The final section is an 18-page set of mostly double-page "travel" maps of U.S. regions, giving road-atlas information.

The ready-reference section has two major subsections: a "Gazetteer of the World," illustrated with small black-and-white photographs and providing thumbnail descriptions of countries and territories as well as some basic statistics, and a 64-page alphabetical list of U.S. counties and cities that gives population (1980 census figures where available) and (for cities) zip codes. There are guides to select major cities (world and U.S.) that give brief tourist information such as average temperature, selected hotels and restaurants, banking hours, and information sources. (The world cities guide has an entry for Calcutta but none for Bombay or New Delhi.) Other items found in the ready-reference section include world and U.S. time-zone maps, the latter showing area codes as well; air distances between world cities; tables showing largest world and U.S. metropolitan areas; several pages of data about the U.S. and individual states; railroad distances between U.S. cities; lists by state of colleges and universities and major military installations; a glossary of map terminology; a metric conversion chart; and a list of abbreviations.

The $6^1/2$-by-$9^1/2$-inch desk-dictionary page is hardly an ideal size for cartographic presentation. The political maps seem especially cramped and cluttered when reduced to this compass. Scale is generally shown on the atlas maps only by mile/kilometer bars, and the "Cosmopolitan" page-per-state or -province treatment for most of North America—with California and New Jersey getting the same single-page coverage despite their disparate areas—precludes comparability. Libraries will prefer atlases at least the size of *Goode's* and will have other, fuller sources for the kinds of geographic information included in the ready-reference section of this volume. Considerations of convenience and the need for desktop access to the types of maps and data included in this volume may make it an appropriate purchase for home or office.

Hammond Discovery World Atlas. Hammond, 1988. 228p. illus. indexes. tables. hardcover $17.95 (0-8437-1224-4); paper $13.95 (0-8437-1223-6).

912 Atlases I Zip code—U.S. [CIP] 88-675304

The Times Family Atlas of the World. 1st ed. Salem House, 1988. 224p. illus. index. tables. hardcover $24.95 (0-88162-346-6).

912 Atlases [CIP] 88-675200

Two major atlas publishers have each brought out a new world atlas designed for home use. They offer an unusually clear choice between styles of cartographic presentation.

The characteristic Hammond approach is reiterated in the introduction to its new atlas. One governing principle is separate maps for separate subjects; the main maps stress political information and do not depict physical relief, which is covered by separate inset-size maps and in a separate section on the continents. Another principle is the treatment of all information on a country or region as a unit. This means bringing together on pages adjacent to the basic political map all related material such as inset-size thematic maps, place-name indexes to the maps, and capsule factual data for individual countries along with the flag in full color.

Also characteristic of the Hammond approach is the "equal" treatment accorded to each state and Canadian province, which in most cases get a full-size basic map, regardless of area. Given the 9-by-$10^3/4$-inch page size and the rigid assignment of a single page per state, the result is a spacious and legible map for a smaller state like Connecticut compared with cramped and cluttered maps for large, populous states like California and Texas. Curiously, there is no place-name indexing for the state maps (though there is for the Canadian provinces). Since the place-name index at the back is extremely limited in scope (fewer than 6,000 names), indexing of U.S. place-names is exceedingly skimpy.

The new *Times Atlas* has a single index at the back of some 30,000 place-names and confines other kinds of supplementary information to sections separate from the main maps. A 40-page section at the front furnishes capsule factual data on nations and territories along with a full-color flag and brief descriptive paragraph. Following the main atlas is a section with maps of 50 major cities. On the New York City map, Roosevelt Island, which appears correctly on an inset map of Manhattan, is shown under its long-abandoned name of Welfare Island.

The main maps in the *Times Atlas* are 9-by-$11^1/2$-inch physical/political maps, which depict relief by means of layer tints. Quite a few are double-page. The maps for a particular continent are introduced by a political map showing individual countries outlined, in the Hammond manner, in contrasting pastel shades. (The *Hammond Atlas*, oddly, does not contain a political map of the entire continent in the case of either Africa or South America; these are sliced into northern and southern segments.) The *Times Atlas* has seven detailed regional maps of the U.S., four of them double-page and five at the uniform scale of 1:5 million. (The *Hammond Atlas* indicates scale only with mile/kilometer bars, not as a fraction.) In general, the *Times Atlas* favors regional coverage at a limited number of comparable scales to the Hammond state-per-page approach regardless of area. This means that the coverage of the world is more balanced in the *Times Atlas*, while the *Hammond Atlas* devotes almost half its pages to North America. The *Times Atlas* also has a section of physical maps of the continents, of the "as seen from space" variety with names added. The corresponding Hammond maps were created by a technique developed by the company that involved photographing previously prepared three-dimensional models. A few other distinctive features of the two atlases may be noted. The boundaries of political subdivisions are clearly outlined on the Hammond maps; the map of Ireland in the *Times Atlas*, by contrast, names the counties, but the boundaries are difficult to discern. The *Hammond Atlas* has a larger section of world thematic maps showing population, production, climate, and other features. There is some discrepancy in the population figures given for countries, even in the case of the U.S. The Hammond figures are closer to 1980 totals, the *Times* closer to mid-1986 estimates; the difference can be marked for countries with a high annual natural increase. A special feature included in the *Times Atlas* is a brief dictionary of geographic terms.

Both of these new atlases are products of reputable and reliable atlas publishers and can be recommended for home use. Libraries are likely to already have larger, more detailed world atlases but may want to add one of these relatively inexpensive titles if they need additional coverage.

Past Worlds: The Times Atlas of Archaeology. Hammond, 1988. 319p. bibliog. charts. illus. index. hardcover $85 (0-7230-0306-8).
912 Archaeology—Maps [CIP] 88-675201

This breathtakingly beautiful new atlas is the third collaborative effort between Times Books of London and Hammond of New Jersey. Previously copublished books have included the widely praised *Times Atlas of World History* in 1978 and *The Times Concise Atlas of World History* in 1984. Times Books, the publishing arm of the *London Times*, is well known for its other outstanding atlases: *The Times Atlas of the World*, *The Times Atlas of the Bible*, and *The Times Atlas of the Oceans*. Hammond, the American partner in the project, has produced more than 2 billion maps since its founding in 1900. More than 100 academic consultants, chiefly from Great Britain but including experts from the U.S., Australia, Sweden, Japan, France, and Nigeria, were involved in the preparation of this new atlas, a project that consumed eight years and cost more than $1 million.

The end product more than justifies the time and expense. The book is oversized (10 1/2 by 14 1/2 inches), as are many of the maps. There are 750 original maps, illustrations, photographs, and site reconstructions, all in color. The main physical maps provide full regional and physical identification and list up to 150 sites. About 60 percent of the colorplates also have secondary maps. All of the reconstructions of sites appear as pictorial illustrations, and some of these are quite magnificent, appearing virtually three dimensional. Among the most spectacular are "Tonglushan: A Chinese Copper Mine" from the Bronze Age; Roman water mills at Barbegal, France, fourth century A.D.; and Chang'an, the capital of Tang China in the eighth century A.D. All maps are drawn to scale (although scales are not always indicated) and include longitude and latitude. Site reconstructions are also drawn to scale, some as small as 1 3/8 inches to the foot. All photographs of objects are dated, and size is indicated in centimeters.

The book includes a detailed table of contents, a 10-page comparative chronology, a glossary, an up-to-date bibliography organized by general subject, and a 29-page index by place-name and subject (for instance, *Shang dynasty*, *boat burials*). The main body of the atlas is divided into seven sections. Chapter 1 provides discussion and examples of dating, excavation, settlement, burials, food, textiles, underwater sites, food, disease, warfare, valuables, and ritual. Chapter 2 describes man and his ancestors from 16 million to 10,000 B.C. Succeeding chapters describe "The Agricultural Revolution," "The First Cities and States," "The Empires of the Old World," and "The New World." The final chapter focuses on the period A.D. 650 to 1800. Coverage is broad-based and balanced.

As is typical in a volume of this detail and complexity, some errors have crept in, generally errors of omission. A map describing "The Demise of the Big Game Hunters" fails to mention the Head-Smashed-In site in western Alberta, which has recently seen the development of a multimillion-dollar commemorative area. The map "Colonisation of the Americas" lists Pensacola and St. Augustine as colonial capitals, but not the much larger New Orleans. A map detailing sites of shipwrecks lists the *Nuestra Señora de Atocha* as the "Atoche" and states it is undated, when the date is known to be 1622. In comparison with other more specialized archaeological atlases like M. I. Finley's *Atlas of Classical Archaeology* (1977), *Past Worlds* provides representative sites rather than a comprehensive portrait of a period.

Overall, *Past Worlds* is one of the most spectacular atlases of the decade and is certain to prove popular among specialists and the general public alike.

Student's World Atlas. Rev. ed. Rand McNally, 1988. 96p. illus. index. paper $5.95 (0-528-83286-7).
912 Atlases [BKL] 87-62450

This slender atlas is aimed at upper elementary and junior high school students. It begins with essays on the solar system, map projections and imagery, a glossary of geographic features, and directions for the use of an atlas. The essays are accompanied by drawings and satellite photographs. Then, for each continent, there are a series of one-and two-page maps: terrain, environment, a thematic map showing the distribution of animals, a map of countries and major cities, and a physical/political map. For large continents, there are several physical/political maps. For instance, there are separate two-page maps for Canada, the U.S., and Mexico and Central America. The maps indicate coordinates and scale (continents are drawn to approximately the same scale) and are accompanied by text and attractive color photographs. Comparisons are made to help the reader equate an unknown with something familiar. An example of this technique is "The entire United States could be placed in just the Sahara Desert." In the essays accompanying the countries and cities maps, language groupings are defined and explained.

Appendixes include world facts and comparisons, principal cities and their populations, an index of major places, and a glossary. The index refers to maps only, not textual materials.

Unlike Warwick Press' *Illustrated World Atlas* [RBB Ag 88] and *The Facts On File Children's Atlas* [RBB F 1 88], this book concentrates on geographic aspects of continents, not individual countries. More text is found here, and the reading level is also more difficult. This attractive atlas offers a good overview of the continents at a very reasonable price and would be a good addition to library collections serving the upper elementary/junior high student.

World Atlas of Nations. Rand McNally, 1988. 208p. illus. index. hardcover $34.95 (0-528-83315-4).
912 Atlases [BKL] 88-60112

The *World Atlas of Nations* presents its maps in a unique, nontraditional fashion: alphabetically by country, not geographically. The arrangement and contents give the atlas an encyclopedic appearance, as text, statistical data, and color photographs are more prominent than the maps. The atlas' purpose is to provide fast and easy access to the 220 independent countries and political entities (territories, possessions, etc.) included. This is facilitated by the table of contents and useful and appropriate cross-references.

The introductory material provides instruction on basic map use and how to best utilize the atlas. A world political map (1:75,000,000), a Pacific and Indian Ocean map (1:48,000,000), and maps of the continents (1:24,000,000) precede the country listings. The atlas concludes with a gazetteer/index of approximately 9,000 place-names. Contrary to the introduction, it does not list "*all* the places on *all* the maps."

A typical entry includes a locator map, country map, and map index (15 small countries have only a country map), official country name and flag, and a "fact block" that provides data on the people, politics, economy, and land of the country. No reference to specific sources is provided for the information contained in the fact block, only the statement in the introduction that the information "is derived from the most current Rand McNally data available." Almost half of the country entries are accompanied by at least one color photograph.

The maps are the same fine quality one has come to expect from

Rand McNally. The scale of the country and continent maps varies, ranging from 1:93,000 (Gibraltar) to 1:30,407,000 (Antarctica). At these scales detailed information is not always possible. Most maps have a copyright date of 1980. Map elevations are metric, and the fact block provides dimensions in both the customary and metric systems of measurements. Only the maps of the world, China, Canada, USSR, and U.S. are double-page maps and bleed into the binding.

The *World Atlas of Nations* is not an essential acquisition for all libraries. If a library has a small book budget, must be selective in its atlas purchases, and has access to sources that provide similar information (encyclopedias, other atlases, U.S. Department of State's *Background Notes*, almanacs, etc.), then it need not acquire this volume. However, the convenience and combination of maps, data, and text, arranged alphabetically in one volume, make the *World Atlas of Nations* an effective ready-reference source for basic information and a quick overview. Map collections, large libraries, and libraries needing to supplement their atlas collection will find this a useful acquisition.

The World Map Directory, 1989. By Aaron Maizlish and William S. Hunt. Map Link, 529 State St., Santa Barbara, CA 93101, 1988. 278p. index. maps. paper $29.95 (0-929591-00-3; ISSN 1040-1687).

912 Maps—Bibliography—Catalogs [OCLC] 89-647115

"I'm planning a trip to Scandinavia and need large-scale, small-scale, city, and recreation maps for Norway, Finland, and Sweden. Can you tell me what is available and where I can purchase them?" The map librarian goes to one source and returns in a matter of minutes with an extensive list of map titles and the addresses of the publishers for the patron. This is a daydream that all map librarians have had more than once: the availability of an equivalent to *Books in Print* for maps. There is still no *Maps in Print*, but *The World Map Directory* (*WMD*) is definitely a step in the right direction.

The purpose of *WMD* is twofold. First, it is the catalog of maps available for sale from Map Link, a map vendor. Some 46,000 cartographic titles are listed, and Map Link indicates that "we try to keep everything listed in stock." It is also an up-to-date cartographic reference source, since it lists topographic and thematic maps, city plans, and atlases and provides coverage for the world, continents, oceans, and most nations. The publishers plan to update *WMD* on an annual basis.

The introduction gives a brief overview on the arrangement of the contents, how to locate specific maps, and an explanation of the items that make up each entry (sheet name, Map Link code, price, scale, and date). Information on ordering materials from Map Link is provided. A clear, concise description of the Library of Congress "G" Schedule, which is used to arrange the map listings geographically, and an explanation of the International Map of the World Numbering System complete the introduction. A list of publisher abbreviations (but not addresses) and a geographic index, with some *see* references, are found at the end of *WMD*.

Between the introduction and the index are 272 pages of map listings that provide extensive, though not complete, coverage of U.S. and international maps. The use of the LC "G" Schedule makes this a very efficient source to use. Index maps, some more detailed than others, are used for almost all of the topographic map series included in Map Link's inventory. Annotations, ranging from one sentence to a page, are provided for most maps and map series and contain useful information on the map publisher and the quality and/or special features of a particular map or series.

WMD is not all-inclusive, and Map Link emphasizes this. Coverage is limited for the Soviet Union, Eastern Europe, Arab countries, and many Third World countries. Coverage is excellent for the U.S., Canada, Mexico, Western Europe, and South America. The U.S. Geological Survey's 7.5-minute topographic map series (1:24,000) is listed only for 11 western states, Hawaii, and the U.S. Territories. Map Link plans to stock the entire U.S. at this scale by 1990. Information on ordering topographic maps is incorrect due to a typographical error; the user is referred to the "G" Schedule's four-digit number of 3201 (World) instead of to 3701 (United States), where the ordering information appears.

The World Map Directory is a must for all map collections and map libraries. It will take a prominent place next to *International Maps and Atlases in Print* (Bowker, 1976), *GeoKatalog* (Geo-Center ILH, 1977–), *World Mapping Today* (Butterworth, 1987), and *The Map Catalog* (Vintage, 1986). Libraries with no map collection, but that receive occasional map questions, will want to consider acquiring this title for their reference collection. It is an excellent source of information at a reasonable price.

The Historical Atlas of Political Parties in the United States Congress, 1789–1989. By Kenneth C. Martis. Macmillan, 1989. 518p. bibliog. charts. indexes. tables. hardcover $150 (0-02-920170-5).

912'.1324273 Political parties—U.S.—History—Maps ‖ U.S.—Politics and government ‖ U.S.—Election districts—Maps ‖ U.S.—History ‖ Local elections—U.S.—Maps [CIP] 88-675270

This is the second of a projected three-volume set produced in part with a grant from the National Endowment for the Humanities Program for Research Tools and Reference Works and edited by a professor of geography at West Virginia University. Volume 1 was *The Historical Atlas of U.S. Congressional Districts, 1789–1983* [RBB N 15 83], which showed in 97 black-and-white maps the changing boundaries of congressional districts from the First through the Ninety-seventh Congresses. The final volume will be *The Historical Atlas of Critical Votes in the United States Congress, 1789–1989*.

Throughout this *Atlas*, Martis illustrates with text and colored maps the geographic structure of U.S. political representation unique to democratic legislative bodies. The volume is divided into four parts. Part 1 is an introduction defining and describing the evolution of political parties in the U.S. The lengthy discussion of sources of information for congressional elections will be very useful for librarians and students. A table of more than three pages traces political divisions by listing the number of seats in each Congress through the One-hundredth and noting the number filled by members of the majority, minority, and third parties. Martis then describes voting-bloc affiliations, major political parties, and third parties throughout our history. The last section of the introduction explains the construction of the maps, including the reasons for the use of particular colors. (The House district maps are from *The Historical Atlas of U.S. Congressional Districts* but are improved considerably with the use of color.) A detailed bibliography completes part 1.

Part 2, the atlas, includes political-party maps for the House and Senate and lists of individual members from the First through the One-hundredth Congress. Maps for early congresses cover half a page. With the Twenty-ninth Congress, as more states were added to the Union, the maps cover a full page. There are inset maps for large cities. Pie charts indicate for each congress the percentage of each political party represented in both the House and the Senate. The last two parts of the *Atlas* are tables of members, congress by congress, showing specific political affiliations (liberal Republican, radical, Jeffersonian Democrat, etc.). Three to six sources were used to verify political affiliation, and affiliations are listed under each source. A subject and name index to part 1 and a name index to part 2 complete the book.

This is a monumental work both physically and in content. The size (17 by 13 inches) is perfect for the maps but makes it difficult to read the text, which is in three columns on each page. The maps clearly illustrate and analyze the membership patterns of two centuries of the U.S. Congress, and it is obvious that the author's six years of research were systematic and complete. Though this volume is considerably larger than the first volume published six years ago, the price is exactly the same. Even with some duplication of *The Historical Atlas of U.S. Congressional Districts*, this volume is a unique source that will be a necessary purchase for academic libraries and medium-size to large public libraries.

A Social and Economic Atlas of India. Oxford, 1988 (c1987). 254p. tables. hardcover $65 (0-19-562041-0).

912'.1330954 India—Economic conditions—1947– —Maps ‖ India—Economic

conditions—1947- — Statistics I India—Social conditions—1947- —Maps I
India—Social conditions—1947- —Statistics [OCLC] 87-900032

This *Atlas* surveys and analyzes contemporary India by means of some 250 multicolor maps, 370 charts, and over 100 statistical tables. All of the maps of India are based on a common projection and have a similar layout. Four scales are employed: full page, 1:15,000,000; half page, 1:21,000,000; quarter page, 1:30,000,000; and inset size, 1:35,000,000. The right-hand page is reserved for cartography; the left facing page contains explanatory text and any accompanying tables. In the lower right-hand margin, below the maps, are bar and pie charts, graphs, or additional tables.

The maps are arranged in nine sections. The first three cover the land (basic physical and political features, administrative subdivisions, parliamentary constituencies); population (distribution, growth, language and religion, literacy, employment); and climate. The fourth and fifth sections deal with natural resources (water resources, land use, minerals) and infrastructure (welfare, education, transportation, communications, irrigation and power, banking). The sixth and largest section covers production (animal husbandry and fisheries, agriculture, industry); most of the quarter-page maps are found in this section. The next section is devoted to tourism, and the eighth section concentrates on major aspects of the national economy (key industrial and fiscal indicators). The last map in this section focuses on the Seventh Five-Year Plan (1985–90). The final section consists of world maps illustrating exports, imports, and aid from and to India. A concluding page of analytical text situates India's developing economy in a global context.

The front matter includes a page of illustrated explanatory notes on how to interpret the more complex graphic techniques employed in presenting data. Source notes appear at the end of the explanatory text accompanying each map, and a transparent overlay sheet is supplied with the atlas showing (for all but the maps at the quarter-page scale) the administrative district boundaries. Lists are provided, by state, of administrative districts and their subdivisions and of parliamentary constituencies. The brief introduction indicates that population figures are based on the 1981 census. No biographical information is furnished about the members of the editorial board.

A wealth of socioeconomic information is presented in fairly limited space through the well-designed, legible, and clearly annotated thematic maps and charts. The accompanying text and tables enable this *Atlas* to serve to a considerable extent as a handbook and statistical abstract as well. It will be a basic reference source on the world's largest democracy and second most populous nation.

Atlas of the Middle East. Ed. by Moshe Brawer. Macmillan, 1988. 140p. bibliog. charts. index. hardcover $50 (0-02-905271-8).

912'.56 Middle East—Maps [CIP] 88-675435

The Cambridge Encyclopedia of the Middle East and North Africa. Ed. by Trevor Mostyn and Albert Hourani. Cambridge, 1988. 504p. bibliog. illus. maps. hardcover $49.50 (0-521-32190-5).

956 Middle East [CIP] 88-10866

The series of Macmillan reference sources on the Middle East continues with this *Atlas* of the region. The editor, a renowned geographer at the University of Tel Aviv, defines the area as the Arabian Peninsula states, Cyprus, Egypt, Iran, Iraq, Israel, Jordan, Lebanon, Libya, Sudan, Syria, and Turkey.

The work is divided into two main sections. The first, "The Region," provides maps, narrative, and tables on geology, climate, fauna and flora, population, oil, and political history. The maps range in size from 1/2 to 1 1/2 pages and present the topics in great clarity (e.g., population density, location of oil and gas fields, pipelines). The two-color maps use browns and grays, with sufficient contrast for easy understanding. Charts, like one on education and literacy rate, are made easily comprehensible through hatching and symbols.

The main section, "The Countries," has a 4- to 7-page article for each of the 19 nations covered. Depending on the size of the country, a fairly detailed (usually 3/4 page) map provides an overview. Boxes at the beginning of each entry list area, population, largest cities, and economic and social indicators. The narrative discusses topography, climate, population, agriculture, minerals, industry, history, and government and politics. Subject maps, tables, and pie charts facilitate understanding of the material.

The Atlas of the Middle East is current, including some early 1988 events. The bibliography and list of further reading include a 1988 title. The index to place-names includes grid references to locations on the maps of the countries.

This *Atlas* can be compared with *The Cambridge Atlas of the Middle East & North Africa* [RBB Ag 88], which includes three additional North African nations. The latter does not treat individual countries; topics are shown on two-color maps of the entire region. It also does not locate cities on the maps; thus there is no index. While there is a lot of overlap in topics treated, there are some unique subjects in each atlas. *The Cambridge Atlas* is useful for those who want to compare countries throughout the region; *The Atlas of the Middle East* is easier to use if one is interested in a particular country.

The Cambridge Encyclopedia of the Middle East and North Africa is a companion to *The Cambridge Atlas of the Middle East & North Africa*. The editors are joined by 80 other academics and journalists, most of whom are British, in providing an overview of various subject areas and then in-depth examinations of the countries. The book defines the region in a broader sense than *The Cambridge Atlas*, including Mauritania on the Atlantic to Somalia on the Indian Ocean and east through Afghanistan. A list of the contributors and their affiliations is presented with their initials at the beginning of the work, and each article is signed. An asterisk by a word in an entry serves as a cross-reference.

Arrangement is in six parts. Part 1, "Lands and Peoples," provides an overview of the region. Suggestions for further reading are included after some entries, and recent titles, mainly British, were noted. Statistics and narrative are fairly current, with some 1986 items noted. Setting the pattern for the rest of the book, some photographs are in color or full-page; all are interesting and reproduced and labeled clearly.

Part 2, "History," is a quick survey by the major periods (e.g., "From Alexander to the Coming of Islam"). Tables of Muslim dynasties are helpful. Inevitably, in a work of many contributors, some information is repeated. For example, the entry on early Islamic history overlaps with the background presented in the section on religions. Part 3, "Societies and Economies," is a broad look at many topics (e.g., irrigation, Islamic banking, the changing role of women, satellite communications). Statistics are drawn from many sources, such as the World Bank.

Part 4 covers "Culture"—religion, literature, the arts, music, and Islamic science. Information on various schools of Islamic law, cuisine, and the many facets of religion in the area are presented in a balanced fashion. Many of these topics are also covered in Macmillan's *Cultural Atlas of Islam* [RBB F 15 87], which is also heavily illustrated with maps, charts, and black-and-white photographs. It is not limited to the Middle East and North Africa, however, but discusses Islam in all parts of the world.

Part 5 on the individual countries comprises nearly 200 pages. The length of each nation's entry ranges from a few pages to seven. The format for all is similar: each begins with a small map and a box of facts on government, society, and economy. Subsequent narrative sections cover the country's geography, peoples, religion, and modern history. A bibliography and photographs accompany longer entries. Lists of Israeli political parties and Lebanese political factions and militias clarify the situations in the two nations today. At the end of "The Countries" section are entries for peoples without a country—Armenians, Kurds, and Palestinians. The information is well presented, and the Palestinian section in particular reflects the balanced writing of the work. Particularly useful will be the pages delineating Palestinian organizations. Part 6, "Inter-State Relations," looks at the region in cross-national, -political, and -military terms. International Islamic movements, the Arab League, and a chronology of the Arab-Israeli problem are very helpful. The book concludes with an index.

These books differ in the way they treat Israel. *The Cambridge Atlas* shows Gaza and the West Bank as occupied territories, and *The Cambridge Encyclopedia* includes the separate entries *West Bank* and *Gaza*. *The Atlas of the Middle East*, on the other hand, shows these regions as part of Israel on the maps, though the text states that they have not been formally annexed by Israel.

Librarians are faced with an outstanding array of reference books on the Middle East from which to choose. Europa's *Middle East and North Africa* (annual) provides surveys of the region and individual countries, though it lacks the handsome illustrations of the books reviewed here. *The Atlas of the Middle East* is complemented by other titles from Macmillan, *A Political Dictionary of the Arab World* [*RBB* Ap 1 88], and *A Political Dictionary of the State of Israel* [*RBB* D 1 87]. The two Cambridge titles also complement each other well. Both of the works under review are well prepared and reasonably priced for the quantity of information and quality of production.

Atlas of Southeast Asia. By Richard Ulack and Gyula Pauer. Macmillan, 1989. 171p. bibliog. charts. illus. index. hardcover $95 (0-02-933200-1).

912'.59 Asia, Southeastern—Maps I Asia, Southeastern—Economic conditions—Maps I Asia, Southeastern—Social conditions—Maps [CIP] 88-17543

Southeast Asia has been an area of turmoil and change for centuries with wars, displaced peoples, and toppled governments being the rule, not the exception, especially since World War II. Geographers Ulack and Pauer present an up-to-date source of information in their *Atlas of Southeast Asia*. The last such publication was the now dated *Atlas of South-East Asia* (St. Martin's, 1964).

The purpose of the *Atlas* is straightforward: "to provide detailed and current maps and information (as of the mid-1980s, when possible) on the Southeast Asian region and on each of the ten nations that comprise the region." This is achieved in a concise, clear, and comprehensive manner. The preface contains valuable information on the sources used, scales of maps, style of presentation, and spelling of place-names. The *Atlas* proper is divided into two parts. Part 1 is an overview of the region with chapters on physical environment and resources, history and politics, culture and population, and urban characteristics. Part 2 consists of 10 chapters—one for each nation (Indonesia, Philippines, Malaysia, Singapore, Brunei, Thailand, Burma, Vietnam, Kampuchea—formerly Cambodia, and Laos). Each chapter begins with a statistical and historical overview and is followed by text on the physical environment, history, economy, transportation, tourism, and people and culture.

The 70 maps (political and thematic), over 60 diagrams and charts, and 50 color photographs are well chosen, and the text and illustrations complement and supplement each other. The scale appears on all of the country and metropolitan maps. It varies from 1:17,600,000 for the regional map to 1:298,000 for Singapore. The metropolitan maps are drawn at a scale of 1:37,500 or 1:75,000, depending on the size of the urban area. The thematic maps do not indicate the scale but are consistent within a chapter. Most map information and data are current as of the mid-1980s. Exceptions to this exist for Vietnam, Laos, and Kampuchea, where the most recent information is unreliable and the only information available is pre-1980s. This is explained in the preface.

The *Atlas* concludes with a selected bibliography of sources and a subject index. The bibliography is arranged by the type of source: atlases and maps, selected works, statistical and government sources, travel guides, and selected periodicals. The index is not a gazetteer, and the lack of a gazetteer or individual map indexes is an inconvenience at times.

Atlas of Southeast Asia is a source most academic and large public libraries will want to add to their reference collections, as it fills a gap that has existed in the literature for many years. The text is well written, the maps are detailed and easy to read, and the diagrams and thematic maps are well chosen and presented. A library owning *Atlas of Southeast Asia* and *Atlas of South Asia* (Westview, 1987) will have coverage of the entire southern portion of the Asian continent.

A Guide to the Archaeological Sites of the British Isles. By Courtlandt Canby. Facts On File, 1988. 358p. illus. index. hardcover $24.95 (0-8160-1570-8).

914.1'04858 Great Britain—Antiquities—Guide-books I Ireland—Antiquities—Guide-books I Excavations (Archaeology)—Great Britain—Guide-books I Excavations (Archaeology)—Ireland—Guide-books I Historic sites—Great Britain—Guide-books [CIP] 88-25068

This book is the first volume in Facts On File's Guides to the Archaeological Sites of Europe and the Mediterranean series. Author Canby is identified as the editor of The Making of the Past, a 20-volume series on archaeology and early history, and the author of the *Encyclopedia of Historic Places*. Canby's audience is the layperson; his purpose is to provide "a reference book for the stay-at-home [and] a field manual for the interested traveler." The material was gathered from "other archaeological guides for particular areas, tourist guidebooks, magazine articles, newspaper clips and so forth...as well as occasional scholarly books for certain sites and for background." He provides no reading list for students or other interested readers.

The more than 750 sites are arranged alphabetically in three sections: England and Wales, Scotland, and Ireland. (The latter section includes the Republic.) The time frame is from the Paleolithic to the Norman Conquest for England and into the twelfth century for Scotland and Ireland. Each section begins with an outline map showing counties and/or regions and a lengthy instructive history (8–15 pages) of each area with an explanation of the types of remains to be found. For example, Canby notes that the over 65 round towers surviving in Ireland "were used as belfrys, as safe storage for the church treasures, as lookouts, as refuges during raids, whether Irish or Viking, but above all as symbols of the aspiration toward God in His heaven above."

The entries range from a few sentences (*Claydon Pike, Memsie Cairn*) to four pages (*Hadrian's Wall, Stonehenge, Boyne Valley Tombs*). The text of the entries (which describe cities and towns, tombs, churches, castles, ramparts, monuments, etc.) is clear, well written, and sufficiently detailed. Sites are located by giving the mileage from the nearest town. The Board's quarrels are with the alphabetical arrangement, the lack of detailed maps, and the quality of the illustrations, as well as the absence of a bibliography. A description of a stone circle in County Cork followed by one of a round tower in County Louth followed by another of a high cross in County Down may be fine for the arm-chair traveler but is not useful for one in a car, or for persons planning an itinerary. The index and lists of sites by county and regions at the end of the volume do not compensate for this flaw. The sites are not even marked on the four outline maps provided. Canby notes in his introduction that travelers will need "detailed Ordnance Survey maps [or] the Reader's Digest *Book of the Road*." The 75 black-and-white photographs do not add much to the *Guide*. Many are gray, unclear, or out of focus. The professionally produced images (British Tourist Office, Irish Tourist Board) are better than those taken by the author, but even these are not well reproduced.

Libraries with holdings in archaeology may want to add Canby's *Guide* for its textual information. While it has some reference value, public libraries serving travelers will not find it a worthwhile addition as a guidebook.

Place-Names in Classical Mythology: Greece. By Robert E. Bell. ABC-Clio, 1989. 350p. bibliog. index. hardcover $48.50 (0-87436-507-4).

914.95'0014 Greece—Gazetteers I Mythology, Greek—Dictionaries [CIP] 88-16870

The geography of classical mythology is treated in this dictionary of approximately 1,000 place-names of importance in Greek religion and mythology. The work serves as a companion volume to *A Dictionary of Classical Mythology: Symbols, Attributes, and Associations* (ABC-Clio, 1982), also by Bell, a librarian at the University of California, Davis. This guide differs from such works as the standard *Princeton Encyclopedia of Classical Sites* (Princeton, 1976) or the *Illustrated Encyclopedia of the Classical World* (Harper, 1975) by focusing on mythology rather than historical events. For example, the entry *Marathon* discusses its place in the legends of Theseus and the worship of Heracles but mentions the famous battle of 490 B.C. only in passing. A traveler to the modern Greek village of Davlia would find in Bell a geographic description of the site, the origin of the ancient name (Daulis), and a recounting of the story of the cruel king Tereus and the sisters Procne and Philomela, with references to the writings of Ovid, Pausanias, and Homer. The *Princeton Encyclopedia* discusses only battles with Persians, the attack of the Thebans, and other historical events. While the author does not consider the work a guidebook, he hopes to enhance mythological interest by providing a geographic context for the legends.

The geographic scope is limited to the boundaries of modern Greece. Entries range from a few lines for a site merely named for a mythological being to several pages for places of great significance, such as Thebes or Delphi. The ancient places are listed alphabetically with the modern name, if any, in parentheses. Transliterations for place-names are those used by the Greek National Tourist Organization. For ancient names Bell has used the transliterations found in the *Loeb Classical Library*. Citations to ancient writers are also to the *Loeb* editions, in standard format for classical works. An appendix lists the modern place-names associated with ancient locations, and a "Guide to Personae" connects significant figures to associated sites. A bibliography of books, maps, and gazetteers is also appended. There are no maps to help the reader locate the places.

Bell notes in the introduction that "in Greece the past and present coexist. Nowhere else can one feel so intensely the infusion of the ancient with the modern." While not a substitute for more general reference works on mythology, this fascinating, well-written dictionary brings to life those ancient places for the traveler or reader and should be considered for purchase by academic and public libraries.

The Oxford Illustrated Literary Guide to Canada. By Albert and Theresa Moritz. Oxford, 1988 (c1987). 246p. illus. index. hardcover $39.95 (0-19-540596-X).

917.1'0464 Literary landmarks—Canada—Dictionaries l Authors, Canadian—Homes and haunts—Dictionaries l Canada—Description and travel—1981– —Guidebooks [BKL]

This illustrated guide to the literary associations of places in Canada contains over 500 entries. These are divided into 12 sections corresponding to the 10 provinces and two territories of Canada. Rather than being arranged alphabetically, the provinces are organized according to their geographical proximity, from east to west. Sections for the Northwest Territories and the Yukon Territory follow the provinces. Within a section, entries for cities, villages, lakes, rivers, and other places are arranged alphabetically. Each entry provides fascinating bits of information about the lives, works, and residences of writers connected with the area. The discussion of a locale follows a chronological sequence based on the period of an individual's association with it. For ease of access, the names of writers treated are highlighted in boldface.

Exceptions to the general chronological approach under a place-name are the two longest entries, those on Montreal and Toronto. Montreal is divided into 19 sections: a general, introductory section, followed by seven sections on English-Canadian writers and 11 on French-Canadian writers. The article on Toronto is composed of seven parts, based on time period and the area of the city.

The compilers, who have written other works on Canada and Canadian literature, recognize not only native Canadians but also literary figures of other nationalities (e.g., Rudyard Kipling and Joyce Carol Oates) who visited Canada, lived there for a period, or wrote about it. In addition to such well-known deceased writers as Robert Service and Lucy Maud Montgomery, entries also cover contemporary Canadian authors such as W. P. Kinsella and Alice Munro.

Readers who have experienced the beautiful full-page color photographs in Oxford's literary guides to Australia and Great Britain and Ireland may be disappointed that no such illustrations appear in this work. However, more than 300 small black-and-white photographs of authors, their homes, and other buildings and places associated with them complement the text. In addition, a number of entries are accompanied by excerpts from literary works describing the particular locale. The compilers apparently assume that users will have an intimate knowledge of Canadian geography, since no maps are provided. Throughout the volume, cross-references appear frequently to guide the user to other entries in which an author is treated. In addition, the index lists all the authors covered, citing both the place-name under which the reference occurs and the page number. The placement of page numbers in the inner margins hinders quick location of a reference, since the volume must be opened practically flat to read them. Unfortunately, there is no index to geographic localities. Therefore, if one does not readily recall that Winnipeg is in Manitoba, locating that entry can be frustrating.

This work is strikingly similar in scope and format to John R. Colombo's *Canadian Literary Landmarks* (Hounslow Press, 1984), which covers more places and includes over twice as many illustrations. However, the Oxford guide is more scholarly and treats over 950 authors, while the Colombo volume covers approximately 500 writers.

If it were not for its size, *The Oxford Illustrated Literary Guide to Canada* would be a handy guidebook for a literary-minded traveler in Canada. It should, however, provide hours of pleasurable reading for those who prefer to do their touring in the comfort of an armchair. Due to its browsable nature, some libraries may want to consider it for the circulating collection rather than the reference collection. Although this work is probably not a necessary purchase for most libraries, particularly if they already have *The Oxford Companion to Canadian Literature* (1983) and the three-volume *Literary History of Canada* (2d ed., Univ. of Toronto, 1976), it will be useful in academic, public, and high school libraries where there is a substantial interest in Canadian literature.

Access America: An Atlas and Guide to the National Parks for Visitors with Disabilities. 1st ed. Northern Cartographic, P.O. Box 133, Burlington, VT 05402, 1988. 444p. spiral-bound $89.95 (0-944187-00-5).

917.3'04 National parks and reserves—U.S.—Guide-books l Recreation areas and the handicapped—U.S. [BKL] 87-072038

Numerous guides have been published for the national parks, and there are several travel guides for the disabled; however, *Access America* is the first publication that deals specifically with the accessibility and usability of our national parks for individuals with disabilities. It provides information for 37 of the country's 49 national parks, listing them alphabetically by park name. The layout, the large-type print, the effective use of maps, charts, and color codes, and the appendixes make this atlas and guide an easy-to-use and informative reference source.

The introduction discusses the methodology used to gather information for the book and describes its format and how one can best utilize its contents. No attempt is made to compare the parks or to rate one park as more accessible than another. This is a decision for the reader, as each individual's needs are different.

A general overview and information on weather, winter visitation, safety, elevation, medical and support services, publications, programs, and transportation are provided for each park. Availability of sign-language interpreters, telephone devices for the deaf (TDD), and rules and precautions for users of guide dogs are also provided.

The maps and charts are clear, easy to read, and an excellent way to obtain a general overview of the park's location, climate, and accessibility. A climate chart provides the mean monthly temperature and precipitation for each park (representative climate charts for 10 major U.S. cities appear in appendix 1 for comparison purposes). A basic facilities chart appears at the end of each park chapter and provides the level of accessibility for telephones, water fountains, and restrooms at visitor centers, campgrounds, hotels, stores, etc.

At least three maps accompany each park narrative. Locator maps show the park's location in a regional setting. Medical and support-services maps show the availability of six types of services or products (e.g., hospitals, dialysis centers, oxygen) within an approximately 100-mile radius of the park. Park maps show the services and the level of accessibility at various locations throughout the park. Maps of visitor centers and area inset maps of developed areas or campgrounds are provided when more detail is needed. Map scales vary and are appropriately chosen. Scales are provided only for the medical and support-services, park, and area inset maps. Visitor center maps are not drawn to scale and are so indicated.

Located throughout the book are 12 essays written by disabled park users that provide a personal and realistic view of park use and accessibility. A directory of independent living centers and a listing of dialysis centers and hospitals for each park are provided in appendixes 2 and 3. A bibliography of books, government documents, and journals follows the appendixes.

The only limitation for libraries may be the book's spiral binding, although it is intended to make the book easier for the disabled to handle. Heavy use, which it will surely receive, will require early rebinding. Northern Cartographic plans to publish several single park excerpts in the future (*Access Yosemite National Park* is currently available).

The information here is current as of late 1987. The editors of *Access America* have compiled a unique and essential reference source. It more than meets the purpose that its subtitle so aptly states: *An Atlas and Guide to the National Parks for Visitors with Disabilities*. The nondisabled will also find the information in *Access America* useful in planning a park visit.

Recommended for all academic libraries, large public libraries, map collections, and any library providing reference service to the disabled.

Cities of the United States. v.1: The South. 1st ed. Ed. by Deborah A. Straub and Diane L. Dupuis. Gale, 1988. 403p. illus. index. maps. hardcover $69.95 (0-8103-2501-2; ISSN 0899-6075).

917.6'04 Southern States—Description and travel—1981— l Cities and towns—U.S. [BKL] 89-659502

This is the first volume in a projected four-volume set. This particular volume surveys 30 cities in 16 southern states, including Washington, D.C. Criteria for inclusion are "largest or fastest growing," historical or industrial significance, or appeal to vacationers and business. The intended audiences are business and vacation travelers, people relocating, and the media.

Arranged alphabetically by state, entries follow a uniform pattern. Each section opens with an outline map of the state. Additional information (e.g., motto, flower, area) is given along with population and economic statistics. Each city section begins with a black-and-white photograph of the skyline followed by a full-page outline map that shows major roads, colleges, airports, and the surrounding metropolitan area. "The City in Brief" highlights information presented in greater detail in the text and includes weather, the cost of housing and living, major colleges, and newspapers. The text treats geography and climate, history, population, municipal government, the economy, education and research, health care, recreation and sightseeing, convention facilities, transportation, and communications. The length of entries for cities varies from 9 to 15 pages.

Although much of the information in *CUS* is available elsewhere, this is a convenient source. Especially useful are the statistics on population and local economies. However, there are some limitations to the work. The recreation and sightseeing parts are almost useless to the traveler because they do not provide addresses and telephone numbers for museums, restaurants, and hotels, and the maps do not show any streets. Despite the stated audience, vacationers will be better served by a travel guide. Equally limiting is the number of cities covered. Eight of the 16 states represented have only one city listed; such prominent places as Jacksonville (the largest city in Florida), Orlando, Chattanooga, Virginia Beach, and Savannah are omitted.

Aside from numerous regional travel guides, a comparable work is *Places Rated Almanac* (Rand McNally, 1985), which covers 329 cities, ranking them on climate, housing, health, crime, transportation, education, arts, recreation, and the economy. A multitude of maps and diagrams illustrates the narrative, and there are citations showing where information was obtained. *Book of American City Rankings* (Facts On File, 1983) is a similar title. In contrast, while far fewer cities are covered, the statistical information in *CUS* is easy to access. *CUS* does not overlap with another Gale publication, *Cities of the World*, which covers only foreign cities.

Public and academic libraries that serve people planning to relocate may find this set valuable.

The Oxford Literary Guide to Australia. Ed. by Peter Pierce. Oxford, 1988 (c1987). 344p. illus. index. maps. hardcover $59 (0-19-554592-3).

919.4'0463 Literary landmarks—Australia—Dictionaries l Authors, Australian—Homes and haunts—Dictionaries l Australian literature—Bio-bibliography [BKL]

Published during Australia's bicentennial year to promote a better understanding of the land and its literature and sponsored by the Association for the Study of Australian Literature, *The Oxford Literary Guide to Australia* provides an illustrated panorama of Australian literature set within a geographic framework, identifying every place that has some kind of literary significance.

The arrangement is by the seven states and territories, given alphabetically. Within these sections, alphabetically listed entries include geographic entities of any size (towns, townships, suburbs, rivers, and mountains) as well as fictional places that have "biographical and imaginative associations" for Australian authors. The authors represented cover the entire spectrum of Australian literature (native, historical, and contemporary) and every kind of writing relevant to the literary history of the continent.

Entries blend descriptions of the geography, history, and literary significance of each place with generous quotations from sources. The text is brought to life through 16 pages of color photographs and 250 black-and-white illustrations. Each entry is keyed to the eight maps included at the end of the volume. The arrangement requires that the reader unfamiliar with Australian geography use these maps, as no index to specific place-names is provided. (*The Oxford Illustrated Literary Guide to Canada* [RBB O 1 88], while similar to this book in many ways, is even more difficult to use, since it lacks maps and its provinces are arranged east to west, rather than alphabetically.) The author index is selective, giving basic biographical information for major writers; index entries are linked to place-names in the main text through cross-references.

The Oxford Literary Guide to Australia is eminently readable. As a reference source it is important for the scope of its coverage, but its references to authors are often tantalizingly brief, and there is no index to titles of individual works. Its handsome format, geographic emphasis, and generous illustrations make it an excellent complement to other reference sources like *The Oxford Companion to Australian Literature* (Oxford, 1985) and *The Oxford History of Australian Literature* (Oxford, 1981). It "explores the notion of place in Australian literature," a necessary dimension if that literature is to be fully appreciated. It should be added to collections that are strong in Commonwealth literature, but not necessarily to the reference collection. It is a book that those planning to visit Australia might well read for the unique perspective it provides on the country and its literature.

BIOGRAPHY, GENEALOGY

V.I.P. Address Book, 1988–1989. Ed. by James M. Wiggins. Associated Media Companies, Ltd., P.O. Box 10190, Marina del Rey, CA 90295-8864, 1988. 800p. bibliog. hardcover $84.95 (0-938731-07-6).

920'.0025 Celebrities—Directories I Celebrities—U.S.—Directories I Social registers I U.S.—Social registers [CIP] 87-33322

According to the introduction, "the purpose of the *V.I.P. Address Book* is to provide readers a means of reaching Very Important People—Celebrities, Government Officials, Business Leaders, Entertainers, Sports Stars, Scientists and Artists." The result is an alphabetical listing of over 20,000 people with addresses and occupation or position tags (for example, actor, businessman, Navy admiral, president of Peru). The introductory material notes that "the category . . .is selected to best describe his/her most noteworthy accomplishment. No distinction is made whether the person still holds that position."

A random sample of the entries reveals that 60 percent of the addresses provided are in care of companies, agents, colleges, government offices, general delivery, P.O. boxes, or publishers. If a library patron knows the affiliation of an individual, the address of the company, government office, etc., can usually be found in other directories. Numerous foreign government officials are included, e.g., "*Lini, Walter* Prime Minister, Vanuatu—c/o Prime Minister's Office, Vila, Vanuatu." Similarly, if the patron knows the position of these persons, the addresses could be found without the *V.I.P. Address Book*. Street addresses *are* given for a few celebrities—e.g., Robert DeNiro, Barbra Streisand, and Pinchas Zukerman—but one wonders if Oscar Brand can really be found at 1 Times Square.

Users are asked to inform the publisher if they find incorrect addresses. "The *V.I.P. Address Book* Updates . . .will publish updated and additional addresses on a regular basis." A subscription to the quarterly updates is $34.95.

A "Bibliography: Other Reference Sources for Celebrities, Dignitaries and Organizations" is appended. It lists 34 directories, including standard Gale and Marquis *Who's Who* publications as well as specialized sources such as *Academy Players Directory* (Academy of Motion Picture Arts and Sciences) and *Kraks BlaBog* (published in Copenhagen). The Board wonders if these directories are the source of the addresses. The introduction does state that unnamed committees of "prominent and knowledgeable people" considered "candidates running into many of [sic] thousands." "The actual task of finding appropriate addresses fell to a worldwide staff of experienced researchers and veteran investigative reporters."

Libraries with a good collection of directories will not need the *V.I.P. Address Book*.

Almanac of Famous People: A Comprehensive Reference Guide to More Than 25,000 Famous and Infamous Newsmakers from Biblical Times to the Present. 3v. 4th ed. Ed. by Susan L. Stetler. Gale, 1989. hardcover $90 (0-8103-2784-8; ISSN 1040-127X).

920'.02 Biography—Indexes [OCLC]

Almanac of Famous People is the successor to *Biography Almanac*, first published in one volume in 1981 [*RSBR* My 1 82] and most recently in the three-volume third edition in 1986. Although the title has changed, the basic purpose has not. The introduction to the *Almanac* states its dual function as "a biographical dictionary and an index to information about famous people."

In its role as a biographical dictionary, it lists more than 25,000 people, historical and contemporary, who have attained fame of one sort or another. The criteria for inclusion, while not spelled out explicitly, are hinted at through Andy Warhol's well-known statement, "Everyone will be world-famous for fifteen minutes," and the note that "fame has neither limitations nor definitions, standards nor rule. It thrives as a result of genius or eccentricity, accident or purpose. The person who has 'made it' in television, sports, business, or science is the prominent person who is included." Leonard Bernstein, Alistair Cooke, Benjamin Disraeli, Sarah Ferguson, John Locke, Josef Mengele, Plato, Dan Quayle, Pat Sajak, three Adlai Stevensons, Mike Tyson, Oprah Winfrey, and Xerxes I, along with named groups (e.g., The Clash, The Platters), are examples of some who meet the criteria. A similar Gale title, *Biography and Genealogy Master Index* [*RBB* Mr 15 88], indexes every entry in every one of the works it covers. The *Almanac*, on the other hand, is selective. Unless a person included in one of the indexed works meets the vague test of fame, he or she is not included.

Each entry notes pseudonyms, nicknames, or other names by which the entrant is known (e.g., Michel Chevreul, "Father of Fatty Acids"); briefly identifies nationality and the nature of his or her fame (e.g., Charles Phillips, "American Manufacturer. Created product which made him nation's largest producer of milk of magnesia, 1873"); and lists birth date and place and, for the deceased, date and place of death. Most, but not all, also give other sources where additional biographical information can be found. Among those whose entries appear sans citations are Caleb D. Bradham, inventor of Pepsi-Cola; Robin Givens, actress; Luc Montagnier, one of the discoverers of the AIDS virus; and Jan Scruggs, the Vietnam veteran who created the concept of a Vietnam vets' memorial.

In all, this edition adds about 2,000 names, most of persons who have attained fame during the past several years. The Board examined the first 205 titles in the list of sources indexed in the *Almanac*; all but 20 were indexed in the third edition. The first volume's key to title abbreviations of indexed sources includes full bibliographic information. The third volume indexes the people in three ways. The chronological index lists each of the 366 days of the year, with persons who were born or died on that date arranged by year. The geographic index lists people by place of birth and death. The last index is by occupation. Occupational categories seem to have been derived from the short identifications. For example, Steven Jobs, formerly of Apple Computers, is identified as a "business executive." Hence his name appears only under that heading in the index and not under *computer executive*, the heading under which one finds Steven Wozniak, cofounder with Jobs of Apple. Such inconsistencies are the exception, however, not the rule.

Almanac of Famous People attempts to play two roles. In functioning as a biographical dictionary, it is not competitive with the various national and international sources with their more detailed entries. The *Almanac* merely summarizes, often telling no more about a person's life than the user already knows. Its real value lies in its second role as an index to other sources. It is far more economical than either *BGMI* or its abridgment, neither of which includes the *Almanac*'s useful chronological, geographic, or occupational indexes. The *Almanac* offers libraries unable to afford *BGMI* a reasonable measure of its power for identifying useful sources of biographical information. Libraries that have *BGMI* and its supplements may want the *Almanac* for the indexes in volume 3.

Great Lives. Comp. by Simon Boughton. Doubleday, 1988. 279p. illus. index. hardcover $17.95 (0-385-24283-2).

920'.02 Biography—Juvenile literature [CIP] 87-22147

"*Great Lives* describes over 1,000 men and women who have shaped history." They come "from all walks of life, including politics and world affairs, religion, science and discovery, philosophy and the arts, entertainment and sports." Many countries of the world are represented, with no bias shown toward Great Britain, where the book was compiled. People from all periods of history are also represented, from biblical figures such as Abraham and Deborah to living people such as South African novelist Nadine Gordimer, Australian writer and feminist Germaine Greer, and Mick Jagger of the Rolling Stones. Many popular figures in the arts and literature are included. The entries are arranged alphabetically, under the familiar name if two exist, such as Mark Twain and Samuel Clemens. Entries range from less than 50 words (Jean Cocteau, Fritz Kreisler) to more than 200 (Lafayette and Martin Luther). Throughout the work are two-page feature articles on major world figures such as Darwin and Lenin. Black-and-white and color illustrations enhance almost every page, making the text interesting for browsing as well as research.

A chronological table of contents places the biographees in historical order from 2800 B.C. to the present and gives the page where the entry for each will be found. The date for the biographee corresponds to the year of the most noteworthy event of that person's life. Some of these would appear to be arbitrary: 1973 for Stevie Wonder and 1971 for Dorothy Day. The nine-page subject index arranges people in the book by events in history, names of their books or paintings, quotations, names of countries, inventions, nicknames, etc. The index listings for Mark Twain, for instance, are *Huckleberry Finn*, *Tom Sawyer*, and *novelists and writers*. Using boldface type for the subject and lighter type for the biographee, the reader is led to the appropriate article.

The people included here can also be found in encyclopedias, often with more lengthy entries. However, the attractive presentation of information will make this book of value in children's collections in public libraries and in schools from the fifth grade through high school.

Index to Collective Biographies for Young Readers. 4th ed. By Karen Breen. Bowker, 1988. 494p. hardcover $34.95 (0-8352-2348-5).

016.92 Biography—Juvenile literature—Indexes ▮ Biography—Juvenile literature—Bibliography ▮ Publishers and publishing—U.S.—Directories [CIP] 88-19410

In her preface compiler Breen, consultant to children's services, Queens Borough Public Library (New York), acknowledges the work of Judith Silverman, who prepared the first three editions of this *Index* (1970, 1975, 1979) in response to young people's need for short biographical material about historic and contemporary figures of note.

The new edition lists 9,773 people, representing the contents of 1,129 collective biographies. Most of the titles indexed in the first three editions have been retained. Out-of-print books are so noted. According to the preface, new to the present edition are 2,528 persons from 187 indexed volumes. Timeliness is indicated by the inclusion of many titles published through 1987.

The titles selected are those considered most suitable for elementary and junior high school reading levels; however, a number of them can also be found in high school libraries. The *Index* aims to be inclusive rather than selective; therefore, the inclusion of a title does not constitute a recommendation. Titles listed in this volume were selected from the following sources: the shelf-list holdings of large public libraries in the New York area; ordering guides of the Board of Education of New York City; *The Elementary School Library Collection* (Bro-Dart); and *Books in Print*. Also, publishers were consulted for titles in their backlists that were appropriate.

Following instructions on how to use the index and a "Key to Indexed Books" is the first major section, "Alphabetical Listing of Biographees," which contains relevant data about birth, death, nationality, and field of activity, followed by symbols indicating in which books the person's biography appears. Most people are listed in only one book, but some have several dozen symbols after their names. The second major section, "Subject Listing of Biographees," lists individuals under fields of activity and nationalities. Among the 25 new subjects added to this current edition are *Eccentrics*, *First Ladies*, *Libyans*, *Martial Arts Figures*, and *Saudis*. As in the third edition, about 90 percent of the subject headings were determined by consulting the Sears or Library of Congress List of Subject Headings. Current usage accounts for the remainder; for example, *Disabled* replaces *Handicapped* and *Native Americans* replaces *Indians, American*.

After the two main sections appear "Indexed Books by Title" and "Key to Publishers." In the third edition, following these two sections was an "Index of Subject Headings." In this edition, a similar list of subject headings is more appropriately placed before the "Subject Listing of Biographees."

As with the earlier editions, the fourth edition of *Index to Collective Biographies for Young Readers* should prove an effective and useful reference for public and school libraries.

Index to Women of the World from Ancient to Modern Times: A Supplement. By Norma Olin Ireland. Scarecrow, 1988. 774p. hardcover $79.50 (0-8108-2092-7).

016.92072 Women—Biography—Indexes ▮ Women—Portraits—Indexes [CIP] 87-35934

This volume, by well-known librarian and indexer Ireland, supplements her index to collective biographies of women. Like the base volume, published in 1970 and still available, the *Supplement* indexes the contents of collective biographies for the purpose of locating information on women of all historical periods and cultures. Many of the entries give further sources for women covered in the first volume; more contemporary figures such as news anchor Diane Sawyer are listed for the first time.

The introduction details the arrangement that, like the original, is an alphabetical list of women with dates of life (if available), nationality, and occupation. Symbols and pages for the analyzed works are given, as well as a useful indication of whether a portrait is included. The 380 books indexed are listed in the front with full bibliographic information. The great majority of the works, which are generally popular rather than scholarly, are from the 1970s and early 1980s. The introduction states that books for young people have been included, but there is no indication of reading level with the bibliographic information; that would have been helpful. The *Current Biography* volumes from 1969 to 1985 are also analyzed.

This *Supplement* and the original volume are handy reference sources for locating information on women from June Allyson or Jane Addams to Palmyran empress Zenobia (fl. circa 260–70). Any library that has found the original *Index to Women* useful may want to acquire the *Supplement*, which can also be used on its own as a guide to more recent collections.

A Dictionary of Irish Biography. 2d ed. By Henry Boylan. St. Martin's, 1989 (c1988). 420p. bibliog. hardcover $39.95 (0-312-02497-5).

920'.0415 Ireland—Biography—Dictionaries [CIP] 88-25142

The first edition of this retrospective biographical dictionary was favorably reviewed in these pages [*RSBR* Ja 1 80]. This edition adds 200 names to that edition's 1,100. Most are of Irish men and women of note who died from 1978 to July 1988. Some new entries are for persons omitted from the first edition. Boylan, career public servant and writer who compiled both editions, "has updated information in the light of new historical evidence and has corrected errors."

The preface to the original edition is retained; it explains the criteria for inclusion. "Birth in Ireland has been taken as the prime requirement but this is modified to admit those who, though born abroad, had an Irish parent, or were of Irish descent, lived and worked in Ireland or made a considerable contribution to Irish affairs." In addition, Boylan includes "Wild Geese," emigrants who won distinction abroad.

Entries range in length from a paragraph for Kevin Barry, medical student executed for IRA activity, and Beatrice Grimshaw, writer of travel books and novels, to 2 pages for Charles Stewart Parnell and 4½ for Éamon de Valera. Side by side with entries for politicians and revolutionaries are those for archaeologists, poets, priests, chess players, and highwaymen. Boylan presents his data (dates and places of birth and death, career, family, publications, etc.) in readable prose and succeeds in giving the flavor of the person. We learn, for example, that Francis Magan, informer, "died unmarried, and by his will required a perpetual yearly mass to be celebrated...for the repose of his soul," and that Marie-Louise O'Morphi, courtesan, became the favorite model and mistress of François Boucher.

Gaelic versions of names (e.g., Ní Chonaill, Éibhlín Dhubh) may be startling to the user, but Boylan assures us that "Irish versions of names are used only when the subjects are known better, or only, thus;

otherwise the English version is used." A standard cross-reference system is used throughout.

Unlike the *Dictionary of National Biography* (with which there is considerable overlap), *DIB* provides no references for individual entries; however, there is an extensive bibliography, which in this edition has been augmented by approximately 30 new titles.

Academic and large public libraries with comprehensive biographical collections will want this revised edition, as will libraries serving a clientele with a strong interest in Ireland.

The Faces of America. Ed. by C. Carter Smith. Facts On File, 1988. 366p. illus. index. loose-leaf $125 (0-8160-1608-9).

920'.073 U.S.—Biography—Dictionaries ‖ U.S.—Biography—Portraits [CIP] 87-6707

The Faces of America is a collection of black-and-white portraits of 311 notable Americans. The subjects were chosen on the basis of the frequency with which their names appear in the indexes of standard history texts. The volume is part of the American Historical Images on File series, which provides copyright-free reproducible illustrations for use by students and others. Other volumes on the Civil War and key issues in constitutional history (e.g., civil rights, labor movement, women's rights) are forthcoming.

The portraits are arranged under nine historical divisions beginning with "The Colonial Era" and concluding with "The Post-War Era." The editors have attempted to achieve a balance of coverage among historical periods. Within each period individuals appear in chronological order according to the first major event in the person's life. Ezra Pound seems misplaced between Barry Goldwater and John Glenn.

Portraits range in size from approximately 4 by 5³⁄₄ to 6 by 8 inches, the majority falling within the upper end of this range. The portraits of subjects who achieved prominence before the advent of photography are reproductions of paintings, engravings, or lithographs, while photographic portraits predominate from about 1850 on. Subjects are usually portrayed during the active period of their careers. Although an effort was made to select illustrations that would reproduce clearly, there appear to be some exceptions (e.g., the portrait of William McKinley). Each portrait is captioned with a biographical note that highlights the subject's principal achievements, and the source of the picture is given.

The index includes entries for each person whose portrait is contained in the volume, as well as persons mentioned in the biographical notes. Thus, while there is no portrait of Walter Mondale, his name is indexed because he is mentioned in the biographical notes that accompany the portraits of Jimmy Carter and Geraldine Ferraro. The index also includes subject entries (e.g., *slavery*), corporate entries (e.g., *Union Pacific*), entries for works of literature (e.g., *Moby Dick*), entries for categories of persons (e.g., *writers*), and so on, with references to portraits of persons associated with them. There are, however, no index entries for pseudonyms or familiar nicknames. Mark Twain is indexed only under *Clemens, Samuel Langhorne*, with "Mark Twain" following his real name. There is no explanatory material describing the various types of entries included in the index. The front matter (table of contents, introduction, and chronology) and the index are bound as booklets and can be kept either in the loose-leaf binder or separate from it.

While portraits of most of the subjects included in the volume can be found in general encyclopedias and illustrated biographical dictionaries, the larger size of most of the portraits in *The Faces of America* and the fact that they can be reproduced legally will make it a useful resource in school and public libraries.

Research Guide to American Historical Biography. 3v. Ed. by Robert Muccigrosso and Suzanne Niemeyer. Beacham Publishing, 2100 S St. NW, Washington, DC 20008, 1988. bibliog. index. hardcover $189 (0-933833-09-1).

920'.073 U.S.—Biography—Handbooks, manuals, etc. ‖ U.S.—Bio-bibliography [CIP] 88-19316

A typical reaction to the appearance of a new biographical dictionary of notable Americans might be to yawn and exclaim, "Not another one!" However, on closer scrutiny, what the editors have created here is far more than a biographical dictionary. It is a well-organized and attractively packaged research guide to sources of biographical information on important Americans. The editors claim that three important objectives dictated creation of the set. First, it was designed to help college and secondary students do term papers. Second, it is intended to be helpful to graduate students and college faculty teaching or researching outside their specialties. Finally, the set is structured to serve librarians as both a ready-reference guide and an acquisitions checklist. In general, it is successful in fulfilling all of these.

The criterion for selection was a simple one. The editors claim that they tried to include individuals most often studied in the fields of politics, statecraft, business and labor, education, journalism, religion, and the military. Literary figures, for the most part, are excluded, since they are covered in another Beacham set, *Research Guide to Biography and Criticism* (1985). All told, there are 278 sketches of some 282 individuals, with several joint entries like *Lewis and Clark*. Chronologically, approximately 32 percent of the individuals were historically significant prior to the Civil War, while the remainder were significant after 1860; all but 11 are deceased. All presidents through Ronald Reagan are included. On the other hand, women and minorities are underrepresented. Only 31 sketches or 11 percent of the total describe women, while there are but nine sketches of blacks and six of native Americans. Areas of the U.S. originally colonized by France and Spain seem underrepresented. There are no entries for Juan Ponce de León, the discoverer of Florida, or Stephen F. Austin, the "father of Texas." The only sports figure included is Jackie Robinson.

For each individual there is a chronology outlining the major events in his or her life, a section on activities of historical significance, and an overview of biographical sources in which scholarly opinion is reviewed and changing interpretations discussed. Most helpful is the evaluation of the principal biographical sources with critical annotations. Sources for younger audiences are also annotated. Primary sources (autobiographies, memoirs, and pertinent documentary and manuscript collections) are described and evaluated. Quite unique is the special section "Fiction and Adaptations," which describes any novels, films, plays, or other creative works about the person. Museums, historical landmarks, and societies that highlight a person's career are listed, and there is a list of important secondary sources. All principal biographical sources are coded *A* for academic, *G* for general, or *Y* for young audiences. The sources listed are very current. For example, under Ronald Reagan, both Donald Regan's *For the Record* and Larry Speakes' *Speaking Out* are listed. Appendixes at the back of each volume group individuals by era, and sites mentioned in the section on museums, etc., are arranged by state. The last volume contains an index that lists the major sources included under each biographee.

Muccigrosso is a historian at Brooklyn College, and contributors include historians, other college faculty, and editors of the major "papers" series. This last group is often the most knowledgeable about particular individuals.

Overall, despite some noticeable omissions among those selected for inclusion and the underrepresentation of women and minorities, this new source should prove a very useful addition to virtually all libraries serving people of high school age and above. It is far superior in scope to Beacham's earlier set on biography and criticism. It is different in coverage from Salem Press's *Great Lives from History: American Series* [RBB O 15 87], which is a collection of 476 biographies that have brief bibliographies appended. Biographical information in *Research Guide to American Historical Biography* is limited to the chronology and activities of historical significance; most of each entry is devoted to the discussion of sources. In many cases this set may serve as an important first source of information for term papers and provide answers to the recurring question, "Which is the best book on. . . . "

PERiodical Source Index, 1847–1985. v.1–2: Places; v.3–4: Families. Ed. by Anne Dallas Budd and others. Allen County Public Library Foundation, P.O. Box 2270, Fort Wayne, IN 46801-2270, 1988. hardcover $300/4v. set; $175/2v. set; $1,400/16v. set in installments.

016.9292 Genealogy—Periodicals—Indexes [OCLC]

Unquestionably, when this index to genealogical periodicals is finished in its final 16 volumes, it will be a major research tool. It is a retrospective complement to the annual volumes of *PERiodical Source Index* (*PERSI*), the first of which the Board reviewed [D 1 87].

These retrospective volumes are arranged basically in the same manner as the annual ones—divided into "Places" and "Families." In this first installment, two volumes are devoted to each index. In the "Places" volumes, articles dealing with the U.S. are listed first and are arranged by state and county or other significant division within the state. Within county listings, the arrangement is by the record type on which the periodical article is based. There are 22 record types ranging from biographies to wills. Major types of note are church records, deeds, directories, census records, obituaries, and vital records. In addition to the U.S., there are sections for Canadian provinces and foreign countries. There is also the section "Research Methodology." The "Families" volumes are arranged by surname, and most names are further identified by state.

A typical entry in both types of volumes includes title of indexed article, journal, volume, number, month, and year. The journals are listed in an abbreviated code with the codes explained at the end of the volume along with a note on the geographic coverage of each journal. A second appendix lists the journals alphabetically by title. Approximately 200 local history and genealogy periodicals are indexed by place and family name in these four volumes, and there are over 120,000 entries. A third appendix lists more than 1,400 journals that are to be indexed when the set is complete. The pages are obviously computer-produced; while the typeface is small, the pages are easy to read.

This work will be published in four installments. Each installment indexes the complete run (from the first issue through 1985) of a unique list of journals. The next four-volume installment is due to be published in mid-1990. No publication dates have been set for the final two installments. The last installment will be in 16 volumes, cumulating the previous 12 volumes and covering additional journals. If a library buys each of the four installments as they are published, the total cost of the set will be $1,400. If a library chooses to wait to buy only the final 16 volumes, the cost will be $1,650.

In our review of the 1986 annual volume of *PERSI*, the Board stated that "libraries with major genealogical collections will find this an absolutely must-buy item. Other public libraries may want to wait until it has more of a publishing history before deciding to purchase." With the publication of the 1987 annual and now this first installment of the retrospective index, the Allen County (Indiana) Public Library has shown that it has a strong commitment to this massive indexing project and the resources to carry it out. All public libraries that provide substantial services to genealogists will want to try to fund this important purchase. Academic libraries that collect the journals indexed to support historical research will want to consider it too.

Genealogical Periodical Annual Index: Key to the Genealogical Literature. v.25: 1986. Comp. by Karen T. Ackermann; ed. by Laird C. Towle. Heritage Books, Inc., 3602 Maureen Ln., Bowie, MD 20715, 1987. 286p. hardcover $17.50 (1-55613-072-4).

929.1'05 Genealogy—Periodicals—Indexes [BKL]

Though previously reviewed by the Board [*RSBR* Ja 15 79], the question is not how this publication has changed over time, but how it compares with the competition. *Genealogical Periodical Annual Index* (*GPAI*) covers 260 genealogical periodicals in this twenty-fifth volume. These publications are contributed by their publishers, and, as new titles are added, an attempt is made to index backfiles. This means that this 1986 volume not only indexes periodical issues for that year but, for some titles, indexes a complete backfile. For instance, indexing for *Kinfolks* covers the first 10 volumes. The list of periodical abbreviations has a notation indicating which volumes and numbers (but not dates) are indexed in this edition of *GPAI*. This list includes the addresses of the journals as well, very useful for tracking down publications not stocked by the local library. The citations themselves note only volume, issue number, and beginning page. For genealogists dependent on interlibrary loan, it may be a handicap to not know the date when requesting a periodical. It was not possible to do an extensive check of the accuracy of the citations, but the few checked were correct.

There is, unfortunately, no sample citation in the prefatory material; the "How to Use . . ." section is more concerned with telling how the index was compiled and that its headings are primarily surnames, localities (state or country), and topics. It is useful to know that certain types of material (society news, reprinted material, etc.) are not indexed, but a sample entry would be helpful for the nonspecialist. At the moment, the major competition is *PERiodical Source Index* (*PERSI*), produced by the Allen County (Indiana) Public Library Genealogy Department [*RBB* D 1 87]. *PERSI* is new and physically not very attractive, but it is an impressive effort. To compare a few features of each: *GPAI* indexes 260 periodicals and *PERSI* indexes around 1,050; *GPAI* is in a single alphabetical arrangement (with localities and the heading *Methodology* pulling a lot of related articles together), and *PERSI* has five sections (places, families, Canadian places, other foreign places, and methodology); *GPAI* looks typeset and *PERSI* is a reproduction of a computer printout.

Picking a sample entry that is in both volumes and seeing how it reads may show differences in approach; bear in mind that both use heavily abbreviated entries and one must always consult the abbreviations lists. *GPAI*: "CHANDLER, Augustus H m1856 w Sarah Ann Benedict, Bible rec OC 23:3:111." *PERSI*: "CHANDLER/*Augustus H*. Chandler fam. Bible recs., NJ CAOR 23 3 September 1986." Is page or date more important to know? Is it more helpful to know Augustus' wife or that he came from New Jersey? Only the user can answer these questions; the librarian can only guess.

The 1987 volume of *PERSI* has just been published, but until it establishes more of a track record, libraries—being conservative—may want to go with *GPAI* because of its long publishing history. Larger institutions with a clear mission to support genealogical research will need both, but smaller libraries may find the less expensive *GPAI* to be adequate—particularly if they don't have a large collection of genealogical periodicals.

Vital Records Handbook. By Thomas J. Kemp. Genealogical Publishing Co., 1988. 231p. paper $19.95 (0-8063-1220-3).

929'.3 Registers of births, etc.—U.S.—Handbooks, manuals, etc. I Registers of births, etc.—Canada—Handbooks, manuals, etc. I Registers of births, etc.—Great Britain—Handbooks, manuals, etc. I U.S.—Genealogy—Handbooks, manuals, etc. I Great Britain—Genealogy—Handbooks, manuals, etc. [BKL] 88-80164

The compiler is president of the American Society of Indexers and author of *The Connecticut Researcher's Handbook* (Gale, 1982). He conceived this book as a way to make it easy for people to obtain copies of birth, death, and marriage records. The *Handbook* provides the information necessary for ordering these records: address and telephone number of the vital records office, fee per document, beginning dates for the office's records, where records are held if not at the state office, and other pertinent information. For example, "If your request is urgent, you may call and charge your certificates to your Visa or Mastercard—there is a $5.00 fee for this service," and "no personal checks accepted" are typical of this additional information. Copies of the application forms used by the offices, which can be photocopied by the person needing a certificate, follow. The arrangement of this material is alphabetical by state, followed by the various U.S. trust territories, Canada (by province), Ireland, and the U.K.

Kemp's is the first book-length publication to be devoted solely to the topic of obtaining vital records. Librarians have long depended upon a pamphlet published by the U.S. government for this type of information. *Where to Write for Vital Records: Births, Deaths, Marriages, and Divorces*, issued by the National Center for Health Statistics, provides information quite similar to that in the *Vital Records Handbook*. In fact, it goes beyond the scope of Kemp's book in that it provides information for obtaining copies of divorce certificates. Also, it gives information on obtaining records for births of American citizens in foreign countries and of alien children adopted by American citizens, as well as death records of American citizens who die in foreign countries and records of births and deaths on ships or aircraft. On the other hand, it does not include copies of the forms used by the various vital records offices (which make up the bulk of Kemp's book) nor does it supply addresses for the vital records office of any foreign countries.

In almost every case, the information in both publications matches, down to addresses, fees, and telephone numbers. Both appear to be up-to-date and carefully prepared. As Kemp admits, this type of information changes rapidly, making any publication on the topic soon out-of-date. At $1.50, *Where to Write for Vital Records* is a bargain that no library should pass up. At $19.95, *Vital Records Handbook* fulfills its purpose of convenience well. Its size will be appreciated by those librarians who find it hard to keep track of the slender *Where to Write for Vital Records*. Its foreign information, limited though it is to a few countries, will be invaluable to those who need it. Its forms, though not necessary in order to obtain the desired records, are a nice addition. Recommended for public and other libraries where the additional information will be useful.

Passenger and Immigration Lists Bibliography, 1538–1900: Being a Guide to Published Lists of Arrivals in the United States and Canada. 2d ed. Ed. by P. William Filby. Gale, 1988. 324p. index. hardcover $100 (0-8103-2740-6).

929.373 U.S.—Genealogy—Bibliography I Ships—Passenger lists—Bibliography I Registers of births, etc.—U.S.—Bibliography II U.S.—Emigration and immigration—Bibliography I U.S.—History—Sources—Bibliography [OCLC] 84-13702

The second edition of *Passenger and Immigration Lists Bibliography, 1538–1900 (PILB)* completely supersedes the first edition (1,309 lists; Gale, 1981) and its supplement (more than 600 lists; 1984) and adds more than 750 new lists. (The first edition replaced Harold Lancour's pioneering classic *Bibliography of Ship Passenger Lists*, as revised by Richard J. Wolfe in 1963, containing 262 sources.) The new edition identifies and provides full bibliographic information for more than 2,550 published passenger and immigration lists, church records, naturalization data, military mustering-out rolls, and other lists, arranged alphabetically by compiler's name or title. Each entry has an annotation describing the contents of the work and often names the original location of the list. Preceding each entry is an item number, a key to the companion set, *Passenger and Immigration Lists Index (PILI*; 3v., Gale, 1981 [*RSBR* My 1 82]; and supplements, 1982–   ). That compilation lists alphabetically the names of passengers from the lists in *PILB* who landed in Canada, the U.S., and the West Indies from the seventeenth through the nineteenth centuries, with age (if known), place and year of arrival, accompanying passengers (if recorded), and source of information precisely identified. Gaps are left in the item numbering in *PILB* to leave room for future additions. Thus far more than half of the sources in *PILB* are not yet indexed in *PILI*, and it will take several more years to publish all the names contained in these sources—which is to say that *PILB* serves "as a first step for researchers until the sources are indexed in *PILI*."

PILB concludes with a detailed subject index that includes placenames of departures and arrivals, places of settlement, nationalities, ships' names, naturalizations, occupations, religious groups, and military units. It is an essential source for research in immigration history, ethnic studies, and genealogy. Recommended for specialized libraries collecting in these areas as well as academic and large public library collections.

A Dictionary of Surnames. By Patrick Hanks and Flavia Hodges. Oxford, 1989 (c1988). 826p. bibliog. index. hardcover $75 (0-19-211592-8).

929.4'2 Names, Personal—Dictionaries [CIP] 88-21882

Since the study of surnames is of potential value to genealogists, historians, philologists, and demographers, one might expect this new *Dictionary* to just complement existing resources, but it does far more than that. While several good surnames dictionaries exist for the British Isles, as lexicographers Hanks and Hodges remark in their prefatory material, "surnames studies are sadly neglected in most of the countries of Europe; the number of reliable reference works is remarkably small." Based on well-structured methodology and sound research, *A Dictionary of Surnames* makes an excellent contribution toward filling this reference vacuum. It identifies and describes the origin and meaning of nearly 70,000 surnames of European derivation found in the English-speaking world.

The majority of names included here are defined as "common" surnames, and many readers will be disappointed to find their surname not represented. The principles for selection were frequency and informativeness. Selection began with a survey of published resources (a bibliography of these is provided), which led to the inclusion of some less-common names for which detailed information was available. The majority of entries were derived from a systematic analysis of the frequency with which names appeared in telephone books from more than 30 cities or areas of Canada, the U.S., and Europe.

The 45-page introduction to the *Dictionary* provides a detailed study of surnames, their origins, and distribution. It describes the methodology used in selection and the kind of information to be found in the entries. A section entitled "Typology of Surnames" defines the broad distinction between monogenetic (names traced to a single family) and polygenetic surnames (those found in many places) and also provides a detailed classification of surnames. Four broad types are patronymics, local names, occupational names, and nicknames, but also described here are many others, such as metronymics (derived from the name of the first bearer's mother) and kin terms, as well as habitation, topographical, ornamental, diminutive, and ethnic names. The study continues with a "Survey of National and Cultural Groups of Surnames" with sections for names of the British Isles, France, the Iberian Peninsula, Italy, German-speaking countries, the Low Countries, Scandinavia, Eastern Europe outside Russia, Greece, and the Soviet Union and for Jewish family names.

Main entries are given in their original European form. Related names (variants, cognates from other languages, diminutives, etc.) are nested within each entry. Every name in the *Dictionary*—main entry or variation—is accessible through the index, essential because of variations in language and spelling. Readers are advised to consult this index first. The information given at the main entries includes country of origin, derivation and type of surname (given name, nickname, habitation name, etc.), etymology, a detailed discussion of history and distribution, cross-references to related names, and variations. A feature of particular interest to genealogists is the inclusion of biographical background when a surname can be traced back to a notable person.

The compilers note that some names remain unexplained and a challenge for further research. They anticipate that future editions of this work will be aided by computerization of source materials. In the meantime, theirs is a significant contribution. *A Dictionary of Surnames* immediately becomes the standard reference source for the information it contains.

Dictionary of Medieval Knighthood and Chivalry: People, Places, and Events. By Bradford B. Broughton. Greenwood, 1988. 774p. bibliog. charts. index. hardcover $55 (0-313-25347-1).

929.7'03 Knights and knighthood—Dictionaries I Chivalry—Dictionaries I Knights and knighthood—England—Dictionaries I Knights and knighthood—France—Dictionaries [CIP] 87-18163

With more than 700 entries for sometimes obscure knights, places, and heroes of various *chansons de geste*, this book contains more entries than are found in a similar work, Dahmus' *Dictionary of Medieval Civilization* [*RBB* Je 1 85]. It is a companion volume to *Dictionary of Medieval Knighthood and Chivalry: Concepts and Terms* (Greenwood, 1986). There are constant cross-references to that volume, which is frustrating to the reader who does not have access to it.

The work is commendable, primarily for its breadth of coverage of Britain and France. Within the confines of the medieval period from about 1050 to the end of the fourteenth century, there is hardly a knight, king, region where they lived, battle, or epic poem telling of their valiant deeds that does not have at least a brief entry. The entries are generally less than one-fourth page, though some, such as those for the King Henrys of England and the King Louises of France, may run to two or more pages. German and Iberian knighthood and romances are also occasionally included. Each entry contains at least one reference, sometimes more, to the bibliography at the end of the book. In addition to the cross symbols referring the reader to the companion volume, asterisks serve as internal cross-references within this volume. There is no pronunciation given. How is one to know that Pontefract (Castle) is generally pronounced, and sometimes spelled, as "Pomfret"? The bibliography lists principally secondary sources, most of them in English, such as Oman's *History of the Art of War in the Middle Ages*, Powicke's *Thirteenth Century*, and Tetlow's *Enigma of Hastings*.

There are some surprising omissions: Shakespeare's King Cymbeline is not cross-referenced to his proper name, Cunobelin; this name does appear in the article *Colchester*. Under the entry for Emperor Frederick, there is no mention of the legend of his beard growing into and through the stone on which he leaned, though some legends are recounted elsewhere, such as the legend of the breastless Amazons. There is no mention of the fictional Esplandián, famous son of Amadis de Gaula, though Amadis himself has an entry. There is no explanation in that entry of where the region of "Gaula" may be, nor in the entry for Wales, of which *Gaula* (or *Gwalia*) is an earlier form.

The appendixes consist of genealogical charts of reigning families; a listing of all the entries arranged by topics (battles, castles, churchmen, romances, etc.); the bibliography (249 items); and a 70-page, double-column index.

Libraries with a readership interested in medieval history, culture, or literature will find this work valuable. For efficient utilization, however, it should be purchased in connection with its companion volume.

HISTORY

Time Lines on File. By the Diagram Group. Facts On File, 1989. various pagings. illus. index. loose-leaf $145 (0-8160-1897-9).
902'.02 Civilization—History—Chronology—Charts, diagrams, etc. I Chronology, Historical—Charts, diagrams, etc. [CIP] 88-26050

Time Lines on File is another in the On File subject series, which now includes a whole series of reproducible materials ranging from maps to software. This latest product is edited by the Diagram Group, which has done several other titles in the series.

Designed for history classes at all levels, *Time Lines on File* consists of 300 illustrated plates suitable for photocopying. Blue tabs divide the seven chapters. Each chapter includes standard timelines as well as "life lines," which show in comparative fashion the lifespans of noted leaders. Many pages have black-and-white illustrations; some are handsome woodcuts, others are ugly drawings like the one of Elizabeth Taylor that bears no resemblance to her.

"World History" includes charts on general world history, the classical world (including a chart on Roman emperors), life lines of world leaders, and charts of major empires. "American History" includes charts of major events, a two-page chart of American presidents, arts events and arts life lines, and life lines for famous Americans. The general historical charts are well done and should prove useful. More subjective and less helpful are some of the arts charts. For example, the chart covering the period 1950–88 includes parallel columns on literature, music, theater, architecture, painting, and sculpture. The literature section lists only 18 novels and one book of poetry in the last 38 years. There are no entries for theater after 1981, none for architecture after 1979, and only five entries for sculpture over the last four decades. Another chart of questionable utility is "Women's Liberation 1793–1988." Since it is only one-half page (the other half is wasted on poor illustrations of a feminist newspaper and the arrest of a birth control clinic owner), there are only nine entries after 1900. While an entry for 1972 notes the ERA was passed by Congress, there is no later entry to note that it was never ratified by a sufficient number of states to be adopted. "European History" includes charts on major events, life lines of important figures in European history, and dynasties listing rulers of England, France, the Holy Roman Empire, etc. Peculiarly there are no charts for Portugal, the Netherlands, or smaller principalities.

"Religion and Ideas" includes charts on Christianity (including a chronology of the popes), the Jewish Diaspora, and Islam, Buddhism, Hinduism, and Sikhism. This last chart is very current, noting the 1988 removal of Sikh terrorists from the Golden Temple. The remaining charts describe Greek philosophers, Roman thinkers, the Middle Ages, the Renaissance, the Enlightenment, and the nineteenth and twentieth centuries. Important events in "Science and Technology" are described in 36 charts. Four of these list key events in space technology since 1900 and manned space flights since 1960.

"The Arts" is the longest and, in many ways, the least satisfactory section of the book. Seventy-three charts describe aspects of the arts from the visual to the dramatic to the literary. This section is the most subjective in the book. For example, a chart describes the "20th Century Movie Industry 1950–1988." While three movies are listed for some years, none are listed for others. Those listed are not necessarily award winners for that year. Similarly, in the movie life lines, marginal talents like Nancy Sinatra and Bo Derek find mention while other more important actors do not.

"Canadian History," coming somewhat out of sequence, seems like an afterthought. It includes charts on major events, prime ministers, and famous Canadians. No one born after 1909 is deemed worthy of mention in this last chart.

Access is provided by a two-page table of contents in the form of a chart, which describes the time lines by period and date, and a 28-page personal-name index that refers to the appropriate chapter and page number. For example, the index entry for Harry Belafonte, popular musician, refers one to chart F5.11. The index entry for James Monroe, U.S. president, refers to three charts.

In sum, *Time Lines on File* brings together a wealth of information in a convenient reproducible format. It combines elements from works like *The Timetables of History* (1975), *The Timetables of Science* [RBB My 1 89], and James Trager's *People's Chronology* (1979), and others from works like William Langer's *Encyclopedia of World History* (5th ed., 1972). Its historical chronologies are helpful, but the life lines are likely to be less utilized. The contemporary charts on the arts need to be expanded, as does the contemporary section on Canada.

This work will be a useful resource for high school libraries and educational resource centers and for those college and university libraries where large sections of American history and Western civilizations are taught.

The Blackwell Dictionary of Historians. Ed. by John Cannon. Basil Blackwell, 1988. 480p. bibliog. index. hardcover $75 (0-631-14708-X).
907'.202 [B] Historians—Biography—Dictionaries [CIP] 88-19361

This is the first substantial dictionary of world historians to be published. The editors claim to have included the historians who are most widely read by British and American students and many others who are frequently cited. There are 450 biographical sketches, ranging from a few lines to more than a page, that describe scholarly reputation, life, and lasting influence. An additional 25 national articles describe the historiography of individual countries or regions, and more than 40 thematic articles describe related disciplines, subdisciplines, and a host of other topics.

Cannon, of the University of Newcastle upon Tyne, served as senior editor and was assisted by one U.S. and two British historians. The contributors are chiefly British (160-plus), with 30 Americans and about nine other countries represented.

European historians, especially those read in the U.K. or the U.S., are reasonably well represented with 60 French historians, 40 Germans, and 20 Italians. There are also 30 classical historians and other important world thinkers like Engels, Marx, and Bacon. Slightly more than 50 living historians are included.

However, this is a dictionary with a profoundly British slant. More than 150 of the biographical sketches focus on the lives of British historians, while about 65 treat Americans. The cast of American historians omitted reads like a veritable "who's who in American history." They include Samuel Flagg Bemis, Arthur Link, Dumas Malone, Alan Nevins, T. Harry Williams, and William Appleman Williams, winners of numerous awards. Perhaps the most grievous omission is William Langer, a Bancroft Prize winner, editor of the valuable Rise of Modern Europe series, president of the American Historical Association, and author of the *Encyclopedia of World History*, the best-selling historical reference work of all time.

The best of the thematic chapters are those on the French Annales school, Byzantine historiography, and Latin American historiography. There are also helpful entries for terms like *cliometrics* and *prosopography*. Less complete are the entries *Demographic History*, which completely ignores the tremendous work of the Berkeley school on the indigenous populations in the Americas, and *Oral History*, which largely ignores its growth in the U.S. While there are the entries *Anthropology and History* and *Sociology and History*, there is none for psychohistory, sports history, or women's history, all popular fields in the U.S. Other entries such as *Constitutional History, British* and *Local History, English* will appeal largely to students of British history. There are no entries for such comparable American subfields as southern history or western history.

Accompanying the biographies are lists of the person's major publications; most entries have brief bibliographies of varying quality. All entries carry the initials of their authors, and there is an alphabetical list of contributors at the beginning of the book. Unfortunately, there is no similarly arranged list of initials, making it tedious to track down individual authors. The volume is well indexed with page references to major entries in boldface type.

In sum, while this is an important tool for the study of historians and a useful reference for history in general, more balanced coverage of non-British historians and traditions would have made it more useful for American libraries. Students seeking additional coverage of American historians can turn to volumes 17, 30, and 47 of the *Dictionary of Literary Biography*, which describe the careers of almost 150 historians, or more specialized tools like the recently published *Historians of the American Frontier* (Greenwood, 1988).

Oxford Illustrated Encyclopedia, Volume 3: World History from Earliest Times to 1800. Ed. by Harry Judge. Oxford, 1988. 391p. illus. maps. hardcover $39.95, $75 for v.3-4 (0-19-869135-1).

909 History, Ancient I History, Modern [OCLC] 85-4876

Oxford Illustrated Encyclopedia, Volume 4: World History from 1800 to the Present Day. Ed. by Robert Blake. Oxford, 1988. 391p. illus. maps. hardcover $39.95, $75 for v.3-4 (0-19-869136-X).

909.8 History, Modern—19th century I History, Modern—20th century [CIP] 87-20408

Volumes 3 and 4 of the proposed nine-volume *Oxford Illustrated Encyclopedia* cover world history from the earliest records to the present day. (Volumes 1 and 2, covering the physical and natural world, were reviewed previously [*RBB* Je 15 86]. A further four volumes plus an index volume will be published over the next three years.) One of the drawbacks in a reference work of this type is the inability to give detailed coverage of major events, ideas, and individuals. The editors acknowledge this difficulty by setting a realistic goal: to concentrate on "accessible, reliable, and clear information" on sharply defined topics. The division date for the two volumes of 1800 was selected arbitrarily by the editor since no one date would provide a clear separation. For persons and events that overlap the eighteenth and nineteenth centuries (Napoleon Bonaparte, for example), entries are included in both volumes. This enables each volume of the *Encyclopedia* to stand alone. Persons and events that would fit better in one of the other volumes will be placed there. William Shakespeare, for example, although important historically, will be covered in a volume on the arts.

The "Users Guide" explains the arrangement of the two volumes. Each entry is alphabetized letter by letter. Cross-references are indicated by an asterisk. Entries average about 200 words, though biographies tend to be briefer, and a few entries are about 500 words.

An average of one illustration per page results in approximately 800 maps, drawings, paintings, charts, etc. Most of these attractive illustrations are in color and are extremely well chosen to illustrate points. For example, the illustrations for *Army* (volume 3) show the evolution of uniforms, equipment, and tactics from Alexander the Great to the mid-eighteenth century. The illustrations in *Navy* (volume 4) show the development of vessels from Nelson's flagship to nuclear submarines. Maps show the path of the Black Death, the major finds of human evolution, and boundaries during the Russian civil war. Tables list important dates in the Hundred Years War and in space exploration.

The work is rounded out by time charts on the endpapers, divided by regions. Volume 3 uses "Asia," "Europe," and "Rest of the World." Volume 4 divides into four regions: "Africa, Near and Middle East"; "America"; "Asia, Australia"; and "Europe." These charts are invaluable in helping the user to place events in the context of time.

William Leonard Langer's *New Illustrated Encyclopedia of World History* (2v., Abrams, 1975), with over 2,000 photographs, maps, drawings, etc., is the closest reference work in scope and content to these volumes of the *Oxford Illustrated Encyclopedia*. Langer's work is arranged chronologically, which makes it more complementary than competitive. Also, the age of Langer's work means many current events and persons such as the Reagan presidency and Ruhollah Khomeini are not covered. Information in Oxford's *Encyclopedia* will update and complement Langer's history.

Whether one decides to purchase all or part of the *Oxford Illustrated Encyclopedia*, volumes 3 and 4 will be useful for any user needing factual historical information presented in an attractive format. Its popular approach makes it appropriate for high school and public as well as academic libraries.

Assassinations and Executions: An Encyclopedia of Political Violence, 1865–1986. By Harris M. Lentz. McFarland, 1988. 275p. bibliog. index. hardcover $29.95 (0-89950-312-8).

909.8 Assassination—History—Chronology I Executions and executioners—History—Chronology [CIP] 87-46383

Political assassinations and executions as well as unsuccessful attempts against major world figures from 1865 to 1986 are described here within the context of political events. Each entry gives brief biographical information on the victim; includes details on the manner of killing, the motive, and the assailant; notes the immediate effects on the political climate of the day; and where known, gives the final fate of the assailant. Lentz is also the author of *Science Fiction, Horror and Fantasy Film and Television Credits*.

The introduction explains that "this book primarily deals with those leaders who have perished as victims of political assassinations, though others who have been merely 'executed' are also included. . . .The inclusion of such executions broadens the scope to include the many victims of the purges of Stalin and Hitler, as well as those Nazi leaders whose crimes against humanity resulted in their justified execution."

The author notes the difficulties in identifying individuals for inclusion in this work. Third World nations presented particular problems since "political violence seems to be a way of political life." Nevertheless, an overview of violent political events and major victims is recorded here.

Entries are listed in chronological order. Related incidents of violence are grouped together even though the violence may have occurred several months apart. The names of targets of unsuccessful violence are noted in roman typeface, while the names of those who perished are in boldface. Entries for individuals range from one sentence to a full page, with longer entries for incidents involving several deaths. While one expects to find individuals such as Louis Mountbatten, John and Robert Kennedy, and Mohandas Gandhi, many lesser-known victims are also included, e.g., Edward King, the mayor of Mount Pleasant, Iowa, who met his fate during a city council meeting, or Ahmed Bassendawah, member of the Supreme Council of Yemen, who was assassinated in 1966. The six-page prologue very briefly surveys other prominent victims of political violence from biblical times through the point at which the book begins in 1865 with the assassination of Abraham Lincoln.

The bibliography lists the 98 books and 10 periodicals used to create this reference work. The index contains the names of the victims and assailants. Within this index, victims are also listed by country of origin, not where they were killed. Trotsky, for instance, is listed under *Russia*, not *Mexico*.

No other reference source offers as complete a listing of these victims arranged chronologically. Recommended for large public libraries and academic libraries supporting history and political science courses.

The Facts On File World Political Almanac. Comp. by Chris Cook. Facts On File, 1989. 453p. index. tables. hardcover $40 (0-8160-1377-2).

909.82 World politics—1945–   [CIP] 88-11208

The author's aim here, as stated in the preface, is to "assemble...as many of the key facts and figures as possible on the major political developments of the postwar world." Since it was impossible to be comprehensive, he concentrates on "countries and events for which the reader is most likely to require information." Countries that the author did not consider important enough to get separate entries include Guyana, Iceland, Kenya, and Lebanon, but some information can be found on them using the index. For the countries he deems important, Cook lists in separate chapters the heads of state since 1945, a description of the legislatures and constitutions, treaties and other diplomatic agreements, political parties, elections, population, and urbanization statistics and trends. If all this information had been grouped together by country, the *Almanac* would have been more useful as a ready-reference source.

Other chapters cover international political organizations and civil conflicts. Also included are a chronology of the nuclear age, a dictionary of political events, and a biographical dictionary.

As might be expected, the population statistics for each country give a variety of years, and some of them are as old as 1983. Sources of some of these statistics are given, while other sources are not. The same is true for election statistics. The only bibliography in the book is a "Source List" of eight items at the conclusion of the elections chapter.

The chapter on wars and civil strife is a good summary of a violent world since 1945. For each event the combatants, key dates, and casualties are included. In addition, the chronology on the nuclear age is an important aspect of the book. There is a table comparing the U.S. and Soviet nuclear arsenals and the number of nuclear explosions by country and year since 1945. Included also are lists of bilateral and multilateral agreements, with a table of countries and whether they adhere to a particular multilateral agreement.

The two dictionaries—political events and biographical—are limited in scope. (Neither George Bush nor the Iran-Contra Affair are mentioned.) The combining of these two dictionaries would have improved the ease of use of the volume.

Much of the information in this source can also be found in the *Statesman's Year-Book*, the *Europa Year Book*, or a general almanac. However, even with the aforementioned reservations, the price ($40) and format (large print, high school reading level) should make the *World Political Almanac* a possible acquisition for high school libraries that cannot afford *Statesman's* ($60) or *Europa* ($350).

The Royals. By Jeannie Sakol and Caroline Latham. Congdon & Weed; dist. by Contemporary, 1988 (c1987). 377p. bibliog. illus. hardcover $19.95 (0-86553-194-3).

941.085'092 [B] Great Britain—Kings and rulers—Biography—Dictionaries I Great Britain—Princes and princesses—Biography—Dictionaries [OCLC] 87-35556

Americans can't seem to get enough of the British royal family, and here is a book that covers various aspects of the lives of Queen Elizabeth and Prince Philip, Charles and Diana, Andrew and Sarah, and the rest. Arrangement is alphabetical, from *Abdication Address of King Edward VIII* to *Zara*, the Queen's only granddaughter (until the recent birth of Andrew and Sarah's daughter). In between, browsers will learn the names of all the royal pets, the tokens of rent Prince Charles is entitled to receive from the inhabitants of the Duchy of Cornwall ("two white greyhounds, a pound of pepper," etc.), the Queen's recipe for barley water, where Diana likes to shop, what Princess Margaret likes to drink, and which women were romantically linked with Prince Charles in his bachelor days. Entries range from one or two lines to three pages. Black-and-white photographs are interspersed throughout the text, but few of the photos are dated, an annoying omission in the case of pictures of family members. There is a brief bibliography but no index or cross-references. When trying to verify the information about the Prince of Wales's token rent, no mention was found in the *Duchy of Cornwall* entry. In browsing, a list of token rents was found under *Annual Rent*. Strictly a browsing item, *The Royals* is not the place to look for authoritative information. There are inaccuracies, arrangement is eccentric, and each entry is defined strictly in terms of its relationship to the royal family. Thus, under *Alice in Wonderland* we find: "*Alice in Wonderland* was a childhood favorite of Prince Philip. Princess Margaret, on the other hand, disliked it intensely."

Despite its limitations as a reference tool, however, the book is great fun for Anglophiles. It might be considered by librarians who are frequently called upon to seek out information on the royals.

Victorian Britain: An Encyclopedia. Ed. by Sally Mitchell. Garland, 1988. 986p. bibliog. illus. index. hardcover $125 (0-8240-1513-4).

941.081'03 Great Britain—History—Victoria—Dictionaries I Great Britain—Civilization—19th century—Dictionaries [CIP] 87-29947

An ambitious work, *Victorian Britain: An Encyclopedia* brings together in one volume information on the period of Victoria's reign, namely 1837 to 1901. Entries include biographies, historical events, descriptions of institutions, groups, and publications, as well as information on art and artifacts. Examples of the wide range of topics treated are *Christmas, Fairy Tales, Plumbing and Sewage Disposal, Restaurants, Tennis, Travel and Exploration,* and *Working-Class Literature*. As the editor notes in her preface, the field of Victorian studies has become complex and interdisciplinary, and, especially in the past 30 years, new scholarly perspectives on culture, women, daily life, and the contributions of less-known individuals have emerged. In order to do justice to the period, 336 scholars from around the world have contributed signed articles to this well-edited volume.

A brief chronology of people and events (an average of 10 items for each year between 1837 and 1901) precedes the main text. The alphabetically arranged entries that follow are concise and factual, averaging about a page in length. Even those on major figures and events are brief, as it is assumed that information on these can be found elsewhere. Each entry is supported by a bibliography of key references. A seven-page annotated bibliography covering basic reference resources for the period is included at the end of the text. The wealth of information is made very accessible through generous cross-references within the text; for example, general subjects are linked to more specific items or to names of individuals or publications. The 75-page index is also well constructed, making this encyclopedia easy to consult and a pleasure to explore.

In its text, *Victorian Britain* conveys the spirit of the century extremely well. The women's perspective is particularly well represented. For a period characterized by distinctive art and artifacts, however, it is not extensively illustrated, with just 41 black-and-white pictures. These cover a good variety of topics such as "Women at Work in the Pen Grinding Room, 1851," an etching of Charles Dickens that appeared in the *Illustrated London News*, and "Rational Recreation and the August Bank Holiday: Blackpool, 1900."

As intended by its compilers, *Victorian Britain* will serve a variety of users. These will include not only undergraduates or general readers beginning to explore the period, but also graduate students and scholars in related fields needing a reliable and well-documented overview with bibliographic references leading to more detailed sources.

The Third Reich Almanac. By James Taylor and Warren Shaw. World Almanac; dist. by St. Martin's, 1988 (c1987). 392p. bibliog. illus. maps. hardcover $24.95 (0-88687-363-0).

943.086'03 Germany—History—1933–1945—Dictionaries ❙ National socialism—Dictionaries [CIP] 88-256

Two British writers have attempted "to walk the tightrope between the fullest possible and the most accessible description of the period." A nine-page chronology of the major events of the period 1933–45 prefaces the work. Events are listed by month only, and acronyms are used that are not explained in the main body of the work.

The rest of the book is arranged alphabetically with a wide variety of entries—people, places, concepts, social factors, government apparatuses, etc. Included are legal terms, resisters to Nazism, and people and events from the period before Hitler and following the fall of the Third Reich. Entries range from a few words to more than seven pages on Hitler. Cross-references are provided, and some black-and-white photographs are in a center insert. Five appendixes give chronologies of various military campaigns of the Third Reich, again by month only. An eight-page list of quotations, a short bibliography (mainly British titles), and a few maps conclude the book.

While the work is in general adequate, it does not include some important topics like the People's Court, although there is an entry on its president. Similarly missing from the work is an entry on Raoul Wallenberg, while far less-important persons are included.

A comparable work is Louis L. Snyder's *Encyclopedia of the Third Reich* [RSBR F 15 77]. The Snyder book is more extensive and has many more entries, a more helpful calendar of significant dates, bibliographic references after some articles, small photographs by many entries, and a 22-page bibliography. Although the Snyder book was not updated in the paperback edition just published, and it does not include some of the topics in the work under review, it will be more useful to students. Secondary school, public, and academic libraries should own one of these two books.

The Blackwell Encyclopedia of the Russian Revolution. Ed. by Harold Shukman. Basil Blackwell, 1988. 418p. bibliog. illus. index. tables. hardcover $65 (0-631-15238-5).

947.084'1 Soviet Union—History—Revolution, 1917–1921—Chronology ❙ Soviet Union—Biography—Dictionaries [CIP] 88-10360

Shukman, director of the Russian and East European Centre, St. Anthony's College, and lecturer in modern Russian history at Oxford, has edited a fascinating history of the Russian Revolution. His introduction emphasizes its specialized scope—it does not cover Russian and Soviet history in general. Forty-six scholars from Western and Third World countries contributed to this work. All articles and biographical sketches are signed, and most conclude with short bibliographies citing scholarly books and articles in Russian and English. A random sampling of bibliographies determined the average length was five citations and currency of materials was as recent as 1986. There are abundant cross-references in boldface print throughout the *Encyclopedia*. Article length is usually several pages but can be as short as a paragraph. A detailed three-page table of contents allows access to the articles, which are not arranged alphabetically but in broad topical chapters arranged chronologically.

The first part of the *Encyclopedia* is a chronological account of events in roughly three time periods: 1905 to 1917, the October Revolution of 1917, and 1917 to 1921. While much emphasis is on political, military, economic, religious, feminist, and ethnic movements, considerable study is devoted to the cultural revolution with articles on literature, art, theater, cinema, music, and ballet. In particular, three Russian writers—Gorky, Blok, and Mayakovsky—are highlighted. Throughout this first part of the *Encyclopedia* are 43 black-and-white illustrations and a number of tables appropriately placed to complement the text.

The second part of the book contains 176 biographical articles, 37 of them illustrated with portraits, and is organized alphabetically. Persons covered in this section represent major historical figures or minor personalities who illustrate important revolutionary movements. The book concludes with an index; major articles are noted by boldface page numbers, and numbers in parentheses refer to illustrations. The endpapers show a map of Russia.

There are three single-volume and one multivolume reference works that are somewhat comparable to *The Blackwell Encyclopedia*. The single-volume works are the *McGraw-Hill Encyclopedia of Russia and the Soviet Union* (1961), the *Cambridge Encyclopedia of Russia and the Soviet Union* (1982), and the *Companion to Russian History* (Facts On File, 1983). They are broader in scope and more general in coverage, have shorter bibliographies and, in the case of the first title, are dated. The multivolume set, *The Modern Encyclopedia of Russian and Soviet History* (Academic International Press, 1976–), is much larger in scope but on comparable topics is equal in detail and length of bibliographies.

The Blackwell Encyclopedia of the Russian Revolution is unique as a reference source devoted to this topic and is a scholarly work that can be highly recommended for academic and large public libraries.

Encyclopedia of Ukraine. v.1 & 2. Ed. by Volodymyr Kubijovyč. Univ. of Toronto; dist. by Libraries Unlimited, 1984– . v.1 with map and gazetteer, $115 (0-8020-3362-8); v.2, $125 (0-8020-3444-6).

947'.71 Ukraine—Dictionaries and encyclopedias ❙ Ukraine—Gazetteers [CIP]

This *Encyclopedia*, providing wide-ranging coverage of Ukrainian history, culture, and society, is a major reference tool for readers seeking information on these topics in English. Two volumes of the anticipated four have appeared to date, covering *A–F* and *G–K*, as well as a separate map and gazetteer supplement. No publication date has been set for the remaining two volumes. The *Encyclopedia* is published for the Canadian Institute of Ukrainian Studies, the Canadian Foundation for Ukrainian Studies, and the Shevchenko Scientific Society. Although in part a translation and revision of a Ukrainian-language work, it also includes important original entries. It is considerably more extensive than the very useful *Ukraine: A Concise Encyclopedia* (Univ. of Toronto, 1963–70, reprinted in 1982), a translation of thematically arranged material from the same project.

Editors and contributors are well-known scholars, and many articles, especially the long ones, are signed. Entries range in length from a paragraph (many biographical entries) to over 32 pages for *History of Ukraine*. Typical articles are *Architecture, Currency, Dissident Movement, Emigration, Grain Production, Higher Education, Humoristic and Satiric Press*, and *Jews*. There are also entries for foreign countries and cities that have large Ukrainian populations, e.g., *Australia, Canada*, and *Chicago*. There are hundreds of black-and-white photographs, and some articles, such as *Byzantine Art, Embroidery*, and *Icons*, are illustrated with colorplates. Other entries, such as *Carpathian Mountains* and *Kiev*, have foldout color maps. Longer articles close with bibliographies listing sources in English, Ukrainian, and other European languages.

With few exceptions, entries and titles appear in English, followed by Ukrainian equivalents. The Library of Congress (in both strict and modified forms) and the International Linguistic transliteration systems are used for rendering Cyrillic-alphabet words and names into the Roman alphabet. Cross-references within entries are indicated by asterisks, and there are also *see* references, some of them to articles in the two final volumes not yet published. The supplement to volume 1 includes not only a fine, large foldout color map with gazetteer, but also valuable statistical data.

This comprehensive and attractive *Encyclopedia* is highly recommended for academic libraries and for public libraries serving Ukrainian populations.

Encyclopedia of Asian History. 4v. Ed. by Ainslie T. Embree. Scribner, 1988. 2,060p. bibliog. illus. index. hardcover $325 (0-684-18619-5).

950 Asia—History—Dictionaries [CIP] 87-9891

Prepared under the auspices of the Asia Society to "make available the highest level of contemporary scholarship on Asia to a nonspecialist audience," this four-volume encyclopedia covers all aspects of Asian civilization from early history to the present, from Iran on the west to Japan, the Philippines, and Indonesia on the east; it excludes the USSR except for the Central Asian Republics. Entries include persons both living and dead, including westerners involved with Asia such as Marco Polo, Francis Xavier, and Douglas MacArthur as well as Asians from Genghis Khan to Corazon Aquino. Also treated are places (*India, Kandy, Kathmandu*); events (*Kabo Reforms, Long March, Deccan Riots, Hostage Crisis*); geographic features (*Jhelum River, Bolan Pass, Caspian Sea, Altai Mountains*); peoples (*Kazakhs, Malays, Karen*); the arts (*Carpets, Ukiyo-e, Chagatai Literature, Tea Ceremony*); periods (*Han Dynasty, Fujiwara Period, Abbasid Dynasty*); and many other subjects both broad (*Language Families, Imperialism, Population*) and narrow (*Koh-i-Nur Diamond*). The length of articles ranges from brief identifications to more than 10 pages. The emphasis is historical, so while there are entries for art, literature, etc., the focus is "on history in its dictionary sense of a chronological record of past events along with an interpretation of their meaning and significance." Entries for westerners cover their involvement in Asian history, not their total life span.

Arrangement is alphabetical, letter by letter, which can be somewhat confusing at times as, for example, one finds *Qin Dynasty* and *Qin Shihuangdi* separated by *Qingdao, Qing Dynasty, Qing Empiricism*, and *Qingtan*. Pinyin is the transliteration used (*Mao Zedong, Chongqing*), and a two-page Wade-Giles/pinyin conversion table is provided in volume 4. All articles are signed, and most have a bibliography appended, with even the short entries having at least one title listed so the reader has a starting point for further information and study. All items listed are in English, but some of them will be found only in libraries having large area studies collections. Both recent and classic titles are noted. While entries are all clearly written and generally can be understood by students and the general reader, some may take a bit longer to digest because of the relative unfamiliarity of most laypersons with these countries and their languages. The article *Tokugawa Period*, for example, uses many terms unfamiliar to the general public but which constitute the best way to delineate the topic; some terms are explained within the entry, but others may have to be looked up elsewhere in the set for better understanding.

There are many *see* and *see also* references, both from articles on related subjects and terms not used to those used instead. A detailed index refers to all main entries and also includes specific page references to other articles where the particular subject is discussed. A "Synoptic Outline" provides a special help to the user by giving first a broad thematic outline of the contents and then listing the specific entries in each category. The alphabetical list of entries in volume 4 lists each entry with its author, and the "Directory of Contributors" lists under each name the author's affiliation and articles written. Contributors are primarily from the U.S. but include scholars from Europe, India, Hong Kong, Australia, Japan, Sri Lanka, and other nations. There are about 160 clearly reproduced black-and-white illustrations and over 60 maps; end papers of all volumes provide a map of the region. Although there are encyclopedias devoted to some of the countries covered here, such as China and Iran, there is no comparable set with such broad coverage.

The *Encyclopedia of Asian History* provides an excellent overview of its subject and will do much to educate the public about this part of the world. Large academic and public libraries will find it a must purchase, and others should consider it for its valuable scholarship and broad coverage.

Historical Dictionary of North American Archaeology. Ed. by Edward B. Jelks and Juliet C. Jelks. Greenwood, 1988. 760p. bibliog. index. hardcover $95 (0-313-24307-7).

970.01 Indians of North America—Antiquities—Dictionaries ∥ North America—Antiquities—Dictionaries ∥ Archaeology—North America—Dictionaries [CIP] 87-17581

Jelks, professor emeritus of anthropology at Illinois State University and a research archaeologist with 35 years' experience, has compiled an impressive and useful archaeological dictionary. By enlisting the combined knowledge and expertise of 13 regional consultants and 138 specialist contributors, most of them U.S. or Canadian faculty or government archaeologists, the editors present a widely representative and authoritative treatment of the most culturally significant North American sites, artifacts, and traditions. Despite its title, this dictionary mainly covers prehistoric periods rather than historic (those with a written record, e.g., colonial) ones.

More than 1,800 entries are arranged alphabetically, with page headers provided for guidance. Each entry is signed by its contributor and varies in length from a sentence to several short paragraphs or, occasionally, a page or two. From tens of thousands of excavated sites, the site entries presented here were selected because each has "contributed uniquely to the essential body of information upon which the current major classifications and interpretations of North American prehistory are based." A typical site entry (*Lovelock Cave*, or *Wupatki Pueblo*) details its location, date(s) of inhabitation, date of excavation, identity of excavators, and the nature of the archaeological evidence found. The associated Indian group or culture is identified, and the site's function, significance, or contribution to archaeological knowledge is noted.

A typical entry for a culture or tradition describes its geographic and temporal distribution, identifying features, relationships to other cultural units, and who defined it and when. Besides names of cultures, traditions, and phases (*Sinagua Division; Woodland; Classic Period, Hohokam Culture*), numerous entries for artifacts, dwellings, tools, and ceramic ware (*Kivas, Fluted Axe, Popes Creek Ware, Core and Veneer Masonry*) flesh out the picture of ancient lifestyles. However, no basic explanations are offered of the underlying archaeological dating techniques, such as stratigraphy, radiocarbon, fluorine, tree-ring (dendochronology), or pollen analysis, upon which so many relative conclusions are based.

Numerous *see* references and the subject index at the back of the book guide the reader to some other entries, but the use of internal cross-references (*q.v.*, and *qq.v.*) apparently interchangeably, without further explanation, is somewhat confusing. The subject index indicates by the use of boldface whether a term has its own entry or is merely a passing reference. The index is uniquely useful in highlighting references to the archaeologists themselves, primarily as the sources of information cited for each entry. By relying solely on the dictionary's subject index and its internal cross-references, however, one might miss finding relevant references. Not all closely related entries are consistently cross-referenced or indexed. The entry *Anasazi Culture*, for example, does not refer to such closely related articles as *Classic Period, Anasazi Culture* and *Developmental Period, Anasazi Culture*, all written by the same contributor.

Each entry cites its major sources of information, many of them published, but unpublished research reports of museums and government surveys are frequently cited as well. The extensive bibliography of sources cited in the dictionary is preceded by a convenient list of journal abbreviations. The bibliography serves as a "single, authoritative, up-to-date list of basic publications and file reports covering the prehistory of the entire continent." The work also has a useful list of the archaeological sites selected, arranged geographically by state or

Canadian province. The preponderance of sites listed for some states and regions highlights the relative paucity of northeastern U.S. sites by comparison. The book lacks a chronology or time line, which would help in relating cultures to one another.

Federal and state cultural resource agencies, college and university libraries, and public libraries emphasizing their regional archaeological resources will find this dictionary especially valuable in its practical identifications and indispensable in reference work and collection development.

The Canadian Encyclopedia. 4v. 2d ed. Hurtig Publishers Ltd., 10560-105 St., Edmonton, AB T5H 2W7, 1988. illus. index. maps. hardcover $225 Canadian (0-88830-326-2).

971'.003 Canada—Dictionaries and encyclopedias I Canada—Biography [BKL]

The second edition of *The Canadian Encyclopedia* has been positively received by librarians and booksellers and the general public. It is, like the first edition [*RBB* My 15 86], edited by James H. Marsh and has been expanded from three to four volumes. The publisher states that the set is "substantially expanded [and] updated." The editor states in the preface that there are over 1,700 new entries, 500 new photographs, numerous new graphs, and over 50 new pieces of original artwork. Most entries are updated to January 1988. Entries vary in length from three to four sentences to essays of four pages. Consultants and contributors to the second edition are primarily the same as in the first: scholars, professors, well-known Canadian writers, and various people who have expertise in diverse fields. Most articles are signed, and the writers' qualifications are listed in the first volume.

The greatest number of additions are place-names and biographies both current and historical; some biographies and place-names have been dropped as well. In its review of the first edition, the Board noted the absence of entries for the Canadian Library Association and the town of Dartmouth. These have been added. There are also additions in what can only be described as the "Canadian" definition of certain issues, philosophies, and policies, such as *Cultural Policy*.

Other new entries include the well-documented essay *Acadia*, the short entry *AIDS*, and the lucid essay *Economy*. Also new are entries on the current topics *Meech Lake Accord* and *Free Trade*, which closes with the signing of the agreement by Prime Minister Mulroney and President Reagan. *West Edmonton Mall* has its own entry in this edition, whereas in the first edition it was part of the entry *Retail*. *Canadian Expatriates in Show Business* treats figures like Raymond Burr and Michael J. Fox.

Publisher Hurtig is well known for his forceful opinions on Canadian politics, which many critics have suggested affected the objectivity of the *Encyclopedia*. There are few instances of this in the second edition compared with the first. For example, in the entry *Continentalism*, the first edition states that "John Turner, a corporate lawyer with close American connections, represented the Liberal Party's return to its continentalist roots." This sentence was deleted from the second edition, changing the nuance of the entry.

The entry *Haida Indians* makes no mention of their contentious land-claims issue. The entry *Land Claims* does not discuss the issue either but sticks closer to a discourse on the concept and legal notions of land claims. One interesting change was discovered. The entry *Fisheries History* includes the same photograph in both editions; however, the captions are different. The 1985 edition states the photograph is a scene on the Grand Banks (Newfoundland); the second edition states it is a scene near Prince Rupert (British Columbia).

Overall, however, the updating is admirable, with sentences added to current topics to reflect changes over the past four to five years. Sports articles have been updated, including championships in the National Hockey League and the Canadian Football League up to 1987. It appears that the publisher's claims for new and updated material are valid.

The index in the second edition has been greatly expanded to 470 pages from 196 pages in the first. The first edition index included only subjects that did not have their own entries. Page and column numbers are now provided in the index. *See* references are indicated in the body of entries by small capital letters.

Physically the set is appealing and easy to read. The three-column format is cleanly set, and many attractive color and black-and-white photographs fill the pages. Charts and graphs are self-explanatory, filling up to a half-page with lots of color. Statistical information is updated to include figures from the 1986 census. Bibliographies, for the most part, have not changed.

The Canadian Encyclopedia, second edition, like the first, is intended to be a general encyclopedia with a distinctly Canadian point of view. The out-of-print *Encyclopedia Canadiana* (11th ed., 1975) should be retained side by side with this set, because it is still valuable in reference departments for its geographic information and historical biographies. Because it has been expanded and updated, *The Canadian Encyclopedia* is a recommended purchase for all Canadian libraries. In the U.S. it is recommended for academic libraries, in particular those offering Canadian studies programs, and large public libraries where there is interest in Canada and Canadians.

Biographical Dictionary of Latin American and Caribbean Political Leaders. Ed. by Robert J. Alexander. Greenwood, 1988. 509p. bibliog. index. hardcover $75 (0-313-24353-0).

972.9'009 [B] Politicians—Latin America—Biography—Dictionaries I Politicians—West Indies—Biography—Dictionaries Iatesmen—Latin America—Biography—Dictionaries I Statesmen—West Indies—Biography—Dictionaries I Latin America—Biography—Dictionaries [CIP] 87-17805

Alexander (a professor at Rutgers) edited *Political Parties of the Americas: Canada, Latin America, and the West Indies* (Greenwood, 1982), a two-volume encyclopedia containing essays on the important parties of 48 nations and territories. This work was favorably reviewed by the Board [*RBB* O 1 83], which pointed out its value for reference librarians and students in "identifying and describing political groups for which scanty data are available elsewhere." While the index to that set provided page references to mentions of persons associated with the parties, *Political Parties* was not a biographical source. Now, Alexander (assisted by 13 scholars with academic affiliations, eight of whom also contributed to the earlier work) has edited a complementary volume of over 450 signed biographical sketches covering the most important nineteenth- and twentieth-century political figures in 41 countries and territories of Latin America and the Caribbean. (Alexander is credited with more than 125 of the essays.)

The entries—varying in length from a few lines to three or four pages—emphasize the political significance of the biographees, giving in addition details on their political careers, family backgrounds, education, and relevant nonpolitical activities. These evaluative essays conclude with selected bibliographies citing a variety of standard general and specialized sources in English, Spanish, and Portuguese: for example, *Facts On File*, who's whos, country histories, *Current History*, *Hispanic American Historical Review*, "Espasa" (the Spanish-language encyclopedia), and the annual *Latin America and Caribbean Contemporary Record*. In light of the fact that the text notes such recent events as the death in August 1987 of Barbadian prime minister Barrow, de la Madrid's presidency of Mexico from 1982 to 1988, Pindling's reelection in 1987 as prime minister of the Bahamas, and numerous events of 1985 and 1986, it is unclear why there are no entries for José Sarney (Brazilian president since 1985), Oscar Arias Sánchez (Costa Rican president since 1986, and winner of the 1987 Nobel Peace Prize), or General Manuel Antonio Noriega (since 1982 commanding general of Panama's defense forces). Appendix A is a chronology of the major events in the region from 1804 to 1985. Appendix B lists entries by country or territory. A detailed index concludes the book.

All in all, *Biographical Dictionary of Latin American and Caribbean Leaders*, despite its omissions, will serve scholars and students of Latin American and Caribbean affairs well, whether they are patrons of academic or large public libraries.

Historical Dictionary of Cuba. By Jaime Suchlicki. Scarecrow, 1988. 368p. bibliog. hardcover $39.50 (0-8108-2071-4).

972.91'003 Cuba—Dictionaries and encyclopedias [CIP] 87-28406

This latest entry (number 22) in Scarecrow's Latin American Historical Dictionaries series deals, as the editor notes in the foreword, with Cuba, a "strategic island that suffers from passions rather than informed judgment." Jaime Suchlicki, director of the Institute of Interamerican Studies at the University of Miami, has published numerous articles and books on Latin America and the Caribbean, most recently *Cuba, from Columbus to Castro* (Pergamon, 1986), and is eminently qualified to produce this reference work.

The *Historical Dictionary of Cuba* begins with a 20-page chronology detailing events from 1492 through 1985. The heart of the work is the alphabetically arranged entries for persons, places, and events. They average one-third to one-half page, but coverage of major topics (*Political Prisoners*; *People's Power*; *Social Structure*; *Castro Ruz, Fidel*; *Roman Catholic Church*; *Poetry*; and *Courts*) ranges from 2 to 6½ pages. The entries are informative, readable, and generally impartial. The emphasis seems to be on events and people in Cuban history with more limited coverage given to social life and customs. Particularly useful are the biographical entries for political leaders, painters, musicians, and writers. We do find the entries *Education*, *Mass Media*, *Music*, and *Welfare* but search in vain for entries on crime, drugs, prostitution, the Mariel exodus, and sports. Part of the problem is the lack of an index, infrequent use of *see* and *see also* references, and the absence of capitals within entries to indicate coverage of related topics. Statistical information is scant and covered within appropriate entries, for example, *Housing*, *Television*, *Nickel*.

Over 900 reference works, monographs, statistical publications, and government documents in both English and Spanish are listed in the bibliography. Imprint information is complete, but items are not annotated. Reference librarians in academic and large public libraries who find insufficient the material on Cuba in general encyclopedias and such sets as the *Encyclopedia of the Third World* and Europa's *South America, Central America and the Caribbean* will want to add Suchlicki's work to their collections.

Encyclopedia of American Scandal. By George C. Kohn. Facts On File, 1989. 381p. illus. index. hardcover $45 (0-8160-1313-6).

973'.003 Scandals—U.S.—History—Dictionaries I U.S.—History—Dictionaries [CIP]

Kohn, author of the *Dictionary of Culprits and Criminals*, has drawn on similar events in this new work. Containing over 375 entries, the *Encyclopedia* covers scandalous people and events from the worlds of politics, sports, movies, business, and high society. From *Plymouth Colony* to *Televangelists*, Kohn describes notable and not-so-notable American scandals. Intended for the browser and the researcher, the *Encyclopedia* is meant to be "both informational as well as enlightening and entertaining."

Entries are arranged alphabetically either by the popular name of the scandal (*Watergate*, *Teapot Dome*) or by the principal player in the scandal (*Janet Cooke*, fabricator of a Pulitzer Prize–winning story, or *Benedict Arnold*). In some cases, a key figure in a scandal is given a separate entry with a *see also* reference to connect the two. In other cases, there is a *see* reference from a personal name to the scandal (e.g., from *Richard Nixon* to *Watergate*, from *Edward Kennedy* to *Chappaquiddick*). If a person is involved in more than one scandalous event, there are separate entries for each scandal (e.g., *Father Divine*, *Warren Harding*).

It is not clear from the author's preface how people or events were chosen for inclusion in the *Encyclopedia*. Mary Todd Lincoln is here, but Ulysses Grant is not, though there are many references in the index to entries where he is mentioned. Lizzie Borden is listed, but not Ted Bundy. And if politics makes strange bedfellows, so too must scandal. Finding John Adams in the same source as Wayne Hays, or F. Scott Fitzgerald with Clifford Irving, is interpreting scandal in its broadest sense.

Though readers may quarrel with some of his choices, Kohn is fair and evenhanded in his treatment of people and events. If allegations of wrongdoing were not proven, this is clearly stated in the article. The writing is concise, clear, and nonjudgmental. Each entry lists pertinent facts, background information needed to understand the event, and the outcome. Sixty black-and-white photographs whet the reader's appetite for more pictures. The index lists mostly personal names. Unfortunately, there are no bibliographies appended to entries or list of sources at the end of the book.

Information on the scandals included in the *Encyclopedia* is available in other sources, but Kohn's work is unique in bringing together scandals from all aspects of life into one volume. The *Encyclopedia* is sure to interest the casual reader, but it also has a place on the reference shelves.

Fallen in Battle: American General Officer Combat Fatalities from 1775. By Russell K. Brown. Greenwood, 1988. 243p. bibliog. index. hardcover $39.95 (0-313-26242-X).

973 Generals—U.S.—Death I U.S.—History, Military I U.S.—Armed Forces—Officers—Death [CIP] 88-5644

Drawing upon 15 years of research, Brown (a retired U.S. Army officer) profiles the careers of 221 American generals and admirals who were combat fatalities from the American Revolution to the Vietnamese Conflict or whose deaths occurred within approximately two years of their wounds. The well-documented introduction critically reviews selected official and unofficial studies on American military history. Perhaps the most startling of Brown's assertions therein is that only since 1941 have the various military departments maintained sufficient data to help the serious student of this subject. Unpublished documents, published registers, and press releases, says Brown, are available for the knowledgeable researcher. However, a serious drawback is that research in official records is hampered by the National Archives' rule that limits the release of information on people who have been dead less than 75 years.

Each biographical entry (one page or less) includes the following: full name, year and place of birth and death, state from which the biographee entered service, branch of service, brief synopsis of preservice and service career, details of the cause and circumstances of death, highest rank held with date of commission, and a short-title list of sources, which are fully identified in the bibliography. Then follow seven appendixes. Appendix A, "General Officer Data," includes a table on general officer deaths by war or campaign (showing that 160 of the 221 deaths were Civil War fatalities), a tally by state or foreign country of the officers' places of birth, and a tally of their principal occupations. Appendix G, like appendix A, is statistical, showing general officer fatalities in selected battles and campaigns (mostly those of the Civil War). Appendixes B through F are lists of individual generals and admirals: combat fatalities, wartime general officer losses from noncombat causes, generals and admirals wounded in action and captured by hostile forces, and miscellaneous facts—highest ranking, oldest, youngest, Medal of Honor recipients, foreign born, etc.

The bibliography precisely identifies a wide variety of current and retrospective general reference titles (e.g., *Appleton's Cyclopaedia of American Biography*, Boatner's *Civil War Dictionary* and *Encyclopedia of the American Revolution*), and military histories (Freeman's *Lee's Lieutenants*, Spiller's *Dictionary of American Military Biography*, unit histories, state military histories, etc.). Appended to the bibliography are lists of periodicals and newspapers and of archives and manuscript collections. Because *Fallen in Battle* has been carefully researched and includes a most useful bibliography, it will be confidently consulted in special, academic, and public libraries by students of American history and by military buffs.

Directory of Popular Culture Collections. By Christopher D. Geist and others. Oryx, 1989. 234p. indexes. hardcover $48.50 (0-89774-351-2).

973'.025 U.S.—Popular culture—Museums—Directories I U.S.—Popular culture—Library resources—Directories I Canada—Popular culture—Museums—Directories I Canada—Popular culture—Library resources—Directories [CIP] 88-28202

The compilers of this *Directory*, all scholars associated with the Department of Popular Culture at Bowling Green State University, have been gathering information about collections of popular culture since the 1970s. They have faced the problems of what exactly constitutes "popular culture," the vast scope of related scholarship, and "a myriad of both substantial and small research collections of possible interest to scholars scattered widely among academic, public, and industrial libraries and museums." For the purposes of this *Directory*, popular culture is defined as "mainstream culture—the arts, artifacts, entertainments, fads, beliefs, and values shared by large segments...of the society." Information on collections in the U.S. and Canada was collected by questionnaires sent to libraries and museums, and members of the Popular Culture Association and the American Culture Association were asked to identify collections. As can be imagined when respondents range from the Library of Congress to the Rosemary Wells Tooth Fairy Collection in Winnetka, Illinois, the 667 entries vary slightly in length (from one-half column to more than a page) and enormously in the detail with which collections are described. To the extent possible, each entry includes address, contact person, telephone number, hours open, whether open to the public or scholars, special restrictions, and narrative description of the collections.

Users of these collections will be interested primarily in two aspects: subject scope and location. The compilers have chosen the second for primary access, relegating the first to an index. Entries are arranged by state or province and city and then alphabetically by collection name. The subject index is based on collection descriptions supplied by the collections themselves. Nevertheless, some headings are too general and consequently have too many entries under them (e.g., *children's books* has more than 80). Subdivision has been applied in some cases (e.g., *sound recordings* is modified by subdivisions like *African music*, *antique*, *Appalachia*, etc.). *See* references link alternative names for the same or similar concepts, and *see also* references list related headings. There is also an index by the name of the collection. Names beginning with personal names are entered inconsistently, sometimes under forename (e.g., *Walt Disney Archives*), but mostly under surname (e.g., *Kennedy, John Fitzgerald, Library*).

The compilers admit this is only a partial listing of collections of potential interest to students of popular culture. They plan future updates and encourage users to supply information on a questionnaire at the end of the volume. All libraries collecting in the area of popular culture will want this *Directory*.

Since 1776: A Year-by-Year Timeline of American History. By Paul C. Murphy. Price/Stern/Sloan, 1988. 208p. paper $6.95 (0-8431-2276-5).

973'.02 U.S.—History—Chronology [OCLC] 88-188547

This revision of the 1975 edition is organized with one page devoted to each year from 1776 to 1987. Each page is divided into columns with the headings *Politics*, *Religion*, *Arts & Culture*, and *Science & Technology*. All headings are not necessarily used every year; *Religion* appears only occasionally in the twentieth century.

Under each heading, events are stated briefly without reference to month and day (e.g., under 1945 *Politics*: "Atomic bombs were dropped on Hiroshima and Nagasaki, Japan," and under 1923 *Arts & Culture*: "The weekly news magazine *Time* was founded in New York"). The events listed are not all of equal importance, as one finds that in 1796 the first elephant arrived in America and in 1977 Buffalo, New York, was paralyzed by snowstorms. Coverage is inconsistent, with sports records and Academy Awards being given for some years and not others.

This book is of browsing interest only. Without an index, its use as a reference tool is limited. Gorton Carruth's *Encyclopedia of American Facts & Dates* (8th ed. [*RBB* Ap 15 87]) is much more comprehensive, is indexed, and is a better choice for reference collections.

The Dictionary of Cultural Literacy. By E. D. Hirsch and others. Houghton, 1988. 586p. illus. index. maps. hardcover $19.95 (0-395-43748-2).

973'.03 U.S.—Civilization—Dictionaries ǀ Civilization—Dictionaries ǀ English language—Dictionaries [CIP] 88-9363

Hirsch's *Cultural Literacy: What Every American Needs to Know* [*BKL* Ap 15 87] advocated a change in our educational system to restore cultural content to the teaching of the basic skills of reading and writing. Appended to the book was a long list of terms, events, phrases, and persons that he felt were essential for any educated person to know. But the reader who could not identify them or did not understand their significance was left in limbo. Now there is a dictionary to briefly explain all those terms and more. (Yes, *limbo* was in the original list and is explained here.) Hirsch's introduction provides a brief explanation of cultural literacy (that shared background knowledge and language that enables us to communicate with one another without constant explanations of the meaning of our terms), followed by an essay on the theory, and directions for using the *Dictionary*.

The work is divided into 23 sections that cover subject areas a student should have encountered either formally or informally by the senior year of high school (e.g., mythology and folklore, world history, American politics). Entries are arranged alphabetically within each section, and running heads give first and last terms for a two-page spread. This makes it easy to browse through related terms, but to look for a specific term, one needs to use the index. Phrases are entered under their "most commonly recognized element." One may need to check several terms in the index, however. For example, in "Proverbs," the entry *lock the stable door after the horse has been stolen, Don't* is indexed under *lock* and *horse* but not under *don't*. There are two other entries indexed under *don't*, however: *Don't fire until you see the whites of their eyes* (in "American History to 1865"), which is also indexed under *whites* and *eyes*, and *Don't give up the ship* (in "Proverbs"), indexed only under *don't*.

Each section is introduced by a brief essay delineating its scope. Entries are defined concisely but usually provide the full essence of the meaning, although one definition seems too short: *Seven Wonders of the Ancient World* is defined as "Seven famous structures of ancient times, one of which was the PYRAMIDS." If the cultural context is not readily apparent, it is given following a symbol: *Pandora's box* is first defined and then continues after the symbol: "To 'open a Pandora's box' is to create a situation that will cause great grief." One definition was noticed to have a fact wrong: *Mikado, The* says the plot concerns "the efforts of a Japanese prince to win the hand of the national executioner's daughter"—Yum Yum was not Koko's daughter but his ward, and he was about to marry her himself when the prince came along. Pronunciation is given when needed, using a key devised for this volume, which becomes quite clear with use although it may be disconcerting at first (e.g., "vair-SEYE" for *Versailles*). Cross-references may be direct, or small capitals may be used for a term that is itself an entry. Some sections are illustrated with small black-and-white pictures and full-page maps.

This is a unique volume presenting definitions in a special light, not attempting to provide complete detail as would be found in literary or geographic dictionaries or encyclopedias. While it can be annoying to have to use the index to find a term, the subject arrangement makes it a delightful volume in which to browse—or to second-guess the compilers. One can quibble about what has been included or excluded, but further meat for discussion of American education is provided. This volume could well find a place in circulating as well as reference collections of high school, public, and academic libraries, as it provides further fuel for the debate.

Directory of Archives and Manuscript Repositories in the United States. 2d ed. Comp. by the National Historical Publications and Records Commission. Oryx, 1988. 853p. indexes. hardcover $55 (0-89774-475-6).

016.091'025 Archives—U.S.—Directories [CIP] 87-30157

The long-awaited revision and updating of this invaluable directory—previously published in 1978 [*RSBR* Jl 1 80]—is at last available. Some 4,225 entries (crafted from responses to a questionnaire mailed to 10,000 repositories in the U.S.) present basic summary information about mostly academic, government, business, and religious repositories containing archival and manuscript material of every kind. Measured against the budget cuts sustained by its compiler, the National Historical Publications and Records Commission, the magnitude of accomplishment represented by publication of the directory is herculean.

Each entry lists institution name, street address, mailing address, and telephone number; days and hours of operation; user fees, if any; general restrictions on access; availability of copying facilities; acquisitions policies; volume of total holdings; description and inclusive dates of holdings; and bibliographic references to other guides and finding aids. Grouped by state and town, then arranged in alphabetical order by repository name, the entries describe repositories in all the states, the District of Columbia, Puerto Rico, and the U.S. Virgin Islands. The Canal Zone, no longer an American territory, is dropped. All entries represent repositories that had responded to the call for information by September 1, 1983, though data reflect conditions as late as 1986. The nearly 1,400 new entries represent a net increase of almost 1,000.

Two indexes—subject and repository—facilitate access to the data in the directory. The index of repositories is arranged in strict alphabetical order, rather than by type of institution, as in the 1978 edition—for most purposes a useful change. The subject index has been improved in general, both in format and in term selection. Subject terms were derived from the narrative descriptions of holdings. It would have been more helpful, however, if the explanatory text for each index had been placed at the head of each, rather than in the general introduction. After all, this is a reference book, not a narrative to be read cover to cover.

This is an essential purchase for academic libraries where there is a need for access to manuscript materials, and should be considered by large public libraries as well.

The Black Resource Guide. 1988–89 ed. By R. Benjamin Johnson and Jacqueline L. Johnson. R. Benjamin Johnson, 501 Oneida Pl. NW, Washington, DC 20011, 1988. 285p. hardcover $40 (0-9608374-6-9).

973'.0496073 Afro-Americans—Societies, etc.—Directories I Afro-Americans—Directories I Associations, institutions, etc.—U.S.—Directories [BKL] 85-91077

The Black Resource Guide has gone through many changes since its first edition (1981 [*RBB* O 1 83]). Each year it has grown, through conscientious and careful additions of new topics and entries. The 1988–89 edition is no exception. Compiled from annual questionnaires sent to each of the entrants, this useful "national black directory" provides listings (including address, telephone number, and director or contact person) for black accounting firms; adoption services; advertising and marketing research companies; architects; bar associations; book publishers and bookstores; business associations; top black businesses in the U.S.; churches; civil rights organizations; higher education institutions; embassies and consulates of black nations; financial institutions; fraternal organizations; hospitals; insurance companies; media (including broadcast and print); museums; resource organizations; science, engineering, and health organizations; and united-fund organizations. Additionally, the names, addresses, and telephone numbers of black public administrators, political office holders, and members of the judiciary are included. As is the case with many directories today, the information in the *Guide* is also available on mailing labels. The volume concludes with a section in which statistical data (from the U.S. Census Bureau) regarding black economic and social concerns are summarized in 16 major categories. Citations to specific census publications are not provided, except for the section that deals with health.

The Black Resource Guide continues to be a useful tool for many public, academic, and business libraries.

Hispanic Resource Directory. By Alan Edward Schorr. Denali Press, P.O. Box 021535, Juneau, AK 99802-1535, 1988. 347p. charts. indexes. tables. paper $37.50 (0-938737-15-5).

973'.04680025 Hispanic Americans—Societies, etc.—Directories [CIP] 88-70503

With the purpose of assisting Hispanic Americans, service providers, government officials, library patrons, business people, and others interested in the Hispanic community in this country, Schorr has compiled this *Directory* of organizations that serve the fastest growing segment of the U.S. population. The volume is organized around a 165-page directory listing 951 organizations nationwide that responded to questionnaires mailed out between January and July 1988. Arranged by state (including Puerto Rico and the District of Columbia) and city, each entry contains at a minimum the address and telephone number of the organization and a coded listing of its services. Where the organization has supplied the data, entries also include the name of a key contact person, date established, size of the staff and/or number of members, number of chapters or affiliates, annual budget, a brief list of ongoing publications, and a narrative statement about the organization's purposes. Specifically excluded from this work are listings for organizations whose focus is on service to refugee and immigrant populations, these groups having been covered by Schorr's *Directory of Services for Refugees and Immigrants* [*RBB* O 1 87]. It is the editor's expectation to publish updates to these two directories in alternate years.

Supplementing the principal directory are nine appendixes and three indexes. Among the appendixes are directories of book publishers and distributors, human rights and equal opportunity agencies, migrant education agencies, bilingual education agencies, and federal Hispanic Employment Program managers. These appendixes add roughly 1,300 additional organizations to the listings in the principal directory. There is also an appendix listing postsecondary educational institutions with 20 percent or more Hispanic enrollment and a 30-page statistical appendix on the Hispanic population, largely drawn from U.S. Census Bureau publications. The volume concludes with indexes by organization name, contact person name, and services provided (legal, education, health, etc.).

With approximately 2,300 organizations, Schorr's work compares very favorably with other directories covering this field. Caballero's *Chicano Organizations Directory* (Neal-Schuman, 1985) lists only 378, and Taylor's *Guide to Multicultural Resources* (Praxis, 1987) lists barely 300. *Minority Organizations: A National Directory* [*RBB* My 15 88] comes closest to matching the coverage of Schorr with its 1,340 entries on Hispanic organizations, yet its single alphabetical arrangement and weak index make it a much less easy-to-use tool than *Hispanic Resource Directory*. Given the volatile nature and highly localized focus of many support and service organizations, it is little surprise that the degree of overlap between *HRD* and other directories is small. Especially strong in *HRD* is coverage of the programs of various religious groups such as the Catholic church.

While there is no shortage of sources of information on organizations focusing on the Hispanic population, well-executed, reasonably priced directories such as this will be welcome additions to reference collections in academic and public libraries serving this clientele.

Index to Afro-American Reference Resources. Comp. by Rosemary M. Stevenson. Greenwood, 1988. 315p. bibliog. indexes. hardcover $45 (0-313-24580-0; ISSN 0742-6925).

973'.0496073 Afro-Americans—Indexes I Reference books—Afro-Americans—Indexes I Blacks—Indexes I Reference books—Blacks—Indexes [CIP] 87-28028]

In response to the proliferation of materials on the black experience, the compiler has developed a subject index to 190 reference tools and classic works in order to guide users to materials on the topic. The primary emphasis is on the U.S., but Canada, the Caribbean, and South America are included. International materials are selectively indexed. Traditional types of reference works (dictionaries, encyclopedias, abstracts, etc.), individual chapters in larger works, and materials that provide reference information have been analyzed and organized by subject.

The *Index* is divided into five parts. The introduction describes the purpose of this work and provides a bibliographic essay on recent publications. "Cited Works" is an alphabetical list by title of the books indexed. The body of the work is the index that provides subject access to those items. There are also author and title indexes that refer the user to the pages in the subject index where the work is listed. These last two indexes are difficult to use because some entries have long lists of numbers under them and because they refer to a page, not an item number, so the user must scan the entire page. For example, the author entry *Perry, Margaret* directs the user to 25 different pages, but the reference is to the same title: *The Harlem Renaissance: An Annotated Bibliography and Commentary*. Blind references are prevalent in the author index and to a lesser degree in the title index.

The most valuable parts of the work are the list of cited works and the subject index. The list is a good current bibliography of works on Afro-American topics. The subject index provides access to the works as a whole and to chapters within them under headings such as *African Cultural Survivals, Amistad Case—Bibliography*, and *Colonization Movements—Bibliography*. It would have been helpful had the compiler stated how the subject headings were determined.

One caution should be kept in mind when using this index. It indexes only books specifically on the black experience. Therefore, if one looks up *Walker, Alice* in the index, only two citations are given, but biographical information abounds on this individual from *Contemporary Authors* to *Current Biography*. As long as this limitation is understood, this work is a useful subject index to works in Afro-American studies and is recommended for those libraries with substantial reference holdings in this area.

Nations within a Nation: Historical Statistics of American Indians. By Paul Stuart. Greenwood, 1987. 251p. bibliog. index. tables. hardcover $45 (0-313-23813-8).

973'.0497 Indians of North America—History—Statistics [CIP] 86-33618

As a compendium of historical statistics on native American tribes, *Nations* will fill a unique niche in most academic and large public libraries with reference or research interests in North American Indian affairs. Drawing upon a wide variety of government documents (mostly federal) and scholarly reports, as cited in his extensive bibliography, Stuart's contribution will appeal to anyone who seeks demographic or economic data about Indians, past or present.

The author, who is associate professor of social work at the University of Alabama and who has written several books and articles about native Americans, notes in his "Introduction, Scope, and Purpose" that *Nations* will be most useful as a statistical overview or starting point for scholarly research into eight major areas: land holdings and climate; population; removal, relocation, migration, and urbanization; vital statistics (e.g., infant mortality, life expectancy) and health; government expenditures; health care and education; employment, earnings, and income; and natural resources (petroleum, lumber) and economic development (trust funds, claims, and land leases). A brief essay introduces each of these topics and is followed by the appropriate tables.

Stuart notes the "relative absence of statistical data from the nineteenth century and the almost complete absence of data from the eighteenth century and earlier." Consequently, his emphasis is on the twentieth century, while whatever earlier data he presents within each chapter are carefully assessed for accuracy and reliability. The author's overall attempt to reconcile seemingly disparate and unequivalent units of measurement facilitates for the student the task of trying to discern consistent patterns in the data.

The statistical tables within each chapter are extensively footnoted as to sources for further information. Tables are presented in either horizontal or vertical formats across the page, depending on the amount of data. Tables are numbered, and headers clearly identify the contents, but the tables appear typewritten and are faint in contrast with the otherwise excellent typeface of the book. While there is no list of tables, their subject matter is indexed. *See* and *see also* references (e.g., "*Employment . . . See also* Indian employment") facilitate quick access. The index uses italics to distinguish between table pages and references to the text. An extensive bibliography conveniently identifies the primary sources for further research.

Nations is a well-crafted, balanced, convenient tool for reference work and will prove useful to many libraries, scholars, policymakers, and tribal groups.

A Hispanic Heritage, Series III: A Guide to Juvenile Books about Hispanic People and Cultures. By Isabel Schon. Scarecrow, 1988. indexes. hardcover $17.95 (0-8108-2133-8).

016.98 Latin America—Juvenile literature—Bibliography I Spain—Juvenile literature—Bibliography I Hispanic Americans—Juvenile literature—Bibliography [CIP] 88-18094

This is the third in a series of bibliographies on people and cultures of Latin America and Spain, and about Hispanics in the U.S. (*Series II* was reviewed by the Board [*RBB* Jl 85].) This volume includes works published since 1984 in English, revisions of earlier works, and recent translations of works not originally published in English, such as Gabriel García Márquez's 1955 *Story of a Shipwrecked Sailor*. Works are grouped alphabetically by the country in which they are set and then alphabetically by author's name. Most of the books are nonfiction works about geography and culture (including titles from the Enchantment of the World, Take a Trip, and Living Here series). Fiction, drama, poetry, and folklore are also included, with adequate representation of women, popular culture, and the poor.

Critical one-paragraph annotations are provided for every listing, with "noteworthy" titles starred (about 60 of more than 200 listed). The author's comments indicate whether a work is "poorly organized" or "has a plodding text," making this useful for collection development. Rarely in books of this sort are annotations as explicit as these: "awkward Spanish translation which is full of spelling, typographical, and grammatical mistakes" or "the patronizing, simplistic text ridicules Aztec culture and beliefs." Suggested grade levels are assigned "for the convenience of some teachers or students," with most titles for ninth grade and up.

There are three indexes (author, title, and subject); subject indexing lacks thoroughness. Although books on these topics are included, no subject headings exist for *women, poetry, drama, Jews, Inquisition*, or *myths*, to list a few. Only the biography of Pancho Villa (not the story about him) is listed under *Villa, Pancho*, and a book about the group Menudo is listed under *Puerto Rico—music*, not *Menudo* or *music*. Names of revisers and translators aren't indexed, although editors and joint authors are.

Another problem is the author's political stance. She repeatedly criticizes books that condemn Reagan's Nicaragua policies as "political rhetoric blaming the U.S." Furthermore, although other lengthy books about history are referred to as "touching" or for "serious students," Schon "can't imagine young adults being interested in long, passionate testimonials about the wonders of the Sandinistas."

This work would be most useful in areas with significant Hispanic populations and/or interest. Many schools and children's collections will not find it necessary because there are relatively few recommended titles. A revised list including the best of the three volumes would be useful.

Jewish Heritage in America: An Annotated Bibliography. By Sharad Karkhanis. Garland, 1988. 434p. indexes. hardcover $57 (0-8240-7538-2).

016.973'04924 Jews—U.S.—Bibliography I Judaism—U.S.—Bibliography I U.S.—Ethnic relations—Bibliography [CIP] 88-25935

A librarian at Kingsborough Community College in New York City has compiled this comprehensive bibliography on the American Jewish experience. The 323 books and 777 articles (from 88 popular and academic journals) date from 1925 through 1987. Some out-of-print monographs are included although the emphasis is on current publications.

The introduction states that "selection of articles and books was based on the significance and treatment of the topic covered and overall balance of distribution of entries within the specified subject areas." Autobiographies, biographies, poetry, and fiction are not included. Selection was also based on the items' general availability in medium-sized public and academic libraries.

The work is divided into seven broad categories: "Reference and Research," "Historical Perspectives," "Antisemitism," "Religious Traditions," "Intellectual and Literary Traditions," "Sociological Impact," and "Political Activism." Subcategories (e.g., "Family Guide-books," "Relations with Christianity," "Intermarriage," "Relations with Israel") facilitate further access. Within subcategories, the books and articles are listed separately in alphabetical order by author, followed by bibliographic information.

The annotations range from one sentence to nearly a page, but the typical entry is several sentences. They are clearly written descriptions but usually not evaluative. There are no cross-references. Separate author, title, and subject indexes provide access to specific numbered entries.

Within the parameters established in the introduction, this book includes most of the standard works in each category. Inevitably, some books are not here that one might expect to find, e.g., *The History of the Jews of Philadelphia: From Colonial Times to the Age of Jackson* (Jewish Publication Society, 1957); *The Jews of Detroit: From the Beginning, 1762–1914* (Wayne State Univ., 1986); and the important *Jewish Catalog: A Do-It-Yourself Kit* (Jewish Publication Society, 1973). One entry discusses the new quarterly *Tikkun*, described as "an alternative voice for Jewish liberals as compared to the [more right-leaning] *Commentary*." However, no articles are included from *Tikkun*. Nor are any articles indexed from the Jewish feminist periodical *Lilith*. Users at different levels of research will find *Jewish Heritage in America* a valuable resource. By including articles and books covering a long span of time, treating a wide range of topics, and including good aids to facilitate access, the author has made a significant contribution. The book will be useful in academic and public libraries and special libraries of Jewish history or research.

Our Vice-Presidents and Second Ladies. By Leslie W. Dunlap. Scarecrow, 1988. 397p. index. hardcover $35 (0-8108-2114-1).

973'.09 [B] Vice-Presidents—U.S.—Biography I Vice-Presidents—U.S.—Wives—Biography [CIP] 88-4123

Biographical sketches of the 43 vice-presidents of the U.S. and their spouses are arranged chronologically here according to administration. The author, a librarian, has written in the field of American history. He states that since the length of time individuals held the office was often brief, information from birth to death was included for a more accurate depiction. He also includes information on women who were the vice-president's second wife or official hostess. The author states in his preface, "Some of my forty-three sketches are brief because of the obscurity of the subject (James S. Sherman and William A. Wheeler) or the scarcity of illuminating source material (John N. Garner destroyed his papers), and others are comparatively long because of the serious work already done (Abigail Adams and Edith Roosevelt), or because of the existence of numerous published letters and memoirs (Harry Truman and Richard Nixon). In a few cases, the availability of a recent definitive study of a minor figure (George M. Dallas) simplified my task; but for several others (Richard Nixon and Lyndon Johnson) the multiplicity of studies obliged me to cut fresh paths through tangled testimony."

Each article begins with an abstract detailing important points in the lives of the biographees. Generally, the information for both the vice-president and his wife is blended within the chapters, which run from 4 to 20 pages. Following the sketch, from one to six "Principal Sources" are given. While some sources are scholarly, many are popular biographies or autobiographies. No footnotes for quotations nor photographs are included.

The author has attempted the difficult task of capturing the personal and public life of these political figures and their spouses on too few pages, duplicating information already found in other books. His choice of what to include seems idiosyncratic, e.g., he neglects to note that Charles Dawes won the Nobel Peace Prize but devotes a lot of space to Nelson Rockefeller's relationship with Megan Marshak.

Libraries will be better served by Robert I. Vexler's *Vice-Presidents and Cabinet Members Arranged Chronologically by Administration* (2v., Oceana, 1975), a more scholarly treatment of the subject that offers more bibliographic citations for further research. Unfortunately, Vexler is out-of-print. Other popular titles on this topic include Klyde Young and Lamar Middleton's *Heirs Apparent: The Vice Presidents of the United States* (Books for Libraries Press, 1969) and Diana Dixon Healy's *America's Vice-Presidents: Our First Forty-three Vice-Presidents and How They Got to Be Number Two* (Atheneum, 1984). But there are few books that include information about Second Ladies. While no other source compiles information about them, there is not enough new here to warrant purchase.

The Civil War Dictionary. Rev. ed. By Mark Mayo Boatner. McKay, 1988. 974p. bibliog. maps. hardcover $29.95 (0-8129-1726-X).

973.7'03 U.S.—History—Civil War, 1861–1865—Dictionaries [CIP] 87-40599

First compiled in 1959 by the distinguished soldier and scholar Boatner, *The Civil War Dictionary* has been revised and issued in a new edition. Although this monograph is intended for the researcher or serious student and provides only essential facts rather than an in-depth analysis, any history aficionado will find this a fascinating reference book. It contains over 4,000 entries with approximately half of those biographical sketches of military and civilian leaders. All Civil War generals are covered, as are scores of campaigns, battles, and skirmishes. Also described are military units, weapons, political issues, terms, and statistics. There are 86 maps and diagrams throughout the text and in an appended "Atlas of Sectional Maps." All maps and diagrams are highly detailed black-and-white line drawings. Unfortunately, some of the maps in the text are of such small size that users will have difficulty reading them. The introduction, the list of "Symbols Used on Battle Maps," and the list of abbreviations, all at the front of the book, are extremely helpful in deciphering the many specialized notations in the text. The front and back endpapers are illustrated with timeline charts of the eastern and western theaters of the war, respectively. Rounding out the work is the 13-page atlas and a five-page bibliography.

A typical biographical entry gives the person's affiliation, military rank, birth and death years, state, year of graduation from West Point, class rank, and assigned service. This is followed by pre–Civil War service and employment history, a detailed chronology of Civil War activities, and frequently a short note on nicknames, family history, character, post-war employment, or retirement dates.

A random comparison sampling of the previous and present editions determined that the bulk of the text has undergone little or no change. As in any massive work, there are sometimes curious omissions; for example, Confederate submarine warfare is discussed, but the leaders H. L. Hunley and George S. Dixon are not covered. There are accurate cross-references given in capital letters throughout the text, but they are not abundant enough; for example, the entry for Harriet Beecher Stowe does not inform the reader that there is the relevant article *Uncle Tom's Cabin*. The bibliography has been updated with only a handful of new additions, the most recent a 1977 publication. Since its original publication, *CWD* has been praised by many subject specialists. The failure to make necessary improvements is thus disappointing. In recent years, several new titles have appeared that are similar in scope and scholarship to *CWD*. First on the scene was *The Civil War Almanac* by Bowman (Facts On File, 1982). Most of that monograph is a day-by-day chronology of the Civil War, but about 200 pages are devoted to succinct descriptions of military weapons and biographical sketches. More extensive is the *Historical Times Illustrated Encyclopedia of the Civil War* by Faust [*RBB* Mr 15 87], which contains over 2,000 entries and almost 1,000 outstanding illustrations. The recent *Who Was Who in the Civil War* by Sifakis [*RBB* O 1 88] presents detailed biographies of all Civil War generals and many other prominent personalities. In comparing these publications, *CWD* obviously provides the most entries. In contrast, the other publications are more current, sometimes more detailed, or complementary to *CWD* in coverage. We recommend *CWD* to all public and academic libraries that do not own the previous edition.

Who Was Who in the Civil War. 2v. By Stewart Sifakis. Facts On File, 1988 (c1987). 600p. bibliog. illus. hardcover $45 (0-8160-1055-2).

973.7'092 U.S.—History—Civil War, 1861–1865—Biography [OCLC] 84-1596

Free-lance journalist Sifakis has compiled an outstanding reference work on the American Civil War. Organized alphabetically, it presents biographies of more than 2,500 people from the Civil War era. Included are all Northern and Southern officers who achieved the rank of general. Also covered are naval officers, diplomats, writers, artists, photographers, physicians, nurses, spies, scouts, politicians, and sundry famous and infamous individuals. Interspersed throughout the text are 249 black-and-white illustrations taken from the author's personal collection, historical archives, and prominent Civil War publications.

A typical entry begins with the biographee's name and birth and death dates in boldface. A brief introduction on the person's prewar life (place of birth, education, activities, etc.) is followed by a detailed accounting of the Civil War years. A short conclusion provides information on postwar employment, cause of death, and so on. Frequently, one or two titles are cited as sources for further information. Within the text, mention is also made of publications written by the person being sketched. While these publication citations are not complete bibliographically, they will prove useful to researchers and enthusiasts. A random check determined that the biographical and bibliographic information is accurate and current. Whenever appropriate, there are cross-references directing users to the correct entry.

Rounding out this work are two appendixes, a select critical bibliography, a list of illustrations with sources designated by codes, and a short glossary of place-names. The first appendix is a chronology of important Civil War events and battles. The second is a list of Union officers who received the thanks of the U.S. Congress.

Three similar general works invite comparison with Sifakis. *The Civil War Dictionary* (1959) by Boatner has 4,000 entries, of which half are biographical. Sifakis argues in his selected bibliography that Boatner has some errors relating to military ranks and people's presence at battles but is otherwise an excellent work. *The Civil War Almanac* (Facts On File, 1982) by Bowman has three parts: a daily chronology, descriptions of accoutrements, and biographies of about 130 persons. Much larger is Faust's *Historical Times Illustrated Encyclopedia of the Civil War* (Harper, 1986 [*RBB* Mr 15 87]). That volume has 2,000 entries, most of which are biographical and illustrated. Bowman and Sifakis are not really comparable, despite the fact that they both have a chronology and biographies. In contrast, Sifakis has approximately 20 percent more biographical entries than Boatner and Faust but fewer illustrations than the latter. Also, Sifakis is superior in citing bibliographic material. We can conclude by highly recommending Sifakis for high school, public, and academic libraries.

Historical Dictionary of the 1920s: From World War I to the New Deal, 1919–1933. By James S. Olson. Greenwood, 1988. 420p. bibliog. index. hardcover $55 (0-313-25683-7).
973.91 U.S.—History—1919–1933—Dictionaries [CIP] 87-29987

This is yet another fine historical dictionary from Greenwood. Compiler Olson is a professor of history at Sam Houston State University. His previous Greenwood books include *Dictionary of the Vietnam War* [*RBB* My 1 88] and *Historical Dictionary of the New Deal* [*RBB* My 1 86]. The present volume focuses on the events of the 1920s in the U.S. Included are more than 700 entries on prominent politicians, important sports figures, labor leaders, radicals, artists, playwrights, novelists, composers, filmmakers, etc. There are entries for important legal cases such as Loeb-Leopold and Sacco and Vanzetti, discussions of important legislation, comments on social issues such as prohibition, discussion of fads such as flagpole sitting and marathon dancing, entries for radio shows like "Amos and Andy" and "Death Valley Days," and even discussion of popular board games like mah jong. The entries vary in length, although they average about one-half page, and each includes suggestions for additional reading. There are numerous cross-references, but some additional ones would be helpful, e.g., from *Prohibition* to *Speakeasies*. A 12-page chronology and an excellent 43-page topical bibliography complement the volume. The book concludes with an index, which is largely to proper names. Subject entries that would list all the articles on a topic such as legislation would be helpful.

This carefully edited work should prove an asset for all reference collections and a useful handbook for students of twentieth-century American history. Because this book lacks illustrations, librarians should also be aware of the well-illustrated Time-Life series *This Fabulous Century*, which has a volume devoted to the 1920s.

New Day/New Deal: A Bibliography of the Great American Depression, 1929–1941. Comp. by David E. Kyvig and Mary-Ann Blasio. Greenwood, 1988. 306p. index. hardcover $45 (0-313-26027-3; ISSN 0742-6828).
016.97391'6 Depressions—1929—U.S.—Bibliography ‖ New Deal, 1933–1939—Bibliography ‖ U.S.—History—1919–1933—Bibliography ‖ U.S.—History—1933–1945—Bibiography [CIP] 87-37568

This unannotated bibliography of more than 4,600 entries (some 1,300 books, 2,500 articles, and 800 dissertations) published as recently as mid-1987 is, according to the preface, the most extensive bibliography of the depression decade ever published, reflecting the continuing "interest in this era by scholars and non-academics alike." This claim appears to be justified when the work is compared to *The Great Depression: A Historical Bibliography* (ABC-Clio, 1983), which lists nearly 1,000 journal articles (no books or dissertations) with abstracts, published during the period 1973–82. Burke and Lowitt's unannotated bibliography of more than 4,200 items, *The New Era and the New Deal, 1920–1940* (Harlan Davidson, 1981), covers the spectrum of socioeconomic, political, and cultural themes of the period, as found in the book and journal literature to 1979. It includes some titles on the Great Depression, most of which are entered in the more recent and more extensive title under review.

New Day/New Deal is a topically arranged bibliography of 13 chapters, most of which are subdivided. In all, 44 separate topics are treated. For example, chapters 5 and 6, covering the Hoover and Roosevelt administrations, are each divided into the categories *General*, *Politics*, and *Policies and Programs*; chapter 7, "The Economy," has five subdivisions (*General*; *Agriculture*; *Banking, Finance, and Monetary Affairs*; *Business and Industry*; *Labor*); chapter 8, "Society," likewise has five categories (*General, Blacks, Immigrants and Ethics, Native Americans, Women*); chapter 10, "Thought and Culture," treats eight topics (*General; Arts; Education; Mass Communication; Popular Culture; Political Ideas and Movements; Religion; Science, Medicine, and Technology*). Other chapters deal with regional, state, and local affairs, constitutional and legal issues, and foreign relations. Chapter 4, "Biography," is particularly interesting for its listings for 167 noteworthy individuals of the period.

Each of the 44 topics is further subdivided into lists—arranged alphabetically by author—of books, articles, and dissertations. Entries in the author index indicate the chapter and section in which an author's work is listed and whether the work is a book (*b*), article (*a*), or dissertation (*d*). Spot checking suggests that both the index and bibliographic references are correct. There is no subject index, so users will need to depend on the table of contents to lead them to the correct section. The cocompilers are, respectively, a professor and a doctoral student in history at the University of Akron.

This bibliography is recommended for students and researchers of the Great Depression using academic and large public libraries.

Encyclopedia of Frontier Biography. 3v. By Dan L. Thrapp. Arthur H. Clark Company, P.O. Box 230, Glendale, CA 91209, 1988. index. hardcover $175 (0-87062-191-2).
978.0092 West (U.S.)—Biography ‖ Frontier and pioneer life—Biography [BKL] 88-71686

This large work, containing biographies of approximately 4,500 western pioneers and native Americans, deserves all the praise it is currently earning. While not competing with the overwhelming quantity of names in Bancroft's *Pioneer Register* for California, it covers all the areas that were affected by the "westward movement," both in Canada and the U.S. Therefore, it contains a few names associated with early French settlements in the seventeenth century, as well as pioneers who settled in Kentucky and other valleys west of Appalachia. But the vast majority of the names are those of men and women who discovered, fought for, governed, or merely lived in the unsettled lands west of the Mississippi.

Each alphabetically arranged entry begins with a descriptor, such as "frontiersman," "desperado," "Army officer," "daguerrotypist," "interpreter," "Indian chief," "cowboy," "writer," or sometimes just "character." Each entry is about one-quarter to one-half page, though some entries, such as those for Fremont or Parkman, run to a full page or more. There are no illustrations, and no pronunciation is given for names.

Each entry, even the briefest, is accompanied by a short bibliography designed to authenticate the information given. (Where the bibliography would become too long, as in the case of Fremont or other well-known persons, there is merely the notation "Literature abundant.") At the front of each volume is a listing of abbreviations of journals and books cited in these bibliographies.

There is an extensive supplementary index of over 70 pages. It does not index the main entries (since they are alphabetically arranged) but is intended to index names of persons within entries. For example, the name *Hickock, James Butler (Wild Bill)* occurs in its alphabetical sequence, but in the index there are 27 citations to other entries in which he is mentioned. General Custer has approximately 100 such citations in the index. This feature of the index adds strength to the reference value of the work. In addition, the index lists topics, such as *buffalo hunting*, *railroads*, *gunmen*, *scouts*, and *guides*, many of them with 50 or more citations.

Coverage is almost as complete as most western history enthusiasts could ask for. One name, for example, that of E. L. Bradshaw, an Arizona "character," is included, though his only claim to fame is that he shot and killed a man in an argument over a shirt. On the other hand, all of the well-known names are here: Mark Twain, Cochise, Chivington of the Sand Creek Massacre, Sacajawea, Escalante, Red Cloud, etc.

Those interested in personalities of California and the Southwest may be disappointed at the paucity of Hispanic names. Of the 142 Hispanic Franciscans who came to California, for example, only a handful are included, chiefly the better-known, earlier arrivals: Serra, Crespi, Palou, Lasuen, etc. On the other hand, whenever a Hispanic or Anglo name is included here, information is generously supplied, in contrast to the brevity of Bancroft's *Pioneer Register*. The missionary/diarist Crespi, for example, gets 27 lines as opposed to only five lines in Bancroft; the trapper Thomas ("Peg-Leg") Smith has 62 lines, but only six in Bancroft.

The Alaskan frontier also appears to be largely overlooked. Neither Bering, Wrangell, nor Rezanov, for example, are included. A few other omissions are surprising: Archbishop Lamy of Santa Fe, U.S. Consul Thomas O. Larkin, and John Marsh, pioneer of 1836 and perhaps the man most responsible—prior to the gold discovery—for persuading his fellow Americans to migrate westward. Also it appears that persons who crossed the Plains in the gold-rush years, such as Edwin Bryant, J. Goldsborough Bruff, or William Swain, are generally not included, even though their diaries subsequently made them famous. Only those persons who became locally prominent after their arrival, whether in California or Oregon, such as Major James D. Savage, appear to be included.

Despite these limitations, the three volumes of this work comprise a wealth of information about persons who lived on the frontier, whether that was the trans-Appalachian frontier, the "wide Missouri" frontier, the mining regions of the Rockies, or the gold-mining/ranching frontiers of California, Oregon, or Arizona. It is suitable for purchase by academic and public libraries alike, especially by any library with interest in western history.

The Bateman New Zealand Encyclopedia. 2d ed. Ed. by Gordon McLauchlan. David Bateman Ltd.; dist. by G. K. Hall, 1988 (c1987). 640p. illus. index. maps. hardcover $49 (0-908610-21-1).
993.1'003 New Zealand—Dictionaries and encyclopedias [BKL]

This one-volume encyclopedia, first published in 1984 [*RBB* F 1 85], covers a broad spectrum of information about New Zealand. Agriculture, the arts, biography, education, geography, geology, history, industry, natural history, sports, and many other topics are covered in short articles about specific topics, arranged in alphabetical order. There are many entries on famous New Zealanders, past and present, and good coverage of Maori history and culture, rugby teams and figures, sheep raising, and geographic locations. While browsing in the *Encyclopedia*, one may be reminded of famous people who are or were New Zealanders—Kiri Te Kanawa, Ngaio Marsh, Katherine Mansfield, Sylvia Ashton-Warner—and may find things that have an association with New Zealand, such as orange roughy, the albatross, and Rhodes scholarships.

Designed to appeal to readers of various ages and educational levels, both students and general readers, the book is described by the editor as popular but also comprehensive and authoritative. The *Encyclopedia* is directed to New Zealanders, as well as to potential visitors from other countries.

Special features include over 500 black-and-white illustrations (mostly photographs); 48 pages of attractive color illustrations of birds, flowers, breeds of sheep, flags, postage stamps, paintings by native artists, Maori artifacts, etc.; and nine color maps: a large, foldout map of New Zealand and eight schematic maps showing soil, land use, vegetation, forests, climate, etc.

There are several aids to finding related information in the *Encyclopedia*, including the usual *see* references. Terms used within an entry that have their own entry are identified by the use of special type. A subject index lists pertinent articles under broad subjects. For example, under *commerce and industry* are listed names of individuals, companies (*Blue Star Line*), industries (*whaling*, *forestry*), products (*peat wax*), government agencies (*Tourist and Publicity Department*), etc. A selective chronology of New Zealand's history offers another way to organize some of the material presented. This second edition of the *Encyclopedia* is little changed from the first. The chronology has been updated through 1987, as have lists of prime ministers and Rhodes scholars; population statistics are now from 1986; and the statistical tables found in the back of the first edition have been dropped. Otherwise, the articles and illustrations appear to be the same. Like the first edition, this book has no bibliographies. It is recommended for libraries of any type and level that don't own the first edition and need material on New Zealand.

Australians: A Historical Library. 11v. Fairfax, Syme & Weldon Assoc.; dist. by Cambridge, 1988 (c1987). bibliog. illus. index. tables. hardcover $495 (0-521-34073-X).
994 Australia—History [BKL]

More than 400 of Australia's leading historians, economists, archaeologists, geographers, librarians/bibliographers, and journalists collaborated in the creation of this major historical work published to coincide with the bicentennial of European settlement in Australia. It avoids a celebratory approach, however, and topics are treated in an objective manner. This remarkably successful work will be of considerable value for both scholars and general readers for many years to come.

The set consists of two parts: five historical volumes and six reference volumes. Volumes are not available individually; they must be purchased as a set. The historical volumes fall outside the scope of the Board's reviewing responsibilities, but, for the record, their titles are *Australians to 1788* (looking at Australian society before the first European settlement); *Australians 1838*, *Australians 1888*, and *Australians 1938* (providing a cross-section of Australian history and society at three 50-year intervals); and *Australians from 1939* (the history of Australia over the past 50 years). Like the rest of the set, these volumes are profusely illustrated, mostly in color. The six reference volumes are reviewed here.

Australians: A Historical Atlas, the first historical atlas of Australia, is the work of cartographers and other scholars. The maps were produced by a team of cartographers at the Division of National Mapping in Canberra. The first section of the atlas, "Place," examines in text, graphs, tables, and photographs the environment, land use, and economic activity (mining, manufacturing, and transportation). The second section, "People," similarly examines aspects of Australia's social history, such as the origins and distribution of the population, and the course of major events, such as wars and the Great Depression. The third section, "Landscapes," shows the impact of European settlement on the continent. A variety of cartographic techniques (pie charts, computer mapping, flow line maps, etc.) have been used successfully. The introduction notes the range of subjects mapped by explorers and government mapping agencies—flora, fauna, topographical features, railways, goldfields, schools, hospitals, outbreaks of disease, recreational facilities, and national parks. All of these sources and others have been used extensively in compiling this atlas. The index includes, besides place-names, entries for topics as varied as aboriginal culture, crops, minerals, diseases, convicts, migration patterns, and names of individuals.

Australians: A Guide to Sources contains over 3,000 references to books, periodical articles, and government publications considered "basic reading for anyone wishing to gain an understanding of the many facets of Australian physical and social conditions and their history." The volume—the work of some 60 scholars—opens with an account of the writing of Australian history and a description of the principal resources for information about Australia (e.g., archives, libraries, museums, pictorial sources, and galleries). Then follow nine sections identifying general reference works (dictionaries, encyclopedias, bibliographies, statistical sources, etc.) and works on Australia's physical environment, aborigines, European discovery and colonization, politics, economy, society, and culture. The cutoff date for this bibliography is the end of 1984. While most titles carry an Australian imprint, a number of British and U.S. publications and a few of other countries are included. The essays introducing each chapter are informative. Tables, illustrations, and photographs throughout the volume add interest. The name index identifies individuals, publications, government agencies, associations, etc.; it is followed by a subject index with numerous cross-references.

Australians: Events and Places is a chronology and gazetteer. The chronology mentions many of the events that earlier chroniclers considered important but also includes incidents that interest a new generation of historians, relating, for example, to the position of women in Australian society and issues in Australian cultural life. Here one can determine the date women first voted in federal elections, the first issue of *Australian Women's Weekly*, the establishment of the Australian Broadcasting Commission, the founding of Australia's first literary periodical, and Australian concerts by Australian-born Dames Nellie Melba and Joan Sutherland. The "Places" section provides a summary history of more than 700 cities, towns, and geographic features. The 32 regional essays in this section place the localities in a wider framework. A personal-name index precedes a place index.

Australians: A Historical Dictionary has over 1,200 biographical and subject entries, covering topics as wide-ranging as Rupert Murdoch, American influence on Australia, literature, the National Library of Australia, New South Wales (and each of the other states or territories), newspapers, the oil industry, and Qantas. Many of the entries are signed and include suggestions for further reading. Shorter entries (some of which also include brief reading lists) were compiled by a team of authors based at the Research School of Social Sciences in the Australian National University. Photographs and other illustrative material and tables are appropriately placed throughout the text. The dictionary complements other volumes in the set, not duplicating information found elsewhere in the series.

It is the intention of *Australians: Historical Statistics*, according to its introduction, to bring together for the first time, in a convenient tabular and graphic form, material from a variety of sources that quantitatively illustrates major aspects of Australian life since European settlement. Its 27 chapters (each with a brief introductory essay) cover immigration and ethnic origin, population, vital statistics, the economy before 1850, labor, transportation and communication, retail and wholesale trade, government finance, manufacturing, crime and justice, education and science, politics, war, religion, and public opinion.

Notes to the tables and endnotes (the latter list the sources and comment on their accuracy and comparability) are essential to interpreting the tables. The index combines access to subjects and names.

The guide portion of the final reference volume, *Australians: The Guide and Index*, contains a number of reference lists: winners of awards and honors in the arts, achievements in major Australian and international sporting events, and officials in federal and state governments (e.g., governors-general of the Commonwealth, state governors, prime ministers of Australia). The names of individual winners of awards and sporting events and government officials do not appear in the index, which makes up the second portion of this volume. Rather, the names of the awards (*Alan Marshall Award*), sports (*cricket*), and government offices (*prime minister*) are indexed. Unfortunately there are many errors in the index pagination of these names. The Alan Marshall Award appears on page 16, not 2; cricket on pages 26–27, not 12–13; prime ministers on pages 43–44, not 29–30.

The general index in this volume "brings together the individual volume indexes to provide a selective but detailed access point for the entire series." It complements and extends—but does not supplant—the individual volume indexes. To illustrate: the index entry *houses and housing* and its eight subentries all with volume and page numbers show that some aspect of this topic is treated in each of the 10 other volumes of this set. Turning then, for instance, to the index entry *housing* in *Australians: Historical Statistics*, one is led to more than 200 columns of data. Similarly, the general index indicates that information on Dame Joan Sutherland also appears in the *Events and Places*, *Historical Dictionary*, and elsewhere in *The Guide and Index* volume. Except for the page references to the reference-list portion of this volume (discussed above), the index appears to be accurate.

In summary, the reference volumes of *Australians: A Historical Library*, approaching Australia's past in different ways, are extremely diverse in purpose and structure, and each volume complements others in the set. By and large, they have been prepared with great scholarly care from original sources and the knowledge of researchers and specialists. They can be recommended for public and academic libraries where interest in Australia, heightened by the coverage of its 1988 bicentennial, is likely to continue into the future.

The Concise Encyclopedia of Australia. 2d ed. Ed. by John Shaw. David Bateman Ltd.; dist. by G. K. Hall, 1989. 848p. bibliog. illus. index. hardcover $54 (0-949135-23-2).

994'.003 Australia—Dictionaries and encyclopedias [BKL]

With an increased awareness of and interest in Australia on the part of the American public today, this one-volume *Encyclopedia* certainly meets a demand. Although its title indicates a quick-reference source, many of the articles included are as in-depth as similar pieces in general encyclopedias. *Aborigines*, for instance, runs $4^{1}/_{2}$ pages, and *Sheep and Wool* 5. The *Encyclopedia* is a highly readable and visually attractive reference work. The illustrations, although mostly black and white and small, enhance the text. Compared with other one-volume encyclopedias, the number of illustrations, maps, charts, and other visual aids is impressive.

The entries are alphabetically arranged. In addition, an excellent classified subject index pulls together related articles under headings like *Literature* or *Sport and Recreation* to give the reader an overview of broad topics. Some larger headings are subdivided. For example, under *Natural History—Botany*, all the entries related to Australian vegetation are indexed under the subheading *Plants, Shrubs and Trees*. This index will be especially useful to American readers, who may not know enough about, say, the exploration of Australia to know the names of specific explorers to look up. There are also cross-references embedded in some entries, and many of the entries provide short bibliographies. The *Encyclopedia* is well balanced with information on a broad range of subjects from the historical/biographical to economics, agriculture, and the arts, with especially good coverage of the natural history of Australia. Appendixes include a chronology; lists of government officials, award winners, and colleges and universities; glossaries of botanical and scientific terms; and lists of extinct or endangered animals and of disasters. Also appended are tables of winners of sporting events.

The Concise Encyclopedia of Australia is highly recommended for all types of libraries, high school level and above, not only as a ready-reference source but for more extensive use as well. Many libraries unable to afford the more expensive Cambridge multivolume *Australians: A Historical Library* [*RBB* S 15 88] will find this *Encyclopedia* quite serviceable.

SUBJECT INDEX

Abbreviations, English
   Concise Dictionary of Acronyms and Initialisms 96
Abnormalities, Human
   Peace of Mind during Pregnancy 114
Abortion
   Psychological and Medical Aspects of Induced Abortion 113
Acquired immune deficiency syndrome
   AIDS 112
   AIDS Bibliography for 1981–1986 112
   AIDS Information Resources Directory 114
   How to Find Information about AIDS 115
Acronyms
   Concise Dictionary of Acronyms and Initialisms 96
Africa
   Place Names of Africa, 1935–1986 164
Afro-American authors
   Black Authors and Illustrators of Children's Books 34
   Black Writers 160
Afro-American children
   Black Children and American Institutions 61
Afro-American dramatists
   Contemporary Black American Playwrights and Their Plays 161
Afro-American entertainers
   Blacks in American Films and Television 142
Afro-American musicians
   Blacks in Classical Music 133
   Heat Wave 137
Afro-American theater
   Contemporary Black American Playwrights and Their Plays 161
Afro-American women
   Women of Color in the United States 62
Afro-Americans
   The Black Resource Guide 186
   Dictionary of Afro-American Slavery 62
   Index to Afro-American Reference Resources 186
Afro-Americans in art
   Images of Blacks in American Culture 123

Afro-Americans in motion pictures
   Blacks in American Films and Television 142
Afro-Americans in the motion picture industry
   Blacks in American Films and Television 142
Afro-Americans in the television industry
   Blacks in American Films and Television 142
Aged
   Crime and the Elderly 80
   National Continuing Care Directory 78
Aged offenders
   Crime and the Elderly 80
Air forces
   Encyclopedia of the World's Air Forces 78
Alcoholics
   Drug, Alcohol, and Other Addictions 81
   The 100 Best Treatment Centers for Alcoholism and Drug Abuse 81
Alcoholism
   Drug, Alcohol, and Other Addictions 81
   Rehab 81
Allusions
   Common Allusions and Foreign Terms 94
Alternative medicine
   Alternative Therapies, Unproven Methods, and Health Fraud 112
American drama
   American Playwrights since 1945 158
   Contemporary Black American Playwrights and Their Plays 161
American fiction
   The Bibliography of Contemporary American Fiction, 1945–1988 159
American literature
   American Women Writers 158
   Dictionary of Literary Biography Yearbook, 1987 154
   Handbook of American Popular Literature 159
   Vietnam War Literature 160
American periodicals
   The Directory of Humor Magazines and Humor Organizations in America (and Canada) 154

American wit and humor
   Comedy on Record 145
Americanisms
   A Dictionary of American Idioms 97
   A Historical Dictionary of American Industrial Language 71
   Webster's New World Dictionary of American English 95
   Webster's New World Guide to Current American Usage 99
Amphibians
   The Completely Illustrated Atlas of Reptiles and Amphibians for the Terrarium 117
Antinuclear movement
   Peace Resource Book, 1988–1989 66
Antiques
   Pictorial Price Guide to American Antiques 128
Aquarium fishes
   Dr. Burgess's Atlas of Marine Aquarium Fishes 117
Archaeology
   Historical Dictionary of North American Archaeology 182
   Past Worlds 167
Architecture
   A Dictionary of Ancient Near Eastern Architecture 127
   Encyclopedia of Architecture 126
Architecture and women
   Architecture and Women 126
Architecture, Ancient
   A Dictionary of Ancient Near Eastern Architecture 127
Architecture, Domestic
   Old-House Dictionary 127
Archives
   Directory of Archives and Manuscript Repositories in the United States 185
Art
   Looking at Prints, Drawings and Watercolours 130
   The Oxford Dictionary of Art 125
   Plain Talk about Art 124
Art, Modern
   Contemporary Artists 125
   Dictionary of Contemporary American Artists 125

Subject Index

Artists
  Contemporary Artists 125
  Dictionary of Contemporary American Artists 125
Artists, Black
  Black Authors and Illustrators of Children's Books 34
Arts, American
  Images of Blacks in American Culture 123
Asia
  Encyclopedia of Asian History 182
Asia, Southeastern
  Atlas of Southeast Asia 170
Assassination
  Assassinations and Executions 179
Associations, institutions, etc.
  The Black Resource Guide 186
  Encyclopedia of Associations: Regional, State, and Local Organizations, 1988–89 52
Astronomy
  The Cambridge Atlas of Astronomy 104
  Earth Science on File 105
  The Guinness Book of Astronomy 104
Athletes
  Biographical Dictionary of American Sports: Outdoor Sports 148
Atlases
  Desk Reference World Atlas 166
  General Reference Books for Adults 38
  Hammond Discovery World Atlas 166
  Student's World Atlas 167
  The Times Family Atlas of the World 166
  World Atlas of Nations 167
Audio-visual materials
  Media Review Digest, 1987 145
Australia
  Australians 190
  The Concise Encyclopedia of Australia 191
Australian literature
  The Oxford Literary Guide to Australia 172
Authors
  Critical Survey of Mystery and Detective Fiction 155
  Index to Literary Criticism for Young Adults 152
  The Nobel Prize Winners: Literature 154
Authors, American
  Dictionary of Literary Biography Yearbook, 1987 154
  The Writer's Directory, 1988–90 150
Authors, Australian
  The Oxford Literary Guide to Australia 172
Authors, Black
  Black Authors and Illustrators of Children's Books 34
  Black Writers 160
Authors, Canadian
  The Oxford Illustrated Literary Guide to Canada 171

Authors, English
  Dictionary of Literary Biography Yearbook, 1987 154
  The Writer's Directory, 1988–90 150
Authorship
  Market Guide for Young Writers, 1988–89 150
Banks and banking
  American Banker Year Book, 1988 69
  The Financial 1000 69
Bereavement
  Books to Help Children Cope with Separation and Loss 55
Bible
  A Dictionary of Quotations from the Bible 56
  The Eerdmans Analytical Concordance to the Revised Standard Version of the Bible 57
  The International Standard Bible Encyclopedia 56
Bibliography
  America as Story 158
  The Bibliography of Contemporary American Fiction, 1945–1988 159
  The Catholic Novel 151
  Fantasy Literature for Children and Young Adults 151
  The Humanities 36
  Music Reference and Research Materials 132
  The Reader's Adviser 35
  A Reader's Guide to the Classic British Mystery 163
Bibliotherapy for children
  Books to Help Children Cope with Separation and Loss 55
Biography
  Almanac of Famous People 173
  Great Lives 173
  Index to Collective Biographies for Young Readers 174
Biology
  The Facts On File Dictionary of Biology 105
Bird populations
  Atlas of Wintering North American Birds 108
Birds
  Atlas of Wintering North American Birds 108
Blacks
  Black Dance 145
  Index to Afro-American Reference Resources 186
Book talks
  Introducing Bookplots 3 34
  Primaryplots 35
  Seniorplots 157
Books
  Young Adult Book Review Index, 1987 39
Books and reading
  Handbook of American Popular Literature 159

Booksellers and bookselling
  The Reader's Adviser 35
Botany
  The Marshall Cavendish Illustrated Encyclopedia of Plants and Earth Sciences 108
Botany, Economic
  The Marshall Cavendish Illustrated Encyclopedia of Plants and Earth Sciences 108
Broadcasting
  The Broadcast Communications Dictionary 89
Brokers
  The Financial 1000 69
Building
  Dictionary of Building 116
Business
  The Basic Business Library 74
Business education
  Bricker's Short-Term Executive Programs 121
Business libraries
  The Basic Business Library 74
Business mathematics
  Barron's Real Estate Handbook 70
Business names
  International Trade Names Dictionary, 1988–89 71
  International Trade Names Dictionary, 1988–89: Company Index 71

Canada
  The Canadian Encyclopedia 183
  Directory of Popular Culture Collections 184
  The Oxford Illustrated Literary Guide to Canada 171
Canadian periodicals
  The Directory of Humor Magazines and Humor Organizations in America (and Canada) 154
Cancer
  Third Opinion 79
Canvas embroidery
  Embroidery and Needlepoint 130
Cards
  The Book of Card Games 147
Celebrities
  V.I.P. Address Book, 1988–1989 173
Censorship
  Intellectual Freedom and Censorship 81
Characters and characteristics in literature
  Imaginary People 157
Chemistry
  The Facts On File Dictionary of Chemistry 105
Chemotherapy
  Orphan Drugs 113
Child development
  Resources for Middle Childhood 61
Children
  Books for Children to Read Alone 34
  Introducing Bookplots 3 34
  Primaryplots 35

Children and death
   The Dying Child 55
Children as actors
   Child and Youth Actors 143
Children as authors
   Market Guide for Young Writers, 1988–89 150
Children's encyclopedias and dictionaries
   Children's Britannica 50
   Raintree Children's Encyclopedia 49
   Young Students Learning Library 49
Children's librarians
   Children's Media Market Place 53
Children's literature
   The Art of Children's Picture Books 34
   Black Authors and Illustrators of Children's Books 34
   Books for Children to Read Alone 34
   Books for the Gifted Child 34
   Children's Media Market Place 53
   Children's Writer's & Illustrator's Market, 1989 150
   Fantasy Literature for Children and Young Adults 151
   Introducing Bookplots 3 34
   Primaryplots 35
Children's literature, American
   Black Authors and Illustrators of Children's Books 34
   Children's Literature Awards and Winners 39
Children's literature, English
   Children's Literature Awards and Winners 39
Children's reference books
   Reference Books for Young Readers 31
Chivalry
   Dictionary of Medieval Knighthood and Chivalry 177
Christian biography
   Lives of Famous Christians 58
Christian fiction
   The Catholic Novel 151
Chronology, Historical
   Time Lines on File 178
Church music
   The Music Locator, 1988 134
   The Recording Locator, 1988 134
Cities and towns
   Cities of the United States 172
Civil service
   Guide to Federal Technical, Trades and Labor Jobs 68
Civilization
   The Dictionary of Cultural Literacy 185
   Time Lines on File 178
Clerks of court
   BNA's Directory of State Courts, Judges, and Clerks 76
Coins, American
   Walter Breen's Complete Encyclopedia of U.S. and Colonial Coins 127
College, Choice of
   The GIS Guide to Four-Year Colleges, 1989 88

Comedians
   Comedy on Record 145
   Laughter on Record 145
Comic books, strips, etc.
   Comic Books and Strips 130
Communication
   International Encyclopedia of Communications 29
Compact discs
   CD Review Digest Annual, Volume 1, 1983–1987 139
Computer adventure games
   Interactive Fiction and Adventure Games for Microcomputers, 1988 147
Computer bulletin boards
   National Directory of Bulletin Board Systems, 1988/1989 30
Computer industry
   The Computer Industry Almanac 72
Computer software
   Survey of Early Childhood Software, 1988 86
Computer-assisted instruction
   Survey of Early Childhood Software, 1988 86
Computers
   McGraw-Hill Encyclopedia of Electronics and Computers 116
Condominiums
   Condo Vacations 120
   Vacation Condominiums for Rent 120
Congresses and conventions
   Seminars Directory 123
Conservatism
   The Radical Right 63
Conservatories of music
   The Schirmer Guide to Schools of Music and Conservatories throughout the World 134
Consolidation and merger of corporations
   Corporate TrendTrac 72
Continuing education
   Peterson's Guide to Certificate Programs at American Colleges and Universities 89
Cookery
   The Cook's Book of Useful Information 118
   Cooking A to Z 119
   The Guide to Cooking Schools, 1989 119
Cookery, American
   The American Regional Cookery Index 119
Cooking schools
   The Guide to Cooking Schools, 1989 119
Corporations
   International Directory of Company Histories 72
   Major Companies of Europe, 1988 73
   The National Directory of Corporate Training Programs 68
Costume
   Fairchild's Dictionary of Fashion 128
   The Historical Encyclopedia of Costumes 90

Costume designers
   Who's Who in Fashion 128
Council of Economic Advisers (U.S.)
   Biographical Directory of the Council of Economic Advisers 73
Courts
   BNA's Directory of State Courts, Judges, and Clerks 76
Creationism
   Anti-Evolution 107
Criticism
   Critical Survey of Literary Theory 149
Critics
   Critical Survey of Literary Theory 149
Crops
   The Marshall Cavendish Illustrated Encyclopedia of Plants and Earth Sciences 108
Cuba
   Historical Dictionary of Cuba 184
Cytology
   Dictionary of Genetics & Cell Biology 108

Decoration and ornament
   Concise Encyclopedia of Interior Design 129
Demonology
   Dictionary of Demons 54
Depressions
   New Day/New Deal 189
Detective and mystery stories
   Critical Survey of Mystery and Detective Fiction 155
Detective and mystery stories, English
   A Reader's Guide to the Classic British Mystery 163
Developmentally disabled
   Directory of Residential Centers for Adults with Developmental Disabilities 79
Devil
   Dictionary of Demons 54
Directories
   International Directories in Print, 1989–90 59
Disco music
   Find That Tune 135
Domestic engineering
   Domestic Technology 118
Domestic relations
   Family Law Dictionary 75
Drama
   The Drama Dictionary 155
   The Facts On File Dictionary of the Theatre 146
   500 Plays 153
   Ottemiller's Index to Plays in Collections 153
Dramatists, American
   American Playwrights since 1945 158
   Contemporary Dramatists 162

Dramatists, English
 Contemporary Dramatists 162
Drug abuse
 Drug, Alcohol, and Other Addictions 81
Drug trade
 Orphan Drugs 113
Drugs
 The American Medical Association Guide to Prescription and Over-the-Counter Drugs 113
Drugs, Non-prescription
 The American Medical Association Guide to Prescription and Over-the-Counter Drugs 113
Earth sciences
 Earth Science on File 105
 The Marshall Cavendish Illustrated Encyclopedia of Plants and Earth Sciences 108
Ecology
 Ecophilosophy 55
 World Nature Encyclopedia 107
Economists
 Biographical Directory of the Council of Economic Advisers 73
Education
 English Language and Orientation Programs in the United States 99
 The Facts On File Dictionary of Education 84
 Who's Who in American Education, 1988–1989 85
 World Education Encyclopedia 84
Education, Preschool
 Survey of Early Childhood Software, 1988 86
Education, Primary
 Survey of Early Childhood Software, 1988 86
Educational equalization
 Resources for Educational Equity 87
Educators
 Who's Who in American Education, 1988–1989 85
Elections
 American Governors and Gubernatorial Elections, 1979–1987 77
Electronics
 The Illustrated Dictionary of Electronics 116
 McGraw-Hill Encyclopedia of Electronics and Computers 116
Embroidery
 Embroidery and Needlepoint 130
Employee selection
 The Guide to Background Investigations, 1988 122
Employees, Training of
 The National Directory of Corporate Training Programs 68
 The Trainer's Resource, 1988 68
Encyclopedias and dictionaries
 Academic American Encyclopedia 40
 Compton's Encyclopedia and Fact-Index 42

 First Stop 44
 Funk & Wagnalls New Encyclopedia 44
 General Reference Books for Adults 38
 The Harper Dictionary of Modern Thought 46
 The Hutchinson Encyclopedia 52
 The New Electronic Encyclopedia 47
Engineering
 Dictionary of Engineering Acronyms and Abbreviations 115
 Encyclopedia of Physical Science and Technology 100
 The New Illustrated Science and Invention Encyclopedia 101
 Van Nostrand's Scientific Encyclopedia 102
English fiction
 Olderr's Fiction Index, 1987 153
 A Reader's Guide to the Classic British Mystery 163
English language
 The Barnhart Dictionary of Etymology 92
 Bernstein's Reverse Dictionary 96
 Book of Roots 93
 Childcraft Dictionary 94
 Common Allusions and Foreign Terms 94
 A Dictionary of American Idioms 97
 The Dictionary of Confusable Words 97
 A Dictionary of Contrasting Pairs 98
 The Dictionary of Cultural Literacy 185
 English Language and Orientation Programs in the United States 99
 The Facts On File Dictionary of Troublesome Words 97
 A Historical Dictionary of American Industrial Language 71
 The Lincoln Writing Dictionary for Children 95
 Morris Dictionary of Word and Phrase Origins 94
 The Oxford English Dictionary: On Compact Disc 91
 Roget's II 98
 The Roots of English 93
 Sports Talk 147
 The Thesaurus of Slang 98
 Webster's New World Dictionary of American English 95
 Webster's New World Guide to Current American Usage 99
English literature
 Dictionary of Literary Biography Yearbook, 1987 154
 An Encyclopedia of British Women Writers 161
 Modern Irish Literature 161
Environmental law
 Guide to State Environmental Programs 83
Environmental policy
 Guide to State Environmental Programs 83

Espionage
 The Encyclopedia of American Intelligence and Espionage 65
Espionage, American
 The Encyclopedia of American Intelligence and Espionage 65
Ethics
 Television & Ethics 56
Ethnicity
 Women of Color and Southern Women 61
Europe
 Major Companies of Europe, 1988 73
 Western Europe, 1989 63
European literature
 European Writers 156
Evolution
 Anti-Evolution 107
Excavations (Archaeology)
 A Guide to the Archaeological Sites of the British Isles 170
Executions and executioners
 Assassinations and Executions 179
Executives
 Moving Up 121
 Training and Development Organizations Directory 121
 Training Directory for Business and Industry, 1989–90 122
Executives, Training of
 Bricker's Short-Term Executive Programs 121
Exhibitions
 Traveler's Guide to Museum Exhibitions, 1989 52
Explorers, Women
 Women into the Unknown 164

Fantastic fiction
 Science Fiction & Fantasy Book Review Annual, 1988 156
Fantastic films
 Revenge of the Creature Features Movie Guide 144
Fantastic literature
 Fantasy Literature for Children and Young Adults 151
Fashion
 Fairchild's Dictionary of Fashion 128
Federal aid to handicapped services
 Financial Aid for the Disabled and Their Families, 1988–1989 82
Federal government
 The State and Local Government Political Dictionary 77
Festivals
 Festivals U.S.A. 90
Fetus
 Peace of Mind during Pregnancy 114
Fiction
 Fiction Writers Guidelines 150
 Olderr's Fiction Index, 1987 153

Film genres
   Handbook of American Film Genres 144
Finance
   Dictionary of Finance 69
Financial institutions
   The Financial 1000 69
Folklore
   The Facts On File Encyclopedia of World Mythology and Legend 59
Food
   Arrow's Complete Guide to Mail Order Foods 118
Food service
   Hotel and Restaurant Industries 74
Football
   The Pro Football Bio-Bibliography 148
Franchises (Retail trade)
   The Rating Guide to Franchises 74
Freedom of information
   Intellectual Freedom and Censorship 81
Frontier and pioneer life
   Encyclopedia of Frontier Biography 189

Games
   The Book of Card Games 147
Gardening
   Gardener's Index for 1987 117
Gardens
   The Traveler's Guide to American Gardens 126
Gas industry
   Oil and Gas Dictionary 116
Gazetteers
   Place-Names of the World 163
Genealogical libraries
   Directory of American Libraries with Genealogy or Local History Collections 38
Genealogy
   Directory of American Libraries with Genealogy or Local History Collections 38
   Genealogical Periodical Annual Index 176
   PERiodical Source Index, 1847–1985 175
Generals
   Fallen in Battle 184
Genetics
   Dictionary of Genetics & Cell Biology 108
Genocide
   Genocide 80
Geography
   Place-Names of the World 163
Geology
   McGraw-Hill Encyclopedia of the Geological Sciences 116
Germany
   The Third Reich Almanac 181
Gerontology
   Dictionary of Gerontology 60
   A Guide to Research in Gerontology 60

Gifted children
   Books for the Gifted Child 34
Gospel music
   The Recording Locator, 1988 134
Gothic revival (Literature)
   The Gothic's Gothic 151
Government, Resistance to
   Revolutionary and Dissident Movements 63
Governors
   American Governors and Gubernatorial Elections, 1979–1987 77
Grants-in-aid
   Financial Aid for the Disabled and Their Families, 1988–1989 82
Great Britain
   A Guide to the Archaeological Sites of the British Isles 170
   The Royals 180
   Victorian Britain 180
   Vital Records Handbook 176
Greece
   Place-Names in Classical Mythology 170
Greek language, Biblical
   The Eerdmans Analytical Concordance to the Revised Standard Version of the Bible 57
Group homes for the developmentally disabled
   Directory of Residential Centers for Adults with Developmental Disabilities 79

Handicapped
   Disability Drama in Television and Film 140
   Financial Aid for the Disabled and Their Families, 1988–1989 82
Handicapped in motion pictures
   Disability Drama in Television and Film 140
Handicapped in television
   Disability Drama in Television and Film 140
Health
   Health Media Review Index, 1984–86 112
   Health Resource Builder 110
Health education
   Allied Health Education Directory, 1988 109
   Health Media Review Index, 1984–86 112
Health occupation schools
   Allied Health Education Directory, 1988 109
Health promotion
   Disease Prevention/Health Promotion 111
Health resorts, watering-places, etc.
   Spas, 1988 111
Health services administration
   The Facts On File Dictionary of Health Care Management 78

Hebrew language
   The Eerdmans Analytical Concordance to the Revised Standard Version of the Bible 57
High interest-low vocabulary books
   High Interest Easy Reading 39
High school libraries
   High Interest Easy Reading 39
   Seniorplots 157
High technology
   Key to High-Tech 109
Hispanic Americans
   A Hispanic Heritage, Series III 187
   Hispanic Resource Directory 186
Historians
   The Blackwell Dictionary of Historians 178
Historic sites
   A Guide to the Archaeological Sites of the British Isles 170
Historical fiction, American
   America as Story 158
Historical libraries
   Directory of American Libraries with Genealogy or Local History Collections 38
History, Ancient
   Oxford Illustrated Encyclopedia, Volume 3 179
History, Modern
   Oxford Illustrated Encyclopedia, Volume 3 179
   Oxford Illustrated Encyclopedia, Volume 4 179
Holism
   Holistic Resources Directory, 1988/89 114
Home economics
   Domestic Technology 118
Horror films
   Horror 155
Horror tales
   The Gothic's Gothic 151
   Horror 155
Horticulture
   Gardener's Index for 1987 117
Hotels, taverns, etc.
   Hotel and Restaurant Industries 74
Human evolution
   Encyclopedia of Human Evolution and Prehistory 106
Humanities
   The Humanities 36

India
   A Social and Economic Atlas of India 168
Indians in motion pictures
   Native Americans on Film and Video 144
Indians of North America
   Historical Dictionary of North American Archaeology 182
   Nations within a Nation 187
   Native American Basketry 130

Information storage and retrieval systems
  Computer-Readable Databases 37
Instructional materials industry
  Children's Media Market Place 53
Insurance
  The Financial 1000 69
  Insurance Dictionary 83
Interior decoration
  Concise Encyclopedia of Interior Design 129
Interior decorators
  Who's Who in Interior Design 129
International relations
  The International Relations Dictionary 65
Ireland
  A Dictionary of Irish Biography 174
  A Guide to the Archaeological Sites of the British Isles 170
Ireland in literature
  Modern Irish Literature 161
Irish
  Irish American Material Culture 62
Irish Americans
  Irish American Material Culture 62

Jazz music
  The New Grove Dictionary of Jazz 138
Jews
  Jewish Heritage in America 187
Judaism
  Jewish Heritage in America 187
Judges
  BNA's Directory of State Courts, Judges, and Clerks 76
Junior high school libraries
  High Interest Easy Reading 39

Knights and knighthood
  Dictionary of Medieval Knighthood and Chivalry 177

Language and languages
  MLA Directory of Periodicals 149
Latin America
  Biographical Dictionary of Latin American and Caribbean Political Leaders 183
  A Hispanic Heritage, Series III 187
Latin language
  The Eerdmans Analytical Concordance to the Revised Standard Version of the Bible 57
Law
  Encyclopedia of Legal Information Sources 75
Libraries
  Intellectual Freedom and Censorship 81
  Video for Libraries 37
Libraries and new literates
  Books for Adult New Readers 87
Libraries, Children's
  Primaryplots 35
  Reference Books for Young Readers 31

Libraries, Young people's
  Reference Books for Young Readers 31
Life care communities
  National Continuing Care Directory 78
  National Directory of Retirement Facilities 120
Literacy
  Adult Literacy/Illiteracy in the United States 86
Literary landmarks
  The Oxford Illustrated Literary Guide to Canada 171
  The Oxford Literary Guide to Australia 172
Literary prizes
  Children's Literature Awards and Winners 39
Literature
  Critical Survey of Literary Theory 149
  MLA Directory of Periodicals 149
  The Reader's Adviser 35
Literature, Comparative
  Dictionary of Literary Themes and Motifs 157
Literature, Modern
  Contemporary Literary Criticism Yearbook, 1987 154
  The Nobel Prize Winners: Literature 154
Local elections
  The Historical Atlas of Political Parties in the United States Congress, 1789–1989 168
Local finance
  The State and Local Government Political Dictionary 77
Local government
  The State and Local Government Political Dictionary 77
Local history
  Directory of American Libraries with Genealogy or Local History Collections 38
Loss (Psychology)
  Books to Help Children Cope with Separation and Loss 55

Man, Prehistoric
  Encyclopedia of Human Evolution and Prehistory 106
Management
  Bricker's Short-Term Executive Programs 121
  Moving Up 121
  Training and Development Organizations Directory 121
  Training Directory for Business and Industry, 1989–90 122
Manufacturing processes
  Product and Process 109
Maps
  The World Map Directory, 1989 168
Marketing research
  Marketsearch 120
Medical education
  Allied Health Education Directory, 1988 109

Medicine, Preventive
  Disease Prevention/Health Promotion 111
Metaphor
  Sports Talk 147
Microcomputers
  McGraw-Hill Personal Computer Programming Encyclopedia 31
Microfilm services
  Microform Market Place, 1988–1989 53
Micropublishing
  Microform Market Place, 1988–1989 53
Middle East
  Atlas of the Middle East 169
  The Cambridge Encyclopedia of the Middle East and North Africa 169
  A Dictionary of Ancient Near Eastern Architecture 127
Minority women
  Women of Color in the United States 62
Mortgage loans
  Real Estate Dictionary 70
Motion picture actors and actresses
  British Film Actors' Credits, 1895–1987 143
  Child and Youth Actors 143
Motion picture industry
  The International Film Industry 142
Motion picture music
  Film, Television and Stage Music on Phonographic Records 133
Motion picture producers and directors
  The BFI Companion to the Western 142
Motion picture remakes
  Cinema Sequels and Remakes, 1903–1987 143
Motion picture sequels
  Cinema Sequels and Remakes, 1903–1987 143
Motion picture studios
  American Film Studios 141
Motion pictures
  The American Film Institute Catalog of Motion Pictures Produced in the United States 141
  Annual Index to Motion Picture Credits, 1987 141
  British Film Actors' Credits, 1895–1987 143
  Child and Youth Actors 143
  Handbook of American Film Genres 144
  Media Review Digest, 1987 145
Municipal government
  The Municipal Year Book, 1988 76
  The State and Local Government Political Dictionary 77
Museums
  Traveler's Guide to Museum Exhibitions, 1989 52
Music
  The Concise Baker's Biographical Dictionary of Musicians 134
  The Literature of American Music in Books and Folk Music Collections 133
  Music 133
  Music Directory Canada '88 132

Music Reference and Research Materials 132
The Norton/Grove Concise Encyclopedia of Music 132
Music, Popular (Songs, etc.)
    Heat Wave 137
Musical revues, comedies, etc
    Catalog of the American Musical 136
    Gänzl's Book of the Musical Theatre 136
Musical revues, comedies, etc.
    Film, Television and Stage Music on Phonographic Records 133
Musicians
    The Concise Baker's Biographical Dictionary of Musicians 134
Musicians, Black
    Blacks in Classical Music 133
Mythology
    The Facts On File Encyclopedia of World Mythology and Legend 59
Mythology, Greek
    Place-Names in Classical Mythology 170

Names, Geographical
    Place-Names of the World 163
Names, Personal
    A Dictionary of Surnames 177
Narcotic addicts
    Drug, Alcohol, and Other Addictions 81
National parks and reserves
    Access America 171
National socialism
    The Third Reich Almanac 181
National songs
    National Anthems of the World 137
Naturopathy
    The Illustrated Dictionary of Natural Health 114
New Deal, 1933–1939
    New Day/New Deal 189
New Zealand
    The Bateman New Zealand Encyclopedia 190
Nobel prizes
    The Nobel Peace Prize and the Laureates 66
    The Nobel Prize Winners: Literature 154
North America
    Historical Dictionary of North American Archaeology 182
    The Penguin Atlas of North American History to 1870 165
Nuclear warfare
    The ABCs of Armageddon 78
Nursing
    Health Media Review Index, 1984–86 112
Nutrition
    The Columbia Encyclopedia of Nutrition 111

Oceanography
    The Facts On File Dictionary of Marine Science 105

Opera
    Opera Annual 136
Operas
    Gänzl's Book of the Musical Theatre 136
Operating systems (Computers)
    McGraw-Hill Personal Computer Programming Encyclopedia 31
Orphan drugs
    Orphan Drugs 113

Pacifists
    The Nobel Peace Prize and the Laureates 66
Paramedical education
    Allied Health Education Directory, 1988 109
Patchwork
    The New Quilting & Patchwork Dictionary 129
Peace
    The Nobel Peace Prize and the Laureates 66
    Peace Organizations Past and Present 66
    Peace Resource Book, 1988–1989 66
Periodicals
    MLA Directory of Periodicals 149
    Ulrich's International Periodicals Directory, 1988–89 32
Personnel management
    The Guide to Background Investigations, 1988 122
    The Trainer's Resource, 1988 68
    Training Directory for Business and Industry, 1989–90 122
Petroleum industry and trade
    Oil and Gas Dictionary 116
Photographers
    Contemporary Photographers 131
Photography, Artistic
    Contemporary Photographers 131
Physical geography
    Dictionary of Concepts in Physical Geography 163
Picture-books for children
    The Art of Children's Picture Books 34
Pictures
    Illustration Index VI 33
Playwriting
    Dramatists Sourcebook 146
Poetry
    Poet's Handbook 53
Police
    The Encyclopedia of Police Science 82
Political parties
    The Historical Atlas of Political Parties in the United States Congress, 1789–1989 168
Politicians
    Biographical Dictionary of Latin American and Caribbean Political Leaders 183
Popular literature
    Handbook of American Popular Literature 159

Popular music
    Encyclopedia of Pop, Rock & Soul 135
    The Great Song Thesaurus 137
    Who Wrote That Song? 137
Power (Mechanics)
    Dictionary of Energy 116
Power resources
    Dictionary of Energy 116
Pregnancy
    Peace of Mind during Pregnancy 114
Presidents
    America at the Polls 2 65
    Records of the Presidency 77
Pressure groups
    Public Interest Profiles, 1988–1989 64
Private schools
    Peterson's Guide to Independent Secondary Schools, 1988–89 86
    Private Independent Schools, 1988 86
Programming languages (Electronic computers)
    McGraw-Hill Personal Computer Programming Encyclopedia 31
Prospecting
    Directory of Treasure Hunting, Prospecting, and Related Organizations 164
Psychical research
    Lives and Letters in American Parapsychology 54
Psychology
    The International Dictionary of Psychology 54
Public administration
    The Public Administration Dictionary 76
Public health
    Disease Prevention/Health Promotion 111
    Health Media Review Index, 1984–86 112
Public libraries
    Video for Libraries 37
Publishers and publishing
    Index to Collective Biographies for Young Readers 174
    Market Guide for Young Writers, 1988–89 150

Quacks and quackery
    Alternative Therapies, Unproven Methods, and Health Fraud 112
Quilting
    The New Quilting & Patchwork Dictionary 129

Radio stations, Short wave
    Passport to World Band Radio 90
Radio, Short wave
    Passport to World Band Radio 90
Readers for new literates
    Books for Adult New Readers 87
Real estate business
    Barron's Real Estate Handbook 70
    The Dictionary of Real Estate Appraisal 70
    The Language of Real Estate 71

Real Estate Dictionary 70
Real property
  The Dictionary of Real Estate Appraisal 70
  The Language of Real Estate 71
Recreation areas and the handicapped
  Access America 171
Reference books
  American Reference Books Annual, 1988 31
  The Art of Children's Picture Books 34
  The Basic Business Library 74
  First Stop 44
  General Reference Books for Adults 38
  Government Reference Serials 67
  A Guide to Research in Gerontology 60
  The Humanities 36
  Index to Afro-American Reference Resources 186
  Information Sources in Science and Technology 102
  Music 133
  The Reader's Adviser 35
  Science and Technology Annual Reference Review, 1989 102
Reference books, Spanish
  Spanish-Language Reference Books 32
Registers of births, etc.
  Passenger and Immigration Lists Bibliography, 1538–1900 177
  Vital Records Handbook 176
Religious biography
  Twentieth-Century Shapers of American Popular Religion 58
Renewable energy sources
  Synerjy 74
Reptiles
  The Completely Illustrated Atlas of Reptiles and Amphibians for the Terrarium 117
Resorts
  Condo Vacations 120
Restaurants, lunch rooms, etc.
  Hotel and Restaurant Industries 74
Retirement communities
  National Continuing Care Directory 78
  National Directory of Retirement Facilities 120
Retirement, Places of
  National Directory of Retirement Facilities 120
Rewards (Prizes, etc.)
  World of Winners 29
Rock music
  Encyclopedia of Pop, Rock & Soul 135
  Encyclopedia of Rock 135
  Find That Tune 135
  The Harmony Illustrated Encyclopedia of Rock 135
  The History of Rock and Roll 140

Scandals
  Encyclopedia of American Scandal 184
School children
  Resources for Middle Childhood 61
School management and organization
  Encyclopedia of School Administration & Supervision 86
School supervision
  Encyclopedia of School Administration & Supervision 86
Science
  Encyclopedia of Physical Science and Technology 100
  The Encyclopedic Dictionary of Science 100
  Information Sources in Science and Technology 102
  McGraw-Hill Dictionary of Scientific and Technical Terms 101
  The New Illustrated Science and Invention Encyclopedia 101
  Science and Technology Annual Reference Review, 1989 102
  Science Experiments Index for Young People 103
  Science Experiments on File 103
  The Timetables of Science 103
  Van Nostrand's Scientific Encyclopedia 102
Science fiction
  More than 100 152
  The New Encyclopedia of Science Fiction 124
  Science Fiction & Fantasy Book Review Annual, 1988 156
Self-help groups
  The Self-Help Sourcebook 87
Seminars
  Seminars Directory 123
Separation (Psychology)
  Books to Help Children Cope with Separation and Loss 55
Serial publications
  Government Reference Serials 67
Sex in mass media
  Violence and Terror in the Mass Media 60
Shakespeare, William
  The Quotable Shakespeare 162
Ships
  Passenger and Immigration Lists Bibliography, 1538–1900 177
Slavery
  Dictionary of Afro-American Slavery 62
Small business
  Free Help from Uncle Sam to Start Your Own Business (Or Expand the One You Have) 77
Social registers
  V.I.P. Address Book, 1988–1989 173
Socialization
  Resources for Middle Childhood 61
Societies
  Encyclopedia of Associations: Regional, State, and Local Organizations, 1988–89 52

Soul music
  Encyclopedia of Pop, Rock & Soul 135
Sound recording industry
  Heat Wave 137
Sound recordings
  CD Review Digest Annual, Volume 1, 1983–1987 139
  Comedy on Record 145
Southern States
  Cities of the United States 172
Soviet Union
  The Blackwell Encyclopedia of the Russian Revolution 181
Spain
  A Hispanic Heritage, Series III 187
Speeches, addresses, etc., American
  We Shall Be Heard 160
Sports
  Biographical Dictionary of American Sports: Outdoor Sports 148
  Guinness Sports Record Book, 1988–89 147
  The Sports Address Book 148
  Sports Talk 147
Sports camps
  The Sports Address Book 148
Sports promoters
  Biographical Dictionary of American Sports: Outdoor Sports 148
State governments
  The State and Local Government Political Dictionary 77
Statesmen
  Biographical Dictionary of Latin American and Caribbean Political Leaders 183
Statistics
  Comparative World Data 104
Stereotype (Psychology)
  Disability Drama in Television and Film 140
Subject headings
  Women in LC's Terms 37
Subject headings, Library of Congress
  Women in LC's Terms 37
Suicide
  The Encyclopedia of Suicide 79

Technology
  Encyclopedia of Physical Science and Technology 100
  Information Sources in Science and Technology 102
  McGraw-Hill Dictionary of Scientific and Technical Terms 101
  Product and Process 109
  Science and Technology Annual Reference Review, 1989 102
Teenagers
  Seniorplots 157
Television broadcasting
  Television & Ethics 56
Television music
  Film, Television and Stage Music on Phonographic Records 133

Television programs for children
  Children's Media Market Place 53
Teratogenic agents
  Peace of Mind during Pregnancy 114
Terminally ill children
  The Dying Child 55
Terrariums
  The Completely Illustrated Atlas of Reptiles and Amphibians for the Terrarium 117
Terrorism in mass media
  Violence and Terror in the Mass Media 60
Textbook bias
  Resources for Educational Equity 87
Theater
  American Playwrights since 1945 158
  The Cambridge Guide to World Theatre 146
  The Facts On File Dictionary of the Theatre 146
Theaters
  Dramatists Sourcebook 146
Theology
  New Dictionary of Theology 57
Trademarks
  International Trade Names Dictionary, 1988–89 71
  International Trade Names Dictionary, 1988–89: Company Index 71
Treasure-trove
  Directory of Treasure Hunting, Prospecting, and Related Organizations 164

U.S.
  Almanac of the American People 68
  America as Story 158
  Business Serials of the U.S. Government 67
  The Civil War Dictionary 188
  The Dictionary of Cultural Literacy 185
  Directory of American Libraries with Genealogy or Local History Collections 38
  Directory of Popular Culture Collections 184
  Encyclopedia of American Scandal 184
  The Executive Branch of the U.S. Government 76
  The Faces of America 175
  Fallen in Battle 184
  Government Reference Serials 67
  Guide to Federal Technical, Trades and Labor Jobs 68
  Handbook of American Popular Literature 159
  The Historical Atlas of Political Parties in the United States Congress, 1789–1989 168
  Historical Atlas of the United States 165

A Historical Dictionary of American Industrial Language 71
Historical Dictionary of the 1920s 189
Jewish Heritage in America 187
New Day/New Deal 189
Passenger and Immigration Lists Bibliography, 1538–1900 177
Population Information in Twentieth Century Census Volumes 60
Research Guide to American Historical Biography 175
Since 1776 185
The Traveler's Guide to American Gardens 126
Twentieth-Century Shapers of American Popular Religion 58
V.I.P. Address Book, 1988–1989 173
Vacation Condominiums for Rent 120
Vital Records Handbook 176
Vital Statistics on American Politics 64
Who Was Who in the Civil War 188
U.S. Congress
  Congress A to Z 67
Ukraine
  Encyclopedia of Ukraine 181
Universities and colleges
  American College Regalia 88
  The GIS Guide to Four-Year Colleges, 1989 88
  Peterson's Guide to Certificate Programs at American Colleges and Universities 89
  Peterson's Higher Education Directory, 1988 89

Vertebrates, Fossil
  The Macmillan Illustrated Encyclopedia of Dinosaurs and Prehistoric Animals 106
Vice-Presidents
  Our Vice-Presidents and Second Ladies 188
Video recordings
  Video for Libraries 37
  The Video Source Book, 1989 33
Video tapes
  Variety's Complete Home Video Directory, 1988 33
Vietnamese conflict, 1961–1975
  Vietnam War Literature 160
Violence in mass media
  Violence and Terror in the Mass Media 60
Visual education
  Media Review Digest, 1987 145
Vocational education
  Peterson's Guide to Certificate Programs at American Colleges and Universities 89

West (U.S.)
  The BFI Companion to the Western 142
  Encyclopedia of Frontier Biography 189
Western films
  The BFI Companion to the Western 142
Wide screen processes (Cinematography)
  Wide Screen Movies 131
Wit and humor
  The Directory of Humor Magazines and Humor Organizations in America (and Canada) 154
  Laughter on Record 145
Women
  Index to Women of the World from Ancient to Modern Times 174
  We Shall Be Heard 160
  Women of Color and Southern Women 61
  Women's Health Perspectives 110
Women authors, American
  American Women Writers 158
Women authors, English
  An Encyclopedia of British Women Writers 161
Women in Judaism
  Women and Judaism 58
Women orators
  We Shall Be Heard 160
Women, Black
  Women of Color and Southern Women 61
Women, Jewish
  Women and Judaism 58
Workshops
  Seminars Directory 123
World politics
  The Facts On File World Political Almanac 180
World records
  Number One in the U.S.A. 50

Young adult fiction, American
  American as Story 158
Young adult literature
  Authors & Artists for Young Adults 156
  Fantasy Literature for Children and Young Adults 151
  Index to Literary Criticism for Young Adults 152
  Olderr's Fiction Index, 1987 153
  Seniorplots 157
  Young Adult Book Review Index, 1987 39
Young adults
  Authors & Artists for Young Adults 156
  Seniorplots 157
Youth
  Directory of American Youth Organizations 83
  Encyclopedia of Good Health 110

Zip code
  Hammond Discovery World Atlas 166

INDEX TO TYPE OF MATERIAL

ALMANACS
   Almanac of the American People 68
   The Computer Industry Almanac 72
   The Facts On File World Political Almanac 180

ANNUALS
   Opera Annual 136
   Science Fiction & Fantasy Book Review Annual, 1988 156

ATLASES
   Atlas of Southeast Asia 170
   Atlas of the Middle East 169
   Atlas of Wintering North American Birds 108
   Australians 190
   The Cambridge Atlas of Astronomy 104
   Desk Reference World Atlas 166
   Hammond Discovery World Atlas 166
   The Historical Atlas of Political Parties in the United States Congress, 1789–1989 168
   Historical Atlas of the United States 165
   Past Worlds 167
   The Penguin Atlas of North American History to 1870 165
   A Social and Economic Atlas of India 168
   Student's World Atlas 167
   The Times Family Atlas of the World 166
   World Atlas of Nations 167

BIBLIOGRAPHIES
   AIDS 112
   AIDS Bibliography for 1981–1986 112
   Alternative Therapies, Unproven Methods, and Health Fraud 112
   America as Story 158
   American Playwrights since 1945 158
   American Reference Books Annual, 1988 31
   Anti-Evolution 107
   Architecture and Women 126
   The Art of Children's Picture Books 34
   The Basic Business Library 74
   The Bibliography of Contemporary American Fiction, 1945–1988 159

Black Children and American Institutions 61
Black Dance 145
Blacks in Classical Music 133
Books for Adult New Readers 87
Books for Children to Read Alone 34
Books for the Gifted Child 34
Books to Help Children Cope with Separation and Loss 55
Business Serials of the U.S. Government 67
The Catholic Novel 151
Comic Books and Strips 130
Crime and the Elderly 80
The Dying Child 55
Ecophilosophy 55
Embroidery and Needlepoint 130
Encyclopedia of Legal Information Sources 75
The Executive Branch of the U.S. Government 76
Fantasy Literature for Children and Young Adults 151
General Reference Books for Adults 38
Genocide 80
The Gothic's Gothic 151
Government Reference Serials 67
Handbook of American Popular Literature 159
High Interest Easy Reading 39
A Hispanic Heritage, Series III 187
Hotel and Restaurant Industries 74
How to Find Information about AIDS 115
The Humanities 36
Information Sources in Science and Technology 102
Intellectual Freedom and Censorship 81
Interactive Fiction and Adventure Games for Microcomputers, 1988 147
Introducing Bookplots 3 34
Jewish Heritage in America 187
The Literature of American Music in Books and Folk Music Collections 133
Marketsearch 120
Music 133
The Music Locator, 1988 134
Music Reference and Research Materials 132

Native American Basketry 130
New Day/New Deal 189
Passenger and Immigration Lists Bibliography, 1538–1900 177
The Pro Football Bio-Bibliography 148
Psychological and Medical Aspects of Induced Abortion 113
The Reader's Adviser 35
A Reader's Guide to the Classic British Mystery 163
Reference Books for Young Readers 31
Resources for Educational Equity 87
Resources for Middle Childhood 61
Spanish-Language Reference Books 32
Synerjy 74
Television & Ethics 56
Vietnam War Literature 160
Violence and Terror in the Mass Media 60
Who Wrote That Song? 137
Women and Judaism 58
Women of Color and Southern Women 61
Women of Color in the United States 62
Women's Health Perspectives 110
The World Map Directory, 1989 168

BIOGRAPHICAL DICTIONARIES
   Authors & Artists for Young Adults 156
   Biographical Dictionary of American Sports: Outdoor Sports 148
   Biographical Dictionary of Latin American and Caribbean Political Leaders 183
   Biographical Directory of the Council of Economic Advisers 73
   Black Authors and Illustrators of Children's Books 34
   Black Writers 160
   Blacks in American Films and Television 142
   The Blackwell Dictionary of Historians 178
   British Film Actors' Credits, 1895–1987 143
   The Concise Baker's Biographical Dictionary of Musicians 134
   Contemporary Artists 125
   Contemporary Black American Playwrights and Their Plays 161

Contemporary Dramatists 162
Dictionary of Contemporary American Artists 125
A Dictionary of Irish Biography 174
Dictionary of Literary Biography Yearbook, 1987 154
A Encyclopedia of British Women Writers 161
Encyclopedia of Frontier Biography 189
The Faces of America 175
Fallen in Battle 184
Great Lives 173
Lives and Letters in American Parapsychology 54
Lives of Famous Christians 58
More than 100 152
The Nobel Peace Prize and the Laureates 66
The Nobel Prize Winners: Literature 154
Our Vice-Presidents and Second Ladies 188
Research Guide to American Historical Biography 175
Twentieth-Century Shapers of American Popular Religion 58
Who Was Who in the Civil War 188
Who's Who in American Education, 1988–1989 85
Who's Who in Fashion 128
Who's Who in Interior Design 129
Women into the Unknown 164

CATALOGS
The American Film Institute Catalog of Motion Pictures Produced in the United States 141
Arrow's Complete Guide to Mail Order Foods 118
Catalog of the American Musical 136
Survey of Early Childhood Software, 1988 86
The Trainer's Resource, 1988 68
Variety's Complete Home Video Directory, 1988 33

CHRONOLOGIES
Assassinations and Executions 179
Domestic Technology 118
Since 1776 185
Time Lines on File 178
The Timetables of Science 103

CRITICISM
American Women Writers 158
Contemporary Literary Criticism Yearbook, 1987 154
Critical Survey of Literary Theory 149
Critical Survey of Mystery and Detective Fiction 155
European Writers 156
Horror 155
Modern Irish Literature 161

DICTIONARIES
The ABCs of Armageddon 78
American Film Studios 141
The Barnhart Dictionary of Etymology 92
Barron's Real Estate Handbook 70
Bernstein's Reverse Dictionary 96
The BFI Companion to the Western 142
Book of Roots 93
The Broadcast Communications Dictionary 89
The Cambridge Guide to World Theatre 146
Childcraft Dictionary 94
The Civil War Dictionary 188
The Columbia Encyclopedia of Nutrition 111
Common Allusions and Foreign Terms 94
Concise Dictionary of Acronyms and Initialisms 96
Concise Encyclopedia of Interior Design 129
Contemporary Photographers 131
The Cook's Book of Useful Information 118
Cooking A to Z 119
A Dictionary of American Idioms 97
A Dictionary of Ancient Near Eastern Architecture 127
Dictionary of Building 116
Dictionary of Concepts in Physical Geography 163
The Dictionary of Confusable Words 97
A Dictionary of Contrasting Pairs 98
The Dictionary of Cultural Literacy 185
Dictionary of Demons 54
Dictionary of Energy 116
Dictionary of Engineering Acronyms and Abbreviations 115
Dictionary of Finance 69
Dictionary of Genetics & Cell Biology 108
Dictionary of Gerontology 60
Dictionary of Literary Themes and Motifs 157
Dictionary of Medieval Knighthood and Chivalry 177
A Dictionary of Quotations from the Bible 56
The Dictionary of Real Estate Appraisal 70
A Dictionary of Surnames 177
The Drama Dictionary 155
Encyclopedia of American Scandal 184
Encyclopedia of Pop, Rock & Soul 135
Encyclopedia of Rock 135
Encyclopedia of the World's Air Forces 78
The Encyclopedic Dictionary of Science 100
The Facts On File Dictionary of Biology 105
The Facts On File Dictionary of Chemistry 105
The Facts On File Dictionary of Education 84
The Facts On File Dictionary of Health Care Management 78
The Facts On File Dictionary of Marine Science 105
The Facts On File Dictionary of the Theatre 146
The Facts On File Dictionary of Troublesome Words 97
Fairchild's Dictionary of Fashion 128
Family Law Dictionary 75
The Harmony Illustrated Encyclopedia of Rock 135
The Harper Dictionary of Modern Thought 46
A Historical Dictionary of American Industrial Language 71
Historical Dictionary of Cuba 184
Historical Dictionary of North American Archaeology 182
Historical Dictionary of the 1920s 189
The Illustrated Dictionary of Electronics 116
The Illustrated Dictionary of Natural Health 114
Imaginary People 157
Insurance Dictionary 83
The International Dictionary of Psychology 54
The International Film Industry 142
The International Relations Dictionary 65
The International Standard Bible Encyclopedia 56
Key to High-Tech 109
The Language of Real Estate 71
The Lincoln Writing Dictionary for Children 95
Looking at Prints, Drawings and Watercolours 130
McGraw-Hill Dictionary of Scientific and Technical Terms 101
Morris Dictionary of Word and Phrase Origins 94
New Dictionary of Theology 57
The New Quilting & Patchwork Dictionary 129
Oil and Gas Dictionary 116
Old-House Dictionary 127
The Oxford Dictionary of Art 125
The Oxford English Dictionary: On Compact Disc 91
The Oxford Literary Guide to Australia 172
Peace of Mind during Pregnancy 114
Plain Talk about Art 124
The Public Administration Dictionary 76
The Quotable Shakespeare 162
Real Estate Dictionary 70
Roget's II 98
The Roots of English 93
The Royals 180
Sports Talk 147
The State and Local Government Political Dictionary 77
The Thesaurus of Slang 98
The Third Reich Almanac 181

Victorian Britain 180
Webster's New World Dictionary of American English 95
Webster's New World Guide to Current American Usage 99
Women in LC's Terms 37

DIRECTORIES
AIDS Information Resources Directory 114
Allied Health Education Directory, 1988 109
The Black Resource Guide 186
BNA's Directory of State Courts, Judges, and Clerks 76
Bricker's Short-Term Executive Programs 121
Children's Literature Awards and Winners 39
Children's Media Market Place 53
Children's Writer's & Illustrator's Market, 1989 150
Computer-Readable Databases 37
Condo Vacations 120
Directory of American Libraries with Genealogy or Local History Collections 38
Directory of American Youth Organizations 83
Directory of Archives and Manuscript Repositories in the United States 185
The Directory of Humor Magazines and Humor Organizations in America (and Canada) 154
Directory of Popular Culture Collections 184
Directory of Residential Centers for Adults with Developmental Disabilities 79
Directory of Treasure Hunting, Prospecting, and Related Organizations 164
Dramatists Sourcebook 146
Drug, Alcohol, and Other Addictions 81
Encyclopedia of Associations: Regional, State, and Local Organizations, 1988–89 52
English Language and Orientation Programs in the United States 99
The Financial 1000 69
Financial Aid for the Disabled and Their Families, 1988–1989 82
The GIS Guide to Four-Year Colleges, 1989 88
The Guide to Cooking Schools, 1989 119
Guide to Federal Technical, Trades and Labor Jobs 68
Health Resource Builder 110
Hispanic Resource Directory 186
Holistic Resources Directory, 1988/89 114
How to Find Information about AIDS 115
International Directories in Print, 1989–90 59
International Trade Names Dictionary, 1988 89 71
International Trade Names Dictionary, 1988–89: Company Index 71
Irish American Material Culture 62
Major Companies of Europe, 1988 73
Market Guide for Young Writers, 1988–89 150
Microform Market Place, 1988–1989 53
MLA Directory of Periodicals 149
Moving Up 121
Music Directory Canada '88 132
National Continuing Care Directory 78
National Directory of Bulletin Board Systems, 1988/1989 30
The National Directory of Corporate Training Programs 68
National Directory of Retirement Facilities 120
The 100 Best Treatment Centers for Alcoholism and Drug Abuse 81
Orphan Drugs 113
Passport to World Band Radio 90
Peace Organizations Past and Present 66
Peace Resource Book, 1988–1989 66
Peterson's Guide to Certificate Programs at American Colleges and Universities 89
Peterson's Guide to Independent Secondary Schools, 1988–89 86
Peterson's Higher Education Directory, 1988 89
Poet's Handbook 53
Private Independent Schools, 1988 86
Public Interest Profiles, 1988–1989 64
The Radical Right 63
The Rating Guide to Franchises 74
Records of the Presidency 77
Rehab 81
Revolutionary and Dissident Movements 63
The Schirmer Guide to Schools of Music and Conservatories throughout the World 134
The Self-Help Sourcebook 87
Seminars Directory 123
Spas, 1988 111
The Sports Address Book 148
Third Opinion 79
Training and Development Organizations Directory 121
Training Directory for Business and Industry, 1989–90 122
Traveler's Guide to Museum Exhibitions, 1989 52
Ulrich's International Periodicals Directory, 1988–89 32
V.I.P. Address Book, 1988–1989 173
Vacation Condominiums for Rent 120
World of Winners 29
The Writer's Directory, 1988–90 150

DISCOGRAPHIES
Comedy on Record 145
Film, Television and Stage Music on Phonographic Records 133
Heat Wave 137
The History of Rock and Roll 140
Laughter on Record 145
The Recording Locator, 1988 134

ENCYCLOPEDIAS
Academic American Encyclopedia 40
The Bateman New Zealand Encyclopedia 190
The Blackwell Encyclopedia of the Russian Revolution 181
The Cambridge Encyclopedia of the Middle East and North Africa 169
The Canadian Encyclopedia 183
Children's Britannica 50
Cities of the United States 172
Compton's Encyclopedia and Fact-Index 42
The Concise Encyclopedia of Australia 191
Congress A to Z 67
Dictionary of Afro-American Slavery 62
The Encyclopedia of American Intelligence and Espionage 65
Encyclopedia of Architecture 126
Encyclopedia of Asian History 182
Encyclopedia of Good Health 110
Encyclopedia of Human Evolution and Prehistory 106
Encyclopedia of Physical Science and Technology 100
The Encyclopedia of Police Science 82
Encyclopedia of School Administration & Supervision 86
The Encyclopedia of Suicide 79
Encyclopedia of Ukraine 181
The Facts On File Encyclopedia of World Mythology and Legend 59
Funk & Wagnalls New Encyclopedia 44
The Hutchinson Encyclopedia 52
International Directory of Company Histories 72
International Encyclopedia of Communications 29
The Macmillan Illustrated Encyclopedia of Dinosaurs and Prehistoric Animals 106
The Marshall Cavendish Illustrated Encyclopedia of Plants and Earth Sciences 108
McGraw-Hill Encyclopedia of Electronics and Computers 116
McGraw-Hill Encyclopedia of the Geological Sciences 116
McGraw-Hill Personal Computer Programming Encyclopedia 31
The New Electronic Encyclopedia 47
The New Encyclopedia of Science Fiction 124
The New Grove Dictionary of Jazz 138
The New Illustrated Science and Invention Encyclopedia 101
The Norton/Grove Concise Encyclopedia of Music 132
Oxford Illustrated Encyclopedia, Volume 3 179

Oxford Illustrated Encyclopedia, Volume 4 179
Raintree Children's Encyclopedia 49
Van Nostrand's Scientific Encyclopedia 102
Walter Breen's Complete Encyclopedia of U.S. and Colonial Coins 127
World Education Encyclopedia 84
World Nature Encyclopedia 107
Young Students Learning Library 49

FILMOGRAPHIES
Child and Youth Actors 143
Cinema Sequels and Remakes, 1903–1987 143
Disability Drama in Television and Film 140
Native Americans on Film and Video 144
Revenge of the Creature Features Movie Guide 144
Video for Libraries 37
The Video Source Book, 1989 33
Wide Screen Movies 131

GAZETTEERS
Place Names of Africa, 1935–1986 164
Place-Names in Classical Mythology 170
Place-Names of the World 163

GUIDEBOOKS
Access America 171
Festivals U.S.A. 90
A Guide to the Archaeological Sites of the British Isles 170
The Oxford Illustrated Literary Guide to Canada 171
The Traveler's Guide to American Gardens 126

HANDBOOKS
Adult Literacy/Illiteracy in the United States 86
American College Regalia 88
American Governors and Gubernatorial Elections, 1979–1987 77
The American Medical Association Guide to Prescription and Over-the-Counter Drugs 113
The Book of Card Games 147
The Completely Illustrated Atlas of Reptiles and Amphibians for the Terrarium 117
Disease Prevention/Health Promotion 111
Dr. Burgess's Atlas of Marine Aquarium Fishes 117
Free Help from Uncle Sam to Start Your Own Business (Or Expand the One You Have) 77
The Guide to Background Investigations, 1988 122
A Guide to Research in Gerontology 60
Guide to State Environmental Programs 83
The Guinness Book of Astronomy 104
Handbook of American Film Genres 144
Images of Blacks in American Culture 123
Primaryplots 35
Vital Records Handbook 176
Western Europe, 1989 63

INDEXES
Almanac of Famous People 173
The American Regional Cookery Index 119
Annual Index to Motion Picture Credits, 1987 141
CD Review Digest Annual, Volume 1, 1983–1987 139
Corporate TrendTrac 72
The Eerdmans Analytical Concordance to the Revised Standard Version of the Bible 57
Find That Tune 135
First Stop 44
Gardener's Index for 1987 117
Genealogical Periodical Annual Index 176
The Great Song Thesaurus 137
Health Media Review Index, 1984–86 112
Illustration Index VI 33
Index to Afro-American Reference Resources 186
Index to Collective Biographies for Young Readers 174
Index to Literary Criticism for Young Adults 152
Index to Women of the World from Ancient to Modern Times 174
Media Review Digest, 1987 145
Olderr's Fiction Index, 1987 153
Ottemiller's Index to Plays in Collections 153
PERiodical Source Index, 1847–1985 175
Population Information in Twentieth Century Census Volumes 60
Product and Process 109
Science Experiments Index for Young People 103
We Shall Be Heard 160
Young Adult Book Review Index, 1987 39

SOURCEBOOKS
America at the Polls 2 65
American Banker Year Book, 1988 69
Comparative World Data 104
Earth Science on File 105
Fiction Writers Guidelines 150
500 Plays 153
Gänzl's Book of the Musical Theatre 136
Guinness Sports Record Book, 1988–89 147
The Historical Encyclopedia of Costumes 90
The Municipal Year Book, 1988 76
National Anthems of the World 137
Nations within a Nation 187
Number One in the U.S.A. 50
Pictorial Price Guide to American Antiques 128
Science and Technology Annual Reference Review, 1989 102
Science Experiments on File 103
Seniorplots 157
Vital Statistics on American Politics 64

TITLE INDEX

The ABCs of Armageddon 78
Academic American Encyclopedia 40
Access America 171
Adult Literacy/Illiteracy in the United States 86
AIDS 112
AIDS Bibliography for 1981–1986 112
AIDS Information Resources Directory 114
Allied Health Education Directory, 1988 109
Almanac of Famous People 173
Almanac of the American People 68
Alternative Therapies, Unproven Methods, and Health Fraud 112
America at the Polls 2 65
America as Story 158
American Banker Year Book, 1988 69
American College Regalia 88
The American Film Institute Catalog of Motion Pictures Produced in the United States 141
American Film Studios 141
American Governors and Gubernatorial Elections, 1979–1987 77
The American Medical Association Guide to Prescription and Over-the-Counter Drugs 113
American Playwrights since 1945 158
American Reference Books Annual, 1988 31
The American Regional Cookery Index 119
American Women Writers 158
Annual Index to Motion Picture Credits, 1987 141
Anti-Evolution 107
Architecture and Women 126
Arrow's Complete Guide to Mail Order Foods 118
The Art of Children's Picture Books 34
Assassinations and Executions 179
Atlas of Southeast Asia 170
Atlas of the Middle East 169
Atlas of Wintering North American Birds 108
Australians 190
Authors & Artists for Young Adults 156

The Barnhart Dictionary of Etymology 92
Barron's Real Estate Handbook 70
The Basic Business Library 74

The Bateman New Zealand Encyclopedia 190
Bernstein's Reverse Dictionary 96
The BFI Companion to the Western 142
The Bibliography of Contemporary American Fiction, 1945–1988 159
Biographical Dictionary of American Sports: Outdoor Sports 148
Biographical Dictionary of Latin American and Caribbean Political Leaders 183
Biographical Directory of the Council of Economic Advisers 73
Black Authors and Illustrators of Children's Books 34
Black Children and American Institutions 61
Black Dance 145
The Black Resource Guide 186
Black Writers 160
Blacks in American Films and Television 142
Blacks in Classical Music 133
The Blackwell Dictionary of Historians 178
The Blackwell Encyclopedia of the Russian Revolution 181
BNA's Directory of State Courts, Judges, and Clerks 76
The Book of Card Games 147
Book of Roots 93
Books for Adult New Readers 87
Books for Children to Read Alone 34
Books for the Gifted Child 34
Books to Help Children Cope with Separation and Loss 55
Bricker's Short-Term Executive Programs 121
British Film Actors' Credits, 1895–1987 143
The Broadcast Communications Dictionary 89
Business Serials of the U.S. Government 67

The Cambridge Atlas of Astronomy 104
The Cambridge Encyclopedia of the Middle East and North Africa 169
The Cambridge Guide to World Theatre 146
The Canadian Encyclopedia 183
Catalog of the American Musical 136
The Catholic Novel 151
CD Review Digest Annual, Volume 1, 1983–1987 139

Child and Youth Actors 143
Childcraft Dictionary 94
Children's Britannica 50
Children's Literature Awards and Winners 39
Children's Media Market Place 53
Children's Writer's & Illustrator's Market, 1989 150
Cinema Sequels and Remakes, 1903–1987 143
Cities of the United States 172
The Civil War Dictionary 188
The Columbia Encyclopedia of Nutrition 111
Comedy on Record 145
Comic Books and Strips 130
Common Allusions and Foreign Terms 94
Comparative World Data 104
The Completely Illustrated Atlas of Reptiles and Amphibians for the Terrarium 117
Compton's Encyclopedia and Fact-Index 42
The Computer Industry Almanac 72
Computer-Readable Databases 37
The Concise Baker's Biographical Dictionary of Musicians 134
Concise Dictionary of Acronyms and Initialisms 96
The Concise Encyclopedia of Australia 191
Concise Encyclopedia of Interior Design 129
Condo Vacations 120
Congress A to Z 67
Contemporary Artists 125
Contemporary Black American Playwrights and Their Plays 161
Contemporary Dramatists 162
Contemporary Literary Criticism Yearbook, 1987 154
Contemporary Photographers 131
The Cook's Book of Useful Information 118
Cooking A to Z 119
Corporate TrendTrac 72
Crime and the Elderly 80
Critical Survey of Literary Theory 149
Critical Survey of Mystery and Detective Fiction 155

Desk Reference World Atlas 166
Dictionary of Afro-American Slavery 62
A Dictionary of American Idioms 97

Title Index

A Dictionary of Ancient Near Eastern Architecture 127
Dictionary of Building 116
Dictionary of Concepts in Physical Geography 163
The Dictionary of Confusable Words 97
Dictionary of Contemporary American Artists 125
A Dictionary of Contrasting Pairs 98
The Dictionary of Cultural Literacy 185
Dictionary of Demons 54
Dictionary of Energy 116
Dictionary of Engineering Acronyms and Abbreviations 115
Dictionary of Finance 69
Dictionary of Genetics & Cell Biology 108
Dictionary of Gerontology 60
A Dictionary of Irish Biography 174
Dictionary of Literary Biography Yearbook, 1987 154
Dictionary of Literary Themes and Motifs 157
Dictionary of Medieval Knighthood and Chivalry 177
A Dictionary of Quotations from the Bible 56
The Dictionary of Real Estate Appraisal 70
A Dictionary of Surnames 177
Directory of American Libraries with Genealogy or Local History Collections 38
Directory of American Youth Organizations 83
Directory of Archives and Manuscript Repositories in the United States 185
The Directory of Humor Magazines and Humor Organizations in America (and Canada) 154
Directory of Popular Culture Collections 184
Directory of Residential Centers for Adults with Developmental Disabilities 79
Directory of Treasure Hunting, Prospecting, and Related Organizations 164
Disability Drama in Television and Film 140
Disease Prevention/Health Promotion 111
Domestic Technology 118
Dr. Burgess's Atlas of Marine Aquarium Fishes 117
The Drama Dictionary 155
Dramatists Sourcebook 146
Drug, Alcohol, and Other Addictions 81
The Dying Child 55

Earth Science on File 105
Ecophilosophy 55
The Eerdmans Analytical Concordance to the Revised Standard Version of the Bible 57
Embroidery and Needlepoint 130
The Encyclopedia of American Intelligence and Espionage 65
Encyclopedia of American Scandal 184
Encyclopedia of Architecture 126
Encyclopedia of Asian History 182
Encyclopedia of Associations: Regional, State, and Local Organizations, 1988–89 52

An Encyclopedia of British Women Writers 161
Encyclopedia of Frontier Biography 189
Encyclopedia of Good Health 110
Encyclopedia of Human Evolution and Prehistory 106
Encyclopedia of Legal Information Sources 75
Encyclopedia of Physical Science and Technology 100
The Encyclopedia of Police Science 82
Encyclopedia of Pop, Rock & Soul 135
Encyclopedia of Rock 135
Encyclopedia of School Administration & Supervision 86
The Encyclopedia of Suicide 79
Encyclopedia of the World's Air Forces 78
Encyclopedia of Ukraine 181
The Encyclopedic Dictionary of Science 100
English Language and Orientation Programs in the United States 99
European Writers 156
The Executive Branch of the U.S. Government 76

The Faces of America 175
The Facts On File Dictionary of Biology 105
The Facts On File Dictionary of Chemistry 105
The Facts On File Dictionary of Education 84
The Facts On File Dictionary of Health Care Management 78
The Facts On File Dictionary of Marine Science 105
The Facts On File Dictionary of the Theatre 146
The Facts On File Dictionary of Troublesome Words 97
The Facts On File Encyclopedia of World Mythology and Legend 59
The Facts On File World Political Almanac 180
Fairchild's Dictionary of Fashion 128
Fallen in Battle 184
Family Law Dictionary 75
Fantasy Literature for Children and Young Adults 151
Festivals U.S.A. 90
Fiction Writers Guidelines 150
Film, Television and Stage Music on Phonographic Records 133
The Financial 1000 69
Financial Aid for the Disabled and Their Families, 1988–1989 82
Find That Tune 135
First Stop 44
500 Plays 153
Free Help from Uncle Sam to Start Your Own Business (Or Expand the One You Have) 77
Funk & Wagnalls New Encyclopedia 44

Gänzl's Book of the Musical Theatre 136
Gardener's Index for 1987 117
Genealogical Periodical Annual Index 176
General Reference Books for Adults 38

Genocide 80
The GIS Guide to Four-Year Colleges, 1989 88
The Gothic's Gothic 151
Government Reference Serials 67
Great Lives 173
The Great Song Thesaurus 137
The Guide to Background Investigations, 1988 122
The Guide to Cooking Schools, 1989 119
Guide to Federal Technical, Trades and Labor Jobs 68
A Guide to Research in Gerontology 60
Guide to State Environmental Programs 83
A Guide to the Archaeological Sites of the British Isles 170
The Guinness Book of Astronomy 104
Guinness Sports Record Book, 1988–89 147

Hammond Discovery World Atlas 166
Handbook of American Film Genres 144
Handbook of American Popular Literature 159
The Harmony Illustrated Encyclopedia of Rock 135
The Harper Dictionary of Modern Thought 46
Health Media Review Index, 1984–86 112
Health Resource Builder 110
Heat Wave 137
High Interest Easy Reading 39
A Hispanic Heritage, Series III 187
Hispanic Resource Directory 186
The Historical Atlas of Political Parties in the United States Congress, 1789–1989 168
Historical Atlas of the United States 165
A Historical Dictionary of American Industrial Language 71
Historical Dictionary of Cuba 184
Historical Dictionary of North American Archaeology 182
Historical Dictionary of the 1920s 189
The Historical Encyclopedia of Costumes 90
The History of Rock and Roll 140
Holistic Resources Directory, 1988/89 114
Horror 155
Hotel and Restaurant Industries 74
How to Find Information about AIDS 115
The Humanities 36
The Hutchinson Encyclopedia 52

The Illustrated Dictionary of Electronics 116
The Illustrated Dictionary of Natural Health 114
Illustration Index VI 33
Images of Blacks in American Culture 123
Imaginary People 157
Index to Afro-American Reference Resources 186
Index to Collective Biographies for Young Readers 174
Index to Literary Criticism for Young Adults 152
Index to Women of the World from Ancient to Modern Times 174
Information Sources in Science and Technology 102

Title Index

Insurance Dictionary 83
Intellectual Freedom and Censorship 81
Interactive Fiction and Adventure Games for Microcomputers, 1988 147
The International Dictionary of Psychology 54
International Directories in Print, 1989–90 59
International Directory of Company Histories 72
International Encyclopedia of Communications 29
The International Film Industry 142
The International Relations Dictionary 65
The International Standard Bible Encyclopedia 56
International Trade Names Dictionary, 1988–89 71
International Trade Names Dictionary, 1988–89: Company Index 71
Introducing Bookplots 3 34
Irish American Material Culture 62

Jewish Heritage in America 187

Key to High-Tech 109

The Language of Real Estate 71
Laughter on Record 145
The Lincoln Writing Dictionary for Children 95
The Literature of American Music in Books and Folk Music Collections 133
Lives and Letters in American Parapsychology 54
Lives of Famous Christians 58
Looking at Prints, Drawings and Watercolours 130

The Macmillan Illustrated Encyclopedia of Dinosaurs and Prehistoric Animals 106
Major Companies of Europe, 1988 73
Market Guide for Young Writers, 1988–89 150
Marketsearch 120
The Marshall Cavendish Illustrated Encyclopedia of Plants and Earth Sciences 108
McGraw-Hill Dictionary of Scientific and Technical Terms 101
McGraw-Hill Encyclopedia of Electronics and Computers 116
McGraw-Hill Encyclopedia of the Geological Sciences 116
McGraw-Hill Personal Computer Programming Encyclopedia 31
Media Review Digest, 1987 145
Medical Reference Tools for the Layperson 1
Microform Market Place, 1988–1989 53
MLA Directory of Periodicals 149
Modern Irish Literature 161
More than 100 152
Morris Dictionary of Word and Phrase Origins 94
Moving Up 121
The Municipal Year Book, 1988 76
Music 133
Music Directory Canada '88 132
The Music Locator, 1988 134

Music Reference and Research Materials 132

National Anthems of the World 137
National Continuing Care Directory 78
National Directory of Bulletin Board Systems, 1988/1989 30
The National Directory of Corporate Training Programs 68
National Directory of Retirement Facilities 120
Nations within a Nation 187
Native American Basketry 130
Native Americans on Film and Video 144
New Day/New Deal 189
New Dictionary of Theology 57
The New Electronic Encyclopedia 47
The New Encyclopedia of Science Fiction 124
The New Grove Dictionary of Jazz 138
The New Illustrated Science and Invention Encyclopedia 101
The New Quilting & Patchwork Dictionary 129
1988 Annual Encyclopedia Update 5
The Nobel Peace Prize and the Laureates 66
The Nobel Prize Winners: Literature 154
The Norton/Grove Concise Encyclopedia of Music 132
Number One in the U.S.A. 50

Oil and Gas Dictionary 116
Old-House Dictionary 127
Olderr's Fiction Index, 1987 153
The 100 Best Treatment Centers for Alcoholism and Drug Abuse 81
Opera Annual 136
Orphan Drugs 113
Ottemiller's Index to Plays in Collections 153
Our Vice-Presidents and Second Ladies 188
The Oxford Dictionary of Art 125
The Oxford English Dictionary: On Compact Disc 91
Oxford Illustrated Encyclopedia, Volume 3 179
Oxford Illustrated Encyclopedia, Volume 4 179
The Oxford Illustrated Literary Guide to Canada 171
The Oxford Literary Guide to Australia 172

Passenger and Immigration Lists Bibliography, 1538–1900 177
Passport to World Band Radio 90
Past Worlds 167
Peace of Mind during Pregnancy 114
Peace Organizations Past and Present 66
Peace Resource Book, 1988–1989 66
The Penguin Atlas of North American History to 1870 165
PERiodical Source Index, 1847–1985 175
Peterson's Guide to Certificate Programs at American Colleges and Universities 89
Peterson's Guide to Independent Secondary Schools, 1988–89 86
Peterson's Higher Education Directory, 1988 89

Pictorial Price Guide to American Antiques 128
Place Names of Africa, 1935–1986 164
Place-Names in Classical Mythology 170
Place-Names of the World 163
Plain Talk about Art 124
Poet's Handbook 53
Population Information in Twentieth Century Census Volumes 60
Primaryplots 35
Private Independent Schools, 1988 86
The Pro Football Bio-Bibliography 148
Product and Process 109
Psychological and Medical Aspects of Induced Abortion 113
The Public Administration Dictionary 76
Public Interest Profiles, 1988–1989 64

The Quotable Shakespeare 162

The Radical Right 63
Raintree Children's Encyclopedia 49
The Rating Guide to Franchises 74
The Reader's Adviser 35
A Reader's Guide to the Classic British Mystery 163
Real Estate Dictionary 70
The Recording Locator, 1988 134
Records of the Presidency 77
Reference Books for Young Readers 31
Reference Tools for Literary Criticism: A Selected Guide 14
Rehab 81
Research Guide to American Historical Biography 175
Resources for Educational Equity 87
Resources for Middle Childhood 61
Revenge of the Creature Features Movie Guide 144
Revolutionary and Dissident Movements 63
Roget's II 98
The Roots of English 93
The Royals 180

The Schirmer Guide to Schools of Music and Conservatories throughout the World 134
Science and Technology Annual Reference Review, 1989 102
Science Experiments Index for Young People 103
Science Experiments on File 103
Science Fiction & Fantasy Book Review Annual, 1988 156
Selected Reference Sources on Gardening 18
The Self-Help Sourcebook 87
Seminars Directory 123
Seniorplots 157
Since 1776 185
A Social and Economic Atlas of India 168
Spanish-Language Reference Books 32
Spas, 1988 111
The Sports Address Book 148
Sports Reference Books 21
Sports Talk 147
The State and Local Government Political Dictionary 77
Student's World Atlas 167

Survey of Early Childhood Software, 1988 86
Synerjy 74

Telephone Books as Reference Sources 24
Television & Ethics 56
The Thesaurus of Slang 98
Third Opinion 79
The Third Reich Almanac 181
Time Lines on File 178
The Times Family Atlas of the World 166
The Timetables of Science 103
The Trainer's Resource, 1988 68
Training and Development Organizations Directory 121
Training Directory for Business and Industry, 1989–90 122
The Traveler's Guide to American Gardens 126
Traveler's Guide to Museum Exhibitions, 1989 52
Twentieth-Century Shapers of American Popular Religion 58

Ulrich's International Periodicals Directory, 1988–89 32

V.I.P. Address Book, 1988–1989 173
Vacation Condominiums for Rent 120
Van Nostrand's Scientific Encyclopedia 102
Variety's Complete Home Video Directory, 1988 33
Victorian Britain 180
Video for Libraries 37
The Video Source Book, 1989 33
Vietnam War Literature 160
Violence and Terror in the Mass Media 60
Vital Records Handbook 176
Vital Statistics on American Politics 64

Walter Breen's Complete Encyclopedia of U.S. and Colonial Coins 127
We Shall Be Heard 160
Webster's New World Dictionary of American English 95
Webster's New World Guide to Current American Usage 99

Western Europe, 1989 63
Who Was Who in the Civil War 188
Who Wrote That Song? 137
Who's Who in American Education, 1988–1989 85
Who's Who in Fashion 128
Who's Who in Interior Design 129
Wide Screen Movies 131
Women and Judaism 58
Women in LC's Terms 37
Women into the Unknown 164
Women of Color and Southern Women 61
Women of Color in the United States 62
Women's Health Perspectives 110
World Atlas of Nations 167
World Education Encyclopedia 84
The World Map Directory, 1989 168
World Nature Encyclopedia 107
World of Winners 29
The Writer's Directory, 1988–90 150

Young Adult Book Review Index, 1987 39
Young Students Learning Library 49